The Necronomicon Files

The Necronomicon Files

The Truth Behind Lovecraft's Legend

Daniel Harms

and

John Wisdom Gonce III

Boston, MA/York Beach, ME

First published in 2003 by
Red Wheel/Weiser, LLC
York Beach, ME
With offices at:
368 Congress Street
Boston, MA 02210
www.redwheelweiser.com

Library of Congress Cataloging-in-Publication Data
Harms, Daniel.
The Necronomicon files : the truth behind Lovecraft's legend / Daniel Harms
and John Wisdom Gonce III.
p. cm.
Includes bibliographical references and index.
ISBN 1-57863-269-2 (alk. paper)
1. Occultism. 2. Lovecraft, H. P. (Howard Phillips), 1890-1937. I. Gonce, John Wisdom. II. Title.
BF1999.H37515 2003
133—dc21
2003008089

Typeset in Minion and Univers Condensed

Printed in Canada

TCP

10 09 08 07 06 05 04 03
8 7 6 5 4 3 2 1

DEDICATED TO

Lord Ganesa, Protector of Books,
Inanna/Ishtar, Queen of Heaven

*

To our families and
The Gentleman of Providence Plantations, late of Earth

Contents

Preface: The *Necronomicon*—Shadow in the Mind

    (Donald Tyson)   ix

Introduction (Daniel Harms)   xv

Initiation (John Wisdom Gonce III)   xx

Acknowledgments

    (Daniel Harms and John Wisdom Gonce III) xxiv

Part I: THE *NECRONOMICON* AND LITERATURE

Chapter 1: H. P. Lovecraft and the *Necronomicon*

    (Daniel Harms)   3

Chapter 2: "Many a Quaint and Curious Volume . . .":

    The *Necronomicon* Made Flesh (Daniel Harms)   29

Chapter 3: Evaluating *Necronomicon* Rumors

    (Daniel Harms)   61

Part II: THE *NECRONOMICON* AND OCCULTISM

Chapter 4: The Evolution of Sorcery: A Brief History

    of Modern Magick (John Wisdom Gonce III)   71

Chapter 5: Lovecraftian Magick—Sources and Heirs

    (John Wisdom Gonce III)   85

Chapter 6: A Plague of *Necronomicon*s (John

    Wisdon Gonce III) 127

Chapter 7: Simon, Slater, and the Gang: True Origins

    of the *Necronomicon* (John Wisdom Gonce III) 173

Chapter 8: The Chaos of Confusion (John Wisdom Gonce III). . . 197

Chapter 9: The *Necronomicon* and Psychic Attack

(John Wisdom Gonce III) 215

Part III: THE *NECRONOMICON* AND ENTERTAINMENT

Chapter 10: Unspeakable Cuts: The *Necronomicon* on Film

(John Wisdom Gonce III) 225

Chapter 11: Call of the Cathode Ray Tube: The *Necronomicon*

on Television (John Wisdom Gonce III).................. 281

Conclusion (Daniel Harms) 297

Appendix: History of the *Necronomicon* (H. P. Lovecraft) 303

Endnotes... 307

Preface

The *Necronomicon:* Shadow in the Mind

—DONALD TYSON

Everyone involved with the occult for any length of time hears rumors about lost keys that unlock the ancient mysteries of ceremonial magic. Usually the key takes the form of a book. Such books are legend in the history of the occult. When Adam emerged from the Garden of Eden, he is fabled to have carried a book of angelic wisdom. A similar book is said to have been given to the patriarch Enoch after he was drawn up, still living, into heaven. Moses supposedly recorded the mystery teachings of Egypt that he acquired from the magicians of Pharaoh. King Solomon was reputed to have set down the angel-inspired method by which he commanded and restrained the seventy-two demons that constructed the First Temple at Jerusalem. Christ spoke in private to his disciples and conveyed to them a hidden teaching that was too sacred and too dangerous for ordinary men—who is to say that it was never written down?

Even if all these tales are untrue and such primordial books of wisdom never existed, it was inevitable that men would write books and apply these and other great names to them to lend them authority. Sometimes the writers claimed a direct link to God or the angels, or presented their works as the inspired teachings of the spirits of Enoch or Moses. There was always a market for wisdom books. No matter how incredible their claims or how vague their teachings, many were eager to pay large sums to acquire copies and to sing their praises.

When the alchemist Edward Kelley sought out the Elizabethan mage John Dee, he carried under his arm the *Book of Dunstan*, an ancient manuscript reputed to contain the veritable secret of transmuting base metals into gold. Years prior to the meeting, Dee had written a work called the *Hieroglyphic Monad* during a thirteen-day frenzy of inspiration. This book, he had confidently assured everyone who would listen, including Queen Elizabeth herself, contained the key to every occult and religious mystery. When Dee and Kelley became partners and talked to a hierarchy of spirits representing themselves as the same angels that had instructed Enoch, the angels dictated to the two men a new book of angelic magic, which they asserted to be the true magic of Enoch lost to humanity after the Flood.

Whisperings about forbidden books of occult power did not stop with the dawning Age of Enlightenment. The mysterious Comte de St. Germain had his *Holy Trinosophia*, Eliphas Levi his *Nuctemeron of Apollonius*, Madam Helena Blavatsky her akashic *Book of Dzyan*. The primary leader of the original Hermetic Order of the Golden Dawn, Samuel MacGregor Mathers, revealed in a letter to members of the Order that his occult teachings had in part been copied "from books brought before me, I know not how, and which disappeared from my vision when the transcription was finished."[1] Mathers's most infamous student, Aleister Crowley, received the text of his *Book of the Law* directly from his holy guardian angel, Aiwass.

These books of power usually share certain traits. Either they are very difficult to obtain or, when examined, extremely hard to understand. Often, as in the case of Dee's *Hieroglyphic Monad* and Crowley's *Book of the Law*, books that are purported to act as keys to occult wisdom themselves require a key before they can be used. In the absence of this key, they appear little more than nonsense riddles for children. It is claimed, however, that when the key is applied, they open like an intellectual Chinese box to reveal their secrets. Those who acquire such books without knowing how to open them remain frustrated, or consider them of little worth and discard them.

Some books, however, have a more sinister reputation. They are believed to be evil talismans that carry with them a dark energy that infects anyone who handles or possesses them. This is said of the *Goetia*, a grimoire that catalogs the appearance, nature, and use of the seventy-two demons of hell, bound and sealed by Solomon beneath the sea in a vessel of brass. A similar hellish contagion is reputed to accompany copies of the *Book of the Sacred Magic of Abramelin the Mage*, a French grimoire that claims on its title page to have been a gift from God to Moses, Aaron, David, Solomon, and "other Saints, Patriarchs and Prophets." The book was translated into English by MacGregor Mathers in 1898. Even to possess one of its magic squares without understanding its meaning is rumored to carry the most dire consequences.

Into this fertile mythic field of fact and fancy that extends to the horizon of the dim past, the writer of supernatural fiction Howard Phillips Lovecraft planted the black seed of his *Necronomicon*. Speak the name *Necronomicon*—the very music of the word sends a chill of dread anticipation down the spine—the "Book of Dead Names," as it is often called, penned by a mad poet. It is whispered that no one can read it and remain wholesome. The very words blight the mind and leave it twisted and deformed, praying for a release from horror that may not even come after death. Of all the keys of magic remembered in the modern age, none is more Stygian than the *Necronomicon*.

The very obscurity of the tome magnifies its fatal fascination. Although it is said to be more than 800 pages long, Lovecraft referred to it in only thirteen stories, at most quoting a few lines or a paragraph of the text. Is it a natural history of other worlds? A sacred scripture devoted to obscene Gods? A practical grimoire of spells and incantations? Or is it the key to an occult gateway that will open on the eve of the final annihilation of the human species? Lovecraft was not explicit, and in his ambiguity lies power. Because he did not reveal the nature of the *Necronomicon*, others are free to speculate about its function. It is a book of possibilities.

The most virulent speculation raging over the book is whether it has any objective reality. Those who possess more enthusiasm than critical judgment maintain that the book is a real text—that Lovecraft had access to an esoteric tradition in which he learned about the *Necronomicon* and its contents, perhaps even acquired a copy of the book. Others maintain that he uncovered the secrets of the book during visionary dreams, as a browser amid the stacks in the akashic library, and carried them with him into the land of the waking. More skeptical critics flatly assert that the book does not exist and never has existed, that it was nothing more than a plot device created by Lovecraft for his stories and carried on by him because it tickled the fancies of literary colleagues such as Frank Belknap Long, Robert E. Howard, and Clark Ashton Smith.

Complicating the history of the *Necronomicon* is the recent spate of apocryphal texts bearing the same title. The general public inevitably confuses these fakes with Lovecraft's *Necronomicon*—indeed, this is the intention of their authors and publishers. To those possessing knowledge of occult literature, these fakes are obvious, but the average person who picks such books off the shelf can be forgiven for assuming them to be genuine, in the absence of any indication to the contrary.

At the most prosaic level, the production of bogus *Necronomicon*s is driven by simple greed. They earn money for those who concoct and publish them, or they would not be published. The Simon *Necronomicon*, one of the most infamous of these hoaxes, has been continuously in print for more than two decades, and for all that time has been lining the pockets of those responsible for it. But greed is not the only factor that keeps the forgeries on the racks. Fakes exist to supply a real market that cannot be supplied in any other way. The public wants the *Necronomicon* to exist—indeed, it demands that it exist. There is an unconscious psychological need for the *Necronomicon* and similar fabled keys to the eternal mysteries to be real.

The book is a universal symbol of knowledge, and knowledge is power. The fabled forbidden knowledge of the *Necronomicon* is the power to unleash and control dark forces of chaos that will bend the laws of nature for the benefit of the possessor of the book. This evil power can only be gained at great risk, with the threat of madness, death, or damnation ever present. Yet there are always human beings eager to take such a risk for their own advantage, believing that they are clever enough to avoid paying the terrible price for hubris. Indeed, those who would never dream of actually attempting to use the book feel a need for such a key in the world, even while deploring its existence.

The impulse to believe in the reality of the *Necronomicon* is, in part, the same impulse that gave rise to the witch-hunting frenzy that gripped Europe from the 15th to the 17th century. It was responsible for the myth of the Black Mass, the McCarthy Hearings to expose Communists in the 1950s, and the widespread reports of Satanic child molestations in the 1980s. Not only is there a need to believe in the existence of keys that unlock the mysteries of the occult, there is an equally deep-seated need in the human psyche for a manifest presence of evil. In its own little way, the *Necronomicon* satisfies both needs.

Many people, particularly fundamentalist Christians, have the notion that the magical grimoires are wicked books overflowing with monstrous blasphemies and horrors too terrible to consider. Uninformed critics of the occult have reinforced this view in their writings. When you actually read the dread grimoires, you find that they are tedious and confusing recipe books and collections of prayers. Even those with the very worst reputation for evil, such as the *Picatrix* and the *Grand Grimoire*, seem remarkably tame to modern eyes. Their reputation has been inflamed because we have an abiding, but largely unrecognized, need for books of evil power. In the case of the ancient grimoires, it was easy for critics to inflate their reputation, because so few readers had actually seen or read the texts. The same mechanism was at work in the history of the *Necronomicon*, where it was easy to magnify the fell repute of the book precisely because it does not exist, and therefore no one could put the lie to extravagant claims about it.

If the *Necronomicon* were a genuine occult text from the 8th century, as Lovecraft reported it to be in his fanciful history of the book, I have no doubt whatsoever that it would consist of a tiresome collection of prayers, prosaic instructions about diet and hygiene, incomprehensible names, and lists of ingredients for potions. It would be like all the other true grimoires, largely unusable by the average person unable to fill in the missing details of rituals and spells. What makes the *Necronomicon* a perennial book of wonder and terror is precisely that it does not exist, has never existed, and will never exist, in the ordinary sense. It will always remain a magical thing, immune from library classification and deconstructive scholarly analysis. In this sense, the *Necronomicon* is like magic itself. In its intangibility lies its power.

When a butterfly is pinned to a corkboard, it ceases to be a butterfly and becomes a lifeless husk. If the Jewish Second Temple were ever rebuilt in Jerusalem, it would lose the mystique it has carried with it for 2,000 years and become nothing more than a building. Similarly, should a true edition of the *Necronomicon* be discovered in some dusty library or book shop, it would be deprived overnight of its power to attract and repel and would become nothing more than an uninteresting old book. What protects the *Necronomicon* from this ignoble fate is its lack of reality, its very nonexistence.

I confess to mixed feelings about debunking the *Necronomicon*. The modern mythology that has grown up around it is so alive and widespread that it almost seems like the murder of a magical being to expose it. Instead of tarnishing the reputation of the book, as might be expected, the numerous fakes have only added to its authority by their bewildering number and conflicting versions. However, every day hundreds of individuals buy copies of bogus *Necronomicon*s under the mistaken belief that they hold in their sweating palms the genuine article, and this is nothing other than a kind of fraud on the part of the publishers and authors. Those with an interest in the history of the book have a right to know about its origins and evolution, to say nothing of its unreality.

Daniel Harms and John Wisdom Gonce have done an excellent job setting forth the facts surrounding the whole *Necronomicon* phenomenon. In these pages, you will find as much of the truth as is known about Lovecraft, his imaginary grimoire, its place in literature and popular culture, and the cottage industry that has arisen over the past three decades to supply the continuing demand for a book that does not exist.

Harms focuses on the history of the *Necronomicon*, both the apocryphal history concocted by Lovecraft to lend the book verisimilitude in his fiction, and its history as a kind of icon within the literary circle of Lovecraft's friends and colleagues, who added to the book's legend by referring to it in their own writings. Harms provides an excellent overview of the modern social hysteria surrounding the book. Gonce places the *Necronomicon* within the context of Western magic, and evaluates the numerous pseudo-*Necronomicon*s published in recent decades for their worth as practical textbooks of magic. He devotes particular attention to the Simon *Necronomicon*, which has become the most popular of the bogus editions. Gonce also examines the place of the mythic book in cinema and television.

There is considerable value in this twofold approach to the phenomenon of Lovecraft's literary homunculus. Harms answers the questions that will be in the minds of most readers who are interested in the *Necronomicon* merely as a part of the landscape of American popular fiction, and Lovecraft's tales and letters in particular. Those who need to know what role the *Necronomicon* played in Lovecraft's short stories, and in the stories of pulp fiction writers contemporary to him will find what they seek here. By contrast, the portion of the book written by Gonce will be of greater interest to anyone attracted to the *Necronomicon* as a practical textbook of magic. Thousands who have bought the Simon *Necronomicon* and other fakes have used them, or attempted to use them, for ritual occultism. Gonce reveals how much value these false editions have as grimoires of magic.

It seems almost a crime to debunk the living and growing myth of the *Necronomicon*, but it is arguably a still greater crime to sell books claiming that they are the genuine *Necronomicon* when no such text has ever existed. Confusion breeds confusion and, if allowed to run unchecked, escapes all control. This book is necessary to set forth in a clear and unambiguous way the bare facts of the whole matter. To their credit, Harms and Gonce also manage to preserve much of the romance and fascination that surrounds the *Necronomicon* in our modern culture.

Perhaps I should not worry about killing the myth of the book. There will always be many who are more than willing to believe that it was written by a mad Arabian poet in the 8th century at Damascus and that it contains the secrets to the power of the mysterious Old Ones who lurk beyond the gates of time and space, and that if only they search long enough, and hard enough, they will find a copy of one of the original, true editions, and gain access to its terrible and wonderful secrets.

Donald Tyson
Bedford, Nova Scotia
25 April 2000

Introduction
—Daniel Harms

You walk into a huge room dimly lit with bulbs that flicker with each step. Stretching off into the distance are row upon row of metal bookshelves, crammed with volumes of all sizes and shapes. You give little thought to most of these as you run through the stacks gripping the pass it took you months to obtain. The library's classification system seems designed to make it harder to find what you seek, and you often double back, peering at the tiny cards pasted to the tops of the shelves.

The row you seek is engulfed in shadows, and you approach with a mixture of anticipation and dread. You peer at the shelves, noting many rare titles only mentioned in whispers—but you bypass them in search of your true quarry. There's the spot on the shelf—and it's empty! No, wait—it's there, on the one above it, wedged between two massive volumes. With great care, you pry it out. After one long look at the cover of what you have sought so long, you slowly open its brittle cover . . .

Compelling, isn't it? If you're like many people, this would be the ideal culmination of years of research into a problem. What if a book existed that gave the answers to everything you've ever wondered? How much effort would you put into finding it? What would you do to get it?

Rumors about such books have been with us for millennia. The Babylonian *Tablet of Destiny*, owned by the God Enlil, and the Egyptian volumes of magick attributed to the God Thoth may be included among them. Generally, these books are said to have great power—those who control them not only have the answers they seek but can use this knowledge to transform themselves and their world. Such books are usually rare (otherwise, our world would be transforming all the time), and are either hidden in secret places or kept secretly by powerful groups of priests or officials. This is not to say that these books do not exist; some of them do. However, as any scholar of magick knows, none of these has ever lived up to its reputation. Yet in some way, these books seem to call for their own existence; many times, a book that has been rumored to exist does turn up decades or centuries after the first tales, written by an unscrupulous individual who wants to influence others or make some fast money.

One of the latest of these works is the *Necronomicon*, which, according to most authorities, was created by the science fiction author H. P. Lovecraft. Authorities justify their suspicions on several grounds: there is no mention of the book previous to Lovecraft's references, and Lovecraft himself, who had no particular motivation to say otherwise, admitted the book was a hoax. Yet there are thousands of people who believe that the *Necronomicon* has existed for centuries, that its existence has been hidden even by those who speak of it (!), and that anyone who finds it will be able to call Lovecraft's "Old Ones" back into existence. They generally respond to contrary claims with assertions like:

- Read Lovecraft; since he wrote about it with such force, the *Necronomicon* must be real;
- You can tell the *Necronomicon* is real if you read between the lines of Lovecraft's writing;
- Lovecraft kept the book's existence a secret because he knew it was dangerous;
- Lovecraft saw the book once, but was traumatized by the experience and forgot that it existed—but he wrote about it anyway;
- A cult spirited away all copies of the *Necronomicon* so that no one could find it;
- You can't prove that it doesn't exist!

Largely due to those who believe, the *Necronomicon* has appeared in fiction, music, art, film, games, occult books, on the Internet, and in many other media. Every sign indicates that this trend will continue in the new millennium.

Who We Are

This book had its origin in the campus radio station of Vanderbilt University. While working on my first book, the *Encyclopedia Cthulhiana*, a large contingent of authors and fans devoted to the works of H. P. Lovecraft encouraged and cheered me on my way. One of these turned out to be a local DJ, the Reverend Doctor Johnny Anonymous, who invited me to his late-night show. It was there that I met an imposing, exotically dressed gentleman named John Gonce, whom I soon learned was looking for a person with a background in Lovecraft studies. He had discovered a book called the *Necronomicon* that he thought was magickally dangerous. I, along with most Lovecraft fans (including Mr. Gonce himself), knew the *Necronomicon* to be a hoax, but had not thought of it much. I started to research the topic, however, and turned up more facts, more possibilities—and a great number of *Necronomicon*s previously unsuspected.

John and I also quickly found that even those who claimed expertise in the fields of literature and the occult had been fooled. James Randi, a.k.a. The Amazing Randi, a famous debunker of the paranormal, included the *Necronomicon* in his *Encyclopedia of Claims, Frauds, and Hoaxes of the Occult* with a list of real grimoires, or books of black magick, that date back to the Middle Ages.[1] On the other end of the spectrum,

Bob Larson's *Satanism: The Seduction of America's Youth* provided a section on the *Necronomicon* that hopelessly muddled two different hoaxes,[2] and even stated that Lovecraft himself wrote the book.[3] And if the experts were of little help, their followers were often less so. It was clear that someone had to reevaluate the evidence and compile it in one place to provide a full look at the phenomenon. The process took a great deal of time and effort, but it seems to have paid off.

We did approach the project with our own preconceived views and opinions, and some will charge us with not being "open-minded." It has been my experience, however, that those who call for "open-mindedness" most loudly are those who rarely practice it. Indeed, I've yet to meet one of those objective, open-minded observers I keep hearing about. What drives a long, intense research project such as *The Necronomicon Files* is not objectivity, but a strong commitment to one's views. We were successful in our work for two reasons. First, we did our best to check all viewpoints, going back to the primary sources and questioning even our own ideas. Second, while we have the same overall views with which we entered the project, many of our discoveries still surprised us and forced us to change some of our ideas. That may not be good enough for some, but we feel we have provided enough evidence for you to go back and check our information for yourself.

The Nature of Belief

Why do people believe in the *Necronomicon*? Indeed, why do people believe anything? A number of factors seem to lead to belief.

> **Trust:** Despite our culture's popular admonition to "think for yourself," no one spends much time doing it. After all, no one can spend all of their time checking up on everything that their family, friends, community, and the mass media tell them. We may trust some sources more than others, but we trust most of what we are told, so long as we don't hear evidence to the contrary. Even if we do receive conflicting information, other factors may influence our judgment.

> **Conditioning:** We are all products of the place in which we live, the people we know, the political and religious systems to which we are exposed, and other factors. This means that each person engages in a filtering of information. This does not mean, as some have proposed, that we can only perceive what we believe in; otherwise, we would never see anything new. At the same time, information that fits our sense of the world tends to be remembered, while information that does not is often downplayed, forgotten, or argued away. (Then again, unusual information is often remembered because it is unusual, but is rarely brought into our worldview.)

> **Experience and perception:** If someone came to me and tried to convince me that dogs don't exist, I'd laugh at them. After all, I've seen dogs since I

was born, and my family even owned one. Much of what we have been told is also backed up by what we experience, whether through the senses, logic, or our emotions. Of course, our conditioning affects this; we may experience what to us seems to be one phenomenon, while in fact it is another. We may yield to persuasion, but it will probably take a new set of perceptions to bring this about.

Repetition: A standard advertising ploy is to repeat a fact until the consumer accepts it. This is present, on a larger scale, in all our lives. If we receive the same information over and over, we are more likely to believe its validity. The effectiveness of repetition is increased if we hear the same thing from different sources. If one of my friends tells me five times that a movie is good, it isn't as believable as if five of my friends tell me once that it's good.

None of these factors are, in and of themselves, bad things. They allow us to function in our day-to-day lives, and give us a basis for convincing others that certain things are true. The danger comes when these factors are used to coerce us into doing something dangerous. Throughout history, there have been those who have made use of these techiques for their own benefit, or to push an ideological opinion onto others. There's nothing wrong with making money from information (otherwise few people would write books), or with putting forth an opinion, as long as those who hear it are getting the information they want.

The goal of this project is to give you a crash course in all aspects of the *Necronomicon*—its significance in literature, history, occultism, and cinema. Occultists and Lovecraft scholars alike will deplore the amount of space spent on each other's ideas. Readers new to the debate will have to be careful to get the details straight, while experts in their fields may find the discussions simplistic. I think that the approach taken here is necessary, however, since the *Necronomicon* phenomenon is widespread and complex. If you have heard of the *Necronomicon*, no matter from what source, you will find in the debate an explanation of others' positions.

This is a book about the different realms of experience and knowledge that come together to create the "*Necronomicon* phenomenon." For most people, these realms remain distinct. Most Lovecraft fans do not believe in magick, many practitioners of magick don't practice Lovecraft-inspired magick, and many movie fans have no knowledge of either. It would be wrong to assume that everyone who reads Lovecraft practices magick or that every person who uses magick reads Lovecraft. What makes this book special, I believe, is that it reaches across these boundaries to describe the legend of the *Necronomicon* in all of its dubious glory, in ways that most who come into contact with it never realize.

This book is not the definitive *Necronomicon* research. No book can be completely accurate, and new versions and rumors constantly appear. For those who disagree with us, we can say only this: Read through our *Files*, and if you're still convinced that our views are incorrect, by all means, construct new theories from what we have given you and do some investigation of your own.[4] But no matter what the outcome, be willing to go where the information takes you.

Buffalo, New York
4 October 1997

Initiation
—John Wisdom Gonce III

Nervously, you look back over your shoulder into the darkness as you rush down the rain-slick sidewalks in one of the older sections of the city. You know you really shouldn't run—that attracts attention—but you are afraid the jealous guardians of the book may already know what you've done. Unconsciously, you tighten your grip on the book satchel clutched under your arm. You know what's in there . . . and you hope no one else does.

You look up the street and see the old, familiar, 19th-century building, revamped as an apartment house. Almost home! You rush past the coffeehouse, the metaphysical bookstore, and the pub. No time for anything but the book. Finally you reach the entrance door and fumble for the key. As you put the key in the lock, a kind of flickering shadow sweeps over you. Startled, you jerk your head around to see what it was. Nothing! Maybe it was just a cloud passing before the Moon. But if it was a cloud, how could it have darkened the street-lights? Shivering as though a lizard of ice had slithered up your back, you shove the entrance door open and rush inside. Running up the flight of steps to your little studio apartment, you know you haven't much time. Inside at last! There is still a layout of tarot cards on your desk. "Children's toys!" you think, and impatiently sweep them onto the floor to make room for the book. With great care, you take the book out of the satchel and place it on the desk. For a moment, you simply gaze down at the single word engraved on its dark, leather cover in faded gold leaf:

NECRONOMICON

How long have you dreamed of this moment? How many sages and wizards of the past would have given anything to be where you are now, with this forbidden book? How many sorcerers would have died on the Inquisitor's rack for a chance to hold it in their hands? At your fingertips is the key to undimensioned forces of unspeakable cosmic power. For this is more than a book; it is the dark treasure house that holds the secrets of the ages. Secrets that transcend the time and dimensions we know, and stretch back through untold eons to the distant reaches of the cosmos where the black planets roll without aim.

Gently, slowly, you open its brittle cover. The vellum is as dry as a mummy's skin and just as delicate, threatening to crack at the slightest pressure. Suddenly it does crack! To your utter horror, a piece of the cover breaks off in your hand. The spine of the book crackles with a sound like dry autumn leaves crushed under foot and breaks away from the rusty iron hinges that once held it together. Desperately, you try to turn one of the decaying parchment pages, but it crumbles in your fingers like the wings of a dead moth. You try to turn another page, and it too crumbles away like a veil of ash. A cold fist of panic clinches your throat as you try to pick up the book, thinking you will store it somewhere until you can find a way to keep it from decomposing. But the entire volume disintegrates in your hands, leaving you with a fistful of dust. Your dreams of limitless power and forbidden wisdom are . . . gone!

Frustrating isn't it? But if you have ever been enamored of one of the several published versions of the *Necronomicon* on the market today, you have probably had a similarly frustrating experience—though perhaps a bit less dramatic than the one described above. For it seems that all these books are ultimately disappointing to their readers, for reasons that you will understand as you read on.

The Necronomicon Files Team

Though it makes no claim to reveal the hidden secrets the cosmos, the book you are holding in your hands at this moment is remarkable in its own way. While there are many books *about* magick, few books can claim to be the product of magick itself. *The Necronomicon Files* is, however, such a book.

For several years, while I was active in the overlapping worlds of the Renaissance Fair circuit, the Neopagan community, and alternative music and art, I occasionally encountered someone who sincerely believed in the authenticity of the *Necronomicon*. "Poor deluded soul!" I thought. As a lifelong fan of the works of H. P. Lovecraft, I knew that Lovecraft had created the idea of the *Al Azif* out of his own imagination and used it as a literary prop to spice up his horror fiction. As a practicing occultist, I knew enough about historical grimoires (spellbooks) to know that there was no *Necronomicon* extant in the Middle Ages or the Renaissance. As a worshiper of the Goddess Inanna/Ishtar and a practitioner of Mesopotamian magick, I knew that the most popular of these *Necronomicons* was not really an ancient Sumerian grimoire.

Because of this, and because of my native arrogance and complacency, I was totally blindsided when I discovered that there were people out there who actually used one of the published *Necronomicon*s to practice magick. There were even groups of practitioners who formed "cults" around one of these published *Necronomicon*s! When this information finally filtered its way through my thick skull, I felt as though I had taken a lance blow to the head from Sir William Marshall himself. As a WWF wrestler might say; "Who'da thunk it?"

I realized I needed to research this whole *Necronomicon* issue seriously if I were going to deal with it intelligently and be able to answer the questions of some of the people who occasionally came to me for a kind of informal "exit counseling" relative to their involvement with destructive cults.[1] One of the most important elements I needed for this research project was someone with a much more extensive background in Lovecraft scholarship than I had at the time. So I began a series of meditations to attract someone into my life who could help me with this project. Since I didn't want to interfere with the free will of that individual, it had to be someone who *wanted* to do this work. It had to be someone with a vast knowledge of the Lovecraft Mythos. It had to be the perfect person for the job

Enter Daniel Harms, author of *The Encyclopedia Cthuliana,* who appeared one night (as if by magick) at one of my favorite haunts, the campus radio station of Vanderbilt University, where my close friend and fellow Lovecraft fan the Reverend Dr. Johnny Anonymous was doing his 91 Noise Show. When the good Reverend introduced me to Daniel, it was, to quote dialogue from *Casablanca,* "the beginning of a beautiful friendship."

My good friend Dru Myers, also an ardent Lovecraft fan, had already given me a great deal of help with this project, but neither of us had the background in Lovecraft studies that Daniel could provide. When the three of us got together (as if by magick), *The Necronomicon Files* was born. We decided to launch a two-pronged attack on the project: to explore both the occult and the Lovecraftian sides of the *Necronomicon* enigma. I hope you enjoy the results.

Some Lovecraft fans and scholars may be impatient with the amount of space devoted to the occult in this text. They should realize that one of the goals of this book is to vindicate Lovecraft, to exonerate him from guilt by association with the various hoax versions of the *Necronomicon* that exploit his name. I daresay that every fifteen minutes someone picks up a copy of one of the hoax *Necronomicon*s and believes that H. P. Lovecraft either wrote it or believed in it. Occultists may think too much time is spent discussing Lovecraft and his Circle. They should understand that such a background is essential to an understanding of the roots of Lovecraftian magick, and the origins of the *Necronomicon* legend.

Those who think that a deconstruction of the *Necronomicon* hoax amounts to "much ado about nothing" should read on, and check out the accounts of destructive activities, magickal backlash, and even murders associated with the book. This hoax has a body count!

So, read through the information we offer, examine it for yourself, and analyze our conclusions. Then, do something that people in our society often tell you to do, but seldom do themselves: Think for yourself.

Nashville, Tennessee
6 December 2001

Acknowledgments

Daniel Harms:

This book could not have appeared without the help of many different people. First, thanks should be given to H. P. Lovecraft, without whose genius our planet would have been a poorer place. Thanks should also be given to Dru Myers, whose unearlthy tastes in fiction and music brought the authors together. John Halperin, Centennial Professor of English at Vanderbilt University, advised me in the formative stages of this project as an independent study. In my researches, the interlibrary loan departments of the Heard Library at Vanderbilt and the Altoona Public Library provided valuable resources. In the early stages, we thought about this project as a website; Samantha Copeland helped us with starting out, while Az0th, E. P. Berglund, Cindi Brown, and M. A. al-Ahari commented on the initial drafts. Philip C. Robinson promised us a home twice, and we left him hanging as the project turned into a book. Marc Michaud, Tim Maroney, Lynn Willis, Darrell Schweitzer, S. T. Joshi, and the former members of the Miskatonic Alchemical Expedition all provided encouragement and valuable information. Oriana Reyes helped with a translation from the German, and David Payanopulos, Steven Marc Harris, Christophe Thill, David Gartrell, David Cantu, and Scott Eaken called valuable material to our attention. Some of our findings have been presented at NecronomiCon '97 and '99 and on the Usenet forums *alt.necronomicon* and *alt.horror.cthulhu*. All of these have provided us with new information and interpretations.

Khem Caigan, Kenneth Grant, Peter Levenda, and Colin Low were all willing to discuss their roles in the *Necronomicon* controversy with us, and the International Guild of Occult Sciences deserves credit for being quicker than a camel caravan with our orders. Gabriel Landini, Jim Reeds, Rene Zandbergen, and the other members of the voynich-l mailing list provided help with that part of the manuscript. Steven Anderson sent us *The History of the Necronomicon and the Sword* at the last minute, and Dan Clore has been a source of both criticism and inspiration.

Special thanks go to my family, Monika Bolino, Donovan Loucks, Steven Kaye, Steven Marc Harris (who thought I'd leave him out again), and John Wisdom Gonce, who all waited anxiously for the appearance of this book.

John Wisdom Gonce III:

Thanks to all those without whom this book would never have been. Thanks to the Old Gent from Providence, Grandpa E'ch-Pi-El, whose work has enriched my life and whose ghost has politely hounded me to clear his name for the past few years. To the staff of Hollywood Wholesale, to Craig Ledbetter of European Trash Cinema, to Ken Kaffke, to Sam Mallory at Blockbuster, to Chris at Tower, and to Richard Cornwell for helping me to find movies. Thanks to Bernadette Hyner of the German Language Department at Vanderbilt University. Thanks to the Interlibrary Loan Department of the Metropolitan Nashville/Ben West Library, and to the Heard Library at Vanderbilt University for helping me find forbidden books and hidden lore. Thanks to Toren Atkinson for his splendid artwork. Thanks to Roy and Kate Cox, and all elements of the Freelancers Jousting Company for releasing me from my 1996 contract. (Maybe the pen really is mightier than the sword—or the lance.) To Mr. Kenneth Grant for allowing me to reprint and quote from his works extensively.

Thanks to those who went beyond mere assistance and beyond the usual boundaries of friendship. To my parents, John Wisdom Gonce II and Leone Stubblefield Gonce, who lost their lives at the time this book was being born. To Lord Ganesha. To Lady Inanna. To Tish Gattis and those crafty Wise Ones who hang out at the Goddess and the Moon. To Pagan Dave, Barbara Lutz, and all those who helped with "The Armitage Working." (I don't see any tentacles yet, thank the Goddess!) To Lishtar, Priestess of Inanna, and Webmistress of Gateways to Babylon, for her tireless encouragement and for her friendship. To Ian Corrigan and the good folk who manage the Starwood Festival for being kind enough to invite us to speak there. To Donald Tyson for his generosity, for his faith in this project, and for writing the preface to this book. To Audrey. To the artist James Christopher. To Cameron Marshall— here's to those wee hours at Kinko's. To Liz Parrot, for her legal skills and her friendship. To Tony Kail of the Subculture Project for his valuable research assistance. To all elements of the local SE2600, especially to Dr. Jonnyx, Maverick, Rattle, Decius, Jonnydarke, and Cybervox. To Mrs. Frankie Blakely for all her help. To Day Star*, Priestess of Inanna, for helping me beat the deadliest of deadlines. To Richard L. Cornwell for inspiration from an age of heroes. To Marty McTier. To my techsupport team of Dru Myers, Scott Nelson, and Matt Coleman; their computer skills are valuable, but their friendship is priceless. Special thanks go to my long-suffering collaborator Daniel Harms, and to Dru Myers, who was part of this project before it became a book. These are the friends and the tribes who stood by me in my darkest hours. Without them, Daniel and I would have stood alone against an empire of lies. May all of the above triumph over all that lurks below.

PART ONE

The *Necronomicon* and Literature

H. P. Lovecraft and the *Necronomicon*
—Daniel Harms

1

As for the Necronomicon, it appears that
Lovecraft used it as a back door or postern gate to
realms of wonder and myth . . .
—FRITZ LEIBER[1]

The *Necronomicon* has become one of the most controversial books of the 20th century. People have debated its existence for decades, and there seems to be no end in sight to the confusion. In the middle of this controversy lies H. P. Lovecraft (1890–1937), a horror writer who gained unbelievable popularity after his death, and is even considered Poe's equal in the genre.

Despite the fact that Lovecraft left dozens of stories and tens of thousands of letters behind him, he is perhaps one of the most poorly understood authors of our time. Some critics have labeled him as "sick" and decadent, though he believed the only true way to cope with an uncaring universe was to follow traditional standards of morality and taste. Others have portrayed him as an occultist and magician, but he was an absolute materialist in every sense of the word. He has been criticized for his racist, almost paranoid, attitudes by those quick to forget that such views, if not particularly enlightened, were the norm for many in his time and place. In many ways, Lovecraft was the most human of humans. His unpopular stances and eccentricities are more than equaled by his literary gifts and the kindness he displayed toward others. Any consideration of the *Necronomicon* must begin with an analysis of this most unusual of men.

The Writer's Early Life

Howard Phillips Lovecraft was born to Sara Susan Phillips Lovecraft and Winfield Scott Lovecraft on 20 August 1890. His mother was the middle of three sisters and came from one of Providence's most distinguished families. Winfield was a traveling sales representative from Rochester, New York, who worked for a silverware company.[2] Howard was their only child. The couple had been married for a year when Howard was born, and they planned to build a house in Auburndale, Massachusetts.

This vision of domestic tranquillity was not to be. On 21 April 1893, Winfield had a nervous breakdown in a Chicago hotel room, running about and shouting that the maid had been rude to him and that his wife was being assaulted on the floor above. He was committed to Providence's Butler Hospital, where he died five years later. Though the cause of his illness is unknown, current medical knowledge has established a probable diagnosis of syphilis. Despite theories to the contrary, no evidence exists that he passed the disease on to Susie and Howard.

Lovecraft's father has become the center of an unusual rumor. According to an essay by Colin Wilson,[3] Winfield Lovecraft had been a member of an Egyptian Freemason lodge that entrusted him with secret lore—including information about the *Necronomicon*. After becoming insane, Winfield allegedly spent a great deal of time at home, and in his ramblings, it is alleged, he revealed his secret knowledge to Howard. The young author supposedly later found some magickal manuscripts among his father's papers, and used them as inspiration for his writing. Wilson has since admitted that this is a fabrication, but it is one that has circulated for so long that it is generally accepted as true.

Can any of this be possible? It is not known whether Lovecraft's father was a Freemason. However, Lovecraft mentions that his maternal grandfather, Whipple Phillips, founded a Masonic lodge in the town of Greene (then Coffin's Corner), Rhode Island.[4] This raises the possibility that Winfield was himself a Mason—though many businessmen throughout U.S. history could make that claim. Even if he had been a Mason, however, Winfield's age and undistinguished occupation (which required him to be out of town for great stretches of time) make it unlikely that a secret society trusted him with highly dangerous information. Even if we assume, for the moment, that Winfield had such information, he could hardly have passed it on to Howard, as he was committed to an asylum soon after his breakdown. Lovecraft later stated that he "was never in a hospital till 1924,"[5] even as a visitor, and his letters show that he did not know the nature of his father's illness. Finally, Lovecraft seems to have been unfamiliar with Freemasonry, and no one has found any link between his writing and its beliefs and practices.

After his father was committed, Howard went with his mother to live with her father, Whipple Phillips. Phillips became a father figure to Howard and did much to encourage his interests in literature and science. His mother became overprotective, even following Howard down the street when he rode his bicycle. Perhaps to please both of them, Howard spent much of his childhood reading his way through his grandfather's library. Those who expect Lovecraft's early reading fare to be filled with horror and black magick will be surprised. Lovecraft read a vast range of books, ranging from the *Iliad* to detective dime novels. He especially liked the works of such 18th-century authors as Alexander Pope and Jonathan Swift, and gained a love for that period that lasted for the rest of his life. Still, it may be possible to find the roots of the *Necronomicon* in his grandfather's library.

When Lovecraft was five, he encountered the *Thousand and One Nights*. Inspired by its tales of Arabian thieves and sorcerers, he declared himself a Muslim and convinced his mother to buy a number of Middle Eastern objects. During this period, he adopted the name "Abdul Alhazred," either through his own invention or that of Alfred Baker, the family lawyer.[6] Some say that this name was inspired by the Hazards, an old Providence family known to Lovecraft's relatives.[7] It could also be that "Alhazred" was a pun on "All-Has-Read," which seems fitting, given Lovecraft's precocious reading. It should be noted that "Alhazred" is not even a proper Arabic name and means nothing in that language whatsoever. Lovecraft was, nonetheless, so taken with it that, twenty-five years later, he named the *Necronomicon*'s author "Abdul Alhazred."[8]

Donald Eric Kessler has suggested another source from this library as an inspiration for the *Necronomicon*. The key may lie in this passage from Lovecraft's letters:

> When I was 6 or 7 I used to be tormented constantly with a peculiar type of recurrent nightmare in which a monstrous race of entities (called by me "Night-Gaunts" ...) used to snatch me up by the stomach ... and carry me off through infinite leagues of black air over the towers of dead and horrible cities ... The "night-gaunts" were black, lean, rubbery things with bared, barbed tails, bat-wings and no faces at all. Undoubtedly I derived the image from the jumbled memory of Dore's drawings (largely the illustrations to *Paradise Lost*) which fascinated me in waking hours.[9]

For more than a year, Lovecraft was terrified of the night-gaunts, and desperately attempted to stay awake each night to avoid them.[10] These nightmares eventually tapered off by the age of eight and ceased entirely when he was ten or eleven,[11] but the terror remained with him for years afterward. His dream-monsters later appeared in such works as the sonnet "Night-Gaunts" and "The Dream-Quest of Unknown Kadath."

The illustrator of this book, Gustave Doré (1832–83), was tremendously popular and known for his woodcuts. Cassell and Company of London published his edition of John Milton's poem *Paradise Lost* in 1866.[12] The origin of Lovecraft's night-gaunts may be seen in such plates as "Satan's Council," which depicts a horde of winged demons with their faces averted from the observer's view. This book, which both fascinated and horrified Lovecraft, may indeed have served as a template for the *Necronomicon*.

This possibility aside, Lovecraft's first experience with the darker side of fiction came at the age of eight, when he discovered Edgar Allan Poe (1809–49). Not only was Poe's vision compelling to Lovecraft, his interest must have been strengthened when he found that Poe had lived in his beloved Providence for a short time. Lovecraft's attraction to Poe continued throughout his life.

Those looking for the *Necronomicon* may find more hints of it in Poe's work. As Lovecraft himself observed in *Supernatural Horror in Literature*, the Gothic tradition, in which old crumbling manuscripts were important plot elements, was a major influence on Poe. In *The Fall of the House of Usher*, the narrator and Roderick Usher spend much of their time reading a library of forbidden lore:

> We pored together over such works as the Ververt et Chartreuse of Gresset; the Belphegor of Machiavelli; the Heaven and Hell of Swedenborg; the Subterranean Voyage of Nicholas Klimm by Holberg; the Chiromancy of Robert Flud, of Jean D'Indagine, and of De la Chambre, the Journey into the Blue Distance of Tieck; and the City of the Sun of Campanella. One favorite volume was a small octavo edition of the *Directorium Inquisitorum*, by the Dominican Eymeric de Gironne; and there were passages in Pomponius Mela, about the old African Satyrs and Aegipans, over which Usher would sit dreaming for hours. His chief delight, however, was found in the perusal of an exceedingly rare and curious book in quarto Gothic— the manual of a forgotten church—the *Vigiliae Mortuorum secundum Chorum Ecclesiae Maguntinae*.[13]

All of these books are real, yet this reads much like one of the libraries Lovecraft later described in his fiction. The last book is especially interesting, as one author has translated its title as "Vigils for the dead according to the use of the church of Mainz."[14] Indeed, the narrator remarks on "the wild ritual of this work, and of its probable influence" on Roderick Usher.[15] A book dealing with the dead that contains strange rites—could this be the inspiration for the *Necronomicon*? There is no way of telling, but Lovecraft did consider the story one of his favorites.

Coming of Age

Lovecraft's grandfather died in 1904, and Lovecraft, his mother, and his two aunts were forced to leave their ancestral home. The family entered a state of genteel poverty, living off a few of Whipple Phillips's investments and their dwindling bank account— going to work would have cost the survivors the respect of their peers, a commodity that was all-important for the family. Lovecraft considered this as his fall from Paradise, and it left him feeling aimless and depressed. Though Lovecraft later claimed he completed high school, he never did so due to a series of physical and emotional "breakdowns."[16] He did write during this time—mostly poetry with a few short stories— but it was not until he joined the amateur press in 1914 that his literary career took off.

The amateur press movement is a minor footnote in literary history, yet it attracted a large number of members. Through the amateur press, aspiring authors could publish their work—whether essays, articles, fiction, or poetry—in a number of member-edited journals. In doing so, they hoped to receive praise and advice on improving their writing, most often in that order. Lovecraft was invited to join after a spirited defense of his literary tastes in the letters column of the fiction magazine *Argosy*, and he quickly became friends with many of its members, including the poet Samuel Loveman and the political activist James Morton. Lovecraft was soon publishing his own journal, *The Conservative*, and publishing a few short stories in others' magazines.

One of these stories, "The Statement of Randolph Carter" (written in 1919), has been hailed as the *Necronomicon*'s first appearance. The title character is a student of the mystic Harley Warren. Warren owns a "fiend-inspired book . . . written in characters whose like [he] never saw again."[17] Though George T. Wetzel proposed that this book is the *Necronomicon*,[18] S. T. Joshi points out that the book came from India and, according to the narrator, cannot be in Arabic, Greek, Latin, or English—the four languages in which the *Necronomicon* is found in later sources.[19] As a result, his book is not the *Necronomicon*, but it may have been a literary ancestor of sorts. Warren and Carter find horror when they follow the book's hints to a graveyard in the dead of night.

In the same year, Lovecraft made an unusual note in his commonplace book. As do many authors, Lovecraft kept a notebook of facts, anecdotes, and brief plots he might use in his stories. On looking over a reprint of this book, I found an entry dated 1919 that said simply, "Book or MS. too horrible to read—warned against reading it—someone reads and is found dead. Haverhill incident."[20] Haverhill is a town in Massachusetts, and Lovecraft is known to have had a friend there.[21] I have yet to hear, however, of any event or rumor fitting this description. It is of arguable significance, as no one in Lovecraft's stories dies from reading the *Necronomicon*, but it is an intriguing possibility that bears investigation.

The *Necronomicon* itself is first quoted in "The Nameless City," which appeared in the amateur press magazine *Wolverine* in November 1921. Here, an explorer makes a solitary journey to a lost city in the Arabian desert. Following low-ceilinged tunnels deep underground, he finds a number of mummified reptilian beings and murals depicting the decline of the city as the desert grew around it and outsiders attacked its people. The explorer denies what is obvious—that these beings built the city—until he reaches the lowest level, where he spies the ghosts of its former inhabitants.

As our narrator approaches the city, he observes that

> . . . it was of this place that Abdul Alhazred the mad poet dreamed on the
> night before he sang his unexplainable couplet:
>> "That is not dead which can eternal lie,
>> And with strange aeons even death may die."[22]

Though Lovecraft never mentions the *Necronomicon* by name, he does build up an atmosphere of mystery and horror around its author—in actuality, Lovecraft's playname brought to life.

While exploring the city, the narrator remembers passages from his outré reading, including "sentences from Alhazred the Mad Arab, paragraphs from the apocryphal nightmares of Damascius, and infamous lines from the delirious *Image du Monde* of Gauthier de Metz."[23] Damascius and de Metz are real authors, while Alhazred is Lovecraft's creation. This demonstrates one of the keys to Lovecraft's success as a horror writer: his ability to blend reality with fiction so thoroughly that readers are unsure which is which, making them willing to accept his creations as facts. Lovecraft later told his fellow writer Clark Ashton Smith why he did so:

> My own rule is that no weird story can truly produce terror unless it is devised with all the care & verisimilitude of an actual hoax. The author must forget all about "short story technique," & build up a stark simple account, full of homely corroborative details, just as if he were actually trying to "put across" a deception in real life . . . as carefully as a crooked witness prepares a line of testimony with cross-examining lawyers in his mind. I take the place of the lawyers now & then—finding false spots in the original testimony, & thereupon rearranging details & motivations with a greater care for probability.[24]

As other authors have demonstrated, this is not the only way to write a horror story, yet Lovecraft mastered this technique. This is why the *Necronomicon* has taken such a hold on so many people's imagination.

The Creation of the *Necronomicon*

While the death of Lovecraft's mother in 1921 saddened him, Lovecraft was ready to move on. The many friendships he had formed in the amateur press circles heartened him considerably. His stories and articles garnered him considerable status in these circles, and soon his friends encouraged him to become a professional writer. The market for Lovecraft's preferred subjects was much smaller than it is today, but, in 1923, Lovecraft found his niche at *Weird Tales*. *Weird Tales* was one of the first magazines to specialize in science fiction and horror. It would later attract many rising stars in the field, including Ray Bradbury and Robert Bloch. Though Lovecraft later submitted stories to other magazines, he gave most of his business to *Weird Tales*. In April 1923, Lovecraft sent five stories to the magazine. One of these was "The Hound," the first story to feature the *Necronomicon*.

"The Hound" tells of two young men who have plumbed the depths of evil in art, literature, and deed. Having exhausted all legal avenues to satiate their passions, they decide to take up grave-robbing, bearing their grisly trophies home to a museum in their basement. The pair visit Holland to dig up the body of a condemned wizard and find an amulet depicting a winged hound on the corpse. The figure is not unfamiliar to them:

> Alien it indeed was to all art and literature which sane and balanced readers know, but we recognized it as the thing hinted of in the forbidden *Necronomicon* of the mad Arab Abdul Alhazred; the ghastly soul-symbol of the corpse-eating cult of inaccessible Leng, in Central Asia. All too well did we trace the sinister lineaments described by the old Arab daemonologist;

lineaments, he wrote, drawn from some obscure supernatural manifestation of the souls of those who vexed and gnawed at the dead.[25]

The two thieves own a copy of the *Necronomicon*, and they consult it upon their return, reading a great deal "about [the amulet's] properties, and about the relation of ghosts' souls to the objects it symbolized . . . "[26] In the end, none of the book's dark lore does the pair any good. The wizard's corpse, melded with a cloud of bats into a houndlike monster, is soon howling outside their mansion. The Thing tears apart one of the graverobbers, and the other decides to kill himself to escape its vengeance. Lovecraft tells the story in an overblown, Poe-like style, and the text is filled with so many references to other horror writers' works that some critics call it a parody.[27]

What was Lovecraft's inspiration for the name *Necronomicon*? Lovecraft later claimed that he first heard the name in a dream. This is not surprising; many of Lovecraft's stories had their roots in dreams, even though he often modified them to suit his literary needs. Lovecraft scholar George T. Wetzel mentions one source of inspiration: the *Astronomicon*, an unfinished astronomical poem by the 1st-century Roman poet Marcus Manilius. Lovecraft had read Manilius's poem as early as 1915, as he quotes it in an amateur astronomy column he wrote for the *Asheville Gazette-News*.[28] It is likely that Lovecraft's subconscious mind filtered this knowledge to create the book's title.

Once Lovecraft dreamed the book's Greek title, he attempted to translate it. Lovecraft's Greek was less than perfect, however, and he decided that "Necronomicon" meant "An Image [or Picture] of the Law of the Dead."[29] Apparently, the narrator in "The Hound" has broken one of these laws and must pay the penalty. Since then, almost every Lovecraft commentator has offered their own translation, ranging from *Guide to the Regions of the Dead*[30] to *The Book of the Laws/Advocate [Lawyer] of the (Violently) Dead*.[31] The difficulty comes with the "nom" section of the word, which may be interpreted in a number of ways. The most accurate translation is probably S. T. Joshi's: *A Consideration of the Dead*.[32] Still, Lovecraft's vision of the *Necronomicon* would take it far from the implications of its title.

If the *Necronomicon* is Greek, however, why did Lovecraft attribute it to the "mad Arab Abdul Alhazred"? The simple answer is that Lovecraft was fond of Abdul and wanted to put him into another story. As a book-lover and historian, Lovecraft knew that many Greek books were later translated and retitled in Arabic, so he turned the tables in a whimsical sense of fair play.[33] He never explained this in "The Hound." For a man who could make a resurrected wizard's corpse believable, however, it was not difficult to distract readers from this historical sleight-of-hand.

Returning to "The Hound," note that the *Necronomicon* is not yet a book of spells.[34] It contains no incantations to call or ward off the horror, but merely states the significance of the amulet and thereby informs the characters of their doom. The exact nature of the book is left uncertain. Alhazred is described as a "demonologist," one who studies and catalogs demons, but this has been a profession of wizards and clergymen alike. Lovecraft expands on this information in later tales.

The Development of a Legend

Lovecraft's next *Necronomicon* story was "The Festival" (1923). The hero walks to Kingsport, Massachusetts to attend his family's age-old Yuletide festivities. At his ancestors' colonial house, he finds a mute old man who invites him to wait inside until the festival begins. The narrator sees a pile of books on a table and is shocked when he looks through them:

> [t]hey included old Morryster's wild *Marvells of Science*, the terrible
> *Saduscismus Triumphatus* of Joseph Glanvil, published in 1681, the shock-
> ing *Daemonolatreia* of Remigius, printed in 1595 at Lyons, and worst of all,
> the unmentionable *Necronomicon* of the mad Arab Abdul Alhazred, in
> Olaus Wormius' forbidden Latin translation; a book which I had never
> seen, but of which I had heard monstrous things whispered.[35]

Here, Lovecraft groups the *Necronomicon* with three other books. Two of them, Joseph Glanvil's *Saduscismus Triumphatus* ("Triumph of the Sadducees," referring to a Biblical sect that denied the existence of the soul) and the *Daemonolatreia* ("Demon-Worship") of Nicolas Remy ("Remigius"), are churchmen's accounts of the doings of witches and wizards and how these evil people may be detected and punished. In fact, Remy (1530–1612) was one of the most infamous witch-hunters of all time, and Glanvil (1636–80) was a defender of witchcraft beliefs during the Age of Reason. By its association with these two books, we might assume that the *Necronomicon* is a treatise on witchcraft.

The first book mentioned, Morryster's *Marvells of Science*, is not a real book at all. It was the creation of the journalist and horror writer Ambrose Bierce (1842–1914?) for his story "The Man and the Snake," which tells of a snake that hypnotizes its prey. Bierce used this sort of invention in his stories "The Death of Halpin Frayser" and "An Inhabitant of Carcosa," both of which are introduced with a quote from the philosopher "Hali." This citation of imaginary people and books may have convinced Lovecraft to provide lengthy quotes from the *Necronomicon* in his stories.

The main character of "The Festival" reads the *Necronomicon* for some time. At the time for celebration, his host picks up the book and escorts the narrator to a church on a hill. During the blasphemous rites that follow, the worshipers display "groveling obeisance"[36] whenever the book is held aloft. The narrator flees the ceremony after he finds that his host's face is nothing more than a mask. He turns up in the bay outside Kingsport and is confined in the hospital at the soon-to-be-infamous Miskatonic University. The library at that school has a copy of the book, so his doctors show it to him to prove that he had only imagined the rites. Instead, he finds the same quote that he had read in Kingsport:

"The nethermost caverns," wrote the mad Arab, "are not for the fathoming of eyes that see; for their marvels are strange and terrific. Cursed the ground where dead thoughts live new and oddly bodied, and evil the mind that is held by no head. Wisely did Ibn Schacabao say, that happy is the tomb where no wizard hath lain, and happy is the town at night whose wizards are all ashes. For it is of old rumour that the soul of the devil-bought hastes not from his charnel clay, but fats and instructs the very worm that gnaws; till out of corruption horrid life springs, and the dull scavengers of earth wax crafty to vex it and swell monstrous to plague it. Great holes secretly are digged where earth's pores ought to suffice, and things have learnt to walk which ought to crawl."[37]

Thus, Lovecraft continues to develop the *Necronomicon*'s history. In "The Festival," he tells us of Olaus Wormius' Latin translation, and that a copy exists in the (fictional) Miskatonic University Library. Yet Lovecraft wavers on the book's exact nature. As Robert M. Price observes, it is difficult to tell whether this book is meant to be a witch-finder's manual or a scripture for the cult.[38]

The New York Sojourn

It was in 1924 that Lovecraft surprised many of his friends by marrying. Sonia Greene was a fellow member of the amateur press movement whom Lovecraft had known for some years. The two moved to New York; Sonia started a hat shop while Lovecraft sought work. The move did have its advantages—it brought Lovecraft near to many of his friends from the amateur press, and he was able to explore the libraries, museums, and back alleys of the city to his heart's content. Yet Lovecraft's New York period was filled with disappointments. His self-effacing and shy personality, as well as his lack of experience, kept him from finding any sort of steady work. He also felt intensely nostalgic for Providence, where he had spent his entire life. He wrote little fiction while in New York, and some of the pieces that survive ("He," "The Horror at Red Hook") show him at his xenophobic worst, filled with decaying buildings and cults of evil foreigners.

Two years later, Lovecraft separated from Sonia and moved back to Providence. He seems to have seen New York and his marriage as personal defeats. He had few kind things to say about the city, and rarely mentioned Sonia thereafter in his letters. At the same time, his return to Providence sparked a period of great creativity. In the next few years, he turned out several of his best short stories, as well as two novel-length pieces that were only published after his death.

Lovecraft's next *Necronomicon* piece, "The Descendant" (1926?), was probably one of these post–New York works. It was never finished, but contains some important information for those interested in the book. The narrator, who is in search of the *Necronomicon*, learns that the churches and governments of the world have destroyed most copies. He is told that only five remain in various libraries around the world. Then he happens to find an Olaus Wormius edition at a used-book store in London! He takes it to Lord Northam, an aged neighbor of his, for assistance in translation. Northam reacts with great fear and starts to discuss his own experiences with the book—including a trip to the Nameless City! Lovecraft stops the story before we learn why Lord Northam found the book so important. Nevertheless, he makes use of the "facts" from this story in later works.

In "The Call of Cthulhu" (1926), one of Lovecraft's most famous stories, he elaborates on the *Necronomicon*'s link to the cults of the "Old Ones" hinted at in "The Festival." An anthropologist comes into possession of the notes of a late uncle, George Gammell Angell, who was investigating the cult of the God "Cthulhu." At one point, Angell talks to a police detective who participated in a police raid on a cult meeting in the bayous of Louisiana. The captured members claimed that the *Necronomicon*'s passages, and especially the poem from "The Nameless City," refer to their sleeping God Cthulhu, who lies in the corpse-city of R'lyeh beneath the Pacific Ocean. Reading this along with "The Festival," we might assume that Alhazred was a demonologist or clergyman who was a secret cultist, hiding messages to his fellows in his work. Still, Lovecraft made yet another change in his focus that would render this assumption false.

Lovecraft: Occult Delver?

One of the most controversial subjects in Lovecraft scholarship is his knowledge of the occult. Some authors downplay any such influence upon his work, and others make Lovecraft into a magician with access to vast knowledge of forbidden lore. Before we examine the accuracy of these viewpoints, we should note that Lovecraft himself had no belief in any aspect of occultism or parapsychology. "I am, indeed, an absolute materialist so far as actual belief goes; with not a shred of credence in any form of supernaturalism," he confessed in a letter to his friend Clark Ashton Smith written in 1925.[39] As we will show, however, this does not mean Lovecraft was not aware of such material.

Lovecraft did learn about a few occult subjects early in his career. In 1914, for example, he mounted an attack upon astrology in a local newspaper, and thereby gained some background in the subject.[40] The Salem witch trials held a special fascination for him, and he was especially fond of the works of Cotton Mather. Mather (1663–1728) was the New England minister who wrote accounts of witch trials, ghostly appearances, and other marvelous occurrences in his *Magnalia Christi Americana*, a copy of which was the crown jewel of Lovecraft's library. Still, Lovecraft's understanding of the occult was spotty at best—at least until 1925, three years after he had created the *Necronomicon*.

It was on October 9th of that year that Lovecraft wrote to Clark Ashton Smith to ask for help. Following the lead of such horror writers as Algernon Blackwood, he had been trying to make references to conventional occultism in his work and thereby add to the horrific atmosphere. Lovecraft's "The Horror at Red Hook," a tale of black magick in modern New York, had shown how incomplete his knowledge of magick and other subjects was. In the end, he resorted to referring to a few conventional demons and copying his devil worshipers' all-important spells and prayers from the *Encyclopedia Britannica*'s article on magic. After confessing to Smith that he was "appallingly ignorant"[41] of such things, he went on to say:

> I'd like to draw on less obvious sources if I knew of the right reservoirs to tap. Do you know of any good works on magick & dark mysteries which might furnish fitting ideas & formulae? For example—are there any good translations of any mediaeval necromancers with directions for raising spirits, invoking Lucifer, & all that sort of thing?[42]

From this passage, it is clear Lovecraft had little contact with any sort of magickal literature at this time. He may, however, have had a pressing motivation for learning about the subject. A letter to Wilfred Branch Talman[43] indicates that he was gathering information on magick and witchcraft for an article to be cowritten with the conjuror Harry Houdini. Lovecraft had ghostwritten the story "Under the Pyramids" for the popular escape artist, and the two had also collaborated on a series of articles on astrology. With the assistance of Providence author C. M. Eddy, the two began *The Cancer of Superstition*, of which only a few chapters were completed. Houdini died before the project could be completed, but I believe that this interest was important for the *Necronomicon*'s development.

Unfortunately, we cannot be absolutely sure what Lovecraft read after his return from New York. He rarely saved the letters he received, so any replies from Smith or his other friends have been lost.[44] We do know that he read such classics as Frazer's *The Golden Bough* and Margaret Murray's *The Witch-Cult in Western Europe*, but neither of these includes references to books that might have inspired the *Necronomicon*'s transformation. Most of the information we have on Lovecraft's occult readings comes years later. In a list of his library's contents, sent to Robert Bloch in 1933, he provided a list of his works on mythology and the occult,[45] none of which seem applicable to our project. Finally, in 1936, he responded to a question from Willis Conover on the same subject:

> If you want to see what the actual "magical" rites and incantations of antiquity and the Middle Ages were like, get the works of Waite—especially his *Black Magic* and *History of Magic*. . . . Other stuff can be found in Waite's translations of "Eliphas Levi." There is a more popular history of sorcery by "Sax Rohmer" (Arthur Sarsfield Ward), whose title I forget.[46]

Arthur Edward Waite (1857–c. 1940), the first author Lovecraft mentions, was a one-time member of the Hermetic Order of the Golden Dawn, an occult organization that may have been the most influential of modern times. Eliphas Levi (1810–75) was the pseudonym of the French magician Alphonse Constant, and Sax Rohmer (1883–1959) was a fiction writer and amateur occultist who created the criminal mastermind

Fu Manchu. This may seem to provide us with the list we need, but Lovecraft in fact did most of his occult reading after 1933, when the New York amateur H. C. Koenig made his own library available to him.[47] In 1926, Lovecraft did tell Talman that he could not find "the Waite book,"[48] without referring to the one he sought.

Though some may consider this to be a stretch, this occult reading may have been the impetus for another shift in Lovecraft's idea of the *Necronomicon*.[49] Previously, the *Necronomicon* held the lore of demons and ghosts, but, as "The Hound" shows, it did not provide a means to deal with them. In his next few stories, Lovecraft portrays the book more as a grimoire, or book of spells, such as the *Key of Solomon the King* or the *Armadel*. These books, which have circulated in the Western world for millennia, are almost always of spurious origin, were often suppressed, and are the subject of chilling anecdotes of the misfortunes that befell those who tampered with them. Around this time, the *Necronomicon* starts to take on these same qualities.

One of the longest pieces Lovecraft wrote at this time is his novel *The Case of Charles Dexter Ward*. A young scholar from Providence, Ward discovers the secret history of his pre–Revolutionary War ancestor, the merchant Joseph Curwen. Curwen's dabbling in sorcery became a matter of rumor in Rhode Island, partly due to the evidence of the wealthy townsman John Merritt. Curwen invites Merritt to his lab, where he finds a wide variety of books by magicians such as Albertus Magnus and Hermes Trismegistus. The crowning horror comes when he takes down the book "Qanoon-e-Islam"[50] and finds that the cover conceals

> the forbidden *Necronomicon* of the mad Arab Abdul Alhazred, of which
> he had heard such monstrous things whispered some years previously
> after the exposure of nameless rites at the strange little fishing village of
> Kingsport.[51]

This is, of course, a reference to "The Festival." Soon thereafter, a committee of prominent men intercept Curwen's correspondence to determine his motives. According to these letters, he and two other magicians used sorcerous information from the *Necronomicon*'s seventh book to resurrect the dead, learning secrets for blackmail or occult power. Their suspicions confirmed, the committee organizes a midnight raid and kills Curwen in his laboratory. Yet Ward soon finds that the affair is not over.

This story proves that Lovecraft was somewhat successful in his search for occult material. At one point, Lovecraft quotes two incantations his sorcerer uses to attack his enemies. These bear striking resemblance to those on a single page in Waite's *Mysteries of Magic*, a translation of excerpts from Levi's work.[52] Since "Ward" was finished on 1 March 1927, we know that Lovecraft had read at least one of the books he sought.

I should end this discussion on a note of caution. Despite my emphasis here on Lovecraft's occult readings, they by no means make him an expert on the subject. Most of the works he read are popularized books that play up the lurid side of occultism. As his letters show, his knowledge of other subjects—history, architecture, literature, chemistry, politics and others—was encyclopedic. Comparatively, Lovecraft did not read much occult literature—he had no money to spend on it! Even after reading these books, Lovecraft never wavered from a belief in a universe without supernatural forces of any kind.

The Legend Comes to Life

In 1927, Lovecraft drew up his "History of the *Necronomicon*," a pseudo-scholarly essay detailing the book's history, so he could keep his "facts" straight in his stories. His first notes on the subject appear in a letter to Clark Ashton Smith on 27 November 1927.[53] Lovecraft altered a few points, possibly at Smith's suggestion.

According to the "History," Abdul Alhazred was a well-traveled poet from Sanaa, the capital of the present-day Republic of Yemen. Alhazred visited the ruins of Babylon and Memphis, and put much of their lore into his book *Al Azif. Azif* (which Lovecraft used only once, in a revision of Adolphe de Castro's "The Last Test") refers to the buzzing of insects thought to be the calls of djinn, or spirits, an idea that was taken from a footnote in Samuel Beckford's pseudo-Arabian epic, *Vathek*.[54] In 738, an invisible monster tore Alhazred apart in Damascus, but his book survived. The (fictional) Byzantine scholar Theodorus Philetas translated the book into Greek in 950, providing the title *Necronomicon*. In 1228, Olaus Wormius made a Latin translation, which is the most common version. The Greek edition was published in Italy in the 16th century, and the Latin translation was printed twice, once in 15th-century Germany and again in 17th-century Spain.[55]

Despite its multiple printings, the book's subject matter made it a target of ecclesiastical and governmental censorship. Patriarch Michael of Constantinople burned many copies, and Pope Gregory IX banned it in 1232. Though a few copies of the Latin translations still exist in libraries and private collections, all of the Arabic and Greek editions were lost or destroyed.[56] All of this is told in a dry, scholarly style with no hint of humor.

Lovecraft's "scholarship" seems impressive, but it has its flaws. In his letter to Smith, Lovecraft states that Pope Gregory IX placed the book on the *Index Expurgatorius*, a list of banned literature not compiled until centuries after that pope's reign. Lovecraft does not include this in the final essay, and might have caught the error beforehand. A more glaring error comes in his discussion of the Latin translator, Olaus Wormius. A Danish physician of that name did exist—but he was not born until 1588. As S. T. Joshi has pointed out, this is probably the result of Lovecraft's misreading of a passage in Hugh Blair's *A Critical Dissertation on the Poems of Ossian*.[57]

Lovecraft wrote these notes to keep his *Necronomicon* background straight for his fiction, but it is interesting that he never treated any of his other fictional books or characters in this way. If Lovecraft had found Arthur Waite's *The Book of Black Magic and of Pacts* (1898), it may have inpired him to write his "History." Waite's book includes profiles of several of the most infamous grimoires, including their publication histories, locations of copies, and their contents. At any rate, the notes were probably never intended for publication, as Lovecraft sent them to interested colleagues on the front and back of an old letter[58] and made no effort to publicize their contents. The essay was printed after his death, and has appeared often since then.

In his next story, "The Dunwich Horror" (1928), Lovecraft made full use of his new information on the *Necronomicon*. The story begins with the tale of Wilbur Whateley, a precocious young man from the town of Dunwich, Massachusetts. Wilbur's grandfather is a curious old man, a reputed sorcerer who boards up the attic of his house after Wilbur is born. On his deathbed, Old Whateley raves to Wilbur to "open the gates to Yog-Sothoth with the long chant that ye'll find on page 751 *of the complete edition.*"[59] This "complete edition," it turns out, is a reference to the *Necronomicon*.

Wilbur does have a copy of the Elizabethan wizard John Dee's English translation of the book, but this is not enough for his purposes. He finds that there are copies at the Bibliothèque Nationale in Paris, the British Museum, the Widener Library at Harvard, the University of Buenos Aires, and, of course, Miskatonic University in Arkham, Massachusetts. Since the latter is closest, he decides to try there first. The aged librarian Henry Armitage lets him see the book, and is chilled when he reads one of its passages:

> "Nor is it to be thought," ran the text as Armitage mentally translated it, "that man is either the oldest or the last of earth's masters, or that the common bulk of life and substance walks alone. The Old Ones were, the Old Ones are, and the Old Ones shall be. Not in the spaces we know, but between them, They walk serene and primal, undimensioned and to us unseen. *Yog-Sothoth* knows the gate. *Yog-Sothoth* is the gate. *Yog-Sothoth* is the key and guardian of the gate. Past, present, and future, all are one in *Yog-Sothoth*. He knows where the Old Ones broke through of old, and where They shall break through again. He knows where They have trod earth's fields, and where They still tread them, and why no one can behold Them as They tread. By their smell can men sometimes know Them near, but of Their semblance can no man know, saving only in the features of those They have begotten on mankind; and of those are there many sorts, differing in likeness from man's truest eidolon to that shape without sight or substance which is Them. They walk unseen and foul in lonely places where the Words have been spoken and the Rites howled through at their Seasons. The wind gibbers with Their voices, and the earth mutters with Their consciousness. Kadath in the cold waste hath known them, and what man knows Kadath? The ice desert of the South and the sunken isles of Ocean hold stones whereon Their seal is engraven, but who hath seen the deep frozen city or the sealed tower long garlanded with seaweed and barnacles? Great Cthulhu is Their cousin, yet can he spy Them only dimly. *Iä! Shub-*

Niggurath! As a foulness shall ye know Them. Their hand is at your throats, yet ye see Them not; and Their habitation is even one with your guarded threshold. *Yog-Sothoth* is the key to the gate, whereby the spheres meet. Man rules now where They ruled once; They shall soon rule where man rules now. After summer is winter, and after winter summer. They wait patient and potent, for here shall They rule again."[60]

Whateley asks Armitage if he can take the *Necronomicon* out of the library, but Wilbur's appearance and behavior disturb the librarian, who refuses even to allow Wilbur to copy passages from the book. Later, Wilbur returns to Miskatonic University to steal the book, but a guard dog kills him and his corpse dissolves, revealing his inhuman nature. Shortly thereafter, the Whateley house explodes as the creature Wilbur had been keeping rampages through the Dunwich countryside. Armitage decides to fight fire with fire, and uses the incantations from the *Necronomicon* and Remy's *Daemonolatreia* in an attempt to dispel the horror.

Keen-eyed readers will notice one addition to the *Necronomicon* myth here—Doctor John Dee's English translation of the book. John Dee (1527–1608) was a real occultist who sometimes gave astrological advice to Queen Elizabeth. He is known for his purported conversations with spirits, from whom he transcribed the angelic language of "Enochian." There is a good reason why Lovecraft did not include this translation in his essay—it was not his creation. To understand why requires an understanding of what has been called the Cthulhu Mythos.

The most popular aspect of Lovecraft's work is a fictional pantheon of beings called the "Old Ones," "Great Old Ones," or "Elder Ones." Though these titles refer to different beings in different stories, they always seem to be creatures that ruled this planet before humanity's arrival, and that may do so again at some unspecified time in the future. Both alien species and cults among humans serve the Old Ones, and hope to bring back their masters. Lovecraft took the same care with this idea as he did with the *Necronomicon*, mingling references to real people and places with his fictional creations. Lovecraft never named his pantheon, but his correspondent August Derleth later dubbed it the "Cthulhu Mythos" after the monstrous creature in "The Call of Cthulhu." Some have debated the appropriateness of this label, as Lovecraft himself did not attach central importance to Cthulhu or keep his body of myth coherent. Nevertheless, the label has remained.

Lovecraft's fellow writers liked his creations, and decided to pay him tribute in their own writing. They borrowed the gods and books from Lovecraft's stories and included them in their fiction. When Lovecraft noticed this, he did the same with their creations. This started a literary game of sorts, in which these authors submitted stories to *Weird Tales* using each other's books and characters. To complicate matters, Lovecraft made money by revising or ghostwriting stories for other writers, often inserting his creations during the rewrites. *Weird Tales* printed his clients' stories under their names rather than Lovecraft's, muddying the waters further. Readers who had no idea about the writers' behind-the-scenes communication assumed that these stories were based on a real background. This confusion later contributed to the *Necronomicon* myth.

The Dee *Necronomicon* marks the beginning of this process. Frank Belknap Long, a young man Lovecraft had met through the amateur press movement, wrote a story called "The Space Eaters," first published in *Weird Tales* in July 1928. Although the tale itself does not contain any items from Lovecraft's stories, Long began it with this quote:

> The cross is not a passive agent. It protects the pure of heart, and it has often appeared in the air above our sabbats, confusing and dispersing the powers of Darkness.—John Dee's *Necronomicon*[61]

Evidently, Long intended this to be a translation of the *Necronomicon* unmentioned in Lovecraft's own work. Even though this quotation did not appear in the story's publication in *Weird Tales*, Lovecraft did read the manuscript that included it. He was flattered, and not only included Dee's edition in his next story, but also penciled Long's edition into "History of the *Necronomicon*."

With this precedent set, Lovecraft's other correspondents borrowed the *Necronomicon* for their own stories. His friend Robert E. Howard, the creator of Conan the Barbarian, mentioned the *Necronomicon* in his short story "The Children of the Night" (1931). Another writer mentioned earlier, the California author Clark Ashton Smith, made more extensive use of the book. The first of his *Necronomicon*-based tales was "The Return of the Sorcerer" (1931). In that tale, a wizard murders his twin brother and fears a horrid revenge from beyond the grave. To avert his fate, he hires a translator to see if an answer lies in his copy of the *Al Azif*. Surprisingly, Smith was one of the first people to see Lovecraft's "History," but included a copy of the Arabic manuscript that Lovecraft said no longer existed.[62] Another story, "The Nameless Offspring," contains an epigraph from the *Necronomicon* that displays Smith's ability as a poet:

> Many and multiform are the dim horrors of Earth, infesting her ways from the prime. They sleep beneath the unturned stone; they rise with the tree from its root; they move beneath the sea and in subterranean places; they dwell in the inmost adyta; they emerge betimes from the shutten sepulchre of haughty bronze and the low grave that is sealed with clay. There are some that are long known to man, and others as yet unknown that abide the terrible latter days of their revealing. Those which are most dreadful and the loathliest of all are haply still to be declared. But among those that have been revealed aforetime and have made manifest their veritable presence, there is one that may not openly be named for its exceeding foulness. It is that spawn which the hidden dweller in the vaults has begotten upon mortality.[63]

Even as the *Necronomicon* gained popularity as a book of spells and evil lore, however, Lovecraft shifted the nature of his favorite creation.

A Cosmic Vision

Lovecraft's supernatural fiction had gained some popularity, but after "The Dunwich Horror," he decided to change his approach. What prompted him to do this is unknown; perhaps he felt that he could no longer say what he wanted by using the trappings of sorcery. As he was to tell Willis Conover later with regard to occult books:

> But you will undoubtedly find all this stuff very disappointing. It is flat, childish, pompous, and unconvincing—merely a record of human childishness and gullibility in past ages. Any good fiction-writer can think up "records of primal horror" which surpass in imaginative force any occult production.[64]

Because of this, Lovecraft turned to science fiction. His Old Ones were no longer Gods or demons, but extremely powerful aliens who had come to Earth in the distant past. Magick might still appear, but it took the form of an alien science that humans could barely comprehend. Hints of these ideas had appeared in his earlier fiction, but now Lovecraft pursued them in earnest. Even as he changed his fictional philosophy, he did not leave behind his earlier creations—including the *Necronomicon*—but adapted them to his new approach.

At times, Lovecraft portrayed the *Necronomicon* as a collection of supernatural lore; it is briefly mentioned as such in "Medusa's Coil" (1930), a revision of a tale by Zealia Bishop. The new direction for the *Necronomicon* became even more evident in "The Whisperer in Darkness" (1930). The hero of this tale is Albert Wilmarth, a folklorist who teaches at Miskatonic University. Wilmarth becomes involved in a controversy over the remains of strange beings sighted in the flooded rivers of Vermont, insisting that they are only the products of a superstitious imagination. He receives a letter from Henry Akeley, a recluse living in the hills, who reveals that these beings are fungous invaders from the planet Yuggoth, or Pluto. What he has found, Akeley writes, should be familiar to a man of Wilmarth's interests:

> I suppose you know all about the fearful myths antedating the coming of man to the earth—the Yog-Sothoth and Cthulhu cycles—which are hinted at in the *Necronomicon*. I had access to a copy of that once.[65]

Wilmarth himself has read the *Necronomicon*, and knows of its descriptions of "worlds of elder, outer entity."[66] Convinced that he is being told the truth, Wilmarth goes to Akeley's home in Vermont, where his sickly friend speaks of Gods hinted at in the *Necronomicon*, including Tsathoggua and Azathoth. Despite Wilmarth's deep knowledge of these myths, he is unable to help Akeley escape his fate.

Lovecraft continued in this vein in "At the Mountains of Madness" (1931), his longest story ever published in his lifetime. An expedition from Miskatonic University sets out for the Antarctic to search for fossil samples. When Professor Lake of the Biology department goes on a survey expedition, he discovers a mountain range higher than the Himalayas and the bodies of a starfishlike species unknown to science. Lake loses radio contact with the base camp and, when the others arrive, they find one man and dog missing, the rest dead, the complete alien specimens gone, and the damaged ones buried beneath a five-pointed mound of snow. Professor William Dyer, who leads the expedition, and a graduate student named Danforth take a plane to survey the other side of the mountains, where they find the ruins of a prehuman city.

The text is riddled with references to the *Necronomicon*. While the members of the expedition considered the book to be myth, they understand its relevance when confronted with solid evidence of the "Old Ones," as the alien beings are dubbed. Alhazred gave hints at the existence of such beings and their servitors, the formless shoggoths. Even the mad Arab, who specialized in demonic lore, insisted that no shoggoths existed on Earth outside of the dreams of the drug-crazed, but Dyer and Danforth confront them in all of their hideousness. While the professor makes it home safely, Danforth goes insane when he looks back as they fly away from the city. It is hinted that this is because the assistant is "among the few who have ever dared to go completely through that worm-riddled copy of the *Necronomicon* kept under lock and key at the college library."[67] Lovecraft never explains why so many Biology and Geology professors have such a deep knowledge of a book of pre-human mythology, but it makes for an excellent story.

Another story that demonstrates the use of the *Necronomicon* as a piece of history and science is "The Dreams from the Witch-House." Walter Gilman, a young mathematics student at Miskatonic University, spends much of his spare time reading the *Necronomicon* and other books, until his professors forbid it as detrimental to his nervous temperament. When the witch Keziah Mason and her rat familiar, Brown Jenkin, attack him, he understands his peril, but is unable to escape them. In "Dreams," Mason's ability to travel through space and time is explained as the product of highly advanced mathematics; Lovecraft never used this to explain his previous references to the *Necronomicon*'s magick, but he may have thought of it in these terms.

The Close of an Era

The mid-1930s seemed to observers to be the high point of Lovecraft's career. He sold many stories to *Weird Tales* and other science fiction magazines, and was gaining a large number of fans. For most of his life, he had remained in Providence, but now he made a number of travels by bus and train as far away as Florida and New Orleans. He had dozens of correspondents from all over the country, and a young fan published his first book, *The Shadow over Innsmouth*. All outward signs indicated that Lovecraft was well on his way to a better life.

One of Lovecraft's greatest contributions to horror and science fiction is his support of younger writers. He was willing to read their stories, provide them with criticism, and help them publish their works. Because of this, their early stories bore the hallmarks of Lovecraft's influence—and many of their stories included the *Necronomicon*. Robert Bloch, the author of *Psycho*, was one of these young writers, so it was unsurprising that he mentioned the *Necronomicon* in his first published story, "The Secret of the Tomb," as well as in several that followed. Henry Kuttner, a young man living in California, included a copy of the *Necronomicon* at Salem's fictional Kester Library in "The Salem Horror." Robert Barlow, who later became Lovecraft's literary executor, wrote "A Dim-Remembered Story," in which each section was titled with a quote from Alhazred's infamous couplets.[68] Others of Lovecraft's creations were also adopted, but none seems to have had the popularity of the *Necronomicon*.

With all of these stories appearing in *Weird Tales*, it is no wonder many readers became uncertain whether the book was real or not. If it had only appeared in the works of one author, it might have been accepted as imaginary; but when it appeared in the works of several, the matter became less clear. It is likely that this confusion led to the book's later fame. *Weird Tales* received so many letters that editor Farnsworth Wright published a notice in the magazine telling the readers that it was Lovecraft's creation.[69] Lovecraft received many letters from fans who wanted to know where they could find copies of the book. Others in the same situation might be tempted to continue the joke, but Lovecraft was always conscientious:

> Regarding the dreaded *Necronomicon* of the mad Arab Abdul Alhazred—I must confess that both the evil volume & the accursed author are fictitious creatures of my own.[70]
>
> Now about the "terrible and forbidden books"—I am forced to say that most of them are purely legendary. There never was any Abdul Alhazred or *Necronomicon*, for I invented these names myself.[71]

Some have said that Lovecraft was a conscious hoaxer, but his letters tell otherwise:

> I am opposed to serious hoaxes, since they really confuse and retard the sincere student of folklore. I feel quite guilty every time I hear of someone's having spent valuable time looking up the *Necronomicon* at public libraries.[72]

Lovecraft's protégés did not always help him with his mission. In one letter, Lovecraft mentions that one of them—"young Bloch" being the prime suspect—inserted a paragraph in a publication advertising the *Necronomicon* for $1.49.[73] I have yet to find this, but it may be one of the first attempts to hoax the existence of the dark book.

People even suggested that Lovecraft write the *Necronomicon* itself. That he did so is undoubtedly one of the most persistent rumors among Lovecraft fans, but

Lovecraft himself turned down the project many times. The first questioner was Robert E. Howard in 1932. Lovecraft took kindly to his friend's suggestion:

> As for writing the *Necronomicon*—I wish I had the energy and ingenuity to do it! I fear it would be quite a job in view of the very diverse passages and intimations which I have in the course of time attributed to it! I might, though, issue an abridged *Necronomicon*—containing such parts as are considered at least reasonably safe for the perusal of mankind![74]

About a year before his death, Lovecraft received another letter from James Blish and William Miller Jr. asking whether he would write a *Necronomicon*. Once again, Lovecraft turned them down:

> As for bringing the *Necronomicon* into objective existence—I wish I had the time and imagination to assist in such a project . . . but I'm afraid it's a rather tall order—especially since the dreaded volume is supposed to run to something like a thousand pages! . . . Moreover, one can never *produce* anything even a tenth as terrible and impressive as one can awesomely hint about. If anyone were to *write* the *Necronomicon*, it would disappoint all those who have shuddered at cryptic references to it.[75]

Lovecraft did leave open the possibility of an "abridged and expunged *Necronomicon*,"[76] but he never wrote it. Lovecraft had one of the best-documented lives in all of history, and could never resist mentioning his projects to his friends. Not only would any "abridged *Necronomicon*" have been found in his notes, no hint can be found anywhere in his correspondence.

While all this was going on, however, Lovecraft was facing his greatest challenges. Despite his success in selling his work, the pulp magazines paid too little too late, and his grandfather's inheritance was almost gone. Lovecraft's health began to fail and, while his fiction from this period rose in quality, its quantity diminished greatly. His revision business continued, but its demands interfered with his writing, until near the end he composed only one story a year.

During this time, Lovecraft never completely abandoned the *Necronomicon*, but its significance in his stories tapered off. In "The Horror in the Museum" (1932), a revision of a Hazel Heald story, the narrator speaks briefly of "the dreaded *Necronomicon*."[77] An evil wizard in "The Thing on the Doorstep" (1933) finds a spell in the book that allows him to transfer his mind between bodies, and the title character of the William Lumley revision, "The Diary of Alonzo Typer" (1935), finds a Greek copy in an old house in upstate New York. Other references appear in "Out of the Aeons," "The Shadow Out of Time," and "The Haunter of the Dark." It is interesting to note, however, that, in most of these cases, the book is only mentioned briefly, and Lovecraft adds little if anything to the *Necronomicon*'s background.

One story, "Through the Gates of the Silver Key," breaks this mold, even going so far as to give another quote from the *Necronomicon*:

"And while there are those," the mad Arab had written, "who have dared to seek glimpses beyond the Veil, and to accept HIM as a Guide, they would have been more prudent had they avoided commerce with HIM; for it is written in the Book of Thoth how terrific is the price of a single glimpse. Nor may those who pass ever return, for in the Vastnesses transcending our world are Shapes of darkness that seize and bind. The Affair that shambleth about in the night, the Evil that defieth the Elder Sign, the Herd that stand watch at the secret portal each tomb is known to have, and that thrive on that which groweth out of the tenants within—all these Blacknesses are lesser than HE Who guardeth the Gateway; HE Who will guide the rash one beyond all the world into the Abyss of unnamable devourers. For HE is 'UMR AT-TAWIL, the Most Ancient One, which the scribe rendereth as THE PROLONGED OF LIFE."[78]

This passage, however, was the work of writer E. Hoffman Price, who roped his Providence friend into collaborating on the story. Though Lovecraft discarded much of Price's plot, he made only a few superficial changes in this quote.[79] Other than this, nothing new on his book appears in his fiction. It may be that Lovecraft felt attached to the *Necronomicon*, and continued to use it even though it was no longer an important element in his stories. Perhaps Lovecraft would have stopped using the book later, but he was running out of time.

Soon, Lovecraft became ill. He tried to avoid trips to the doctor due to his finances, so he did not seek medical assistance until it was too late, and he had to be admitted to the hospital. The diagnosis was cancer of the intestine, probably brought on by poor diet, complicated by Bright's disease, an infection of the kidneys.[80] Lovecraft kept a brave face on things, even taking notes on his symptoms in hope of helping the doctors, but he quickly grew worse. On 15 March 1937, Howard Phillips Lovecraft died.

The Master's Legacy

Lovecraft's death affected his circle heavily, and some members stopped writing fiction, or at least horror fiction. His literary estate was passed on to his executor, Robert Barlow, whose age and circumstances left him unable to promote Lovecraft's fiction actively. Lovecraft's friend August Derleth took the first steps in making Lovecraft known. He and another writer, Donald Wandrei, created a publishing house called Arkham House dedicated to the works of H. P. Lovecraft and other authors from the pulps. Their first collection of Lovecraft's stories, *The Outsider and Others*, took years to sell out, but since has become a collector's item worth thousands of dollars. At any rate, Derleth took it upon himself not only to promote Lovecraft's fiction, but to publish his poetry, essays, letters, and other documents of interest.

Derleth himself turned out a great deal of Cthulhu Mythos fiction, much of it dealing with the *Necronomicon*. Though Derleth was a more-than-capable writer, as his "Sac Prairie" novels show, his attempts at Lovecraftian fiction were less successful, and were most likely turned out to bring in money to finance other projects. Debates still rage as to whether Lovecraft would have been discovered without Derleth's influence—yet there is no way to tell one way or another. The fact that Lovecraft can be found in major bookstores across the United States, however, is largely due to August Derleth.

Even now, more authors have come to read and enjoy Lovecraft. Stephen King's story "I Know What You Need" has the *Necronomicon* as a central plot element, and nearly every other horror writer since then has written Cthulhu Mythos stories. Lovecraft's fiction has influenced the works of such diverse authors as Umberto Eco[81] and Jose Luis Borges.[82] It is this wide exposure that has resulted in the *Necronomicon* becoming as popular as it has.

Unlikely Sources

Over the years, a number of theories as to the *Necronomicon*'s origins have been given. Recent research has rendered many of them unlikely. Here are a few of the most popular ideas, and the arguments against them.

- **The *Picatrix*:** This work is perhaps the most famous magickal book in Arabic, and was supposedly written by "Norbar the Arab" or Picatrix himself, whoever that is. Legend has it that the book dates back to the 12th and 13th centuries, though it is not mentioned in European magickal writings until the 16th century. In his *History of Magic and Experimental Science*, Lynn Thorndike devoted an entire chapter to this work, referring to it as "a confused compilation of extracts from occult writings and a hodgepodge of innumerable magickal and astrological recipes."[83] The *Picatrix* has been translated into both Latin and German, and two or three English editions are in the works (and have been for some years).

  It has been suggested that Lovecraft may have come across mention of this book in his reading, perhaps in Thorndike's work (published in 1923). The history of the book, with its multiple translations and suppressed nature, seems to fit the work of the mad Arab.[84] However, this is true of many grimoires, and Lovecraft did not have such a detailed history of the *Necronomicon* thought out when he invented the book. In fact, the only factor that favors the *Picatrix* is that it was originally in Arabic, yet Lovecraft only chose this language due to the large number of works translated from Greek into Arabic. While the *Picatrix* is known in occult circles, I can't understand why Lovecraft would have had such a great knowledge of it in the early 1920s, while being ignorant of most other aspects of the occult.

- **Nathaniel Hawthorne (1804–64):** This New England author is best remembered for his novels *The Scarlet Letter* and *The House of the Seven*

Gables. Lovecraft was familiar with Hawthorne's *Tanglewood Tales* and *Wonder Book* by the age of six.[85] Around 1920, however, Lovecraft set out to read all of Hawthorne's work—stories, novels, letters, and even the published edition of a notebook in which Hawthorne kept his notes for possible tales. The latter is interesting for our purposes, as Lovecraft later kept his own "Commonplace Book" of story ideas.

Some Lovecraft scholars hold that Hawthorne's notebook may hold the *Necronomicon*'s inspiration. Lovecraft scholar Don Burleson has found the following entry: "An old volume in a large library,—every one to be afraid to unclasp and open it, because it was said to be a book of magic."[86] Based on this, some consider Hawthorne a likely source of inspiration. I remain skeptical, however; if this were the source, why did the *Necronomicon* not become a full-fledged "book of magic" until 1927? I believe that Lovecraft's reading in the occult during this period was a much greater influence than a sentence in the "Commonplace Book"— though future evidence may prove me wrong.

• **Robert W. Chambers (1865–1933):** Chambers was a New York-born author who became known for his historical novels and romances, so Lovecraft was surprised to discover an early book of his called *The King in Yellow* (1895), a collection of short horror stories still praised today. The tales center on the fictional play "The King in Yellow." The words of this play are of the purest evil and exert a terrible fascination over its readers, many of whom go mad after reading it. Because of this, "The King in Yellow" is condemned by church and state, but is still popular with artists and writers. For example, in the story "The Repairer of Reputations," a man named Hildred Castaigne reads the book and is driven to overthrow the government and become King of America. In "The Yellow Sign," an artist and his model find the Yellow Sign mentioned in the play and are killed when its guardian comes for them.

The most commonly cited source for the *Necronomicon*'s inspiration has been Chambers's imagined play "The King in Yellow." Lovecraft himself is partially responsible for this conclusion, as he tells us in "History of the *Necronomicon*" that the *Necronomicon* inspired Chambers to write about his play. However, Lovecraft did not encounter this book until May of 1927, while writing his massive essay on "Supernatural Horror in Literature."[87] In fact, reading Chambers seems to have affected Lovecraft's vision of the *Necronomicon* very little, as the two books have almost nothing in common. One is a manual of forbidden lore, magick, and prehuman history; the other is a play. Some say that both have a basic concept—the book that drives its readers mad—but this is not the case. Lovecraft never stated that the *Necronomicon* drove its readers mad. Rather, when the characters in his stories experienced uncanny events, the *Necronomicon* allowed them to place their experience within a terrifying system of belief, and in doing so hastened their descent into insanity. The truth of the matter is that Chambers's influence on the *Necronomicon* was minimal.

- **Madame Helena Petrovna Blavatsky (1831–91):** This eccentric Russian was the founder of the Theosophical Society, one of the most influential occult societies of the late 19th century. Her books, such as *Isis Unveiled* and *The Secret Doctrine*, are considered either supernaturally inspired books of wisdom or collections of balderdash, depending upon whom you ask.

  In *The Secret Doctrine* (1888), Blavatsky introduced her readers to the *Book of Dzyan*, a document from a higher dimension that her spiritual teachers, or Secret Chiefs, showed her. According to Blavatsky, the book was written on palm leaves in the forgotten Atlantean tongue of Senzar, which the Secret Chiefs translated for her. Later examination has shown that parts of the *Book of Dzyan* bear considerable resemblance to the Indian *Rig-Veda*.

  Several authors have mentioned the possibility that the *Book of Dzyan* inspired the *Necronomicon*, but I doubt this is the case. Lovecraft did have some contact with Theosophical literature, such as W. Scott-Elliot's *The Story of Atlantis and the Lost Lemuria* and Alfred P. Sinnett's *Esoteric Buddhism*. On the other hand, he did not learn about the *Book of Dzyan* until his occultist friend E. Hoffman Price told him about it in February of 1933.[88] Even then, Lovecraft never saw any of Blavatsky's material until late 1936, when Henry Kuttner lent him a "Blavatsky opus"[89]—from the context, probably *The Secret Doctrine*. Lovecraft went on to tell Kuttner that he hadn't found out more about it than Price had told him.[90] Four months later, Lovecraft was dead, having written no fiction in the interim. Lovecraft was intrigued by the *Book of Dzyan*, but it appears only in his very last tales. Seekers after the source of the *Necronomicon* should look elsewhere.

- **The Hermetic Order of the Golden Dawn:** Perhaps the most influential occult order of the 19th century was the Golden Dawn, a group that taught ceremonial magick from a combined Judeo-Christian/Egyptian tradition. Samuel Liddell "MacGregor" Mathers, William Westcott, and W. R. Woodman founded the Golden Dawn in 1888, based on a charter from Anna Sprengel, supposedly a member of the Die Goldene Dammerung (Golden Dawn) in Germany. The Dawn had a stormy history, due to personality conflicts and the eventual revelation of the group's spurious origins. Several groups tracing their lineage back to the Golden Dawn still exist, and many of the Order's rituals and lectures have been published by Aleister Crowley, Israel Regardie, and others.

The Golden Dawn operated during Lovecraft's life, so some have formed connections between him and the secretive organization. For the most part, most authors have done nothing more than suggest possible, and unlikely, links. However, "Simon," the author of one of the hoax *Necronomicon*s, goes much further:

[W]e know that Lovecraft was friendly with Arthur Machen, and Algernon Blackwood, among others, who were initiates of the Golden Dawn.... It is my belief because the society itself, the Golden Dawn, hinted at a secret Arab manuscript that was only available to higher initiates, that there was knowledge of the Necronomicon among the Golden Dawn, and that Machen, Blackwood, and some of the others dropped these hints to Lovecraft in the course of their correspondence with him or just in talking at the Kalem Club they used to belong to in Brooklyn Heights.[91]

It is difficult to know where to begin correcting these misconceptions. Lovecraft was a great fan of these writers—both Machen and Blackwood were writers of weird fiction known even today. It is true that they were members of the Golden Dawn, at least for a short time. Lovecraft, however, never corresponded with them, being too respectful or shy to bother them. When he went to see a reading by Lord Dunsany, one of his greatest influences, he failed to even ask for an autograph.[92] In all of his thousands of letters, Lovecraft never mentions corresponding with either of these men, or any other known member of the Golden Dawn. He certainly never met them at the Kalem Club, an informal group of Lovecraft's friends who started meeting in Brooklyn in 1924—none of the members of the club ever mentioned a visit by these men. The link between Lovecraft and the Golden Dawn is wishful thinking.

- **Sumerian mythology:** This is not so much a source of inspiration of the *Necronomicon* as a theory put forth in Simon's *Necronomicon*, published by Avon Books in 1979. This book proposed that Lovecraft was a student of the mythology of ancient Sumer. According to this theory, he incorporated his knowledge into his writing, and this may have inspired the *Necronomicon*.[93]

This theory is most commonly held by those who know little of Sumerian mythology or of Lovecraft. We cannot rule out some knowledge of Sumerian myth on Lovecraft's part, as he was familiar with the legends of many different cultures. However, a look at Lovecraft's writing, both fiction and correspondence, reveals only a few Sumerian placenames and no mention of the Gods or demons of that culture's pantheon. Even if Lovecraft knew something of Sumer, he did not seem to have any great understanding of it.

Conclusion

Many have insisted that the *Necronomicon* is portrayed so realistically that it must have existed before Lovecraft. Those who say this deny the power of human imagination and creativity, both of which Lovecraft possessed in abundance. The irony is that Lovecraft foretold this situation in one of his letters to Willis Conover a few months before he died:

> If the *Necronomicon* legend continues to grow, people will end up believing in it and accusing me of faking when I point out the true origin of the thing![94]

He was more right than he could have imagined.

"Many a Quaint and Curious Volume . . .": The *Necronomicon* Made Flesh —Daniel Harms

2

If the Necronomicon *actually existed, it would be out in Bantam paperback with a preface by Lin Carter.*

—T. E. D. KLEIN[1]

Almost three years ago, I wrote a book describing the monsters and books of H. P. Lovecraft's Cthulhu Mythos. Writing my book and having it published was an indescribable thrill for me, and I have since found myself the focus of some attention from those who have appreciated the volume. At one time, I considered all this to be wonderful, but recently this has been tempered with unease as I feel my work slip from my grasp. On one occasion, a young person insisted that one of the entries in my encyclopedia had to be correct, even though it was deliberately contradicted by Lovecraft's original story—it said so in the "standard reference work," and that was that! At another time, I was informed that one individual had built up his own system of ritual magick based mostly on information from my book. These incidents and others have forced me to accept that a literary work is not an extension of the author, but rather exists apart from their intentions and can sometimes travel in surprising directions.

Reading Lovecraft's letters, in which he discusses the *Necronomicon*, I feel a sort of kinship with him, even though his situation was more serious than mine. Lovecraft and his friends created a fictional pantheon filled with alien Gods and centered in a blasphemous tome called the *Necronomicon*. They intended nothing but fun; while they tried to make their pantheon internally consistent for each other, they had no idea that anyone would take it seriously. Many readers did, however, and wrote Lovecraft asking him where they could find the *Necronomicon*. Although perhaps tempted to ignore these correspondents or lead them on, Lovecraft's letters show that he gave each a careful and conscientious answer. At the same time, the steady stream of these requests made him realize that he had started something that was now beyond his control, and that the rumors of his creation would grow faster than he could contain them.

Under these circumstances, it is not surprising that a few hoaxes, or even a fake volume, appeared. The reality of the situation, however, is that *Necronomicon* hoaxes cropped up often, and almost a dozen books entitled *Necronomicon* appeared. The transition from the figment of an author's imagination to an actual volume took less than thirty years, and the trend has grown since then, creating a fan's dream and a bibliographer's nightmare. The following entries detail some of the more important events that took place in the *Necronomicon*'s journey from fantasy to reality.

The Faraday Review

This particular *Necronomicon* hoax appeared near the end of Lovecraft's life and, as far as I can tell, it was the first attempt to portray the *Necronomicon* as a real book. The hoax was perpetrated by Donald A. Wollheim (1914–90), one of Lovecraft's younger correspondents who published an amateur science fiction magazine called *The Phantagraph*. Wollheim later became the founder of DAW Books and a famous publisher of fantasy and horror fiction. At some point in the 1930s, Wollheim submitted a book review of the *Necronomicon* to the *Bradford Review and East Haven News*, a small-town Connecticut newspaper. Unfortunately, no one is sure of the date the article was published. I have looked over back issues of the paper from mid-1934 until Lovecraft discovered the hoax in September of 1936, and have found nothing. A partial copy of the review did appear in *Lovecraft at Last*, a book by another of Lovecraft's young correspondents.[2]

Wollheim's review critiques a supposed translation of the *Necronomicon* privately printed by W. T. Faraday. This, Wollheim claimed, was the first English translation of the *Necronomicon* ever made, and was only the second publication of it since the Latin edition of Olaus Wormius. (Wollheim had not seen Lovecraft's "History of the *Necronomicon*," so the "facts" in his article are not consistent with Lovecraft's stories.) According to Wollheim, the book "purports to be the account of the Spheres of the Occult and their dealings with mankind."[3] Faraday's book is only a third as long as the original, as the translator excised the manuscript "for safety's sake."[4] Nowhere within is Lovecraft mentioned, but the author mentions at the end that the book inspired Ambrose Bierce and Robert W. Chambers.[5]

Wollheim's article was published without Lovecraft's knowledge, and the author kept it a secret from him during their correspondence. I'm not sure why; perhaps Wollheim felt embarrassed in retrospect and didn't want his idol to find out. He later sent the clipping to Willis Conover, who forwarded it to Lovecraft. If Wollheim was worried, he shouldn't have been; Lovecraft joked with Conover, "I must get hold of this Faraday translation, even though it is probably a fake."[6] He seems to have considered the article harmless, and I agree; those few who read the review in the small-town newspaper probably didn't give it a second thought.

Cultus Maleficarum (The Sussex Manuscript)

After Lovecraft's death, his small yet loyal body of fans continued. Today, these individuals would probably be posting on their own Internet groups; at the time, they contented themselves with publishing fan journals and fiction. Not surprisingly, a few even tried to write their own *Necronomicons*. During the 1940s, the fantasy writer Lin Carter saw a leatherbound collection of quotes from the *Necronomicon* that had been published in fiction works up to that time.[7] Only one of these volumes has surfaced from obscurity—Fred L. Pelton's *Cultus Maleficarum*, better known as the *Sussex Manuscript*.

We know very little about Fred Pelton, but his writing makes it clear that he was a great fan of Lovecraft. Few people were even aware of Pelton's work when he died in 1950,[8] but he was nonetheless a prolific author. By the end of his life, he had written the book-length treatise *A Guide to the Cthulhu Cult*[9] and two (as-yet unpublished) works on the linguistics of prehuman tongues, in addition to the *Sussex Manuscript*. Pelton put a great deal of energy into his manuscript, including many references from the Mythos fiction of various authors.

The introduction to the *Sussex Manuscript* states that it is an English translation of Olaus Wormius's Latin text made in 1598 by a "Baron Frederic I" of Sussex. (For the record, Sussex was never a barony.) The book draws a great deal from the works of August Derleth, the founder of Arkham House, who wrote many tales of the "Cthulhu Mythos" modeled on Lovecraft's after his death. Derleth decided that the universe was ruled by Lovecraft's "Great Old Ones" (who were irredeemably evil), and by a group of friendly creators called the "Elder Gods." Some of Lovecraft's stories carry a hint of this good/evil dichotomy, but Derleth makes this cosmic battle into the central theme of his stories.

According to the *Manuscript*'s first section, the Elder Gods sent down their messengers to Earth to begin cults among the prehuman inhabitants. The Elder Gods' influence was dependent upon a ritual performed every thousand years that would continue their cycle of rule. The kings responsible for this, including such Mythos beings as Ithaqua, Shub-Niggurath, and Lloigor, betrayed the Elder Gods and usurped the ritual's power, thereby summoning up Cthulhu.

The second book tells how Cthulhu and his kings seized control of the world and set about destroying the worshipers of the Elder Gods. Some of their priests escaped in secret, and eventually were able to call the Elder Gods down upon their rebellious kings and imprison them. As they did so, these Gods created humans, a species that had the spark of the gods within them and so could become the guardians the world. To counter this, the Great Old Ones sent forth Ilyth'la to establish cults among men dedicated to reestablishing their role. (Readers of the *Sussex Manuscript* will notice that, in this section, the narrator turns from subtle praise of the Elder Gods to outright worship of the Great Old Ones.)

The third book speaks of the history of the cult and the glories that await those willing to join it. Of course, such rewards are commensurate with the dangers involved, so the book describes the initiation ceremonies of the cult, in which the neophyte must resist all manner of temptations and punishments—many of which it is difficult to believe any person could survive. The fourth section includes histories and prophecies regarding the cycles of Earth. This section cuts off mid-word; twenty-three blank pages follow. Perhaps Pelton was growing tired of the project, or was just unable to complete it.[10] The whole is written in a difficult pseudo-archaic style, and includes so many of Pelton's imagined places and monsters that it is almost impossible to understand.

Pelton, not content with merely writing the *Necronomicon*, went so far as to create a leatherbound illuminated text. He sent a transcript to August Derleth, who was so enthusiastic about the book that he considered it as an Arkham House publication. He even advertised it by mentioning the *Sussex Manuscript* in his story "The Gorge Beyond Salapunco," published in *Weird Tales* in 1949. Donald Wandrei, Derleth's partner in Arkham House, was less than enthusiastic about the project, and Derleth eventually scrapped the idea. The book lay forgotten until Lovecraft scholar Edward P. Berglund set out to find it. Eventually, he contacted Fred Pelton's son, who sent him a photocopy of the manuscript. Berglund obtained permission to have the manuscript published in the fan magazine *Crypt of Cthulhu*, and later in the Price *Necronomicon* (see p. 55) and Pagan Publishing's edition of *A Guide to the Cthulhu Cult*. Berglund later lost touch with Pelton's son, and the original document has vanished like so many of its fictional predecessors.[11] Berglund did manage to retrieve a set of transparencies of the book, however. On the whole, the *Sussex Manuscript* is more a literary curiosity than anything else. Due to its obscurity and late date of publication, few people outside of Mythos fan-dom have even heard of it. Moreover, its style has kept it from becoming popular. Despite this, the book is worthy of admiration for the amount of work that Pelton lavished upon it.

The *Necronomicon* For Sale

The *Necronomicon*'s journey from fantasy to reality was first felt in the world of bookselling. The first sign of this may have come in the 7 July 1945, issue of *Publishers' Weekly*. In its "The Weekly Book Exchange," where booksellers across the nation advertised for titles, the Grove Street Bookstore in New York requested, along with a number of real books, the *Necronomicon*, Ludvig Prinn's *De Vermis Mysteriis*, and Mycroft's *Commentaries on Witchcraft*.[12] (The latter two books are the creations of Robert Bloch, and all three appear in that author's short story "The Mannikin.") When this curious request was brought to the attention of Jacob Blanck, a columnist in the magazine, he saw the humor in it, but asked future hoaxers to "consider that poor wretch the unimaginative bibliographer."[13]

Mr. Blanck's plea seems to have been ignored. In his summer 1946 (#78) catalog, the late New York bookseller Phillip Duschnes advertised another *Necronomicon*. Item 511 in his catalog is a Wormius translation of the *Necronomicon* priced at $375.

The catalog sagely notes that only two other copies in the United States exist, one at Miskatonic University and the other "in the Library of J. Pierce Whitmore,"[14] who was probably intended to be an unnamed "celebrated American millionaire" mentioned in Lovecraft's "History of the *Necronomicon.*" When Winfield Townley Scott noted the entry in his column in the *Providence Journal*, Duschnes confessed that it was a hoax, saying "I think I may be excused on the basis that a little laugh now and then is worth having."[15]

Two other notable hoaxes appeared in the *Antiquarian Bookman*, a periodical for bibliophiles and dealers. In 1962, Walter Baylor placed an ad for "The Necronomican,"[16] and in 1966, a Wormius copy was advertised for $25,000.[17] Of course, there was no *Necronomicon* for these potential buyers to purchase, but all this was soon to change.

Druillet's Leaves from the *Necronomicon*

Philippe Druillet is a French illustrator whose work has been featured in *Heavy Metal* magazine. At one point in his career, Druillet created his own imaginative pages, which he jokingly claimed were pages from the *Necronomicon.* Three of these appeared in the magazine *Anubis;*[18] later more were printed in a special Lovecraft issue of *Heavy Metal.*[19] Five more plates turned up in the French edition of that magazine *(Metal Hurlant),* and were recently posted to the World Wide Web.[20] For some unknown reason, only one page from *Anubis* was reprinted in the *Heavy Metal* publication. The pages themselves are unreadable, but feature a great deal of mystical-looking calligraphy and sketches of alien monsters with bat-wings and inhuman faces.

The *Heavy Metal* and *Metal Hurlant* appearances of these pages were printed without comment, but the *Anubis* printing gives us more information. The introduction tells us that these particular pages were chosen for reprinting because they "would mean little to the uninitiated."[21] The "complete" book was to be printed by Editions du Terrain Vague of Paris, though a recent bomb attack on that establishment is purported to have set the project back considerably. When the editor states that C. Auguste Dupin, Poe's fictional detective, is "on the case,"[22] the fiction behind it all becomes clear. (For the record, the promised book was never published.) This particular hoax seems not to have fooled many people, though it is difficult to be sure, given its wide distribution.

The *Necronomicon:* A Study

In 1967, another book-length *Necronomicon* appeared, this time out of science fiction writer Jack Chalker's Mirage Press in Baltimore. The book is usually listed under Mark Owings's name in catalogs, but I have been informed that Owings researched the book and Chalker wrote it based on his notes.[23] The book was published in a limited edition of six hundred copies. According to an agreement with Arkham

House, Mirage Press could not sell the book for more than $1.95,[24] which probably made it infeasible to put out more copies.

The Necronomicon: A Study is a fascinating piece of work. Among other items, the pamphlet includes Lovecraft's pseudo-scholarly essay "History and Chronology of the *Necronomicon*," as well as quotations taken from Cthulhu Mythos stories and novels. Its centerpiece is "The Existing Copies: A Bibliobiography," which correlates material about the *Necronomicon* from dozens of stories by different authors into a rough chronology. At the beginning of the essay, Owings tells us that these writers "masked their chronicles as fiction"[25] and based their work on their incomplete knowledge of the *Necronomicon*. He lets his readers in on the joke by the end, citing the aforementioned catalog hoaxes as proof of his claims and ending the essay with the mock-solemn proclamation, "As it was with [Sherlock] Holmes, so let it be with Lovecraft."[26] The piece builds up a complete history of the book, but then lets us know that it is all meant in fun.

This *Necronomicon* was not only the first book of this title ever published, but also features the first disclaimer placed on a published *Necronomicon*. It has become a habit for the authors of such books to warn the reader of the terrible wrath of the Old Ones that will visit itself on anyone who reads or uses the book. Owings's book featured an even more terrible warning:

CAUTION!
The title *The Necronomicon* is a literary property and may not be used without the permission of the Estate of H. P. Lovecraft.[27]

This warning would not hold its power for long.

De Camp's Al Azif

The mid-1970s witnessed a resurgence of Lovecraft's work, with the appearance of biographies, paperback printings, and fan fiction inspired by the master. The exact reasons behind this remain unclear, though the mass-market paperback releases of Lovecraft's fiction and August Derleth's death in 1971 were probably important factors. During his life, Derleth had kept tight reins on the production of Lovecraftian criticism and Mythos fiction alike, often preferring that it be published through Arkham House (with his approval) or not at all—the fate that befell the *Sussex Manuscript*. The warning of legal action in Owings's book seems to have been forgotten, perhaps because the post-Derleth staff of Arkham House realized that Derleth's claim to the "Estate of H. P. Lovecraft" was almost nonexistent. The publishers of the 1970s could not reprint Lovecraft's work without Arkham House's permission, but authors were free to pursue their own creative projects on Lovecraft and the Cthulhu Mythos—for better or for worse. One of the most famous (or infamous) of these works was Owlswick Press's *Al Azif* (1973).

Lyon Sprague de Camp is well known as a popular writer on archaeology and lost continents. His *Lovecraft: A Biography* (1975) remained the definitive work on Lovecraft's life for more than twenty years. As de Camp told it later,[28] George Scithers of Owlswick Press asked him to write a preface to a "Necronomicon." The book, Scithers told de Camp, consisted of Arabic-appearing calligraphy designed by Robert Dills.[29] De Camp wrote up the introduction, drawing on an actual trip he had made to Iraq and adding an incident in which a government official is alleged to have sold him the manuscript of *Al Azif* in the (fictional) language of Duriac. A friend from Lebanon later told de Camp that three Iraqi scholars in succession had attempted to translate the book, but each vanished from their homes soon after they began— most likely because they had a habit of reading aloud as they translated! The Iraqi authorities became dismayed and arranged to have de Camp buy it so it could wreak havoc among U.S. scholars in retribution for that country's Middle Eastern policies. The book was published in a limited edition of 348 copies that rapidly sold out.

The book, bound in red and blue, follows the style of Arabic texts—written right to left, with the pages arranged in the same fashion.[30] The pages at the beginning and end of the "Duriac" manuscript differ widely from each other, but those in the middle repeat a sequence of sixteen pages, half of these differing from the other half only by a few characters at the ends of some lines. De Camp warns us that the publishers "take no responsibility whatever for any extraordinary occurrence which may attend upon or result from the translation, transliteration, or vocalization of said matter."[31] Since the pages within are in an imaginary language, however, casual readers need not fear.

Owlswick proved to be much more conscientious in its marketing of the book than later publishers of hoax *Necronomicon*s. As George Scithers told me, he received orders from people who clearly thought the book was real. In each case, the person's check was returned. At one point, a student wrote them stating that he thought the book contained real spells and that he was writing a thesis that would prove the book authentic. Failing to make the student believe that it was a fake, Scithers was forced to write the young man's thesis advisor and tell him what was going on.[32] Few people have ever considered this to be the "real" *Necronomicon*—but the fact that it is often kept under tight control in the special collections departments of libraries has shocked more than a few.

For readers today who want to see the *Al Azif* without spending hundreds of dollars, the book has reappeared as a print-on-demand work from Wildside Press. In addition, I have located a pirated edition, bound in black, that reproduces the original, plus a one-page commentary by "the Rev. Yaj Nomolos, S. P."[33]

It may have been the success of the de Camp book that started the *Necronomicon* publishing craze that followed. It is impossible to be sure about this, but at least de Camp proved that such a book was marketable and (since it included no Arkham House disclaimer) legal. Whatever the case, I believe that it was certainly a premonition of things to come.

The Necromantic Grimoire of Augustus Rupp

Another book to come out of the occult craze of the 1970s was a curious volume called *The Necromantic Grimoire of Augustus Rupp*. The individual who seems to be responsible for this production is Anthony Raven, of whom I know nothing save that he wrote a pamphlet entitled *The Occult Lovecraft*[34] and a short work of fantasy called *The Ruby Toad* (whose author is listed as both Raven and Rupp!). At any rate, Bob Lynn of Waldwick, New Jersey, published this tiny black-bound book in 1974, in a limited edition of 500 copies.

According to the introduction, this book was originally the work of Augustus Rupp, a professor of Mesopotamian history at Stuttgart University who died in 1849.[35] In 1846, Rupp published his own grimoire, or book of magic, based on material taken from the *Grimoire of Honorius* (a real-life book of 17th-century extraction), the *Heptameron* of Peter de Abano (supposedly dating from the 14th century), and the *Necronomicon*.[36] In the 1890s, Cambridge professor Carter Stockdale rediscovered the book and had it translated and re-published.[37] This latest edition, Raven tells us, was published in response to demands by scholars and magicians alike.[38]

To allay some reader's suspicions, there is ample evidence that the work is a hoax. First, a search of the On-Line Computer Library Catalog turns up no evidence of a previous edition in any library. The book mentions that Rupp fled his dwellings "only moments before the arrival of the inquisitors."[39] Rupp's haste seems unwarranted, as members of the Inquisition would have been rare in 19th-century Protestant Germany. Later, it is noted that, following Stockdale's republication of the *Grimoire*, he returned to Cornwall to live with his uncle "William Pigwiggin."[40] I have not found the name "Pigwiggin" anywhere but in the comic poem "Nymphidia" by Michael Drayton (1563–1631), in which it signifies a wasp-knight who is the lover of the Queen of the Faeries.[41] Add to this the fact that Augustus Rupp shares his initials with Anthony Raven, and it seems likely that the latter is the book's author.

The first part of the book consists of a bestiary of sorts, describing vampires, ghouls, werewolves, demons, the Devil, succubi, incubi (demons who have sex with humans), and Asmodeus and Lilith (two powerful demons from Judaic tradition). Each entry is given a single page, and the information given could be gleaned from a ten-minute trip to any library or a few weeks watching the Late Late Movie. The second part of the book details the various diagrams used in summoning evil beings. Some are taken from other sources; others are original to this source. Among these is the "Tishku Circle," which is used to call upon planetary power if its guardian "Hastur, King of the Abyss" can be avoided.[42] A few pages later, an ornate diagram appears labelled the "*Cthulhu Circle* from the hideous *Necronomicon* (Spanish edition—Madrid 1630)," along with the instruction that "when used with the *Key* the Necromancer can *call* dead *Cthulhu* who waits dreaming in his house at *R'lyeh*."[43] The third section contains summonings and banishings for the beings mentioned previously.

Even though this book only mentions the *Necronomicon* briefly, it is notable on two counts. First, it treats the *Necronomicon* as a real book, and purportedly much of its material is taken from that tome. Second, the book shares with the later "Simon" *Necronomicon* an emphasis on Mesopotamian myth. This is most noticeable in the book's references to Namtar, a plague God who was the attendant to Ereshkigal, Queen of the Underworld, and the son of the God "Mulge." The only references I have found to Mulge (as well as Tishku) are in Francois Lenormant's *Chaldean Magic: Its Origin and Development* (1877), an English translation of the *Science Occult: La Magie chez les Chaldeens,* mentioned in the Simon book's bibliography (p. lvi). I am uncertain whether the makers of the Simon book had any contact with this book or its authors, but it is nonetheless an intriguing possibility.

Rupp's Grimoire has had little or no influence on the occult scene. It is seen only in a few library collections and used-book stores, and its subject matter—a curious mixture of Lovecraft, Mesopotamian mythology, medieval grimoires, and cinematic wisdom—is not integrated enough to create an actual system of magick.

The Culp *Necronomicon*

During the 1970s, a large number of new Lovecraft fans and critics emerged. Perhaps the most famous group dedicated to Lovecraft (which survives today) is the Esoteric Order of Dagon, an amateur press organization named after the infamous cult from Lovecraft's "The Shadow over Innsmouth." The members of the EOD, who generally number around twenty-four, mail each other small pamphlets containing essays, poetry, and fiction. One such work, found in the February 1976 mailing, was Robert C. Culp's version of the *Necronomicon*. I know very little about Mr. Culp, other than that he lived in Fort Myers, Florida, and traveled to many foreign locales.[44] He had published a few other pieces in EOD fanzines in 1975, and one of his other pieces, "The Papyrus of Nephren-Ka," was recently reprinted.[45] He published no new Cthulhu Mythos fiction after his *Necronomicon* appeared, a fact true believers may consider significant.

Culp's *Necronomicon* begins with a quote by "Olaus Wormius" stressing the heretical nature of the magick contained within and the dangers of its use. Following this are two short sections that detail the wonders and dangers of dealing with the Great Old Ones. The bulk of the manuscript is taken up by a tale of an evil priesthood's search for the secrets of eternal life. The hunt becomes almost comical, as they search tombs and lost cities for the elusive scroll that contains the spell, those who moved it leaving mocking notes behind them.[46]

While he allows the story to trail off in confusion, Culp's writing does at times convey the sense of cosmic fear that has become Lovecraft's trademark. Unlike subsequent hoaxes, which reached a wider audience, it is improbable that the booklet deceived the select group of Lovecraft fans who received it.[47]

H. R. Giger's Necronomicon

The years 1977–78 saw the appearance of three different *Necronomicon*s. Some of these volumes' authors have claimed that they were the "first" *Necronomicon* and that the others are only imitators, but Owings's and de Camp's books had been released well before all of them. Each of the three was published in a different country, and (so far as I can tell) the authors had no knowledge of what the others were doing. The first of these to appear was H. R. Giger's *Necronomicon*.

The Swiss artist Hans Rudi Giger (1940–) has become known worldwide for his paintings depicting dark mechanical landscapes and cybernetically altered beings. The artist received critical acclaim for the creature and sets in the classic science fiction film "Alien," and has gained a devoted following among horror fans as well. Sphinx-Verlag of Basel, Switzerland, published a portfolio of this artist's works entitled *Necronomicon* in 1977, and French and German editions appeared in the fall of that year. Giger's *Necronomicon* has since appeared in many languages from different publishers. *Necronomicon II*, another collection of Giger's work, followed in 1985, and some have called his third book, *Biomechanics,* "*Necronomicon III*."

Giger first encountered Lovecraft's work through his friend Robert B. Fischer, who asked Giger to illustrate his journal, *Cthulhu News*. As Giger tells it, when he needed a name for his latest collection of artwork, his mentor, Sergius Golowin, suggested "The *Necronomicon*."[48] I think that Giger's memory may be faulty here, as he shot an art film called "H. R. Giger's *Necronomicon*" two years before the book's appearance. It is likely that Golowin suggested the name for the film, and then Giger used it later as the book's title. Giger does seem to have a genuine appreciation of Lovecraft and his work, even though he mentions that Lovecraft's father is a Freemason,[49] a rumor started in the Hay *Necronomicon* (see p. 49).

Giger gives only a little information about his vision of the *Necronomicon*, most of it appearing on the title pages to *Necronomicon* and *Necronomicon II*. At the beginning of the *Necronomicon,* it seems that Giger is discussing an existing ancient manuscript. He translates the word *necronomicon* in an unusual way as "the types or masks of death,"[50] and mentions the hideous illustrations within. In the end, he writes that, through his book, the *Necronomicon* "has become reality for the first time."[51] The paragraph in *Necronomicon II* is not as interesting. It is mostly a reprint of information from Lovecraft's "History of the *Necronomicon*," with a few changes in spelling—Lovecraft's Gods "Cthulhu" and "Yog-Sothoth," for example, become "Cthullu" and "Yoxodo."[52] This is the extent of the *Necronomicon*-related material in both books—the rest of these texts discusses Giger's life and his inspirations for the prints within.

When Giger calls his books "*Necronomicons,*" he seems to be referring to a book from literature that he feels is complementary in tone to his art, not insisting that they are manuscripts written by a mad Arab. It would be difficult to mistake Giger's book for any sort of ancient manuscript that might have inspired Lovecraft.

The Simon *Necronomicon*

The next *Necronomicon* to appear became the most popular and is still seen in many bookstores today. The book was translated and edited (or written, depending on who you ask) by a group associated with the Magickal Childe bookshop, then known as the Warlock Shop. Though now closed, this store was for many years the center of New York City's occult community. The shop's owner was Herman Slater, a showman-occultist of the old school. The book's translator—if he can be referred to as such—was a man known only as "Simon." Simon wrote a number of books for Magickal Childe, including the *Necronomicon Report* (later rereleased as the *Necronomicon Spellbook*), a guide to the use of the *Necronomicon*'s chapter on the names of Marduk. Two of his other books, *The Gates of the Necronomicon* and a translation of the French grimoire *The Red Dragon*, were scheduled for publication in 1992, but the death of Herman Slater seems to have put these plans on hold.

The origins of the Simon *Necronomicon* remain a mystery, since those responsible for it have given two different versions of events. The introduction to the book itself relates how a monk of unknown origin[53] provided the original manuscript to Simon, an individual involved in both the translation of rare manuscripts and international espionage.[54] Someone gave Simon and Magickal Childe the manuscript to translate and publish, but would not allow them to show the original to others.[55] Little else about Simon is explained in the book.

For those who are unsatisfied with this explanation, *The Necronomicon Spellbook* gives a different version of events. The author (who is presumably Simon, yet refers to himself in the third person) tells us that Simon was no spy, but a bishop with a great command of languages who ministered to the poor of New York. In the spring of 1972, two of his fellow monks brought him a 9th-century Greek manuscript of the *Necronomicon* that they had acquired through their thefts of documents from libraries and collections across the nation.[56] The monks were captured shortly thereafter. This part of Simon's story checks out—to a point. Two monks from the Autocephalous Slavonic Orthodox Catholic Church were captured in March of 1973 after having stolen books from college libraries across the country, including those of Harvard, Yale, Chicago, and Notre Dame.[57]

Some might call this convincing, but it is problematic on several counts. The two thieves concentrated on taking highly valuable 16th- and 17th-century atlases, instead of old Greek manuscripts. Considering that they were able to smuggle these huge volumes out of the libraries under their robes, they could have had their pick of the collections' books. Why, then, would they choose a Greek manuscript that—according to Simon himself[58]—they were not sure was worth anything at all? It should also be noted that the two monks were willing to help track down the books they had resold, which seems at odds with Simon's account of their silence about the manuscript. Finally, the logical "bishop" to receive the manuscript would have been their denomination's Bishop of New York. At the time, the Autocephalic Church had only one bishop of New York, whose biography, as given in the *New York Times*, [59] contradicts the background given in the *Spellbook*. That bishop passed away in 1984, though all those who worked on the book insist that Simon is still alive. Finally, we have the monk's own motivations—instead of turning the book over to its owner or the police, why would he have provided it to a small occult bookshop to be printed in a limited edition?

Whatever the background, "Simon" claims to have translated the book and to have given it to Magickal Childe.[60] A large group of contributors then went into action. In an on-line essay, Khem Caigan (formerly Khem Set Rising) describes his role in the book's production. Jim Wasserman, the head of Studio 31 Graphics, brought him into the project while the two were working for publisher Samuel Weiser. Bonny Nielsen's Feint Type handled the typesetting, and Larry Barnes was responsible for printing the book under the Schlangekraft ("Serpent Power/Strength") imprint. No less a figure than William S. Burroughs stopped in to view the book's printing. Khem, who was brought into the project at a relatively late date, was given the task of designing the cover and touching up the sigils in the book. (If the typescript in his possession is any indication, the manuscript's drawings were in sore need of this.) He attempted to base his designs on magickal documents, and even put together a list of Lovecraft quotes from the *Necronomicon*.[61] No one seemed to care, however; they were more concerned that he finish his work quickly.[62]

A limited leatherbound edition of 666 copies, and a clothbound edition of 1275 copies[63] were published under the Schlangekraft imprint in December of 1977. There was at least one other hardback printing of 3,333 copies, followed by additional printings and a paperback released by Avon Books in 1980, which has not been out of print since.

The identity of Simon has remained a mystery, with half of the New York occult community being accused at one time or another. I have met a number of people who say that they have met Simon, and I have no reason to doubt their veracity. However, the copyright forms for the *Necronomicon Spellbook* list two authors, both writing under the pseudonym "Simon"![64] It is likely that one of these individuals acted as the public face of Simon—an assumption that places us no closer to the mad monk's identity. Another clue may be found in the *Books of Rune & Magickal Alphabet & Cypher*, published by Earth Religions Supply in 1975. The series editor is given as Simon,[65] while the book itself is edited by "Levender, Slater, and Goulavitch."[66] The last name on this list is most likely the "Vladimir Gulevitch" responsible for the book's third section,[67] so we are left with Herman Slater and "Levender" as candidates for Simon.

The most likely candidate here is Peter Levenda. Sources disagree on his role in this process. The acknowledgments mention him only as one of a staff of five translators.[68] In an interview for the magazine *Dagobert's Revenge*, Levenda states that his " involvement was on the translation side"[69] and that his "modest contribution was recognizing that some of the Greek was an attempt to phoneticize Babylonian and

Sumerian words."[70] When I talked to Mr. Levenda a few years ago, however, he had
this to say:

> My role in the *Necronomicon* affair was as a general editor of the translated
> text. I also did much of the background research . . . . I researched Sumerian
> lore at the NY Public Library, for instance, and provided some of the bib-
> liography for Simon's introduction.[71]

Levenda also wrote a short promotional article on the *Necronomicon*, which has
turned up at the American Religions Collection at the University of California at
Santa Barbara's Davidson Library. Next to his byline, someone has written in "Simon
(Editor of Necronomicon)."[72] Levenda was receiving half of the royalties from the
Simon book,[73] so he must have had an important hand in the work.

The most fascinating aspect of this book is its link to the Sumerian civilization,
which began around 3500 B.C. between the Tigris and Euphrates rivers. When the
Simon book was published, the origin of the Sumerians was a mystery, but now they
are believed to have sprung from the earlier Ubaid culture from the same region.
Instead of a single state like those of modern times, Sumer was made up of city-
states, including those of Ur and Kish. The hallmarks of this civilization included
cuneiform writing and huge brick pyramid-shaped temples known as ziggurats.
These city-states spent a great deal of time in conflict with one another, leaving them
open to brief conquests by the Elamites (circa 2700 B.C.) and Akkadians (2371 B.C.).
Later, Babylon, a city formerly controlled by the Sumerians, conquered its masters
and adopted a great deal of Sumer's mythology and religion for its own. The Simon
Necronomicon is thus linked with one of the oldest traditions of magick in the world.

Simon presents his *Necronomicon* as a work of Sumerian magick with one twist:
some of the demons and spirits within the *Necronomicon* bear a striking resemblance
to those in Lovecraft's fiction. For example, Lovecraft speaks of the sea God "Cthulhu,"
and the *Necronomicon* includes "Kutulu," a name that, according to Simon, means
"Man of the Underworld" in Sumerian.[74] These creatures, along with other Sumerian
creatures of evil, are classified as "Azonei," and pitted against the more beneficent
planetary deities, such as Inanna and Sin, known as the "Zonei." The book provides
formulae that place humanity in a position to influence this cosmic war.

The manuscript begins with "The Testimony of the Mad Arab," in which the
unnamed author describes his great feats of magick and the terrible beings he has seen.
He describes his simple life as a shepherd, which was disrupted when he witnessed
a rite of the Ancient Ones and narrowly escaped the fury of their worshipers. His
doom arrives and he must record all that he has learned before the forces he once controlled overcome him.

The next few sections of the text present a series of rituals called "the Walking
of the Gates." Each of these gates is the domain of one of the Zonei and is connected
with a planet, a color, and a sphere of influence. After a lengthy period of purification, the magician walks through each of these gates in sequence, gaining more power

as he passes each one. The enterprising wizard may also travel to the underworld at one point, to become master of the forces of that realm. Two spells used in the ritual, one to call up the Fire God and the other to summon a guardian spirit called the Watcher, appear after the main incantations.[75]

The next sections of the book are much less systematic than the first three, and contain spells for every contingency, from calling up the dead[76] to restoring sexual potency.[77] The "Maqlu Text" is a collection of exorcisms, while "The Book of Fifty Names" reveals the fifty epithets of the God Marduk that may be invoked for a variety of purposes. The proper use of these spells is sometimes obvious, but at other times the exact methods employed are left unclear.

In "The Magan Text," the mad Arab ceases his discussion of magick to give two of the most important myths connected with the book's Gods. The first is a creation myth, in which the God Marduk slays the evil mother-Goddess Tiamat to establish his dominion. The second tells of the love-Goddess Inanna's journey to the underworld. She becomes trapped there, but is later freed as part of a story that suggests the traditional cycle of the seasons. The author returns to his purpose in "The Urilia Text" as he describes the names and powers of the demons he opposes. Though he charges the reader not to have anything to do with these beings, he nonetheless provides a few hymns and rituals dedicated to the "Ancient Ones."

The book ends with another chapter of the mad Arab's testimony. The demons lurk outside the circle, lying in wait for him; the Zonei have deserted him. He becomes disorganized, jumping from one admonition to another as though fearful of not getting everything down. As demons converge from outside his protective barrier, the Arab scrawls "this is the Book of the Servant of the Gods . . ."[78]

Unlike the other *Necronomicon*s I have covered, this book's goal is not to pay homage to Lovecraft but to provide an actual magickal system for occult practitioners. The book includes everything from love spells to invocations of the Azonei, though Simon cautions repeatedly that this is an "advanced" book and that nothing called up through it can be effectively banished.[79] The magickal aspect of the *Necronomicon* is one of its most controversial, and I will leave it to someone more experienced in such matters to evaluate it in this regard.[80] Instead, I will concentrate on the matter of the book's authenticity.

Usually, I would begin with the manuscript itself, but since this is unavailable, the book must be evaluated solely upon its contents. This is complicated by Simon's statement that any similarities in doctrine or phrasing between this book and "later" non-Sumerian sources may be because they both have the *Necronomicon* as their source.[81] Even if we ignore these, a number of discrepancies between the Simon book and more traditional sources on Sumerian myth turn up.

First, much of the book derives, not from the myths of Sumer but from those of Babylon and later cultures. The most glaring example of this involves the God Marduk. Aside from the "Fifty Names of Marduk," the book also mentions him as the "God of Jupiter," one of the seven major Zonei,[82] and includes the tale of the God's

defeat of Tiamat in "The Magan Text." Marduk was the patron God of Babylon, however, and did not become important until that city's rise, long after the time of Sumer.
Likewise, the demon Pazuzu does not appear in myth until Assyria's rise in the first
millennium B.C., long after Sumer's prime.

Some of the lettering in the seals of the gates, especially those on pages 39 and
45, contain lettering more reminiscent of Greek characters than Sumerian, and the
dagger on page 114 is clearly in Greek characters. This may seem like hair-splitting,
but it is nonetheless significant that Simon claims a Sumerian origin for a book that
obviously dates from a later time.

Also of interest are the Lovecraftian inclusions, such as the gods "Kutulu" and
"Azag-Thoth." Despite Simon's elaborate and creative etymologies of these names,[83]
no other work, past or present, contains any mention of "Kutulu" or any of Simon's
other demons whose names resemble Lovecraft's monsters. Lovecraft himself never
included any mention of Sumer's Gods or demons in his stories or letters.[84] In fact,
Lovecraft seems to have known very little about any civilization older than Greece
or Egypt. If the Simon book is an authentic work of Sumerian magick, it would be
unusual for such references to be found only in this work and those of a 20th-century
horror writer who had no interest in Sumer.

In addition to these objections, the role of the book's evil beings differs from
both that of the Sumerian demons and Lovecraft's Old Ones. In our culture, which
is influenced by Judeo-Christian religion, we tend to think of evil beings as directly
opposing the forces of good. This view is reflected in the Simon book, with its "Azonei"
fighting the "Zonei" for the rulership of the universe. For the most part, however,
the evil spirits of the Sumerians were not the enemies of the Gods, but often served
as instruments of their vengeance.[85] The monsters of Lovecraft's work, on the other
hand, are not evil, but vastly powerful and amoral beings that could crush humanity as casually as a person might swat a fly. Thus the beings of the Simon *Necronomicon*
bear little resemblance to either Sumerian myth or Lovecraftian fiction.

If this were not enough, a closer look at the manuscript reveals many other discrepancies. Humwawa is presented in the *Necronomicon* as a monster who is the lord
of filth, but the "Epic of Gilgamesh" lists him as a giant who serves the God Enlil
and protects forests.[86] Pazuzu (the demon behind "The Exorcist") becomes an
undoubtedly evil being, while in antiquity he was considered to be the protector of
newborn children, as well as a plague-God.[87] It is true that the significance of mythological beings can change over time, but no other document suggests that these
unusual interpretations are part of any alternative Sumerian tradition.

The Gates in the *Necronomicon* are accurate material—but only so far as the
Gods and the planets match up. An examination of the ritual suggests that the author
of the Simon *Necronomicon* had a vastly different view of cosmology than the people
of Mesopotamia. The Sumerians, and later the Babylonians, did conceive of a heaven
with seven layers, and they believed that seven planets (including the Sun and the
Moon) moved through the sky. However, a scheme in which each planet traveled in

An Assyrian bronze figurine of the demon Pazuzu circa 800–600 B.C.E. Courtesy of the Oriental Institute of the University of Chicago.

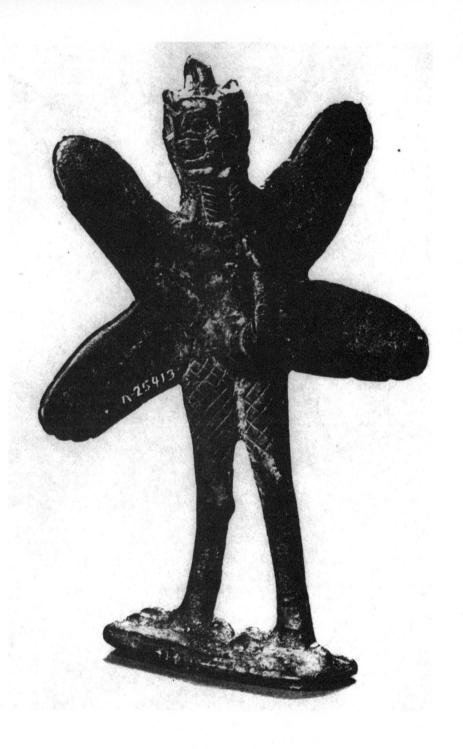

one of these heavens did not appear until much later. Babylonian and Sumerian astronomers believed that the planets all moved at the same distance from Earth.[88] This casts considerable doubt on a Mesopotamian origin for Simon's scheme, in which the magician moves through a series of gates, each defined by a planet, to get to "the furthest reaches of the stars."[89]

This is not the only historical difficulty with the Gate Walking ritual. According to Simon, each stage of the Gate Walking ritual is connected with a particular deity, color, and metal. For example, the fifth gate is associated with the Babylonian Sun God Shamash, whose color and metal are gold.[90] While this may accord with the correspondences between these items in traditional systems of Western magick, Babylonian magicians saw things differently. For them, the metal gold did not signify Shamash, but Enmeŝarra, the father of Enki, or Ea,[91] or the God Enlil.[92] Likewise, Simon's attribution of copper to Ishtar is false, as that metal is the property of Enki.[93] A glance at these charts reveals that, aside from a link between lead and the God Ninurta (or Ninib), no connection between the deities mentioned in the Simon book and the metals given therein exists in the Babylonian literature.

What of the color schemes? In a set of tapes sold at Magickal Childe, Simon discusses the ziggurats, or step-temples, of Mesopotamia:

> A normal human type . . . was not allowed to enter the ziggurat beyond a certain level, depending on your degree of initiation. . . . It is believed according to the Sumerian texts that have been translated that each level was painted a different color . . . Each color corresponded to a different planet. The Sumerians were aware of seven planets, and each level of the ziggurat corresponded to one of the seven planets.[94]

The problems here are legion. First, not all ziggurats had seven steps. While seven was the preferred number of floors, some had as few as three or as many as nine.[95] Second, the colors of the ziggurat are not mentioned by Sumerian sources. Instead, early scholars of this region took the historian Herodotus's description of the colored walls of Agbatana (Ecbatana), an 8th-century town of the Medes in the Zagros Mountains, and decided that the ziggurats were colored in the same scheme. Then again, the scheme in the *Necronomicon* does not reflect Herodotus, being closer to the Queen color scheme utilized by the Hermetic Order of the Golden Dawn. Finally, Morris Jastrow notes "that these colors were brought into connection with the planets, as some scholars have supposed, is highly improbable."[96]

In short, the Gate Walking ritual in the *Necronomicon* does not reflect the beliefs of the Sumerians or Babylonians. Perhaps coincidentally, it best resembles the ideas about Mesopotamian belief put forth by 19th-century scholars who filled in the gaps in their data with material from Greek, Mithraic, Mandaean, Jewish, and other sources.[97]

Comparison of the Simon book to the books mentioned in its bibliography reveals even more damning evidence. An initial look shows that many of the passages in the books coincide with those in the *Necronomicon*. In fact, they often match not only in content but in matters of phrasing. Those who own the Simon book might look to page 161, and compare Part II to a passage from R. C. Thompson's *The Devils and Evil Spirits of Babylonia*:

Incantation: Cold and rain that minish all things, . . .

They are the evil Spirits in the creation of Anu spawned.
Plague Gods, the beloved sons of Bel,
The offspring of Ninkigal.
Rending in pieces on high,
Bringing destruction below,
They are the Children of the Underworld.
Loudly roaring of high,
Gibbering below,
They are the bitter venom of the gods.[98]

If unconvinced, turn to page 199 and read the "Hymn to the Ancient Ones" in conjunction with this piece from Pritchard's *Ancient Near Eastern Texts Relating to the Old Testament*:

They are lying down, the great ones.
The bolts are fallen; the fastenings are placed.
The crowds and people are quiet.
The open gates are (now) closed.
The gods of the land and the goddesses of the land,
Shamash, Sin, Adad, and Ishtar,
Have betaken themselves to sleep in heaven.
They are not pronouncing judgment;
They are not deciding things.
Veiled is the night;
The temple and the most holy places are quiet and dark.[99]

The piece in Pritchard is a ceremony used for divination at night, and it is difficult to tell how it became a prayer to the "Ancient Ones" unconnected with that purpose.

These are only a few of the examples that could be given. Some might cite this as evidence that the Simon book is real, but consider this: Translations from one language to another are rarely the same between translators, as such individuals often differ in their command of the language, their poetic ability, or their choice of words. For example, much of the material in Thompson's *Devils and Evil Spirits of Babylonia* has been retranslated by Markham Geller for his *Forerunners to Udug-Hul: Sumerian Exorcistic Incantations*. I suggest that interested readers turn there to see how many differences can exist between two translations.[100] A large number of the phrases from these translations and the Simon book are identical—surprising, considering how Simon's 9th-century Greek author and the 19th-century scholars manage to make the same mistakes. For example, Thompson, in the passage above, (and Simon) mention "plague gods," when the original makes it clear that the reference is to a single God—Namtar.[101]

All of this evidence makes it unlikely that the book's translators and staff would have failed to notice that the book originated in a much later period. Nevertheless, the only hint in the Simon *Necronomicon* itself that this may not be authentic Sumerian magick comes in the prefatory notes, which state that "although some of the characters found in these pages can be traced to Mandaic and Demotic sources, and are evidently of a much later date than the Rites of Sumer, the overall appearance of the seals is quite unusual, almost surreal."[102] It may be true that the seals are unusual, but I'm not sure why that justifies their post-Sumerian origins. Later, the *Spellbook* did address some of these problems, but only by putting forth a highly unlikely scenario: "[I]t was the magick of the NECRONOMICON that gave spawn to the religion of Sumer."[103] A letter recently sent to me by Peter Levenda, the project's general editor, suggests that the book is the product of a group of magicians from a later period who preserved the Sumerian myths.[104] He did not suggest from which culture these wizards might have come, and I wonder why no one on the project pointed this out to begin with.

When the circumstances surrounding the book's appearance are examined, the differences between the two stories show that something is not right. Two commentators who claim to have known the individuals involved have stated that these stories shouldn't be taken seriously.[105] They do not state why this is the case, and some might debate whether they met Simon at all. Their words should be considered nonetheless. Evidence within the *Necronomicon*'s preface seems to back this up; one of the people involved regrets "setting foot or tentacle"[106] inside Magickal Childe, and Simon wears "a suit of some dark, fibrous material"[107] when first met. Those who take the Simon book very seriously would do well to note these comic touches.

In the end, we must accept that the Simon book is a unique manuscript. While it has been claimed that this is a book of Sumerian origin, it differs greatly from all previous sources on the subject, and it even fails to follow Lovecraft's own pantheon. It might be easier to evaluate the book if we could find and retranslate the supposed original, but its owners' changing stories and their refusal to make it available only adds to the general suspicion. These discrepancies make it almost definite that the book is a modern hoax. I would normally be more harsh on the authors of such a work, but I will say this: out of all the books covered in this essay, the Simon *Necronomicon* is the only one that even comes close to giving off the atmosphere of dread that would accompany a reading of Lovecraft's *Necronomicon*. If only for this, the authors of this work deserve commendation.

The Hay *Necronomicon: The Book of Dead Names*

A year before the publication of the Giger and Simon books, another *Necronomicon* was being written across the Atlantic. Central to the publication of this book was Colin Wilson, a man of extraordinary talents and opinions.

Wilson is a controversial English writer who began writing as a literary critic. His first book, *The Outsider* (1958), was hailed as a literary masterpiece, but he was soon a pariah in the same literary community that had praised him. His critical reputation nearly destroyed, Wilson nonetheless found a market for his later works of criticism, fiction, biography, and occultism. Wilson's first reaction to Lovecraft appeared in his *The Strength to Dream* (1962), a work giving his interpretations of various imaginative writers in light of his own philosophy. Wilson expressed grudging admiration for Lovecraft's story "The Shadow out of Time," but branded the man as a "sick" individual who used "inauthentic forms of expression" (whatever that means), and even went so far as to compare Lovecraft to the Marquis de Sade and Peter Kurten, the Dusseldorf serial killer. After August Derleth voiced his outrage over these spectacular misinterpretations, Wilson back-pedaled considerably, and wrote three enjoyable Cthulhu Mythos novels: *The Mind Parasites*, *The Philosophers' Stone*, and *The Space Vampires*. Though he has often commented on H. P. Lovecraft since then, he seems still to consider Lovecraft an "unhealthy" writer, and is constantly attempting to interpret Lovecraft in light of his own philosophy and theories, overlooking any evidence to the contrary.

According to the introduction, Wilson first became interested in the book's possible existence when his friend L. Sprague de Camp "found" the Owlswick Press *Necronomicon*. Even though the manuscript could not be translated and was thought to be a hoax, Wilson was intrigued. Soon, he came into contact with two individuals: Robert Turner and George Hay. Turner was head of a group of magicians called the Order of the Cubic Stone and was looking into the possibility that Lovecraft received his inspiration from ancient grimoires. Hay was editing a collection of essays on the *Necronomicon*. Wilson did not believe that the *Necronomicon* was real, but he set out to find the answers for himself.

The break came when Wilson's friend Carl Tausk mentioned to him that an occult scholar from Austria, Doctor Stanislaus Hinterstoisser, might have some information. Wilson wrote Hinterstoisser, who informed him that Lovecraft's father, Winfield, had been an Egyptian Freemason. While most U.S. Masonic lodges are largely social clubs, Hinterstoisser maintained that the Egyptian Freemasons possessed secret knowledge passed down from the charlatan Cagliostro (1745–93), and, in the distant past, from the Greeks, Egyptians, and Sumerians. Winfield Lovecraft saw some of this material at his lodge, and was taught to read (or decipher) it by a man named "Tall Cedar." The doctor later told Wilson that one of the books Winfield saw was the *Necronomicon*, but he inconveniently passed away before he could give any more information.

Encouraged, Wilson and his friends set out in search of the *Necronomicon*. Since Lovecraft mentioned the Elizabethan wizard John Dee as a translator of the book, Robert Turner went to the British Museum to look through Dee's papers. There, he found Liber Logaeth (or Logaeath), a manuscript made up of squares filled with letters. Turner sent these to David Langford, a computer programmer and cryptographer, who deciphered the manuscript and discovered the text of the *Necronomicon* there. Hay changed the plans for his book, and *The Necronomicon: The Book of Dead Names* was published in 1978, with a paperback from Corgi Books emerging two years later.

At least, this is the story Wilson tells in the book. He admitted, in *Fantasy Macabre* for 1980, that the piece was a "spoof."[108] Later, in an article written in the Saint John's Eve 1984 issue of the fanzine *Crypt of Cthulhu*, Wilson gave the full story. It began with Neville Armstrong, the founder of Neville Spearman Limited, a publishing company that reprinted the fiction of such Lovecraft contemporaries as Robert E. Howard and Clark Ashton Smith. Armstrong asked his friend George Hay to compile stories to create an authentic-looking *Necronomicon*. After collecting some material, Hay turned to the literary critic and occultist Colin Wilson for help. Wilson was unimpressed with much of the volume, and asked Robert Turner to write the actual text of the *Necronomicon*. An explanation of the volume's origins was still needed, but Wilson had his background in fiction to help him. He had a German friend write him a letter, addressing it from the fictional "Doctor Hinterstoisser." This helped him give the background; he filled in the rest with his imagination. Armstrong liked the book, and published it.[109]

One of the most unfortunate aspects of this *Necronomicon* is the brevity of the "*Necronomicon*" section itself. The book contains a system of magick that is modeled on those of actual grimoires such as the *Key of Solomon* and the *Goetia*, but is based around the creatures of the Cthulhu Mythos instead of more conventional demons. Along with paragraphs describing the nature of the Old Ones, the book describes how to make altars, ceremonial swords, incense, and the other trappings of the magician. The actual rites call upon Gods such as Yog-Sothoth, Shub-Niggurath, and Cthulhu (all described in a way consistent with Lovecraft and other Mythos authors) to bring the caster wealth and knowledge.

It is interesting to contrast the Hay *Necronomicon* with the Simon book. After its publication, the Hay book soon went out of print. Wilson estimated that no one involved in his project made more than one hundred pounds (about $150 at current rates) on it.[110] On the other hand, the general editor of the Simon book tells me that the *Necronomicon* has been in print ever since its publication[111] and, in my experience, has enjoyed greater popularity than Hay's book. One important reason may be the purposes behind the texts. The Hay *Necronomicon* is intended as a semischolarly joke. What few rites it contains are time-consuming and require expensive incenses, woods, and other materials. The Simon book is a book for would-be magicians. It includes a large number of rites, many of which require no components whatsoever. Wilson and his compatriots treat their *Necronomicon* as a literary curios-ity, while Simon's book is filled with premonitions of doom that heighten the book's reputation in the eyes of those who read it. The fact that the Hay book was never available in the United States may also account for this disparity.

Robert M. Price believes that this prank was done in "innocent fun."[112] I would suggest otherwise. In his *Crypt of Cthulhu* article, Wilson points out that "*Necron-omicon*" does not mean "The Book of Dead Names," so "anyone with the slightest knowledge of Latin will instantly recognize it for a fake."[113] Lars Lindholm, author of *Pilgrims of the Night,* has pointed out that "*Necronomicon*" is Greek in origin and wonders how the book's less-educated readers are supposed to understand the etymology if Wilson himself cannot master it.[114] Still, I would be more willing to dismiss the matter as a simple case of high-brow leg-pulling if the book hadn't been rereleased.

In 1992, Skoob Esoterica reprinted the Hay *Necronomicon* in a paperback edi-tion that has been released in the United States. The book is usually found in the occult department, and no hint is given anywhere in it that Wilson admitted it was a fraud. It was even followed by a sequel, *The R'lyeh Text* (another imaginary Mythos book, this one from the fiction of August Derleth). *The R'lyeh Text* gives a few more pages from the *Necronomicon,* along with some essays on the occult. Perhaps having learned their lesson, the authors are more sensationalistic in this book, foreseeing all manner of dooms presaged by its appearance. Still, no hint of Wilson's *Crypt of Cthulhu* article emerges. In one passage, Robert Turner even ridicules one of the opponents of his *Necronomicon* by speculating upon "the author's motives for such an expenditure of verbiage on a subject that most of the public would consider mean-ingless."[115] Since Wilson has already admitted that the work is a hoax, his and Turner's own "expenditure of verbiage" here hardly seems justifiable.

Das Necronomicon

The trio of *Necronomicon*s from 1977–78 has been translated a number of times. Although it does attest to these books' popularity, it is otherwise uninteresting from my standpoint. There is one such work that should be mentioned, however, for its fascinating nature.

My search of an interlibrary database turned up *Das Necronomicon,* translated by Gregor A. Gregorius and published by Verlag Richard Schikowski of Berlin in 1980. When I obtained it, it proved to be the Simon book translated almost word-for-word into German, with a translation of *The Goetia,* a medieval grimoire used to call up demons, filling out the rest of the volume. No mention of Magickal Childe or Simon appears anywhere in the book. The English version's introductory mate-rial is missing, but the unnamed commentator tells how the partially encoded man-uscript of this *Necronomicon* was found in the notes of the dead occultist Gregor A. Gregorius. I later discovered that Gregorius was actually Eugen Grosche (1888–1961), the head of the German occult lodge Fraternitas Saturni ("Brotherhood of Saturn").

This group was a branch of the Ordo Templi Orientis, or OTO, which refused to accept Aleister Crowley's takeover of the group in 1925, and which was later banned by the Nazis along with other lodges and fraternities.[116] As best I can tell, they are an exclusive and traditional order, and if the attribution is correct, it is a testament to the Simon *Necronomicon*'s popularity that even an order like this considers the book to be of importance.

The book's forward is so brief and vague that it seems to have been an after-thought on the translator's part to justify plagiarism. With the explosion of information technology since then, they needn't have bothered. Anyone with access to the Web can find a reasonably complete copy of the Simon or Hay book within five minutes, and I have yet to hear of anyone being sued for this. *Das Necronomicon* may be the earliest example of a trend in which these books, like Frankenstein's monster, have escaped their creators and assumed a life of their own.

The Elizabeth Ann Saint George *Necronomicon*

Elizabeth Ann Saint George is (or was—I have no idea whether she is still alive) a London occultist trained in the ceremonial tradition. According to her brief biography in her *Casebook of a Working Occultist*, Ms. St. George grew up in the West Indies and, though she claimed London as her home, she spent a great deal of time traveling around the world on a shoestring budget. After marrying, she settled down and started her own psychic investigation firm, called Spook Enterprises.[117] The rest of this book ranges from a serious account of her initiation into a Western mystery school to tales of chasing KGB agents with her family and friends, their dogs, and an archangel. Though I am hesitant to make such judgments, I believe that much of it was written in fun.

I have discovered more than thirty titles under the Spook Enterprises imprint, one of which is—horror of horrors—the *Necronomicon*. In a brief note, the author comments that the work is also known as "The Book of Shades," and that it is "a copy of a manuscript which was in Peru, in a private collection in 1964."[118] The *Necronomicon* was translated by a "Madam Ruzo," the wife of a deceased private collector who lived at a Peruvian *estancia*, and St. George, though the latter admits that her Arabic "extends nowhere at all."[119]

This *Necronomicon* is not attributed to Abdul Alhazred, but to a magician named al-Raschid of Sothis. (Sothis is another name for the star Sirius, and probably an in-joke.) The book's few pages give instructions on all manner of deeds, ranging from helping women in labor to summoning an army of angels. The simplest of these makes use of concepts such as hygiene and medicine, while the most complex usually have some hard-to-find or impossible requirement ("the secret incense of earth," "the six-sided figure of death," or starlight). The manuscript is unusual among *Necronomicon*s in that it attempts to portray Alhazred as someone who knows of Islam, and the text is peppered with pious mentions of Allah and his prophet.

The book is too short to truly fulfill its intention. At some points I found myself shaking my head—why would a man from the Middle East like al-Raschid consider irrigation a hidden secret? Yet the Saint George *Necronomicon* betrays a concern to construct a *Necronomicon* that a person of that time might actually have written. Medieval authors often included material that we would consider scientific with that many would consider magickal or superstitious. In that sense, this *Necronomicon* is more faithful to the time and place of Alhazred than most others.

Merlyn Stone's *Necronomicon*

Merlyn Stone is a precocious young wizard who self-published four instructional manuals on modern sorcery while still in his teens. The fourth of these is Stone's own version of the *Necronomicon*, a small paperbound pamphlet with a green cover, issued in 1999.

The book's subtitle is "A Compendium of Ceremonial Magick," and it strives mightily to live up to it. The first magickal operation given within is a protective rite—the Opening of the Watchtowers—followed by instructions for calling up spirits. We are then treated to lists of these spirits, a few from a number of medieval grimoires—plus some from the Simon *Necronomicon*. The book goes on to include sundry rites of ceremonial magick, a description of the Black Mass, a brief explanation of the Kabbalah, and a question-and-answer page regarding the author's other works. In all, the book contains material from Jewish mysticism, medieval books of black magick, Satanism, Druidic (?) practice, and the Simon book, all assembled under one cover.

This book is confusing on several points. It is uncertain whether this book was issued by Sacred Grove or Crystal Dawn Press—both are listed as the publishers at different points. In the introduction, Stone tells us that the *Necronomicon* is "merely an archetypal symbol,"[120] yet later states that Crowley saw a copy,[121] and that the original (wherever it is) has been carbon dated to 6000 B.C.[122] Even having asked the author for clarification, I am still baffled as to his sources for these statements. Further, the work's stated purpose is that "these rites and the knowledge within will not be lost due to the overly political organizations, greedy companies, and the like."[123] This sentiment is admirable—and it would be even more so if most of the collected material had not been available for decades in paperback! Stone has since explained that the book served to bring together materials he didn't have room for in his other works,[124] which makes more sense to me.

The last two examples typify a phenomenon that will most likely grow in years to come: the writing of *Necronomicon*s, not for money or fame, but out of an occultist's desire to make his or her own vision of the book tangible. It is likely that many more such *Necronomicon*s exist of which I am not aware, so be on the lookout, and do not assume that a book is authentic merely because it is not listed here.

The Carter *Necronomicon*

One of the longest *Necronomicon*s ever published was that of Lin Carter (1930–88). Carter was a fantasy writer known for his "Thongor" books, a series that describes the voyages of a barbarian from the lost continent of Lemuria. Carter's legacy in the fantasy genre is less due to his fiction than his role as an editor of the Ballantine Adult Fantasy line and a number of paperback anthologies.

Lovecraft was one of Carter's favorite authors, and he managed to write a large number of tales using the "Cthulhu Mythos." Instead of trying to horrify his audience, Carter saw his Mythos fiction as a way of systematizing the information provided by other authors. If there were gaps or contradictions, Lin would try to resolve them in his stories, sometimes writing tales solely for this reason. As such, his stories are often catalogs of the Cthulhu Mythos, with little attempt at characterization, plot, or atmosphere. His works are largely unknown outside of the Lovecraftian community.

Since Lin Carter was the "Grand Systematizer" of the Cthulhu Mythos, one can see why he would write his own *Necronomicon*. Rumor has it that he got his start at a fantasy convention back in the 1950s, where he showed a few gullible fans a few fake pages from the *Necronomicon* he had concocted.[125] Later, while working on his *Lovecraft: A Look Behind the Cthulhu Mythos*, Carter wrote a few short stories meant to be chapters of the *Necronomicon*. The first of these was "The Doom of Yakthoob," which describes the death of Abdul Alhazred's teacher, Yakthoob. "Doom" was published in the summer 1971 issue of Derleth's magazine, *The Arkham Sampler*, and other sections of the book showed up occasionally in small press fanzines. It was not until after Carter's death that his *Necronomicon* was published in its entirety, first in *Crypt of Cthulhu*[126] and then in Robert M. Price's *Necronomicon*.[127]

Carter pretended his book was a "Dee translation" he had found and annotated. The first part, "The Book of Episodes," is a series of nine short pieces describing the adventures of the mad Arab Abdul Alhazred. All of them are cautionary tales in which Alhazred's investigations go awry with horrible consequences. The next section, "The Book of Preparations," tells of the glories of service to the Old Ones and the precautions to be taken before one invokes them. "The Book of the Gates" describes ways of seeing and traveling through both time and space, and "The Book of Dismissals" includes several different methods of sending away That Which is Called Up. The manuscript has several inconsistencies, and is missing an entire section—"The Book of Rites"—that Carter never got around to writing, though some parts of it are said to exist.[128]

Recently, a few people have pointed out the connection between Carter's material and that in the Hay *Necronomicon*. Not only does Carter's manuscript mention the "Scimitar of Barzai"[129] and the "Runes of Nug-Soth,"[130] both of which are original to the Hay book,[131] but his section "Of the Times and Seasons to Be Observed"[132] is a rewrite and expansion of the same section in the other *Necronomicon*.[133] My guess is that Lin Carter, in his bid to bring together the entire Cthulhu Mythos, decided to make his own work an extension of the Hay book. Unfortunately, the book was left incomplete, so there is no way of knowing if Carter would have tried later to include material from the Simon *Necronomicon* or the *Sussex Manuscript*.

I don't think Carter was writing this with the intent of fooling anyone. Since most of his Mythos fiction appeared in the small press, it is likely that Carter planned the same for it. Although his rather bland style fails to incite any horror in the reader, Carter nonetheless has made a valiant effort to create a *Necronomicon* of proper length with direct ties to the Cthulhu Mythos.

The Price *Necronomicon*

During the 1980s, interest in Lovecraft subsided once again and *Necronomicon* publishing became less lucrative. Recently, however, another upsurge in Lovecraftian material has begun. Numerous anthologies of Lovecraft's stories have appeared, and Skoob Esoterica reprinted the Hay *Necronomicon* and released it, along with *The R'lyeh Text*, in the United States for the first time. Chaosium Books, a role-playing game company best known for their *Call of Cthulhu* game based on Lovecraft's works, has joined many others in the business in branching out into fiction, putting out a line of paperback Cthulhu Mythos anthologies. In November 1996, they published their own *Necronomicon*, a collection of stories and articles edited by Robert M. Price, a New Testament scholar and editor of *Crypt of Cthulhu*. "Hexes and Hoaxes," his excellent article on the *Necronomicon*, appeared in the December 1984 issue of *Rod Serling's The Twilight Zone Magazine* and established Price as something of an expert when it comes to the *Necronomicon*.

Price's book begins with a brief look at the *Necronomicon* from the standpoint of deconstructionist literary criticism. A key idea from the deconstructionists is that of deferral of meaning. A word can never be defined, for example, for to define it would require other words that in turn must be defined, and so on. In the same way, a text can only be understood by referring to other texts, which cannot be understood without referring to other texts, and so on. Price argues that the *Necronomicon* itself is an example of this deferral, as the book's vagueness and references to other works point us to other meanings. This is an unusual and somewhat appropriate way for dealing with the *Necronomicon*, considering the mysterious way in which Lovecraft often alludes to it, though I wonder how many of Price's readers will be both pulp fiction fans and deconstructionist critics interested in this line of thought.

The book itself is a fascinating piece for those who enjoy the Cthulhu Mythos. Along with stories from the Cthulhu Mythos, the book reprints the *Sussex Manuscript*, Lin Carter's *Necronomicon*, and Price's own "A Critical Commentary on the *Necronomicon*," which endeavors to interpret various passages from the book and determine which are "original" using the same methods as Biblical criticism. A quote on the back cover asserts that "true seekers into the esoteric mysteries of the world"[134] realize that the book exists, but none of the pieces within is credited to their authors and they are not presented as parts of an authentic *Necronomicon*.

Black's *Necronomicon*

One of the latest *Necronomicon*s to appear has little to do with Lovecraft, but deserves a mention nonetheless. This book comes out of Creation Press, a British publisher that links horror, magick, and eroticism in their works, and which has published a Lovecraft tribute anthology (*Starry Wisdom*) and their own collection of Lovecraft's stories (*Crawling Chaos*). Creation then issued Book One of *Necronomicon: The Journal of Horror and Erotic Cinema* in May of 1996. The editor, Andy Black, states that this was originally a magazine that has been expanded into book form.[135] The book shows only one link to Lovecraft—an essay by Black on Lovecraft's influence on the film genre—but it is interesting as a journal that attempts to look at horror and erotic films in a scholarly manner.

The *Necronomicon* On-line

I mentioned earlier that many of the published *Necronomicon*s have turned up in one form or another on the Internet. The new global computer network has also proven to be a showcase for individuals to display their own creativity, and create their own *Necronomicon*s. One of these is John Opsopaus's *Necronomicon Novum*. This may not be the best example, as the piece was originally published in the November 1995 issue of *Mythos* magazine. I have yet to find any mention of that magazine elsewhere, however, so it is evident that this particular version would not have achieved the same circulation if conventionally printed.

The *Necronomicon Novum* is one of the most unusual of these pieces I have ever seen. Mr. Opsopaus admits that he doesn't "remember how much [Lovecraft] said about the content of the *Necronomicon*," and that he was forced to create its contents from scratch, "mostly spun out of no more than the name *Necronomicon*."[136] Instead of drawing on the Cthulhu Mythos, he collected material from Greek, Roman, and Etruscan myths relating to the Gods of the underworld and various demons, and presented all of them as emanations of the collective unconscious. The piece is brief, but it displays the versatility and uniqueness writers have brought to the concept of the *Necronomicon*.

Another *Necronomicon* that has appeared on the Web is a project by Phil Legard, an English chaos magician, known as *Grimoirium Imperium, or the Book of the Old Spirits, being the Book of the Law and Practices of the Sleeping Dead Learned by Doctor John Dee from the works of Abd al-Hazred*. As of 1999, Legard has transcribed four books of ten, and I eagerly await the other six.

According to the book's introduction, this work was owned by the wizard John Dee. Dee received this book in 1581 from Barnabas Saul, who claimed to receive revelations by gazing into a magick mirror. Dee thought little of the gift, and Saul left shortly thereafter, to be replaced by the infamous Edward Kelley. In 1601, Dee rediscovered the manuscript in his papers and decided to translate it, finding himself led on by an irresistible compulsion.[137] In 1606, Dee sold many of his magickal manuscripts because of debt, and this one numbered among them.[138]

As the book begins, the wizard Abd Al-Hazred tells how a demon called Ebonor approached him with an offer of magickal knowledge. Al-Hazred accepted, but found that the knowledge he gained alienated him from the rest of humanity. He reveals the initial set of these secrets—a number of seals for invoking different aspects of the Lovecraftian God Nyarlathotep.[139] The second chapter is similar, describing the beings that coincide with different parts of the zodiac.[140] This is followed by a series of instructions for creating the tools—including a sword, wand, dagger, robe, diagram, and ring—required for the operation. Such objects are constructed according to the methods of ceremonial magick, with the pieces being made at certain times out of the proper materials and inscribed with curious diagrams.[141] The last piece that has been transcribed describes the circle of power that protects the magician from the spirits he conjures.[142]

Legard's work is difficult to evaluate from any perspective. On one hand, its attribution to John Dee is clearly false, and Legard has admitted as much. On the other, this is a modern magician's book of spells that, as best I can tell, does have some foundation in actual practice. (Another ritual, Legard's *Liber Muqarribin*, tells of the calling of Abdul Alhazred, a rite he has described as a working of his own.) No further chapters of the *Grimoirium Imperium* have appeared for some time; I hope that the project will be picked up again soon.

An Italian Trio

Italy has recently been the site of considerable interest in Lovecraft's fiction, as well as the *Necronomicon*. In the past six years, in fact, no less than three different books claiming to be the *Necronomicon* have surfaced in Italy. Since I do not read Italian, I have been unable to evaluate their contents, but some general comments can be made.

The trend was started with *La Magia Estelar: El Verdadero Necronomicón* by Frank G. Ripel (1988), the Italian head of the Ordo Rosae Mysticae. From a friend's description,[143] this book seems to be Lovecraft's Mythos mixed with a liberal helping of the occult works of Aleister Crowley. In subsequent works, published by Rome's Il Trigono Libreria Esoterica, Ripel has claimed that the *Necronomicon* is merely a less powerful work derived from the *Sauthenerom*, a work lost with the destruction of Atlantis.

The next such book to appear was Pietro Pizzari's *Necronomicon* (1993). It is supposedly taken from a manuscript in the Vatican Library. Following a series of brief introductions, Pizzari gives us six sections of the "Book of the Names of the Dead." Given a quick scan of the text, the material does look original and more faithful to Lovecraft than most—but the magickal symbols appear to have been drawn freehand with a magic marker.

In 1994, Fanucci Editors of Rome have released an Italian paperback version of the *Necronomicon*. From the information given at their website,[144] this book is the most complete *Necronomicon* ever published, containing new Sumerian information found in 1990 that was translated by Venustiano Carranza, a professor at the (fictional) University of Mexico City. (Carranza was actually Mexico's first president. Since he died in 1920, it is likely that his contribution to this volume was minimal.) From what I have seen, the book was originally intended as an Italian reprint of the Hay book (which occupies the rear of the volume), and had some supplementary material—including artwork from the Simon book—tacked on later, with a detailed explanation. The same publisher is now offering a sequel—*Necronomicon 2: The Tomb of Alhazred*—that supposedly includes material buried in the tomb of Abdul Alhazred himself, in Yemen!

The *Necronomicon* Project

In my discussion, I have tried to distinguish between those hoaxes that seem to have been done in innocent fun and those in which other factors seem to have been at play. I feel that this is an important consideration, but I don't want to be too harsh on those who have perpetrated either type of hoax. My conclusions in this regard have been based mostly upon the works themselves. The authors may, however, have other motivations that I have been unable to determine. Besides, I myself am not entirely guiltless when it comes to fake *Necronomicon*s.

A few years ago, Laurent Alquier announced that he was putting together a French "*Necronomicon* Project" website. The project was opened to the public, and anyone who wanted to contribute a passage from the dread volume could. When I found out about it, I was intrigued enough to write up my own contribution, an invocation to the Mythos God Daoloth.[145] In a recent letter to an electronic gaming magazine, Mr. Alquier announced that he had time to revise the project, and noted that he had even been approached by people who wanted to know whether this was the real *Necronomicon*.[146] It was something of a surprise to me. On his home page, Mr. Alquier had included links to both a project statement that clearly defined the work as fictional, and a contributor's page giving each person credit for the part they had written. Since then, Mr. Alquier has placed a very prominent warning informing those who visit the site that it is fake, but it remains to be seen whether anyone still takes it seriously.

This incident should serve to point out two elements of *Necronomicon* hoaxes. One is that there are people who will believe anything is real without bothering to look at it carefully, a fact that anyone preparing to put together a hoax should consider. The other is that performing a *Necronomicon* hoax is so enjoyable that even a debunker can easily be caught up in the fun. I hope that if any future debunker writes about the *Necronomicon* Project, they will be as merciful about it as I have tried to be.

Conclusion

When I first wrote this chapter, I was certain that I had covered all of the *Necronomicon*s that could be found. Recent events, however, have proved me wrong. More and more

*Necronomicon*s have turned up, largely because of the growing influence of the Internet, a medium that permits these books to be widely disseminated—or at least, for forged copies to be bought and sold.

The new flood of *Necronomicon*s comes primarily from two different sources. The first is the occult community. As seen above, many occultists are intrigued enough by the *Necronomicon* to create their own interpretations of the book. A key example of this is *Liber 555* by the artist Michael Bell, which is written entirely in meaningless hieroglyphs, yet, through its vivid depictions, manages to be more faithful to Lovecraft's vision than most of the works I have described. In addition, magicians from many traditions take it upon themselves to record their dreams, experiences, and favorite magickal workings in private journals. Within the Wiccan tradition, these records are known as "Books of Shadows"—but I wouldn't be surprised if a few humorists choose to put "*Necronomicon*" prominently on the cover.

The second source for these *Necronomicon*s is the live-action role-playing (LARP) games. Players in LARPs engage in what can be described as structured improvisational theater, with players dressing as and taking the roles of characters who return to an ongoing story with every session. To make the game come alive for the players, the directors of these events often create elaborate props—including beautiful and authentic-looking *Necronomicon*s. I have seen a few of these show up on online auctions from time to time—thankfully, they have always been labeled as stage dressing, rather than the works of Abdul Alhazred.

Under these circumstances, providing a complete list of *Necronomicon*s is fruitless. Such an attempt might even be misleading, as items not mentioned here might be considered real by default. I urge caution on the part of those who would buy such works, hoping against hope that they are getting the "true" *Necronomicon* for their troubles.

Evaluating *Necronomicon* Rumors —Daniel Harms

3

Reason, v. i. To weight probabilities in the scales of desire.
—AMBROSE BIERCE, *THE DEVIL'S DICTIONARY*

So far, the search for the *Necronomicon* has brought us through some strange territory—horror writers, mysterious cults, black magick, countless B-movies, and cycles of ancient myth. By this time, some readers have dismissed the *Necronomicon* as a mass delusion brought about by authors and hucksters, a product of the superstitious times into which civilization is slowly sliding. Others have decided that all of this is merely an elaborate smokescreen, that my coauthor and I are pawns of some shadowy organization dedicated to keeping the secret of the *Necronomicon* to itself. And a number are probably sitting on the fence.

Most of the people who read this book will put it aside and never give the issues another thought. That's perfectly fine—they got what they came for, and there are more important matters in life than the *Necronomicon*. Still, there will be those who want to go further, and take a look for themselves. Unfortunately, training people to think critically is not a high priority in most societies. Much as we like to think of ourselves as free individuals, we are nonetheless conditioned to hold certain views and are rarely taught how to question them, save in the light of another, largely unquestioned belief system. Unlike many "debunking" books, the goal of *The Necronomicon Files* is not to produce believers, but to give you the tools to investigate for yourself.

Seven Guidelines for the Evaluation of *Necronomicon* Hoaxes

Here are some guidelines for looking into these questions.

1. *Be your own worst critic.* We are often told that it's best to "keep an open mind" and "wait until the facts are in" to pass judgment. In reality, all the facts rarely come in, and most people make up their minds on such

questions quickly. Anyone who has taken the time to read our book this far most likely has opinions or beliefs about the *Necronomicon*— pro or con.

The key to investigation is not to avoid believing anything, but to use your beliefs as a springboard. Examine them critically, and be prepared to argue both for and against them. Even though John and I do not believe in a pre-Lovecraft *Necronomicon*, we spent a great deal of time operating as if we did—following up rumors, checking library catalogs, and researching in such a way that some have mistaken us for supporters of the *Necronomicon*'s existence. This provided a number of interesting avenues to explore, and left open the possibility of finding information that contradicts what we hold dear.

2. *Get back to the original sources.* Always try to follow the rumor as far back as you can. *Necronomicon* rumors have a tendency to become entangled with both fact and fiction as time goes on. The original source is likely to have more information that will help you evaluate the claim—or may be willing to let you in on the joke. I am always surprised by the people who pontificate on what Lovecraft said about the *Necronomicon*, then admit they've never read his stories!

3. *Go to alternate sources for corroborating information.* Does Lovecraft say that John Dee translated the *Necronomicon*? Start looking for biographies of John Dee, descriptions of his library, and so forth. Too many people have placed their trust in a single source without investigating whether it is true. The Internet is a useful source for this sort of cross-checking, but requires a great deal of judgment.

4. *Break the rumor into smaller parts, and verify each part individually.* Taking their cue from Lovecraft, many hoaxers blend fact with fiction, and it is necessary to evaluate each statement individually. Just because John Dee was a real person doesn't mean that he translated the *Necronomicon*. Even if you do find out that one part is false, it often helps to do more research to bolster your argument.

5. *If you can't be certain, assess the probabilities.* It is almost impossible to disprove the existence of anything. A few people have asked skeptics to prove that a pre-Lovecraft *Necronomicon* doesn't exist. This is impossible; one would have to search every place on Earth where such a book might be hidden at the same instant (to make sure no one moved it around while the search was going on). Still, hundreds of people have searched for it for three-quarters of a century, and no such book has ever been found, so it is quite improbable that it exists. It is better to ask if anyone has any proof that such a book *does* exist.

6. *Recognize your limitations.* I've been looking over *Necronomicon* hoaxes for years, yet if someone brought me a Greek or Latin manuscript and said it was the *Necronomicon*, I would be unable to evaluate it for myself. Know when you need to call in someone else to help you.

7. *Don't burn bridges for others.* Be polite, return books and documents to their collections, and make your research into a pleasant experience for everyone involved. Sometimes, we become so engrossed in our own doings that we forget we're dealing with other living, breathing people, with whom someone else might want to deal in the future. If someone won't talk to you, or you can't take that treasured book home, don't ruin the chance for someone else to do so next week or a few years down the road.

I should also comment on two other "ways of knowing" that may come up in a *Necronomicon* search. One of these is a knowledge that comes from within us, whether through intuition, contact with a higher power, or divination and fortune-telling. These can be the source of deep personal revelation and significance, and should not be dismissed lightly. However, don't expect this knowledge to be accepted by anyone else. Too many people have a spiritual realization and then are disappointed that everyone else doesn't accept it on their authority. Some substitute one improbability for another; one person told me that the best way to learn if the *Necronomicon* exists is to summon a demon! If you do have an experience like this, and want to convince others, look for proof in the physical world.

The other type of information that may present itself is secret knowledge. On one hand, you may be stonewalled by a person who refuses to talk, or who gives their justification as, "That's a secret we've been told to keep." On the other, you may learn something, on the condition that you keep it to yourself or not divulge your source. Unfortunately, when it comes to convincing others, most such evidence is useless without a source to back it up. While you may be tempted to pry into others' lives or give out such information, this is always a bad idea. When John and I have been given secret pointers, we have asked, "How else could we find this out?" and tried to find it another way. If we couldn't, we didn't use it.

Investigating *Necronomicon* Hoaxes

It may be helpful for me to provide examples of some of the hoaxes I've looked in to, to give some idea about how these work in practice. You'll notice that I don't always follow these guidelines, but when I don't, I point out how things might have been made easier if I had. The important thing to remember is that all of the following could have been done by anyone willing to invest a little time into checking it out. Even though some areas may be beyond your field of expertise, this does not mean you have to sit back and let the experts (whoever they are) figure everything out for you.

The Colin Low Anti-FAQ

One of the most infamous *Necronomicon* hoaxes is Colin Low's Anti-FAQ. A FAQ, or Frequently Asked Questions file, is an Internet document that provides quick answers to questions people ask about a single topic. I'm not sure what an anti-FAQ is; its intent may be to leave a person even more confused than before. Colin Low is an Internet occultist who has also written a book-length article on the Qaballah, which seems to be respected by other practitioners on the Web.

According to the Low FAQ, the *Necronomicon* was indeed the work of Abdul Alhazred, who used ceremonial magick and drugs to send his mind to view distant times and places. Olaus Wormius did translate the book, but instead of being Lovecraft's Danish doctor, he was a clerk serving the Spanish Inquisition who was burned when his superiors discovered what he had done. Doctor John Dee translated the book into English, and the mystic Nathan of Gaza rendered it into Hebrew. The notorious occultist Aleister Crowley later saw Dee's copy in the Bodleian Library at Oxford, and the book had a profound influence on his later writing and beliefs.

The FAQ states that Lovecraft encountered the *Necronomicon* through Aleister Crowley and Sonia Greene. Before Sonia met Lovecraft, she supposedly met Crowley on his trip to New York and the two had an affair. When she became involved with Lovecraft, she passed on her knowledge of the *Necronomicon* to him. Since Lovecraft only had third-hand information, his fictional version differs considerably from the "real" one. Unfortunately, the Nazis later hunted down every known copy of the *Necronomicon*, and those that they did not find were hidden away from the general public and remain so half a century later. Low denies that any of the *Necronomicon*s currently on the market are authentic, and states that he himself has no idea where a copy may be found.

When I began my investigation of the Anti-FAQ, I couldn't find Colin Low, so I examined the facts in the essay. Since I had never found anything factual on the *Necronomicon* or Alhazred before, I tried to start from the parts I knew were factual and work backward. John Dee, Nathan of Gaza, and Aleister Crowley were all real, but no link between them and a "*Necronomicon*" can be confirmed in works on their lives. I found no mention of Low's "Olaus Wormius" in the library's books on the Inquisition. Given the bulk of material on the subject, this is not surprising, but I was skeptical of this Spanish Inquisitor with a Scandinavian name. As for the Crowley-Lovecraft link, neither Lovecraft nor Crowley reported an affair between Sonia and Crowley, and no biographer of either man has mentioned it. Since I could find no corroborating information, I grew suspicious of the essay.

My feelings were confirmed when I examined the material more closely. It seemed surprising to me that the author spent so much effort researching the background material, yet gave no sources for the information on the *Necronomicon*. In fact, the only source Low cites in the article is "*The Book of the Arab*, by Justin Geoffrey, Starry Wisdom Press, 1979." Justin Geoffrey was an imaginary poet mentioned in the stories of Robert E. Howard, one of Lovecraft's friends, and Starry Wisdom is a cult named in Lovecraft's "Haunter of the Dark." No entry for *The Book of the Arab* exists in the On-line Computer Library Catalog (OCLC), an on-line catalog of hundreds of libraries across the country, and I have yet to find this or any other books from Starry Wisdom Press. Low's story became less likely the more I researched.

Then I had a breakthrough. I found a post by Colin Low on the alt.magick newsgroup, and was finally able to write to him and ask whether he cared to comment on the essay. I was surprised when he wrote me back and told me it was a hoax of his own invention. Low had become annoyed at those who either dogmatically asserted or denied that the *Necronomicon* existed. As he told me, he hoped that

> those that really knew their stuff would see through it instantly and enjoy
> it (in the spirit of Lovecraft's own pseudo history), while those who were
> insulting others for the sport of it would be cast into doubt and confusion.[1]

At another time, Low said, "extending the hoax to a completely ridiculous extent is the first step in weaning [believers] off credulity."[2] With all respect to the author, I think he has overestimated the rationality of his readers. One of the most common questions I get about the *Necronomicon* is whether the Low FAQ is a reliable source. I should note that Mr. Low now includes on his website two articles that discuss the *Necronomicon* in a more critical light.

The Philosopher's Stone

Aside from his key role in the Hay *Necronomicon*, Colin Wilson has unwittingly created a few other *Necronomicon* hoaxes through his fiction. Of all the authors who have followed Lovecraft in writing Cthulhu Mythos stories, Wilson is perhaps the most skilled at mixing fact and fiction, until the reader can hardly tell one from the other. One of the most famous of these is the *Voynich Manuscript*.

The *Voynich Manuscript* is a real book, kept at Yale's Beinecke Library, that was once thought to be the work of the philosopher Roger Bacon. The manuscript first surfaced in the 16th century, and has baffled the best cryptographers in the world ever since. For his purposes, Wilson decided that the manuscript was actually a commentary on the *Necronomicon* written by a monk named Martin Gardner. This has been a rather popular hoax, and I continue to meet people who think the *Voynich Manuscript* is the *Necronomicon*. There is another fictional elaboration of Wilson's I would like to deal with, however.

Several years ago, I was reading Wilson's novel *The Philosopher's Stone* and came across a rather unusual passage. It told the story of Benjamino Evangelista (or Benny Evangelist), a faith healer and cult leader who lived in Detroit. On 3 July 1929, an unknown attacker decapitated Evangelista and his family with a machete. Police who entered the house found an altar with curious figurines in the basement, along with other ritual paraphernalia. The police could never determine the murderer's identity, and eventually dropped the case. According to Wilson, this was not all. Before he died, Evangelista had published a book called *The Oldest History of the World*

Discovered by Occult Science in Detroit, Mich. In that confused, pseudo-Biblical work, Evangelista referred several times to a book with the title *Necromicon* or *Necremicon*— and since this was the first of three such volumes he wrote, these references appeared before those in Lovecraft.

My first impulse was to discard this rumor completely, but then I decided to check it out. In his foreword, Wilson referred to some of his creations as fictional, but neither Evangelista nor *The Oldest History* was among them. I looked in the *New York Times Index*, and discovered an article describing Evangelista's murder just as Wilson said it had happened. I then discovered that *The Oldest History* was an actual book published by Evangelista. I was beginning to doubt my belief that the first appearance of the *Necronomicon* did not predate Lovecraft.

I might still be confused to this day if Colin Wilson's novel hadn't provided page numbers for the *Necronomicon* occurrences in Evangelista's book. I took those references to the interlibrary loan staff and requested that any library owning a copy of *The Oldest History* should photocopy the relevant pages and send them on to me. When they arrived, I was relieved to find that the pages had nothing about the *Necremicon*—or any other variant spelling of the word—or for that matter, anything that Colin Wilson claimed was discussed there.

To tell the truth, I felt foolish about this, and almost chose not to include it here at all. After all, it was clearly fictional, and no one would take it seriously. Then, at a horror convention, someone asked me about it, wanting to know whether it was true that the *Necronomicon* was mentioned in Evangelista's work before Lovecraft's! Even for someone who has researched such hoaxes for years, it is easy to forget just how fragile the lines between fiction and fact can be, and how seriously people can take stories written solely for entertainment.

The Quine *Necronomicon*

The most convoluted *Necronomicon* hoax I ever investigated is certainly the "Quine *Necronomicon*." My investigation began with a rather innocuous post to the alt.horror.cthulhu Usenet group, in which someone quoted from the "Quine translation" of the *Necronomicon*. In the ensuing discussion, the original poster gave out more information. The book's translator was Antonius Quine, the child of a missionary in Central America. Quine went on to attend Yale and Princeton, but gave up his teaching career to live in isolation in Colorado. Along with his 1972 English translation of the *Necronomicon*, he was also responsible for a translation of von Junzt's *Unaussprechlichen Kulten* and a manuscript entitled *The Last Ten Million Years*. Quine had become very eccentric in the past few years, the poster informed us, but had avoided close scrutiny of his life for quite some time.[3]

There was a great deal of bantering on the newsgroup, including a few "announcements" of Mr. Quine's untimely death. It sounded like the usual joking, but I've always been exceedingly cautious in such matters, which serves to keep my wits sharp. One promising sign of a hoax was the mention of *Unaussprechlichen Kulten,* a book created by Robert E. Howard. While many have claimed that the *Necronomicon* exists somewhere, very few insist that Von Junzt's 1839 treatise on exotic cults did. I had already searched OCLC for every *Necronomicon* entry, and had found no Quine translation. I even used a computerized database to check on his Standish, Colorado, address, only to find that no Antonius Quine—or, for that matter, anyone else— lived in a town of that name. It was probably safe to say that the Quine book was a joke and nothing more.

A few months later, the Quine *Necronomicon* took on a new dimension when a poster started asking questions about it. When his questions were met with disbelief, this person insisted that the Quine *Necronomicon* was real, and that he had proof that it existed. A number of people immediately said that he was lying, others believed him, and one insisted that people check the evidence (but showed no sign of looking into it himself). To assess what was going on, I posted to the group and asked the individual defending the treatise's existence to back up his claims. In a private e-mail, he provided an impressive list of evidence. He knew fourteen people who had seen the book, and the library records at Macotta University backed up his claims that a Sumerian copy of the *Necronomicon* had been checked out from them and later returned. He also noted that the *National Union Catalog*, a book detailing the holdings of many different libraries, had an entry for Antonius Quine's work. It was an impressive array of facts—or at least it seemed to be.

This person's story added a new element to the Quine saga—a Sumerian copy of the *Necronomicon*. This immediately got my attention. I might accept that a "Quine *Necronomicon*" published by a Lovecraft fan existed, but a (presumably) pre-Lovecraft Sumerian edition was just too much. I started to go over his evidence with a fine-toothed comb. First, I asked the person if he could give me the names and addresses of some of the people who had seen it. Next, I tried to locate Macotta University, only to find that it was not listed in any of the college directories at my library. Then I looked for the *National Union Catalog*, and discovered that it had been largely superseded in 1982 by the OCLC database I was using. His evidence was rapidly falling apart.

I was curious about my friend's motivations; it could be that someone was feeding him misinformation, and I wanted to be as gentle as possible. Unfortunately, this was not the case. He proved unwilling or unable to send me the names of those who had seen the Quine *Necronomicon*. When I pointed out that no one had connected the *Necronomicon* with Sumer before Simon's *Necronomicon* appeared, he told me that the earlier letter had contained a "typo" and that the original was either Latin or Arabic—he forgot which. After this, it was abundantly clear that someone was putting me on.

My suspicions confirmed, I posted to alt.horror.cthulhu and alt.necronomicon with my own hoax, a tale of how I had found the Quine *Necronomicon*. I had made the trip to Hatuna-Macotta (a word meaning "many troubles") and made it to the library, only to find that the original *Necronomicon*—either Latin or Arabic, I forgot which—had been returned, along with Quine's translation. The latter included passages from Lovecraft's fiction, the fiction of William S. Burroughs, and the *Book of Mormon*—all illustrated with "The Far Side" cartoons. I tacked on a typical Mythos ending, in which I continued to type even as a slimy monster devoured me. Since I knew that the entire history of the *Necronomicon* was filled with such jokes, I was careful to make it utterly absurd, and no one seemed to take it otherwise.

My informant wrote me and berated me for "throwing me off the track." I am rarely harsh, save toward those who are clearly trying to deceive others. I replied that he had referred me to an imaginary book with an imaginary translator from an imaginary town at an imaginary library, seen by imaginary people, and as such he wasn't the only one who had been misled. I never heard from him again.

A few days later, I received a letter from one of my informant's friends. He was just as baffled as I about the actions of the hoaxer, but he did shed some light on how his friend had put together the hoax. "Macotta University," for example, came from mention of a website for the fictional "Mankato University" in a phone conversation. There was yet another twist, however—my new pen pal had talked to a book dealer at a local convention who said he had seen a copy of the Quine *Necronomicon*, and would try to get it for him!

My conclusion is that the Quine *Necronomicon* is a joke that got out of control. The poster who started the whole discussion recently published a letter from "Antonius Quine," who seems to be doing all right for an imaginary dead man. I'm not sure why the "Macotta University" hoaxer went to such lengths to fool me; perhaps he wanted to see how long he could deceive me. There seems to have been more than this involved, however, as he continued to insist to his friend that the Quine book really existed—though, at last count, the number of people who had seen it had dropped to two. My guess is that the bookseller mistakenly recalled another *Necronomicon* as the Quine version, or just wanted to attract another regular customer. The entire affair was proof of how quickly fiction can be turned into fact. It served as a clear reminder to me that even when the stakes are as low, as in the *Necronomicon* debate, there are those who have no qualms about falsifying evidence to bolster their claims.

PART TWO

The *Necronomicon* and Occultism

The Evolution of Sorcery: A Brief History of Modern Magick —John Wisdom Gonce III

4

Nam et ipsa scientia potestas est. (Knowledge itself is power.)

—FRANCIS BACON

. . . the matter hath come to such a pass that every trick of a buffoon is believed to be Magic . . .

—THE BOOK OF THE SACRED MAGIC OF ABRAMELIN THE MAGE [1]

. . . so I'm doin' it the hard way, like a post postmodern man.

—DEVO

To explain the relationship between modern (or postmodern) magick and the *Necronomicon* fully, we should examine the nature of magick itself and its recent history. This thumbnail history is merely the observation of one man. It focuses primarily on the English-speaking world; it will undoubtedly be biased; it will concentrate on certain magicians, authors, and movements, while ignoring others of equal or greater importance who simply have no bearing on this issue.

Aleister Crowley defined *magick* as "the Science and Art of causing Change to occur in conformity with the Will."[2] However, this definition could apply to any effort that causes change, even a physical act. So we will expand this definition for the purpose of this thesis in this way: Magick is the science and art of causing change to occur in conformity with the will, by means that are nonphysical and preternatural (that is, ways that are not fully understood by science). I am perfectly aware that there are even more definitions of magick than there are magicians and I don't expect everyone to agree with me. This definition is merely an expedient to enable us to start from a common point of departure. Like Crowley, I have adopted the archaic spelling of magick with a "k" in order to differentiate it from theatrical illusions or sleight of hand.

Chivalry and Sorcery: Early History of Magick

To understand modern magick, we must first meet two gentlemen from the 16th century. The first is Heinrich Cornelius Agrippa von Nettesheim (1486–1535), knight, theologian, medical man, and magician. In his magnum opus, *Three Books of Occult Philosophy*, he managed to combine all previous systems of occultism—Neoplatonism, the Hermetic magick of the ancient and Classical world, planetary magick, medieval magick, and folk magick probably derived from witchcraft sources. Agrippa integrated them all with the Hebrew Qaballah into a complex, but workable, system. It was largely thanks to him that the Qaballistic Tree of Life became the accepted model of the universe for Western occultists. His was the first modern, organized philosophy and system of magick, and his book was the magickal encyclopedia of the Renaissance. For almost five centuries, it was the single most important textbook of European occultists.[3]

The second gentleman is Doctor John Dee (1527–1608), perhaps best known as the court astrologer to Queen Elizabeth I; he was also a renowned scholar, mathematician, geographer, linguist, alchemist, cryptographer, and probably an espionage agent.

With the help of Edward Kelley, his scryer (one who practices divination by gazing into crystals, mirrors, etc.), he received the Enochian System of Angel magick. Dee and Kelley supposedly did their scrying on a special "shew stone," supposedly of gold-mounted obsidian,[4] the true identity of which has been "reinterpreted" by modern Satanists and *Necronomicon* theorists, as we shall see later. Some scholars

The two magicians whose work served as the foundation for the "Magical Revival" and of Hermetic Order of the Golden Dawn.

Heinrich Cornelius Agrippa: knight, doctor, theologian and magus. The great synthesizer and organizer of Renaissance magick.

Doctor John Dee: court astrologer of Queen Elizabeth I, alchemist, mathematician, geographer, and pioneer of Angel magick.

speculate that Dee's Enochian language was actually a code he used to relay intelli-gence information during his reputed career as a spy at the court of Emperor Rudolph of Bohemia. We will encounter Dr. Dee several times in the course of these studies.

From Dust to Dawn: The Golden Dawn

When Francis Barrett published *The Magus* in 1801, he created an enormous stir and opened the way for the "Occult Revival" of the 19th century. *The Magus*, how-ever, was only a butchered form of Agrippa's *Three Books* with a few sections from the spurious *Fourth Book of Agrippa* and d'Abano's *Heptameron* thrown in.[5] Nevertheless, *The Magus* was the inspiration for numerous occult lodges of the Masonic or Rosicrucian type in the English-speaking world, its influence culminat-ing in the foundation of the celebrated Hermetic Order of the Golden Dawn in 1888. It has been well established that Samuel Liddel "MacGregor" Mathers drew sub-stantially upon *The Magus* (i.e., Agrippa) for the rituals of the Golden Dawn. Mathers also worked the Enochian system of Dr. Dee into the curriculum of the Golden Dawn, making it compatible with the Qaballah and using a Masonic-type system of grade levels corresponding to the Sephiroth on the Qaballistic Tree of Life. This grade system was the first of its kind and has been imitated by countless ceremonial lodges ever since.

I do not mean, however, to give the impression that the Golden Dawn sprung to life entirely from the indirect influence of two Renaissance mages by way of Mathers's scholarship. The spiritual environment of Victorian England was already fertile soil for the growth of such an occult society. As the 19th century drew to a close, the Spiritualist movement, which had widened the metaphysical horizons of all classes of British men and women, had begun to bore Victorian occultists. The lodges of Freemasonry and Rosicrucianism opened their doors to a few upper-class Englishmen, but probably disappointed them with their comparative lack of mag-ickal lore. Some of the books of Eliphas Levi (Alphonse Louis Constant, 1818–75), translated into English by A. E. Waite, revived interest in ceremonial magick and sought to reconcile it with Christianity. The French Decadent movement had aroused a somewhat morbid interest in magick with its blasphemous, quasi-Satanic occultism, as exemplified by the artwork of Felicien Rops and the writing of J.-K. Huysmans (1848–1907), whose novel *La-Bas* (*Down There*, 1891) contains the most famous description of a Black Mass ever written.[6] (At the time the Golden Dawn was being established in Britain, the infamous magickal war of Huysmans and Boullan against the Marquis de Guaita was being waged in France.[7]) The romantic age of archaeol-ogy and the vast holdings of the British Empire had also made information about the magickal practices of ancient civilizations and foreign cultures available to the British public. British occultists had, for a while, been enamored of the Eastern mysticism of Madame Helena Petrovna Blavatsky's Theosophical Society, but the love affair was soon marred by competition from the Golden Dawn, which promised to reveal the buried secrets of a distinctly Western tradition.

The occultism of the Decadent movement was characterized by morbidity, sexuality, blasphemy, and quasi-Satanism—as illustrated in this etching by Felicien Rop. To H. P. Lovecraft, Aleister Crowley was only a throwback to the Decadents.

Dr. William Wynn Westcott, Coroner of London, Master Mason, and member of the Rosicrucian Society, founded the Golden Dawn upon the "authority" given to him in forged letters from an imaginary Fraulein Anna Sprengel, supposed head of a fictional German Society called *Die Goldene Dammerung* (The Golden Dawn). The letters authorized Westcott to open an English branch of the legendary German society. Wescott recruited Dr. W. R. Woodman and S. L. Mathers to help him create the society. Woodman seems to have served only as a figurehead for the Dawn, and took little part in its actual creation. It was Mathers whose hard work and scholarship built the ritual structure of the Dawn upon the foundations of Agrippa and Dee, and the grimoires of the Renaissance. The Hermetic Order of the Golden Dawn was not so much a magickal order in the typical sense as it was an occult university. Much of the educational process in the Dawn was accomplished by means of written "Knowledge Lectures" provided for each grade, and by Flying Rolls—essays composed by Mathers, Westcott, and others of the Order, and mailed to Inner Order members. Flying Rolls dealt with a wide variety of subjects, from translating occult ciphers, to Qaballistic correspondences, to the morality of magickal workings.

The God, The Cad, and The Ugly: Aleister Crowley

Besides Mathers himself, the most notable members of the Golden Dawn were William Butler Yeats, Arthur Edward Waite, and Aleister Crowley. After the collapse of the Golden Dawn, only Crowley would go on to found his own magickal societies,[8] pursue further magickal experiments, and gain a scandalous reputation in the process. Crowley's notoriety was based mainly on his sex-positive, anti-Christian stance (he called himself the Great Beast 666, or the Master Therion), and his wildly irresponsible behavior toward his disciples and mistresses, which was even more wildly exaggerated by the British press.

Though Crowley's magickal system was still based upon the framework of the Golden Dawn and Mathers (and therefore upon Agrippa and Dee), he placed the emphasis on sex as the ultimate magickal power source. Crowley prophesied that semen would replace blood as the vehicle of magickal power in the coming Aeon of Horus. He also removed the all-powerful Qaballistic\Hebrew Godhead from the supreme position of his magickal system and stated: "There is no God but Man."[9] Crowley's magick put emphasis on "the attainment of the Knowledge and Conversation of the Holy Guardian Angel," a goal that would allow the magician to fulfill his own "true will" and realize his own divinity.

In Crowley's *Liber Al vel Legis—The Book of the Law*, he states his Law of Thelema: "Do what thou wilt shall be the whole of the Law." While many have interpreted this as license to do anything, Crowley's *Magick in Theory and Practice* states that this refers to the magician's need to follow a true purpose or "true will," a personal destiny that does not harm another, as long as that *other* is also doing his *true will*. This is a concept similar to Dharma in Hinduism and Buddhism. (Whether Crowley and his followers actually practiced this ideal is debatable.)

Aleister Crowley, the Master Therion, makes the Vir sign.

Crowley's contribution to modern magick certainly cannot be ignored. He was one of the earliest exponents of yoga in the West, and some of his most brilliant writing is on that subject. He was also a pioneer of Eastern sexual magick, Tantra, and Taoist alchemy. He was one of the earliest Western occultists to use the I Ching system of divination. An exhibitionist rather than a secretist, Crowley published much material that was previously hidden from the public.

Crowley's contribution, however, was a rather mixed blessing at best. The Master Therion's scandalous escapades and deliberate courting of the tabloid press reflected poorly on the entire occult community.[10] His approach to sex magick was chauvinistic, often using women for sexual rituals without their understanding, and his misogynist attitudes are well documented.[11] Though lauded as a great revealer of traditional magickal secrets and systems, Crowley sometimes bastardized those systems to accommodate his personal idiosyncrasies. For example, the traditional Qaballistic number of Sephiroth is ten. Anything beyond ten is heretical and outside the system.[12] So Crowley made the number of his system eleven by adding Daath, the gateway in the Abyss, as an extra Sephirah for his version of the Tree of Life. (See chapter 5 for more information on this.) Crowley's reputation as a magickal innovator has also been exaggerated. It was not Crowley who introduced sex magick to European lodges, but an African American named Paschal Beverly Randolph.[13] And 777, that incomparable book of magickal/Qaballistic correspondences that Crowley published, was not written entirely by him, but in all likelihood by Mathers and others, and was originally a Flying Roll only for the private use of Golden Dawn members.[14] Though Crowley did much to popularize magick; it was probably his scandalous headline-making that ultimately helped to discredit it.

Crowley began his career during the 19th-century intellectual renaissance of occultism. It is probably no coincidence that, by the end of his career, Western occultism had been exiled to a kind of intellectual ghetto. By the early years of the 20th century, most of the finest minds shunned the occult simply to preserve their reputations. Modern occultists cannot seem to agree whether Crowley was a great genius, a flagrant charlatan, or a self-indulgent hedonist. He was probably all three at different times. Perhaps Neopagan author Isaac Bonewits has the most balanced view of Crowley: "He was a genius whose brilliance was matched only by his neuroses. . . . Crowley was not evil, but he was tremendously irresponsible."[15]

H. P. Lovecraft was aware of Crowley (as was anyone who read the newspapers). With the clear perception of an outsider, Lovecraft sums up Crowley in a letter to a friend: "In the 1890's the fashionable Decadents liked to pretend that they belonged to all sorts of diabolic black mass cults & possessed all sorts of frightful occult information. The only specimen of this group still active is the rather over-advertised Aleister Crowley . . . who, by the way, is undoubtedly the original of the villainous character in H. R. Wakefield's 'He Cometh and He Passeth By.'[16] From Lovecraft's historical perspective, Crowley was not a magickal innovator of the future but an overrated throwback to the Satanic naïveté of the 19th-century Decadents.

Catechism and Dogma: The Second Magickal Revival

After World War II, there occurred a kind of second occult revival in the form of the Neopagan Witchcraft movement inspired by the writings of Robert Graves and the discredited anthropological theories of Margaret Murray. This movement was synthesized by Gerald Gardner with ideas from Theosophy and Tantra, and with rituals from Aleister Crowley and the Golden Dawn. Today, Janet and Stewart Farrar have maintained the momentum of modern Wicca with rituals that are perhaps less influenced by the Golden Dawn tradition. Modern Neo-Wiccan, Druid, and Asatru groups practice their crafts as religions, not just systems of magick. Today, Neopagan groups evoking Goddesses and Gods of Indo-European, Mesopotamian, Native American, Norse, Slavonic, Celtic, African, and Greco-Roman pantheons abound. Polytheism has something for everyone.

Satanism continues to thrive under different philosophical justifications, though outwardly little changed from its medieval roots as a rebellion against the Roman Catholic Church. Many modern Satanists are essentially atheistic and claim that they don't believe in a real or personal "devil," but merely use Satan as a symbol for the principle of self-indulgence. Satanic institutions range from totally secret groups and deadly serious organizations like the now-defunct Process Church, to purely theatrical enterprises like Anton Szandor LaVey's Church of Satan and organizations that fall somewhere in between, like Michael Aquino's Temple of Set. At the low end of the scale are random "dabblers," most of whom are teenagers who form their practice from books, movies, and their own imaginations. Satanic magick seems to be a rather negative form of ceremonial magick (Golden Dawn or Crowley-esque), though LaVey's brand is blended with fictional/dramatic elements and dispenses with the protective circle of magickal tradition—a practice considered foolhardy by many magicians, especially where serious workings are concerned—because the Satanist is supposed to be "one with the forces of darkness" he invokes. When accused of ritual murders, sex crimes, grave robbing, and other criminal activities by law-enforcement officials and the Christian and Neopagan communities, the various Satanic lodges unanimously chorus, "It wasn't our group!"

Ancient shamanic and yogic techniques of visualization, meditation, chakra therapy, breath control (pranayama), and others have been repackaged as the New Age movement. The only thing "new" about these magickal practices is that they are now being offered to CEOs and car salesmen to boost their skills and lower their blood pressure. A Neotantric movement also blends the yogic sex magick practices of India, Tibet, and China with so-called New Age practices, many of which date from the dawn of human history.

Quantum (Meta)Physics:
The Scientific Sorcerers of Future Past

Currently, the magickal community is going through twin phases of scientific futur-
ism and historical revisionism—simultaneously reaching forward into the future
and back to the ancient past. In the Middle Ages and the Renaissance, men like Roger
Bacon, Agrippa, Paracelsus, and Dr. John Dee could be both scientists and magicians. However, the rationalism of the 18th century (the so-called Age of Reason)
created a split between science and magick. Even so, some occultists later tried to
reclaim the mantle of science. The Theosophists tried to appropriate the scientific
method in the 19th century, and even Crowley claimed that his was "the method of
science, the goal of religion." These bygone magicians were still all victims of the
materialistic superstition of the Victorian era.

At the end of the 19th century, scientists were smugly confident that they understood almost everything there was to know about the universe, which they conceived
as a kind of gigantic clockwork mechanism that strictly followed the rules of
Newtonian physics. The emergence of quantum physics dealt a deathblow to the
old-fashioned mechanistic view of the universe so popular during the Industrial
Revolution. And it is quantum physics that provides many modern occultists with
their explanations of why and how magick works. Science fiction author Arthur C.
Clarke has observed that any sufficiently advanced form of technology would be
indistinguishable from magick. It could be just as valid to say that a sufficiently
advanced form of magick would be indistinguishable from technology. At this tran-
sitional point in history, that singular creature—the scientist/magician—may once
again take the stage.

One pioneer of the scientific approach to modern magick is the highly respected
Neopagan author Isaac Bonewits, who often defines *magick* as "folk parapsychology." Bonewits has worked to bring magickal theory in line with the discoveries of
parapsychology and physics. In his 1971 book *Real Magic,* he published some twenty
"Laws of Magic" and discussed them as a scientist might explain the laws that govern
electricity. In his book *The Holographic Universe* (1992), Michael Talbot used the
holographic model to explain paranormal and mystical phenomena. Possibly following Bonewits's lead, ceremonial magician Donald Michael Kraig articulated
"Sixteen Theorems of Magick and Sex Magick" in his 1998 book *Modern Sex Magick.*
New Age healing guru Dr. Deepak Chopra frequently invokes the principles of quantum physics to explain his approach to Ayurvedic medicine and (for lack of a better
word) magick. Chaos magicians have also jumped on the scientific bandwagon, con-
ceptualizing their brand of magick in terms of psychology, chaos theory, Heisenberg's
uncertainty principle, and so on.

While technology is not synonymous with science, the two are closely associated,
and the growing scientific bias of modern occultism has encouraged many magick
users to become technology users as well. Some magicians now seem to spend more

time in cyberspace than on the astral plane. Violating their stereotype as techno-phobic barbarians, many young Neopagans, who humorously call themselves "cyber-pagans," are very active on the Internet, starting websites, newsgroups, and e-mail lists. Ceremonial magick has also made itself known in cyberspace, where a profusion of occult groups have their own websites. There is even a *Mage's Guide to the Internet* as well as an *alt.magick* newsgroup, a Satanism FAQ (Frequently Asked Questions), and a *Necronomicon* FAQ, to which we will devote more attention later.

An equally important occult trend is historical revisionism. Modern Pagans and occultists have grown leery of "traditions" that claim great antiquity, but only date back to the 19th or the mid–20th century. Neopagans, like the above-mentioned Bonewits, founder of Ar nDriocht Fain (ADF), and Ian Corrigan, the ADF's National Preceptor, have done exhaustive research to recover the authentic beliefs and prac-tices of ancient Indo-European religion and adapt them to the needs of Neopagans. Kenneth Johnson, unsatisfied with the apocryphal writings of Gardner and Murray, based his book *Witchcraft and the Shamanic Journey* on authentic sources from his-tory, anthropology, and folklore. In his book *Enochian Magic for Beginners, The Original System of Angel Magic,* cutting-edge ceremonial magician Donald Tyson has thoroughly restored the Enochian system based on historical sources, so that modern magicians can use Dr. Dee's system in its original form, free of the errors of the Golden Dawn and Aleister Crowley. Tyson has also edited and annotated the first complete English edition of Agrippa's *Three Books of Occult Philosophy,* cor-recting representations of Agrippa's original sigils, seals, magick squares, and geomantic diagrams, some of which had never been published before. This landmark work makes Agrippa available to modern readers free of the plagiarized mistakes of Barrett.

"Truth" has become a relative concept in the new paradigms of magick. A cer-tain statement may be "true" on one level and "untrue" on another, just as an elec-tron may behave as both a particle and a wave. This kind of relativism shows itself in Bonewits's *Law of True Falsehoods*, which, he says, "refers to data which contradict one's usual metapattern but which nonetheless work."[17] He goes on to explain, "In any other system this would lead to great anxiety or even insanity. In magick, how-ever, we have the Law of Synthesis, so that two truths may be held without strain until a final decision can be made."[18] It is no wonder that, in the overlapping occult and Neopagan communities, the widely held belief is that "all paths are valid."

The Age of Chaos: Austin Osman Spare

All of the previously examined magickal styles and groups—ceremonial, Neopagan, Satanist, and New Age—can generally be classified as dogmatic magick. They all base their practices on a tradition, whether ancient or modern. Many openly claim—with varying degrees of legitimacy—to be following guidelines laid down by their predecessors. For many, the influence of the Golden Dawn is inescapable, especially for Neopagans. (I recently saw a book on Wiccan magick that instructed the witch to cast a circle using the Lesser Banishing Ritual of the Pentagram complete with the names of the Hebrew archangels.) LaVey and Michael Aquino, also influenced by Crowley, cannot avoid certain traditional Golden Dawn elements. In Aquino's Temple of Set, members are given a course of basic instruction called Lesser Black Magick, or LBM. The similarity in terminology, if not concept, to the Golden Dawn's Lesser Banishing Ritual of the Pentagram, or LBRP, is unmistakable. Even Crowley, for all his pretensions of rebellious innovation, was essentially a dogmatic magician in the Golden Dawn tradition.

For dogmatic magicians—and until recently that meant *all* magicians—two elements are especially important: tradition and mystery. The dogmatics feel that the older a ritual is, the more power and legitimacy it has. Medieval authors of books on magick rarely gave their names, instead attributing their works to semi-mythic figures of the past like Moses and Solomon. (Dee and Agrippa were exceptional for claiming their own books.) A magickal group rarely forms without claiming to be the resurrection of a previous tradition, ranging from the Rosicrucian Brotherhood to the secret lore of the Freemasons. An otherwise honest old gentleman like Dr. Westcott couldn't stand to start an occult society like the Golden Dawn without pretending that its origins stretched back to a venerable predecessor in Germany. Even today, many groups fight to be known as the "true" Order of the Golden Dawn or Ordo Templi Orientis, putting forth convoluted arguments as to how their lineage from the original group came about. For centuries, the hallmark of the magician was tradition.

The other element, mystery, determines which traditions the magicians choose to follow. For example, three major orders of knights emerged from the Crusades: the Templars, the Hospitallers, and the Teutonic Knights. The Templars were the most mysterious because they were accused of secret blasphemous rites of unclear nature, and their leader was burned at the stake in 1314. As such, they have inspired a minor cottage industry of occult works, and many occult fraternities claim to have rediscovered the rites of the Templars. In contrast to the Templars, the Hospitallers (Knights of St. John) and the Teutonic Knights have survived into modern times as honorary orders, and have consequently been substantially ignored by occultists. The more mysterious and suppressed the tradition, the more appeal it has, and the less likely it is that anyone will be able to question its authenticity.

The first modern magician to actually break with dogmatic tradition was Austin Osman Spare, the father of modern chaos magick. Once an associate of Aleister Crowley, Spare soon parted company with the Great Beast to pioneer his own brand of magick: the Zos Kia Cultus. In the early 1970s, Spare's ideas were adopted by an organization called the Illuminates of Thanateros (IOT), of which, Peter J. Carroll is the best-known spokesman.

Spare had been affiliated with Crowley's group, the A.˙.A.˙., and had become disillusioned with the elaborate, complex nature of ceremonial magick. He ultimately denounced it as an expensive waste of time, for the same reason that he denounced all religion and science: In his view, all systems of belief must be false in a universe that cannot be defined or even described. Since man is a part of that universe, he is already "God" and thus, in Spare's belief, there is no use in the practitioner trying to contact "God" (himself) through complex magickal rituals. He should instead get in touch with his own subconscious mind by whatever means necessary, ergo the maxim of chaos magick: "Nothing is true. Everything is permitted."[19]

Critics of Spare have cited similarities between Spare's magickal philosophy of chaos and Asian philosophies such as Tantra and Taoism, and have accused him of simply rewording them with his own nihilistic twist. For example, Spare's word for universal energy is "Kia," a word with no definition in any Western language, but unmistakably similar to the Japanese word "Ki," which has a similar meaning. The Taoist maxim "The Tao which can be defined is not the Tao" is likewise used by Spare, substituting the word "chaos" for the word "Tao."

Spare was convinced that the true source of a magician's power was his or her own subconscious mind. Therefore, the only workable system of magick was one that had meaning to the subconscious of the individual magick user. Old spells from dusty grimoires were useless, according to Spare, unless their symbology could be incorporated into the subconscious mind of the mage. Why not take the far-easier route of building one's own system of magick or divination, taking symbolism from any source that had significance to the individual magician? Thus a modern chaos magician, evoking an entity for protection, might evoke a comic book superhero from his or her childhood rather than a Qaballistic archangel or a Goddess from an ancient pantheon.[20] This explains the popularity of fantasy and horror writers like Michael Moorcock and H. P. Lovecraft with some chaos practitioners.

Critics of chaos magick insist that the reason why dogmatic systems work is precisely because they *do* call upon timeless archetypes—Goddesses, Gods, angels, sigils, yantras, and the like—archetypes that have existed in the collective minds of all humans from time immemorial, a concept close to Jung's "collective unconscious." These beings and symbols from the collective unconscious are reckoned more powerful than subjective symbols from the individual mind of the lone chaos practitioner. Isaac Bonewits, in his convincing "Switchboard" theory, states that generations of magicians, using the same spells or evoking the same entities, set up powerful magickal currents or "circuits" that can be tapped by anyone using the same methods.[21] Because of this, they claim, chaos magicians are going to a great deal of trouble for very little result.

While chaos magicians enthusiastically claim that they do not rely on the use of many magickal tools or elaborate rituals, traditionalists say that they have merely "reinvented the wheel." They point out that magickal systems such as yoga, shamanism, and witchcraft have long achieved their results with little or no paraphernalia. Chaos magicians, on the other hand, say that this is beside the point. While dogmatic magicians tend to label magick that makes changes in the material world as "sorcery" or "low" magick and refer to magick of the more mystical type intended to contact one's "Higher Self" as "high" magick, chaos magicians refuse such prejudicial labels,[22] and prefer to judge magick by its results rather than its intentions.

Genesis P. Orridge, drummer for Throbbing Gristle and a practicing chaos magician, established Thee Temple ov Psychick Youth (TOPY) in 1981. Taking its cue from William S. Burroughs, who once said, "We intend to destroy all dogmatic verbal systems. . . ." Thee Temple incorporated deliberate misspellings into its name and documents. TOPY is less an occult society than a loosely organized, international fellowship of like-minded individuals. In a one-page manifesto reprinted in an Australian newsletter, TOPY is described as a "Magickal Order" dedicated to the belief that "all repressive elements, whether they are social, personal, or whatever, should be seen as obstacles on your path that you should seek to remove with Joy."[23] Though the group is said to be influenced by sources as diverse as Satanism, Crowley, Nietzsche, anarchism, and, of course, chaos magick, their activities have become so legendary that the truth is hard to ascertain. When Scotland Yard mistook one of Orridge's videos for an actual videotape of ritual crime, the resulting tabloid scandal made it unclear whether the outrage was the result of actual crime or the Puritanical mentality of the British legal system.

Many chaos magicians, like Peter J. Carroll, seem to tend toward the dark. The reasons for this are more complex than simple rebellion against the unnatural Christian system of sexual morality that characterizes most basic forms of Satanism. Carroll and his colleagues are seeking what they see as the primitive, amoral, shamanic essence of magick. There is, perhaps, more of the tribal witch doctor than the sophisticated occultist in the chaos magician, though he may draw ever-so-much influence from quantum mechanics, chaos theory, complexity theory, and the like. Atavism, rather than evolution, seems to be the primary concern of the chaosist.

Showing verbal influence from TOPY, Internet magician Haramullah nevertheless criticizes the darkside chaos magicians, finding them just as dualistic as the dogmatics they disdain, because they have simply replaced "Ordur" with "Kaos," rather than balancing the duality. Influenced by Buddhist thought, Haramullah recommends what he calls the "Midul Path."[24]

Some modern magicians have synthesized chaos with dogmatic techniques in a number of ways. Tantric yogini Margo Anand has combined Spare's method of constructing and charging sigils with her system of Tantric sex magick.[25] Isaac Bonewits has developed an original color system for designating types of magick relative to his form of Neopagan Druidism.[26] Apparently, chaos works best when balanced with order—what Haramullah would call the "Midul Path" between the cosmic forces of creation and dissolution.

If dogmatic magick is usually moralistic, chaos magick tends to be amoral. If dogmatic forms are usually theological, chaos magick is essentially agnostic and existential. If dogmatic magickal systems that have surfaced (or resurfaced) since the Golden Dawn can be called "modern," perhaps chaos magick should be called "postmodern." The term *postmodern*, however, like the term *chaos* itself, has gradually become an overused, catch-all term with conflicting definitions, and may be in danger of becoming nearly meaningless. All the terms, labels, and categories I have used in this essay are artificial—but essential—aids to understanding the world of modern occultism. Definitions are, at their best, a method by which humans can break large, difficult subjects down into smaller categories and learn more effectively. At their worst, definitions can become a trap by which language can be used to rob us of truth. It appears to this observer that dogmatic and chaosist magickal systems have more in common than either side's practitioners would care to admit.

It would be easy to conclude, at this point, that magick is simply at a crossroads between dogmatic and chaosist systems, if it weren't for what Lars B. Lindholm calls "a whole third and enigmatic variety."[27] By this I mean Lovecraftian/*Necronomicon* magick, which is the subject of my next chapter.

Lovecraftian Magick: Sources and Heirs —John Wisdom Gonce III

5

Certainly, the medieval storyteller and the sorcerer worked in parallel trades, manipulating words and phrases to achieve their effects, and the medieval Islamic sorecerer was pre-eminently a man with a book.

—ROBERT IRWIN, *THE ARABIAN NIGHTS: A COMPANION*

The field of Lovecraftian magick is wide and confusing, and has been the subject of innumerable debates that may seem inaccessible or irrelevant to the nonoccultist. Hopefully, this chapter will make the subject more accessible to everyone by examining possible influences from occult literature that may have shaped Lovecraft's thinking when he invented his imaginary grimoire as a literary device to spice up his horror fiction.

Lovecraft Among the Sorcerers

Any study of the *Necronomicon* should begin with an examination of the man who created it, Howard Phillips Lovecraft (1890–1937). Many believe him to be the greatest horror fiction writer of the 20th century. Lovecraft revolutionized (and existentialized) the modern horror story, much as Ernest Hemingway advanced the modern novel. Since the *Necronomicon* (if it ever existed) is supposed to be an occult book, the first question is this: What occult knowledge did H. P. Lovecraft really have?

Lovecraft knew both more and less about the occult than either Lovecraft scholars or Lovecraftian occultists have led readers to believe. The tendency of Lovecraft scholars and occultists in this area is toward equal, but opposite, extremism. Lovecraft scholars have maintained a "conspiracy of silence" relative to any knowledge that he might may have had about magick or the supernatural. In his splendid biography, *H. P. Lovecraft: A Life*, scholar S. T. Joshi is meticulous in uncovering all the source material and influences for each of Lovecraft's stories, and deals with all the minutiae of Lovecraft's life, down to the most trivial incidents. Yet in spite of all this careful research, Joshi overlooks Lovecraft's letter to Clark Ashton Smith asking for source material on the occult, and ignores his subsequent studies of historic grimoires (books of magickal spells). In the same book, Joshi devotes three pages to the theft of Lovecraft's suits from his New York apartment! We could more readily excuse Joshi, de Camp, Mosig, and other students of Lovecraft for ignoring his studies of occult literature if those studies had had no effect on his fiction. But the evidence shows that Lovecraft definitely used information and ideas gleaned from occult sources in his tales.

Why would Lovecraft scholars overlook—or willfully ignore—his studies of magick and the supernatural? I believe there are two main reasons for this. The first is that many Lovecraft scholars seem to share his mechanistic/materialistic view of the universe—they simply don't believe that any inquiry pertaining to the occult could be worthwhile. The second reason relates to the agenda of many Lovecraft scholars, which is to win for Lovecraft the long-overdue recognition that he deserves as one of the great American authors of the 20th century, and one of its most original philosophers. Perhaps Lovecraft scholars fear that any taint of occultism—even a casual study of it—might compromise Lovecraft's reputation as a serious writer and thinker. While securing recognition for Lovecraft is an admirable goal, I believe that this need not be accomplished at the expense of the truth.

The occultists themselves—no conspiracy of silence for them!— have taken full advantage of this "blind spot" in Lovecraft studies, and indulged in wild speculation about Lovecraft as a closet alchemist and delver into magickal mysteries. Most offer highly imaginative theories but little evidence to support them. Perhaps the most notable writers in this vein are W. H. Muller, who believes that Lovecraft had knowledge of the highest levels of alchemical lore,[1] and Kenneth Grant, who sees Lovecraft as a natural adept whose only fault was that he balked at crossing the Abyss.

Occasionally, a serious writer will take a stab at assessing Lovecraft's occult knowledge, but will do a botched job because of poor research. This is what happened in Anthony Raven's book *The Occult Lovecraft*, wherein Raven dismisses Lovecraft as having little or no learning about magick. Raven bases his assessment of Lovecraft's knowledge entirely on "The Horror at Red Hook,"[2] a story that Lovecraft wrote before he began a serious study of magickal lore.

Since most Lovecraft scholars are unwilling (or afraid) to tackle the controversial issue of what Lovecraft knew about the occult—and occultists are all too willing to write unfounded nonsense about it—the time has come for someone to impartially evaluate Lovecraft's knowledge of the occult. I hope this discussion will fill a lamentable gap in current Lovecraft studies. I offer it not as an exhaustive study of Lovecraft's knowledge of occult topics, but as a groundbreaking introduction to it. I trust hands more skilled than mine will follow this with more thorough research.

The truth is that Lovecraft was fascinated with the occult, just as he was fascinated with so many other subjects, including astronomy, chemistry, paleontology, mythology, and history. Before his death, he became, in a modest sense, an occult scholar. Any investigator trying to determine how much Lovecraft knew about magick and the occult (or any other subject) is immediately faced with two sizable problems.

The first is that the sheer vastness and variety of Lovecraft's reading makes it impossible to be sure of all his sources or the full extent of his knowledge. Unquestionably a genius, Lovecraft learned to read at the age of four and was an omnivorous reader from childhood to the end of his life. S. T. Joshi calls him one of the greatest autodidacts (self-educated persons) of the 20th century. Most of our biographical knowledge about him comes from the multitude of letters he wrote to his friends, most of whom were also writers and would-be writers who formed a literary clique now known as the Lovecraft Circle. While Lovecraft often commented in letters about books he was reading, there is no reason to assume that he always did so. And most of Lovecraft's letters have never been published.

This brings us to the second problem: The five volumes of Lovecraft's *Selected Letters* published by Arkham House, the small collections of letters printed by Necronomicon Press, and the magnificent epistolary biography *Lord of a Visible World* edited by S. T. Joshi and David E. Schultz represent only the proverbial tip of the iceberg of Lovecaft's vast correspondence. Estimates of Lovecraft's total output of letters vary between 75,000 and 100,0000. Some of these letters ran up to fifty pages of fine, closely spaced handwriting. Even his postcards often contained more text than the average letter.[3] Only a small percentage of these letters has survived. Most are kept in carefully guarded collections at Brown University, in other college and museum libraries, and in private collections around the country. Even the epistles published in *Selected Letters* were often heavily abridged and censored by August Derleth,[4] and usually left out the drawings with which their author often illustrated them. In the introduction to *Selected Letters I,* Derleth gives us a teasing mention of these, as well as a hint of Lovecraft's possible occult knowledge: "Sometimes he drew signs of cabalistic ritual or magick, or the characters of a Russian word, or even strange whorls and seraphs of some unknown language of his own invention."[5] All of this makes it difficult to prove absolutely what Lovecraft knew or didn't know about magick.

Nevertheless, there are some facts about Lovecraft of which we can be sure, and some definite sources we can trace. Let us begin with the source of Lovecraft's earliest and most formative impressions of magick and the supernatural: *The Arabian Nights.*

A Thousand and One Arabian Nightmares

At five years of age, Lovecraft read an English version of *The Arabian Nights* available in the 1890s. We cannot be sure which of the several competing editions he read. Many of them were abridged and heavily bowdlerized for young readers. Of his early fascination with the *Nights* Lovecraft writes:

> Then again—how many young dream-Arabs have the Arabian Nights bred!
> I ought to know, since at the age of 5 I was one of them! I had not then
> encountered Graeco-Roman myth, but found in Lang's Arabian Nights a

gateway to glittering vistas of wonder and freedom. It was then that I invented for myself the name of Abdul Alhazred, and made my mother take me to all the Oriental curio shops and fit me up an Arabian corner in my room. Had I not stumbled upon Graeco-Roman myths immediately afterward, my sense of dream-placement might easily have been with the Caliphate of Bagdad.[6]

As S. T. Joshi points out, Lovecraft could not have read the Lang edition at five (circa 1895), since it was not published until 1898 (London: Longmans, Green). The Lang edition found in his library was a later gift from his mother, and this was probably the source of the confusion. S. T. Joshi guesses that Lovecraft probably read the version translated by Edward William Lane. At any rate, Lovecraft's fascination for the *Nights,* though it began in childhood, was a life-long obsession. In another letter, Lovecraft elaborates on the origins of the name of his Arab alter ego, Abdul Alhazred:

> I can't quite recall where I did get Abdul Alhazred. There is a dim recollection which associates it with a certain elder—the family lawyer, as it happens, but I can't remember whether I asked him to make up an Arabic name for me, or whether I merely asked him to criticize a choice I had otherwise made.[7]

Lovecraft scholars have twisted themselves into knots trying to puzzle out the derivation of Abdul Alhazred. Some speculate that Alfred Baker, the family lawyer, derived the name from the Hazards, an old family of Providence well known to the Lovecrafts. My own opinion is that Alhazred was a pun on "All-Has-Read," which seems appropriate in view of young Lovecraft's voracious reading habits. (Sometimes the simplest explanation is the best, but don't tell that to a Lovecraft scholar.) After all, the name Abdul Alhazred means nothing in Arabic. Joshi observes that it also violates Arabic grammar with its redundancy, and that a better version "would have been Abdel Hazred, although this doesn't have much of a ring to it."[8] At any rate, Lovecraft was fond of this childhood play-name, and went on to use it as the name of the fictional "mad Arab" who authored the imaginary *Necronomicon* in his tales of horror.

From his readings of *The Arabian Nights,* Lovecraft learned more than he realized about the magick of the medieval Arab world. Most modern readers of the *Nights* do not fully understand that many of the stories recorded in the *Alf Layla wa-Layla* (or *One Thousand Nights and a Night*) were not necessarily viewed as fantasy by medieval Muslims. Astounding as it may seem, some of the supernatural tales that are presented in the *Nights* as entertainment are recorded in other medieval Arab literature as absolute fact. An entire genre of medieval Muslim literature called "marvel tales" (*aja'ib*) existed, in which whole books were compiled of fantastic stories presented as nonfiction. Part travelog, part historical treatise, and part grimoire, these books were helter-skelter collections of unlikely information about the wonders of Egypt, India, the far-reaching cosmos, cyclopean monuments and lost civilizations of antiquity, feats of magick, and the magickal powers of certain stones, plants, and animals. Many of the marvels originally found in nonfiction works on magick and cosmology eventually found their way into the *Nights*. Devout Muslims had no doubts about the existence of the djinn and the power of magick, for the Prophet himself attested to them in the Koran:

> ...they follow what the Satans recited over Solomon's kingdom. Solomon disbelieved not, but Satans disbelieved, teaching the people sorcery—(vol. II, verse 96).

As Robert Irwin comments in his excellent book *The Arabian Nights, A Companion*: "In this sort of social and intellectual context, the frontiers between occult fiction and non-fiction were so weak as to be more or less indistinguishable." Consequently, medieval Arabs would have viewed the tales in the *Nights* not as fantasy stories, but as fictional accounts of possible events. Robert Irwin also points out "we find tales that would not be out of place in the *Nights* embedded in such 'non-fictional' works as sorcerer's manuals." He points to such examples as a frightful tale of magickal dismemberment from the 11th-century grimoire *Ghayat al-Hakim* (*The Goal of the Sage*, later translated into Latin as *Picatrix*[9]) and to a magickal treatise entitled *Suns of the Lights* by Ibn al-Hajj, which contains a spell by which a man can have sex with the daughter of the White King of the Djinn.[10] The parallels between real Arab grimoires and tales from the *Nights* are sometimes uncannily close. For example, the above-mentioned *Ghayat al-Hakim* gives a formula for making a severed human head speak prophecies and, in the *Nights* story "The Tale of the Wazir and the Sage Duban," the sage claims to have a book containing a spell to make a severed head speak. This is undoubtedly why Aleister Crowley advised his students to read the *Nights* in *Magick in Theory and Practice*, where he described it as "Valuable as a storehouse of oriental magick-lore." Thus a careful reading of the *Nights* must have provided Lovecraft with a fairly accurate view of medieval Islamic metaphysics—at least as it was imagined by the coffeehouse crowds of Cairo, Damascus, and Baghdad.

Lovecraft's fascination with *The Arabian Nights* definitely carried into his adult life, leading him to do further research into Islamic history and folklore, as indicated by books in his library: *The Calif Haroun Alraschid and Saracen Civilization* by Edward Henry Palmer, and *Tales of the Genii* by Sir William Charles Morrell (pseudonym). Knowing Lovecraft's passion for research, it is quite probable that he went on to read Sir Richard Burton's unabridged and unexpurgated version of the *Nights* when he reached adulthood. What would Lovecraft have learned from such studies? He would have learned about a fascinating menagerie of Islamic genies and monsters: a subspecies of djinn known as the ghoul (*ghul*) that dwells in cemeteries and deserted places and eats human flesh, an Arab werewolf (or perhaps were-hyena) called the *qutrub* that is a man or woman who transforms into a beast at night and eats corpses. (The ghouls in Lovecraft's "Pickman's Model" may have been inspired by both of these creatures, since he describes them as being doglike.) Lovecraft may also have learned about the *udar* (a sort of homosexual ghoul that raped men in the desert and left them to die with worm-infested rectums), the *nasnas* (a humanoid creature with only half a body, divided laterally), the *peri* (a beautiful female spirit), and the *diw* (a Persian genie of evil and darkness).[11] The *rukh* (or "roc"), the giant bird of Persian folklore that flew away with Sindbad the Sailor, may have been the inspiration for Lovecraft's Shantak bird, found in "The Dream-Quest of Unknown Kadath."

Lovecraft's readings of the *Nights* and related lore taught him the Arab sorcerer's concept that spirits could be controlled by the correct manipulation of magickal objects (rubbing magickal lamps, etc.), and spirits could be imprisoned in objects (genies confined in lamps, flasks, rings, and stone pillars). Robert Irwin surmises that this idea "probably derives from a debased form of loosely Neoplatonic ideas popular in late antiquity concerning theurgy, or the practice of magick through the control of spirits."[12] Neoplatonism was also the underlying philosophy of Western ceremonial magick and of the Qaballah. From the *Nights*, Lovecraft may also have learned of Arab methods of divination—geomancy, as used in "Aladdin," and astrology, as used in "The Third Dervish's Tale." It was here that Lovecraft also learned of the crucial role of words and books in the practice of magick. In the tales of the *Nights*, knowing the "magick words" can literally be a matter of life and death: Ali Baba survives only because he remembers the magickal password "Open Sesame" to gain entrance to the treasure cave of the Forty Thieves. In "The Story of the Sage and the Scholar," the sage controls genies and performs magickal feats through his knowledge of the supernatural power of letters. Not surprisingly, one of the most important practices in Islamic occultism was "letter magic" (*ilm al-huruf*), which was similar to the use of letters and names of power in the Hebrew Qaballah. Surviving medieval Arab magickal texts often show Jewish influences, such as the manipulation of letters, use of Solomon's seal, and spirits with Hebrew-sounding names. Some tales of the *Nights* feature Jewish sorcerers, such as the evil Azariah in "The Adventures of Mercury Ali of Cairo," though most sorcerers were depicted as Maghribis (Berbers from North Africa or Spain) or as Persians.

As Robert Irwin observes "the medieval Islamic sorcerer was pre-eminently a man with a book."[13] The formative influence of the *Nights* undoubtedly fired Lovecraft's imagination with a fascination for ancient spellbooks, and the conviction that such mildewed tomes were essential for the working of powerful sorcery. In the tale "Judar and his Brethren," the Magribi sorcerers squabble over a grimoire entitled *Fables of the Ancients* "whose like is not in the world . . . for in it are particulars of all the hidden hoards of the earth and the solution of every secret."[14] There can be no doubt that the Islamic wizards Lovecraft encountered in the *Nights* were the fictional ancestors of his imaginary Abdul Alhazred, and that their legendary spellbooks were the fictional forebears of his equally imaginary *Necronomicon*.

A Pagan in Providence—Early Influences

Undoubtedly, many of Lovecraft's ideas about magick and the supernatural came from his studies of mythology and folklore. Lovecraft discovered the world of classical Greco-Roman myth at age six through his readings of Hawthorne's *Wonder-Book* (1852) and *Tanglewood Tales* (1853), Thomas Bulfinch's *The Age of Fable* (1855), and Sir Samuel Garth's 1717 translations of Ovid's *Metamorphosis*. His grandfather Whipple Phillips also fostered in Lovecraft a love of ancient Rome by showing him pictures and antiquarian souvenirs brought back from his trips to Italy. Of his grandfather, Lovecraft wrote, "He loved to muse amidst the ancient ruins of the city, & had brought from Italy a wealth of paintings, & other objets d'art whose theme was more often classically Roman than Italian."[15] Some Roman coins that Whipple brought back from his travels seemed to precipitate in Lovecraft what might be interpreted as a past-life experience: "I cannot begin to suggest the feeling of *awe* and *anomalous familiarity* which those coins—the actual products of Roman engravers and mints, and actually passed from Roman hand to Roman hand twenty centuries ago—awaked in me."[16] Whether this was a genuine past-life experience or the product of Lovecraft's fertile imagination, I cannot say.

One very poignant example of the magickal influence of mythology on Lovecraft comes from this period of his childhood. In one of Lovecraft's letters, he recalls those juvenile days of enchanted worship:

> When about seven or eight I was a genuine pagan, so intoxicated with the beauty of Greece that I acquired a half-sincere belief in the old gods and nature-spirits. I have in literal truth built altars to Pan, Apollo, Diana, and Athena, and have watched for dryads and satyrs in the woods and fields at dusk. Once I firmly thought I beheld some kind of sylvan creatures dancing under autumnal oaks; a kind of "religious experience" as true in its way as the subjective ecstasies of a Christian . . . whose unimaginative emotionalism and my unemotional imaginativeness are of equal valuelessness from an intellectual point of view. If such a Christian tell me he has felt the reality of his Jesus or Jahveh, I can reply that I have seen hoofed Pan and the sisters of the Hesperian Phaethusa.[17]

Lovecraft describes this as "my last flickering of religious belief." Interestingly, he also states, in the same letter, "I was, and still am, pagan to the core."[18] Perhaps, with the proper spiritual guidance, Lovecraft might have grown up to be what we today would call a Neopagan. In a privately circulated publication called *Lovecraft: Sorceror* [sic], Paul F. Memoli uses this example to argue in favor of Lovecraft as an unlikely and unconscious priest of Pan, compares his devotion to Pan to that of Aleister Crowley ("Hymn to Pan"), and cites Lovecraft's love of Arthur Machen's story "The Great God Pan" as further evidence.[19]

But the young Lovecraft lived in a spiritual void. After the death of his mother,

Sarah Susan Phillips Lovecraft, in 1921, Lovecraft wrote: "Like me, she was an agnostic with no belief in immortality, and wished for death all the more because it meant peace and not an eternity of boresome consciousness."[20] It's odd that Lovecraft should characterize his mother as an agnostic in view of the way she dutifully shunted him off to Sunday school at the First Baptist Church of Providence when he was a boy. In his Sunday school classes, Lovecraft made such a heretical nuisance of himself by sympathizing with the Roman persecutors instead of the Christian martyrs that he was eventually allowed not to attend. That he was allowed to skip Sunday school, rather than being punished for his iconoclastic attitude, indicates to me that church attendance was not really all that important to Susie Lovecraft. (My own parents were devout Southern Baptists for whom nonattendance of church was not an option.) Lovecraft's mother apparently sent him to Sunday school, not because of any deep-seated religious faith, but because it was the proper thing for genteel New Englanders to do—a mere social convention.

It appears that the spiritual convictions of the Lovecraft family were shallow at best, and nonexistent at worst. C. S. Lewis once remarked that, after his conversion to Christianity, he found that he was a "converted Pagan among apostate Puritans."[21] "Apostate Puritans" seems to me a pretty apt description of Lovecraft's family; they seem to have embraced all the superficial, hypocritical rubbish associated with Christianity—a prissy hatred of sex, fatuous notions about "public decency," patriarchal contempt for independent women—but none of its spiritual bedrock. Lovecraft's compulsive conservatism, his abstinence from alcohol and tobacco, his severe dress code, and his Puritanical, anti-sexual attitudes were probably all remnants of his early "Christian" training, and they seemed to have stuck with him, even though an actual belief in the Christian God did not. As the above-quoted Lewis would have said, Lovecraft's formal religious training was neither Christian nor Pagan, but simply "modern."

It isn't surprising that Lovecraft rejected the spiritually bankrupt belief system of fundamentalist Christianity. What *is* unusual is his adoption of Greco-Roman Paganism based on his study of books. Even more interesting to the occultist is his account of having seen "some kind of sylvan creatures dancing under autumnal oaks." From the perspective of the magician, this might not have been the product of an overactive imagination, but rather the ability to see into the spirit realm (clairvoyance) that is often exhibited by children. This clairvoyant ability is something most of us lose as we grow older. It is entirely possible that Lovecraft was able to see creatures in the astral realm at the age of seven. If this was an early manifestation of clairvoyant ability, Lovecraft surely lost it as he "matured" and was inculcated with a materialistic adult worldview. Any psychic abilities that the young Lovecraft may have had were probably stifled, as was his sexuality and his faith in his own physical strength, by the suffocating influence of his neurotic mother and the paranoiac conservatism of turn-of-the-century New England.

Algernon Blackwood: Wizard of the Backwoods

Lovecraft discovered the works of Algernon Blackwood (1869–1951) as early as 1920, and considered Blackwood's story "The Willows" the best weird story ever written in the English language. Blackwood himself was a strange combination of mystic, magican, and outdoorsman. Like Yeats and Machen, he had been involved in the Golden Dawn, but had managed to avoid its political disputes. He also delved into studies of Rosicrucianism and Buddhism.

Critics have observed that Blackwood saw himself, first and foremost, as a mag-ickal/mystical instructor, and that this often usurped his role as an artist, forcing him to "over explain" events in his stories. Like any good teacher, he used repetition. Rather than being satisfied with ominous hints, he wanted to make sure his audience would "get it." Blackwood's vision has been compared to that of the Romantic poets, but with a sinister twist—he often represents the forces of nature as alien and indifferent, even hostile, to humans. This concept was obviously not lost on Lovecraft.

Arthur Machen: Black Magick in Fairyland

One of the foremost "fictional occult" influences on Lovecraft was Arthur Machen (1863–1947), whom some biographers have described as having a life and personality that rivaled those of the strange characters in his own stories. Machen was associated with the Outer Order of the Golden Dawn, though he was never, as some occultists suppose, an inner initiate. As with many authors with Pagan or occult leanings, Machen seeded his stories with concepts from his own belief system. Most prominent in Machen's tales is the idea that powerful, ancient forces lie just behind the surface of nature, or the facade of daily life. As Phillip Van Doren Stern has said: "Machen dealt with the elemental forces of evil, with spells that outlast time, and with the malign powers of folklore and fairytale."[22] Although Lovecraft did not discover him until 1923, Machen's ideas obviously affected him profoundly.

Sax Rohmer: Cthulhu Manchu

Arthur Henry Sarsfield Ward, better known by his pseudonym, Sax Rohmer (1883–1959), was the creator of the popular fictional villain Fu Manchu. It is a great pity that Ward/Rohmer is remembered only for this character, since he was capable of writing much better fiction. Rohmer's "Limehouse thrillers" of the 1920s and '30s were perhaps the closest British equivalent to the pulp fiction craze going on in the United States during the same period.

Rohmer had a substantial influence on Lovecraft, though most Lovecraft scholars seem unaware of it. This is probably because most of Lovecraft's references to Rohmer are found in unpublished letters and obscure sources. In an unpublished letter, for example, Lovecraft remarks that he read Rohmer's novel *Batwing* (1921) at a time before he wrote "The Call of Cthulhu" in 1926. *Batwing* isn't a supernatural thriller, but has scary overtones relative to Voodoo and Afro-Caribbean magick. One of its chapter titles is "The Call of M'kombo," which is unmistakably similar to

Lovecraft's "The Call of Cthulhu." The plot of *Batwing* also involved a Voodoo cult set in Cuba, similar in description to Lovecraft's Cthulhu Cult set in Louisiana, which Lovecraft described as "voodoo of a more terrible sort than they had ever known."[23] Both authors conformed to silly racial stereotypes and common misconceptions about Afro-Caribbean religions; both cults practiced human sacrifice and were set in forbidding swamps. Lovecraft also read Rohmer's *Brood of the Witch Queen*. Although he dismissed it as just another vampire story in *Supernatural Horror in Literature*, he was more candid in his admiration of it in a letter to Robert Bloch dated 1933: "The best thing Rohmer ever did, though, is 'Brood of the Witch Queen.' That is what I call a story!"[24] Lovecraft read *Brood* in 1927, the same year he wrote *The Case of Charles Dexter Ward*, and he may have been influenced by the novel, since both stories involve the resurrections of ancient sorcerers who return to plague the modern world. The evil Egyptian wizard Hortotef in *Brood* is armed with a spell-book called "The Book of Thoth," which takes its name from a magickal book in Egyptian mythology and folklore. Rohmer's Hortotef uses this grimoire in ways comparable to the ways Lovecraft's evil sorcerers use the *Necronomicon* in his stories. Lovecraft may even have named his title character after Rohmer's real name, Arthur Sarsfield Ward, which is arguably similar to Lovecraft's *Charles Dexter Ward*. Though most Lovecraft scholars have alternate explanations for the origin of this fictional name, we know that Lovecraft was aware of Ward/Rohmer's real name, since he mentioned it in a letter to Willis Conover in 1936.

There was no correspondence between Lovecraft and Rohmer, but they may have shared a mutual acquaintance. Lovecraft was a friend of Harry Houdini, and ghostwrote "Under the Pyramids" for him in 1924. Rohmer was supposedly also acquainted with Houdini according to some sources and, if this is true, Houdini may have mentioned each man to the other.

There can be little doubt that Rohmer was a sincere occultist. He was fascinated with ancient Egypt, and Eastern cultures and mysticism, though he subscribed to the stupid racial and cultural stereotypes that were common in his day. Contrary to some unreliable sources, Rohmer/Ward was never a member of the Golden Dawn, since he would have been only five years old when it was established in 1888; when it fell apart around 1901, he would have been all of eighteen and still struggling at odd jobs in London. He might have had Rosicrucian connections, however, and there is no reason why he could not have been affiliated with one of the offshoots of the Golden Dawn, such as Dion Fortune's Society of the Inner Light. In *Master of Villainy: A Biography of Sax Rohmer*, his wife, Elizabeth Sax Rohmer, related an anecdote in which she interrupted one of his magickal rituals, insisting that he stop lest he "go barmy."[25]

In 1914, Rohmer/Ward wrote *The Romance of Sorcery*, which served Lovecraft as a sourcebook of information about the history of magick. From it, Lovecraft must have learned about the exploits of Apollonius of Tyana, Nostradamus, Dr. John Dee, and others. Rohmer's book was almost literally a "romance," however, in that it offered a very glamorized version of the lives of these semi-legendary magicians.

The Devil and H. P. Lovecraft: Satanism and the Decadents

The closest known parallel to modern Satanism in Lovecraft's day would have been the Decadent movement of the late 19th century. Judging from Lovecraft's comments about Crowley, as quoted in the previous chapter, Lovecraft had no higher opinion of the Decadents than of any other branch of the occult: "In the 1890s the fashionable Decadents liked to pretend that they belonged to all sorts of diabolic black mass cults & possessed all sorts of frightful occult information."[26] Further evidence of Lovecraft's familiarity with the worldview and occult orientation of the Decadents is shown in his story "The Hound" (1922), in which the two protagonists turn to grave-robbing and black magick in their goofily Gothic pursuit of every imaginable form of evil-doing.

The Error at Red Hook: Crib Notes from Britannica

Perhaps one of Lovecraft's worst fictional forays into occultism was "The Horror at Red Hook." His knowledge of magickal lore was so sketchy in 1925, when he wrote the tale, that he was reduced to cribbing information from a source so obvious as the entries for "Magic" and "Demonology" in the *Encyclopedia Britannica*. It was there, in the ninth edition, which he owned, that he found the incantation he used in "Red Hook," where he called it a "demon evocation." This is the incantation that Malone, the police detective, finds on the wall of the dance hall/church used as a ritual site by the foul cultists of the tale. The author of the *Britannica* article, E. B. Tylor, got it from a German text called the *Pneumatologia Occulta de Vera*, which was published in Georg Conrad Horst's *Zauber-Bibliothek, oder von Zaberei, Theurgie und Magik* (Mainz, 1821). The relevant incantation appears in volume 2, page 90. Tylor left out the parts in German before and after, keeping only the bastardized Hebrew. Though Lovecraft ignorantly called it a demon evocation, it was actually an incantation used for treasure hunting.

Lovecraft further embarrassed himself by trying to translate the incantation in a letter (probably written to Wilfred Branch Talman). It was the humiliating defeat of "Red Hook," however, that brought about a turning point in Lovecraft's research.

Clark Ashton Smith: Sorcerous Sources

Clark Ashton Smith (1893–1961) was probably the writer whom Lovecraft respected most among all those in his circle of friends. In 1912, at the age of eighteen, Smith had gained fame as a poet with the publication of his first book, *The Star-Treader and Other Poems*. This popular acclaim lasted only until 1918, however, at which point Smith's style of metered, rhymed, romantic verse was considered obsolete. Smith might have lapsed into obscurity but for Lovecraft's suggestion that he try his hand at writing fiction for the pulp market.

On 9 October 1925, after the debacle of "The Horror at Red Hook," Lovecraft wrote to Smith asking for sources for background material on magick; "... any good translations of any mediaeval necromancers with directions for raising spirits, invoking Lucifer, & all that sort of thing?"[27] We have no record of Smith's reply to Lovecraft, but we do have the record of a letter Smith sent to fantasy illustrator Virgil Finlay on 13 June 1937, answering a similar request. Smith probably recommended similar sources to Lovecraft:

> Aside from fiction, I recommend the books of Montague Summers, such as *The Geography of Witchcraft*, *The History of Demonology and Witchcraft*, etc. Grillot de Girvy's *Witchcraft, Magic, and Alchemy* would interest you greatly, since it contains more than 350 illustrations, many of which are taken from rare prints and cuts; but the book is rather expensive, costing at least 5 or 6 dollars.[28]

Smith may also have recommended the books of Arthur Edward Waite (1857–1940), and Eliphas Levi (1810–75) to Lovecraft, since Lovecraft, in turn, recommends them as source material to Willis Connover in a letter dated 29 July 1936. These included Waite's *Book of Black Magic* and Waite's translations of Levi's books. In fact, Lovecraft used two incantations in *The Case of Charles Dexter Ward* that came from a single page in Waite's Levi compendium, *The Mysteries of Magic*. It can be no coincidence that, by 1927, the *Necronomicon* had become a full-fledged grimoire rather than just a book of imaginary folklore.

In the same letter to Conover mentioned above, however, Lovecraft described the medieval grimoires he studied as "flat, childish, and unconvincing."[29] Lovecraft was looking for material to help him terrify his readers. The purpose of the grimoires was not to terrify, but rather to practice magick—something that works much better when the magician is *not* terrified. While truth may be stranger than fiction, it is seldom as entertaining. Lovecraft became convinced that he could devise much more interesting and frightening visions of dread from his own imagination. And he was right.

Dreams in the Witch-Cult: Lovecraft on Witchcraft

Lovecraft seems to have been enormously influenced by Margaret Murray's landmark anthropological work, *The Witch-Cult in Western Europe*, first published in 1921 by Oxford University Press. The book proposes that the cult of witchcraft in Europe had its origins in an ancient pre-Aryan race that was forced underground by subsequent conquerors, but continued in remote corners of the world. Its beliefs were supposedly uniform, and its practices virtually unchanged among the peasantry. Modern anthropologists have discredited Murray's theories, but in Lovecraft's day they were still accorded some credibility. Lovecraft accepted the theory of the universal witch cult because it meshed with some of his favorite literary themes: the relative unimportance of humanity in the history of Earth, and the existence of a conspiracy of subhuman or alien races lurking on the fringes of civilization, practicing black magick, and worshiping the Great Old Ones. This idea blended well with his theme of the Cthulhu Cult.

Stories like "The Festival" (1923), which he wrote immediately after reading

Murray's book, and "The Dreams in the Witch House" (1932) were heavily influenced by *Witch-Cult*. It is ironic that some followers of the Wiccan religion believe that this ancient cult (if it ever existed) thrived in a pastoral, utopian age of matriarchal harmony, whereas Lovecraft saw it as a nightmare of subhuman barbarism. As they say, it takes all kinds.

Houdini, Howard, and the Cancer of Superstition

Ehrich Weiss, better known as Harry Houdini (1874–1926), was not only the greatest escape artist and stage magician of his (or perhaps any other) era. He was also a staunch crusader against phony spirit mediums and occult charlatanism of all kinds. In fact, Houdini was just as great a skeptic as Lovecraft himself, so it is no wonder that the two men got on well together. Lovecraft ghostwrote a story for Houdini, "Under the Pyramids," which was first published as "Entombed With the Pharaohs" in the 1924 anniversary issue of *Weird Tales*. By all accounts, Houdini was favorably impressed with the story, and probably also saw in Lovecraft a useful literary ally in his fight against what he saw as supernatural humbug. Once, when Lovecraft was down-and-out in New York, Houdini even offered to help him find work.

Later, when Houdini was performing in Providence in 1926, he asked Lovecraft to write an article attacking astrology. In fact, Lovecraft already had some knowledge of astrology—enough to mount attacks against it in small newspaper articles. Later, Houdini offered Lovecraft the job of writing, or revising, *The Cancer of Superstition*, which was to be an attack on all "superstition" as Lovecraft and Houdini understood the word. Houdini himself had written some works of this kind, most notably *A Magician Among the Spirits,* a signed copy of which he had given to Lovecraft. What Houdini wanted now, however, was something with more in-depth scholarship. The only surviving text of *Cancer* is an outline by Lovecraft and the introductory pages of the book as written from the outline by his collaborator, C. M. Eddy.[30] It examines the supposed origin of superstition in primitive times, and draws upon Frazer's *Golden Bough* and Fiske's *Myths and Myth-Makers*, indicating that Lovecraft may have been familiar with both books. Houdini's tragic death on 31 October 1926 brought the project to an end.

The Haunter of Theosophy

Some Lovecraft scholars rhapsodize about how he supposedly "demythologized" his Cthulhu Mythos as his literary career progressed. In fact, Lovecraft persisted in using mythic and occult elements in his fiction to the end of his days, though he often offered science fiction explanations for the existence of his Mythos "demons." He never divorced magick from his fiction; he simply married it to science. Even Theosophy was pressed into service as a source of "forbidden lore." Lovecraft would have learned about H.P. Blavatsky from Rohmer's *The Romance of Sorcery*. His first literary mention of Theosophy is found in his famous tale "The Call of Cthulhu" (1926), in which he wrote:

Theosophists have guessed at the awesome cycle wherein our world and human race form transient incidents. They have hinted at strange survivals in terms that would freeze the blood if not masked in bland optimism.[31]

Lovecraft's interest in Theosophy was really sparked when he heard about *The Book of Dzyan* from his friend E. Hoffman Price. In a 15 February 1933 letter to Price, he wrote:

> What you say of your new tale, and of the Pushkara-Plaksha-Kusha-Shalmali-Mt. Wern-Senzar-Dzyan-Shamballah myth-cycle which you have dug up, interests me to fever heat: and I am tempted to overwhelm you with questions as to the source, provenance, general bearings, and bibliography of all this unknown legendry. Where did you find it? Why isn't it mentioned in ordinary works on comparative folklore? What—if any—special cult (like the theosophists, who have concocted a picturesque tradition of Atlanteo-Lumerian elder world stuff, well summarised in a book by W. Scott Elliott) cherishes it? For gawd's sake, yes—send along those notes, . . . I'm quite on edge about the Dzyan-Shamballah stuff. The cosmic scope of it—Lords of Venus, and all that—sounds so especially and emphatically in my line.[32]

In a letter written on 18 February 1933 to Clark Ashton Smith, Lovecraft wrote:

> Price has dug up another cycle of actual folklore involving an allegedly primordial thing called *The Book of Dzyan*, which is supposed to contain all sorts of secrets of the Elder World before the sinking of Kusha (Atlantis) and Shalmali (Lemuria). It was kept at the holy city of Shamballah, and is regarded as the oldest book in the world—its language being Senzar (ancestor of Sanskrit), which was brought to earth 18,000,000 ago by the Lords of Venus. I don't know where E. Hoffman got hold of this stuff, but it sounds damn good . . .[33]

Note the word "allegedly" in the letter above. Lovecraft must have known—or at least suspected—that *The Book of Dzyan* was as fictional as any story he had ever written for the pulps. And indeed it was, for Madame Blavatsky herself wrote the book from sources like the *Vedas*. Naturally, Lovecraft's only interest in these works was as material for his fantastic fiction. In "The Haunter of the Dark" (1936), Lovecraft lists *The Book of Dzyan* alongside such imaginary books as the *Necronomicon* and *De Vermis Mysteriis*.

Lurkers in Lovecraft's Library

At the time of his death, Lovecraft's library yielded several books related to magickal, mythological, and supernatural subjects.[34] I don't have space here to discuss all of these works in detail, and analyze how they might have affected Lovecraft's work. Of special interest, however, is Lewis Spence's *Encyclopedia of Occultism*. Lovecraft may have only skimmed over the book, or occasionally used it as a reference work. Knowing his passion for research, however, he may have read it from cover-to-cover. If he did, he would have found some useful information about everything from "Abaddon" to "Zulu witch-finders." There is an entry for Arab sorcery, astrology, and alchemy on page 34 of the 1920 edition, which Lovecraft owned. Oddly, on the facing page is a reproduction of a medieval painting showing a "Group of Arab magicians repenting of their sorceries." In the picture, a Christian saint is preaching to the Saracen sorcerers; in the foreground to the right, one wizard is tearing the pages out of a large book. The book is undoubtedly a grimoire he is destroying as an act of repentance. I wonder if this illustration was a further inspiration for Lovecraft in the ongoing saga of his imaginary *Al Azif*, and its fictional author, Abdul Alhazred.

Lovecraft—The Ultimate Skeptic

However much research Lovecraft may have done on magick, it never changed his basic worldview of atheism and materialism. Even in his own lifetime, some of Lovecraft's fans believed him to be privy to cosmic secrets disguised as fiction. One of these was William Lumley, a marginal member of the Lovecraft Circle, for whom Lovecraft revised "The Diary of Alonzo Typer." In his letter of 3 October 1933 to Clark Ashton Smith, Lovecraft lampoons Lumley as

> an unique survival from the earth's mystical childhood—a combination of priceless credulity and gorgeous Munchausenism. . . . He is firmly convinced that all our gang—you, Two-Gun Bob, Sonny Belknap, Grandpa E'ch-Pi-El, and the rest—are genuine agents of unseen Powers in distributing hints too dark and profound for human conception or comprehension . . . Indeed—Bill tells me that he has fully identified my Cthulhu and Nyarlathotep . . . so that he can tell me more about 'em than I know myself.[35]

Till the end of his days, Lovecraft described himself as an atheist and a "mechanistic materialist."

Pathways of Power

Many occultists know of Lovecraft's skepticism, yet still find fertile ground for their magickal practices in his fiction. In Lovecraft's fictional worlds, magickal power and supernatural entities impose themselves upon mundane reality by three main avenues: words, geometry, and dreams.

Words have a force far beyond that of ink stains on pages or spoken sounds. The idea of a fearful power intrinsic to language itself permeates Lovecraft's fiction. In Lovecraft's universe, the *Necronomicon* is more than an antiquarian collector's item, it is a leather and paper bomb filled with verbal shrapnel. Whether written or spoken, language found in forbidden books can warp space-time and tear the fabric of reality. In *The Case of Charles Dexter Ward*, a man with no magickal training absentmindedly reads an incantation aloud and sets supernatural events in motion. The magick works apart from the will, the intent, or the understanding of the speaker, as automatically as pulling the trigger of a gun. Perhaps this is a reflection of Lovecraft's attitude as a mechanistic materialist. Practically all modern magicians would say that magick could never work, no matter what "words of power" were used, without the magickal will of the practitioner.

There is some precedent for this mechanistic approach in real traditions. Some schools of mantra yoga teach that the yogi has but to "vibrate" the mantra correctly for the right number of repetitions (japa) and he will get results, whether he understands the Sanskrit words or not. Early Qaballists were often called by the title *Ba'al Shem* (Master of the Name) and maintained strict secrecy about the correct pronunciation of the Tetragrammaton, the most powerful Name of God. They feared that if the Name were unworthily spoken aloud, either by accident or in blasphemy, it would automatically bring terrible results. Unspoken words in "blasphemous" books were deemed an unspeakable threat and were banned and burned by the medieval religious hierarchy to preserve the structure of society, if not the natural order of the universe.

Geometry, in the hands of our dark dreamer, becomes mathematical magick opening doorways into alien dimensions, as it did for the witch Keziah Mason in "The Dreams in the Witch House." Cyclopean, non-Euclidean architectures give birth to "obscene" angles that swallow living men into unseen dimensions, as in "The Call of Cthulhu." This use of occult mathematics, preternatural angles, and hyperspatial geometry, though intended for surreal horror fiction, finds a similarity in the "sacred geometry" of Tantric yantras and mandalas, geometric patterns believed to have mystical power. Gods and Goddesses can be meditated upon and contacted by yantras whose configurations are keys to the powers of those divinities. In both East and West, magicians have long used sigils believed to have power over spirits because of their very shape.

Dreams are an invasion route often used by Lovecraft's creatures from "Outside." In "The Dreams in the Witch House," "Beyond the Wall of Sleep," and "The Haunter of the Dark," dreams become psychic attacks leading to possession states not unlike those of Voudon celebrants. Lovecraft's Dreamlands series is a complete cycle of tales about a world visited by humans in dreams.

Here again, there is a reflection of actual magickal practices in Lovecraft's fiction. Dream control has long been used by magicians for contact with the dead and with nonhuman entities, for Qaballistic pathworking, and for astral travel of all sorts, as we shall see. Something must be said here about Lovecraft's own admission that vivid dreams and nightmares were the source of several of his fictional creations. For this reason, Lovecraft scholar Dirk Mosig associates Lovecraft's frightening dream experiences with what Jungian psychologists call "cognitive dissonance." To Mosig, Lovecraft was an "oneiric writer" who transformed his nightmares into creative fiction to reduce their "dissonance"—their disruptive power over his life.[36] In his book-length essay, *Supernatural Horror in Literature,* Lovecraft projected this tendency of his on humanity at large and used it to explain the origins of religion and magick: "The phenomenon of dreaming likewise helped to build up the notion of an unreal or spiritual world . . . we need not wonder at the thoroughness with which man's hereditary essence has become saturated with religion and superstition."[37]

Occultists have probably exaggerated the intensity of Lovecraft's dream life, and Lovecraft may very well have exaggerated it himself. "It came to me in a dream!" is a time-honored excuse for authors who wish to hide their true sources of inspiration. Bram Stoker, for instance, claimed that a night of indigestion inspired *Dracula*, when in fact he had done a great deal of research into Transylvanian geography and folklore before writing it. Simple research could also be the true source of the name *Necronomicon* itself, rather than something Lovecraft supposedly found beyond the wall of sleep.

I believe that all the apparently genuine metaphysical principles that appear in Lovecraft's work are coincidental. In some cases, the occult elements in his fiction seem to have a ring of truth because they were based on research—even though a closer examination shows that the "research" may have consisted of skimming books for useful names and fragments, and that the magick is poorly understood and misrepresented as often as not. If the magick in Lovecraft's stories appears convincing, it is only because Lovecraft, like any good writer, had the ability to write convincingly about things with which he had no experience, and make his readers suspend their disbelief. Occultist readers not only suspend their disbelief, however, they hang it by the neck until dead. They *want* to believe that Lovecraft's tales are secret tracts on magick disguised as fiction, and even the faintest similarity between Mythos fiction and real magick will be seen as proof positive. Given an inch of coincidental similarity, they will take a mile of magickal doctrine from the fiction of their favorite writer.

My verdict is that, though Lovecraft may have had a certain amount of "head knowledge" about the occult, he never really understood the mechanics of magick—the underlying principles that make it work. Like many writers of horror fiction, all magick was "black" for H. P. Lovecraft. In truth, magick itself is neutral, like electricity, and only its application—to heal or to harm—makes it "white" or "black." Furthermore, Lovecraft never understood the principle of "will" or "intent," which must be trained and developed to focus magickal energy, just as an athlete trains and develops her strength or endurance. In *The Case of Charles Dexter Ward,* Lovecraft has Dr. Willet, a man untrained in magick, use an incantation he learned the day before against Joseph Curwen, a powerful sorcerer who had practiced magick for some two hundred years. Of course Willet, Lovecraft's hero, effortlessly wins this magickal duel. The crowning absurdity of this exchange is that the villainous Curwen uses a Qabballistic incantation that is actually a list of Hebrew God names, while Willet, our hero, uses an invocation to the abominable Cthulhu Mythos monster, Yog-Sothoth.

Despite these objections, it is clear that some magickal practitioners have found a great many occult ideas in Lovecraft's fiction. For a long time, however, this went unnoticed, until the English occultist Kenneth Grant began his literary career.

Kenneth Grant: Aleister Crowley and the *Al Azif*

Very little is actually known about Kenneth Grant, as he seems to have taken care to provide as little information about himself as possible.[38] Most of what is known about him comes only through his relationship with Aleister Crowley.

Grant first met Aleister Crowley in 1944, when Grant was then only twenty years old. Crowley was sixty-nine and would be dead in three years. During that brief association, Grant believes himself to have inherited the spiritual mantle of Crowley. Grant also assumed leadership of one branch of the OTO after the Master Therion's death in 1947. As the man many Thelemites (followers of the teachings of Aleister Crowley) consider the most legitimate leader of any Crowley group functioning in the world today—perhaps the only one with a direct imprimatur from Crowley himself—Mr. Grant's opinions cannot be ignored.

Grant's published works begin with *The Magical Revival* in 1972. It is in this work that he first presents the idea of H. P. Lovecraft as a magician and of his Cthulhu Mythos as occult revelation disguised as fiction. Here also, Grant begins to draw parallels between Lovecraft and Crowley, attempting to show that both men channeled their work from astral sources filtered through their subconscious minds.

It is undoubtedly Grant who is the progenitor of all the attempts by current occultists to link Lovecraft with Crowley—what Crowley historian Sandy Robertson calls "The Lovecraft/Crowley Axis."[39] One has only to look at the "Chart of Comparisons" on page xxxix of Simon's *Necronomicon* and then compare it to the same kind of comparison chart on pages 115–6 of *The Magical Revival*, published five years earlier, to see where Simon got his ideas.

In truth, some of Grant's Lovecraft/Crowley parallels seem too close to be coincidental. Lovecraft's *Al Azif, Book of the Dead* sounds similar to Crowley's *Al vel Legis, the Book of the Law*, and also to Crowley's *The Ab-ul-Diz Working* (*Liber 60*). Lovecraft writes of "Kadath in the Cold Waste" while Crowley uses the name "Hadith" to describe himself as "The Wanderer in the Waste." Lovecraft's Yog-Sothoth sounds like Crowley's (actually Grant's) Set-Thoth. Lovecraft's supposedly pentagram-like "Elder Sign" carved in gray stone is similar to Crowley's "Nuit's Star," a five-pointed star with a circle in the center.[40] And the list goes on.

Naturally, all of this could be circumstantial evidence, but it makes Grant's argument for a Lovecraft/Crowley link look more convincing. Less convincing is Grant's assertion that both men wrote about a group of beings called "the Great Old Ones." On Crowley's side of the equation, the reference is to "The Great One of the Night of Time," which was actually taken from a Golden Dawn ritual rather than Crowley's own work. Some of Grant's other correspondences are also a bit uneven. It must be remembered, however, that this word play of correspondences in *The Magical Revival* represents Grant's earliest attempt to draw parallels between Lovecraft and the Great Beast. Any creative author can find apparent parallels between any two sufficiently large, though unrelated, bodies of work (say, for example, Adolf Hitler's *Mein Kampf* and C. S. Lewis's *Chronicles of Narnia*). Grant's true genius lies, not in his ability to contrive superficial "correspondences," but rather in his knack for actually detecting common themes and ideas in the works of both Crowley and Lovecraft, as he does in his later books.

Grant is well aware of Lovecraft's skepticism toward the supernatural, and does not style him as a secret initiate. Nor does Grant ever argue in favor of an actual physical meeting between Lovecraft and Crowley. He believes instead that both men unknowingly tapped in to the same magickal current. In Lovecraft's case, the process was supposedly unconscious. In *Aleister Crowley and the Hidden God*, Grant states "Crowley's Aiwass Current, Spare's Zos Kia Cultus, and Lovecraft's Cthulhu Cult are different manifestations of an identical formula—that of dream control. Each of these magicians lived their lives within the context of cosmic dream myths which, somehow, they relayed or transmitted to man from other dimensions."[41]

Grant's belief in the *Necronomicon* is likewise freed from dependency upon a physical book of paper and ink. "The Necronomicon does not exist as a book in the mundane world, but it does exist in the dream state and is available to those who are able to penetrate the Veil and the Abyss and break open the seals of the *qliphoth* which guard it."[42] Grant conceives of the *Necronomicon* as an "astral book" existing only in the Akashic Records and therefore only accessible through dreams, astral travel, and Qaballistic pathworking. (The *Akashic Records* is originally a Hindu/Buddhist/Tantric concept of a repository of the memories of all past lives stored on the astral planes.)

The Tree, the Abyss, and the Gate

It is impossible to understand Grant's writings on Crowley and Lovecraft without some background in the Kabbalah (or Qaballa, or Cabala) and the system of Sephiroth on the Tree of Life. The Qaballah was originally a system of Hebrew mysticismthat was appropriated by gentile mystics and magicians during the Middle Ages and the Renaissance. As Richard Cavendish says, any statement made about the Qaballah will be an oversimplification,[43] but this explanation should suffice for our purposes.

For about five hundred years—or at least since Agrippa—the Sephirothic system of the Qaballistic Tree of Life has been *the* model of the universe in Western occultism. Each Sephirah on the Tree represents an aspect of existence and/or magickal consciousness. The Sephiroth also correspond to the traditional "philosophical" planets of the system of planetary magick. Each Sephirah is identified with a Hebrew name of God, ruled by a specific Hebrew archangel, and identified by a list of magickal correspondences that help the pathworking magician recognize when he or she reaches the correct Sephirah or Sphere. For example, the Sephirah Netzach (Victory) is seventh on the Tree of Life, ruled by the archangel Haniel, identified

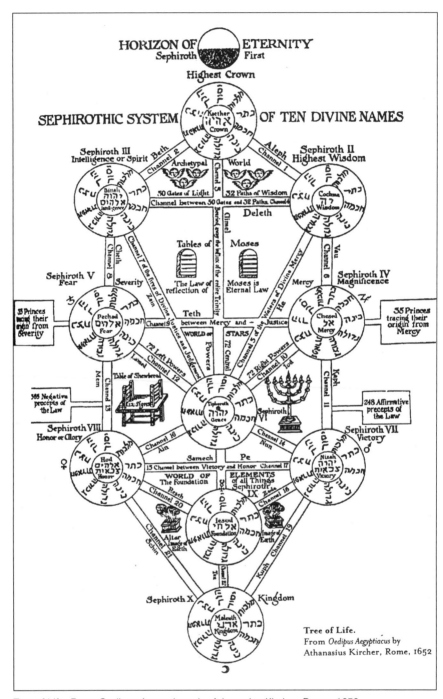

Tree of Life. From *Oedipus Aegyptiacus* by Athanasius Kircher, Rome, 1652.

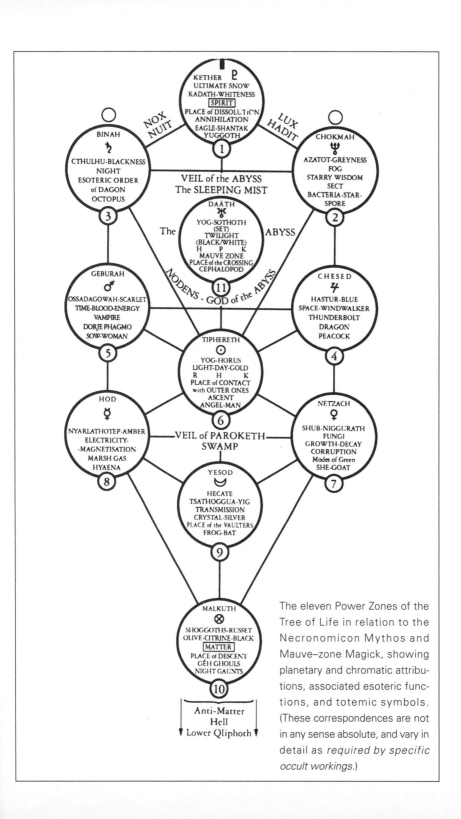

The eleven Power Zones of the Tree of Life in relation to the Necronomicon Mythos and Mauve–zone Magick, showing planetary and chromatic attributions, associated esoteric functions, and totemic symbols. (These correspondences are not in any sense absolute, and vary in detail as *required by specific occult workings*.)

with the planet Venus, the color green, the metal copper, the gemstone jade, the incense sandalwood, and so on. Each Sephirah is an "emanation" of God; each represents an archetypal idea, a realm of creation.

Below the Tree of Life is the Tree of Death, from which hang the ten Qlippoth, or "Shells," the shattered worlds of disease and evil. Each Sephirah has its corresponding Qlippah and the planetary correspondences are the same for both. This idea was part of the Hebrew Qaballistic system, but was later expanded upon and mapped by subsequent gentile magicians.[44] The traditional view of the medieval Qaballists was that the Qlippoth formed an upside-down Tree, hanging below Malkuth like a malignant root system beneath the Tree of Life. As such, the "Tree of Death" of the Qlippoth was the lowest part of the Asijjah (Lower World) and was to be avoided as a realm of gross materiality and evil spirits. Kenneth Grant, however, places the Qlippothic Tree *behind* rather than *below* the Tree of Life, a kind of darkside mirror image of the Sephirothic Tree. Moroever, Grant does not believe that this Qlippothic realm should be avoided. He sees the denizens of these Qlippothic realms not as "evil" beings per se, but as atavistic forces whose energies can be tapped by the magician.

In Qaballistic magick, the goal of a pathworking magician is to journey from Sephirah to Sephirah, learning from each and traversing the paths between in an ongoing quest for enlightenment, knowledge, and power. Separating the top three Sephiroth on the Tree (Kether, Chokmah, and Binah) from the lower seven Spheres, however, is an Abyss, a vast gulf that the ancients pictured as a huge expanse of desert. Crossing the Abyss is considered the highest achievement of an adept, and essential to transcending illusion.

Located in the center of the Abyss is a non-Sephirah called *Daath*. Daath is to a Sephirah as a black hole is to a star. *Daath* means "knowledge," because it represents an interface between the Sephirah of Binah (Wisdom) and the Sphere of Chokmah (Understanding) and, according to the Grant/Crowley system, the gateway of Daath is the opening of a pathway through the Abyss. Grant elaborates on this, referring to the Daath area as the "Mauve Zone" and explaining it as a kind of Sephirothic worm-hole allowing access not only to the Qlippoth, but also to other nonhuman worlds, as we shall see presently.

In his Enochian writings, Dee briefly mentions a demon called "Coronzon" (or "Choronzon"), who he says may interfere with the magician's work.[45] Crowley found this reference and stated that the demon Choronzon, the "Breaker-Down of all Thought and Form," was the guardian of the gateway of Daath. Though Bill Whitcomb, author of *The Magician's Companion*, considers Choronzon to be the equivalent of Nyarlathotep (intermediary and messenger of the Great Old Ones in the Cthulhu Mythos),[46] Kenneth Grant identifies him with Lovecraft's Yog-Sothoth, "the key to and the guardian of the gate."[47]

In March 1912, Aleister Crowley published *Liber CCXXXI* (231) in his magazine *The Equinox*.[48] Here he presented the names and sigils of "the genii of the 22

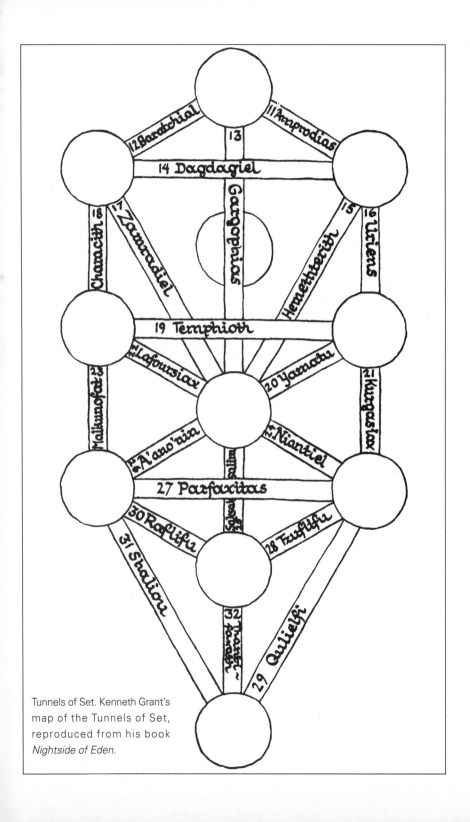

Tunnels of Set. Kenneth Grant's
map of the Tunnels of Set,
reproduced from his book
Nightside of Eden.

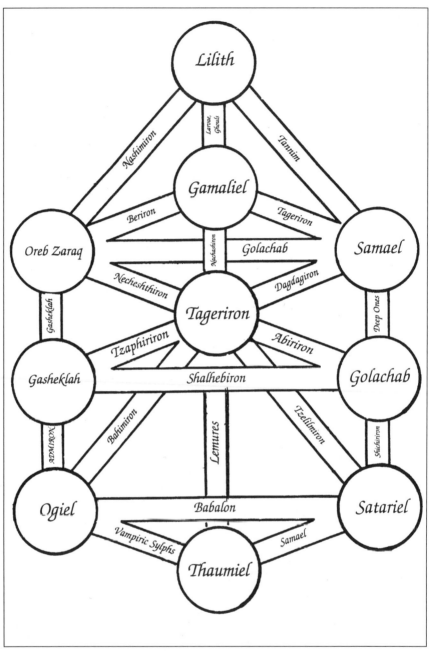

Tree of Death. This is my version of the more traditional upside down Qlippothic "Tree of Death" mapped by the medieval Qaballists. A similar version of this Qlippothic Tree was incorrectly attributed to Kenneth Grant by a well-known occultist who specializes in Qaballistic lore. Notice that it conflicts with Grant's map of the Tunnels of Set in his diagram of the Qlippothic Tree reproduced in *Nightside of Eden*.

scales of the serpent of the qlippoth." In *Nightside of Eden*, Kenneth Grant extrapolated these into the twenty-two Tunnels of Set, part of the Qlippothic universe reached through the gateway of Daath. This universe is apparently infested with disease, horror, and danger, as well as with swarming demons. Grant himself refers to Crowley's *Liber CCXXXI* as "an extremely sinister grimoire."[49] As effectively mapped by Grant in Part Two of *Nightside of Eden*,[50] these twenty-two Tunnels of Set underlie and correspond to the twenty-two paths on the Tree of Life. Just as the Paths of Wisdom connect the radiant Sephiroth on the Tree of Life, the Tunnels of Set connect the hideous worlds of the Qlippoth on the Tree of Death.

According to Grant, the universe of the Tunnels is perceived as evil only by those who are unenlightened about their real importance. In Grant's view, the abhorrent entities lurking in the Tunnels of Set are not "evil spirits" per se, but primal atavisms within the human consciousness, which the magickal practitioner can access by means of sex magick rituals utilizing the sigils in *Liber CCXXXI*. In Grant's system, the twenty-two Tunnels of Set also serve as symbolic descriptions of—among other things—twenty-two vaginal secretions (kalas) released in sex magick rituals. Part Two of *Nightside of Eden* is essentially a grimoire providing instructions for meeting the inhabitants of each Tunnel.

The main point of all this is that Grant considers Lovecraft a natural adept with the ability to travel astrally in dreams and traverse the Spheres of the Qaballistic universe. Grant's view is that Lovecraft, in crossing the Abyss, was drawn through the gateway of Daath and pulled down into the Tunnels of Set and the Qlippothic realms of horror. In those nightmarish Tunnels of Set, Grant believes, Lovecraft found the *Necronomicon*. An ominous quote from "The Dunwich Horror" calls this to mind: "Yog-Sothoth knows the gate. Yog-Sothoth is the gate. Yog-Sothoth is the key and the guardian of the gate."[51] Grant believes that Yog-Sothoth is none other than the demon Choronzon, guardian of the gate of Daath. Could an encounter with Choronzon, the Breaker-Down of all Thought and Form, he asks, have caused Lovecraft's obsession with non-Euclidian geometries and the breakdown of Newtonian physics?

From Lovecraft's story "The Horror in the Museum" comes a description of Yog-Sothoth: "Imagination called up the shocking form of fabulous Yog-Sothoth—only a congeries of iridescent globes, yet stupendous in its malign suggestiveness."[52] Grant believes those "malignant globes" to be Lovecraft's dream recollection of the shattered Spheres of the Qlippoth, confused with the entity that guards the way to them. August Derleth's Lovecraft pastiche, with the tantalizing name "The Lurker at the Threshold,"[53] contains a similar description of Yog-Sothoth. In Grant's view, Yog-Sothoth/Choronzon is the "Lurker" at the "Threshold" of Daath. From this perspective, it is no coincidence that Lovecraft's Mythos horrors are described as coming, not from the stars (Sephiroth), but from the dark void (Daath) between the stars.

Grant describes Lovecraft as having "snatched from nightmare space his lurid dream-readings of the Necronomicon"[54] and also cites Lovecraft's account of the title presenting itself to him in a dream as evidence that the *Necronomicon* is an astral book. Grant further states that, not only Lovecraft, but probably Mathers, Blavatsky, Crowley, and others "are reading from an akashic grimoire."[55] He cites Madame Blavatsky's *Book of Dzyan* (thought by some to be an influence on Lovecraft) as such a "transmitted" book, with its descriptions of "an elder world of monstrous phenomena."[56] Grant also mentions Chambers, Ambrose Bierce, and Arthur Machen as perhaps having "glimpsed the akashic Necronomicon."[57]

When Grant uses the term "Necronomicon Gnosis," he is not just using "gnosis" in its more conventional sense as knowledge revealed by intuition or supernatural means. *Daath*, the name of the gateway in the Abyss, is Hebrew for "knowledge"; in Greek it would be "gnosis." For Grant, the Necronomicon Gnosis is literally a knowledge revealed through the black hole of Daath. Grant declares, "Surely if it exists at all, the Necronomicon, like The Book of Thoth and the Book of Dzyan, exists as ever in the Tunnels of Set."[58] In *Beyond the Mauve Zone* (1999), Grant states that the *Necronomicon* represents an individual magickal current, whose number is 555, as distinct from Crowley's "Therionic" current, whose number, naturally, is 666. Also in *Beyond the Mauve Zone,* Grant uses the term "Necronomicon Mythos" in a way that seems interchangeable with the more typical term "Cthulhu Mythos"—the blanket term for Lovecraft's monstrous Gods—Azathoth, Yog-Sothoth, and so on. This could be interpreted to mean that he sees the *Necronomicon* as the key to Lovecraft's imaginary universe—a universe that Grant perceives as not as imaginary as most of us think.

In both his book *Outside the Circles of Time* and an article appearing in *Man, Myth and Magic,* Grant also suggests reincarnation as a possible link between Lovecraft and the *Al Azif.* "It would seem far more likely that in some previous existence Lovecraft was well acquainted with the Necronomicon."[59] He further speculates that the nightmares from which Lovecraft suffered were the result of crimes committed in a previous incarnation "in which he practised black and abysmal sorceries."[60] In a letter, Grant told me that it was Lovecraft himself who first mentioned the idea of reincarnation. However, I have found only two references to reincarnation in Lovecraft's *Selected Letters:* One was a jocular letter stating that Robert Bloch was a reincarnation of Ludvig Prinn.[61] The other was from a letter to Clark Ashton Smith in which Lovecraft emphatically states, "I am, indeed, an absolute materialist so far as actual belief goes; with not a shred of credence in any form of supernaturalism—religion, spiritualism, transcendentalism, metempsychosis, or immortality."[62] ("Metempsychosis" is the transmigration of the soul into another body after death.) Though Lovecraft signed all his letters to E. Hoffmann Price as "Abdul Alhazred," this was obviously a whimsical joke, and not intended as a confession that he believed himself to be the reincarnation of the mad Arab. (It was typical of writers in the Lovecraft Circle to be referred to as the authors of the imaginary books they created.) The theme of reincarnation does show up in Lovecraft's earlier fiction; his poem entitled "Nemesis" appears to be devoted to the subject of a man remembering past lives as a magician, and the stories "Polaris" and "Beyond the Wall of Sleep" deal with this theme as well. However, I am unsure how seriously we should take these as evidence of Lovecraft's actual beliefs.

As bizarre as Grant's theories may appear to the non-occultist, they actually constitute the best argument in favor of Lovecraft as an authentic, albeit unintentional, magus. Grant's speculations may rely overmuch on the unprovable supernatural, but at least they are not built on a foundation of disprovable rubbish: Winfield Lovecraft as an Egyptian Freemason, secret occult lore passed from Aleister Crowley to Sonia Greene, hidden tomes at Brown University, and so on.

The only problem is that Grant's theories depend on the notion that Lovecraft was a "natural adept." In my opinion, there is no such thing as a natural adept. You cannot be a natural adept anymore than you could be a natural computer programmer or a natural neurosurgeon. Adepthood requires not only native psychic ability, but careful study, discipline, and unwavering faith. (Lovecraft never even passed the faith hurdle.) Raw magickal aptitude without practice will not make you an adept any more than a high IQ without study will earn you a college degree.

Satanic Mechanics: Michael Aquino and Anton LaVey

In 1972, the same year that *The Magical Revival* came on the scene, another landmark in Lovecraftian magick came with the publication of *The Satanic Rituals*. Whereas Grant's writings were concentrated on broader issues of theory and offered little in the way of ritual for the would-be practitioner, the *Rituals* delivered two ceremonies: "The Ceremony of the Nine Angles" and "The Call to Cthulhu."

While not mentioned anywhere in the text, these rituals were in fact the work of Michael Aquino, former head of the Temple of Set—a continuation or offshoot (depending on whom you ask) of the Church of Satan. Aquino joined the Church in 1970, and came to the attention of Anton LaVey, the head of that organization. LaVey was already a great fan of Lovecraft and a friend of Lovecraft's correspondent Clark Ashton Smith. Aquino has stated that LaVey often used the incantation from "The Horror at Red Hook" at the beginning of ceremonies.[63]

While reading Lovecraft's works, Aquino became intrigued by Lovecraft's ability to evoke realistic terrors while distancing himself from them in his personal philosophy. He set out to express these tensions in a ritual form, and composed the "Ceremony of the Nine Angles," complete with concocted prehuman language fragments. Upon seeing this, LaVey asked Aquino for a "water" ritual to balance what he saw as the "fire" basis of the rite, and "The Call to Cthulhu" was born. LaVey touched up the rituals and an introductory essay by Aquino, and had them published.[64]

"The Ceremony of the Nine Angles" refers to the number nine, a significant numeral within the Church of Satan's symbolism. In the ceremony, a masked group stands in dim light before a trapezoid as they evoke Azathoth, Yog-Sothoth, Nyarlathotep, and finally Shub-Niggurath. The last of these appears (or rather, we hope, a celebrant playing that role appears) and leads the participants through an enumeration of the powers and properties of the Nine Angles.[65] The "Call to Cthulhu" should take place on the shores of a lake or other body of water, and "summons" the Great Old One Cthulhu, to whom the congregation delivers a paean and a promise that he shall no longer return to his watery home.[66]

Though it is not labeled as such, a third Lovecraftian ritual exists within the *Rituals*. This ceremony, called "Die elektrischen Vorspiele," is said to be taken from a "Black Order" whose practices informed Nazi occultism at a later date. The elaborate ceremony involves the production of a highly charged electrical field, white noise, and a pentagram lined with neon tubing.[67] During this ritual, the invoker calls the forces of darkness to emerge "through the gates of the Shining Trapezohedron,"[68] and warns of the "Hounds of the Barrier" who "move only through angles."[69] The Trapezohedron is a key element in Lovecraft's "The Haunter of the Dark," while the hounds who travel through angles are familiar to Mythos fans as taken from Frank Belknap Long's "The Hounds of Tindalos."

When asked about this ritual, Aquino mentioned that he had nothing to do with the rite, and that Long had been shocked that his creation might have appeared in a Nazi-inspiring ritual.[70] Long need not have worried. The ritual bears a striking resemblance to the eighth section of the *Emerald Tablets* by Morris Doreal, a believer in the hollow-Earth theory and founder of the Brotherhood of the White Temple. Doreal's influence from the *Weird Tales* authors is evident. Elsewhere, his work mentions "Yog Sog-Thoth"[71] and a description of an attempt by serpent-men to take over Earth matches Robert E. Howard's short story "The Shadow Kingdom" in an amazing number of details.[72] As for LaVey, it seems likely that the rite was more inspired by such works as William Hope Hodgson's *Carnacki, Ghost-Finder*, whose hero makes extensive use of an electric pentagram made of glowing tubing, than by any occult practices of the Third Reich.

The use of trapezoid symbolism in this rite is common within the Church of Satan's philosophy. In *The Devil's Notebook*, LaVey mentions his study of "haunted geometry," of places with histories of hauntings, "jinxes," madness, and murder. According to LaVey, his investigations showed that, "in each case angles were present that violated either topographical and architectural symmetry and perfection."[73] The presence of these angles—whether in a house, a military monument, or a Mayan temple—seemed to lead to psychological extremes in those who viewed them. Coupling this with the works of Lovecraft and Long, LaVey formulated his "Law of the Trapezoid," which stated that such images might be used productively to raise emotional energy for ritual. To actualize this theory, LaVey formed the Order of the Trapezoid within the church, but maintained it as a strictly administrative body. When Aquino founded the Temple of Set, he created a new Order, dedicated to its own brand of "chivalry" and magickal research.

What is the point of these rituals? It would be incorrect to say that LaVey and Aquino were 20th-century Cthulhu worshipers who devoutly believed in the titanic squid-God's literal existence. In the introduction to the book, LaVey tells us that conventional religion is based on the harnessing of imagination. Within the Church of Satan, "fantasy is utilized as a magick weapon by the individual rather than by the system."[74] The rituals in the book, then, are best seen as experiments in the channeling of emotional energy outside of an orthodox context of belief. LaVey is silent as to what ends this might serve, save as a rhetorical argument against Christianity.

Outside of the church and the temple, however, little has been done with these rituals. While many magicians I have consulted are familiar with them, we see few cases in which they are used, and even fewer in which they have inspired other works. So, while these calls to the Great Old Ones are widely circulated, Grant remains the most potent influence on Lovecraftian magick, though Aquino and LaVey undoubtedly rank as two of its forgotten pioneers.

Cthulhu Voodoo: Michael Bertiaux

Another major figure in the Lovecraftian magick scene was Michael Bertiaux, head of the Chicago-based Monastery of the Seven Rays. Born in 1935, Bertiaux began his life at Catholic schools, then entered the Anglican ministry. Teaching in Haiti in 1963, he was contacted by members of the Voudon (better known to the public as Voodoo) societies of that island, and asked to help spread their religion. After reflection, the minister realized that his calling lay elsewhere, and he became initiated into the Voudon priesthood and the Martinist Order tradition by Doctor Lucien-Francois Jean-Maine. He returned to the United States, and began his work of bringing Voudon to a non–African American audience.

Bertiaux also claims membership in the Ecclesia Gnostica Catholica, the Memphis-Misraim rite of Freemasonry, the Ordo Templi Orientis Antiqua (an OTO said to predate the split Crowley instigated), the Choronzon Club, and Le Couleuvre Noire (or Black Snake Order), among others. His Confraternity of Oblates of the Monastery of the Seven Rays, based in Chicago, is an umbrella organization for some of these groups and many others. While Bertiaux clearly has a local group with whom he practices, the bulk of his teaching is done through a colossal, multiyear correspondence course. Magickal Childe printed a fraction of these documents in *The Voudon-Gnostic Workbook*, a work of more than six hundred pages, in 1988.

I hope that Bertiaux and his students will be merciful when it comes to my description of their doctrines. Most of his material is hard to come by (even the *Voudon-Gnostic Workbook* does not always give all the lessons in the courses covered) and couched in obscure language. As a result, I am not sure what crucial elements of Bertiaux's system have been omitted from the material covered.

Neville Drury states that Bertiaux's system "resembles the Kabbalistic Tree of Life except that the Hebrew God-names are replaced by their Voodoo counterparts."[75] As discussed earlier, this Tree of Life is of central importance for Western ceremonial magick. In my opinion, Drury's statement is not accurate, as it implies that Bertiaux uses Qaballah as the organizing principle for his system. Rather, the Chicago occultist starts with Voudon, and then uses it to assemble and arrange a wide variety of philosophies and systems, a process referred to as "Voodootronics." For example, while Qaballah is based around the number 10, Bertiaux gives the number 16 primary importance. Bertiaux's system of magick resembles a ceremonial magick assembled by Voudon priests, rather than Qaballists. As such, it has a darker tone than Qaballism, as the loa of Voudon are more ambivalent in nature than the Hebrew God.

From this base, Bertiaux expands his instruction to incorporate all manner of belief systems, ranging from Crowley-esque sex magick to Theosophy to Shinto. Some individuals may be better suited to some of these courses than others, and their learning is tailored accordingly. Racial heritage and astrology determine a person's fitness for certain courses, and women are excluded from many. Bertiaux does not portray this as unfitness for magick in general—others will simply be more fulfilled in other magickal groups. The goal of these numerous processes is to master a set of machinery—which may exist as physical objects, symbols, mathematical equations, or other power centers[76]—to master the energy of the cosmos in an approach that seeks to be a science of occultism. Within this system, animal sacrifice is hardly mentioned, while sexual energy or "radioactivity," along with energy from stellar sources beyond the planets normally utilized by occultists, becomes the driving force behind many of the rites.

Kenneth Grant and Michael Bertiaux began corresponding before Grant wrote his *Cults of the Shadow* (1975). Whether both of them were practicing Lovecraftian occultism, or if this displays Grant's influence, is unknown, but *Cults* gives an account of Bertiaux's experiments in this field. Bertiaux set up a "Lovecraftian Coven" that sought to unite the aquatic energy brought with the Deep Ones in "The Shadow over Innsmouth" with that of the half-human creatures from "The Dunwich Horror." This coven carried out a set of rituals using the powers of Lovecraft, including aquatic rites—of a disturbingly sexual nature—near a lake in Wisconsin (possibly Devil's Lake near Baraboo) where August Derleth claimed Mythos beings dwelt.[77]

In performing these rituals, Bertiaux seeks to understand the Meon, or Universe B, a zone of "non-being" that acts as a mirror to the reality we know. This alternate reality is supposedly not threatening in itself, but when this alternate universe touches our own, it creates zones of uncertainty, which, according to Bertiaux, can lead to the creation of what we know as *evil*. According this belief system, Lovecraft noticed this discord, but did not understand its true source. Bertiaux's approach to this other universe is twofold: to explore its nature, and to guard against incursions that magicians who do not understand the system may unwittingly stir up. The impression Grant gives of Bertiaux's activities in *Cults of the Shadow* makes Le Couleuvre Noire sound like an American version of his New Isis Lodge—complete with beautiful priestesses copulating with scaly Mythos monsters on the shores of deserted Midwestern lakes.

Since this time, Grant and Bertiaux have gone their separate ways magickally, but the use of Grant's concepts remains important in Le Couleuvre Noire, and Bertiaux recognizes Grant as "a constructive and most creative adept of cosmic process and scope."[78] The Adytum Azothos Lodge is an active group that works within Bertiaux's OTOA. Their website includes "Into the Depths of Severity and All Beauty" by Rev. Nicholaj Frisvold, which describes a series of rites in which messages from such Gods as Dagon, Nyarlathotep, and "Chthulu" are received.[79] It would be easy, however, to overestimate the importance of Lovecraft's creations within this philosophy. Mentions of the Old Ones are outweighed by concepts from Voudon, Tantra, Ifa, and other such systems, and form a small part of a much wider set of mystical techniques. In his interview with Neville Drury, Bertiaux states that he still thinks of himself as an Anglican. I wonder what the Ecumenical Council would think of that!

Bertiaux's magickal correspondence courses are rumored to be priced at more than a hundred dollars yearly for a period of several years, and there is no agreement in the occult community as to their true worth. One observer declared that Bertiaux's *Voudon-Gnostic Workbook* was about the size of the Chicago telephone book—and contained about as much esoteric lore!

The Spawn of Grant: The EOD

Occult groups practicing Lovecraftian magick have proliferated since the publication of Grant's books. The most famous of these is the Esoteric Order of Dagon, or EOD. The order was founded by Steven Greenwood in 1980, under the influence (and with the encouragement) of Kenneth Grant.[80] It was self-described as "an association of initiates exploring the connections between the fiction of H. P. Lovecraft and other occult concepts."[81] The EOD attracted a great number of occultists and, during the 1980s, became a loose network of lodges pursuing work in Spain, England, and the United States. The order claimed to have "no ceremonial mummery, special handshakes, obsessive secrecy, nor paper claims to historic lineage."[82] Yet in *Starry Wisdom* (I, 1), Frater Tenebrous states that "the Esoteric Order of Dagon (EOD) is an occult Order descended from the Sirius-mystery cults of ancient Egypt, Babylon and Sumeria" and describes Lovecraft as "the High Priest 'Eich-Pi-El' the Prophet of the coming Aeon of Cthulhu."[83] While perpetuating the Lovecraft/Crowley Axis originated by Grant, members of the order were not required to be avowed Thelemites—"acceptance of *Liber Legis* is helpful but not mandatory as the Elder Gods are known by many different means . . ."[84] Those who demonstrated common interests with the order were invited to join.

According to Frater Tenebrous in a document entitled *The Aeon of Cthulhu Rising*, perhaps the most important task of the EOD was "the Opening of the Gate of Yog-Sothoth" and warned that those who tried "must be prepared to undertake this most dangerous descent into the Abyss of Daath (the so-called 'false knowledge')."[85] Tenebrous claims that "it is here that this 'false knowledge' (glyphed by Lovecraft as the grimoire, Necronomicon) can be found . . . brought back through the vortex of Daath, and finally given actual, concrete manifestation in the Outer."[86]

The EOD publication "Starry Wisdom," actually the internal newsletter of the

Dunwich (UK) Lodge, featured numerous fascinating essays and outlines for rituals, including a "Cthulhu Invokation" [sic] and a "Rite of Communion With Cthulhu" complete with a chalice of salt water in lieu of communion wine. The member of the group who acted as a "Host" to be possessed by Cthulhu was seated on the west side (the direction of R'lyeh[87]) of the Trapezoid of Invokation, facing inward. The priest or priestess performed the "primary Banishment" by tracing the Elder Sign (upright pentagram) at each of the four cardinal points, beginning at West and moving in a counterclockwise rotation. A variant on Lovecraft's phrase spoken by the Cthulhu cult, "Ph'nglui mglw'nafh Cthulhu R'lyeh wgah'nagl fhtagn," was used as a "Mantra of Invocation." "At the moment of possession," reads the instructions, "the power and identity of the Great God Cthulhu will be drawn into the body of the Host."[88] An editor's note at the end of the instructions stated that this was a "speculative" ritual that had not yet been conducted as a group working by members of the EOD as of the 1990 date of publication. The R'lyeh Lodge of the EOD had a library of such submitted works, including occult artwork, called the Library of Daath, of which it seems that very little has since come to light.

In 1991, the Order's "Yaddith Lodge" announced that the EOD was entering a "Period of Silence" in which only the three top members (Steven Greenwood, Nina Crummett, and Peter Smith) would remain active,[89] a proclamation that many members found surprising.[90] That same year, however, the three members of Yaddith Lodge started the Miskatonick Society, a group that republished the "Starry Wisdom" pamphlet and appeared to be pursuing the same lines of research. Notice that "Miskatonick" is spelled with a "k" to distinguish it from Lovecraft's fictional university. Like its namesake, however, the society was essentially an organization dedicated to study. "Research papers which are by nature speculative and concentrate on rediscovering curious and forgotten lore with relevance to the Mythos, are published in the irregularly-issued Journal of the Miskatonick Society, 'The Silver Key,'" according to Nina Crummet (Soror Azenath) in her "Introduction to the Miskatonick Society."[91] It seems they were no longer circulating ritual material, but concentrating on essays on Lovecraft's work and occult topics instead.

As of this writing, it appears that the Period of Silence has now ended, and the EOD has reemerged as of the Vernal Equinox of 20 March 1997 with an announcement by one Frater Bokrug XIII of the opening of a new lodge by the Esoteric Order of Dagon. It was further announced that "on the date of 20 August 1997 e.v., a New Director of the Order will be appointed by the Yaddith Lodge (comprising the Three Ex-Directors). At this time, the Director shall receive possession of the Great Seal of the Order, and with it the power to re-open the R'Lyeh Grand Lodge, and to inaugurate further Lodges."[92] The new newsletter of the EOD is called *Cthulhu Rising: The Official Organ of Esoteric Order of Dagon.* Lovecraft fans will note that August 20th is Lovecraft's birthday, which I am sure is the reason that date was chosen for the reestablishment of the EOD. Unfortunately, 20 August 1997 fell during a retrograde of Mercury, which most astrologers would agree is a disastrous time for beginning new projects. According to "The Call of Cthulhu" (1926), Cthulhu is supposed to rise when "the stars come right," not when the stars come *wrong!* We shall see.

Sects, Drugs, and Rock 'n Roll: The Miskatonic Alchemical Expedition

Another occult organization with roots in the EOD is, or rather was, the Miskatonic Alchemical Expedition founded by Bill Siebert, also known as AShT ChOzar Ssaratu. Siebert was, by his own admission, expelled from Kenneth Grant's Typhonian branch of the OTO in 1985, whereupon he founded the Cthonic-Auranian OTO, "a wholly new manifestation of the Order claiming no imprimatur from Crowley."[93] During this same period, he became a regional coordinator of the Esoteric Order of Dagon and cofounded Math of the ChRySTAL HUMM, "a Shamanic/Alchemical Thelemic Powerzone based in an old rundown farmhouse with 23 acres of rolling fields & woodlands (our ritual space) in upstate New York."[94] As a result of this cross-fertilization of disparate occultic influences, the Miskatonic Alchemical Expedition, or MAE, "birthed itself at Math of the ChRySTAL HUMM somewhere in 1986 or 87."[95] Although members of the MAE did not have to be affiliated with the Cthonic-Auranian OTO, Siebert did "strongly urge" those with longterm involvement in the MAE to apply for membership in the Esoteric Order of Dagon. Every applicant to the MAE was assumed to be a "functional Thelemite whose understanding/apprecia-tion of the Mythos is based upon direct personal magickal experience with outer energies," not a mere interest in weird fiction. The objective of the MAE, according to Siebert, was to "create an environment in which dreams/phantasies/visions are projected outward within our working group (Circle)."[96]

The primary method by which expedition members "projected outward" was by means of a drug/sacrament called the "entheogenic elixir," usually composed of a concentrated grain-alcohol distillate of Psilocybe Mexicana (hallucinogenic mush-rooms) diluted with Chambord raspberry liqueur and Coca-Cola. Sometimes cannabis infusions in ethanol or a drop or two per person of liquid LSD (1000–2000 mcgs!) would be added to the cup, as well as human "kalas"—consecrated sexual fluids (eeewww!). The estimated dose of psilocybin given to expedition members at MAE gatherings was approximately 75–300 mgs per person. While Siebert admits that "traditional ethnopharmacologists claim 50 mgs to be the maximum useful dose of psilocybin, I have found that doses far in excess of this to be efficacious in the right Set-&-Setting . . . some persons regularly consumed 3 or 4 servings over a 4–8 hr period."[97] While drugs *are* used as an adjunct to some forms of Shamanism, I believe that their only usefulness—if any—is in the early training of some practitioners, and should never be adopted as a mainstay. At any rate, increased dosage of hallu-cinogens only produces brain damage, not enlightenment.

Siebert claims that "conscious & deliberate use of sex, entheogenic sacrament and ritual . . . all assist the rational mind to gently step aside" into a drug-induced "samadhi." (Here again, I think there is a big difference between having your mind "gently step aside," and having it run over by a truck.) Expedition members were encouraged to contact whatever deities of different backgrounds they found to be useful, including those of the Cthulhu Mythos. According to Siebert, "a Lovecraftian mage may experience sexual union with Cthulhu or discover that s/he is at one with the chaos of Azathoth."[98] As for copulating with Cthulhu, the thought of catching unspeakable alien STDs scares me more than anything Lovecraft ever wrote.

Though Siebert doesn't provide an exact date for its demise, the MAE apparently closed in 1988, and the banks foreclosed upon the "powerzone" property at Math of the ChRySTAL HUMM. The Cthonic-Auranian OTO still existed as of 1994. It is easy to assume that Siebert's group, the MAE, existed solely as an excuse for sex orgies and drug-taking, and the hierarchy of the Esoteric Order of Dagon must have assumed just that, since they first tightened their control of their lodges, and then disbanded the order subsequent to Siebert's activities in the late 1980s. However, there were undoubtedly members of the Miskatonic Alchemical Expedition who were sincere seekers after the Great Work, no matter how misguided their leadership may have been.

Bloodsuckers for Cthulhu: The Temple of the Vampire

Another occult organization with Lovecraftian leanings is the Temple of the Vampire, which claims to be

> an ancient religion now registered with the federal government of the United States and possessing international membership. Shrouded in secrecy, the Temple has been known in historical times by many different names to include... in ancient Sumeria HEKAL TIAMAT (The Temple of the Vampire Dragon Goddess Tiamat).[99]

The latter would seem to be an influence from the Simon *Necronomicon*. The term "Ancient Ones" is a direct lift from the Simon book, and is Simon's version of the Lovecraft Circle's "Great Old Ones." The TOV also claim to be in contact with these Ancient Ones, whose very presence can turn the devotee into a vampire.

The Gates of Chaos

This sort of experimentation is not confined solely to organized groups, as many individual practitioners have made inroads into Lovecraftian occultism. One of these is chaos magician Tyagi Nagasiva, a regular poster on the alt.magick newsgroup. In his Internet document "Kathulu Majik: Luvkrafting the Roles of Modern Uccultizm," Tyagi claims that most Western magick is too hierarchical, too moralistic, too biased in favor of the forces of order and too habituated to structured language. Tyagi champions the Simon *Necronomicon*/Chaos connection, and believes that, without the destabilizing force of "Kaos," the magician will stagnate. "One may become balanced through exposure to Kathulu."[100] Tyagi's deliberate misspellings show the Burroughsian influence of Genesis P. Orridge's Thee Temple ov Psychick Youth.

With an elaborate twist on Grant's idea of the *Necronomicon* as an Akashic book, Tyagi Nagasiva has tried to associate the *Necronomicon* with the tradition of *terma* literature found in the Nyingma branch of Tibetan Buddhism.[101] As we will see later, this possible association between terma literature and the *Necronomicon* was articulated much earlier in an article by witchcraft pioneer Doreen Valiente, though Tyagi Nagasiva probably thought of it independently. Termas are writings that are considered to be ahead of their time by the Buddhist sages, and so are hidden away, perhaps for centuries, until the time is right to reveal them. Some termas supposedly exist exclusively in akashic form to be revealed only in dreams. Some are even reputedly written in the alien languages of the Dakinis or Nagas. There are also reputed to be "false termas," books of black magick and evil that can deceive the seeker. The *Bardo Thodol,* or *Tibetan Book of the Dead,* is the most famous of all termas, unless, like Tyagi Nagasiva, you include "Concerning the Dead," better known as *Necronomicon.*

The highly respected chaos magician Phil Hine has worked extensively with Lovecraftian magick, which he considers uncharted magickal territory allowing for high levels of personal innovation. Hine does not attempt to fit the Cthulhu Mythos into traditional, ordered systems such as Qaballah and the tarot, which he sees as missing the point of their chaos and wildness. His exegesis of Mythos magick is entitled *Pseudonomicon*[102] to show how our conventional need to name things breaks down when applied to the Great Old Ones. Hine's approach seeks instead to escape Western ideas of magick, and contains no prescribed rites, as experience of the Mythos is personal. Though Hine perceives the Great Old Ones not as a plurality, but as a unity that exists in nature and projects itself according to the magician's conceptions, he nevertheless makes an attempt to define them individually; Nyarlathotep is the gateway into the Gnosis of the Old Ones Cthulhu is the force of Beast-Consciousness submerged within the human psyche, and so on. Presenting the concept of "Purposive Disintegration," Hine advises the practitioner how to allow insanity into his or her life—letting it run its course while calmly, intellectually evaluating it, and eventually arriving at a point where madness and sanity can no longer be distinguished. Methods recommended for the practice of Mythos magick include (but are not limited to): liminal gnosis (scrying in which the scrying mirror becomes a gateway), dream control, emotional engineering, shape-shifting, glossolalia, use of obsessive fetish ("any object or item which becomes associated with a resonant state of consciousness,"[103]) frenzy, and sexual magick.

In *Pseudonomicon*, Hine presents an outline for a kind of initiatory psychodrama called "The Ghoul's Feast"[104] intended to make the participants escape their egos and unleash their atavistic desires, a process he identifies with the many transformations of characters in Lovecraft's fiction. He also presents a scenario for a guided pathworking in which the practitioner shape-changes into a Deep One and swims through the ocean depths to encounter Cthulhu in sunken R'lyeh. Hine mentions the "Dark Zones," or secluded places that serve as gateways to the power and presence of the Old Ones. While Hine advises the mage to attune his or her spirit to such a spot, he warns against the dangerous practice of trying to raise its power for selfish reasons.

Danger, Dunces, and Diabolism

Critics of Lovecraftian occultism often wonder why anyone who bases his magick on fiction would choose Lovecraft's horror stories as a paradigm. Why not base a magickal system on Tolkien's *Lord of the Rings* or Baum's *Oz* books rather than the horrors of the Cthulhu Mythos? In Lovecraft's tales, worshipers of the Mythos "Gods" always seemed to suffer from a cosmic case of masochism. They seek to help the Great Old Ones break through and regain control of Earth so that they, the devotees, can be swallowed up and annihilated in the resulting mind-blasting chaos and horror. It doesn't make good sense! Why on Earth would the magician want to invoke terrifying alien beings who yearn to reconquer the planet and destroy it by remaking it in their own hideous images? Michael Aquino wrestled with this question when he set about writing the Lovecraftian rituals for Anton LaVey's *The Satanic Rituals:* "Why should such 'gods' be worshipped by human beings at all—particularly if they were malignant? Was HPL expressing contempt for humanity by illustrating its morbid desires for self-obliteration . . . ?"[105] Phil Hine soberly warns his readers with a disclaimer, stating that "working with the Cthulhu Mythos current is dangerous, due to the high risk of obsession, personality disintegration or infestation by parasitic shells."[106] So the lingering question about Necronomiconian or Lovecraftian magick is not so much "how?" as "why?"

A ritual published in the *Cincinnati Journal of Ceremonial Magick* entitled "Return of the Elder Gods"[107] may hold the answer. The author states that the "Elder Gods" are going to instigate the world crisis that he believes is coming, but that they can also "provide the energies for successfully dealing with it."[108] The magician who wrote the article is obviously a Thelemite heavily influenced by Grant; he quotes Crowley's *Liber Al vel Legis* at the beginning of the essay and Crowley's Law of Thelema at the end, and describes himself as using the "Current of Maat," a magickal current that appears in some of Grant's works. The author claims that the macrocosmic forces he calls the Elder Gods are reflected microcosmically in the set of primitive survival drives (hunger, aggression, sex) that exist in the "individual and Racial Unconscious," which he calls the Forgotten Ones. The Forgotten Ones will seem dark and Qlippothic and there is a "certain danger in contacting them; but there is sure disaster in neglecting to do so . . . to effectively counter a planetary invasion by the Elder Gods, the Forgotten Ones must be summoned to consciousness."[109]

The ritual itself seems to be a shamanic invitation to possession, but it is possession by forces that supposedly already exist within on a very primal level. "They will come through the gateway of his hunger, devouring him, forcing his body to its knees."[110] Though the name of Lovecraft is never mentioned, the Elder Gods, whom the writer describes as having once been in control of Earth with humankind as their slaves, are obviously the same as Lovecraft's exiled Cthulhu Mythos entities. Thus, calling upon such entities to defend against others may be a necessary undertaking—or at least in the opinions of some magicians.[111]

Phil Hine also considers contact with the Great Old Ones to be valuable for a number of reasons. Not only does their native antinomianism allow us to step outside our ordinary value systems and look at ourselves through alien eyes, but Hine actually once effected a *healing* by invoking Tsathoggua! (Hine also admits that he was violently ill afterward.[112]) Perhaps one reason why Hine can achieve such positive results with his brand of Lovecraftian magick is that he conceives the Gods of the Cthulhu Mythos not as demonic entities to whom he must enslave himself with a Faustian pact, but as personifications of natural forces whose energies can be tapped.

Defenders of Lovecraftian magick insist that it is dangerous precisely because it is a "powerful" system of magick that "really works." Once one accepts the idea that valuable things can sometimes be dangerous, however, it is too easy to slip into the sophomoric notion that all dangerous things are valuable. I think a fine distinction needs to be drawn between things that are valuable but potentially hazardous, like electrical power, and things that are just plain hazardous with no redeeming value, like nuclear waste. Frankly, I have never quite understood the line of reasoning that insists that a style of magick that is dark and dangerous must automatically be more effective than one that is brightly lit by the White Light and relatively safe. Those who are fairly intelligent don't seem to use this kind of "danger = efficiency" equation in daily life. For example, hitchhiking from New York to Michigan would not only be a dangerous way to travel but also slow and inefficient. Driving in a car or taking an airline flight would not only be safer but much faster and more effective. If danger equals efficiency, why don't automobile corporations use that idea to sell cars? ("Buy the new *Titanic* mini-van! Guaranteed to crash every time you take it on the road!") The obvious answer is that danger does *not* equal efficiency, in either magick or the mundane world. Yet this idea is as ancient as it is asinine. Philosophers of the past have sometimes wrestled with this suicidal brand of Faustian foolishness. G. K. Chesterton, in his essay "War of the Gods and Demons," remarked:

> There was a tendency in those hungry for practical results . . . to call upon spirits of terror and compulsion; to move Acheron in despair of bending the gods. There is always a sort of dim idea that these darker powers will really do things, with no nonsense about it. . . . And it is their faith that the only ultimate thing is fear and that the very heart of the world is evil. They believe that death is stronger than life, and therefore dead things must be stronger than living things; . . . The Punic power fell because there is in this materialism a mad indifference to real thought. By disbelieving in the soul, it comes to disbelieving in the mind.[113]

The Love-Call of Cthulhu: Lovecraftian Sex Magick

One of the most controversial subjects in Lovecraftian magick is the blending of Lovecraftian ritual with sex. This process turns up on many different levels. A recent anthology called *Starry Wisdom*, printed by London's Creation Press, brings together a large number of artists, authors, and occultists in a tribute to Lovecraft, and places a strong emphasis on sexuality in his life and work. The book is a fascinating piece of interplay, but its obsession with linking Lovecraft to sex makes it about as credible as a porn video based on the life of Mother Teresa.

Yet does this reflect magickal ritual at all? The answer here would have to be "yes." A common theme in many of the ceremonies we have collected is the explicit combination of sexual acts and Lovecraftian deities. The most influential work on this subject is undoubtedly *Hecate's Fountain* by Kenneth Grant. In this book, Grant describes a number of rituals done by his New Isis Lodge, which must have been theatrical masterpieces in which scenery, props, and special effects combined to create an astounding experience. The plot is always the same: the ritual is going well, then a mistake is made. As a result, the priestess presiding over the rite engages in a sex act with a creature "from beyond the spheres we know." Given that this happens several times—and only to the priestess (who is invariably young and beautiful)—one has to ask just how "accidental" all of this is!

In one such incident, an Asian priestess of New Isis Lodge called Li was conducting a ceremony called the "Rite of the Ku" (Grant describes the Ku as a sort of Oriental incubus/succubus). The ritual was conducted around "a tank filled with tinted fluid in which swam several delusively realistic devices suggestive of the Deep Ones or Their minions." At the climax (no pun intended) of the ritual, Li strips and dives into the tank only to be gang-banged by its slimy denizens—or, as Grant describes it:

> As her form clove the waters eight phallic feelers reached up and seized her. They engaged her in a multiple maithuna in which each tentacle participated in turn. . . . The eightfold orgasm that finally convulsed her was registered by the votaries around the throne. Violent paroxysms displaced the black hoods, revealing shining heads and the protuberant eyes of the batrachian minions of Cthulhu.[114]

I wonder what kind of condoms one uses to fit those "phallic feelers." At any rate, this kind of ritual will seem bizarre to most readers, so an understanding of the role of sex in magick may help place this in context. In Western society, two perspectives on sexuality dominate. One is that sex is for procreation, and that the goal of intercourse is to make a child; the other is that sex is a recreational activity for the pleasure of the participants and any voyeurs who enjoy watching. These two positions (no pun intended) are not necessarily incompatible, despite the claims of their most fanatical defenders, yet they define most debates on the topic.

The magickal use of sex is closer to the former. A conventional heterosexual coupling may create a child, but any sexual act, even masturbation, releases psychic energy that can produce a so-called magickal child on a spiritual, mental, or physical level. Much of our understanding of this has come from Eastern magick, and from the mystery religions and fertility cults of the ancient world. Even if Black Masses with naked women on the altar and orgies at witches' Sabbats never occurred, their presence in Christian folklore nevertheless acknowledges the power of ritual sex.

But what does sex magick have to do with Lovecraft? If we examine the man's life, the answer is . . . *nothing!* "Lovecraftian sex magick" is an oxymoron. Lovecraft had little or no interest in what he termed "amatory phenomena." For him, sex was purely about biology, and ranked in importance somewhere between social reform and garbage disposal. Lovecraft's wife, Sonia Greene, described him as an "adequately excellent lover," which could be interpreted two ways, depending on whether you concentrate on the "adequate" or the "excellent."

Lovecraft's stories often have sexuality as one of their themes, but the author rarely concentrates on the sex act itself, as he does in his revision of C. M. Eddy's "The Loved Dead," which deals with (gasp!) necrophilia. Even here, Lovecraft mercifully spares us the prurient (or morbid) details. Typically, Lovecraft only shows us the aftereffects of deviant sex—the spawn of evil. Mating between the people of Innsmouth and the Deep Ones, under the watchful eye of the Esoteric Order of Dagon, results in the fish-faced horrors of "The Shadow over Innsmouth." In the hills of Massachusetts, "The Dunwich Horror" is birthed when a half-witted woman bears twin children for the hideous Yog-Sothoth. Sometimes the reference is subtler; Cotton Mather's account in *Magnalia Christi Americana* of the offspring of man and beast inspired Lovecraft's "The Unnamable." Though Charles Dexter Ward is not a monster, his sorcerous legacy from Joseph Curwen is passed down through the generations until it bears its final fruit. Perhaps Lovecraft treats sex as a secular Original Sin, which results in insanity and murder down through the ages.

Aleister in Wonderland

I cannot help but wonder what Aleister Crowley would think of the profusion of Lovecraftian occultists and *Necronomicon* users of today. Moreover, how would the Great Beast feel about the way many of these Lovecraftians have identified themselves and their practices with his 93 current of Thelemic magick? I strongly suspect he wouldn't approve. Nevertheless, some Lovecraftians might claim to be carrying on an obscure Thelemic "tradition" by using elements of fiction in their magick. Crowley himself tried his hand at writing occult fiction (with at least one disastrous side-effect, as we shall see), some of which may have reflected his own beliefs and practices. As discussed earlier, some occultists were also writers of fantasy and horror fiction, and seeded their stories with magickal concepts. So why shouldn't the influence flow in the opposite direction—with fiction influencing magickal practice?

At first glance, Crowley himself appears to be influenced by fiction in his practice of magick. His love of the poetry of Lord Dunsany is no secret, and in *Magick in Theory and Practice*, he recommends as reading "of a generally helpful and suggestive kind" such fictional works as Marjorie Bowen's *Black Magic,* Bram Stoker's *Dracula,* Sir Edward Bulwer Lytton's *A Strange Story,* George MacDonald's *Lilith,* and even Lewis Carroll's *Alice in Wonderland.* However, he also warns his readers that these works are "not to be taken, in all cases, too seriously," but should be read merely to "give him . . . a general familiarity with the mystical and magickal tradition."[115] Some might also accuse Crowley of participating in the "tradition" of writing fake grimoires, since the Master Therion entitled his textbook on the tarot *The Book of Thoth,* after the legendary grimoire described in the ancient Egyptian tale of *Setna and the Magick Book.* This too would be a misrepresentation of Crowley and his motives. While Crowley *did* use the title of the mythic spellbook for his work on the tarot, he claimed its authorship for himself, and he never pretended it was actually a translation of *the* original papyrus scroll written by the ibis-headed Egyptian God of magick. This is a far cry from writing a fake *Necronomicon* and attributing its authorship to a fictional mad Arab.

Of course, we'll never know for certain what Crowley's reaction would have been, since he never lived to see the beginnings of Lovecraftian magick. Or did he? One of Crowley's magickal protégés was a man named Jack Parsons. John (Jack) Whiteside Parsons (1914–52) was an undisputed genius, a pioneer of rocket science for the Allies during World War II, the inventor of the JATO (jet-assisted take-off rocket), and a pioneer of space rocketry. Parsons was also an active member of the California Agape Lodge in the American OTO, and Crowley chose him to lead that organization. In letters, Parons often addressed Crowley as "Most Beloved Father." It seems there was just one problem with Jack Parsons—his obsession with pulp fiction.

Parsons was a life-long fan of fantasy, horror, and science fiction, and attended many meetings of the Los Angeles Science Fantasy Society (LASFS). He often played host to notable sci-fi/fantasy authors and illustrators of the day. Among all these connections to fantasy and sci-fi, there are also a few possible Lovecraft connections. Parsons may have met E. Hoffman Price, a notable member of the Lovecraft Circle. Parsons was also known to have been in contact with people in Pasadena who were acquainted with Clark Ashton Smith, another of Lovecraft's regular correspondents, and the one who advised him about where to find sources for research on magick. At one point, Parsons was intimately (and disastrously) acquainted with science fiction writer L. Ron Hubbard (future founder of Scientology), who may have met Lovecraft on one occasion. John Carter, author of the excellent Parsons biography *Sex and Rockets, The Occult World of Jack Parsons,* speculates that Parsons probably read the Lovecraft story "The Colour Out of Space" as published in the September 1927 issue of *Amazing Stories,* and may also have read *Weird Tales,* the pulp magazine that featured most of Lovecraft's published work.

Fantasy fiction was not just entertainment to Parsons, however; it also had a profound influence on his practice of magick. Parsons was convinced that Jack

Williamson's 1940 novel *Darker Than You Think*, a tale of atavistic shape-changers and their bid to reconquer Earth (which shows a remarkable degree of Lovecraftian influence), was a prophecy of the coming of Babalon, the Scarlet Woman Goddess of Thelemic lore. Williamson, like Lovecraft, was surprised whenever he encountered occultists who took his work too seriously. In his autobiography *Wonder's Child*, Williamson wrote:

> I met John Parsons. An odd enigma to me, he was a rocket scientist with unexpected leanings toward the occult. He wanted to meet me because I'd written *Darker Than You Think*—a good many people have taken it more seriously than I ever did; witches now and then have taken me for a fellow Wiccan.[116]

Darker Than You Think also had a profound effect on Parson's ill-fated Babalon Working, which I will examine in a moment.

Parsons once conducted a forty-day magickal working called "The Black Pilgrimage," the title of which he probably got from the M. R. James story "Count Magnus" (1904), which had a great influence on such Lovecraft stories as "The Call of Cthulhu," "The Rats in the Walls," and "The Diary of Alonzo Typer." In "Count Magnus," the villainous count of the title is described as making a Black Pilgrimage to Chorazin (Chorazin—or Choronzon—is a name with profound meaning in both Thelemic and Lovecraftian magick, as previously discussed). Parsons probably based his Black Pilgrimage partially on Crowley's Abyss Working (in which Crowley encountered the demon Choronzon, reputed guardian of the gateway of Daath). In his *Book of Babalon*, Parsons wrote; "For thereby I have taken the Oath of the Abyss, and entered my rightful city of Chorazin."[117] It could be that Parsons also got the idea of making a "Black Pilgrimage to Chorazin" from a "revision" story Lovecraft ghostwrote for his occultist friend William Lumley entitled "The Diary of Alonzo Typer" (1935). In the tale, the hapless Typer makes a "pilgrimage" of his own to a sinister town called "Chorazin" in upstate New York, and enters the abandoned van der Heyl mansion nearby, where he finds, among other forbidden works, a Greek version of the *Necronomicon*. Typer's goal is to find "that Forgotten One who is Guardian of the Ancient Gateway,"[118] which sounds a lot like Crowley's and Grant's conception of the demon Choronzon, whom Crowley called "The Dweller in the Abyss." Ultimately, Typer disappears forever—dragged down into the basement of the decrepit van der Heyl mansion by a hideous Cthulhu Mythos monster. Of course, the original town of Chorazin (or its ruins) was located in Israel, which Parsons was planning to visit.

In 1946, Parsons began his infamous Babalon Working, using science fiction writer L. Ron Hubbard as his magickal assistant. Inspired by Crowley's own occult novel *Moonchild*, Parsons and Hubbard attempted to bring Babalon, the Scarlet Woman, into this world using a combination of sex magick and Enochian evocation. Parsons may also have been influenced by Lovecraft's "The Dunwich Horror," and also by the story that inspired Lovecraft's tale, Arthur Machen's "The Great God

Pan." Parsons and Hubbard used a woman named Marjorie Cameron (who will be mentioned later in the chapter on the *Necronomicon* in film) as the magickal vessel for the Babalon Working. The side-effects of this working may have included Parsons's untimely death, caused by an explosion in 1952—what Kenneth Grant would call a "tangential tantrum." Babalon herself apparently prophesied this fiery death in a channeling. In March 1946, Parsons wrote, "And in that day [the coming of Babalon] my work shall be accomplished, and I shall be blown away on the breath of the father." Blown away indeed!

What did Aleister Crowley think of Parsons's pulp fiction approach to magick? Not much! In a December 1943 letter to the actress Jane Wolfe, Crowley commented on Parsons's fictional delusions:

> Jack's trouble is his weakness, and his romantic side—the poet—is at present a hindrance. He gets a kick from some magazine trash, or an occult novel (if he only knew how they were concocted!) and dashes off in wild pursuit. He must learn that the sparkle of champagne is based on sound wine, pumping carbonic acid into urine is not the same thing.[119]

When Parsons wrote to Crowley regarding his Babalon Working, Crowley replied in a letter dated 19 April 1946:

> You have got me completely puzzled by your remarks about the elemental—the danger of discussing or copying anything. I thought I had a most morbid imagination, as good as any man's, but it seems I have not. I cannot form the slightest idea what you possibly mean.[120]

During this same period, Crowley wrote to Karl Germer and ranted, "Apparently he, or Hubbard, or somebody, is producing a Moonchild. I get fairly frantic when I contemplate the idiocy of these goats."[121] In January 1946, Crowley ousted Parsons from leadership of the Agape Lodge, naming his successor in a letter. Crowley's last recorded comment on Parsons—his obituary, if you will—is as prophetic as it is telling: "I have no further interest in Jack and his adventures; he is just a weak-minded fool, and must go to the devil in his own way. *Requiescat in pace.*"[122]

So what would the Master Therion think of the modern Lovecraftian occultist? Would he see him as a courageous magickal pioneer, or as a "weak-minded fool" who "gets a kick from some magazine trash"? I leave you to decide for yourself, based on the best evidence at hand. *Requiescat in pace!*

A Plague of *Necronomicons* —John Wisdom Gonce III 6

From Lovecraft's heyday as a pulp fiction writer in the 1920s and 1930s, through his posthumous cult figure status with horror fans and intellectuals in the 1950s and 1960s, there had never been any proof that his fictional *Necronomicon* was a real book. Then, in the 1970s, as Lovecraft's popularity dramatically increased, the shelves of ordinary bookstores fairly groaned under the weight of said "proof" when not one, but *four* books called *Necronomicon* saw the light of print, three of which claimed to be *the* "real" *Necronomicon*. Over the decades, as "Necromania" swept over the Western world, even more *Necronomicon*s slithered out of various publishing houses the world over. There was Jack Chalker's and Mark Owings's 1967 *Necronomicon*, de Camp's *Necronomicon*, Robert C. Culp's *Necronomicon*, H. R. Giger's *Necronomicon*s (volumes I & II), the Simon *Necronomicon,* the Hay/Wilson/Turner *Necronomicon*, the Lin Carter *Necronomicon*, the Price *Necronomicon*, the Elizabeth Ann St.George *Necronomicon*, the German *Necronomicon* pirated from the Simon version, and the three Italian versions of the *Necronomicon*. So many *Necronomicon*s, so little time!

Out of this plague of *Necronomicon*s, only three books are of any real interest from a magickal point of view: the de Camp *Al Azif/Necronomicon*, the Hay/Wilson *Necronomicon*, and the Simon *Necronomicon*. And of these three, the Simon book is the only version unanimously agreed to be of any use to the magickal practitioner. The de Camp version, despite its warning against using the book for calling up spirits, is an untranslatable, illegible, but decorative joke. To my knowledge, no magician has ever used this volume for anything other than a paperweight.

The Hay/Wilson/Turner *Necronomicon*, purportedly a fragmentary translation by Doctor John Dee, is supposedly decoded from a cipher in the manuscript *Liber*

Grimoires of dubious authenticity were much in vogue with occultists of the Decadent movement, as shown by this poster advertising the *Grand Albert,* a book falsely attributed to Albertus
Magnus. To judge by the attitude of the lady in the illustration, shifty spellbooks were just as
useful for seducing the gullible in those days as they are today.

Logaeth[1] by a cryptography expert named David Langford using a giant mainframe computer. The spells and rituals of the book are allegedly "reconstructed" by Robert Turner, who is actually a practicing magician. Turner was probably recruited for this project because of his reputation for Dee scholarship; he translated and edited an edition of Dee's *De Heptarchia Mystica* published in 1983–86. Turner's involvement in this hoax is particularly ironic in view of the way he spent a large portion of his book *Elizabethan Magic* railing against the Golden Dawn for adding inauthentic elements to Dee's Enochian system. Now Turner, the impeccable purist, is peddling the Hay/Wilson *Necronomicon* as the decoded text of Dee's cipher manuscripts! How have the mighty fallen!

Outside of the self-conscious, melodramatic use of archaic spellings and King James Bible phraseology, the writing in the Hay *Necronomicon* bears little resemblance to Dee's work as seen in published editions of his writings on angel magick from Sloane mss. 3188 and 3191. Enochian scholar and Dee historian Geoffrey James calls the Hay *Necronomicon* ". . . an elaborate hoax proving that some people have a great deal too much time on their hands."[2] Kenneth Grant rightly calls it "a feeble pastiche composed of spells and incantations drawn mainly from well-known medieval traditions . . . all of which derive from the *Shemhamphorasch* of *The Book of the Goetia of Solomon the King*."[3] While I agree with Grant's assessment of the spells themselves, I find that the "tablets," talismans, and sigils in the Hay book are made to look more like the sigils in *The Grimoire of Armadel*.[4] The crude "mystic runes" comprising "Ye Alphabet of Nug-Soth" look like an uninspired imitation of the alphabet of Dee's Enochian language. And why would a Middle Eastern Arab like Abdul Alhazred use a Germanic term like "rune"! Maybe Abdul was a survivor of some long-lost tribe of Norse Arabs. (Just kidding!)

In 1993, George Hay, published a sequel to his *Necronomicon* called *The R'lyeh Text,* which purports to be "Hidden Leaves from the Necronomicon." Now, in the world of Lovecraftian fiction, *The R'lyeh Text* was invented by August Derleth after Lovecraft's death—Lovecraft himself never wrote about it. Moreover, Derleth never claimed that the *Text* was part of the *Necronomicon*. Hay, Wilson, Turner, and company, on the other hand, don't seem to know any more about Lovecraft than they do about magick, and so they use this inappropriate title for the next episode in their occult soap opera, claiming that the *Text* is a previously "lost" portion of the *Necronomicon*. None of that really matters, however, since *The R'lyeh Text* is every bit as silly and useless as its lame predecessor—from the pointless, rambling introduction by Colin Wilson, to the obscure concluding essays of Patricia Shore and someone named "Arnold Arnold," to the unworkable "spells" sandwiched in between. The most interesting thing about the book is the crocodile on the cover.

The Hay *Necronomicon* and its sequel, *The R'lyeh Text,* are similar to the grimoires of the Renaissance and medieval periods in that the tools and materials described as essential for the spells are often unobtainable and/or prohibitively expensive. The workings can only be done in specific locations with regard to terrain,

The cover of the Hay *Necronomicon,* Skoob Books, 11a-17 Silician Avenue, Southampton Row, London Wc1A 2QH. UK price £5.99.

and they can only be done on special dates on the magickal calendar. (For example, Cthulhu can only be evoked on Hallowmass, Shub-Niggurath at Beltane, etc.) To turn this mess into a workable system, or to make it compatible with any other system, would be a Herculean and worthless effort.[5] Perhaps these are intentional safeguards to keep anyone from misguidedly attempting to use these books. Perhaps additional safeguards should be put in place to keep anyone from misguidedly *buying* the books. Nevertheless, gullible consumers have a right to buy the Hay/Wilson *Necronomicon* instead of wasting their money on silly things like food and rent.

The Simon *Necronomicon*

At this point, we've narrowed things down a bit, and it appears that the Simon book is the only *Necronomicon* that requires serious attention.

Simon Says

The Simon *Necronomicon* borrows enough from the principles of real magickal systems that some find it useful. The sections "Of the Zonei and their Attributes," "The Incantations of the Gates," and "The Book of Entrance, and of the Walking"[6] are based on nothing more or less than planetary magick and astral pathworking, two of the most venerable types of Western magick. The reference to the seven planetary "gates" as a "Ladder of Lights" on page 17 is an obvious lift from the Qaballistic description of the ten Sephiroth as a "Tree of Lights." The use of gates as magickal symbols may be an emulation of early gnostic texts, like *The Book of the Great Logos*, which speak of the "opening of gates" into different mystical/magickal realms, as do the angelic writings of Dr. John Dee.[7]

Throughout the introduction of the Simon *Necronomicon*, there are attempts to associate both Lovecraft and Simon's book with Aleister Crowley and Thelemic magick. The book is even dedicated to the Great Beast: "On the One Hundredth Anniversary of the Nativity of the Poet Aleister Crowley 1875–1975." In the acknowledgments, the editor thanks "the demon PERDURABO, without whose help the presentation of this book would have been impossible."[8] "Perdurabo" was the magickal name Crowley adopted when he joined the Golden Dawn. (Like all G. D. names, it is a Latin motto; it translates as "I will endure to the end.") The copyright is in the name of a certain "Schlangekraft, Inc."; this name is German and means "serpent power," which is interesting because of its possible reference to the OTO (Ordo Templi Orientis), originally a German lodge taken over by Crowley. The OTO practices a Tantra-like form of sex magick involving the arousal of the serpent of kundalini, the primal power coiled at the base of the spine—ergo, "serpent power."

Even the choice of the name "Simon" as a pseudonym is probably a tribute to Crowley. *Simon Iff* was a fictional character created by Crowley as an idealized version of himself and used as the hero of a series of short stories and of the novel *Moonchild*.[9] Considering all the other links to Crowley in the Simon *Necronomicon*, this seems a more likely explanation than the obvious allusion to Simon the Sorcerer in the New Testament (Acts 8:9–23), who tried to buy the gifts of God from the Apostle Peter. Though Crowley himself may have named Simon Iff after the infamous biblical magus, the nom de plume of Simon, the *Necronomicon* author, is probably meant as a bow to the Great Beast.

Will the Real Simon Please Stand Up?

One of the enduring mysteries about the Simon *Necronomicon* is the question of exactly *who* Simon—its enigmatic author—really is. As with virtually every other issue concerning the book, there is little agreement and much controversy as to the actual identity of the author. The scanty biographical material in the *Necronomicon* styles Simon as a sort of James Bond–like espionage agent, whereas the *Necronomicon Spellbook* makes him sound more like a Montague Summers–type clergyman. Some of our Internet informants have insisted that Simon is/was none other than "Horrible" Herman Slater, the now-deceased founder and owner of Magickal Childe in New York, and the original publisher of the Simon *Necronomicon*. Others insist that Simon is a real individual unknown to the public.

We have managed to communicate with Mr. Peter Levenda, the well-known writer whose work on the Simon book was known (or at least suspected) for some time in occult and literary circles. Mr. Levenda proved to be quite friendly and helpful, and was willing to talk openly about his involvement with the Simon *Necronomicon*. According to Levenda, he was both the "general editor of the translated text" and a researcher into Sumerian lore at the New York Public Library. Unusual as it may seem, Levenda described the "Necronomicon 'group'"as "more of an ad hoc assembly of friends and like-minded people than it was a purely commercial arrangement between translators, editors and researchers, etc."[10] In this group, one person often did a number of jobs. If Peter Levenda cannot claim to be Simon, then perhaps no one individual can. Simon may simply be the pseudonym of a staff of writers. At the end of the manuscript for a promotional article written in 1977 to plug the *Necronomicon*, however, the name of Peter Levenda is typewritten. Beside Levenda's name is a signature and note that reads, "(Simon) Editor of Necronomicon." This signature exactly matches the autograph found in a signed copy of the hardbound first edition of the Simon book. To most, this would seem to be a "smoking gun"—proof positive that Peter Levenda and Simon are one and the same. However, I have reason to believe that Levenda is not the "one and only" Simon, and that the name Simon is a composite pseudonym for two or more authors. I will elaborate on my reasons for this later.

At least two reliable sources, however, substantiate the authentic existence of an actual Simon. Robert M. Price, editor of Chaosium's *Call of Cthulhu* fiction series, says he met Simon about ten years ago in New York. Price described Simon as "surprisingly young" with black hair and a beard.[11] Khem Caigan—alias Khem-Set Rising, illustrator of the Simon book—told the authors that Simon is indeed a real person who once offered classes in his *Necronomicon* "at the Magickal Childe over on 19th Street between 5th and 6th Avenues."[12] Later, we'll examine Simon's classes on the *Necronomicon* in detail.

Manuscript Masquerade

Another haunting question about the Simon book relates to the manuscript from which it is supposedly translated: Where is it!?

According to the account in the *Necronomicon Spellbook*, the manuscript was one of several hundred antiquarian texts stolen in 1972 by two monks who looted universities and private collections all across America in the "biggest rare book heist in the history of the United States." After the two monks went to federal prison, Simon was somehow left in possession—at least temporarily—of the sinister manuscript. The manuscript was supposedly written in Greek "in a large, cursive hand," apparently an old grimoire or "book of spells dating from the ninth century, A.D."[13] The text supposedly contains frequent "copyist's glosses"—anachronistic references inconsistent with the period in which the book was supposedly written.[14] The author of the text—the "Mad Arab"—never gives his name (he is never called "Abdul Alhazred"), whereas most medieval Arab authors provide not only their names but also their genealogies. Daniel Harms succeeded in tracking down the above-mentioned news story, only to discover that the two monks, Steven Chapo and Michael Huback, tried for grand theft in 1973, stole mainly rare atlases from the 17th, 18th, and 19th centuries. There is no mention of any medieval "book of spells." The *New York Times* article also says that the two convicted thieves were very helpful in assisting authorities with tracking down the stolen books.[15] If we are to believe Simon, the two defrocked monks somehow forgot about a 9th-century manuscript written in Greek. As Dan Clore has remarked, the whole account is too much like a bad Cthulhu Mythos story to be credible.

On page li of the introduction is "A WORD CONCERNING THE ORIGINAL MANUSCRIPT," in which the publishers and editor explain that they cannot grant permission to anyone to view the original manuscript of the *Necronomicon*. Their reasons are more creative than credible: The first excuse is that the manuscript is not the property of the editor and publishers. They were given the right to translate and publish the text, but not to display the manuscript for public inspection. Excuse number two is that most requests to see the manuscript might be the frivolous queries of fearful practitioners who suspect that certain sigils were not copied correctly. Last, but not least, the supernatural hazards of coming into physical contact with the original manuscript of the *Necronomicon* supposedly include frightening hallucinations, "physical incapacities," and "emotional malaise." According to the introduction, "A great deal of misfortune accompanied the publication of this book,"[16] supposedly including an editor suffering a collapsed lung, L. K. Barnes being plagued by the constant messages of the "extraterrestrial intelligences" who guarded the book and oversaw its publication, and production designer Jim Wasserman being harassed by poltergeist activity. Even the typesetters were beset by swarms of rats. Because of the dangerous nature of the manuscript, it was deemed unwise to expose the general public to it.

Skeptics find it suspicious that the original manuscript of the *Necronomicon* is conveniently unavailable for appraisal by epigraphers and other scholars who could establish authoritatively whether it is genuine or not. Even if the publishers of the Simon *Necronomicon* were to produce a physical manuscript, it would be no guarantee of authenticity, since the history of literary antiquities is rife with spectacular fakes. Any ancient inscription not found in a controlled excavation is automatically suspect. An outstanding example is the case of Moses Wilhelm Shapira who, in 1883, offered the British Museum fifteen fragmentary scrolls, which he claimed to be the oldest written biblical text in the world, a version of *Deuteronomy* possibly written by Moses himself. Within the year, the scrolls were declared to be fakes and Shapira committed suicide from humiliation.[17] In reality, a team of translating scholars would never work directly from a 9th-century manuscript for fear of damaging a priceless artifact. Instead, they would use a set of photographic prints of the original manuscript. The publishers of the Simon book, however, cannot even produce a set of manuscript prints to support their claims of authenticity.

Khem Caigan, or "Khem-Set Rising," who illustrated the Simon *Necronomicon*, told us that he never saw the original manuscript from which the book was supposedly taken. Khem worked from drawings in a typewritten copy of the "translation." He was given permission to change and re-create the author's crude sketches. It seems a trifle odd that scholars translating an ancient magickal text would not want to reproduce the original seals and diagrams exactly as they appear in the manuscript. The illustrations, sigils, and diagrams—including the beautiful quasi-pentagramic "Elder Sign" on the front cover—were all created or developed by Khem himself, not taken from an ancient text. (Incidentally, Khem claims that Avon Books used his art from the Magickal Childe edition without giving him any credit.) Nor does Khem remember any plagues of rats or poltergeist activity accompanying the "translation" of the book; "I can't say that anything untoward happened during the job or after that I can honestly attribute to the 'Simonicon.' Manhattan being what it is, you've got trouble coming every day."[18]

All of this casts considerable doubt on the Simon *Necronomicon* being an ancient work. Later, we will hear another account of its origins that supports the misgivings that many occultists have about the book and its magickal usefulness.

Sumer or Later : The (Un)Common Soil of a (Non)Tradition

In the introduction to his *Necronomicon*, Simon claims that H. P. Lovecraft and Aleister Crowley met (at least mentally) on the "common soil" of Sumer. Simon also quotes Aleister Crowley as saying: "Our work is therefore historically authentic; the rediscovery of the Sumerian Tradition."[19] So, how important was the Sumerian Tradition to Crowley? Daniel and I have both searched diligently for this quote and haven't found it yet, though we have sifted painstakingly through our considerable libraries and enlisted the help of mages on the alt.magick newsgroup on the Internet, many of whom are dedicated Thelemites with a knowledge of Crowley's writing that exceeds our own. Crowley was so prolific that his published work presents a challenge to even the most dedicated reader, but the fact that even the Crowleyan occultists can't find it indicates that the quotation is obscure and that Simon is deliberately exaggerating its importance. Here are the only references to Sumer that we were able to find in Crowley's writing. (It's worth noting that Crowley seldom uses the term "Sumer" and often refers to it by the now-obsolete term "Chaldea."[20])

- In *Magick Without Tears,* Crowley discusses the "White School" of magick and observes that "the only religion which corresponds to this School is that of ancient Egypt; possibly also that of Chaldea."[21] (Notice that Crowley puts "Chaldea" in a very minor light compared to his beloved Egypt, mentioning it only as an afterthought.) Crowley also briefly mentions "Chaldean" astrology in the same work.

- On the second page of Crowley's published edition of Mathers's translation of *The Goetia: The Lesser Key of Solomon* is a curse against Mathers printed in Greek that is actually taken from the *Leyden Papyrus.*[22] One of the names of power in the curse to strike down Mathers is the Sumerian Goddess Ereskhigal, but her presence there is purely incidental and the source is Egyptian and not Mesopotamian.[23]

- In "The Cephaloedium Working," Crowley writes his "Holy Angel his Guardian is Aiwaz 93, the God first dawning upon Man in the Land of Sumer."[24] This is the only reference to Sumer in that work and, again, there is no mention of a Sumerian Tradition.

- *Liber Aleph vel CXI: The Book of Wisdom or Folly* includes a mention of "Sumer, where Man knew himself Man" (whatever that means). However, this is a mere passing reference in a section dealing with the Sphinx of Egypt ("De Sphinge Aegyptiorum").[25]

We should remember that these four mentions come from literally thousands of pages of Crowley's writings, which covered a period of roughly half a century and hundreds of topics.

When we asked Peter Levenda, who edited the Simon *Necronomicon,* where the quote came from, he said it was taken from one of Kenneth Grant's early books.[26] Perhaps there is no greater living scholar on the subject of Aleister Crowley than Kenneth Grant, who once served as Crowley's secretary, and, thanks to his working relationship with Crowley's literary executor, John Symonds, has access to *all* of Crowley's written works, both published and unpublished. If the "Sumerian Tradition" quote came from Grant, it could easily be from one of Crowley's unpublished letters or magickal diaries, which only further underscores its insignificance.

Presumably, we are to believe that the Simon *Necronomicon* represents the ultimate grail of Crowley's alleged quest, the supposed rediscovery of the Sumerian Tradition. The introduction itself continuously attempts to link Lovecraft to Crowley on the "common soil" of Sumeria, even though ancient Sumer was a time and place in which Lovecraft had little or no interest and for which he had no personal affinity whatsoever. In a 1927 letter to Bernard Austin Dwyer, Lovecraft declares that "behind the Roman world my sense of personal identity cannot be projected [imaginatively]; so that the dimmer, vaster, and more terrible dawn-world of Gnossus and Nineveh, Ur and Babylon, Memphis and Thebes, Ophir and Meroe, must remain to me a thing existing only on paper as objective historical fact."[27] So acute was Lovecraft's fascination with Imperial Rome that he barely took an interest in any other ancient civilization.

Crowley, for his part, rarely seems to have practiced magick or channeled revelations from any ancient civilization other than Pharaonic Egypt—as in the case of his *Book of the Law* revealed in Cairo by the spirit Aiwass. Kenneth Grant claims that Crowley believed the Yezidi "devil worshipers" of northern Iraq to be the descendants of the Sumerians, but there is no proof of this. If Crowley were so devoted to the Sumerian Tradition, why didn't he call his coming age the "Aeon of Enki" and not the Aeon of Horus?

In his introduction, Simon spares no stratagem to link two men who never met with a civilization neither cared about. On page xxxix is a "Chart of Comparisons" that attempts to draw parallels between Lovecraft, Crowley, and Sumer. This calls to mind Grant's Lovecraft/Crowley links in *The Magical Revival*. On pages xli and xlii is another chart of correspondences, this one between zodialogical signs and planetary spheres and their Assyro-Babylonian equivalents. The title of the chart, "Supplementary Material to 777," links it to the Golden Dawn book of correspondences Crowley published. Most of the information, however, comes from chapter XXIV of E. A. Wallis Budge's book *Amulets and Talismans*.[28] As such, the Simon *Necronomicon* is a compendium of material from many other sources, with an Assyro-Babylonian overlay. All of its attempts to link up with either Crowley's Thelemic 93 current or Lovecraft's fiction are shallow and unconvincing.

Cracked Axis: Theobald versus the Therion

Simon's attempt to link Lovecraft (or "Uncle Theobald," as he sometimes called himself) with Crowley is just one of the more recent (and moronic) attempts to develop a "Lovecraft/Crowley Axis"—a connection proving that both men were tied into the same magickal current. If Lovecraft and Crowley had ever met—astrally in Sumer, or under any other circumstances—the only result is likely to have been a fistfight.

We have already discussed Lovecraft's views on occultism and supernaturalism, yet this was not the only difference between the two men. Crowley grew up in a strict Plymouth Brethren household, while Lovecraft was allowed to indulge his interests as a child. The English wizard openly indulged in alcohol and heroin, while the American author was a strict teetotaler. Lovecraft had virtually no interest in sex, while Crowley embraced a wide variety of sexual practices, and partners of both sexes. When Crowley had money, he spent it on luxuries until it was gone; Lovecraft kept himself at a level of genteel poverty through scrimping and saving. Lovecraft considered himself a patriotic Englishman; Crowley had to backpedal from his writings supporting the Germans in World War I. It could be argued that all of these are minor details, yet three major differences existed between Lovecraft and Crowley.

First, the two men disagreed considerably on the role of humanity in the universe. Crowley's view centered on the concept of the will. Each person had a sacred duty that should be fulfilled, and by enacting this will, they became the center of irresistible power—"every man and woman is a star." In Lovecraft's scheme, life and humanity are only accidental chemical reactions within an uncaring cosmos. For the Providence writer, we have no destiny other than inescapable death, and the best that can be done is to seek beauty and meaning in tradition.

Second is their attitude toward publicity. Lovecraft was shy to a painful degree. He remained a recluse for most of his life and approached others with much trepidation, even in his letters. When Lord Dunsany, one of his favorite authors, read at the Copley Plaza Hotel in 1919, Lovecraft refused even to get an autograph, insisting that he disliked "fawning upon the great." By contrast, publicity was Crowley's meat and drink. He performed a number of stunts intended to impress the papers, such as burning his passport (in a conveniently unopened envelope) before journalists. If the media weren't paying attention, he even tried such stunts as suing people for calling him "wicked"! His self-aggrandizing manner was the exact opposite of Lovecraft's unassuming one.

Finally, both men treated those around them in entirely different ways. Lovecraft had a wide circle of penpals, to many of whom he wrote for twenty or more years. He took it upon himself to aid young correspondents in their writing and, while he vigorously defended his views, Lovecraft had few real enemies. Crowley, on the other hand, left a swath of jilted lovers, disgruntled friends, and shattered organizations in his wake. Those who idolize Crowley may want to look at Kenneth Grant's memoir *Remembering Aleister Crowley*. Much of the Crowley-Grant correspondence is filled with Crowley griping about Grant's lack of spiritual attainment, his inability to fill out everything on Crowley's shopping lists, his reluctance to become Crowley's unsalaried secretary, and so forth. Don't forget, this was at a time when Crowley wanted Grant to be his magickal heir!

While Crowley knew nothing of Lovecraft, Lovecraft was aware of Crowley, not only from the newspapers—as I discussed in the previous chapter—but also through the secondhand anecdotes of his personal friend Frank Belknap Long, who was acquainted with the editor T. Everett Harre, who had actually met the Great Beast. In an unpublished letter to Clark Ashton Smith dated 11 February 1934, Lovecraft comments on Long's descriptions of Crowley, and of how Harre—a man not known for squeamishness—was nauseated by the encounter. Lovecraft analyzes the Master Therion as a loathsome, degenerate character who nevertheless had literary talent and scholarship, though he put them to perverted use. In an unpublished letter to Richard E. Morse dated 25 April 1936, Lovecraft remarks that the question of whether a "mass of psychological putrescence" like Crowley should be allowed to remain unconfined was a question too hard for a mere layman like himself. Obviously it doesn't take the proverbial "rocket scientist" to see that there isn't much room here for a Lovecraft/Crowley Axis.

The Public Awaits

Some current authors on occult topics are not completely silent on the subject of the Simon *Necronomicon*. Attitudes vary. Some have shown admiration, some impartiality, some have been disarmingly frank in their disapproval, while others have practically bent over backward to be diplomatic about the issue of whether the Simon book is authentic, and whether its brand of magick is workable or valuable (two very different issues). The remarkable thing about all this is not so much what has been said about the Simon book, as what *hasn't.* As you read this list of comments, you will notice that the opinions of many notable occultists, New Agers, and Pagans are conspicuous by their *absence.* Perhaps these savants thought the "*Necronomicon* question" was unworthy of their attention, or perhaps they were just afraid of (shudder!) offending someone. At any rate, here is a sampling of reactions:

- Though not usually considered an "occultist," one author who was apparently fascinated with the *Necronomicon* was cutting-edge writer William S. Burroughs. According to Peter Levenda, Burroughs discovered the Simon *Necronomicon* being printed by his own printer, and called it "a dangerous book . . . the theological equivalent to a loaded gun."[29] Khem Caighan (illustrator of the Simon book), whom I mentioned earlier, tells a less romantic—but perhaps more believable—version of this story:

  It was about that time that William Burroughs dropped by, having caught wind of a "Necronomicon" in the neighborhood. After going through the pages and a few lines of powder, he offered the comment that it was "good shit." He might have meant the manuscript too—check out the "Invocation" on page xvii of his Cities of the Red Night. *Humwawa, Pazuzu, and Kutulu are listed among the Usual Suspects.*[30]

  Indeed, Burroughs *does* seem to have been somewhat impressed with the Simon book, so that in the Invocation at the beginning of his surrealistic tribute to pulp fiction, *Cities of the Red Night* (1981), Burroughs dedicates the novel to:

  the Ancient Ones, to the Lord of Abominations, Humwawa, whose face is a mass of entrails, whose breath is the stench of dung and the perfume of death, Dark Angel of all that is excreted and sours, Lord of Decay.[31]

  He also dedicates the work to—among others—Pazuzu, *Kutulu,* "the Akhkharu," *Lalussu,* the *Great Old One,* the *Star Beast, Pan,* and "To all the scribes and artists and practitioners of magick through whom these spirits have been manifested. . . ."[32] The novel itself involves such

Necronomiconian themes as astral projection, ceremonial magick, ancient civilizations, private detectives who use occult techniques, and a revolution of sorcerers.

Does this mean that Burroughs was a great believer in the magick of the Simon *Necronomicon*—or perhaps that he considered it great literature? Well, not exactly. On 7 April 1978, Burroughs wrote a brief essay entitled "Some considerations on the paperback publication of the NECRONOMICON," which he sent to L. K. Barnes, who designed (and possibly helped write) the Simon *Necronomicon*. In this essay, Burroughs states: "With some knowledge of the black arts from prolonged residence in Morocco, I have been surprised and at first shocked to find real secrets of curses and spells revealed in paperback publications for all to see and use." Burroughs goes on to observe that he shouldn't have been shocked since, with universal literacy, "There are no secrets anymore." He gives the example of a college student who designed a nuclear weapon from unclassified information. Burroughs continues with some unflattering statements about the sort of person who might be attracted to the magick in the *Necronomicon*:

Is there not something skulking and cowardly about this Adept hiding in his magick circle and forcing demons to do the dirty jobs he is afraid to do himself, like some Mafia don behind bulletproof glass giving orders to his hitmen? Perhaps the Adept of the future will meet his demons face to face.[33]

Burroughs finishes by saying that it is good that these secrets are being revealed to the public, if only to keep them from being monopolized by corporate and government agencies. His point here is freedom of information, not endorsement of the Simon book. At no point in this essay does Burroughs refer to any specific printed version of the *Necronomicon*—Simon's or anybody else's. On the copy Burroughs sent to Schlangekraft, Larry Barnes scribbled an unhappy note to J. Gordon Melton (a columnist for *Fate* magazine) saying, "Unfortunately Burroughs does not speak much of the hardcover book or its contents [sic] which is where your review will be greatly appreciated."[34] In fact, Burroughs says *nothing* about any edition of the Simon book or any other *Necronomicon* hoax in his essay. He simply uses the *Necronomicon* as a metaphor for hidden secrets revealed. Barnes and company were obviously expecting Burroughs to write a "review" plugging the Simon book, and were bitterly disappointed. Burroughs's apparent endorsement of the Simon book in *Cities of the Red Night* is probably the result of his enjoyment of anything antinomian or repulsive. In any case, he treats the book as pulp horror fiction, which is probably what he considered to be its only real value.

Proudly displayed as a blurb on the back cover of nearly all paperback editions of the Simon *Necronomicon* is a truncated version of a quote from Burroughs's essay: "Let the secrets of the ages be revealed. The publication of the Necronomicon may well be a landmark in the liberation of the human spirit." What Burroughs actually wrote is:

Let the secrets of the ages be revealed. This is the best assurance against such secrets being monopolized by vested interests for sordid and selfish ends. The publication of the NECRONOMICON may well be a landmark in the liberation of the human spirit.[35]

For some reason, the publishers saw fit not to print a somewhat more sarcastic and less approving observation later attributed to Burroughs: " . . . the *Necronomicon*, a highly secret magickal text released in paperback."

- In the spring of 1978, columnist J. Gordon Melton wrote a review of the Simon *Necronomicon* for *Fate* magazine. L. K. Barnes had sent Melton a hardbound copy of the book on 27 January of that year, and had diplomatically nagged him to write a review of it ever since. Melton complied with a review that, at first, seemed to go along with the Simonian party line. He begins by seemingly accepting Simon's origin story, and stating that "Lovecraft may not have created the *Necronomicon* out of pure imagination."[36] Gradually, however, by dropping a few dubious hints, Melton shows himself to be less than firmly in the Simon camp. For example, he states that some will see the book as "an expensive if sophisticated attempt to cash in on the Lovecraft mania." In the same paragraph, he comments that "some magick leads to fanciful escapism, some to manipulative power grabbing and some to the borderlands of insanity. The new *Necronomicon* borders on the latter."[37] He concludes by warning his readers that the book may be dangerous. (And Barnes thought he had a problem with Burroughs!) Ironically, in the same issue, Melton commented on how frustrated he was with the way "the psychic community deals with fraudulent works such as those by Carlos Castaneda who has spent a decade selling us a fictional colleague, Yaqui magician Don Juan." Barnes probably got more (or less) out of this review than he bargained for.

- *Earth Religion News*, Magickal Childe's "official" publication, which Herman Slater touted as "The Only Pagan Tabloid Magazine Dedicated to the Practice and Study of Paganism," published several advance advertisements for the Simon *Necronomicon*. One of these was found by my friend Tony Kail of *The Subculture Project* (an investigative and educational organization that seeks to inform both Pagans and law-enforcement professionals about the realities of occult crime). Tony turned up a June 1974 issue with a melodramatic advertisement for the Simon book with a header that read "PUBLIC NOTICE":

In the fall of 1968, in the nave of a quiet little church in the Bronx, of a denomination with an esoteric lineage, three men met and exchanged a briefcase. One of these was a priest. The other a scholar. The identity of the third man, with the briefcase, is unknown. . . . Today, some five years later, the contents of the briefcase are disclosed, in print, fo[sic] the first time ever. The pastor of the little church is dead; the scholar is in hiding; the unknown man remains unknown, and the priest can only be known by a pseudonym here, lest he be defrocked for the role he has played in the publication of

THE NECRONOMICON[38]

The ad describes the book as "The inspiration of Lovecraft's 'Cthulhu Mythos'stories" and calls it "a Pagan grimoire replete with spells and incantations for the summoning of dark forces from the 'Outside.'" It also promised "Advance orders for this first edition of *Necronomicon* are being taken now by Herman Slater of the Warlock Shop, in Brooklyn, New York (a store devoted to the needs of Pagans, Witches, and Magicians alike)." The author of the book is referred to as "Fr. Simon." Interestingly, the same issue featured two articles written by Simon— one entitled "A Short Primer on Pagan Ceremonial Magick," the other "Black Magic and Politics"![39]

Lest anyone imagine that Herman Slater was just trying to palm the Simon book off as a harmless fake, another advertisement for the *Necronomicon,* probably dated to 1976 or 1977, states that it is "Not a phony, or a cleverly composed forgery."[40]

- In his introduction to the 1980 Weiser edition of *The Grimoire of Armadel,* Francis King states that any desired magickal text, "even an imaginary one," will ultimately be supplied to its market/audience, even if it must be forged. King cites the example of Edward Kelley—John Dee's scryer—who claimed to have found the fictional alchemical tome, the *Book of St. Dunstan,* which contained instructions for transforming base metal into gold. Within fifty years, three different forgeries of the book were on the European market. King compares these historical forgeries to the *Necronomicon,* which has led to "two printed versions [the Simon and Hay books]—amusing hoaxes which will probably become collectors' items."[41]

- In the November 1984 issue of *Twilight Zone* magazine, there appeared an article by horror fiction editor Robert M. Price entitled "Hexes and Hoaxes: The Curious Career of Lovecraft's *Necronomicon.*" Though Mr. Price devotes most of this article to Lovecraft, his Circle, and their literary heirs, he does make some comments about some of the *Necronomicon* hoaxes, including the Simon opus. Regarding the "Simonicon," Price observes, "So far all our Raiders of the Lost *Necronomicon* have pulled their pranks in innocent fun. . . . But this may not be the case with *The Necronomicon* brought out by Schlangekraft and Barnes Graphics in 1977 and by Avon in paperback, in 1980." Price observes, with some obvious dismay, that the Simon book is "no less a fake than the others, but Simon seems to want it taken seriously. It is intended for real occult rituals; the author even teaches classes on how to use it."[42] (Later, I'll be examining those classes in detail.) Since Price has a background in both Lovecraft scholarship and biblical textual criticism (and, no doubt, the history of the Ancient Near East), he proceeds to pick apart some of the most glaringly idiotic mistakes in the Simon book. He concludes his article with the wry observation that "ironically the *Necronomicon,* which was originally conceived as forbidden, suppressed, and nearly impossible to obtain, has now become a mass-market paperback!" and jokingly guesses this may have been the vision of the future that drove Alhazred mad.

- Stage magician and self-appointed high priest of the skeptic cult, James "the Amazing" Randi, briefly mentions the *Necronomicon* in his *Encyclopedia of Claims, Frauds, and Hoaxes of the Occult.* One might have expected him to comment on the falsity of the Simon book and other *Necronomicon* hoaxes. The most "amazing" thing here, however, was Randi's lack of scholarship. He ignorantly included Lovecraft's imaginary book in a list of historical grimoires. No wonder nobody takes him seriously anymore.

- In Kenneth Grant's later works, *Hecate's Fountain* (1992) and *Outer Gateways* (1994), he refers to the Simon *Necronomicon* as the "Schlangekraft recension"[43] and even quotes the Simon book[44] and includes it in the bibliographies of both works. Mr. Grant now uses the term "Necronomicon" to mean alternately Lovecraft's literary device, the akashic *Necronomicon* existing in the Tunnels of Set, and the published *Necronomicon*—particularly the Simon book. In *Beyond the Mauve Zone* (1999), Mr. Grant includes the Simon book in his bibliography under "Necronomicon," but curiously places it last on the list, behind the Hay/Wilson version, and even Giger's artbook version. Whether this is the result of alphabetical order, or the books are prioritized according to importance, I'm not sure.

- One of the first prominent occultists courageous enough to confront the "*Necronomicon* question" was Donald Tyson. In his website *Donald Tyson's Supernatural World* at *http://dontyson.tripod.com/index.html,* he includes a list of links on occult topics, including one for "Necronomicon." In this essay, Tyson provides a good account of the fictional origins of the book in Lovecraft's imagination. He also comments briefly on the Hay/Wilson and

Simon versions. He sums up all published *Necronomicon*s by saying: "By all means purchase, read, study, memorize and take to heart any and all of the books found in the stores with the title *Necronomicon*, but for heaven's sake remember as you do so that they are phonies, each and every one."

- Black Moon Publishing, an independent occult publishing house that advertises on the Internet, claims as its goal "the generation and radiation of nightside magickal currents." In addition to republishing documents of the EOD and various works related to the Lovecraft/Crowley Axis, Black Moon has published several Simon *Necronomicon*-related items, including *Liber Azif: A Study of the Avon Necronomicon* by one Fra Ollar Ethanzi (1990) and a "Cuthonic Tarot" or *Tarot of the NecronomIcon* by one Mat-A.

- Bob Larson, host of the Christian radio show *Talk-Back,* is the author of many alarmist books designed to tweak the worst fears of the Fundamentalist Christian community. In *Satanism, the Seduction of America's Youth,* Larson includes a section on the *Necronomicon,* but confuses the Hay/Wilson version with the Simon version. This shouldn't be too surprising, since Larson doesn't know the difference between Satanism and Paganism either. He also states that Lovecraft "concocted" the book himself (possibly hinting that he wrote his own version of it). One of Larson's more ridiculous statements seems to put him on common ground with Simon in the realm of Assyriological ignorance:

The Sumerian civilization has been closely aligned with Aryan ideology, and their language resembles Hindu Sanskrit. Their religion was a complex system of ritual magic, including the summoning of evil powers.[45]

Of course, the Sumerian language has no known linguistic descendants, and has no known relationship to Sanskrit. Sumerian cuneiform, which is composed of wedge-shaped markings, bears no resemblance to the Sanskrit alphabet. The ancient Mesopotamians never accorded demons the sort of devotion they did their Gods and Goddesses, and, while there are plenty of cuneiform texts devoted to exorcising evil spirits, there are none with incantations designed to invoke them. Perhaps Bob should stick to disc-jockeying, and leave research to the big boys.

In his book *Extreme Evil, Kids Killing Kids,* Larson claims that teenaged murderer Sean Sellers (executed 4 February 1999 for the murder of a convenience store clerk) was influenced to read the *Necronomicon* and begin a life of crime as a result of hearing a "witch" (no doubt a Wiccan) speak at a school assembly. First, I think Larson is misidentifying cause and effect here—I wonder if there are any statistics on teen crime following the appearances of Christian preachers at school convocations. Second, I have never known any Wiccan (and I have many Wiccan friends) to recommend the *Necronomicon* to anyone. Larson has never been one to let a little thing like the truth stand in the way of an opportunity for some good anti-Pagan propaganda.

- In the third edition of his *Godwin's Cabalistic Encyclopedia,*[46] David Godwin lists the Cthulhu Mythos entities Azathoth and Cthulhu, complete with spellings of their names in Hebrew, but no entry for "Necronomicon." Apparently, discretion is the better part of valor.

- Bill Whitcomb's *The Magician's Companion* has a long entry under "Cthulhu Mythos," giving definitions of Cthulhu, Azathoth, Nyarlathotep, Hastur, and Shub-Niggurath, along with a thumbnail sketch of Lovecraft. Whitcomb seems to echo the chaosists when he says, "It does not matter where a magickal system came from if it is believable and elegant in form."[47] Critics of Simon's book would probably take exception to both the words "believable" and "elegant." Although Whitcomb says the Mythos "seems to be a rapidly evolving, coherent and powerful magickal system,"[48] he side-steps the issue of whether the various *Necronomicon*s are forgeries or authentic, and what the intentions of their authors are with a noncommittal "I cannot say."[49] If the author of an encyclopedia on magick cannot give his opinion, then one wonders who can.

- On the Internet, the *Necronomicon* FAQ (Frequently Asked Questions), compiled by Kendrick Kerwin Chua, is as impartial as possible. Acting as a discussion moderator and avoiding flamewars, Kendrick continually states that "discussion is at best educational, but usually leads to no concrete conclusions or new ideas." My only question is—What's the point?

- In his article "Calling Cthulhu" for the fall 1995 issue of *Gnosis,* Erik Davis is a bit less deferential. He calls the Simon *Necronomicon* "a grab bag that contains far more Sumerian myth than Lovecraft," but later observes that "magicians with strong imaginations have claimed that even the Simon book works wonders."[50]

- Lars B. Lindholm departs from diplomacy completely in *Pilgrims of the Night.* "There's just one problem with the [Simon and Hay *Necronomicon*s]. It seems it's all lies. The writers of these works have been confronted with opposition and attacks to the point that their scholarship and ethics have been challenged."[51] He declares that he does not see the humor in passing off "forgeries" as authentic literature. He also makes the point that, just because the magick seems to "work" does not mean the book it was taken from is the real *Necronomicon.*

- Konstantinos, in his book *Summoning Spirits*, is equally frank. He warns his readers that, in order to evoke entities from the *Necronomicon*, they will probably have to create them themselves, as they would any egregore.[52] (An egregore is a thought-form created by the magician by means of his/her will and visualization. It is a mental image solidified into astral substance. According to Konstantinos—and to Isaac Bonewits—it is much easier to use a preexisting egregore than one that the magician has to create.) He calls the Simon book "probably a well-researched hoax"[53] and observes that the rituals work because they are based "to some extent" on real occult practices. He advises his readers to contact some of Marduk's Legion of Fifty if they want to experiment with the book. Marduk, of course, is a real Babylonian God, unlike the fictional creatures of the Cthulhu Mythos. Of the Hay/Wilson/Turner *Necronomicon* he remarks that none of its material "is even remotely based on occult practices"[54] and that he cannot imagine why anyone would try to use it.

- Highly respected chaos magician Phil Hine, in his book *Pseudonomicon*, flatly states:

  There are no *Necronomicon*s .... there are several published necronomicons [lower case "n" is Hine's], but none of them for me do justice to that sense of an "utterly blasphemous tome" which drives you insane after a thorough reading.[55]

  Hine sees the *Necronomicon* as a symbolic "cipher" for an overwhelming magickal experience that reverses the magician's worldview like a religious conversion. For Hine, publishing a book called *Necronomicon* is missing the point, since the *Necronomicon*'s power comes from its "mythic nature," in which one hopes to find it "in the depths of some dusty shop" rather than in the occult section of a modern bookstore. He also seems to accept Grant's idea of the *Necronomicon* as an astral book that "escaped from the library of Dream,"[56] but not as a literal book, and especially not as a mass-market paperback.

- *Fate* magazine, in a special "millennium issue" for January 2000, listed the publication of the *Necronomicon* as one of the hundred most important metaphysical events of the past century. I have only one question: Which *Necronomicon* are they talking about? I find it hard to understand why any of the "Necrohoaxes" should outrank the publication of a book like *The Holographic Universe* (which, to the best of my memory, wasn't mentioned in this list of milestones). Silly me!

- In the second edition of his book *Modern Magick: Eleven Lessons in the*

High Magickal Arts, Donald Michael Kraig includes an appendix consisting of questions and answers. In one of these, he deals with the *"Necronomicon* question," and declares, "There are many books which claim to be THE *Necronomicon.* They all have just one thing in common: they are nothing but inventions of contemporary authors."[57] Of the Simon book, Kraig writes, "The most popular version is loosely based on Sumerian religion—very loosely."[58] He comments that much of the Simon book (which he doesn't mention by name) seems to be taken from the works of the Assyriologist Francois Lenormant. He also points out that, according to Lovecraftian fiction, the beings of Lovecraft's Cthulhu Mythos are dangerous and malevolent, with a desire to take over or destroy our world. He concludes by ominously asking the reader: "Are you *prepared* to chance that?"[59]

I think it is fair to point out that the first edition of *Modern Magick* contained no such confrontation of the *Necronomicon* hoax. The second edition, with the above comments, did not appear until 2001, after I met Don Kraig at the 1999 Starwood Festival at Brushwood, New York, and took the opportunity to speak with him. Later, I was honored when he attended a workshop Daniel Harms and I did there called "Magick and the *Necronomicon.*" Like many serious magicians with a traditional background, Mr. Kraig probably never thought the *Necronomicon* problem was worth addressing, until somebody pointed out how many people take it seriously.

So much for the opinions of the critics (or the lack thereof)! Now let's examine the actual historical, mythical, and magickal framework upon which the Simon book is built.

A Mess of Mesopotamia

Dagon an' Ashtoreth—Belial an' Beelzebub—Golden Caff an the idols o' Canaan an' the Philistines—Babylonish abominations—Mene, mene, tekel, upharsin

—OLD ZADOK ALLEN TO ROBERT OLMSTEAD,

H.P. LOVECRAFT, "THE SHADOW OVER INNSMOUTH"

Like the demented ravings of Old Zadok Allen in Lovecraft's story, the Simon *Necronomicon* presents a hopeless mishmash of ancient cultures: Sumerian, Babylonian, and Assyrian, and even some Canaanite, Greek, and Egyptian elements. But Old Zadok was drunk, illiterate, senile, and frightened of the Deep Ones, so what was Simon's excuse?

Any magickal system may be workable if its users believe in it. In my experience, however, a system will be more useful if it is actually based upon some existing culture or pantheon, as Bonewits's "Switchboard" theory suggests.[60] So how well does the Simon *Necronomicon* "plug into" the magickal circuit of ancient

Mesopotamia? I am in an especially good position to assess how well (or poorly) the Simon book depicts Mesopotamian magick, since, as a Neopagan, I am a worshiper of the great Goddess Inanna/Ishtar, and practice authentic elements of Sumerian/Mesopotamian magick and religion based on years of careful research from genuine academic sources.

Since the Simon *Necronomicon* claims to be a Sumerian grimoire, the first question we should ask is: Who were the Sumerians? The Sumerians descended from the older Ubaid culture (5500 to 4000 B.C.E.) of the ancient Near East. They were the first literate inhabitants of Mesopotamia—the land between the Tigris and Euphrates Rivers in what is now southern Iraq. The Sumerians invented writing toward the end of the Late Uruk Period (3500 to 3100 B.C.E), named after the important city of Uruk in southern Sumer that was closely associated with the Goddess Inanna, and where much of the monumental architecture of that period has been excavated. The Sumerians were also the first to establish urban centers of civilization in Mesopotamia. During the subsequent Early Dynastic Period, Sumer consisted of a group of independent and sometimes warring city-states, each with its own patron or matron God or Goddess. Each city was considered the property of a deity. Sumerian artists were apparently the first to depict the human form in a highly representational manner, particularly in the holy city of Nippur, where art was primarily an expression of religious devotion. Even after the Sumerians were absorbed ethnically by other peoples invading the crossroads of Mesopotamia, their agglutinative, ergative language survived as a liturgical and scholarly language, much as Latin survived in medieval Europe. Sumerian religious beliefs, legal records, and literature have also come down to us largely through the ancient Semitic language of their conquerors, the Akkadians. Sumero-Babylonian magick has survived in the form of incantations and spells recorded in Sumerian and Akkadian, and sometimes in other languages like Elamite or Hurrian.[61]

In terms of Sumerology (the study of ancient Sumer) and Assyriology, as the general study of ancient Mesopotamia has come to be called, there are a vast number of criticisms that can be leveled against the Simon *Necronomicon*. Though Simon claims that his book represents Sumerian magick, much of its material is actually bastardized from Babylonian sources. The Semitic Babylonians were actually of a later period and had a somewhat different culture and political structure. To better understand the differences between the two, think of the Sumerians as differing from the Babylonians as the Greeks did from the Romans. The Babylonians emulated the earlier Sumerian culture, but spoke a different language (Akkadian), and though they had the same basic religious beliefs, they worshiped the same Gods and Goddesses by different names.

Most critics agree that the Simon *Necronomicon* does not correctly reflect the magickal/religious atmosphere of ancient Mesopotamia. The book presents a struggle between the good Gods, or "Zonei," of the standard Mesopotamian pantheon, and the evil "Azonei," or Ancient Ones, derived (after a fashion) from Lovecraft's Cthulhu

Mythos. In Mesopotamian mythology, however, there is no cosmic struggle between the forces of good and evil as found in Zoroastrianism, Judaism, Christianity, and Gnosticism. Demons and genies of all types were called "good" or "evil" depending on their effects on humans; there are even references to "evil Gods." The Babylonian God Marduk's defeat of Tiamat, for example, is now believed to have been the tale of Babylon's battles with other city-states, not of a battle of good against evil. This is not to say that the Mesopotamians had no morality; their society had definite concepts of right and wrong, good and evil, clean and unclean, and was bound in taboos. Examples of ancient literature like the *Epic of Anzu*, in which an evil being uses trickery to attain power only to be defeated by the heroic God Ninurta, indicate that the ancient Mesopotamians were more "moral"—and fair-minded—than we had thought. Ironically, the Simon book is a work of amoral darkness, focusing only on the strength and wit of the practitioner to subdue rebellious entities

Scholars who can read and translate ancient Mesopotamian languages, and who have read the Simon *Necronomicon*, have observed that it contains some words and even a few phrases of Sumerian and Akkadian. Most of these words are not arranged in grammatical order, however, and are simply strung together seemingly at random.[62] Admittedly, magickal works are among the most difficult to translate, but these are not magickal formulae or anything else coherent. Ancient Mesopotamian magickal spells and rituals were always written coherently—though sometimes slightly garbled; they were never complete "mumbo jumbo."[63] The fact that they are supposed to be incantations does not justify the gobbledygook nature of the Simon texts. Some fragments appear to some scholars to be authentic, but don't appear to have been understood by the author himself. This has led dogmatic magickal practitioners to speculate that the authentic fragments may have intrinsic power of their own, making the book unexpectedly dangerous.

Simon's most infamous violation of Sumerian syntax is probably his claim that Lovecraft's Cthulhu is found among the ancient Mesopotamians in association with the town of Kutu (sometimes known as Cutha), which he refers to as "KUTU." Simon further states that "KUTU" is a Sumerian name for the underworld. Thus he claims that "KUTU-LU" or "Cuthalu" means "the man of the underworld" or "man of Cutha." First, the proper Sumerian idiom would be LU-KUTU. Second, while there was a real city of Kutu in Babylonia, where Nergal was worshiped at a temple called E-meslam (or Meslam House), its only association with the underworld was that its patron deities were Nergal and Ereskigal, Lord and Lady of the underworld. And third, no God—even one with tentacles on his face—would be referred to by the humble title of "Lu" or "Man."[64]

Simon may have gotten his reference to Kutu, or Cutha, from a rather common grimoire called *The Sixth and Seventh Books of Moses*. Falsely attributed to the biblical prophet, this book claims to be "translated for the first time from the Cuthan-Samaritan language into English."[65] The so-called translator's preface of this spellbook further states:

The language and manuscript of this rare and eternal monument of light, and of a higher wisdom, are borrowed from the Cuthans, a tribe of the Samaritans, who were called Cuthim in the Chaldee dialect according to the Talmud, and they were so called in a spirit of derision. They were termed sorcerers, because they taught in Cutha, their original place of abode, and afterward in Samaria, the Kabala or Higher Magic (Book of Kings). Caspar, Melchior, and Balthasar, the chosen arch-priests, are shining lights among the eastern Magicians. They were both kings and teachers—the first Priest-teachers of this glorious knowledge, and from these Samaritan Cuthans— from these omnipotent priests of the fountain of light, who were called Nergal.[66]

This fanciful explanation for the origin of the spurious *Sixth and Seventh Books of Moses* was undoubtedly inspired by some passages in *II Kings* in the Old Testament:

And the king of Assyria brought men from Babylon, and from Cuthah, and from Ava, and from Hamath, and from Sepharvaim, and placed them in the cities of Samaria instead of the children of Israel: and they possessed Samaria, and dwelt in the cities thereof. Howbeit every nation made gods of their own, and put them in the houses of the high places which the Samaritans had made, every nation in their cities wherein they dwelt. And the men of Babylon made Succothbenoth, and the men of Cuth made Nergal . . . (II Kings 17:24, 29, 30).

Now it's interesting that this association of Cutha, or Kutu, with black magick and idol worship (or, in this case, Cthulhu worship) may have come into the Simon book through *The Sixth and Seventh Books of Moses*, which has a sinister reputation of its own, not unlike that of the *Necronomicon* itself. Some traditional sources claim the *Sixth and Seventh Books* was written in the 16th century and published under the patronage of that shifty pontiff, Pope Julius II (1503–13). Others attribute it to an unknown monk in the German city of Erfurt. In the 19th century, elements from the infamous French grimoire *The Red Dragon* were added to *The Sixth and Seventh Books of Moses*. (Simon, incidentally, also edited the edition of *The Red Dragon* published by Magickal Childe.) Apparently, the book has been translated into every Western language, and is known as "the Devil's Bible" in some areas. The book has been especially popular in Germany, where, in 1925, a man named Angerstein was convicted of seven or eight murders allegedly associated with the *Books*. Earlier printings of the *Sixth and Seventh Books* were reputed to contain a seal that was supposed to give its possessor great riches after he had killed nine people. Angerstein was arrested just before the last murder. (Daniel and I have researched all available editions of the *Sixth and Seventh Books*, and have found no such seal.) From 1945 thru the 1950s, there were fifty-six lawsuits involving the book.[67] Lutheran minister, author, and all-around anti-occult alarmist Kurt E. Koch claims that the book is exceedingly dangerous, and advises those who own copies of it to burn them, stating that "houses in which this book is kept are accident and disaster prone."[68] (I wonder if any of those houses burned as a result of people setting fire to their copies of *The Sixth and Seventh Books of Moses* in accordance with the good reverend's advice!) For those who have read of the supernatural plagues supposedly accompanying the production of the Simon *Necronomicon*, as recounted in Simon's preface to the second edition, this "urban legend" should sound familiar.

While there is abundant proof that there are no Great Old Ones, no Elder Gods, and no "Kutulu" anywhere in ancient Mesopotamian mythology or folklore, there has been speculation that the Sebittu, or "the seven" found in Babylonian mythology, correspond to the Great Old Ones. One Babylonian incantation describes them as:

> Bred in the depths of the ocean; not male or female are they, but are as the roaming wind-blast . . . knowing neither mercy nor pity, they hearken not to prayer. They are horses reared amid the hills, the evil ones of Ea; throne bearers to the gods are they.[69]

A corrupted version of this incantation is featured on pages 79–80 of the Simon book with the tacked-on verse, "They are the vengeance of the Ancient Ones."[70] One problem with this notion is that the passage refers to another group of Sebittu, who are subordinate to Ea as sons. Later in the passage, these Sebittu are described as being "throne bearers to the gods"—a humble servitude totally unlike Lovecraft's Great Old Ones. Other parts of the book are composed of existing translations of Mesopotamian religious texts with names of Lovecraftian critters inserted wherever the original tablet was illegible. My extensive reading in this field leads to the obvious conclusion that all references to Lovecraftian entities are grafted onto the texts artificially.

For ceremonial magicians, a major point of contention with the Simon *Necronomicon* is its virtual lack of instructions on the casting of a protective circle. This totally contravenes Mesopotamian magickal texts, which routinely instruct the magician to demarcate a circle on the floor or ground by sprinkling flour (the Akkadian word *zisurru* literally means "flour which makes a boundary").[71] Rituals were carried out from inside the circle where the magician was protected from certain types of demons. Other circles were cast in whitewash or blackwash beside doors or around figurines of deities. There are even ancient commentaries that explain how the circle is symbolic of certain protective deities.[72] The Simon book only tells the practitioner to cast a circle on page 71 in "The Conjuration of the Watcher" (in flour) and on page 100 in "The Book of Calling" (in lime, barley, or white flour, "or dug into the ground with the Dagger of INANNA of Calling. Or embroidered in the most precious silk, or expensive cloth"). Even then we are not given any instructions as to how to magickally *ward* the circle to protect ourselves from attack. Without actual warding—like that provided by, for example, the Lesser Banishing Ritual of the Pentagram—the circle is not a bulwark against psychic attack, but just a line of flour on the floor. The *Necronomicon Spellbook* dispenses with the circle entirely, telling its readers to just ignore any strange things they feel or hear. This type of negligence was rarely seen in medieval grimoires, and never in the ancient cuneiform texts of Mesopotamia, of which the Simon book pretends to be representative.

Another hot topic of the Simon book is the melodramatic warning on page liii that "there are no effective banishings for the forces invoked in the NECRONOMICON itself." Some practitioners agree that this is sound advice, particularly for the magician trained in the "Good versus Evil" paradigm, who now still relies on his "goodness" to control entities from an "amoral" paradigm. In this "amoral" system, entities are supposedly only controlled by the skill, strength, and cleverness (trickery) of the magician. To others, this warning on banishings is a load of codswallop, which nevertheless makes for good horror fiction. One big problem with the "no effective banishings" warning in a supposedly Sumerian grimoire is that it conflicts with actual magickal practices of ancient Mesopotamia, in which there were plenty of effective banishings for all classes of evil spirits. Spells of the Neo-Assyrian period, which some current scholars call the "demonic phase"—when evil spirits were depicted in all their horror—contain simple banishings like "Get out evil *rabi su!*"[73] Based on my experience, I believe the notion that humans can evoke entities that cannot be banished is puerile nonsense. While some things are harder to banish than others, anything that can be summoned can be banished.

One of the more authentic bits and pieces of magick in the Simon book doesn't seem to derive from Mesopotamian sources at all. On page 111 is a short spell entitled "To Win the Love of a Woman," which instructs the practitioner to pronounce the given chant three times over a piece of fruit and give it to his intended love object. However, the original spell—minus the Simonian wording—is taken from a 9th-century Coptic Egyptian papyrus, Berlin 8325.[74] The source is early medieval Christian Egypt and not ancient Sumer. One of the most authentic spells in the book is the other ritual on page 111, entitled "To Recover Potency," because it features a form of knot magick like that actually practiced by the ancient Mesopotamians.

The seals of the Zonei and the "Gates" presented in the book resemble nothing in ancient Mesopotamian art or magick/religion. However, their rectangular shape and scribbled characters bear a probably-more-than-coincidental resemblance to a couple of Greek (page 5) and Arabian (pages 77 and 78) amulets reproduced in Idres Shah's *Oriental Magic*, a book actually mentioned in the "Bibliography and Selected Reading List" on page lvi of the Simon book. The Gate of Nanna in "The Book of Entrance" is a direct derivation of "The First Pentacle of the Moon" in *The Key of Solomon* (*Clavicula Salomonis*) as reproduced by Idres Shah on page 51 of *The Secret Lore of Magic*. The seals for the "Abominations" in the "Urilia Text" look similar to the seals of demons from the *Goetia* as incorrectly reproduced by A. E. Waite in his *The Book of Black Magic*. The fifty names of Marduk in "The Book of Fifty Names" were (mostly) derived from the *Enuma Elish*, the Babylonian creation epic, but neither the commentary nor the seals, both of which also look like contrivances from the seals of Goetic spirits in the *Lesser Key of Solomon*, were. I'll say more about Simon's wretched rendering of Marduk's fifty names a bit later.

The tools that the Simon *Necronomicon* instructs its users to make in the section called "The Book of Calling" (pages 95–120) are nothing like the actual tools used in Sumerian and other Mesopotamian magick. For example, there are no instructions for making or using a bell, even though ancient Mesopotamian magickal texts often refer to the ringing of a bell as a method of repelling evil spirits, and there are surviving examples of Neo-Assyrian copper and bronze bells cast with images of protective spirits that were undoubtedly used in rites of exorcism.[75] There are no instructions for making a wand, even though the copper wand may have been one of the primary magickal tools of magicians in the ancient Near East—as evidenced by the beautiful and intricate specimens excavated at Nahal Mishmar.[76] However, "The Book of Calling" does tell the practitioner to carry a "rod of lapis lazuli," but never says how to use it or what purpose it serves. Many of the magickal tools used by ancient Mesopotamian wizards were based on ordinary objects and household items. For example, purification rites may have been conducted using a simple water bucket with a pine or fir cone as an aspergillum (water sprinkler), as Neo-Assyrian art depicts benevolent genies purifying the bodies of kings and the precincts of dwellings with bucket (*banduddu*) and cone (*mullilu*, literally "purifier").[77] Other tools of Mesopotamian magick were perfectly ordinary objects like a stove or brazier, tamarisk and date branches, reeds, onions, cedar or juniper, incense, salt, flour, and sea salt. The magician or priest consecrated these for magickal work by chanting (literally "enchanting") over them. What we *are* given in "The Book of Calling" are crude drawings and vague instructions for making three basic items. The first is the "Crown of Anu of Calling," which is made of beaten copper and looks like some kind of fez—so that its wearer would look more like a Shriner than a Sumerian wizard. Next is the "Frontlet of Calling," made of "fine cloth" in black and white, and decorated with Simonian signs that don't look like anything found in Mesopotamian art. The last item is the "Copper Dagger of Inanna of Calling," which unaccountably has the Goddess's name written on the blade in English, in the letters of the Roman alphabet rather than cuneiform. The Simon book also tells us to make the seals of the Gods Nergal and Marduk out of iron and brass, respectively, even though the metal iron was rare and the alloy brass was unknown in ancient Sumer.

Some of the most flagrant anachronisms and misappropriations of mythology in the Simon book are found in the Gate Walking sections. The first problem is that Simon modeled his Gate Walking initiation after Western planetary magick. While the ancient Mesopotamians did practice a kind of "star magick," it was never as elaborate as the system of planetary magick practiced thousands of years later in the Western ceremonial tradition, which has Gods, Goddesses, personifying planetary spirits, demons, and elaborate correspondences associated with each of the planets, the Sun, and the Moon. As Jeremy Black and Anthony Green remark: "Although some deities have connections with stars or planets, many do not, and the idea that Mesopotamian religion was astral in origin is untenable."[78] Notice the mention of the God NINIB on page 32. "Ninib" was a name that 19th-century scholars mistakenly attached to the God Ninurta, and it is interesting that the author of this supposedly "ancient" text makes the same mistake. While our earliest records of astronomy/astrology come from the Babylonians and date from about 750 B.C.E., and Babylonian astrologers were casting horoscopes on a regular basis by at least the 5th century B.C.E., the planetary cosmology presented in the Gate Walking rituals was unknown in Sumer and did not appear until circa 150 C.E. with the work of the Greek astronomer Ptolemy. And as if all that weren't bad enough, the metals that Simon ascribes to the Gods of the Gates are derived from the Qaballistic correspondences of Western ceremonial magick, as found in *777*, so they won't work in the Mesopotamian magickal current. For example, Simon assumes that gold should be associated with the Sun God, Utu/Shamash, whereas the ancient Assyrians and Babylonians associated gold with the God Enmeshara.[79] Simon jumps to the conclusion that Inanna/Ishtar should be associated with copper, since She rules the planet Venus. The ancient Mesopotamians, however, associated copper with the God Enki/Ea.[80] I will deal with Simon's misuse of planetary magick and Mesopotamian mythology in greater detail a little later.

The next to the last chapter of the *Necronomicon* is "The URILLIA Text," which is a kind of Simonian version of the *Goetia,* in that it contains a list of nasty (mostly imaginary) demons, their goetic-looking sigils (which resemble nothing found in Mesopotamian art), and instructions for evoking them. This kind of magickal text is not found anywhere among the cuneiform tablets of ancient Mesopotamia—and for good reason. Evil demons were seen only as sources of death, disease, and disaster, were reckoned as worse than useless, and no Sumerian *maš maššu* or Babylonian *ashipu* (incantation priest) would want to evoke them. The references to evil spirits found in cuneiform magickal texts come in the form of exorcisms and banishings. The quaint medieval notion that evil demons must be evoked to grant desires for wealth, sex, or power is largely a side-effect of Christian and Islamic theology, in which God is seen as unwilling to bestow such advantages, and unyielding in his impossible moral standards. If God would not provide the medieval sorcerer with what he desired, he would use divine angelic authority to call up and coerce Qlippothic demons that would. The Sumerians and Babylonians, on the other hand, had but to ask their Gods and Goddesses for wealth and sexual pleasure (Inanna and Dumuzi), magickal power (Enki), or the strength to defeat enemies (Ishtar, Nergal, or Ninurta). In ancient Mesopotamia, magick and religion were completely intertwined. When your Gods will give you everything you want, there is no need to make a "pact with the devil." Even when demons were seen as agents of divine retribution, they were not placated. The *ashipu* or *maš maššu* sought instead to banish the evil spirit, while removing the cause of the Gods' anger, be it a broken oath or a violated taboo. The only exception was the Assyrian/Babylonian demon-God Pazuzu, who was sometimes

used to fight off Lamashtu, a creature even worse than himself. Otherwise, the evil
udug, maskim, gidim, and *galla* were fit only to be driven away.

Oddly, the demons listed in "The Abominations" section of "The URILLIA Text"
aren't good for much either. I suppose you could use "HUMWAWA" for a diabolical
air freshener, since he exudes "the horrid perfume that is the odor of death." And
then there's "PAZUZU," the "Lord of all fevers and plagues"—you never know when
a case of leprosy will come in handy. And of course there's "XASTUR," the "foul
demoness who slays Men in their Sleep"—not exactly my idea of a wet dream. As in
other parts of the *Necronomicon*, we find here the refrain, "MAY THE DEAD RISE
AND SMELL THE INCENSE!" Anyone who wants to evoke these things needs to
wake up and smell the coffee.

Haphazard misrepresentations and blending of deities and demons from different historical periods and national pantheons further destroy the illusion of
authenticity. The God Marduk, for example, did not achieve the status He is accorded
in the Simon book until Babylonian times, after the fall of Sumer. Simon's pseudo-
Sumerian demon, Azag-Thoth (Azathoth), never existed at all. While there was a
hideous Sumerian demon called *Asag* (Akkadian *Asakku*), Thoth is a Coptic version
of the name of the Egyptian God Tehuti. Simon never explains how a Sumerian
demon and an Egyptian God separated by hundreds of miles and years could have
made such an unlikely fusion. Undoubtedly, he stuck the two names together in an
act of mythographic gene-splicing to get a pseudo-historical name that sounded like
Lovecraft's "Azathoth." Azathoth was the "blind, idiot God of chaos" in the Cthulhu
Mythos, however, and not at all like Thoth/Tehuti, the Egyptian God of wisdom.

In the previously mentioned section of "The URILIA Text" called "The Abominations" (pages 186–202), we are given a sigil for "Humwawa" and sketchy instructions for evoking him. He is described as having a face composed of coiled intestines
and is called "Lord of Abominations" and "Dark Angel of all that is excreted."[81] In fact,
however, "Humwawa"—or more properly "Huwawa" (Akkadian *Humbaba*)—was
no angel or genie, but a mortal ogre, the giant "king of the Cedar Mountain"[82] who
served the splendid God Enlil. Far from "Dark," Huwawa was described as protected
by seven layers of frighteningly dazzling radiance. The idea that Huwawa's face is
composed of intestines—thus causing his breath to smell like dung—is a miscon-
ception based upon clay plaques from the Old Babylonian to Neo-Babylonian periods that depict Huwawa's face formed by a pile of entrails. These plaques were
intended to serve only as reference guides for diviners (fortune-tellers) who performed divinations by *expisticy* —examining the intestines of disemboweled animals. The model plaques are usually inscribed with instructions such as, "If the
entrails look like the face of Huwawa . . ."[83] They were probably not intended as literal depictions of Huwawa's normal appearance.

Huwawa was killed and beheaded by the heroes Gilgamesh and Enkidu in Tablet
V of the *Epic of Gilgamesh*.[84] One wonders what benefit the magician could possibly
derive from summoning the shade of a decapitated monster. While it is true that, in

the Old Babylonian period, Huwawa's image was used on amulets, this was probably only because of his association with Enlil—one of the most important Gods of
the Mesopotamian pantheon. While dead Gods were sometimes believed to retain
some power in ancient Mesopotamia, I'm not sure if this was the case with dead
monsters. Being a good Neopagan, I cannot help but wonder how the Gods—assuming they exist—feel about having their servants slandered, and their names indiscriminately (blasphemously?) bandied about and glued onto the names of lesser
demons.

The "URILIA Text" also states that "Humwawa" and the demon Pazuzu (of *The
Exorcist* fame) are brothers. No Mesopotamian mythical or magickal text ever links
these two beings in any way—and certainly not as brothers. Huwawa and Pazuzu
are not only beings of two vastly different classes, but of two different ethnic cultures and historical/archaeological periods.[85] Huwawa was Sumerian and Akkadian,
first appearing in the *Epic of Gilgamesh,* which dates from as early as the third millennium B.C.E. Pazuzu was Neo-Assyrian and Babylonian and dates from only about
the 7th century of the first millennium B.C.E. But what are a few thousand years
between friends?

All of the above indicates that Simon's version of Sumero-Babylonian magick
is not merely "dumbed down," but totally inaccurate. Evidently, the more informed
the magician is about ancient Mesopotamia, the more difficult it will be for him or
her to use the Simon *Necronomicon* effectively. In this case, ignorance is, if not bliss,
at least an expedient.

Simon versus Sumer

Peter Levenda, who did research for the Simon book, candidly admits these short-
comings, but offers his own explanations:

> Yes, much of what passes for Sumerology in the *Necronomicon* is at vari-
> ance with what has been generally disseminated in public forums. I feel
> that the confusion is the result of two factors: in the first place, so few of
> the Sumerian texts have been translated and made readily available to the
> public; at best, much of this has been left to technical journals inaccessible
> to non-academics. . . . In the second place, the *Necronomicon*—while incor-
> porating many Sumerian motifs in its pages—is a work of a much later
> magician or magicians . . . yet it does seem to remain loyal to a Sumerian
> cosmology.[86]

Levenda now claims that the Simon *Necronomicon* should be read as the attempt of
a medieval mage to interpret a Sumerian magickal system, perhaps one passed down
orally by a Middle Eastern mystery cult. He admits that this sounds unlikely, but
cites such examples as Graham Hancock's discovery of an ancient branch of Judaism
still practicing animal sacrifice in Ethiopia.[87] If such ancient survivals can exist, why
couldn't a Sumerian tradition survive as well?

A medieval Arab mage like Abdul Alhazred may well have been inconsistent in his interpretation of an ancient magickal system whose records had been garbled in their transmission across the millennia. For those who are willing to accept it, I suppose this is the best possible justification for the historical and mythological errors in the Simon *Necronomicon*. Medieval grimoires are famous for their corruptions and bastardizations of earlier mythologies. In the *Goetia*, for example, the beautiful Canaanite Goddess Ashtoreth is transformed into "Astaroth" a treacherous male demon who "appeareth in the Form of an hurtful Angel," rides "an Infernal Beast like a Dragon," and has "Noisome Breath."[88] If the editors of the Simon book had provided some pseudo-scholarly footnotes—what Lovecraft would have called "mock scholarship"—claiming that all the mistakes in the Sumerian material were supposed to be medieval glosses from an ancient oral tradition, the hoax would have been much more convincing. However, I must point out that this new explanation of the *Necronomicon* as a medieval corruption of Sumerian magick does not appear in the introduction of the Simon book itself, and Mr. Levenda did not suggest it until after we had refuted the only two other possibilities: that it was authentic Sumerian magick, or that it was pre-Sumerian magick. Perhaps only a highly skilled psychic can predict the *past* of the Simon *Necronomicon*.

Why would Simon label a distinctly non-Sumerian book as being Sumerian? The two traditional values of dogmatic magicians—*tradition* and *mystery*—come into play here: When it comes to traditional magickal systems, the motto of dogmatic magicians is "the older the better." Sumer is one of the oldest civilizations known to us; while older settlements have been found, none are as complex or wondrous as the land between the Tigris and the Euphrates. Sumer was also the first civilization to invent writing, so instead of guessing about their beliefs from artifacts, we have their songs and poetry to tell us of their Gods. Thus, a Sumerian magickal tradition may be seen as more valid and powerful than any other because of its great age.

Besides their glamorous antiquity, the Sumerians are also something of a mystery to us. While some material has been published on Sumer, many more sources exist for Egyptian or Greek civilization. Many of the books in Simon's bibliography date back to the turn of the 19th century and have been long out of print; some are unavailable in English. Perhaps more important are popular (mis)conceptions of the ancient land. Sumer is barely even mentioned in our educational system, and only conveys a sense of remote antiquity to most people. Furthermore, the current political unrest in Iraq hinders archaeological work and makes any revival of popular interest in Sumerian culture unlikely. Although some experts can see glaring errors in Simon's attribution, most people who pick up the *Necronomicon* will believe it to be an accurate work of Sumerian mythology and magick, and that's all Simon wants.

Lovecraft Unloved: The Not-So-Great Old Ones

Simon doesn't seem to have gone to any more trouble to understand Lovecraft's Mythos than he did to research Mesopotamian mythology and magick. In the introduction, Simon claims that his URILLIA Text (or "URILIA Text"—it's spelled both ways in the book) is possibly "Lovecraft's *R'lyeh Text.*" Except that Lovecraft never wrote about the *R'lyeh Text.* August Derleth created it after Lovecraft's death. Nor was the *R'lyeh Text* ever considered to be part of the *Necronomicon*, an error both Simon and Robert Turner, who gave that title to the Hay sequel, perpetuate. On page xiii of the introduction, Simon claims that "Lovecraft created a kind of Christian Myth of the struggle between opposing forces of Light and Darkness." Current Lovecraft scholarship reveals this as a description of Derleth's rather than Lovecraft's version of the Mythos. Lovecraft's cosmos was fundamentally amoral, with the Mythos entities destroying humankind with an attitude of indifference, rather than calculated evil.

Dan Clore, proprietor of *The Dan Clore Necronomicom Web Page,* points out, "Simon would like us to see great similarities between both his Mesopotamian material and the magick of Aleister Crowley, and the Lovecraft Mythos, but provides essentially no correspondences between them."[89] For example, Simon insists on a similarity between the Greek word *stele* (as in Crowley's Stele of Revealing) and the name "Cthulhu." In the right Greek typeface, *stele* does look sort of like CTH^H. Other "correspondences" are equally wrong-headed. Simon cites Shub-Niggurath's Sumerian name as ISHNIGGARAB and associates both with Crowley's Pan, even though Shub-Niggurath is female. One of Simon's correspondences is unintentionally comical: He associates Crowley's Aiwass (who dictated *Liber Al* to him) with Lovecraft's Azathoth, the "blind idiot god" of chaos. Does this mean that Aiwass was an "idiot," that Crowley was idiotic for listening to him, or that the *Book of the Law* is an idiotic book? This is as close to blasphemy as a Thelemite can get.

One of the primary Gods of the Cthulhu Mythos—Nyarlathotep—is conspicuously absent from Simon's *Necronomicon.* I suppose Simon couldn't think of a "correspondence" for him, even though he is very similar to Crowley's Aiwass in appearance and behavior. Simon must have flunked spelling in grammar school, because even when he casually mentions Lovecraftian entities without fake correspondences, he usually misspells their names. And, for some reason, he decided to refer to the Cthulhu Mythos as the "Ancient Ones" rather than the "Great Old Ones."

Dan Clore further points out a paragraph in Simon's introduction in which practically every statement is incorrect:

> Lovecraft's mythos deals with what are known as cthonic dieties [sic], that is, underworld gods and goddesses, much like the Leviathan of the Old Testament. The pronunciation of cthonic is "katonic," which explains Lovecraft's famous Miskatonic River and Miskatonic University, not to mention the chief diety [sic] of his pantheon, Cthulhu, a sea monster who lies "not dead but dreaming" below the world; an Ancient One and supposed enemy of Mankind and the intelligent Race.[90]

The problems with this statement are as follows: First, *cthonic* is pronounced "thah-nick"; the "ch" is silent (at least in English). Second, Leviathan was a sea monster, not a deity, and sea monsters are not cthonic. Third, most *Bible* scholars would say that Satan was the only truly cthonic character in the Old Testament. Fourth, Lovecraft's *Miskatonic* was probably meant to sound like a Native American derivation. Fifth, Cthulhu is an alien entity that predates humanity by eons, and whose name cannot be properly pronounced by human vocal organs, according to Lovecraft.[91] His name cannot derive from the Greek word *cthonic* (though Lovecraft himself may have been inspired by the word). Sixth, the above derivation conflicts with the "Kutu-Lu" version used elsewhere in the book. Seventh, Cthulhu is not the chief deity of Lovecraft's Mythos; he is important to humans because he is confined on Earth. Eighth, Cthulhu is not a sea monster, he is an extraterrestrial creature trapped under the ocean.

To make matters even worse, the lack of Lovecraftian lore in the Simon book seems not to have been based on accidental ignorance, but on deliberate contempt for Lovecraft and his works. Khem Caigan described the way his own attempts at Lovecraftian scholarship were willfully ignored by the publishers of the Simon book: ". . . not much Lovecraft was in evidence either—except for a pretty lame intro and ending. I'd made up a concordance of all the 'Necronomicon' quotes from HPL and his circle of Mythos contributors, but they weren't interested."[92]

All of these examples should make it clear that there is no correspondence between Lovecraft's Mythos, Crowley's Thelemic magick, or Simon's pseudo-Sumerian mangled mythology. Therefore, any magickal system emerging from the Simon book will have very little or nothing to do with Lovecraft, Crowley, or Sumer.

The Grimoire That Time Forgot

There are several popular cultural influences that seem to have motivated the writer (or writers) of the Simon book. In the mid-1970s, the occult was "in," and had been since the 1960s. Lovecraft was also "in," since his works were being published not only by Arkham House, but also in cheap paperback editions. He had caught on with new generations of readers, and his popularity was booming. As his popularity increased, so did the suspicion that Lovecraft had been a closet magus, and that his *Necronomicon* was a real book. *The Occult Lovecraft,* by Anthony Raven, published in 1975 by Gerry de la Ree, addressed this very question. Also, a tiny book entitled *The Necromantic Grimoire of Augustus Rupp,* which claimed to be a sort of abridged version of the *Necronomicon,* came out during the same period, from the same publisher. *Necronomicon* hoaxing was inevitable and promised to be popular, and Simon probably wanted to get in on the trend.

The enormous popularity of the movie *The Exorcist* (1973) was probably another big influence, and may explain why Simon decided to dress his *Necronomicon* up in the garb of ancient Mesopotamia. The real star of *The Exorcist* was arguably the Assyrian/Babylonian demon Pazuzu, and the movie was so popular that it sired two obnoxious sequels, one of which came out in 1977, the year the Simon book was first published. The nominal hero of the film was Father Karras, a Roman Catholic priest, which might also account for why Simon is presented as a sort of renegade clergyman. Both priestly exorcists and Mesopotamian demons were "in" in the 1970s.

There are other factors that link the Simon book unmistakably with the era of eight-track tapes and bell-bottom pants. The book reveals an appalling amount of misinformation about Assyriology, but Simon probably figured that was no problem. There wasn't much information available about ancient Sumer at that time. Today, Sumerology and Assyriology have made considerable advances, so it is now easier to catch Simon's mistakes than it was in 1977.

Whatever the cultural influences that led to the Simon *Necronomicon*, its magick bears a closer examination. So lets go right to the heart of the matter in this next section.

The Gates That Lead to Nowhere

The very heart and soul of the Simon *Necronomicon* would seem to be what its enthusiasts call "the Gates." This is comprised of three chapters: "Of the Zonei and Their Attributes," "The Book of Entrance, and of the Walking," and "The Incantations of the Gates." As previously mentioned, use of "Gates" as metaphors for entrances into magickal realms shows apparent influence from Gnostic writings, Dr. Dee's Enochian magickal writings, or both. Since Magickal Childe published a facsimile edition of Meriç Casaubon's *A True and Faithful Relation* as early as 1974, Simon may have been influenced by it. It is also likely that Simon was influenced in his use of "Gates" by older works on Gnostic texts like G. R. S. Mead's *Fragments of a Faith Forgotten* (1910). Perhaps it is worth mentioning that some scholars believe that Edward Kelley's scryings were fraudulent and that Kelley merely plagiarized Gnostic texts to give Dee his supposedly "angelical" revelations. Geoffrey James, among other Dee scholars, believes this to be unlikely, and I concur. Another influence from Enochian magick on Simon probably came through Aleister Crowley's writings, specifically *Liber 418, The Vision and the Voice*.

As I mentioned earlier, Simon's Gate Walking rituals are just a "dumbed down" version of the kind of planetary magick found in the Western ceremonial tradition. The correspondences in the Simon book make it obvious that these seven Gates are openings into planetary spheres—magickal worlds of the seven "philosophical" planets and of the Gods—or Zonei—associated with those planets. This would seem to be a good choice for writing a supposedly ancient grimoire, since planetary magick is one of the oldest systems of magick and is foundational to most systems of Western magick, from the Qaballah to esoteric herbalism. Occult scholar Donald Michael Kraig believes planetary magick is at least as old as Babylon, and forms a bridge between natural magick (like Wicca) and ceremonial magick (like the Golden Dawn), and between ancient and modern systems.[93] So let's look at how Simon makes use of this tradition.

In the "Of the Zonei and Their Attributes" chapter of Simon's *Necronomicon*, the reader is first instructed to make a series of seven seals or sigils, corresponding to the seven gates. Each seal is to be made of what Simon guesses to be an appropriate metal to its planetary and deity rulership; copper for Inanna/Venus, silver for Sin/the Moon, etc.—one for each of the seven gates.

In the "Book of Entrance," the reader is instructed to prepare for a seven-month initiation of "gate walking," or astral pathworking, among these seven planetary spheres. The practitioner is given instruction as to the correct invocation to be used at each gate, as well as the appropriate seal to wear on his body while his astral body is traveling. The reader is warned that the gates must be entered in order and that, once the magician begins the Gate Walking enterprise, he must see it through to the end or deal with an attack from "Without that must surely come."[94]

In preparation for the Gate Walking, the practitioner is never told to cast a protective circle. (He/she is told to do so for the Conjuration of the Watcher, however.) This is comparable only to *The Book of the Sacred Magic of Abramelin the Mage*, which, alone among Western grimoires, demands that the magician rely upon purity for protection rather than upon the circle. Whereas *Sacred Magic* calls upon the magician to pray and purify himself by physical cleansing, perfuming his chambers with incense, and abstaining from intercourse for "four moons," the Simon *Necronomicon* demands no more "purity" from the magician than not ejaculating semen for one lunar month prior to each Gate Walking ritual. (Note also the intrinsic chauvinism in both cases.) There is some precedent among present-day magick users for not using a protective circle, as in the case of practitioners of Maat magick, a form of Thelemic magick taught by a former disciple of Grant known as *Nema*. Most modern practitioners, however, consider practicing magick without a warded circle to be suicidal. As one Wiccan friend of mine puts it, "There are too many things in the universe that will eat you like an hors d'oeuvre."[95]

In lieu of a warded circle, the practitioner is told to summon and leave behind a "Watcher" to protect his body so that it will not be killed and his spirit left to "wander throughout eternity the dark spaces between the Stars."[96] (A cheerful thought!) The practitioner must also bind the Watcher to himself via a sacrifice of "new bread, pine resin, and the grass Olieribos"—I'll explain what "olieribos" is a bit later. The Watcher is capable of taking a variety of appearances (page 70) and can turn hostile and even attack and kill the practitioner should he make a mistake in the incantations or neglect to make the proper sacrifice. Simon apparently based his "Watchers" on a race of foul creatures from Lovecraft's fiction called "shoggoths" that appear as fifteen-foot-long, slimy, black blobs that extrude sense organs and tentacles at need. Shoggoths were known to turn on their masters (the Elder Things) and devour them at the slightest opportunity. This may explain the violent, unstable nature of Simon's Watchers. (The term "Watcher" is part of other traditions, such as the *Book of Enoch*, but the *Necronomicon* uses it in a totally different sense.) Az0th insists that pursuing this system without the Watcher would be a "serious mistake," its use being a minimum safeguard against "possession or worse."[97] The sacrifice is not so much bribery, in his opinion, as the mere observing of "formalities."

Some precedent exists for this type of astral entity outside the *Necronomicon*. D. J. Conway, in her book *Astral Love*, writes of a creature that she calls the "Terror of the Threshold" (an oddly Lovecraftian-sounding name). This is an astral creature composed of the deepest fears of the practitioner. If the practitioner can meet the Terror and face it in the proper manner, she can turn it into a powerful ally. One duty of the Terror is to guard the body of the astral traveler from harassment by astral entities. A Qaballist might very well laugh at all these desperate measures, simply evoking the archangel Sandalphon, who governs the affairs of Malkuth, and asking for the protection of an angelic guardian. Although the Watcher may be useful, many believe that there are easier ways to accomplish its purpose.

Now, with a Watcher to guard his body (and hopefully not eat it), the magician is supposedly ready to project astrally into the realm of the Gates, armed with the proper seal and incantation to open the first portal. So far, so good! But magickal practitioners like myself evaluate such material, not by looking at it in isolation, but by comparing it with actual Mesopotamian mythology, other systems of magick cross-culturally, and their own experience.

The closest ancient Mesopotamian parallel to the Gate Walking procedure is found in the myth of *Etana*. Etana was a king of Kish, who yearned for a magickal herb that would give him a son. The Sun God, Shamash, told him to go to a pit, where he found an eagle that had been imprisoned for oath-breaking and blaspheming against the God. Somehow, Etana makes the eagle sprout wings, and the two become friends. Etana describes a dream to the eagle in which he ascends to heaven, passes through the seven gates of the Gods, and makes his plea before Inanna. The eagle proposes to make the vision a reality, and the two fly up to the heavens. In one version, Etana panics and asks to return to Earth, but another ends after he arrives in heaven and just as he passes through the fourth gate. The text of the original tablet is broken off at this point, but, according to the Sumerian king list, Etana had a son named Balih, so it seems his quest to ask for Inanna's favor was successful.

Does this support Simon's Gate Walking procedure? Not really. Here are the lists of the Gods from each system:

Etana	*Necronomicon*
Anu	Nanna (Sin)
Enlil	Nebo
Ea (Enki)	Inanna (Ishtar)
Sin (Nanna)	Shammash
Shamash	Nergal
Adad	Marduk
Ishtar (Inanna)	Ninib

As you can see, four Gods in *Etana* are not among Simon's guardians, and none of the others occupy the same location in both systems. Notice that, in the original *Etana* version, Inanna/Ishtar, not Ninurta (whom Simon ignorantly calls "Ninib"), occupies the highest level—that of the seventh gate—making Her literally the "Queen of Heaven." Perhaps Simon's displacement of the Goddess from Her rightful status marks him as, not only an Assyriological ignoramus, but a male chauvinist as well.

Several other details are troubling here. The Simon book fails to mention the small matter of a friendly eagle willing to fly the magician to heaven before the process begins. None of the trappings that Simon adds—the bowl of "olieribos," the sword, the calling of the Watcher—are here. None of the gates are linked to any colors, metals, or planets. Etana passed through all of them at once—there was no wait of a month between each gate—and the only prerequisite is that he show "obeisance," or respect, at each one, not that he have a mystical seal or a secret password. The most important difference for the *Necronomicon*'s defenders, however, is that Etana gains no magickal powers from entering any of the gates—he simply gets his one specific wish granted by the Goddess.[98]

Even Simon's use of planetary magick in the Gate Walking initiation is bogus. As I mentioned earlier, while the Mesopotamians did practice a form of star magick, as outlined in the *Maqlu Text*, their system does not correlate with the kind of planetary magick used in the Western ceremonial tradition. The *Maqlu* ritual is performed during a two-day period (not seven months) at the end of the month of Abu, the time of year when spirits move freely between the netherworld and this world, similar to the Celtic period of *Samhain* (Halloween, or All-Hallows-Eve). The ritualist travels in a shamanlike trance into the heavens as a messenger to the Gods, then into the underworld to bring judgment against evil sorcerers. During this process, the ritualist identifies himself with (or transforms into) a star in the night sky. The purpose of the *Maqlu* ritual is to destroy evil sorcerers and ghosts, not to acquire specific magickal powers. Here again, there are none of Simon's seals or passwords, no metal correspondences, no lag time of months, and no seven levels of gates. As I mentioned earlier, even Simon's correspondences of metals and colors for the Gods are wrong for ancient Mesopotamian magick.

Perhaps Simon was influenced by faulty turn-of-the-century scholarship. Scholars of the late 19th century, like Anz and Bousset, once thought that the idea of seven heavens in Jewish mysticism was associated with seven planetary star Gods, and that this cosmology of seven planetary spheres was borrowed from the Babylonian tradition. Ioan Culianu disproved this theory when he showed that the idea of seven planetary heavens could not have been derived from Babylonian religion, because the Babylonians believed that the stars and planets were all the same distance from Earth.[99] Greek astronomers from the time of Plato were the first to believe that the planets moved at different distances from Earth. Aristotle was the first ancient scientist to go on record as proposing that the planets traveled in concentric circles, but Ptolemy of the 2nd century C.E. was the first astronomer to list them in the order in which they appear in traditional planetary magick (as well as in the Simon book); that is, the Moon-Mercury-Venus-the Sun-Mars-Jupiter-Saturn. Since the Babylonians never conceived of the planets orbiting Earth at different distances, they never found any link between the levels of heaven and the planets. Not only did the Babylonians not identify the different levels of heaven with planets, but Babylonian cosmology recognized a variable number of heavens, from one to nine, with the exception of six, which also conflicts with Western planetary magick.[100]

Aside from Anu's heaven, the only other place in Sumero-Babylonian mythology that has seven gates is *the underworld*.[101] While the Sumerian underworld was not an especially pleasant place, there is little corollary between it and the Christian Hell. And yet Simon seems to equate the underworld with the Judeo-Christian *Gehenna*, a place of perpetual misery. This has led to speculation that the only place the Gate Walking rituals are likely to lead the practitioner is to the lower astral realm, or "astral hells"! Simon may not have been acquainted with *Etana* at all, and it appears that he based his Gate Walking initiation on a bastardized version of *The Descent of Inanna* (something that I, as a worshiper of the Great Goddess, consider somewhat blasphemous). This is quite likely, since Herman Slater, who definitely played a role in the publication of the Simon book, used *The Descent of Inanna* as a model for a Wiccan initiation ritual in one of his books on witchcraft. It is interesting to note that, in the Hebrew Qaballah, there are also seven Hells just as there are seven gates to the underworld in the Babylonian system. These seven Hells also correspond to the first seven Sephiroth and their Qlippoth on the "Tree of Death." These Qlippoth are opposite, negative, poisonous versions of the Sephirothic realms on the Qaballistic Tree of Life. Even more interesting, the planetary associations for the first seven Qlippoth are the same as they are for the first seven Sephiroth. This means that each of these hellish Qlippothic realms is associated with one of the planets. For example, the Sephirah Yesod is associated with the Moon, but so is Gamaliel (the Obscene Ones), the Qlippah of Yesod.[102]

I am not alone in this theory. Some occultists have connected the seven-gated levels of the Babylonian underworld, the seven Hells of Hebrew Qaballism, the first seven Qlippoth—the demonic "shells" or shattered realms of a former creation—of the Qaballah, Grant's Tunnels of Set, and the hellish lower astral realms described by both modern occultists and Tibetan and Indian yogis. What if these Gate Walking rituals of the Simon *Necronomicon* are engineered, either by accident or design, to take the practitioner into these infernal spirit realms?

Oddly enough, Simon himself may be suggesting this. The *Necronomicon* ends with the following quote from the *Chaldean Oracles of Zoroaster*:

> Stoop not down unto the Darkly-Splendid World; wherein continually lieth a faithless Depth, and Hades wrapped in clouds, delighting in unintellible images, precipitous, winding, a black ever-rolling Abyss; ever espousing a Body unluminous, formless and void.[103]

If we consult the translation Simon uses, that of "Sapere Aude" (or William Westcott), we find this passage followed by another:

> Stoop not down, for a precipice lieth beneath the Earth, reached by a descending Ladder which hath Seven Steps, and therein is established the Throne of an evil and fatal force.

Notes from the Underworld

As bizarre as this theory may sound, there has been some practical experience on the part of *Necronomicon* users to substantiate it. On Friday, 20 October 1995, there was a sobering posting on the alt.magick newsgroup: From: Sun@Sun (sorcery trouble) Subject: Re: Simon's Necronomicon. The practitioner was asking for advice and recounting the frightening experience he had with the Gate Walking ritual. He had been trying to cross into the sphere of the Moon or of the God Sin.

> I will elaborate, the vibrations which haunted me had also the effects that it felt as if parts of my soul and body were dead. (This is difficult to explain.) At times I was afraid that some evil parts of myself, which seemed to thrive on the emanating vibrations would become powerful enough to possess me. It was sometimes like being trapped in one of Baudelaire's poems. But colder.[104]

Az0th, a well-respected magician who is active on the Internet and was trying to advise this practitioner, speculated that he had opened the wrong gate somehow, that he had "breached Ganzir" or "worse." The practitioner, however, insisted that "the energy I think could be described as dark and negative moon energy. Sometimes I thought that the vibrations were perhaps better described not as insectoid but as shellfish (a la lobster, crab, crayfish, shrimp)."[105] It is interesting to note that crustaceans are classic magickal correspondences for the Moon: the crab symbolizing the astrological sign Cancer, ruled by the Moon, the lobster or crayfish pictured on the tarot trump card, The Moon. From the impressions and correspondences cited by the hapless practitioner, there is every reason to believe that he had made contact with the Sphere of the Moon, as he had intended. Only it was the frightening, hellish, Qlippothic side of that Lunar Sphere.

The "Ganzir" to which Az0th refers is an ancient Sumerian name for the underworld[106] that is also used throughout the Simon *Necronomicon*.[107] The inference of Az0th is that the hapless mage had accidentally opened the gate to Ganzir instead of the Lunar Sphere. If the Simon book never sends anyone who uses it to any place *other* than Ganzir, however, what of the Qlippothic correspondences the practitioner reported? The Simon book itself describes the Underworld of Ganzir thusly: "for a broken star is the gate of GANZIR, the Gate of Death, the Gate of the Shadows and the Shells."[108] The Hebrew word *Qlippoth* is translated literally as "shells," which would seem to offer us evidence from the Simon book itself of the Sephirothic/Qlippothic nature Simon's version of Ganzir.

Another intriguing piece of correlating evidence comes from "The Book of Entrance" (page 49), which warns the astrally traveling mage to beware of "the ALLU, frightening dog-faced demons." Both Robert A. Monroe, in *Journeys Out of the Body,* and an anonymous woman narrator quoted by Denning and Phillips in *The Llewellyn Practical Guide to Astral Projection* reported being attacked during astral projection by demonic entities that resembled dogs. These doglike assailants were also exclusively dwellers of the lower astral! One would be unlikely to find them in the upper astral realms of the planetary spheres. I have also had the experience of being attacked by a doglike being while out-of-body and I was not traveling in the astral realms, but merely through Earth-bound space.[109]

Az0th, who has experimented with the Gate Walking rituals, has told the authors that he considers the process comparable to practices found in both Shamanism and Gnosticism, and considers it "nearly unique in modern times in revealing an egregore whose boundaries and ultimate nature remains a mystery."[110] (As mentioned earlier, an egregore is a thought-form created by the magician by will and visualization, a mental image solidified into astral substance.) So Az0th, an experienced magician, believes the astral realm of the Gate Walking to be a created thought-form, one that he believes "ultimately has nothing to do with either Akkadian mythology or Lovecraft."[111] If Az0th's assessment is true—and I believe it is—then Simon's so-called initiation of walking the Gates will lead the hapless practitioner into what is only a large thought-form created by a modern magician or, more likely, a group of magicians, whose aims seem somewhat suspicious, to put it charitably. Why, however, does this Gate Walking egregore (or thought-form) seem deliberately designed to fry the circuits of anyone who uses it? That is a question I will answer a bit later.

Knocking on Ganzir's Door

Another objection to the practice of the Gate Walking rituals also relates to my theory that the Gates lead either into the hellish Qlippothic realms, or into an equally hellish man-made thought-form. It also relates to themes from Lovecraft's own Mythos fiction: If users of the *Necronomicon* succeed in opening the Gates and traveling through, won't the Gates then be opened for entities from outside to enter the Earth plane and make a bid to take over (or retake) our dimension of reality?! Obviously, any doorway, once opened, will allow traffic to pass through from either side. Simon himself seems to confirm this through the supposed words of the "Mad Arab" on page 19, when he warns of "the attack from Without that must surely come."

One poster to the *alt.religion.wicca* newsgroup had her own eloquent way of expressing her theories regarding the dangers of the book. Though convinced the book is a modern production with "no historical basis," she believes the magick of the Simon book will work, "and I would never touch it with a 10,000 foot pole."[112] She cites cases in her experience in which:

anyone even the slightest bit other-sensitive who has read it reported a similar thing to me ... odd dreams where they would hear of a knocking on a door, or dreams of a brick wall crumbling ... It's my thought that someone a tad lame-brained invented some sigils that did inherently have some meaning. That there is some kind of Cthulu [sic] thing out there in the flotsam and jetsam of universes, and it's icky, and it is behind a wall of sorts. That every time that book is read, a brick falls out. Kinda ominous, but that's my little theory.[113]

I too have heard cases of individuals using—or just reading—the Simon *Necronomicon* who experienced frightening dreams of something large and powerful knocking on a wall. It is intriguing to compare this phenomenon with Donald Tyson's theories regarding the potential dangers in Dr. John Dee's system of Enochian magick. Tyson believes the supposed Angels who communicated the Enochian system to Dee through Kelley's scrying had a sinister agenda to bring about the Apocalypse, as described in the biblical *Book of Revelation*.[114] Practice of the Enochian system is not ordinarily dangerous, according to Tyson, but it can open the minds of humans to be controlled by these so-called angels, thus bringing about their own destruction. Tyson once remarked that, among humans, the Enochian system was like a modern pistol that has fallen among primitive tribesmen who, having never seen a gun before, use it as a hammer to crush nuts.[115] While it may be useful as a tool, Enochian magick, like a firearm, can also do much more, and be unexpectedly dangerous.

The Necronomicon Meme

Perhaps some of the problems caused by the Simon book can be explained by what I call the "*Necronomicon* meme." Oxford zoologist Richard Dawkins defines a *meme* as a set of ideas that can replicate itself like a virus and spread from one human brain to another. His viral analogy is apropos, since evidence shows that a meme can spread through a population in a way that is mathematically similar to the epidemiological expansion of a plague. In 14th-century Europe, the bubonic plague wiped out a vast portion of the population in just a few years. Memtic "contagion" may act more slowly, but have results that are just as dramatic. In *The Lucifer Principle,* Howard Bloom points out that the meme of Christianity spread throughout the Roman Empire in only three hundred years, and the meme of Communism, carried by Marx's *Das Kapital,* "infected" more than a billion people throughout the world. In *The Einstein Factor,* Win Wenger and Richard Poe observe that a meme, like a virus, "has a blind, unthinking desire to reproduce at any cost." They point out that memes do not recognize good or evil, and are "just as efficient at spreading bad or trivial ideas as good ones." Sets of concepts like democratic government, Nazism, the Internet, rap music, the Dewey decimal system, and Beatlemania are all memes that have infected—or still infect—human minds at one time or another.

So what of the "*Necronomicon* meme," an "information virus" that seems to be spreading rapidly through our own population? I believe that new memes can splice themselves onto older ones—even those that have existed in the remote past, and still exist as archetypes in the collective unconscious. Magick itself is an information virus of ancient lineage. Almost as old as magick itself, however, is the archetypal concept (meme) of a forbidden magickal book or artifact that seems to offer great power, but only brings suffering to those who use it. The oldest surviving example of this kind is probably the ancient Egyptian folktale of *Setna and the Magic Book*, thought to date from the 19th Dynasty, which tells of the adventures of a sorcerer who steals the *Scroll of Thoth* from a tomb in the necropolis at Memphis. Setna has to give up the scroll after a series of disasters. A more modern example is found in "The Monkey's Paw," a short story by W. W. Jacobs, in which the user of the "paw" gets his wishes technically "granted," but only in ways that bring tragedy and misery. Wenger and Poe believe that extinct memes from the past can be revived by "faithfully reproducing their memetic codes." I believe that the *Necronomicon* meme has grafted itself onto the memetic code of the archetypal concept of the forbidden magickal book. The unexpectedly dangerous nature of the Simon *Necronomicon* can perhaps be explained in light of this subconscious meme.

Lovecraft once said that it would be impossible to write a satisfyingly scary version of the *Necronomicon*, since no written text could equal the terror invoked by a few ominous hints. And the ominous hint was the secret of Lovecraft's power as a horror writer. Though critics sometimes railed at him for his use of nonspecific adjectives, it was his refusal to describe the horror in too great a detail that unleashed the imaginations of his readers. Lovecraft knew that the subconscious mind of the reader could make a hint more horrible than a graphic description. I believe that the ancient meme of the deadly grimoire also operates on the subconscious minds of many of the users of the *Necronomicon*. While the user may consciously believe he has found the path to power, his subconscious mind knows he is using a book that is reputed to bring madness and death to those who even dare to read it. And most modern magicians believe the subconscious mind is the true source of magickal power. Thus, the *Necronomicon* meme may work on the human mind in the same way a computer virus locks up the files and wipes out the hard drive.

Necronomicon: Puzzle or Pipe Bomb?

The *Necronomicon* may be a snare to the unwary and inexperienced, not because of what Simon put in the book, but because of what he may have left out. One mage on the alt.magick newsgroup defends this lack of completeness in a reply to an inquiry by someone who was interested in experimenting with the Simon book:

> Whoever wrote the thing had real and personal experience of the ritual procedures and did NOT include every single, significant detail in the published account . . . Most of the theoretical "why" is also conspicuously absent. Filling in the missing bits, as must be done with any real grimoire, is a

challenging and risky business, but not without its rewards; knowing what's important only comes with experience.[116]

I agree that some things simply cannot be taught, but must be learned by experience. Nevertheless, I see this apologetic for the *Necronomicon* as a terribly diplomatic way of saying that the author(s) left out vital pieces of instruction and information, whether through negligence, ignorance, or deliberate malice. The practitioner is expected to be brilliant and erudite enough to fill in the gaps for himself. If not, he can fall by the wayside and devil take the hindmost.

This occult version of Social Darwinism should have gone out of style with the demise of the Holy Inquisition. In medieval and Renaissance grimoires, there is some excuse for deliberate secrecy and exclusion of information. In some cases, the author is just trying to stay off the rack, the wheel, or the stake. At other times, the "grimoire" consisted of the personal notes of the author, who only needed an outline and could fill in the details from his memory. Secrecy was also the stock-in-trade of magickal lodges and secret societies. In the postmodern era of revealed knowledge, however, those antiquated magickal bureaucracies are lumbering toward extinction, as their occult "secrets" pour out of the woodwork like multiplying termites. Now the studying practitioner has a right to expect thorough and complete information at every level. In this Information Age, the notion that certain knowledge must be kept out of peoples' hands for their own good has fallen into disrepute. While some occult secrets may not be understood by everyone who hears them, this does not mean that those secrets themselves should be withheld. Knowledge is power, and anyone who withholds it does so only out of self-interest. Authors can no longer use a need for secrecy as an excuse to hide their ignorance or selfishness.

Most of the people I have seen take an interest in the Simon *Necronomicon* have not been experienced occultists skilled at "filling in the missing bits," but youthful "dabblers" not yet out of their teens. This can make the lack of completeness not only negligent but criminal, since leaving parts of instruction out of magickal books does not render them harmless, anymore than failing to provide adequate instruction in the use of a rip saw will keep the (mis)user from cutting off his or her fingers. In all fairness to the mage being consulted, he did not give the inquirer unconditional encouragement, but asked him why he wanted to experiment with the Simon book, as "there are easier ways to spend your time."[117]

Oddly, Mr. Peter Levenda, general editor of the *Necronomicon*, agrees with me on this subject, stating that it "does not give full information, making it dangerous for dabblers" and that it "may be more trouble than it's worth!" for those who want "a kind of 'quick fix' occultism."[118] He believes, however, that it does have some value, pointing to Kenneth Grant's OTO, who he claims "have all done some really fine work with the *Necronomicon* (both from a practical and a 'speculative' angle)."[119] He goes on to make a surprising statement:

The *Necronomicon* is NOT the "Witches Spellbook"! If anything it is the "Anarchist's Cookbook" of grimoires. Dangerous? Of course. Important? Absolutely. I am afraid I cannot apologize for it.[120]

Since most terrorists would consider using *The Anarchist's Cookbook* a good way for them to blow themselves up because of its faulty instructions, Levenda's metaphor takes on a perhaps unintentionally sinister, yet goofy, quality. Whether the Simon text is comprised merely of pieces of a jigsaw puzzle, or jagged chunks of flying shrapnel, is a question I will address next.

Nitro-nomicon, the Antipersonnel Grimoire

I am not alone in my belief that the Simon book is potentially dangerous. A group of people in the United Kingdom calling themselves "The Cthulhu Survivors Clinic" recently left a message on the guestbook of our website, *www.necfiles.org*, saying that they have had "some pretty scary experiences with the Book" and are currently writing a website where others can share the stories of their misadventures with the *Necronomicon*. Our British poster confessed: "We're poor occultists, and have to admit we can see no reason why it should be so dangerous, but it is." Even the defenders of the Simon book, including its general editor, admit that it is dangerous—"dangerous but valuable," they claim. Other critics don't see any value in the Simon book—to them it's just a metaphysical minefield! In fact, a careful examination of the Simon *Necronomicon* by a trained occultist will show that its rituals were deliberately engineered to blow up in the faces of its users.

A few moments ago, I examined the hazardous nature of the Gate Walking initiation, a process whose goals can be attained more easily and safely by means of conventional planetary magick or Qaballistic pathworking. There are more subtle booby traps hidden in the Simon *Necronomicon*, however, waiting to frag the hapless practitioner. Some of these magickal land mines can be found in "The Incantations of the Gates," which are comprised of a few Sumerian and Akkadian words mixed with a lot of meaningless Simonian gibberish. Even the few lines of ancient text are incorrectly translated and are, in any case, inappropriate to the goal of the ritual. Take, for example, "THE INVOCATION OF THE SHAMMASH GATE" on pages 56 and 57. Shamash is the Babylonian Sun God, so the practitioner must invoke Him in order to open the solar Gate at this stage of the Gate Walking initiation. For this purpose, Simon provides the practitioner with an incantation, one line of which reads: "ZI DINGIR UDDU-YA KANPA!" Simon says this means "Spirit of the Sun, Remember!" What it actually translates into is "Spirit, Utu (the Sumerian name of Akkadian/Babylonian Shamash), be thou exorcised!" Since this "invocation" is actually a banishing, the practitioner who is trying to win the favor of the God Shamash by using this incantation could end up in deep horse dooky. Hopefully, the worst he'll get is a bad sunburn.

Another of these teratological tripwires can be found in "The URILLIA Text II:

The Abominations" section of the Simon book. "The Abominations" is a section dedicated to the evocation of a repulsive crew of pseudo-Lovecraftian (KUTULU), pseudo-Sumerian (HUMWAWA), and uniquely Simonian (XASTUR) demons. These Qlippothic uglies are described as "the ensnarers, the liers-in-wait, the blind fiends of Chaos, the most ancient evil," and their nasty toilet habits and antisocial tendencies are described in lovingly gruesome detail. Their Goetic-looking sigils are also provided, along with sketchy instructions for evoking them. On page 191 of "The Abominations," we are told "to summon these and other Demons, the herb AGLAOPHOTIS must be burnt in a new bowl that has a crack . . . And it must be the Evil Times, and at Night."[121]

Aglaophotis is actually none other than the peony plant (*Paeonia officinalis*), which is well known in esoteric herbal lore for *driving away* evil spirits! According to *The Greek Herbal of Dioscorides:*

> Peonia, or Glycyside, some call it Pentoboron [ye male Peonie, some Orobelium, some Orobax, some Haemagogum, some Paeseden, some Menogenion, some Menion, some Paeonium, some Pantheceratos], some Idaei dactyli, some Aglaophotis. . . . [The herb Peony is plucked up in the heat of the dog days before the rising of the sun & it is hanged about one & is good against poisons & bewitchings & fears & devils & their assaults, & against a fever that comes with shivering, whether by night or by day, or a quartan. And it is said that sometimes growing on a hill where there are devils, it drove them away].[122]

Agrippa also comments on the peony in his *Three Books of Occult Philosophy* in a list of natural things that can be used for magickal invocations of divine beings (not demons): "The like doth the herb aglauphotis do . . . as saith *Pliny*, and the which magicians use."[123] Just as Agrippa claimed, Pliny also confirmed the divine nature of the peony, or aglaophotis. Mrs. M. A. Grieve, a modern authority, corroborates the findings of the ancient and medieval sages, adding that the peony is good for "driving away evil spirits and averting tempests."[124] Paul Beyerl, in his *A Compendium of Herbal Magick*, comments that the peony is ruled by the astrological sign Leo, and associated with both the light of the Sun, and the magick of the Moon. In fact, the name "aglaophotis" means "bright light," clearly making it unsuitable for use at "the Evil Times, and at Night," as the Simon book advises.

Since all the authorities, ancient and modern, agree that demons have an allergic reaction to peonies (alias aglaophotis), I must ask what would happen to the hapless Necro-nerd who summons a demon while burning aglaophotis as Simon advises. Would it simply refuse to answer your summoning because you were burning peonies? Or would the summoned demon react like a pitbull would if you rubbed poison ivy in its eyes, and retaliate by chewing off your face (metaphysically speaking)? The best-case scenario is that nothing happens. The worst-case scenario is that they send you home to mother in a plastic bag.

Let's say that your summoning was "successful"—that you have evoked a demon from "The Abominations" but now it is furious because you are burning peonies in a cracked bowl, and the smoke is irritating its eyes and sinuses like the magickal equivalent of tear gas. If you believe the warning in the introduction of the Simon book—that there are no effective banishings for demons evoked from the *Necronomicon*—you are now trapped inside your circle by an angry demon that you cannot banish. That's assuming you were sensible enough to cast a circle—there are no instructions in "The Abominations" telling you to cast one. So there you are—cornered by an irate demon, with no protective circle, and no way to banish it. At this point, your best bet is to keep burning peony—and lots of it—in the hope that the fumes will drive the demon away. As Simon Orne warned Joseph Curwen in Lovecraft's *The Case of Charles Dexter Ward,* "do not calle up That which you can not put downe; either from dead Saltes or out of ye Spheres beyond. Have ye Wordes for laying at all times readie."[125] In the same antiquated vernacular, I would add: Do not pisse off That which ye calle up out of a cheap pulp fictione grimoire!

Those who insist on dealing with the Watcher may be interested to know what Simon says about it in his first publication on the subject. In his article "A Short Primer on Pagan Ceremonial Magick," found in an issue of *Earth Religion News* (the newsletter published by Magickal Childe), Simon makes the following statement on the nature of the Watchers:

> The Watcher represents an evil race of beings that seem set to destroy the human society and make the world their own. We cannot really see them, or know their characteristics long enough to recognize them, but the image is sufficiently strong to enable people like the Sons of Jared to label anyone they don't like as a "Watcher."[126]

Simon goes on to quote Budge's translation of the *Egyptian Book of the Dead* on the subject:

> Deliver me from the Watchers who have slaughtering knives and have cruel fingers, and who slay those who are in the following of Osiris. May they never overcome me, may I never fall under their knives.[127]

Based on Simon's own words, is this the sort of creature you want to invite to tea—much less have guarding your soft, fleshy parts?

While it may be fun to catalog various ways in which the Simon book can turn its users into recipients of the Darwin Award, it doesn't answer the basic question of *why* the Simon *Necronomicon* was deliberately designed to be dangerous. Why would anyone intentionally engineer a grimoire to backfire on its users? And how could an apparently reputable occult publishing house like Magickal Childe have published such a spellbook? To answer these questions, we must examine the origins of the Simon book (its real origins, not the nonsense written in its introduction), the motives of the person (or persons) who wrote it, and the personality of the man who first put it into print.

Slater, Simon, and the Gang: 7
True Origins of the *Necronomicon*
—John Wisdom Gonce III

As I told you longe ago, do not calle up That which you cannot put downe; either
from dead Saltes or out of ye Spheres beyond. Have ye Wordes of laying at all times
readie, and stopp not to be sure when there is any Doubte of Whom you have.
—HOWARD PHILLIPS LOVECRAFT, *THE CASE OF CHARLES DEXTER WARD*

Magic, n. An art of converting superstition into coin.
—AMBROSE BIERCE, *THE DEVIL'S DICTIONARY*

There are several possible explanations for why the Simon book is so potentially dangerous. One possible reason for the Simon *Necronomicon*'s built-in
snares may be its influence from shifty grimoires like *The Lesser Key of Solomon*
and *The Book of the Sacred Magic of Abramelin the Mage*, two spellbooks that have bad
reputations for landing their users in deep guano.

The enormous influence of Aleister Crowley on the writer(s) of the Simon book
could be another explanation. Crowley himself occasionally inserted "traps" into his
written works. As Neopagan writer Isaac Bonewits (who is himself an OTO initiate)
observes:

> While it would be worth your time to study the theoretical works of Crowley,
> most of his baroque-rococo rituals have rotten stage directions, along with
> the usual sexual references and occasionally dangerous practical jokes. . . .
> They are not booby traps for the experienced, who understand the para-
> doxes involved, only for the beginner, who will take things literally.[1]

Bonewits also comments that "the majority of his (Crowley's) books are *not* suit-
able for beginners, despite his frequent claims to the contrary."[2] If Simon worshiped
Aleister Crowley as passionately as the dedication, preface, and introduction of the
Simon book indicate, he may have seen nothing wrong with inserting a few Crowley-
style traps into his *Necronomicon*.

These theoretical speculations as to why the "Simonicon" was designed to put
its users behind the eight ball are fine as far as they go. However, there is also historical

evidence—both direct and circumstantial—to indicate why the book ended up in the hazardous shape it's in, and how it got written and published in the first place.

According to an informant of mine who claims he was around during the heyday of Herman Slater's occult shop/publishing house, Magickal Childe, and who wants to be known only as "Nestor," the Simon *Necronomicon* was created as the result of a party—and lots of alcohol! Back in the early 1970s, when the Magickal Childe was known as the "Warlock Shop" and located at 400 Henry Street in Brooklyn, there was a big beer/wine bash held one evening on that site. This party may have been a celebration after one of the regular lectures on magick and the "craft" given at the nearby Unitarian Church by various members of the Warlock Shop/Magickal Childe crew.[3] As Nestor tells it, most of the partygoers were Lovecraft fans, and had read many of Lovecraft's works. As the partying (and drinking) continued, Ed Buczynski, who was Herman Slater's lover and part owner of the shop at that time, told the crowd at the Warlock Shop that H. P. Lovecraft had once lived in an apartment just up the block from where they were. Suddenly, the party chatter turned into a discussion of all things Lovecraftian. This is the way Nestor tells it:

> The topic of his (Lovecraft's) stories and the characters in them became more lively as the wine and other spirits flew [sic]. Soon the question of just how much people would believe from fiction stories was being debated hot and heavy. Eddie and I maintained that because people were hopping into the "occult" and other practices without having any idea of scientific methods or learning psychology, or even a good basis in ancient history, these people were offering themselves up as victims of any wild idea which came along. Herman Slater, Leo Martello, my ex-wife, and most of the others said that people could naturally tell the difference. One of the others who was present was a ceremonial magician and member of the OTO called "Simon Peter" (I don't know his real name) mention [sic] some of what he consider [sic] to be absurd in the tales of the Mad Arab's "Necronomicon" and how some people had taken it for real. Well that started it—several cases of good wine were bet on just how gullible people were when it came to magick. . . . As the wine and other substances flowed, ideas were offered and passages for [sic] other grimoires were parodied and altered . . . Eddie suggested that since we were doing this so close to H.P. Lovecrafts [sic] place of writing that it should be put in a form as if it was the "Necronomicon" of the Mad Arab from Lovecrafts [sic] novels.[4]

This casual reference to Lovecraft's fictional *Necronomicon* by the mysterious "Simon Peter" was apparently the catalyst that led the crowd at the Warlock Shop to write their own *Necronomicon*. The initial process apparently consisted of Ed Buczynski taking notes as members of the group made suggestions "as to what a . . . newly comprised grimoire should contain (one that people who had do[sic] research on magick would realize was a fake) . . ."[5] According to Nestor, the influences that made up the Simon

Necronomicon were many and varied, including ideas from the Golden Dawn, Leland's *Aradia, The Egyptian Book of the Dead*, some of the works of Samuel Noah Kramer on ancient Mesopotamia, and certain concepts from "that booby-trap of magickal booby-traps," *The Book of the Sacred Magic of Abramelin the Mage*, "plus a good healthy dose of wild wine sodden imaginations."[6]

As Nestor tells it, the Simon *Necronomicon*, at this embryonic stage, was conceived, not only as a fun-but-harmless hobby for the Magickal Childe crew, but also as a teaching device to help train neophytes studying magick:

> We wanted to make it so that anyone with a basic background would clearly see that the rites and material were rigged to self-destruct and might even flash back on the user. I mean how many people could be that stupid? But just in case Eddie was going to use it later for a training exercise to show people what to look out for. Some people had already caught on that some of Crowley's works were rigged the same way for the unwary.[7]

In a later e-mail, Nestor pointed out some of the specific problems in the Simon text, and what he said sounded uncannily like some of my own conclusions about the book:

> As far as things backfiring—if you have some magickal training and use some common sense; when you look at the Necro you will see that protections which a ceremonial magician might use are either lacking in some cases or incomplete. In addition since the material itself was a mixture of cultures and practices its internal unity is at best missing. The result would be that people using the book would open themselves up to forces which could not be handled (even if you see them just as parts of the unconscious or archetypes).[8]

So the original aim of the gang who wrote the Simon *Necronomicon* was to deliberately fill it with mistakes and pitfalls, then give it to neophytes to read in order to see if they could recognize the errors in the text, in order to evaluate their level of magickal knowledge. If they could pass the "*Necronomicon* test" they were presumably judged to have advanced beyond the stage of total ignorance—or, as Nestor would say, "how many people could be that stupid?" Unbeknownst to him, book-sale statistics would soon provide Nestor with an unexpected answer to that question.

The notion that the Simon book was put together by a circle of casual friends rather than by a formal staff of writers is borne out by Peter Levenda's previously quoted statement that the "*Necronomicon* group" was "an ad hoc assembly of friends and like-minded people." The contributions Nestor and most of the other partygoers made to the Simon book seem to have begun and ended at that historic party, and no one really seemed to expect the project to go beyond the stage of an in-house hobby. Certainly, none of them could have foreseen it becoming a publishing phenomenon. I'll let Nestor tell the rest of the story in his own way:

> Well the party went on to the wee hours of the dawn (as they often did at

the Warlock Shop—Gods how the neighbors must have hated us!) When we left Eddie said he would work it all up and let us know what happened. That was the last that most of us thought about it. (Maybe some of us ask [sic] how it turned out with Eddies [sic] and Hermans [sic] students—I might have asked for a body count on the people foolish enough to believe in it and try to use it!). Then suddenly there it was "The *Necronomicon*"! In print!!! The joke had turned around and become a nightmare!!!! Herman Slater had taken Eddie's writing and had it copywrited [sic] and published! Eddie swore that he didn't know about it until Herman gave him one of the first copies, and I would take Eddie's word for it. Herman started publishing it and using it as a hook. . . . He made a bundle off it. The Gods only know how many people have been hurt with this joke that went bad.[9]

It appears that Herman Slater rushed the book into print before anyone could get wind of what he was doing and try to stop him. Khem Caigan, the artist who drew and refurbished the seals, illustrations, and other graphics for the Simon *Necronomicon* gives corroborative testimony that Slater and his cohorts, Jim Wasserman and Larry Barnes, were anxious—maybe desperate—to get the book published quickly. "I offered to do more, but they were in a king-hell hurry to get it to press, so it's not exactly as I'd have liked it to be."[10] Why were Slater and company in such a rush to get their *Necronomicon* into print? Could it be that they were racing against time to keep the various contributors from the "*Necronomicon* party"—held on that fateful night at the Warlock Shop—from finding out that their harmless in-joke was about to become a published hoax—and a public menace?

Why, on the other hand, would Herman Slater have published a deliberate (and possibly dangerous) hoax? Didn't he realize that publishing the Simon *Necronomicon* would be like putting an ebola virus victim in a kissing booth? And why would Magickal Childe Publishing, which had reprinted the works of Pascal Beverly Randolph and Gerald Gardner, and published hardbound facsimile editions of the diaries of Dr. John Dee (Casaubon's *A True and Faithful Relation*) now stoop to printing a spurious *Necronomicon*?

Perhaps the main answer to this question can be found in one word: M-O-N-E-Y—lots of M-O-N-E-Y—more M-O-N-E-Y than Magickal Childe Publishing had ever made before! Some "old timers" of the occult scene acquainted with Slater attest to the fact that, while Slater may have had a sincere belief in Thelemic magick, Paganism, and the occult, he was definitely in business to make money. Norman Fleck, an OTO initiate and collector of occult books and curios who now lives in Buffalo, New York, recalls, "I would walk into the shop (Magickal Childe) and Herman would either ignore me or just grunt at me with a frown on his face. Then, when I would walk out buying a big arm-load of stuff, he would be all smiles and say it was great to see me again."[11] Norman had no problem believing that Slater was capable of publishing someone else's work without their consent—particularly if there was big money involved. Nestor agrees with the view that Herman's motives were largely financial. "Herman and Simon had some disagreement (well, who didn't with Herman Slater). It might have been over financial matters, as Herman was a great con artist and was completely unprincipled when it came to financial dealings."[12] Dick Sells, who was vice president and a Seventh Ring Priest of the Church of All Worlds, elder of Ravenwood, a member of the Brotherhood/Sisterhood of Wicca, and High Priest of Unicorn Grove during the time he knew Slater, also attests to Herman's contradictory (and sometimes mercenary) personality traits:

> Herman had a heart as big as all outdoors, he was very generous and compassionate to his friends . . . but if you left a manuscript lying around he would rush it into print with his name on it, if he thought he could make money from it.[13]

> "Gossip" was that Herman made a lot of poor choices in friends and lovers . . . my observation was that this was true in at least two cases. In my observations of him and experience with him, though, he was a "hard" business man and was reported to have "borrowed" much he claimed as original . . . I know of several items that were claimed by others, but what is original????[14]

Another possible motive for Slater's publication of a hoax *Necronomicon* could have been his sense of humor. Herman was apparently quite a trickster, who enjoyed doing and saying the most outrageous things. As Sells recalls, "[Slater] often, early on, described himself as a screaming faggot. . . ."[15] This was quite an inflammatory statement to make in the early 1970s, and seemed to be fueled as much by over-the-top humor as by out-of-the-closet gay militarism. As an occult chameleon, Slater was reputed to delight in changing his persona at will—when talking to a witch, he was the most devout of Wiccans; among Satanists, he was the most ardent devil-worshiper, when hanging out with Thelemites, he became a hardcore Crowley fan. Perhaps the publication of the Simon hoax was intended to push the envelope, as well as fill the cash register. In light of his rampant absurdist humor, Herman may have thought that publishing a faux *Necronomicon* was not only a moneymaking enterprise, but jolly good fun. Slater probably quelled any ethical doubts he may have felt by telling himself that people would surely be able to see through the hoax. If so, his faith in the wisdom of the reading public was certainly misplaced.

And what of the mysterious "Simon Peter" mentioned earlier? Was he the Simon who was ultimately given credit (or blame) for editing the *Necronomicon*? This is Nestor's assessment of the Simon question:

> Now if there was a Simon attached to the book (and knowing Herman he could have either just decided to use the name to sell the book or he wanted to involve Simon Peter) it may have been Simon Peter who was involved with the Brooklyn OTO chapter at the time. Now I didn't know Simon Peter

all that well but he haunted the back room of the Warlock Shop at 400 Henry Street with the rest of us. His status was not really clear except that he was involved with ceremonial magick and he claimed to be a "Bishop" in a Ukrainian Orthodox Rite church.[16]

This sounds remarkably like the thumbnail biography of Simon in the *Necronomicon Spellbook*, where he is described as "a consecrated bishop of his Eastern Church . . . coming from a Slavic background . . ."[17] Whatever else one may say about him, I must admit it takes talent to turn a harmless beer bash into "The Horror at Red Hook."

As mentioned above, Nestor claims that there was some sort of dispute between Herman Slater and Simon. He guesses it may have been about money. I wonder if they might have been fighting over the publication of the book itself. Simon may have opposed Slater's covert printing of the *Necronomicon*, but once the book was out— with his name on the title page—he was trapped! He was forced either to publicly denounce the book, or play along with the farce now that there was no turning back.

The picture that emerges from all this testimony indicates that the Simon *Necronomicon* was actually compiled by a group of friends, and was intended as a joke. Filling the book with deliberate mistakes—making it the Three Stooges' approach to magick—was part of the humor. This would mean that those who actually assembled the book—Peter Levenda, Ed Buczynski, and all the rest—were originally acting in good faith. They composed a faux grimoire inspired by the fiction of their favorite horror writer for fun. They never intended it to be used for the actual practice of magick. Later, they tried to put it to practical use as a training tool. Ultimately, a greedy publisher bamboozled them out of it. By the time they realized they had been duped by a metaphysical version of "bait-and-switch," it was too late.

While we have not been able to confirm all the details of Nestor's testimony, his story dovetails neatly with what we already know from other verifiable sources. Some details of his testimony, however, don't quite add up. For the writers of the Simon book to have been shocked to see it in print, they must have neglected to read their own newsletter, in view of all the advance advertisements for the *Necronomicon* Slater published in it. Because it has been circulated through the occult community as a supposed document of warning, I present it here so that our readers can evaluate the evidence and make up their minds for themselves. Since there is no other handy spokesman from the original "*Necronomicon* gang," I suppose it is fitting that I close this section with the words of Nestor himself: "Please tell people what really happened! Tell them not to buy or use that book! It is a trap!! It is rigged to flash back on them and get out of hand quickly!!!"[18]

Cliff's Notes of the *Necronomicon:* Sinister Supplements

After its initial publication, it became obvious to the magick-using public that the Simon book was incomplete in many ways. Since the first publication of *The Necronomicon Files*, and the establishment of our website at *www.necfiles.org*, Daniel and I have been besieged with e-mails from people who want to know where they can find more in-depth information about the ways and means of performing the rituals from the Simon book. The publishers of the Simon *Necronomicon* (and other opportunists) also saw a need (probably financial) for "filling in the missing bits" themselves with supplemental material—a sort of diabolical *Cliff's Notes* for the dreaded *Necronomicon*. Those supplements published by Magickal Childe, Avon Books include:

> Simon, *Report on the Necronomicon* (New York: Magickal Childe, 1981)
> Simon, *Necronomicon Spellbook* (New York: Magickal Childe, 1987)
> Simon, *Necronomicon Spellbook* (New York: Avon, 1998)

The *Necronomicon Spellbook* was the first published attempt to flesh out the bare bones of the Simon book. This book was out-of-print when we wrote the first edition of *The Necronomicon Files*. As of October 1998 (the same month that our book was first released), the *Necronomicon Spellbook* was reprinted by Avon Books.

Since I already had a copy of the original version of the *Spellbook* published by Magickal Childe and a photocopy of the *Report*, I bought a copy of the current edition by Avon in order to compare the three. After an extensive search of the texts, I found no detectable difference between them whatsoever. So the good news is there is no reason for readers to hunt down both editions to find some imaginary bit of "forbidden lore" they may have missed. The bad news is that, since there wasn't much to the *Spellbook* to begin with, both versions are equally useless. The *Report* was twenty-four pages, while the 1987 edition was a disappointingly slim volume of 169 pages of large double-spaced type. Though the formatting of the Avon edition is more honest, it cuts down the page-count even further, so that the book should probably be entitled the "*Necronomicon* Spell-Pamphlet." The *Spellbook* is obviously modeled after the *Goetia: The Lesser Key of Solomon the King* and is merely an expanded version of "The Book of Fifty Names" in the Simon *Necronomicon*, elaborating on the use of the fifty names of Marduk. It lists the names with their accompanying sigils and words of power by which to evoke them.

The important difference in this book lies in the instructions for evocation that the author provides. Practitioners are instructed to make a copy of the seal of the name/aspect of Marduk they wish to evoke, on fresh paper. The spell should make use of white candles, incense, and a visualization technique. The readers are then instructed to focus their gaze on the seal, while controlling their breath with three deep inhalations; simultaneously, they are to mentally picture their goal. Then comes the incantation to invoke the desired entity, in which they chant the "word of power" like a mantra.[19] In short, these are simple (downright minimal) visualization and evocation techniques. I guess if you were totally inexperienced, and had never read anything about magick other than the Simon *Necronomicon*, this stuff might be useful, but for those with even a minimum of learning and experience, the *Spellbook* will be about as informative as a kindergarten coloring book.

The *Spellbook* also inherited some glaring, uncorrected errors from the Simon *Necronomicon*. Marduk, as I mentioned earlier, was not as important to the Sumerians as He was to the Babylonians, and the way He is presented in both the *Necronomicon* and the *Spellbook* is derived from the Babylonian *Enuma Elish*. The fifty names of Marduk are not to be "evoked" like goetic demons, but are more like the divine Names of God used as words of power in the Qaballah. (Perhaps the ancient Hebrews adopted this idea from the Mesopotamians, which would account for the way the Names of God are used in Qaballistic magick.) As in the *Necronomicon*, the functions attributed to the fifty names have little or nothing in common with the *Enuma Elish*—the Babylonian creation epic recorded in cuneiform on seven clay tablets—where the fifty names are found. For example, military power is attributed to Asarualimnunna (Asar-Alim-Nuna) in the *Spellbook*, whereas the name was actually associated with wealth and food production in the *Enuma Elish*. Worse yet, Simon botched the order in which the names are given, incorrectly listing "Marduk" as first, so that the authentic first name, "Marukka," is given as second, and so on down the line. Because of this numerical cluster-hump, the actual fiftieth name, "Enkurkur" (Lord of the Lands), does not appear in either of the Simon books. Simon's cranium was also deeply implanted in his rectal cavity when he composed the rest of the list. For example, he drops the thirty-fifth name from the *Enuma Elish*—"Gish-Numun-Ab"—for no apparent reason, and substitutes the name "Lugalabdubur" just for laughs. The forty-second name, "Lugalugga," is *not found* in the *Enuma Elish*, and is apparently just a piece of Simonian gobbledygook. The "seals" of the names, as I mentioned earlier, are not found anywhere in the annals of ancient Mesopotamian art and magick, so Simon (or whoever) must have made them up out of whole cloth. Defenders of the *Spellbook* may object that, even if the book is a hoax and the seals are made up by the author, they may still have magickal power, as do the contrived seals from venerable hoaxes like *The Lesser Key of Solomon,* which was never written by Solomon himself. I must point out here that, in the old grimoires, even those falsely attributed to legendary authors, the actual seals and names of spirits were received from the spirit realm by scrying and gematria. The seals in the Simon books, on the other hand, were made up by brainstorming to look scary and magickal, and, of course, to make a quick buck.

There is still no mention in the *Spellbook* of casting a protective circle or of banishing spirits. The practitioner is told simply to ignore any "eerie feelings" or "odd sounds" that may accompany the rituals. According to the author, these are "unevolved psychic entities trying to disrupt your ritual. They are not worthy of your attention."[20] In my opinion, the *Necronomicon Spellbook* is also pretty "unevolved" and likewise "not worthy of your attention."

A second supplemental volume, *The Gates of the Necronomicon* by Simon, is also rumored to be in print. According to the people at Magickal Childe in New York, however, the book has never gone into publication. Mr. Peter Levenda shed more light on the situation:

Gates was never published in any form that I know of; it was set in type and ready to go to press when Herman Slater—the owner of Magickal Childe Publishing—passed on; since that time, nothing has happened. In fact, I know that everyone is looking for the ms. at this time since no one knows where it wound up eventually.[21]

Theoretically, this book would have taken the practitioner step-by-step through the Gate Walking rituals, explaining the process in much greater detail. I say "would have taken" because Magickal Childe closed permanently on 1 March 1999 and is therefore unlikely to publish anything ever again.

A more obscure *Necronomicon*-related book published by Magickal Childe is *The Magickal Formulary,* edited by Herman Slater and printed in 1981—the same year as the *Necronomicon Spellbook.* This book can't really be considered a "supplement" to the Simon *Necronomicon,* since it contains only one reference to the supposed book of the Mad Arab. On page 90 is a formula for something called "STARRY WISDOM OIL." Whatever its purpose, this odious ointment must have stunk like Cthulhu's underwear, since it contained a discordant blend of pine, camphor, nettles, jasmine, and musk (whew!). Though the *Formulary* never tells us what this oil is supposed to be used for, it does claim that the recipe is "From the *Necronomicon.*"[22] Oddly, this malodorous concoction is never mentioned in either the Simon *Necronomicon* or *The Necronomicon Spellbook.* Then again, Slater may have been planning a "*Necronomicon* Cookbook." Who knows!

Necronomicon Knock-offs

At this point, I must discuss some other supplemental guides to the Simon *Necronomicon* not published by Magickal Childe or Avon Books.

The Necronomian: Workbook Guide to the Necronomicon by Darren Fox (Brother Moloch 969). Available for $49.95 from the International Guild of Occult Sciences. Copyright © by Darren Fox and I.G.O.S. Research Society. The table of contents page gives the alternate title of *The Necronomian: The Workbook to the Avon Necronomicon.* The volume itself is in black hardcover with the title in gold leaf and looks like a very thin high school yearbook. It purports to be the only useful guide to open the secrets of the Simon book. The author repeatedly calls his own work "a book of hard-hitting sorcery" (in fact that's the title of chapter 3), and continuously plugs I.G.O.S. correspondence courses.

The main problem with this book is that it scarcely even follows the Simon *Necronomicon* at all. When it does, its advice is out of step with both the Simon book and traditional magickal systems. For example, Brother Moloch gives us the Fifty Names of Marduk, but with new sigils formed by the author himself using gematria. Whether this was done out of magickal ingenuity, or from fear of copyright violations is anybody's guess.

In a section of chapter 4 entitled "The Zones or Seven Gates," he writes, "these gates are equivalent to the seven planets and Sephiras [sic] of the Tree of Life."[23] He claims to have skipped over the book's "long drawn out process of conjuring the Gates"[24] and advises the reader to rush through the entire Gate Walking initiation in a week—one gate per day starting with the Moon on Monday and taking the optional excursion to the underworld on Friday. One of the many reasons why this will not work, in my opinion, is that the days of the week corresponding to the planets do not fall in corresponding order to the consecutive Gates. In other words, following Monday (the Moon) is Tuesday, the day associated with Mars, but the Gate of Nergal, or Mars, is the Fifth Gate, not the second. The Simon book warns the reader that he must walk the Gates "each in its place and one at a time, and that thou must enter the Gates in the lawful manner, as is put down in the Covenant; else, thou art surely lost."[25] If this is true, Moloch's readers will surely end up adrift in the abyss. Brother Moloch also advises the reader that he can dispense with the Watcher if he likes. I suppose the reader could also dispense with his body if it isn't guarded from forces trying to take over his unprotected carcass—as the Simon book warns. One wonders why Fox bothered to write a guide to the *Necronomicon* at all if he feels that so much of it can be discarded.

Among the sublime and spiritually evolved spells in this grimoire is an evocation of Humwawa "To Cause Death To An Enemy." The most interesting thing in this dopey opus, however, is a copy of Kenneth Grant's "*Necronomiconian* Tree of Life," reproduced—without the author's permission—from *Hecate's Fountain*.

This atrocious little book is printed in double-spaced type, illustrated with infantile drawings, poorly written, peppered throughout with misspellings and grammatical mistakes that do *not* appear to be typographical errors, shows the literary influence of Beavis and Butthead, and appears to have been thrown together by a gang of enterprising junior high students in a high school annual department after class. My mail-ordered copy of *The Necronomian* was accompanied by an I.G.O.S. catalog that offered, among other things, a purported time-travel device called "the Time Transposer" consisting of bedsprings that the user wraps around his head and copper plates that he glues to his belly! As I mentioned earlier, I.G.O.S. stands for "International Guild of Occult Sciences." After reading this book, I think it should probably stand for "Ignorant of Goetic Operations and Sorcery"!

The Hidden Key of the Necronomicon by Alric Thomas. Palm Springs, CA: International Guild of Occult Sciences. 1996. Copyright by Alric Thomas and I.G.O.S. Research Society, $39.95, ISBN 1-57179-057-8.

Author Alric Thomas claims to be affiliated with a magickal society called the Silent Dragon, which has supposedly used the information in this book for "many years." Perhaps this is an allusion (or should I say *illusion*?) to the "Cult of the Dragon" described on page 208 of the Simon book as a cult of death that worships the "Ancient Ones." This volume closely resembles *The Necronomian* in format—same black hard covers with gold leaf title—but the pages are all of green stock held together with a velo binding, both of which will look familiar to Kinko's customers. Page 3 offers a ritual for evoking the Scorpion Man mentioned on page 209 of the Simon book, along with a copy of his sigil, also reproduced directly from the Simon *Necronomicon*. The practitioner is advised that the Scorpion man can give knowledge of the "Outside" when working with "*Necronomicon* Powers."

The most remarkable feature of *The Hidden Key* is author Thomas's reproduction of the diagrams of the Gates from the third chapter, "The Book of Entrance, and Of the Walking," with the seals of the Zonei from the second chapter, "Of The Zonei and Their Attributes," inserted into their centers. The centers of the diagrams of the Gates were left blank in the Simon *Necronomicon* itself, presumably to indicate open doorways. Apparently, the insertion of these seals into the Gates is meant to be the "hidden key" that will "unlock" the Gates for users of the Simon book. Page 14 of *The Hidden Key* features Thomas's version of the MANDAL OF CALLING on page 119 of the *Necronomicon*, in which he fills in the blank spaces on the Mandal with the names of the Gates and seals of Ganzir and the Zonei in what he believes to be their correct positions.

Though *The Hidden Key* claims to provide *Necronomicon* users with the long-awaited thorough instructions they crave, author Thomas dumps all responsibility back into the lap of the practitioner with the following cop-out: "Some may feel that the book is incomplete, because of a lack of instruction. Meditation and hard work will prove that it is more than complete."[26] One wonders if practitioners would be better off going straight for the "meditation and hard work," thereby saving $45. The book begins with a warning in which the author and publisher disclaim any responsibility for any injury that may occur to the practitioner from using the material in *The Hidden Key*. I can certainly see why!

Necronomicon Revelations Book I by Tahuti. Palm Springs, CA: International Guild of Occult Sciences. 1996. Copyright by Tahuti and International Guild of Occult Sciences, $60, ISBN 1-57179-065-9.

This book was a mystery to us for some time. We saw mentions on websites and in *Books in Print*, but the book itself never materialized. By sheer accident, Daniel found a copy at an occult bookstore. This rarity may not be evidence of the book's usefulness, however, as we shall see.

In his introduction, Tahuti tells us that "*NECRONOMICON REVELATIONS* picks up the torch of enlightenment and runs away."[27] The reader, after taking one look at this amateur production, should also run away—in the opposite direction. Tahuti goes on to say that "this work is the result of vast and extensive research, countless hours of study, many an untold sleepless nights [sic], and a dedication and determination to find a workable method for the use of the seals of the Fifty Names of MARDUK."[28] The trouble is that the author was not the one whose research, study, insomnia, and dedication went into this work. I am reluctant to make such charges, but in this case they are justified—most of the book is reprinted without permission from the *Necronomicon Spellbook*! I have a feeling that this may account for its rarity.

To be fair, the author does include some material of his own in this work. We are presented with a new method for working with the Fifty Names of Marduk, involving a strobe light and a set of flash cards, as well as suggestions on when to use the "Mandal of Calling" from the Simon book. That's it folks—strobe lights and flash cards—the only original ideas in the book! As with most I.G.O.S. books, the techniques offered are nothing that a practicing magician couldn't develop with a little ingenuity. Like the other I.G.O.S. works, this one is cheaply bound, filled with typos, and is certainly not worth the price of admission.

The Sorcerer's Handbook by Merlyn Stone. Denver, CO: Crystal Dawn Press. 1998. Copyright by Merlyn Stone, $19.95, No ISBN.

I'm not sure why this male author decided to swipe the name of Merlin Stone, the lady who wrote *When God Was a Woman*. One is often tempted, however, to do strange things during adolescence, and "Merlyn Stone" was a high school student when he wrote this book. Stone states in his biography that he is "Founder of the new Order of the Crystal Dawn." (For what it's worth, Crystal Dawn was the name of a porno actress in the 1980s.) Stone claims he was "unseated from the Order of Bards, Ovates, and Druids in England because of his compulsion for magick power rather than time wasted on useless study." Looking at his *Handbook* one can see where a little more "useless study" would have helped a great deal.

Chapter 12 (the last chapter) of the *Handbook* is devoted to the Simon *Necronomicon*, which Stone claims is a powerful magickal system. Like the authors of the I.G.O.S. books, he encourages his readers to violate that system, because he considers it unworkable as presented in Simon's original book. On page 62, he says, "To perform the ritual of the Walking, d nt[sic] perform the ritual as it indicates in the book or you will be greatly unsatisfied. I tried them many times over. I did all the things listed and I ended up feeling really stupid." Apparently, it took Stone a while to understand that he was supposed to undertake the Gate Walking in astral form.

Though Stone adds various bits and pieces of his own to the Simonian system (he casts the circle of Calling moving clockwise rather than counterclockwise), this chapter is mostly a simple rehash of material from the Simon book. The Fifty Names of Marduk, and the other "usual suspects" are predictably recycled. Stone's ethical bent ("bent" is a good word for it) is rather toward the nasty side of things, since he has a special section on using the URILIA Text to put curses on people you don't like. This is about what you might expect after reading his previous chapter on Necromantic magick, in which he instructs the reader to break into a crypt.

In any case, Stone's loyalty to the Simon book is questionable since, in 1999, he published his own version of the *Necronomicon*—a humble pamphlet of forty-five pages, published by "Sacred Grove Press." (Stone must have changed the name of his publishing company from "Crystal Dawn" after seeing some of her old videotapes.)

The Sorcerer's Handbook is definitely an amateur production; the diagrams (including the Seals of the Gates of the Watchtowers) are drawn by hand, the pages are photocopied on one side only, and are held together by a plastic ring binder of the type found at Kinko's. The overall quality isn't much worse than that of the I.G.O.S. books mentioned above, however, and the price, at least, is much lower. Looking at this book makes me glad that I wasn't able to get anything published when I was seventeen. Like the I.G.O.S. books, this is essentially the Beavis and Butthead approach to magick. (Hunn! Hunn! Demons are cool!)

Hex, Lies, and Audiotape: The *Necronomicon* Workshops

Perhaps the most rare and intriguing supplement to the Simon book is a series of three audiotapes of Simon himself conducting workshops on the use of his Necronomicon. I did not deal with these "*Necronomicon* Tapes" in the previous section because they deserve a section of their own. These tapes were recorded at Magickal Childe in 1981, the same year the *Necronomicon Spellbook* was published, and a year after the first paperback printing of the Simon Necronomicon from Avon Books. Simon's voice sounds rather youthful and shows evidence of formal speech training. The gentleman conducting these lectures is not, in my opinion, the "whole Simon," but merely the public face, or "mouthpiece," of Simon. As I noted earlier, "Simon" is apparently a composite pseudonym of two or more individuals. More important, the questions and answers are recorded so we can hear Simon being pinned down on controversial issues. Please excuse the *Mystery Science Theater 3000* nature of my commentary.

Tape #1 Simon begins his workshop by introducing himself as "the famed and notorious, and much maligned editor of the *Necronomicon* . . . Simon." As he says this, we can hear laughter from the workshop audience in the background. One student snickeringly asks his name. (Why are these people laughing? Could it be that they realize the book is a hoax?) Simon promises to examine the book "in pretty close detail as to the Sumerian origins of most of it" and of the "later Gnostic accretions" that he claims were added to it. He also promises to discuss the "cosmic" scope of the book, and to examine how the *Necronomicon* fits into Western occultism. He also promises to give pronunciation guidelines.

Simon then recycles the same origin story of the book found in the introduction to the *Necronomicon Spellbook*. He claims that others told him the mysterious manuscript was the fabled *Necronomicon,* since he had never heard of it, and had no knowledge of Lovecraft. (From reading the Simon book, I have no problem believing that he was completely ignorant of Lovecraft.) He adds that Sumerian words were transcribed phonetically in the Greek manuscript and identified by accident. He then comments on the supposed historical, anthropological, and archaeological importance of the book, claiming that it indicates that someone in the 12th century C.E had knowledge of Sumer, a civilization that was not rediscovered until the turn of the 19th into the 20th century. Simon states that the *Necronomicon* is "not a medieval book—it's not written in the Neo-Platonism of the time," which contradicts the explanation that Peter Levenda later offered to Daniel and me that the *Necronomicon* was the product of a medieval sorcerer's version of the Sumerian magickal system. It also seems to contradict the book itself, which is arranged in a rather strict Neoplatonic hierarchy of gates subordinate to other gates, demons subordinate to Marduk, and so on. Simon claims that his *Necronomicon* differs from medieval grimoires in that its magick isn't connected to Judaism, Christianity, or Islam, but rather to the religion and philosophy of ancient Sumer, and possibly also to that of Manicheanism and Zoroastrianism (both of which have little in common with ancient Mesopotamian beliefs).

According to Simon, the *Necronomicon* is really about a war between two alien races battling for control of Earth—a war in which humans will eventually be forced to choose sides. Simon must have decided to whitewash his book's evil reputation, because he then claims that "the rituals of the *Necronomicon* are supposed to serve as a kind of defense against this abuse of our planet." I'm not sure how invoking nasty demons from the *Necronomicon* is supposed to save our planet, but that was Simon's alibi-of-the-week back in 1981, and he stuck to it at least for the duration of this workshop. Simon then compares this sci-fi cosmology with Manicheanism and Zoroastrianism, though it sounds more like August Derleth's version of the Cthulhu Mythos.

Simon follows this with a dumbed-down version of the Babylonian Flood story. He then puts his own Manichean twist on the *Enuma Elish*—the Babylonian creation epic—in which he interprets the war between Marduk and Tiamat as a Mesopotamian version of the struggle between the Elder Gods and the Great Old Ones from August Derleth's version of the Cthulhu Mythos. Simon later discusses the Fifty Names of Marduk briefly, and backpedals from his previous statement about the non-Neoplatonic nature of his *Necronomicon* by saying that the use of the Fifty Names in the book is "somewhat Neo-Platonic."

Next, Simon discusses the Goddess Inanna/Ishtar, and says, "this is where the magick part of the Sumerian religion and culture comes into play, with Inanna." I agree partially with this statement, though it ignores Enki/Ea, who is properly the God of magick in the Mesopotamian pantheon. Simon then gives his own bogus, blasphemous version of *The Descent of Inanna into the Underworld*. My careful study of ancient Mesopotamian theology has led me to the conclusion that, rather than carelessly loosing demons on the world, Inanna's victory over the underworld gave Her power over death and demonic forces—a power that She could share with Her worshipers. She was a kind of "savior Goddess" whose story of death and resurrection probably served as a template for Persephone, Mithra, Jesus, and other latecomers. A discussion of Mesopotamian soteriology is outside the scope of this book, so suffice it to say that Simon's interpretation of *The Descent of Inanna* is a travesty of Her heroic triumph over the underworld. Simon admits, in a way, that this story of Inanna's journey through seven gates into the underworld is the model for his Gate Walking initiation (suspicions confirmed!) in that it "mirrors the initiation ceremonies for someone who wishes to master the underworld."

Simon explains that the square sigils of the Gates given in his *Necronomicon* are to be drawn on the floor, claiming that each one constitutes a kind of do-it-yourself ziggurat for the magician, who must carry out the Gate Walking procedure with his or her body inside the drawn "Gate." He compares this to the Indian and Tibetan use of mandalas. (You've got to be kidding!) He goes on to explain that the Gate of Nanna is the most important, since it is the first, and that the magician walking the Gates can only get the password to the next Gate by first going through the previous Gate. He claims that this is the "failsafe" built into this system of "self initiation," and that the Gate Walking system of the *Necronomicon* cannot be abused. (I suspect Sun@Sun, AZ0th, and others might take exception to that statement.) Simon then lists the Gates in the order in which they appear in the *Necronomicon,* and comments that the last Gate—that of Ninib, called "Adar"—is similar to the Gate of Nanna. Unlike the other gates, however, the magician does not actually enter the Gate of Ninib. Simon hints ominously that, at the last Gate, "*something* comes through that doorway to greet you" (perhaps the ghost of Herman Slater with discount coupons for the next *Necronomicon* knock-off). I wonder if the "*something*" that comes through the doorway to meet the hapless Gate Walker is the "evil and fatal force" mentioned in *The Oracles of Zoroaster.* On this creepy note, Simon begins answering questions about particulars, such as how the seals should be made. He says the seals should only be made on wood or paper if the appropriate metal is not available.

Simon states that "subtle changes take place in the psyche of the magickian" during the Gate Walking initiation. (I'll bet! Like, perhaps, insanity.) He compares the process to that found in *The Book of the Sacred Magic of Abramelin the Mage.* (Suspicions confirmed!) Simon also states that once you have passed through the Marduk Gate, you can reenact Inanna's descent into the underworld, and "exert power over the demonic forces." This is an odd statement, in view of Simon's previous claim that Inanna originally released all those demonic forces into the world. Simon ends by warning his listeners that they are not allowed to evoke demons until after they have passed the Marduk Gate. In my opinion, the only thing Simon should have to pass is a lie detector test.

Simon spouts so much nonsense on this tape that I only have room to deal with his most flagrant Assyriological boners. Simon Says:

- The *Oracles of Zoroaster* was of Sumerian origin. (It wasn't.)

- No Sumerian gold or jewelry has ever been found. (Magnificent finds—including harps covered with hammered gold—were excavated by Sir Leonard Wooley at the "Royal Tombs" of Ur.)

- All Sumerians were short and fat with huge round eyes, wore only clothing made of leaves, and were of extraterrestrial origin! (This stuff is only funny for so long.)

- Sumerian civilization grew up in only a hundred years. (Try several *thousand* years!)

- Oannes, legendary bringer of civilization to the Mesopotamians, was an extraterrestrial alien. (The tale of Oannes [Sumarian *Uan,* Akkadian *Adapa*] comes from *The Babyloniaca* of Berossos from the 4th or 3rd century B.C.E. Simon's version has more in common with *Chariots of the Gods* and Zecharia Sitchin.)

- Sumer was a peaceful civilization "totally unprepared for warfare." (In fact, the Sumerians—inventors of the war chariot, bronze weapons, and tactical infantry formations—were not only prepared for war, they *invented* it.)

- All ziggurats had seven levels. (Some had three, some nine.)

- Each level was associated with a planet. (Wrong again.)

- Each of the seven cities of Sumer was associated with one of the planets. (There were more than seven, and none were associated with any particular planet.)

- Inanna was a "Sumerian Pandora" who released all the underworld's demons on Earth. (A small group of demons [*galla*] followed Her against Her will, and returned to the underworld as soon as they found a victim to take Her place.)

- The phrase MAY THE DEAD RISE AND SMELL THE INCENSE is found in the *Enuma Elish*. (It isn't.)

- The Sumerian script is called "hieroglyphics." (It is actually called *cuneiform*.)

- The Sumerian word for "temple" is *Bar*. (The Sumerian word for "temple" was *E*, which also means "house," as in *E-anna*, the "House of Heaven," which was the name of the Temple of Inanna at Uruk.)

- The Sumerians built their temples over places of evil. (They should have built one over Magickal Childe!)

Tape # 2: Simon starts with a rehash of material from the previous workshop, and some wisecracks about the war between Iran and Iraq. He reemphasizes that the Gate Walking initiation is the heart of the system of his *Necronomicon*. At one point he says, "The Mad Arab, or whoever composed this book . . ." and is immediately drowned out by laughter from the workshop crowd (who apparently know it's all a fraud). Simon goes on to claim that the author of the *Necronomicon* was writing around 800 C.E. in Damascus, and that his knowledge of Sumerian magick was handed down to him by "underground cults thousands of years old." He claims that he "writes darkly about hidden cults that worship the Ancient Ones," including the ancient Goddess Tiamat, whom Simon equates with the Cthulhu Mythos, and also with Leviathan in the *Book of Job* (which he misquotes). I can see now why he hides behind the pseudonym of "Simon"; he's probably running from lynch mobs of Goddess worshipers and Bible scholars.

One of the workshop students asks Simon about Aleister Crowley's knowledge of the *Necronomicon*, and Simon strangely contradicts all the carefully contrived Crowley links in his book by saying, "I don't know if Crowley was aware of Lovecraft or the *Necronomicon*." He speculates that Mathers may have hidden the existence of the book from Crowley after they "became bitter enemies." Simon states that "Crowley never once mentions this book, except for Kenneth Grant's famous quote. . . ." This is the same "Sumerian Tradition" quote I mentioned earlier, which is found on page xi of the *Necronomicon*, where it is attributed to Crowley, not Grant. He then parrots Grant's theory that the Sumerian tradition is found among the Yezidi "devil wor- shipers" of Iraq, and is the basis of Crowley's 93 current of magick. But then he backpedals by saying, "But that's just conjecture at this point, no one's really cer- tain." Why did Simon suddenly decide to trash all the false associations between Crowley, Lovecraft, and the *Necronomicon* that had been so carefully built into the book? Perhaps this about-face was the result of pressure from Thelemites who wanted him to quit dragging Crowley into his hoax.

Then Simon discusses the Watcher, and its care and feeding. He says the origi- nal Watchers were created by Marduk "as mindless automatons." (Later, he contra- dicts this by saying Tiamat created them.) He states that the Watchers are completely amoral, and will carry out any task "with no concern for—the shedding of blood, for instance." After offering this engraved invitation to magickal murder, Simon goes on to warn his students "should the priest slip up in his dealings with the Watcher, he will be destroyed by the Watcher." (With friends like the Watcher, who needs ene- mies?) Simon then elaborates on the methods and tools used to invoke the Watcher; the use of the sword (which is the symbol of the Watcher), and the "new bowl" (which must be inscribed with the "appropriate sigils" given on page 69 of the Simon book). In the bowl, certain sacrifices must be burned to summon the Watcher. These are "new bread," pine resin, and "the grass Olieribos." Simon then reveals that "olieri- bos" is actually nettle. The Sword of the Watcher must be engraved with the last of the three signs found on page 69 of the book. According to Simon, the Watcher actu- ally inhabits the sword when invoked.

Simon then says that the Watcher sometimes appears as a fierce dog, and some- times as a man with staring eyes—which he compares to a character in Marvel

Comics. (I swear I'm not making this stuff up!) Simon reminds his listeners that, if they bungle the incantations, omit the sacrifices, act "in defiance of the covenant" or otherwise screw up the ritual, the Watcher will devour them, and not even the Elder Gods can stop it. And as if all that weren't bad enough, Simon also warns that some Watchers are "lawless" and await the return of "the Ancient Ones to once more rule the Cosmos." (Great! Now all you need to conjure up is something to watch the Watcher.) Simon says "The Conjuration of the Watcher" must be performed "at the darkest hour of the night." A double circle of flour is to be poured around the ritual space, no altar is used, the Conjuration of the Fire is made, the bowl—with burning sacrifices in it—is placed between the two circles in the northeast. The practitioner is told to wear a black robe and cap, and not to stick the sword into the ground until the Watcher is actually summoned. Simon then gives instructions on the pronunciation of the Incantation of the Watcher by reciting it himself. He emphasizes that, at the last three words of the incantation (on page 71), the sword is to be thrust into the ground, at which point the Watcher is supposed to appear. The Watcher can be dismissed by striking the sword, after which it should be removed from the ground. He warns that you cannot leave the circle until after the Watcher has departed. (Don't drink prune juice before the ritual.)

The Lesser Banishing Ritual of the Pentagram (LBRP) is a Qaballistic method of creating sacred space by drawing the upright banishing pentagram in the air in all four directions, evoking the four archangels of the four quarters, and invoking the presence of God. Qaballists derived this ritual from ancient Hebrew prayers like the *Kaddish*. Many scholars now believe that the Hebrews in turn derived the *Kaddish* (as well as the concept of angels, Cherubim, and Seraphim) from ancient Mesopotamian sources.

In a Q&A session, Simon claims that the LBRP is insufficient to guard your body during the Gate Walking. This is ironic, since the LBRP has more in common with Mesopotamian magick than all of this Watcher nonsense. Take, for example, the invocations of four Gods for the four quarters in the *Forerunners to Udug-Hul.*[29] Modern day Mesopotamian Pagan Bell Murru has found the LBRP so compatible with Sumero-Babylonian magick that he has composed his own version of it, Kibratu— A Sumero-Babylonian Pentagram Ritual.[30] I have even composed my own version, which I presented for the first time at the Starwood Festival of 2001, using the eight-pointed star of Inanna. Simon advises against doing an LBRP with the Watcher present. (Probably because you'd end up with flambé-of-Watcher when the Archangels of the four quarters arrived and recognized it as a nasty little Qlippothic demon.)

The session concludes with a discussion of other handy-dandy uses for the Watcher, including self-defense. (Oops!) Ethical considerations are discussed about the use of the Watcher as a metaphysical hitman. (Ouch!) Simon assures the audience that his *Necronomicon* is "a complete system" that cannot be abused. (Terribly comforting to families of the victims of various cult crimes, I'm sure.)

Simon's howlers this time around include the following false statements:

- Assurbanipal was an early Babylonian king. (Assurbanipal was a late Assyrian king.)

- He comments on what he calls "the Sumerian *Maqlu Text.*" (The *Maqlu* was actually Babylonian.)

- Lovecraft learned about the *Necronomicon* from Algernon Blackwood and Arthur Machen, whom he says were close friends of Lovecraft, and members of his Kalem Club in New York. (Though Lovecraft admired the works of both men, he never met either one. And neither of these two great writers ever belonged to the Kalem Club, whose heyday lasted from about 1924 to 1926, and consisted only of a circle of Lovecraft's friends living in New York City. Blackwood had lived unhappily in New York from about 1892 to 1899, when Lovecraft was still a child in Providence, then returned to England and never went back. Machen never seems to have lived outside Great Britain.)

- Blackwood and Machen learned about the *Necronomicon* from the Golden Dawn, which he claims, "hinted at a secret Arab manuscript that was only available to higher initiates." (Blackwood and Machen were both members of the Golden Dawn, but they were in the Outer Order, and not "higher initiates." No study of the history and literature of the Golden Dawn has ever yielded any hints of a "secret Arab manuscript.")

- The Goddess Tiamat was synonymous with Mummu. (Mummu was a male God.)

- Nettles are associated with Saturn. (Nettle [*Urtica dioica*] is actually associated with Mars.)[31]

- The words in the Incantation of the Watcher are all Sumerian. (One of them is Akkadian—*sarratu,* which, oddly enough, means "falsehood."[32])

Tape #3 In this tape, Simon deals with "The Book of the Calling" (page 95), and says, "Not to be outdone by other medieval grimoires," the *Necronomicon* includes a book on evocation. (Remember when he said it wasn't a medieval grimoire in the first tape?) He then quotes part of the text from pages 95 and 96, which advises the practitioner to purify himself and his ritual area by sprinkling salt water, which is actually authentic for Mesopotamian magick. He quotes the passage following this, which promises that "honor, dignity, wealth and happiness" can be obtained from the Elder Gods, and the "submission" of the Ancient Ones, but also warns the reader to avoid these things because they are a trap leading to death. (Yeah, right!) Simon points out that medieval grimoires will always provide rituals "that you must never perform," and that these prohibitions are actually a kind of invitation to do the forbidden. This assertion is partly correct. Some of the medieval grimoires—even those replete with vile curses—were attributed to biblical prophets and kings, and claimed that their authority came directly from God, even when offering spells to kill your neighbor, make his cows go dry, or violate his daughter. With his usual oiliness, Simon implies that really advanced initiates can possibly evoke nasty demonic critters with no ill effects. He quickly reminds his listeners that beginners shouldn't try it at all. A questioner from the audience points out the ambiguity of all this, and Simon admits, "You could unknowingly become a worshiper of the Ancient Ones and unknowingly open a gate." (This guy has gates on the brain!) He reiterates that you shouldn't try this until after passing the Marduk Gate. Simon then states that the job of the initiate working the system is to guard one particular gate against an invasion from those nasty Ancient Ones. (Why, then, does the book contain a chapter on evoking them?) He compares all this to Lovecraft's "The Dunwich Horror."

Simon then discusses the weird little glyph at the top of page 99, which is supposed to be the sign of Enki, which the "Mad Arab" calls the "Elder Sign" on page 12. And again, Simon mentions the sign of the Watcher. He claims that these two signs, together with the pentagram (as shown on page 69), are an unbeatable combination. (Khem Caigan superimposed all three to make the "Elder Sign" on the cover of the book.) Simon says that tracing the symbols mentioned above in the air should be effective against most attacks. He then digresses into a discussion of the type of "new bread" that should be offered to the Watcher; unleavened church communion wafers versus cornbread, and the reasons why nettle is burned. Simon discusses the tools and vestments illustrated on pages 112–14, elaborates on their supposed mythological and cultural significance, and talks about ways of making the dagger of Inanna out of copper plate. Only the colors white (for Inanna) and black (for Ninib) are to be used, because Ninib (Ninurta) "knows the Outer Regions and the ways of the Ancient Ones" and because Inanna "subdued the Underworld and vanquished the Queen thereof." (At last Simon gives Inanna Her due!) The "eight-rayed star" on Simon's little copper Shriner fez (the Crown of Anu) looks more like a chaos rune, however, than the star of Inanna/Ishtar. Someone asks about the amulet on page 11, and Simon says it should be made of pure silver. He describes the frontlet as being wide and long "like a Russian Orthodox stole" and suggests it be done in white with black inscriptions. Simon warns not to use the tools or vestments for any purpose other than magick. Someone asks about the cleaning of these vestments, and Simon sarcastically replies that the Sumerians weren't that picky about cleanliness, but does allow that they could be hand-washed. He points out that the seals of the four gates at the four quarters given on pages 115–18 are asymmetrical, and claims the asymmetry of these Simonian seals causes stress on "the forces around you," and are designed for "causing a gate to open through stress." According to Simon, the lines of energy bounce off each other, creating a vortex in the ritual space. He contrasts this to medieval grimoires in which you are safe from alien forces within the circle. Using these seals at the four quarters creates an opening or "gate" through which you will meet "other intelligences."

Simon discusses the type of deserted place where these evocations should be performed—preferably in the mountains. He emphasizes that the place should be "purified by supplications to thine particular God and Goddess," your patron deity. Amazingly, the concept of a personal God or Goddess is actually authentic to Mesopotamian magick and religion. (It's amazing that some authentic Mesopotamian concepts made it into Simon's book.) He then reads the part about offering pine and cedar incense, bread, and salt. This too is surprisingly authentic. Then Simon reads the incantation of exorcism, and says he found something similar at "the Sumerian Collection" in New York, in which the exorcism was used together with the bread and salt as a house banishing. Proceeding to page 100, he points out that the bread should be burned in a bronze brazier, and the salt scattered about the room. A circle—"not a square this time"—must be drawn on the ground in which the practitioner must stand while reciting the incantation. Simon points out the warning in the text not to venture outside the circle "lest thou be consumed by the invisible monsters" as a tradition from medieval grimoires. Reading from page 101, he says that you should put down your circle and call your personal God or Goddess, but that "their images must be removed from the altar . . ." unless you are calling Marduk. Then the "perfumes" are to be burned in the brazier "after the calling of the fire" as per the Conjuration of the Fire God. Then the Watcher is summoned "after Its fashion." According to Simon, you start the invocation of the four gates in the north and work your way around the circle counterclockwise. (Why am I not surprised?) After all these circumambulations and incantations, if you're not totally exhausted, you recite a fifth invocation of all four gates all at once.

After briefly discussing the second Mandal of Calling on page 120, Simon discusses what kinds of entities may be called using this formula, including the invocation of the dead on page 104, in which you must invoke Ninnghizhidda. He warns that you must not free the spirit, or make a pact with it, since this would (gasp!) violate the covenant. If you do, the Watcher will "jump on you"! Then he proceeds to the "GREAT CONJURATION OF ALL THE POWERS" on pages 106–8, which is to be used mainly for emergencies (which I'm sure are quite common in this brand of magick). Someone in the crowd asks Simon if these incantations could be set to music, and he allows that this is possible, but that it might lead members of the audience to mental illness. Moving on to page 109 and "WHAT SPIRITS MAY BE USEFUL," Simon points out that the safest to call are the spirits of the Fifty Names of Marduk, particularly for beginners. Reading down the list, he mentions the "Spirits of the Seven [Planetary] Spheres," and says that you cannot evoke a Planetary spirit until you have entered its Gate via the Gate Walking initiation. A student asks Simon about the magickal passwords received at the Gates, and he replies that: "you'll either see it written or you'll hear it spoken." Simon claims that people have used the system and looked up the words, and found that they were authentic Sumerian. Simon then skips lightly over the two little spells on page 111, and jokingly remarks that, if you've worked this system for long, you may need the spell to regain sexual potency.

Simon concludes with "the part of the *Necronomicon* that is considered most vile"—The URILIA Text, which begins on page 183. Simon reads the part that says "the Curse of ENKI" will be upon anyone who shows these words, and jokingly points out that he "blew it" by publishing them. To coach his students on pronunciation, Simon recites part of the incantation of "the ANCIENT ONE" on page 185, and immediately gets drowned out by laughter from the class, since his pronunciation of the next-to-last line on the page sounds like the quacking speech of the big-brained aliens in *Mars Attacks*. Simon claims that his "IAK SAKKAKH" represents Lovecraft's Yog-Sothoth. (No comment!) Simon proceeds to "The Abominations" on page 186, and claims that "here we are talking about *the* Gate, the Gate of 'The Dunwich Horror,' the Gate that Lovecraft feared so much!" He says that this is the Gate behind which the Ancient Ones dwell, waiting to break through at the slightest opportunity. These Gates must be opened at "the darkest hour of the night" and must not be left open after sunrise. Beyond that point it can't be closed until nightfall the next day. One of the students asks what it would be like if the Ancient Ones broke through to retake our world. Simon's reply is: "Did you ever see *Night of the Living Dead*?" Another asks: "Would it affect the environment?" Simon answers that it would. (Well, duh!) One of his more perceptive students points out that someone crazy enough could use this information to "just do in the world!" Simon counters that this would be breaking the covenant, and the Watcher would eat the malefactor. But then someone else would have to close the Gate, and Simon never exactly explains how that would be accomplished. Someone asks if his system is more powerful than Enochian magick, and Simon hedges by saying that they are just different. He then discusses the ugly entities in "The Abominations," and one of his students points out the moral ambiguity of this part of the book. Simon counters that the Mad Arab presented these demons and their seals purely as a warning. He goes on to claim that followers of the Ancient Ones evoke these beings, and that those followers dwell among us, but are not quite human. (Sounds like the Young Republicans!) Simon says that the mere act of invoking these creatures means that you have switched sides to the Ancient Ones. When asked about the Watcher's dispassionate enforcement of the covenant, Simon compares it to Gort, the killer robot, in *The Day the Earth Stood Still*. Someone asks Simon about this oft-mentioned covenant, and Simon replies that you won't understand the covenant until you have (you guessed it!) gone through the Gate Walking initiation. Somebody points out the potential dangers of this system, and Simon responds that the system was probably not as dangerous in ancient Sumer when everybody understood all this stuff. The problem, he says, is that this system is so ancient and alien from our traditional forms of magick, and that these Gods and demons haven't been evoked for so long. The initiation of the Gates, he claims, is very "positive" and "wholesome." His feeling is that the Gate Walking initiation should be gone through first, before using anything else in the book, so that "you will intuitively understand the dangers in the rest of the book." When asked how long the initiation process should take, he says a year would be safest. At least a month must come between each Gate, but most people, he claims, need more than a month of recovery time. (In a comfy padded cell, no doubt.)

Simon's howlers on this tape include the following disinformation:

- He says the pentagram represents a plow. (Most Pagans agree that it represents an upright human.)

- He says the Sumerian word for "plow" was *ar*. (The Sumerian word for "plow" was *apin*.)

- Simon claims the Sumerians called themselves "the people of the plow." (They called themselves *sag-gi-ga*, which means "black-headed.")

- The pentagram, Simon states, is the sign of the human race. (I thought he said it represented a plow!)

- Simon infers that the Sumerians were "Aryans." (They were probably Asiatics—they did not speak any language of the Aryan language group.)

- Simon suggests that the practitioner use *777* to discover which correspondences to use for Sumerian deities. (Oops!)

- Simon states that the "hieroglyph" of the eight-pointed star on his "Crown of Anu" is the Sumerian symbol for "God(s)." (The eight-pointed star was normally the exclusive symbol of Inanna, and of Her planet, Venus. There was also an eight-pointed cuneiform sign for *Dingir*, or "God," that consisted of four cuneiform wedges joined at the center.)

- He says Pazuzu was Sumerian. (He was Assyrian/Babylonian.)

- Simon claims that "mandal" is an Arab word for circle. (It is obviously a corruption of the Sanskrit word *mandala*. Though he calls it a "circle," the MANDAL OF CALLING on page 119 is square with a cross in the middle.)

- Simon claims that his asymmetrical seals are totally different from the symmetrical seals in Western medieval magick. (In fact, the seals for goetic demons in European grimoires—like the seal for Furcas in the *Goetia*, for instance—are often asymmetrical.)

- Simon claims that his system is related to the Qaballah, even though he insists that Mesopotamian magick is totally alien to current magickal systems. (Much of the magick of both East and West shows Mesopotamian influence.)

So ends the series of Simon's taped workshops on his *Necronomicon*. Much of the material presented in this workshop was probably intended to go into *Gates of the Necronomicon,* the never-published sequel to the first Simon book. To fully point out the flaws in these teachings would require another entire volume, so I have merely "hit the high spots." From listening to the tapes, you can tell that some of the workshop students have tired of this endless game of "Simon says," and that the question they would really like to ask is: How much of this stuff is, well . . . you know . . . *real?* One of Simon's biggest problems is his utter failure (or willful refusal) to grasp either the solid historical facts or the spiritual essence of ancient Mesopotamian magick and religion.

Simon's moral ambiguity is more frightening than any of the sci-fi/horror elements in his pulp fiction spellbook. If the sacred duty of the Simonian initiate is to guard the dreaded Gate of the Ancient Ones, why does the book give tantalizing instructions for opening that Gate? Why does Simon advise his readers to use the Watchers for protection after he called them "a race of evil beings" in an article he wrote earlier? It would be simplistic to glibly dismiss Simon as just another intellectual swindler, or as one more in the long line of charlatans that have plagued the history of magick. He is actually something worse. He is like a politician who will not commit to either side in a war, but sells guns to both, while telling each that they have his exclusive support. His double loyalty to both the Light and the Dark actually amounts to a double betrayal.

The Chaos of Confusion —John Wisdom Gonce III 8

Beat your black wings, and prance with cloven feet
With hideous rites the friends of Chaos meet!

—HOWARD PHILLIPS LOVECRAFT

D evotees of Simon's book champion it because "the magick works." But if modern occultists have learned anything by now, we have learned that, in the hands of an able operator, *anything* can work. As a Wiccan high priestess of my acquaintance says, "You can summon demons by chanting Mother Goose rhymes if you have sufficient intent."[1]

So now we return to a quasi-chaosist notion of a system of "no-system." If only the belief of the practitioner is important, the "raw material" of the spells or the magickal system itself is insignificant. Or is it? I believe that the nature of the system used will always affect the results of any working in subtle or not-so-subtle ways. The raw material is always significant. A bowl of soup made from fresh spring water will taste very different than one made from water that came out of a mud puddle, or, for that matter, a cesspool. Among computer users there is an old proverb: Garbage in, garbage out.

Necronomicon magick must be classified as a third branch of postmodern occultism, mainly because there is nothing else to do with it. Attempts to integrate the Simon book and its users into the chaos community have been less than satisfying, in spite of rumors that the book was co-authored by Peter J. Carrol or some other well-respected chaos magician. It seems that the only kind of "chaos" *Necronomicon* users can lay claim to is *confusion*. The conceptual confusion is such that devotees, desperate to integrate the *Necronomicon* into a system, have contrived progressively more far-fetched scenarios for meetings between Lovecraft and Aleister Crowley, two men who would have despised each other on sight. Perhaps my favorite of these is Colin Low's "Sonia Greene scenario." (Low has since admitted to the authors that it is a fiction of his own invention.)[2] Here again, the result is not always convincing, to put it charitably.

Nor can we say that the magick of the Simon book is what Internet mage Haramullah would call the "Midul Path," incorporating dogmatic and chaosist systems into one. Rather than synthesizing chaos with dogma, the Simon *Necronomicon* practitioner simply vacillates between the two. He cannot claim to be a chaos magician because he relies upon a tradition. But the "tradition" on which he relies is demonstrably spurious, meaning that his is not a dogmatic system. He claims that it doesn't make any difference that his tradition is based on a pulp fiction hoax—after all, "nothing is true, everything is permitted." Yet he continuously tries to establish some sort of legitimacy for his "tradition" by trying to link Lovecraft to Crowley. Yet it was not Crowley, but Austin Osman Spare, who was the true father of chaos magick. Like a man who can't live with his wife and yet can't leave her, the *Necronomicon* devotee shuffles back and forth between magickal paradigms, unable to establish himself anywhere. This is less the fault of the practitioner than of the text; the Simon *Necronomicon* cannot be a Sumerian grimoire because it was written in the 1970s, but it cannot be a chaos magick text because it pretends to be a Sumerian grimoire.

The Satanic Connection

Guilt by association with Satanism has not helped the reputation of the Simon *Necronomicon* in some quarters. Some have even speculated that either Anton LaVey or Michael Aquino may be the true author of the Simon book. One cannot help but see certain parallels between Anton LaVey's *The Satanic Bible* and *The Satanic Rituals*, and the Simon *Necronomicon*. All three books were published in paperback by Avon in a similar format in the seventies (*The Satanic Bible* actually had its first edition in 1969). All three are often linked by authors of works on cult crime and Satanism. All three have rather ranting introductions that rival the main body of the work. And all three contain elements of pseudo-Lovecraftian occultism.

In *The Satanic Bible*, LaVey claimed that Edward Kelley, the scryer for Dr. John Dee, used Lovecraft's Shining Trapezohedron for a scrying stone (supposedly the actual "shew stone" written of in connection with Dee and Kelley). According to LaVey, Dee and Kelley received the Enochian language from the "Outside" of Lovecraft's Old Ones, not from heaven. LaVey printed his own Satanic "translation" of the Enochian Calls, claiming that Enochian should be called the language of the "angles," not of the Angels. Colin Low's "Necronomicon Anti-FAQ" was undoubtedly influenced by LaVey in its associations between the Great Old Ones and the fallen angels and Nephilim of the Bible. Low's ideas about Dee and the shewstone may also be inspired by LaVey.

In spite of the circumstantial evidence, neither Anton Szandor LaVey nor Michael Aquino could have written and published the Simon *Necronomicon* anonymously. LaVey in particular was an incurable publicity addict who would have shouted it to the skies if he had been responsible for such a well-known book. And while Aquino was once a member of the EOD—where he was known as Frater Set 0*—there is no evidence of his having had anything to do with writing the Simon book. But the

Simon *Necronomicon* is now firmly associated in the minds of many Christian activists, writers on cult-related crime, and law enforcement personnel with Satanism and all its works. Larry Kahaner's book *Cults That Kill: Probing the Underworld of Occult Crime*, mentions that the *Necronomicon* and *The Satanic Bible* were given to police investigators to study by consultant Jim McCarthy.[3]

Peter Levenda, who, as we have seen, has his own stake in the *Necronomicon*, makes several references to the dread grimoire in his book *Unholy Alliance*. He observes that LaVey's books, plus the Simon *Necronomicon*, have been "found at cult sites in the United States and have been—rightly or wrongly—featured on various radio and television talk shows on the dangers of Satanism." I guess he considers any publicity good publicity. Author Michael Newton considers it important as well. In his book *Raising Hell: An Encyclopedia of Devil Worship and Satanic Crime*, he lists a black-and-white illustration of the pseudo-pentagram sigil seen on the front cover of Simon's *Necronomicon*. His caption under the sigil reads "Demonic symbol used in the *Necronomicon* and worn by some occult worshipers in southern California." In her well-researched, but slightly paranoid, book *The New Satanists*,[4] Linda Blood drags both the *Necronomicon* and Lovecraft into the issue of Satanism on page one of the introduction! In chapter 4, she cites the case of a fifteen-year-old girl entangled in a destructive cult situation. The girl's mother searched her room and discovered "the usual literature: *The Satanic Bible*, *The Satanic Rituals* and the *Necronomicon*. The latter is a paperback volume of ersatz demonic spells that are actually based on the works of horror writer Howard Phillips Lovecraft. It is immensely popular with teenage dabblers."[5] And plumbing the darkest depths of ignorance is *Painted Black*, in which author Carl A. Raschke declares that both H. P. Lovecraft and Edgar Rice Burroughs (?) were "practicing occultists."[6] Fans of Lovecraft doubtless resent seeing him held responsible for the Simon *Necronomicon* and having his name dragged relentlessly through what they see as the Satanic mud. Nevertheless, such is the popular conception of those who use the *Necronomicon*.

One organized Satanic group that strongly displays its roots in the Simon book is the "Order of the Absu," headed by Paul Nehib. This organization believes that power comes through exploration of the body's capacities for pain and pleasure.[7] Its manifesto, "The Book of the Absu," tells how "the waves of the Absu rage and the Demons it vomits forth impale the accursed nazarene a thousand times over."[8] Members of the order should spend less time on invective and more on research. Despite the Simon book's declaration that the "Absu" is the Sumerian equivalent of hell, it was actually a vast underground freshwater lake that was distinct from the underworld.[9] Mangled mythography aside, the existence of the Order of the Absu proves that some organized Satanists have adopted the Simon *Necronomicon* as scripture.

The Satanic image of the Simon book is further enhanced by its popularity with quasi-Satanic rock bands.[10] Notably, Marilyn Manson claims he was introduced to the Simon *Necronomicon* as a teenager, saying he witnessed someone use it to invoke

Ninnghizhidda.[11] The most seminal of the "Simonesque" bands, however, are Deicide (signed to Roadrunner Records) and Morbid Angel (started in 1987), both from Florida. Deicide in particular is brazenly outspoken and receive regular publicity-enhancing condemnations from goofy Christian media personalities like Bob Larson, as well as frequent death threats from extremist groups. The lead guitarist for Morbid Angel calls himself Trey Azagthoth and the band produces songs with titles like "Angel of Disease" (an invocation to Nyarlathotep) and "Nar Matturu."[12] Other bands have taken their names directly from the Simon book, like Tiamat (with an album called *Sumerian Cry*), Marduk (from Sweden), Nergal (Switzerland), and Absu (Texas). A Polish band called Betrayer has even released an album called *Necronomical Exmortis*, while the Swedish group Hypocrisy has growled out a cut entitled "*Necronomicon*" on their album *Obsculum Obscenum*. The Dutch death metal band Sinister combines Lovecraftian and Simonian imagery in the lyrics of the song "Awaiting the Absu," from their 1995 compact disc called *Hate*:

> *Necromantic art from*
> *The kingdom of Woe*
> *Cthulhu sleeps and*
> *Dreams the burning pain*
> *Pazuzu plague gods,*
> *Shaped from the blood of Kingu.*[13]

Satanic hype and death metal music notwithstanding, not everyone sees the Simon book as being pivotal to Satanic metaphysics. In *Out of the Darkness: Exploring Satanism and Ritual Abuse*, David K. Sakheim and Susan E. Devine address the issue of "source amnesia" in Satanic cult survivors (SCSs) and what type of occult activity they report. They declare that the type of occult activity practiced by destructive Satanic cults "is not the *Necronomicon* (Schlangekraft 1977),"[14] and refute many other sources as well. What was reported by the survivors was "a variously integrated mix" of ceremonial magick, Qaballistic practices, sex magick, an odd form of Theosophy, and brain-washing techniques, all emphasizing "blood and death rites" in their worship and organized for secrecy.

Those who believe that LaVey and his Church of Satan were involved with the Simon *Necronomicon*, and those Satanists who revere the Simon book—particularly those affiliated with the Church of Satan—have probably never read an editorial written by Simon for the first issue of *Earth Religion News* entitled "To Hell in a Breadbasket," in which he dismisses LaVey's brand of Satanism as nothing but a sexist, racist, and misguided attempt to make money. In this article, Simon mentions that a Satanist publication told its readers that the Warlock Shop in Brooklyn was a gathering place for "white" practitioners, and therefore not a proper place to buy goods. If this is true, Herman Slater must have considered this discouragement of others from spending money in his store the gravest insult imaginable.

On the Internet, the *alt.satanism* FAQ states that critics of Satanism believe that the *Necronomicon* is "an authoritative guide to Satanic practices."[15] The author says that "few Satanists take the book seriously in any way, and none follow it to the letter. This and other things lead non-Satanists to see what simply is not there."[16] Although the FAQ may not reflect the views of all Satanists, it is probably the best source of a "Satanic view" on the Simon *Necronomicon*.

High School Metaphysics

Evidently, the *Necronomicon* is less popular with most serious Satanists and occultists than it is with young "dabblers," and the reasons for this are probably more financial than metaphysical. An impoverished high school student interested in practicing magick could ill afford a fifty-dollar hardbound copy of *The Complete Rituals of the Golden Dawn* by Israel Regardie. A mass-market paperback like the Avon editions of the Simon *Necronomicon* for $5.99 is much more accessible and has a tantalizingly sinister feel that many other occult books lack.

For the adolescent, would-be cult leader with a convincing line of occult babble, the Simon opus represents a ready-made cult book around which to build a nucleus of followers. I have heard of incidents of this type as far apart as California, New York, and Oklahoma, and personally encountered three situations of this type—one in Pennsylvania and two in Tennessee.

In the instance in which I became most involved, the male cult leader and his female victims were all students at the same high school. The leader began his seduction of the intended prey with "intellectual" discussions about ancient Sumerian civilization, which would inevitably lead to a discussion about whether or not there is a "real Necronomicon." At this point, he would convince his intended victim to read the Simon book and promise to teach her astral projection to enable her to practice the Gate Walking initiation—under his supervision, of course. By this time, he had usually managed to have sex with his victim and had already begun a subtle campaign of mind control over her. While he may or may not actually have practiced the Gate Walking rituals himself, he was probably anxious to use his disciples for guinea pigs to find out more about how the system worked. He did, however, possess enough real skill at magick and astral projection to harass his victim psychically and astrally if she proved disobedient.

One of his victims described the astral attacks her erstwhile guru launched against her. After her attempts to distance herself from the cult leader, he appeared in her room in astral form, telling her that he had been watching her for a long time and said, "You are mine and you are going with me!" She described his visible astral body as a "black on black" shadowy form issuing an audible voice. On one occasion, his astral body appeared in her room and attempted to pull her out of her physical body against her will. She described herself as "calling on every God and Goddess I could think of to keep from being pulled out of my body."

Perhaps the most terrifying of all were the nightmare "sendings," or dream attacks, of a decidedly demonic nature. In one of these, the cult leader attacked her in the form of a rotting corpse. In another dream, a huge, black, humanoid creature that she described as being "like a giant spider" pursued her. She described the creature as "absolutely hideous," having four eyes, multiple limbs, skin of a "charred black" color, and arachnid characteristics. I couldn't help but notice the similarity between the creature she described and the "Scorpion-Man," a creature that appears in Mesopotamian mythology, as well as in the Simon book. Fans of the Simonian Mythos may also notice a similarity between the thing that attacked the girl and the female demon Xastur. Though no description of Xastur's appearance is given in the *Necronomicon*, she is believed by nightside magicians to be a spider demon or Goddess, though their description of her may be derived from the spider Goddess Lolth from the *Dungeons and Dragons* role-playing game.[17] On page 194 of the Simon book, Xastur is described as "a foul demoness who slays Men in their Sleep." Apparently she also attacks sleeping teenage girls.

This period of astral attack was also accompanied by an unbelievable "run of bad luck": death in her family, a traffic accident that totaled her car, and the frustration of several important plans. These material disasters, combined with the incidence of attempted "astral rape," convinced her that she was under psychic attack. Though she was hundreds of miles away, I did what I could. When she asked for my help, I gave her instructions for casting warded, sacred space using the Lesser Banishing Ritual of the Pentagram, as well as information about cults and mind-control techniques, and certain background material about the Simon book. Then my allies and I moved to magickally neutralize her tormentor, an effort that was quickly successful.

Contrary to stereotype, the cult leader was not an obviously domineering, charismatic firebrand. More Alan Alda than Aleister Crowley, the unique style of this Necro-nerd was to pose as being very vulnerable and convince his victim that he and she were "soul mates" destined to practice magick together. In the opening moves of the gambit, he even allowed her to believe that she was in control of the "relationship," until such time as she disagreed with him or wanted out, whereupon she discovered who was boss. His victims, ironically, were strong-willed, highly intelligent young women who imagined that no one could ever take control of their lives. Their unshakable belief in their own invulnerability was exactly what made them so vulnerable.

One of the most common misconceptions about destructive cults is that they are always huge organizations like the Unification Church, with thousands of enslaved members. As Steven Hassan reveals in his excellent book *Combating Cult Mind Control*,[18] a destructive cult may consist of only two people: the cult leader and his follower/victim. Hassan has noted abusive marriages that exhibited all the mind-control techniques, fear, and deception of a giant cult like the Moonies. Small size does not make a destructive cult any less destructive. Nor is a high I.Q. any defense against cult mind control, as evidenced by the fact that many cults—both large and small— recruit their members from college campuses and the honor rolls of upper-class high schools.

The objectives of the leader of a dabbler cult may be as simple as seducing every female member of his group, or as complex as long-term extortion. One frequent poster on the Usenet groups told us of his encounter with a member of a *Necronomicon* cult whose leader apparently had a hardback version of the Simon book that he would not allow his disciples to read (presumably to keep them from seeing the copyright date). The cult member claimed that his group used the book as their "bible," and was only "deprogrammed" from his beliefs when a friend quoted passages to him from the Simon *Necronomicon* that he recognized as coming from the cult leader's supposedly secret book. When the cultist finally left the group, the cult leader reportedly accused the deprogramming friend of having "killed one of his children." Reportedly, the parting comment of the disillusioned former cult member was "Man, when I think of all the money I've given them over the years."[19]

For whatever reason, the Simon *Necronomicon* seems to have become the book of the small cult. Certainly, not everyone who uses the Simon book exploits it in this way, but as an inexpensive, underground "bible," the poor man's *Keys of Solomon*, it must be irresistible to the would-be lodge leader intent on surrounding himself with slavish devotees. For decades now, Christian extremists and conspiracy theorists have been chasing the mirage of a vast, global, Satanic conspiracy that is supposedly responsible for child molestations, cattle mutilations, and human sacrifices on a grand scale. This underground cabal is even said to keep harems of "breeders"— female sex slaves whose purpose is to give birth to babies who can not be traced, and so can more conveniently be used for sacrifice. No such organization seems to exist, however, outside of Bob Larson's nightmares and Mike Warnke's sexual fantasies. The best evidence indicates that almost all crime and destructive cult activity related to the *Necronomicon* (or any other kind of occultism) is perpetrated by small dabbler cults, not by a huge, underground conspiracy of Satanists, nor by normative groups in the magick-using community. Usually, these dabbler groups consist of teenagers who got their ideas about magick from the Simon book, Anton LaVey, and bad horror movies. All these years, the conspiracy theorists and Christian fundamentalists who rant about "occult crime" thought they were battling Fu Manchu, the Illuminati, and the Trilateral Commission. In reality, they were up against Beavis and Butthead.

The Vampire Clan: White Trash and Black Magick

Among these odd folk, who correspond exactly to the decadent element of "white trash" in the
South, law and morals are non-existent.

—HOWARD PHILLIPS LOVECRAFT, "BEYOND THE WALL OF SLEEP"

Undoubtedly, the most famous of all *Necronomicon*-using dabblers is Roderick Ferrell, seventeen-year-old convicted murderer and leader of a teen vampire cult. Ferrell's notoriety began after he bludgeoned Richard and Naoma Wendorf to death with a crowbar in their Eustis, Florida, home on 25 November 1996. The Wendorfs were the parents of Ferrell's sixteen-year-old girlfriend, Heather Wendorf. According to investigators, Heather Wendorf had been "crossed over"—or initiated—into Ferrell's vampire cult earlier that same day in a ritual conducted by Ferrell at a local cemetery, in which he and Heather drank each other's blood. After murdering Heather's parents, Ferrell stole the Wendorf's car, a blue 1993 Ford Explorer, and headed for Louisiana with Heather Wendorf and three other cult members in tow: Howard Scott Anderson, sixteen, of Mayfield, KY, Sarah "Shea" Remmington, sixteen, of Murray, KY, and Dana L. Cooper, nineteen, of Murray, KY. All five cultists were arrested in Baton Rouge as they attempted to check into a motel. All were extradited to Florida to stand trial for murder.

A police search of the Wendorf's stolen Explorer yielded hundreds of items, including a blood-stained bed sheet and bloody paper towels, a black-handled hunting knife, dismembered dolls, two teddy bears (one wrapped in a pearl necklace), a copy of the Anne Rice novel *Queen of the Damned*, and a dog-eared copy of the Simon *Necronomicon*. Investigators discovered that, in Murray, KY, where Ferrell stayed with his mother, he was one of the leaders of a thirty-member vampire cult. The cult was implicated in the brutal mutilation and killing of several puppies in an animal shelter in Murray around mid-October. (According to Stan Scott, Sheriff of Calloway County, KY, they tore the legs off one dog and trampled another to death.) The cult regularly met at an abandoned, graffiti-covered building they called the Vampire Hotel, which was hidden in the woods. According to Sergeant Mike Jump of the Murray police, cult members regularly conducted their rituals at the "Hotel," where they sacrificed small animals and inflicted cuts on each other's arms to drink the blood. The ritual activities of the vampire group were also reputed to include drug use, group sex, sexual torture, and supposed communication with spirits. Though police referred to the teen cult as the Vampire Clan, certain waggish reporters christened them "the hemogoblins."

Investigations into the background of Roderick Ferrell revealed that his interest in the *Necronomicon* was far more than casual. His possession of the book at the time of his arrest was no coincidence. According to seventeen-year-old Audrey Presson, a friend of Ferrell's at Eustis High School, Ferrell often discussed the *Necronomicon* with her over the telephone. Presson testified under cross-examination by defense attorney Candice Hawthorne that she and Ferrell had shared an interest in the book, although he took it more seriously than she did. Psychologist Wade Myers III testified that Ferrell "felt he was able to get powers from this book."[20]

It would be difficult to say with any precision what effect, if any, the Simon *Necronomicon* had on the practices of the rest of Ferrell's Vampire Clan. Heather Wendorf reported "talking to spirits" during blood-drinking rituals, definitely indicating some sort of magickal evocation (if not hallucination). She also reportedly claimed to have been a demon in a previous incarnation, indicating some type of invocation or possession, whether real or imagined. The Simon book may also have influenced the clan's sacrifice of animals. "The Conjuration of the Watcher" definitely demands that some type of sacrifice be made to the Watcher on a regular basis.[21] On page 207, the "Mad Arab" advises his readers to make their sacrifices to demons neither too large nor too small for fear that the evil spirits either will not answer when summoned or else grow too powerful. He follows this with an anecdote about a priest from Jerusalem who worshiped the "Old Ones" and sacrificed sheep to demons. Human sacrifice also seems to be encouraged by the Simon *Necronomicon,* as seen on page 19: "strive ever onward . . . though it mean thine own death; for such a death is as a sacrifice to the Gods, and pleasing." This passage may also relate to suicide, which Ferrell told police he had attempted unsuccessfully. Page 210 of the Simon book refers to a "Cult of the Dragon" who "keep not to our laws, but murder quickly . . . their blood covers them." The most vampiric reference to human sacrifice in the Simon *Necronomicon,* however, is a passage found on pages 160 and 161 of "The MAGAN Text," which instructs the reader in the making of a magickal sword for summoning Tiamat. The instructions require the small matter of eleven homicides:

> And the Blood of the weakest here
> Is libation unto TIAMAT
> Queen of the Ghouls
> Wreaker of pain
> And to invoke her
> The Red Water of Life
> Need be spilt on a stone
> The stone struck with a sword
> That hath slain eleven men
> Sacrifices to HUBUR
> So that the strike ringeth out
> And call TIAMAT from Her slumber

All of this may have had an influence on Ferrell's own obsession with human sacrifice. Ferrell's ex-girlfriend, April Doeden, nineteen, told reporter Kate Halfpenny that he had talked about sacrificing her baby boy. "He wanted to give his father [Satan] the ultimate gift."[22] John Goodman, a member of the Vampire Clan, said Ferrell "had become possessed with opening the Gates to Hell, which meant he would have to kill a large number of people in order to consume their souls. By doing this, Ferrell believed he would gain super powers."[23] Ferrell often called himself Vassago, a name he must have taken from the Satan-worshiping murderer who opens the Gates of Hell in the 1995 movie *Hideaway.*[24] The letter "V" surrounded by circular marks was burned into Richard Wendorf's body—presumably the "V" stood either for "vampire" or for "Vassago." We do not know if Ferrell considered his killing of the Wendorfs to be "sacrificial" as such, but we do know that, during his taped confession, he told police the act of killing them made him feel like "a god." Like film villain Vassago, Ferrell believed he could open the Gates of Hell, and that he received supernatural power from killing people. We do not know for certain how instrumental Ferrell may have thought the Simon *Necronomicon* would be in his quest to open the Gates of Hell. We do know, however, of Ferrell's obsession with the book. And we know that the central theme of the Simon book is the *opening of gates*. As discussed earlier, I believe the Gates presented in the *Necronomicon* may open only into hellish Qlippothic realms. Perhaps Roderick Ferrell was only interested in opening Simon's version of the Gate of Ganzir, a place that would correspond to anyone's idea of Hell.

Regarding the homicidal passage from "The MAGAN Text" quoted above, I have not yet heard of anyone murdering eleven people to make the "Sword of HUBUR" in order to summon Tiamat. I hope I never do—but nothing really surprises me anymore. Perhaps the crowbar he used for the two killings was Ferrell's substitute for a sword. If so, he was stopped before he could kill nine more victims to "consecrate" it, and strike it against a blood-covered stone to raise Tiamat, "Queen of the Ghouls" and "Wreaker of Pain."

Attorneys for the defense attempted unsuccessfully to use Ferrell's involvement with Satanic occultism and the *Necronomicon* as a defense strategy. Also cited as mitigating circumstances were Ferrell's medical history, his history as a victim of child abuse, and even his mother's affair with a fourteen-year-old boy. As of the time of this writing, Roderick Ferrell has been sentenced to death for first-degree murder. Heather Wendorf was freed by a grand jury. The other cult members are being tried as principals to murder.

The *Necronomicon* Squat: The Horror at Santa Monica

Circles and pentagrams loomed on every hand, and told indubitably of the strange beliefs and aspirations of those who dwelt so squalidly here. In the cellar, however, the strangest thing was found . . .

—HOWARD PHILLIPS LOVECRAFT, "THE HORROR AT RED HOOK"

Perhaps the next most publicized dabbler-cult crime involving the Simon *Necronomicon* is the murder of Shevawn Geoghegan. Shevawn was a bright fourteen-year-old girl who had become enamored of life on the streets, and among the "squats"— abandoned buildings inhabited by transients, or "squatters"—in Santa Monica, California. One reporter described the environment of the squats as "a deadly mix of teenagers, runaways, and criminal drifters."[25] Shevawn had run away from home numerous times and had been in rehab. By 1998, however, she seemed ready to give up this rebellious but dangerous life.

The last day Shevawn's parents ever saw her alive was 24 February 1998. On that day, Shevawn went to the squat at 1525 Euclid Street, where she spent much of her time. The Euclid squat (which was, ironically, an abandoned mental health facility) was a dark, labyrinthine building of Spanish-style architecture and creepy atmosphere that seemed to lend itself perfectly to sinister doings. The squat at Euclid Street was lorded over by Glen Mason, a twenty-three-year-old drifter who compared himself to Charles Manson. Shevawn had an on-again-off-again relationship with Mason.

The two had sex, after which they engaged in some rough play. Aided by Dennis Ronald Scott and Elizabeth Ann Mangham, Mason tied and gagged Shevawn, after which he strangled her and left her body in a sleeping bag in the squat's basement, surrounded by Satanic graffiti, inverted pentagrams drawn in blood, and corpses of sacrificed animals. It was here that the police found her body two days later.

What was the motivation for this bizarre crime? A number of factors seem to have contributed to it—Mason's troubled childhood, his need for control over the under-age girls who lived in his squat, and concocted allegations that Shevawn was a "snitch." Yet Mason had another reason for the crazed killing. He believed himself to be a priest of Satan who could communicate with him through a pentagram of blood. One of his friends, Jason "Mad Dog" Yoakum, said that "[Mason] wanted a soul. If he could get a soul, it would be a brownie point for Satan and make him stronger." At other times, Mason would claim to be immortal and immune to bullets. He was interested in literature on black magick, including *The Satanic Bible* and the Simon *Necronomicon*.

How much did the Simon book have to do with Mason's bizarre belief system? It is difficult to say from the information that has been given to the public. He did find it important enough that he gave a copy of the *Necronomicon* to Shevawn and her friend, Tanya Zerkov. Tanya later said of the book, "We were scared at first, but we read three pages of it and started laughing." Yet the book seems to have been much more than a joke to Mason. According to another of Shevawn's friends, Kim Calder, "He decided that there really was this race of ancient spirits he was going to summon from below. He was a Satanist. He really believed it." Mason's attorney argued in vain that Shevawn's murder was not sacrificial, since no blood was spilled. He had apparently never heard of the Thugee cult of India, who sacrificed their victims to Kali by strangulation.

The morbid involvement of the Simon *Necronomicon* in these murders starkly belies Peter Levenda's statement, "I have heard of no fatalities from the use of the book; no persons going insane; no dramatic self-immolations."[26] Whether Roderick Ferrell and Glen Mason's involvement with the Simon book was a cause or an effect of their murderous insanity is hard to say. Perhaps it was both. Much of this is admittedly speculation on my part, but it is at least highly educated speculation based on information from reliable news services, on my experience as a magician and as a religious counselor, and on years of study of magickal texts, including, of course, the *Necronomicon*. In my opinion, the Simon book lends itself to this unique form of abuse because it is the only major occult work of the latter 20th century that speaks approvingly of sacrifice—possibly even human sacrifice and/or suicide. While I realize that we live in an age of "blame shifting," in which nobody wants to take responsibility for anything, I cannot think of anyone to blame for this other than the authors of the book.

As I mentioned earlier, the grimoire *The Sixth and Seventh Books of Moses* was implicated in fifty-six lawsuits in Germany from 1945 through the 1950s. Bear in mind that this was in postwar Europe rather than present day America, where this kind of litigation is common. As far as I know, none of the families of the victims of crimes related to the Simon book have ever sued the writers or publishers for damages. Frankly, this surprises me. What doesn't surprise me is the deliberate anonymity of those who wrote and published the book. No wonder they hid behind pseudonyms and dummy corporations like "Simon" and "Schlangekraft Inc."!

"Dark Visions of Dead Fish": The *Necronomicon* and the Occult Community

So who, among legitimate members of the "occult community," uses the Simon *Necronomicon*, and why? Some Satanists, like the Order of the Absu, seem to constitute a following for the book, yet the more reputable, or at least the better publicized, elements of Satanism seem to repudiate the book as the domain of the "dabbler." Some who are attracted to the dark aura of Satanism may also be attracted to the dark aura of the Simon book, but these individuals are clearly not in the majority.

Some chaos magicians who have adopted elements of Lovecraft's Cthulhu Mythos have also shown an affinity for the Simon *Necronomicon*. However, their numbers in the overall chaos community seem to be few. Some chaos practitioners may be attracted to the Simon book purely because of its shifty reputation; after all, "Nothing is true, everything is permitted." I frankly find it difficult to see why advocates of the postmodern make-it-up-as-you-go-along system of chaos magick would wax enthusiastic over a forgery that is a throwback to the old follow-instructions-to-the-letter grimoires of the Renaissance and the Middle Ages. Some chaosists use Lovecraftian elements in their magick with no evidence of influence from the Simon book. Peter J. Carrol, for example, puts an invocation to Azathoth in his book *Liber Kaos*.[27] Phil Hine in particular has evolved a system of Lovecraftian magick, as expounded in his books *Prime Chaos* and *Pseudonomicon*, with no reliance on modern *Necronomicon* pastiches, which, as we have seen earlier, he treats with utter indifference, if not contempt. While all *Necronomicon* magick may be Lovecraftian, all Lovecraftian magick is not necessarily related to the *Necronomicon*. Chaos magicians as a group seem to be more influenced by the fiction of fantasy writer Michael Moorcock than by that of H. P. Lovecraft.

Certain unclassifiable ceremonial magicians with a highly eclectic bias, such as the redoubtable Az0th, have experimented with the Simon book out of curiosity, but hardly seem devoted to it. As mentioned earlier in a quote from Peter Levenda, Kenneth Grant is rumored to have experimented with the Simon *Necronomicon*, but here he seems to be the exception rather than the rule. If the Simon book has any utility in magickal practice, I would say that it definitely belongs in the hands of trained and experienced occultists, like those of Grant's Typhonian OTO, who presumably know what they are doing. The ceremonialist, whether a Thelemite or otherwise, has a lifetime's work cut out for her or him in more reliable and proven systems such as Enochian, planetary magick, Westernized Tantra, Golden

Dawn–related Qaballah, or any combination of these. Why waste time and energy on a possibly useless or dangerous work like the Simon *Necronomicon*?

Wiccans as a group seem to detest the Simon *Necronomicon*. Opinions on the book vary. Some consider it useless rubbish, while others believe it to be quite dangerous—mainly to its users. Image-conscious Wiccans seek to divorce themselves from any taint of Satanism or dark magick. They see the Simon book as a dark, negative grimoire at odds with their role as servants of the Light. Doreen Valiente, who, along with Gerald Gardner, was the cofounder of Wicca, once wrote an article entitled "*Necronomicon*—the Ultimate Grimoire?" that appeared in the April 1982 issue of the metaphysical magazine *Prediction*. In the article, Valiente begins with a cautionary tale about an occultist she once knew who forged and sold documents that he claimed were authentic fragments of the "nefarious and abhorred" *Necronomicon* whenever he was low on cash. She goes on to discuss the origins of the imaginary book in Lovecraft's mind, and speculates that he read Madame Blavatsky's *The Secret Doctrine*. Naturally, she mentions his acquaintance with Murray's *The Witch-Cult in Western Europe*, and guesses at some of the possible occult lore he may have tapped. She mentions Kenneth Grant's ideas at some length, and even ties the Cthulhu Mythos in with Temple's *The Sirius Mystery*. She compares the *Necronomicon* to the *terma* tradition of Tibetan Buddhism (an idea she originated long before Internet mage Tyagi Nagasiva came up with the same concept). Oddly, she cites the megaliths of New England, mentioned in Lovecraft's stories as "supportive evidence."[28] Valiente's emphasis is on the mystery surrounding the book, and the possible over lap of Lovecraft's ideas with real occult theories. Even so, Valiente doesn't seem to take any of this stuff too seriously. She mentions the Giger, de Camp, and Hay books, pointing out some of the flaws in the Hay *Nerconomicon*. But she never mentions the Simon book, which she apparently hadn't read at that point. If she had, she would undoubtedly have roasted it as well. I cannot call Valiente's article a "standard Wiccan response" to the *Necronomicon* question for two reasons: Her article doesn't address the Simon hoax (of which she must have been unaware), and, as far as I know, she is the only notable Wiccan who has ever written an article of this kind. Most present-day Wiccans won't give the *Necronomicon* (Simon's or anyone else's) the time of day.

Other members of the Neopagan community also seem to give the Simon book short shrift. Many of them see themselves as followers of the Light just as much as Christians do, and have no use for a "dark" grimoire. I have heard that a few (apparently very few) Pagans who practice Mesopotamian magick and religion have tried to use the Simon book. One small organization of this type, based in Texas, seems to have passed out of existence. The only notable Neopagan even remotely associated with the *Necronomicon* is the highly respected author Isaac Bonewits, who was (falsely) rumored to have co-authored part of the Simon *Necronomicon* hoax with science fiction writer Marion Zimmer Bradley. The only writing Bonewits has done relative to Bradley is as a research consultant for some of her fiction, and the rumor grew out of a discussion held in response to the Simon book after its publication. Bonewits assured me that, though he occasionally enjoys "throwing Cthulian jokes into overly serious discussions," and has written some Lovecraftian folksongs (!), he does not take those "Dark Visions of Dead Fish" seriously: "I leave that to the Satanists and their groupies."[29]

New Agers seem to ignore the Simon *Necronomicon* completely, not wanting to associate themselves with something so dark and strange. Yet the impartial desire of the New Agers to accept everything and reject nothing makes it unlikely that any New Age author will ever write a scathing denunciation of the book, any more than he or she will write a glowing recommendation of it. The consistent tendency of the New Age is to deny that any such issues exist. As Richard Blow points out in *The New Republic*, New Agers do not tackle difficult issues, they hug them.

All of this raises the obvious question of why I, a Neopagan with a background in ceremonial magick, Tantrism, and the New Age, believe the Simon *Necronomicon* hoax to be such a critical issue. The answer can be found in the same desires I share with the rest of the overlapping Pagan and occult communities. Most Neopagans, whether Wiccan, Druid, Asatru, Neotantric, or whatever, want to see their religions treated with more respect by law enforcement, government, and the followers of mainstream faiths in the greater community. Most occultists want to see the art and science of magick accorded more respect by modern scientists, philosophers, and theologians. Many anthropologists, parapsychologists, and historians want to see the study of magick and its history given more serious attention by academia. None of these happy developments are likely to occur until we in the magick-using community take responsibility for cleaning up the garbage in our own backyards.

Until now, most of us have used what I call the "Ostrich Solution" when confronted by a problem like the *Necronomicon* hoax—we hide our heads in the sand and hope the problem will go away. But the problem hasn't gone away; it has just gotten worse. By not openly addressing the issue of the *Necronomicon* hoax and its association with occult crime and destructive cult activity, we have left the field open for religious fundamentalists to use it as fodder for anti-Pagan and anti-occult propaganda. Worse yet, because silence is interpreted as consent, we have given the impression that we don't care about this mess, or that we approve of it.

One of the real issues with the Simon book is truth in advertising. You can't sell motor oil with a label that says, "Baked Beans"—the FDA would hang you out to dry. Nor should you be allowed to fraudulently market a spellbook you wrote last week as an ancient Sumerian text. Perhaps what we need is a sort of consumer protectionism relative to occult literature. Not that I am volunteering to become a sort of metaphysical Ralph Nader. Nor am I advocating censorship, or the kind of rabid denunciation that one sees from televangelists. Nor do I wish to institute a Pagan version of the Inquisition or the Vatican to "excommunicate" those whose beliefs disagree with mine. What I advocate instead is the deconstruction of unwarranted claims to occult authority. Admittedly, careful deconstruction of an objectionable work is unattractive, because it requires careful work and scholarship. Any moron can throw a book on a bonfire—and many morons do.

Some may object that historical accuracy should not matter within the occult community—after all, it's what works for you that counts. This is to ignore the lessons of human nature. My experience among occultists shows that many people take these phony histories at face value, and become angry when they find out it's all a sham. Some dismiss these people, saying that they don't have the proper level of "spiritual enlightenment" to understand the "real message," but this is dissembling. Any teachers or groups worth their salt should be able to maintain themselves without pretending to have secret teachings handed down from the high priests of Atlantis, or lineages dating back hundreds of years. Since many groups charge in one way or another for their teachings, I think these false antiquity claims amount to a marketing scam, and should be dealt with in the same way as *Consumer Reports* warns customers of shoddy products and services.

The Last Temptation of Cthulhu: *Necronomicon* Fundamentalism

Devotees of the Simon *Necronomicon* often display the kind of fanatical zeal more often associated with Islamic extremists and fundamentalist Christians than occultists. Daniel and I have sometimes been accused of not being "open minded" about the *Necronomicon* question. Our experience has shown, however, that the followers of "Simontology" rarely take a live-and-let-live attitude themselves. Their fanaticism often includes a humorless, hostile intolerance of "heretics" who don't subscribe to their "Old Time Religion." One poster to the guestbook of our website *www.necfiles.org* wrote, "Ishtar damn you" and belligerently proclaimed that the Simon *Necronomicon* was real. (Ironically, Inanna/Ishtar is my personal Goddess, so I leave it to the reader to decide which of us She would be more likely to damn.) My favorite of the handful of "death threats" left on the guestbook is from a character who calls himself Realmwatcher:

> You are full of crap writing what you did about the simon necronomicon. If you do not revoke[sic] what you have falsely stated about it, I will be forced to send the creatures it can conjure after you and your "friend." Then see if it is just a mish-mash of different beliefs.[30]

Another prizewinner came from some creature called "Necrolord" in Finland, who wrote, "YOU F*CKERS! YOU SHALL DIE! No-one[sic] claims the true lord to be myth and survives his hideous curses! I am a true obeyer and you shall die soon!" One character e-mailed me threatening to root my computer, crack all my files, and ruin my life if I didn't reveal the secret of "the grass olieribos" to him. And then there was the evangelical comment made by one "Tia," who stated, "The book has power . . . there is nothing you or anyone else can say to make it anything else." What can you say to a "true believer" whose mind is already made up, and who doesn't want to be confused by facts? (There is no God but Kutulu, and Simon is his Prophet!) After a while, Daniel and I began to feel like Salman Rushdie after he wrote *The Satanic Verses*, and Islamic extremists put a price on his head.

I will not list the various flavors of magickal attack Daniel and I experienced while working on this project—I will deal with that in the upcoming chapter, "The *Necronomicon* and Psychic Attack." Here it will suffice to discuss the mundane lengths to which some defenders of the Simon book were willing to go in order to stall this project. About two years ago, for example, the server that housed our original website mysteriously crashed for reasons that no one has quite been able to explain. Was it the neglect of the Web host, was it hacked, or was it directly or indirectly magickally attacked? Perhaps it was some combination of all the above. But the real *coup de main* came when I was in the crucial stages of preparing this manuscript for publication in its second edition, and someone sent a computer virus to me in an attachment to an e-mail titillatingly entitled "NECMAGIC." Specifically, this was a SirCam virus designed to lock up all executable files in my computer's registry, and ultimately to wipe out my computer's hard drive. (Nasty!) Timely tech support from my friend Matt Coleman, of Javanco, and the use of the state-of-the-art virus application InnoculateIT, quickly averted the disaster. This same tactic was tried, not once, but a couple of times.

In the Cthulhu Mythos fiction of the Lovecraft Circle, the *Necronomicon* never quite made it to the level of a "sacred text." While Abdul Alhazred was called a "mad poet," he was never called a *prophet*. Lone wizards like Joseph Curwen and Wilbur Whateley consulted the book for its magickal instructions, but don't seem to have accorded it any actual reverence. Even the primitive and degenerate humans who ignorantly worshiped the Cthulhu Mythos monsters as "Gods" don't seem to have read the *Necronomicon* as a "scripture"—if they could read at all.

Why, then, do many real-life Necro-nerds canonize the *Necronomicon* as if it were "The Gospel According to Saint Simon"? (What's next? Will they start placing Gideon *Necronomicon*s in hotel rooms?) It is tempting to dismiss these "Necro-worshipers" as being "a few bricks shy of having a load," but I believe the reasons for their behavior may be more complex. Some of these "Simontologists" may be convinced of Simon's alibi that his book offers a defense system against the "Ancient Ones" (assuming the Ancient Ones actually exist). Other "true believers" may be sincere Pagans with a desire to connect with the ancient Mesopotamian magickal current, and misguidedly believe the Simon book is their key to real Sumerian magick. A few Typhonian Thelemites may believe that the Simon book represents the best expression of Kenneth Grant's connection between Crowley and Lovecraft. Some Satanists who, like the Order of the Absu, have adopted the *Necronomicon* as their "scripture," may resent any attempt by "heretics" to discredit it. Others may have more cynical reasons for protecting the Necro-hoax: Cult leaders who use the Simon *Necronomicon* as the nucleus of their groups won't take kindly to anyone who debunks the "sacred text" that enables them to squeeze money, sex, and power out of their followers.

As a Neopagan, I regard religious pluralism (the belief that any one religion is about as good as any other) to be the best stance. Indeed, the maxim that most Pagans and magick-users have inherited from the New Age is, "All paths are valid." While I generally accept this guideline, I have noticed that some things that appear to be "paths" are actually deadfall traps with sharp spikes at the bottom. Even so, I support the right of any person to follow their chosen path—as long as they don't try to force me to join them on that path at gunpoint!

Conclusion, But Probably Not the End

At this point, we have traced Lovecraftian/*Necronomicon* occultism from its origins in Lovecraft's fiction and the speculative writings of Kenneth Grant, through the rise of the *Necronomicon* forgeries of the past three decades, down to the squalid cults of the small-time "dabblers." I wish to make it abundantly clear that I do not hold Mr. Kenneth Grant responsible for the various ways in which his ideas have been misused—including the spurious *Necronomicon*s. That would be like blaming Henry Ford for every traffic accident in American history. Nor do I classify his Typhonian OTO as a "destructive cult." Grant himself seems to be a generous source of encouragement to young occultists in pursuit of the Great Work, and is too much of a gentleman to engage in what he calls "religious or anti-religious hooliganism or other irresponsible or extreme forms of fanaticism."[31]

Critics of Lovecraftian occultism deride it as an outgrowth of pulp fiction—a mere product of "fandom" with no spiritual roots or validity. We may have forgotten that the word *fan* is only an abbreviation of the word *fanatic*, a term whose connotations of religious zealotry are well known. Tim Maroney has pointed out that "if Communism and other secular movements are in a sense 'religions,' then so is fandom."[32] It would seem that the borderline between "fans" and "fanatics," readers and believers, is often thinner than we imagined.

Nevertheless, most Lovecraft fans do not practice Lovecraftian magick. They simply enjoy Lovecraft's literature without using the Cthulhu Mythos as a template for a magickal paradigm. This is what makes the occasional occult crossover even more startling.

The persistence of the *Necronomicon* phenomenon and the stubborn belief of its adherents are less evidence of the persuasiveness of the *Necronomicon* forgeries than they are of humanity's perennial desire for belief. As C. G. Jung warned us, modern man is in search of a soul. Or, more precisely, he or she is in search of a belief with which to feed that soul. This universal hunger for belief is so compelling that, if it is not fed a nourishing diet, it will eat anything, even something poisonous. Modern science, art, and philosophy have conspired to destroy the underpinnings of traditional religious belief, replacing them instead with a kind of hungry agnostic/atheistic void. Modern physics has revealed that the subatomic particles that are supposed to be the building blocks of the universe are, in fact, elusive and unstable, appearing sometimes as particles and sometimes as waves, the atoms themselves composed mainly of void space. Even the comforting superstition of materialism is no longer a reliable belief, as science itself leans toward the ancient Vedic model of the material universe as an illusion. In an illusory universe, the nature of reality is up for grabs. The consensual reality of one given belief system is no better than another.

Some observers have commented that Lovecraft's fiction has a strong appeal for so-called troubled youth.[33] One reason for this could be Lovecraft's ability to distort conventional reality fantastically in his stories. "Troubled youth" have little stake in conventional reality, since it incorporates a socioeconomic ladder on which they occupy the lowest rung. As more and more readers have less and less stake in the consensual reality of traditional culture, the dystopian nihilism of an author like Lovecraft exerts a greater appeal. Only the horror of his work can hurt them enough to reach their media-desensitized feelings, only his cosmic pessimism rings true with their own disillusionment. Better to believe in a horrible something than in absolutely nothing.

Colin Low's belief is that all "great books"—from the Torah to the Koran—are frauds whose origins are legendary and whose authors are unknown, and that, in the *Necronomicon*, we have the opportunity to see the folkloric evolution of a "great book" in action.[34] The fact, however, is that more books on magick have been published in the past two decades than in the previous 2,000 years, and the odds are against any one grimoire emerging from under that avalanche of paper with the title of "great," particularly not any of the *Necronomicon* pastiches. Fake grimoires claiming to be authored by Solomon or Faust (or Abdul Alhazred) are as commonplace as madmen claiming to be Napoleon or the Antichrist. Since most of those forged magickal recipe books date from the Middle Ages, the Renaissance, or the Reformation, the only really exceptional thing about the Simon *Necronomicon* hoax is its recent date of origin.

Yet the desire for magickal solutions is now at an all-time high. In a postmodern world of electronic media and info-tainment, modern explorers of the occult search for magickal systems that have both an air of antiquity and application in day-to-day life. Both magickal reinterpretations of Lovecraft's fiction and latter-day treatments of his fictional *Necronomicon* seem to offer this. Only the individual can decide whether the promise is real or empty.

The *Necronomicon* and Psychic Attack —John Wisdom Gonce III 9

> *Do not expect the enemy not to attack. Instead, assure yourself that the enemy would not be successful in the event of an attack*
>
> .—SUN TZU, *THE ART OF WAR*
>
> *Let them curse it who curse the day, who are skillful to rouse Leviathan.*
>
> —A MISQUOTE OF JOB 3:8 BY SIMON
>
> *Thou brakest the heads of leviathan in pieces, and gavest him to be meat to the people inhabiting the wilderness.*
>
> —KING DAVID, PSALMS 74:14, THE KING JAMES BIBLE

As noted earlier in this work, the Simon *Necronomicon* has been increasingly linked to occurrences of black magickal or psychic attack. While many of those attempting to use the Simon book in this destructive manner are occult dabblers whom I would hardly classify as skilled adepts, this is not always the case. Even so-called dabblers can be remarkably talented, as in the case cited in the previous chapter. Since *Necronomicon* users seem to be prone to obsession and possession, the Necro-nerd himself may have no skill whatsoever, and the creature riding him may be the true source of the power and intent behind the attack. In magickal self-defense, as in most areas of life, it is wise never to underestimate anyone or anything.

First, let me issue a warning. Do not assume you are under magickal attack based on some isolated incident or misfortune. Just because somebody knocks over your coffee cup, do not assume that you are the victim of an occult conspiracy, or that some terrible cosmic force is working against you. Only when you notice misfortunes of an unaccountable nature, and patterned in a certain synchronicity, should you become suspicious. Even then, you should use the most reliable form of divination you have—tarot, the I Ching, runes, and so forth—to double-check your intuition. Remember that the best defense is to take precautions and set up strong magickal wards around your home and workspace. Don't become complacent or lazy where this is concerned—as I often have in the past. When all else fails, *laugh!* The forces of evil can stand almost anything except being the butt of a joke that leads to a good, hearty gale of belly laughter.

Having said all that, let's discuss the types of astral creatures, alias "Watchers," usually used in these sorts of attacks by devotees of the Simon *Necronomicon*. These will generally fall into one of three categories:

- Thought-forms or egregores created entirely from the imagination of the magician;

- Ensouled elementals—thought-forms or egregores into which the creating magician has grafted part of his own soul or personality, or has ensouled by the invocation of elemental essence—sometimes referred to as artificial elementals; and

- Opportunistic Qlippothic entities (demons) that will happily take on any guise for a chance to be evoked into the earthly plane where they can hunt human prey.

Easiest to deal with will be the basic thought-form or egregore. Always remember that these simple thought-forms are a product of their creator's imagination, and have no independent existence or identity of their own. Usually, these entities will be repelled by a basic protective circle or ward (such as that cast by performing the Lesser Banishing Ritual of the Pentagram). A simple visualization process can destroy them outright. The defender has only to visualize the attacking thought-form exploding into fragments like a shattered glass figurine, or bursting into flames and being reduced to ashes. As Dion Fortune has said, "That which is thought into existence by the imagination can be thought out of existence by the imagination."[1]

If you have attempted to destroy what seemed to be a simple thought-form by the visualization technique above and find that it successfully resists your counterattack, you are probably dealing with an ensouled elemental. If this artificial elemental is ensouled with an elemental essence (earth, air, fire, or water), it can be banished by use of the upright banishing pentagram. If the ensouled elemental is imbued with the personality of its maker, a different technique may be required. Dion Fortune, in her book *Psychic Self-Defense*, recommends an absorption method[2] that I consider intolerably dangerous even for a highly accomplished and experienced practitioner. Instead, I advise the practitioner to evoke a powerful Goddess or God form for defense or counterattack. A sufficiently powerful divine entity can annihilate an ensouled elemental with the added bonus of the devastating effect such destruction may have on the attacker, who will feel whatever part of himself he put into the elemental being destroyed.[3] Any benign yet militant Goddess or God with whom you feel sufficient rapport will be appropriate; Christians may call upon Jesus or the Archangel Michael, Norse Pagans upon Odin or Tyr, Wiccans upon Morrigu or Lugh, Hindus or Tantrics upon Durga, and so forth. Use your imagination, as well as your faith! If you have no particular belief, you may need to experiment within the bounds of time limitations caused by the emergency of psychic attack.

Folktales of cantankerous demons irate at being summoned by black magicians are just a load of codswallop.

The classic image of an evil magician evoking a demon. Notice the book face-down inside the circle. From a 19th-century French illustration for the Decadent movement novel *La-Bas* (*Down There*) by J. K. Huysmans.

The demons attacked the magicians because it was fun, not because they were angry. Qlippothic entities like nothing better than to be evoked into the earthly plane where they hope to run amok and cause as much suffering as possible. Denizens of the Qlippoth are willing to adopt the guises of any Lovecraftian critters that suit their natures. (He wants Cthulhu? I'll give him Cthulhu!) Stupid, gullible, or unethical practitioners will sometimes accidentally evoke these Qlippothic entities even when they think they are only creating a thought-form. (He wants a shoggoth? We'll give him a shoggoth!) Interestingly, the Cthuloid disguises forced on some Qlippothic entities by their naive summoners may actually hamper their activities. Lovecraft's Great Old Ones were not actually "Gods" in the sense of divine spirit beings. Despite their ability to travel interdimensionally, the Cthulhu Mythos crowd were essentially a bunch of science fiction space monsters ignorantly worshiped as Gods by primitive or degenerate humans. You can exploit this materialistic Achilles' heel by evoking a militant Pagan God or Goddess (far older and more powerful than the Cthulhu Mythos) to defend you and/or counterattack the Qlippothic entity. The pseudo-Sumerian demons of the Simon book offer a more convenient role for these Qlippothic vermin to assume. (He wants a Watcher? I'll give him a Watcher!) But even the Watcher is no match for the ancient Gods. These demonic/Qlippothic entities may sometimes be easier to deal with than ensouled elementals, since they are almost always susceptible to banishment by use of the pentagram. They may, however, be more persistent, since they are independent creatures with minds of their own. You should be aware that magickal attack may affect not only you, but also members of your family and friends. Try to shield them as best you can! Hunting wolves will circle the herd waiting to pull down and devour its weakest members. Qlippothic spirits will do the same.

Earlier, I recounted the case history of a girl who was attacked in dreams by a hideous spiderlike creature. This arachnid entity could have been either an ensouled elemental or a preexisting demon. The girl tragically lost her grandfather to a sudden illness during this same period of magickal harassment from the cult leader who victimized her.[4] She told me that her grandfather's house was the setting of the dream in which she was attacked by the arachnid creature. Perhaps the house of the dead (murdered?) man was the site of its most recent victory.

Other cases of psychic attack related to the *Necronomicon* are reputed to involve psychic vampirism. In an article for *Fate* magazine, occultist and writer Michelle Belanger cites the case of a young man in the United Kingdom who opened himself to possession by an astral parasite through his use of "a false *Necronomicon*."[5] Belanger never names the version of the *Necronomicon* he used, but since she describes him as using it to "open a spirit gate," it is obviously the Simon book. According to Belanger, the astral parasite used its possessed victim to drain energy from his friends. Often, he would appear to them in dreams, pulling their auric energy into himself.

While Daniel and I were at work on this book, we received e-mail from Peter Levenda with the following ominous warning:

The book [Simon *Necronomicon*] protects itself, I think. It has a life of its own, now, and has not been out of print a day since that fateful December in 1977. What does it want? Where is it going from here? None of us—none of the original band—have the foggiest idea. We have projections; we have hunches. But we don't know.[6]

A life of its own indeed! I will not belabor the reader with an itemized list of the unaccountable depressions, vicious psychic attacks, Fortean overworked coincidences, and occurrences of bizarre—sometimes tragic—synchronicity that have entered my life since Daniel and I began this project. One good example here will suffice: Just as we closed the deal to republish this book in its new revised edition, I found myself grief-stricken over the loss of a close friend. The same week, the hard drive in my computer crashed just as I desperately needed it to make revisions. A friend of mine was on his way to install a new hard drive when both front tires on his car blew out simultaneously as he was driving through a clean, well-paved parking lot at the break-neck speed of 15 miles per hour! These material occurrences can hardly be dismissed as psychological delusions, though they might be written off by the lame and shopworn explanation of coincidence. However, at the same time these seemingly mundane disasters were occurring, a menacing, unclean, psychic entity was detected in the upper floor of my house. The thing had to be rigorously banished by the efforts of several people. What is really interesting here is the synchronicity of these incidents—they all occurred just as the book was about to go back into publication. I must point out that these occurrences have no similarity to the "plagues" that supposedly accompanied the "translation" of the Simon book. The Simon book itself has no power. Instead, these incidents were created by certain individuals with a stake in the Simon hoax and, perhaps, by something else. I believe that the Simon *Necronomicon* is defended by an egregore, probably created by a group of people, rather than by one lone magician. Perhaps further energy has been added to this "*Necronomicon* Egregore" by devotees who have pumped their energy into it over the years since the publication of the Simon book. Like the maddening novel of Sutter Cane from *In the Mouth of Madness*, the Simon *Necronomicon* takes its strength from new readers, new believers.

As Peter Levenda has pointed out, the Simon book has not been out of print a day since the initial date of its publication. That would be remarkable enough when one considers the number of profoundly valuable books on occult topics that have been allowed to slip quietly out of print. When one considers the relative lack of criticism the Simon book has received, however, it is truly amazing. No topic is more overpublished than the occult, and no group of people more outspoken in their opinions than the occult community. And yet, in the twenty years since its publication, no one has written an in-depth, scholarly deconstruction of the book until now—this in spite of the fact that the Simon *Necronomicon* is at once a bestseller and a flagrant hoax! Aside from the casual comments of a few occultist authors, and inconsequential flame-wars on the Internet, there has been little criticism of the book at all! What is everyone afraid of?

Az0th, the magician whom I quoted in the previous chapter, has stated that what he encountered in his experiments with the Gate Walking rituals was an egregore "whose boundaries and ultimate nature remains a mystery, something nearly unique in modern times." In a subsequent personal e mail communication, Az0th warned me that this egregore appears in many respects prehuman and "does have teeth," and, because of its ancient nature, was unpredictable and couldn't be defended against by regular magickal means.[7] I believe that this egregore—or one like it—aggressively defends the *Necronomicon* from its critics. Its primary weapons appear to be fear, hatred, and disease. This *Necronomicon* egregore may seem formidable, but it is hardly invincible and, contrary to Az0th's views, it can easily be defended against by conventional magickal means—provided one doesn't grow lazy or complacent. While I don't usually encourage those defending against psychic attacks to expend their energy on counterattacks,[8] I make an exception in cases involving the Simon *Necronomicon*. I believe that an effective course of action for those who know themselves to be harassed by someone evoking entities from the Simon book, is to launch an attack, not on the human using the book, but on the book itself—or rather on the egregore that guards it. Again, I advise the practitioner to evoke powerful avenging deities against this *Necronomicon* egregore, which, though intimidating, is of pathetically recent origin and low-voltage power compared to the mighty Goddesses and Gods of the ancient Mesopotamian, Indo-European, Hebrew/Semitic, Native American, Asian, and African pantheons. This *Necronomicon* egregore will eventually be broken down and annihilated by a steady bombardment of this type.

The practitioner who must defend himself against magickal attack is encouraged to consult the books listed in the following bibliography. I realize that those embroiled in a magickal war may not have the leisure to run about collecting a library, therefore the books are listed in order of importance, with those most immediately useful listed first.

Spiritual Cleansing: A Handbook of Psychic Protection. Draja Mickaharic. Samuel Weiser, Inc. 1982. ISBN 0-87728-531-4. This is a good book on psychic first-aid techniques.

Psychic Self-Defense. Dion Fortune. Samuel Weiser, Inc. 1996. ISBN 0-87728-381-8. First published in 1930, this is the seminal book on defense against magickal and psychic attack, and still required reading. Violet Firth—alias Dion Fortune—was a survivor of the magickal lodge scene of the post–Golden Dawn period at the turn of the century. Much of the occult skullduggery she describes in case histories will show you that things haven't really changed. Though her Victorian morality will not allow her to name names, you can tell that some of her anecdotes involve occult bigwigs like Crowley and Leadbeater.

The Llewellyn Practical Guide to Psychic Self-Defense and Well-Being. Melita Denning and Osborne Phillips. Llewellyn Publications. 1993. ISBN 0-87542-190-3. A grimoire for Yuppies; it gives good advice on fending off, not only deliberate magickal attacks, but also the constant, stressful psychic noise of modern urban life.

Silver's Spells for Protection. Silver Raven Wolf. Llewellyn Publications. 2000. ISBN1-56718-729-3. Silver makes good use of the Pow Wow system for cleansing and defense.

Castings: The Creation of Sacred Space. Ivo Dominguez Jr. Panpipe. SapFire Productions, Inc. 1996. ISBN 0-9654198-0-0. This book provides good instruction on the casting of protective wards, and covers more than a dozen different types of castings. Though it is written from a Wiccan perspective, the author has a background in Qaballah and other types of ritual.

Modern Magick: Eleven Lessons in the High Magickal Arts. Donald Michael Kraig. Llewellyn Publications. 1993. ISBN 0-87542-324-8. Perhaps the best introduction and training manual for ceremonial magick in print anywhere, it contains the best instructions for performance of the Lesser Banishing Ritual of the Pentagram, as well as good pointers on self-protection. It also contains instructions on the creation of artificial elementals.

Condensed Chaos: An Introduction to Chaos Magic. Phil Hine. New Falcon Publications. 1996. ISBN 1-56184-117-X. This is definitely the best introduction to the new science of chaos magick from its most articulate expositor. Well worth reading for many reasons. Pay special attention to the chapter devoted to the creation of thought-forms, which Mr. Hine calls Chaos Servitors.

Path to Power. Roger Heisler. Samuel Weiser, Inc. 1990. ISBN 0-87728-705-8. Provides good advice on the importance of banishings, as well as a ritual for the creation of artificial elementals.

A Witch's Guide to Faery Folk. Edain McCoy. Llewellyn Publications. 1994. ISBN 0-87542-733-2. Besides advice on approaching the faery folk and making alliances with them, the book contains good instructions for building artificial elementals.

Interceding Against the Powers of Darkness. Kenneth E. Hagin. Faith Liberty Publications. Kenneth Hagin Ministries, 1987. P.O. Box 50126, Tulsa, OK 74150. Aside from being one of the few media evangelists (he's on radio) who is not a fraud, Hagin teaches unique countermeasures to use against Qlippothic entities (demons), particularly by effective use of the powerful name of that ancient magus called Yeshua ha Natzerai, better known as Jesus of Nazareth. Having studied directly under this venerable mage, I can attest to the efficacy of his magickal powers—er, I mean gifts of the Spirit.

Sun-Tzu Speaks: The Art of War. Adapted and illustrated by Tsai Chih Chung. Translated by Brian Bruya. Anchor Books Doubleday. 1994. ISBN 0-385-47258-7. Sun Tzu's advice is good for any kind of warfare— physical or nonphysical. This comic book version of the ancient Chinese classic makes it accessible to even a five-year-old.

Necronomian: Workbook Guide to the Necronomicon. Darren Fox. I.G.O.S. Research Society. 1996. ISBN 1-57179-054-3. Not worth the fifty-dollar price, but will provide valuable insight into the probable worldview and mentality of your attacker. As Sun Tzu said, "By understanding both the enemy and yourself, you can engage in a hundred battles without ever being in danger."

PART THREE

The *Necronomicon* and Entertainment

Unspeakable Cuts:
The *Necronomicon* on Film
—John Wisdom Gonce III   **10**

In this section, I will explore the phenomenon of the *Necronomicon* as it appears
in the movies. No investigation of the impact of the *Necronomicon* on the modern
world would be even remotely complete without an examination of the impact
of the *Necronomicon* on film. Shakespeare's metaphor of the world as a stage has
been supplanted by the postmodern cinematic consciousness of life as a movie.
British rock star/actor Sting once said he believed all Americans secretly think of
themselves as movie actors and of their lives as films. Even serious matters like war
and politics are inseparable from cinema. Legend has it that Nixon decided to invade
Cambodia only after watching *Patton* (1970). Sylvester Stallone complains that three
Presidents of the United States have addressed him as "Rocky," and that Ronald
Reagan quoted dialogue from *Rambo* (1985) as a rallying point for right-wing militarism. (Reagan, himself an old B-movie actor, well knew the political value of
Hollywood grandstanding!) Since the audiovisual deluge of cinema has overwhelmed
all aspects of postmodern life, it would be futile to hope that Lovecraft's fictional
grimoire could escape the flood. The interwoven concepts of Lovecraft's fiction, the
Necronomicon legend, and the nature of magickal practices have all been defined in
the public imagination by the reality-shaping propaganda/entertainment industry
of film.

Even serious magickal practitioners have begun to see their art in cinematic
terms. Chaos magician Phil Hine, when describing the romantic appeal of Lovecraftian

magick, cannot help but compare it to its wicked horror-chic reflection on the silver screen:

> It's glamorous, especially if you still harbour the secret wish that magick is, really, like the business that goes on in the horror movies—you know, blonde virgins, ancient altars, things with tentacles responding to your summoning. . . .[1]

Mr. Hine's description above sounds strikingly similar to a scene from the movie *The Dunwich Horror* (1970). In fact, it sounds more like a Lovecraftian horror movie than like any of Lovecraft's actual tales—none of which featured any "blonde virgins."

Most susceptible to the allure of B-movie metaphysics are the very young, for whom movies are a favorite source of occult disinformation. Teenage vampire-cult leader, murderer, and Simon *Necronomicon*-user Roderick Ferrell often called himself "Vassago"—the name of the Satanist serial killer in the horror film *Hideaway* (1995).[2] A teenage girl entangled in a destructive Simon *Necronomicon*–related cult told me of her plans to be photographed lying nude atop a big tombstone in an old graveyard. I immediately wondered how many times she (or her cult leader) had seen the *The Dunwich Horror,* which I mentioned a moment ago. One Satanist group actually used the movie *Ghoulies* (1985) as a training film to teach their members ceremonial magick.[3] The alarming tendency of real life to become "reel life" is most acute in matters cultic. For this reason, I will examine the use of occult themes in movies featuring the *Necronomicon*, and the connections some of these films have had with real-life occult practices.

Since the *Necronomicon* is inextricably linked to its creator, H. P. Lovecraft, I will also discuss the way Lovecraft's work has been treated by filmmakers.[4] Lovecraft himself seemed to have the kind of love/hate relationship with Hollywood that many Americans feel today. In a 1915 letter to Rheinhart Kleiner, he wrote, "As you surmise, I am a devotee of the motion picture, since I can attend shows at any time." In the same letter, however, he goes on to qualify his approval: "Some modern films are really worth seeing, though when I first knew moving pictures their only value was to destroy time." Lovecraft even wrote a poem to Charlie Chaplin entitled "To Charlie of the Comics" in the same year. In 1917, Lovecraft won an award for his mercilessly panning review of a silent film entitled *The Image-Maker of Thebes.* In a 1933 letter to Richard Morse, Lovecraft emphatically stated, "I shall never permit anything bearing my signature to be banalised and vulgarised into the flat infantile twaddle which passes for 'horror tales' amongst radio and cinema audiences!" Famous last words! At this point in history, there have been numerous film adaptations of Lovecraft's stories, and countless films that show indirect influence from his work.

Rather than trying to present this discussion as one long essay, I deal with it in a film-by-film format, providing a synopsis and review of each movie. I will be examining primarily how the *Necronomicon* is used in the plot of the film, its appearance as a movie prop, and whether its use in the movie agrees or conflicts with the legend of the *Necronomicon* as shown in Lovecraft's work. All films will be listed in chronological order, beginning with the earliest productions. While trying to make this work "scholarly" and "systematic," I have also tried to keep it from being *dry* and *boring!* As you read these reviews, you may occasionally think you have stumbled onto rejected scripts from *Mystery Science Theater 3000.*

The Haunted Palace. 1963. American International Pictures.
Director: Roger Corman. Screenplay: H. P. Lovecraft, Charles Beaumont. Starring: Vincent Price, Debra Paget, Lon Chaney Jr., Frank Maxwell.
The action in this film version of Lovecraft's *The Case of Charles Dexter Ward* begins in preRevolutionary War Arkham, Massachusetts, Lovecraft's fictional town of sinister doings, rather than in Providence, Rhode Island, as in the original story. As the movie begins, Ezra Weeden (Leo Gordon), and Micah Smith (Elisha Cook Jr.), two local yokels, anxiously follow a mesmerized woman as she sleepwalks through Arkham's mist-shrouded streets to the door of the "Haunted Palace" of the title. This sinister palace is the home of the infamous wizard Joseph Curwen, who apparently had the medieval structure transplanted from Europe to the American colonies stone by stone. To Weeden and Smith, however, this regal estate is "the home of Satan himself," as they tell their cronies at the tavern when they report what they saw.

Meanwhile, a bearded, stone-faced Curwen (Price) in elegant 18th-century "small clothes" escorts the dazed woman into his home and down into the cozy family dungeon, where he shackles her to a huge wooden frame. What Curwen has in mind for the girl is not just a bit of harmless B&D, however. For he then opens a round iron grating over a circular pit in the stone floor of the dungeon. This pit is an inter-dimensional worm-hole through which the "Elder Gods" can enter our world to get a piece of the action—and a piece of the ladies of Arkham. The spaced-out girl looks down into the pit as it emits a greenish light and an echoing growl, indicating that the Elder God is abominably amorous. Suddenly she snaps out of her trance and screams.

Weeden and Smith have now rounded up a lynch mob, a meager substitute for the army of privateers described in Lovecraft's original tale. These torch-waving peasants look as if they got lost on their way to Frankenstein's Castle in an old Universal horror film. They descend upon Curwen's "palace," drag him outside, tie him to a tree, and burn him alive. Before they can "light up his life," however, Curwen promises to return and exact vengeance on their descendants.

Next, we flash forward to the 1870s, one hundred and ten years later, where Charles Dexter Ward (Price again) is a stranger newly arrived in Arkham with his wife, Ann (Paget), in order to claim the family palace, a unique fixer-upper opportunity that he has inherited from his great-great-grandfather, Joseph Curwen. The villagers note Ward's uncanny resemblance to his unsavory ancestor, and haven't forgotten how Curwen violated their women by forcing them to mate with Yog-Sothoth, and thereby populate their town with mutants before their ancestors burned him at the stake. The locals try to pressure Ward into leaving before he can visit the palace. Only the kindly Dr. Willet (Maxwell) will even tell the Wards how to get to the old Curwen place. Screenwriter Charles Beaumont then opts to forget about the alchemical raising of Curwen from his essential salts, which occurs in Lovecraft's original novel, and lamely substitutes the device of Curwen's portrait. Upon entering the palace, Ward quickly becomes obsessed with the portrait of his look-alike ancestor, Joseph Curwen, which hangs in the great hall of the castle. The sinister portrait is the avenue by which the spirit of Curwen enters and possesses the body of Ward by a kind of hypnotic metempsychosis. As both the possessed Ward and the possessing Curwen, Price gives an excellent and unusually subdued performance.

Using the body of Ward, his descendant, the evil sorcerer, Curwen, makes contact with his old partner in occult crime, Simon Orne (Chaney), recovers his copy of the *Necronomicon,* and tries to resume his forbidden experiments in forcing human women to mate with the Elder Gods. (Where is Susan Brownmiller when you really need her?) Curwen quickly tries to get rid of Ward's wife in order to pursue his agenda without hindrance. For all her demure Victorianism, however, Ann is not so easily cast off, even when Curwen tries to repulse her with the prospect of kinky sex. She knows the old Charles is still in there somewhere, and her love for him causes her to remain at the palace out of concern for his sanity.

However, Curwen has bigger fish to fry—or should I say *burn*? He goes on a pyromaniacal killing spree, burning the descendants of the people who burned him alive a century before. Curwen's plans for Cthulhian kink are further sidetracked when he resurrects the body of his 18th-century mistress, Hester Tillingast, for a bit of Poe-like necrophilia. Willet and Ann intervene to save whatever's left of Charles's sanity, but Curwen and company take them prisoner and shackle Ann to the big wooden frame in the dungeon. Price, as Curwen, reads incantations aloud from the dread grimoire in his incomparable voice, while the provocatively struggling Debra Paget awaits a fate considerably worse than death—mating (or is it rape?) at the hands (or are they tentacles?) of the abominable Yog-Sothoth. Ann is a good Victorian girl who doesn't approve of casual sex and, even if she cheated on Charles, it probably wouldn't be with a slimy Mythos monster.

History (or at least the screenplay) repeats itself, as the angry villagers gather to light torches—and not for a weenie roast. They plan to burn the Curwen castle and rid themselves of the curse forever. As the orgy of arson ensues, Curwen's portrait is burned, breaking its spell over Charles. It's *coitus interruptus* for Yog-Sothoth, as Charles unchains Ann and they flee the burning palace with Dr. Willet. Once he is safely outside, leaning against the tree where Curwen was burned a century ago, Charles assures everyone that he is his old self again (but how old, and which self?). However, when Price turns around, he is wearing his Curwen makeup again, so it's anybody's guess as to who's who. He promises Dr. Willet that he will *repay* him. (Shudder!)

This is the first film to be more-or-less openly based on a Lovecraft story. It suffers from the title of a Poe poem because American International Pictures (AIP) was trying to work it into their successful series of Poe films. It is obvious from the blurbs on AIP's one-sheets—"Story by Lovecraft, Poem by Poe"—that they didn't trust Lovecraft's popularity to carry the movie alone and wanted to hedge their bets.

Plot inconsistencies abound. Ward is supplied with a wife, and the time is moved from the 1920s Providence of Lovecraft's story, to the 19th century in order to make Ward's situation more Poe-like. Some of the more intriguing and horrible elements of Lovecraft's story are dropped entirely. In the original tale, Ward resurrected Curwen from his essential salts, and Curwen killed Ward to take his place. The storyline may have been "adapted" from Lovecraft's tale, but it didn't adapt well enough to survive. The sets are beautiful, but the special effects are nonexistent; Yog-Sothoth glows like green neon but isn't animated, and looks more like the Creature from the Black Lagoon than any of Lovecraft's descriptions. One of the worst things about this movie is its music. The soundtrack is inappropriate, intrusive, and, at times, just plain nerve-racking. In this film where so many people and things are incinerated, I kept wishing somebody would burn the musical score.

The film also contains the usual Roger Corman sexual obsessions. Not only does Curwen evoke Yog-Sothoth, as in Lovecraft's tale, but he has it mate with human females, a project more befitting the Whateleys! Given his fascination with xenophilia, it is not surprising that Corman went on to film Lovecraft's "The Dunwich Horror" in 1970, with Daniel Haller as director.

Lovecraft might have been flattered to have his work associated with that of Edgar Allan Poe, his literary idol. But he wouldn't have liked the work in question to be *The Case of Charles Dexter Ward*, a story with which he was less than pleased, and which was never published during his lifetime. Nor would he have liked Beaumont, Corman, and Haller's overtly sexual treatment of the story. And I just know he would have cringed when Frank Maxwell, as Dr. Willet, gave a summary of the Cthulhu Mythos that was based more on his disciple August Derleth's ideas than his own. One wonders why the evil Mythos Gods are referred to in the script as the "Elder Gods," rather than by the more proper term "Great Old Ones."

This is the first cinematic appearance of the *Necronomicon*. For its world premiere, the prop *Necronomicon* used in this film is an impressive folio-sized[5] tome bound in covers that appear to be of red buckram secured with hasps of filigreed silver, with gilt-edged pages and the title engraved in slightly faded gold leaf on the front cover. The sorcerers venerate it as though it were the diabolic equivalent of the Talmud. Even the good folk are in awe of it; at one point Mrs. Ward reaches out to touch the book as it lies open on a stand, but Dr. Willet stops her. "Why? It's only a book!" she says. "It's much more than a book," Willet replies. In fact, he seems to know as much about the fearsome text as Curwen himself, having earlier declared that it "held enough secrets to give a man absolute power . . . supposedly contained formulas through which one could communicate with or even summon the Elder Gods, the Dark Ones from beyond who once ruled the world . . . Cthulhu, Yog-Sothoth."

Use of the *Necronomicon* in this atmospheric film is perfectly consistent with

Lovecraft's vision of the dread grimoire as it was used in his actual stories. It is the quintessential sourcebook of foul sorceries and alchemical weird science.

Necronomicon (Succubus). 1967. Trans American Films (Spanish/Italian). Director: Jess Franco. Producer: Adrian Hoven. Screenplay: Pier A. Caminecci. Starring: Janine Reynaud, Jack Taylor, Howard Varnon, Nathalie Nort, Michel Lemoine, Pier A. Caminecci, Adrian Hoven.

The film opens with an S&M scene of a beautiful, red-haired dominatrix in black named Lorna (Reynaud) torturing two "bottoms," a man and a woman who are both tied spread-eagled to X-shaped crosses. Lorna teases, whips, and cuts her victims before apparently stabbing them both to death. The house lights are then turned up to reveal that it is all a nightclub act in the tradition of *Le Grand Guignol*. A darkly handsome man watches Lorna's performance while thinking, "I have done well! She is perfect! A disciple who mirrors my own image, the essence of evil, a devil on earth." As the audience applauds, a man at the bar asks Bill Malway (Taylor), Lorna's lover/manager, "Where did you find her?" Bill replies, "In the most incredible place—Lisbon." We are then shown a flashback of Bill's first encounter with Lorna, when she appears, uninvited, in his hotel room. When he asks how she got into the locked room, she answers cryptically that she can get in anywhere. Too drunk to appreciate her seductive striptease, Bill falls into bed and passes out. Lorna is tearfully incredulous: "But I'm a witch, I'm irresistible."

The movie proceeds in an episodic series of surreal scenes that are all so dreamlike that the viewer is unable to tell whether any given sequence is supposed to be interpreted as real-time, a flashback, a psychotic episode, or a dream sequence. There is a party scene in which the guests are fed LSD-laced sugar cubes by two butlers—one of whom is a dwarf with a silver tray. As the guests begin to hallucinate, a bored psychiatrist reads from a mysterious unnamed book (the *Necronomicon*?): "A spider's foot, a toad's belly, a fox's brain." As the psychiatrist's quotations from the book become more and more sinister, the acid-tripping Lorna's behavior becomes more and more blatantly salacious: "There is no mistake about her. No cloven hooves. But as she is a Greek Goddess, so is she a devil!" Lorna writhes lasciviously on the floor. "In a furnace—in a fiery hell—she will rot!" The other guests crawl over Lorna, kissing her. "A devil who must swallow the living in pursuit of her earth-bound desires. But a devil who must devour the dead in pursuit of her hell-born lust." They seize another girl by her arms and legs and place her on top of Lorna, and the two kiss passionately. "The serpent is venomous to us all," he concludes.

In an even more alarming sequence, Lorna rendezvous with a blond girl (Nathalie Nort) and takes the girl back to a weathered seaside castle where she says she has "always lived." Lorna leads the girl into a room filled with mannequins dressed in sumptuous historical costumes, then to her bedroom where she allows the girl to seduce her. During their lovemaking, Lorna attacks the girl, attempting to kill her. When the blond girl tries to escape, the mannequins suddenly come to life and attack her, like a mob of female golems. Finally, Lorna stabs the girl to death with a sword, then erotically kisses and caresses one of the animated mannequins.

Near the conclusion of the movie, Bill makes a bargain with the mysterious dark-haired man to kill Lorna. In Bill's private studio/loft, Lorna rehearses her S&M-snuff nightclub act seen at the beginning of the film. The same two actors are chained to X-shaped crosses. This time, however, Lorna actually kills them. Bill startles Lorna by turning off the accompanying music. As though awakening from a trance, Lorna realizes what she has done and flees up the steps onto the roof, where she is apparently killed by three gunshots, according to a prearranged signal.

When Bill returns to his apartment, he is startled to find Lorna waiting for him in the nude. She commands him to kiss her and, as he obeys, she stabs him in the back of the neck with a knife. The final scene shows Lorna being driven back to the seaside castle by a chauffeur. A narrator's voice-over reads: "She loved the games men played with death, when death must win. As though the slain man's blood and breath revived Faustine—and you, Lorna, are Faustine."

As the film ends, the viewer is left unsure of a number of issues: Was Lorna a cold-blooded murderess, or was she somehow being hypnotically "programmed" to kill by the Svengali-like dark-haired man? Was she an immortal vampirelike creature, or simply a deluded mortal woman? Were the supernatural events in the movie (animated mannequins, etc.) really happening, or were they dreams or hallucinations? Was the book being read at the party actually the *Necronomicon,* or just an arcane volume being read by a bored partygoer? Was the man reading the passages (spells?) from the book magickally making the events at the party happen, or merely commenting on them? In a film as nonlinear and surreal as this, these questions may not have any relevance. A surrealistic work isn't expected to make sense.

Directed by the infamous Spanish filmmaker, Jess Franco, this bizarre film makes no mention of the Lovecraft Mythos, and has little to do with Lovecraft's fictional grimoire other than its title. I only include it in this section because it *does* use the name "Necronomicon." My first theory as to why Franco chose that name was based on the false assumption that he had released *Necronomicon* in 1970[6] and was looking for a sound-alike title in imitation of Fellini's popular *Fellini Satyricon,* released the same year. Then I discovered that *Necronomicon* was released in 1967, three years earlier.[7] A large number of Italian and Spanish translations of Lovecraft's work had been published in the previous year, so it is likely that Franco's choice had something to do with this.

I find it difficult to comment effectively on the plot of this rare movie, which may not be as big a problem as it seems, since *Necronomicon* doesn't have a plot.[8] Franco essentially used no script while shooting *Necronomicon,* simply making it up as he went along. Much of the screenplay, such as it is, was written by Pier A. Caminecci, a millionaire friend of producer Adrian Hoven who, once he got a good look at gorgeous actress Janine Reynaud, agreed to save the film after Franco and Hoven had run out of money. Though this movie had the biggest budget of any

Franco film, it was still made on the proverbial shoestring. Yet Franco and Caminecci somehow managed to give the film an affluently "decadent" look with a clever use of location shooting. In one scene, the scantily clad Lorna sashays alluringly past a historic cathedral as a group of black-habited, hooded monks stand outside canting a Gregorian chant. They obligatorily cross themselves and try to avert their eyes from temptation. Sex versus death contrasts are at least more elegant in this film, if not any subtler than in current horror movies.

Though filmed on a low budget, *Necronomicon* was, thanks to Caminecci's influence, given a special screening at the Berlin Film Festival, where it was viewed by the great Fritz Lang, among others, and hailed as an erotic masterpiece. Retitled *Succubus* for release in the English-speaking world, it created a sensation when released in the United States, where American men's magazines wallowed in its gloss of European decadence and sexuality—"a film that makes *I Am Curious Yellow* look like a Walt Disney production."[9] The simple-minded censors were probably baffled by its confusing surrealism; it not only blurred the lines between reality and fantasy, sex and death, fun and perversion, but it also confused the distinction between art and pornography. It was rated X in its British release, while the prissy British censors might have axed a less clever film outright.

The name *"Necronomicon"* is only used to lend an atmosphere of the macabre and the forbidden to the film's pornographic surrealism. Though it is unrelated to Lovecraft's work, Franco's film still makes use of Lovecraft's fictional book in its title and, by so doing, typifies the attempts of filmmakers to eroticize the literary ideas of a man who had no use for overt eroticism.

The Dunwich Horror. 1970. American International Pictures.
Director: Daniel Haller. Executive Producer: Roger Corman. Screenplay: H. P. Lovecraft, Curtis Hanson. Starring: Sandra Dee, Dean Stockwell, Ed Begley, Sam Jaffe.
The film opens with Lavinia Whateley moaning in monsterbirth. I would say "childbirth," but that wouldn't be quite accurate. Old Wizard Whateley (Sam Jaffe, who played Dr. Zorba in the *Ben Casey* series) presides at the bedside, since his daughter is actually giving birth to his pet magickal project, the offspring of Yog-Sothoth. Yes, Old Whateley has deliberately pimped his daughter to the Great Old One in order to bring its spawn into this world.

We next flashforward into 1970, where Dean Stockwell plays an amazingly suave, soft-spoken, and seductive Wilbur Whateley, not at all like the hulking, goatish brute of Lovecraft's original story. In fact, Wilbur is so charming and hypnotic that, when he puts his smooth moves on Dr. Armitage's virginal assistant, Nancy Wagner (Sandra Dee), she not only lets him seduce her, she helps him steal the *Necronomicon* and use her as a sexual sacrifice to Yog-Sothoth. (I've heard that love is blind, but this is ridiculous!)

Wilbur goes to the library of Miskatonic University to consult their prized copy of the *Necronomicon*. There, he coolly talks Nancy into letting him read the rare volume instead of returning it to its display case. Dr. Henry Armitage (Ed Begley) is at first delighted to meet a member of the Whateley family ("You've read my paper on Dunwich?"), but refuses to allow Wilbur to study the *Necronomicon*. So Wilbur cons the naive Nancy into giving him a ride back to Dunwich, where he invites her into his pad, a decrepit but genteel old mansion on the edge of town where he lives with his grandfather, Old Wizard Whateley. There, he slips a Cthulhu Mythos mickey into Nancy's tea, disables her car, and offers the drugged girl a guest bedroom at the Whateley manor in order to keep her there for the unspeakable fun and games to come.

Maybe Wilbur put some LSD in Nancy's drink (remember, it's 1970), because she dreams (or hallucinates) of being harassed by naked revelers covered in mud and/or body paint, accompanied by a goat, and wallowing in a wild sexual orgy. Are they worshipers of the Great Old Ones—or just refugees from Woodstock? (This is definitely 1970!)

Nancy's friend Elizabeth (Donna Baccala) tells Dr.Armitage of her disappearance and of her fears that Nancy is with Wilbur, saying, "If he were a straight guy, I wouldn't worry." (Yep! It's 1970 all right!) They drive to Dunwich together, looking for the lost librarian, and are angrily turned away from the Whateley house by Old Wizard Whateley. Armitage and Elizabeth continue their search for Nancy by consulting a physician named Dr. Corey (Lloyd Bochner), the local MD who delivered Wilbur Whateley. Corey spoils Lovecraft's surprise ending by telling Armitage that there were *two* babies born to Lavinia that night—Wilbur was just the more human of the two brothers. Armitage now understands why Wilbur wants the *Necronomicon*. He guesses Wilbur's blasphemous plan to become a cosmic pimp for Yog-Sothoth, and sets out to stop it.

Meanwhile, Wilbur takes the drugged Nancy to a circle of ancient megaliths, or "standing stones," called the Devil's Hop Yard. As he seduces her onto the stone altar, he explains that the place was once used for "fertility rites"(wink-wink, nudge-nudge!). The sedated girl lies back and moans as Wilbur invokes Yog-Sothoth, and cultists in black robes stand around and watch her do the wild thing with the Old One. Wilbur is not content to let old Yog have all the fun, however. He takes off his shirt, obviously intent on a *menage-a-Mythos*, with Nancy in the middle. Disappointingly, the shirtless Wilbur is only covered with "tattoos" obviously painted on. A poor substitute for Lovecraft's description of him as having "the leathery, reticulated hide of a crocodile. . . . The skin was covered with coarse black fur, and from the abdomen a score of long greenish-gray tentacles with red sucking mouths protruded limply." (John Holmes, eat your heart out!)

Back at the Whateley mansion, Elizabeth shoves her way past Old Wizard Whateley, and runs inside looking for Nancy. At the top of the staircase, she opens a huge door, only to find Wilbur's hideously amorphous brother, whose body is a tangle of writhing tentacles or, as one of Lovecraft's backward Dunwichites described it, "made 'o squirmin' ropes . . ." The trans-cosmic monstrosity rapidly attacks, strips, and does Azathoth-only-knows-what to the terrified girl, in a sequence that probably inspired countless scenes of Japanese anime pornography. This incident fills Old Wizard Whateley with uncharacteristic remorse, and he dies trying to stop Wilbur from using Nancy for monster breeding, as he once used his own daughter Lavinia, who now resides at the local mental hospital. (And you thought your family was dysfunctional!)

Wilbur then has Nancy drive him back to Arkham, where he breaks into the library, kills a security guard, and steals Miskatonic's copy of the *Necronomicon*, the "complete edition" with "the long chant that ye'll find on page 751." Then he returns to Dunwich with Nancy for the climactic (no pun intended) ceremony. Back among the monoliths in the Devil's Hop Yard, Wilbur calls to his extradimensional father, Yog-Sothoth, and to his tentacle-sprouting brother, who breaks out of his prison room and invisibly spreads mayhem throughout the countryside.

Barely in time to stop this abominable family reunion, Armitage finds Wilbur about to offer up the drugged-as-usual Nancy, who lies scantily clad on the stone altar with the *Necronomicon* propped open between her legs. With a counter-spell from the forbidden tome, Armitage vanquishes Wilbur's hideous brother (who looks like someone in a rubber mask with medusa-like snakes or tentacles sticking out of it), drives Yog-Sothoth back to the stars, and incinerates Wilbur in a column of flames. Armitage isn't altogether successful, however. In the last scene, a fetus is superimposed over Nancy's belly, showing that she has been "knocked up" by Yog-Sothoth as a result of the Whateley's obscene magickal experiments.

This movie supposedly showed us a blasphemous mating between Sandra Dee and Yog-Sothoth, but what we really see is a marriage between H. P. Lovecraft and Ira Levin. The makers of this movie were heavily influenced by Roman Polansky's popular film version of Ira Levin's *Rosemary's Baby* (1968), and tried to make over Lovecraft's story into a Satanic conspiracy film. Since *The Dunwich Horror*, like *Rosemary's Baby*, was about a woman being impregnated by a supernatural creature, and since it was Lovecraft's most popular tale, AIP probably figured it was their best bet to cash in on Levin and Polansky's box office blockbuster. Films like Alfred Hitchcock's *Psycho* (1960) had already made horror more internal, surreal, and— well—more *personal*, because the terrible things that had once been confined to castle dungeons and mad scientist's laboratories could now happen to you in your own bathroom. AIP was trying desperately to keep up with these trends, and had matured slightly since the days of its first two half-hearted Lovecraftian attempts, *The Haunted Palace* (1963) and *Die Monster Die* (1965). The studio still maintained some of the cliches inherited from Universal horror films of the 1930s and 1940s, however. At the end of the film, the Whateley house predictably burns to the ground in the finest tradition of *Frankenstein Meets the Wolf Man*. One of the most annoying things about this film is the way odd background characters appear and disappear with no explanation, like the black-robed cultists who stand around watching

Wilbur "doing" Nancy on the altar, and the two albino women who attend Lavinia in childbirth. Now you see 'em—now you don't!

The Dunwich Horror is very much a film of its time, as its various "psychedelic" photographic effects and cultural influences show. It is difficult to tell, for example, if the revelers who harass Nancy in her dreams are "pagans" having a Bacchanalian orgy or hippies at a rock festival. It is now the 21st century, and women are expected to display I.Q. as well as T&A, but 1950s throwback Sandra Dee manages to look spaced out even when she's *not* supposed to be drugged. Sometimes the then-trendy camera effects are interesting, as was the sequence that appears to have been shot through dark gauze, and the sepiatone flashback of Old Wizard Whateley (perfectly acted by Jaffe) delivering his prophecy about Lavinia's offspring in Osbourn's General Store. Best of all were the hallucinatory, cartoonish strobe and solarization effects in the sequence where Nancy's friend, Elizabeth, is attacked by Wilbur's tentacular brother—the only truly frightening scene in this film. In other scenes, the effects simply look gimmicky. Overall, however, the psychotropic, drug-like ambience compliments the delirious horrors of Lovecraft's story. Remember that Roger Corman was the guiding hand behind that trendy drug-exploitation movie, *The Trip* (1967).

By casting cute little Dean Stockwell as a smooth-talking, sophisticated Wilbur Whateley, AIP trashed one of the most creative and original elements in Lovecraft's story. Western literature has traditionally granted far too much charisma, wealth, and dignity to villains—the brilliant Professor Moriarty, the aristocratic Count Dracula, the royal Fu Manchu, and the like. Lovecraft deliberately broke with tradition when he made Wilbur and Old Wizard Whateley, not only powerful sorcerers out to unbalance the universe, but also backwoods Yankee rednecks with about as much sophistication as a rerun of *Hee Haw*. Like a diabolical blend of Faust and the toothless, inbred hillbillies in James Dickey's *Deliverance*, Wilbur and his grand-daddy use the *Necronomicon* to make the whole cosmos "bend over and squeal like a pig!" In Lovecraft's tale, Old Whateley's dialect made the *Beverly Hillbillies* sound like the English Lit. Department at Oxford: "Let me tell ye suthin'—*Some day yew folks'll hear a child o' Lavinny's a-callin' its father's name on the top o' Sentinel Hill!*"[10] Wilbur was especially repulsive because of his teratological ancestry. Lovecraft described him as "shabby, dirty, bearded, and uncouth of dialect . . . Almost eight feet tall . . . this dark and goatish gargoyle appeared . . ."[11]

And that's not even counting the quasi-phallic tentacles hidden under his over-alls. Add to this the country-bumpkin crudity of all the Whateleys, for example, the way Wilbur asked for the loan of the *Necronomicon* with all the finesse of a horny Billy goat:

> I calc'late I've got to take that book home. They's things in it I've got to try under sarten conditions that I can't git here, an it'ud be a mortal sin to let a red-tape rule hold me up. Let me take it along, Sir, an I'll swar they wun't

nobody know the difference. I dun't need to tell ye I'll take good keer of it. It wa'nt me that put this Dee copy in the shape it is.[12]

The original Wilbur would have made Gomer Pyle look and sound like James Bond. He may have been hung like a horse (or should I say an octopus?), but Wilbur was not the kind of guy who could talk a girl into becoming a human sacrifice on the first date. By contrast, the desperately miscast Stockwell plays the role as though he were auditioning for James Dean's part in *Rebel Without a Cause*. To Lovecraft fans, he looks like Brad Pitt playing the Elephant Man without makeup.

Still, there were some authentically Lovecraftian touches in this film. Surprisingly, Haller and company brought to the screen one of the most folkloric and lyrical elements in Lovecraft's original tale: When Old Wizard Whateley and Lavinia die, whippoorwills act as psychopomps waiting to carry off the spirits of the dead. The Devil's Hop Yard also had a gratifyingly ominous Lovecraftian atmosphere. Perhaps we owe these additions to screenwriters Lee Hanson, Henry Rosenbaum, and Ronald Silkosky.

The *Necronomicon* seen in this film is a black book. I don't mean "black" purely in the magickal sense; I mean that it is literally *black*. Even the huge, curving, iron hinges with protruding rivet heads that hold the covers to the spine are darkest, stygian black. The folio-sized book never has a chance to get dusty because it is kept in its own glass case, like a Gutenberg Bible on display, in the Miskatonic University Library. As Wilbur Whateley lovingly caresses the pages, we see that the text appears to be written in pseudo-Arabic script. Before Armitage can interrupt him, he reads this passage:

> *Yog-Sothoth is the gate whereby the spheres meet. Only them from beyond can make it multiply and work. Yog-Sothoth is the key, and with the gate open, the Old Ones shall be past, present and future—all are one. The Old Ones walk serene and primal, undimensioned and unseen. The Old Ones broke through of old and they shall break through . . .*

These words are taken almost verbatim from the story itself, and Lovecraft's prose enhances the mood here considerably.

This movie has the dubious distinction of being the only film in which the *Necronomicon* is used as a sex toy. No, really! Stockwell braces the book open between Sandra Dee's (or her body-double's) spread legs as she lies semi-nude on the stone altar waiting to be sacrificed to, or mate with (the distinction is a little blurry), Yog-Sothoth. Stockwell reads incantations from the dread grimoire as she writhes and moans orgasmically. The camera moves in for a close-up of her left hip as her buttocks flex erotically, presumably she is rubbing herself against the spine of the book. Haller and Corman thus explicitly exhume the buried sexuality in Lovecraft's story. Corman's influence probably started the trend of sexualizing film treatments of Lovecraft's tales. All we need now is a series of Lovecraftian porn videos with titles like *Pickman's Nude Model, Wet Dreams in the Witch House, The Call Girls of Cthulhu,* or *Debbie Does Dunwich.*

More intriguing and disturbing yet are the bits and pieces of what appear to be actual occult practices that creep into the ritual Wilbur conducts over the drugged Nancy as she lies on the stone altar in the Devil's Hop Yard. (Nancy's body itself seems to serve as an altar, harkening back to the practices of Anton LaVey's Church of Satan.) The entire ritual seems reminiscent of a working designed to produce a *homunculus* (a human baby with the spirit of a demon) described by Aleister Crowley in both his novel *Moonchild* (1917), and in a ninth-degree OTO document entitled "De Homunculo Epistola"(1914). When he evokes Yog-Sothoth, Wilbur makes the "Vir" sign of the horned beast used by Aleister Crowley, with fists held beside his head, palms facing the ears, thumbs sticking out like little horns. This gesture is used in two Thelemic Rituals of the Pentagram: "The Star Ruby" and "Liber V vel Reguli," also called "The Ritual of the Mark of the Beast."[13] The word *kia* crops up repeatedly in the incantations he chants over the girl's body. As mentioned in chapter 4, the word *kia* has no meaning in any Western language, but in chaos magick the word— as coined by Spare—means "universal energy."[14] The word also appears in the Simon *Necronomicon,*[15] where it is (correctly) defined as "earth" (page xlii). Since this film was released seven years before the Simon *Necronomicon* was published, it's hard to say if the similarity is coincidental or deliberate. According to John Carter, author of *Sex and Rockets*, both Dean Stockwell and Dennis Hopper were said to have once been roommates of Marjorie Cameron, the "Scarlet Woman" of the ill-fated OTO initiate Jack Parsons. Perhaps Stockwell learned some occult lore from her. Cameron is also supposed to have worked with Hopper in Curtis Harrington's 1961 pseudo-Lovecraftian fantasy film *Night Tide*, which featured a "Deep One" playing a mermaid in a sideshow. Could Marjorie Cameron have been an early participant in Lovecraftian occultism? Who knows? But her former magickal partner, Jack Parsons, definitely allowed fiction to influence his magickal practices, and perhaps his fictional sources included Lovecraft. Cameron was also involved in Parsons's "Babalon Working," in which Parsons was trying to create a "moonchild," or homunculus, using the method outlined by Crowley.

Since the makers of this film were trying to emulate Polansky's *Rosemary's Baby,* there is a possibility that the occult elements were deliberate. A popular, but unverified, rumor circulated that the Satanic elements in *Rosemary's Baby* were authentic— the result of serious research. Anton Szandor LaVey spread the false rumor that he served as technical advisor to Roman Polansky during the filming. (He didn't!) Perhaps the makers of *The Dunwich Horror* wanted to have "authentic" occult elements in their film for the sake of competition.

The use of the *Necronomicon* in this film is basically consistent with Lovecraft's ideas: its usefulness in the evocation of Yog-Sothoth, its veiled connection with the monoliths of New England (by which the Devil's Hop Yard was inspired),[16] its reputation as a priceless antiquarian rarity as well as a cult book, and the unwillingness of scholars and institutions to loan it out for study. It is doubtful, however, if Lovecraft ever consciously saw anything erotic in it, nor would he likely have approved of Sandra Dee using it for a magickal vibrator.

The Hunchback of the Morgue. 1972. Eva Film S. L.(Spanish).
Director: Javier Aguirre. Screenplay: Javier Aguirre, Alberto S. Insua. Starring: Paul Naschy, Rossana Yanni, Vic Winner, Maria Elena Apron, Manuel deBlas.
Paul Naschy, famous star of Spanish-speaking horror films, plays Wolfgang Goto, the hunchback of the title. Goto lives in the German town of Feldkirch, where everyone despises him because of his deformity. Everyone, that is, except for a beautiful, but terminally ill, girl named Ilsa who is dying in Feldkirch Hospital, where Goto visits her daily, bringing her flowers. Goto also works at the hospital as a caretaker, and moonlights as a murderer and graverobber, supplying corpses for the illegal cadaver trade run by the hospital medical school. To his credit, Goto usually kills only those who have cruelly abused him or ridiculed Ilsa, his tubercular girlfriend.

The unfortunate hunchback is also befriended by two mad scientists—Dr. Orla and Dr. Tochner, who have just lost their financial backing from the university for their dubious experiments in the creation of artificial life. Orla and Tochner rescue Goto from a mob of evil medical students who try to kick and beat the hapless hunchback to death when he retaliates against one of them for insulting Ilsa. Ilsa meanwhile dies, leaving Goto heartbroken. Goto cannot bear to leave Ilsa's body to be dissected by his enemies, the cruel and vulgar medical students, so he kills two of them while stealing her corpse away to the medieval catacombs below Feldkirch Hospital. Goto later asks Dr. Orla if he can revivify the dead Ilsa and leads him to her body in the catacombs. Orla assures the trusting hunchback that he will, but this is a mere political promise. Orla only wants the old catacombs—once used as headquarters by the Teutonic Knights and as torture chambers by the Inquisition—as the new site of his experiments. Orla also plans to use Goto to obtain "specimens" (of the kicking and screaming kind) illegally.

As the police search for him, Goto provides Orla with corpses to feed the mass of tissue that he and Tochner have created. Orla is exultant over his success at creating artificial life:

> The creature is a primordial, a being that inhabited the earth much earlier than man. Its prototype is the oldest in history. The books of the Dark Ages; the *Necronomicon* and theses written on alchemy and magick are just full of references to this type of creature. . . . This creature is the only bearer of the secrets of all forgotten civilizations, and we're going to reveal those secrets.

Before long, the obsessional Orla demands *living* tissue to feed his growing monstrosity, insisting that Goto kidnap girls from the Feldkirch Women's Reformatory to be fed—alive and screaming—to the creature. Tochner's girlfriend, Dr. Maria Meyer, who runs the reformatory, is beginning to have her doubts about Tochner's involvement with Orla, and talks Tochner into trying to leave. Orla imprisons the reluctant Tochner in the catacombs to retain his scientific services, and when Maria tries to rescue her lover, Orla imprisons her too. Orla continues to lie to Goto with false promises of creating a "new Ilsa" in order to make Goto keep supplying him with reformatory girls as snacks for his monster. All is not bleak for the forlorn hunchback, however, for Dr. Meyer's beautiful blond assistant, criminal psychologist Dr. Ilke, has fallen in love with Goto because of his legendary loyalty to his lost Ilsa. So smitten is she by the hunky hunchback that she not only hides him from the police, but seduces him in a most unlikely nude scene. (This is a great movie for guys who suffer from a poor self-image—if a homicidal hunchback can score with a gorgeous intellectual babe, so can you!) When Ilke spies Goto descending into the catacombs by a secret entrance, she follows him and catalyzes a series of events whereby Tochner and Maria Meyer escape, and the monster smashes through the door to its cell and attacks Orla and Goto. Orla is killed and Ilke is carried away unconscious by Tochner, while Goto and the monster fall together into a vat of sulfuric acid.

Some good horror movies have come out of Spain, but this isn't one of them. This film contains all the staple elements of Spanish-speaking horror films of the '60s and '70s: dubious medical experiments, beautiful women, sadism, and amazingly good atmosphere. Naschy plays the retarded hunchback like a low-rent version of Lenny in *Of Mice and Men*. (Duh, I had a little girlfriend, but she don't move no more!) Practically everything about this cheesy melodrama is gratuitous: lovingly ghoulish close-ups of bodies being dismembered, reformatory girls beating each other with belts, the sadistic humiliation of the hunchback, an improbable coupling between a stunning female psychologist and a deformed murderer, and, last but not least, tortured animals. There is a scene in which Goto is horrified to find rats eating the dead body of his beloved Ilsa, and retaliates by setting them on fire. The shots of burning rats scurrying frantically down the catacombs could not possibly have been faked. Remember that this film was shot in the land that made bullfighting famous!

Use of the *Necronomicon* in this hopeless film is scanty to say the least. The book is never actually shown on screen, but only mentioned by Orla as a reference book to provide an end for his insane means. In the badly dubbed English version, which I own, the actor speaking the English dialog for the Orla character even mispronounces "*Necronomicon*," calling it "the Necromia." Orla's monster, in its earliest bloblike stages, looks somewhat like one of Lovecraft's shoggoths or Formless Spawn, and yet when the creature escapes in the final scene, it is a man in a rubber suit dripping with black slime, who looks more like Uncle Remus's tar baby than one of Lovecraft's cosmic horrors.

Giger's Necronomicon. 1975.

H. R. Giger and J. J. Wittmer. With appearances by Li Tobler and others.

In spite of its tantalizing name, this is simply a forty-minute, 16mm documentary film about the work of Giger from 1972 to 1975. The high point of the movie is the segment involving the last art exhibition of Giger's late girlfriend, Li Tobler, "Schuhwerke" (Shoe Works), in which Li invited guests at the exhibition to appear in surreal art-shoes. H. R. Giger himself appears in shoes made from two loaves of bread, and films the other guests. Li committed suicide later that same year.

The Evil Dead. 1983. Renaissance Pictures.
Director: Sam Raimi. Screenplay: Sam Raimi. Starring: Bruce Campbell, Ellen Sandweiss, Betsy Parker, Hal Delrich, Sarah York.
Five college students go to spend their break in a cabin in the Tennessee hills. In the basement, they find a copy of an old grimoire (not called the *Necronomicon*, though this changes in the sequels), a grotesque magickal/ritual dagger with a skull-shaped pommel, and a tape recorder. These three items belonged to the former resident, an archaeologist. When they play the tape, they discover that it is the diary of the previous tenant of the cabin who had taken his wife there for seclusion while he worked on his discovery (the book). The scientist describes his research:

> A volume of ancient Sumerian burial practices and funerary incantations, it is entitled *Morturom Demonto*, roughly translated: "The Book of the Dead." Bound in human flesh and inked with human blood, it deals with demons and demon resurrection, and those forces which roam the forests and dark bowers of man's domain. The first few pages warn that these enduring creatures may lie dormant but are never truly dead. They may be recalled to active life with the incantations presented in this book. It is through recitation of these passages that the demons are given license to possess the living.

The voice of the researcher on the tape then recites an incantation from the book, which reactivates a creature that was already lurking in a dormant state near the house. The entity attacks and possesses members of the group and forces the possessed members to attack their friends. The friends are then forced to kill the possessed victim in order to survive. By listening to the rest of the recording, they discover what happened to the archaeologist and his wife:

> I know now that my wife has become host to a Kandarian demon. I fear that the only way to stop those possessed by the spirits of the book is through the act of bodily dismemberment. I'd leave now to avoid this horror but for myself, I have seen the dark shadows moving through the woods and I have no doubt that whatever I have resurrected through this book is sure to come calling for me.

Even killing the possessed victim isn't good enough, as the corpse must be cut into pieces or it will reanimate and attack again. The landscape itself has turned hostile, and the trees of the forest are animated by the evil entity to attack the young girls.

One even rapes the girl named Cheryl (Ellen Sandweiss). One by one, they are all killed except for Ash (Bruce Campbell), who must survive to do the sequels. Ash is finally attacked by three demoniacally animated corpses at once, when he throws the book into the fire and burns it—thus destroying the murderous corpses, who then decompose in one of the most disgusting time-lapse deterioration sequences ever filmed.

Though made on a low (almost no) budget, this film is clever, atmospheric, and endlessly creative. The "monstervision" POV (point of view) shots, for example, which give the audience a creature's-eye-view of zooming through the forest and rushing up to pounce on a victim, were created by strapping a camera to a board and having two men run through the woods with it, then speeding up the resulting footage. *Evil Dead* stands out as a splendid example of postmodern, splatterpunk horror cinema, comparing favorably with such revolutionary European monstrosities as the infamous German film *Nekromantik*.

My only complaint about the prop *Necronomicon* used in this film is that it is too small to be the 800–1,000-page grimoire of Lovecraft's tales—too small in fact to be visually imposing on film as a threatening book of black magick, since it is only about the octavo size of a prayer book rather than the folio size of a family Bible. The illustrations, however, are excellent. Tom Sullivan, who made the pen and ink drawings, sigils, and glyphs for this prop receives my compliments. Some of the illustrations are vaguely reminiscent of the work of Austin Osman Spare from such works as his unpublished *Grimoire of Zos*.[17]

The allusion to "Sumerian burial practices" is an obvious lift from Simon's *Necronomicon*. The power of the spoken incantation, however, is perfectly in line with Lovecraft's vision of the *Al Azif*. As mentioned earlier, the idea of a fearful power intrinsic to language itself permeates his fiction. In the Lovecraftian universe, magickal incantations will work apart from the intent or understanding of the speaker, just as they did for Dr. Willet in *The Case of Charles Dexter Ward*. Even a voice from a tape recorder reading an ancient chant can summon demonic entities. There is no mention, however, of any creature associated with the *Necronomicon* or its minions being automatically destroyed when the book is burned. Book-burning never worked for the Inquisition, and it shouldn't have worked for Ash.

Evil Dead II. 1987. Renaissance Pictures.
Director: Sam Raimi. Screenplay: Sam Raimi and Scott Spiegel. Starring: Bruce Campbell, Sarah Berry, Dan Hicks, Cassie Wesley.
This is not really a sequel to the first *Evil Dead* movie, but rather a remake of it. The plot is almost identical, with the same cabin in the forest and the same evil spirits lurking in the woods. As before, Ash (Campbell) takes his girlfriend, Linda (Denise Bixler), on a vacation retreat, but there is no other couple with them. The tape recorder with its fateful message is still a pivotal plot device. The message itself varies only slightly from that of the first film:

> This is Professor Raymond Knowby, Department of Ancient History, log entry number two: I believe I have made a significant find in the Castle of Kandar. . . . It was in the rear chamber of the castle that we stumbled upon something remarkable; Mortuorum Demonto, the "Book of the Dead." My wife and I brought the book here to this cabin where I could study it undisturbed. It was here that I began the translations . . .

Included here are the phonetic pronunciations of these passages: "Kunda astratta montose eargrets gut nos veratoos kanda amatos kanda."[18]

Then begins the hallucinatory, hyper-real roller-coaster ride of delirious grue and demented comedy. Again, we are shown the "monstervision" view of the evil rushing through the woods at high speed. The incantation invokes Whatever-It-Is (a Kandarian demon?) into Linda, turning her into a deadite, and forcing Ash to kill her by decapitating her with a shovel. Ash is zombified in turn, but is transformed back into a human by the sunrise. He tries to leave the forest, but the bridge is out, forcing him to return to the cabin. The dead Linda (animated by stop-motion) crawls out of her grave and attacks Ash. (Talk about your blind dates!) Linda's severed head bites Ash on the hand, infecting it with the zombifying contagion. In a cartoonishly surreal scene of slapstick splatterpunk, Ash cuts off his own demoniacally possessed hand with a chain saw while he rants "Who's laughing now?" Then he traps the still-animated hand under a bucket and stacks books on top of it. The top volume, appropriately enough, is *A Farewell to Arms*. (Let's all give Ash a big hand!) Professor Knowby's daughter, accompanied by her boyfriend and two others, arrives at the cabin via a backwoods trail unknown to Ash. She manages to survive the ensuing round of slaughter long enough to open a cross-time vortex with a spell from the *Necronomicon*. Ash sends the evil through the dimensional doorway, but gets pulled through it himself. At the close of the film, Ash finds himself in either medieval Europe or a pseudo-medieval alternate world, surrounded by armored medieval knights and soldiers who are also fighting the monsters released by the *Necronomicon*, thus paving the way for a sequel.

The film begins with an impressive montage and voice-over narrating the supposed origins of the *Necronomicon*. The dreaded volume hovers in space before us, in the background, the waves of a crimson sea crash on a dark shore. An unseen hand illustrates and inscribes its pages by stop-motion animation, line by line, with disturbing images, sigils and glyphs while Campbell's voice explains:

> Legend has it that it was written by the Dark Ones. *Necronomicon Ex Mortis*, roughly translated "Book of the Dead." The book served as a passageway to the evil worlds beyond. It was written long ago when the seas ran red with blood. It was this blood that was used to ink the book. In the year 1300 A.D. the book disappeared.[19]

The book is bound in some kind of rugose leather—the wrinkled folds converge on the front cover to form an ugly, tortured face. The unspoken visual inference is that it is bound in human skin. Tom Sullivan's fleetingly seen illustrations still have a hauntingly Spare-like look.

There are some basic problems with calling the grimoire *Necronomicon Ex Mortis*. *Necronomicon* is Greek and means "Image of the Laws of the Dead," according to Lovecraft's own faulty etymology, or, more correctly, "Book Concerning the Dead." *Ex Mortis* is Latin and means "from death." This would give us a title that means "Concerning the Dead From Death." Though this title may impress the ignorant, it's a bit redundant and nonsensical, as well as being an indiscriminate mix of languages worthy of Colin Wilson. Though the *Necronomicon* can definitely open passageways to "evil worlds," Lovecraft never described it as being inked in blood in any of its editions. Neither did the book disappear in 1300. In his fictional "A History of the *Necronomicon*," Lovecraft states that, though Alhazred's original Arabic version was lost by 1228, Olaus Wormius's Latin translation was repeatedly printed into the 16th and 17th centuries, and that rare copies of Latin (and maybe some Greek) versions were known to exist in the modern world.[20] And why, pray tell, is the book referred to as *Mortuorum Demonto* at one time, and *Necronomicon* at another? The lack of any reference to Cthulhu, Yog-Sothoth, or any of the other Great Old Ones makes this filmic *Necronomicon*'s place in the Lovecraft Mythos a bit dubious, to say the least. Many Lovecraft scholars and fans would say that it doesn't belong there at all. Still, the forbidden tome makes a good prop for a rip-roaring splatterpunk yarn— which is all the makers really wanted. It is its surreal style and outrageous horror/ humor that save this film from being a more-of-the-same sequel like other series movies in the splatter genre.

Forever Evil. 1987. B&S Productions/United Home Video.
Director; Roger Evans. Screenplay: Freeman Williams. Starring: Charles Trotter, Howard Jacobsen, Red Mitchell, Tracey Huffman.
This film begins as a clone of *The Evil Dead*, with three couples spending vacation time in a secluded cabin, only to be slaughtered by supernatural forces. Even the zoom-up-to-the-victim "monstervision" technique is used. Marc Denning (Mitchell) is the only survivor of the massacre, which included his brother and his pregnant girlfriend. Escaping from the cabin, Marc staggers onto a road where he is hit by a car. Days later, he regains consciousness in a hospital. Old police veteran Lieutenant Leo Ball (Trotter) is investigating the murders at the cabin and recognizes the MO of a ritual murderer, or murderers, whom he has been tracking for years. Leo approaches Marc Denning while he is still in the hospital, not to interrogate him, but to ask him for help in solving his pet homicide case. This series of similar grisly murder stretches back for more than sixty-five years. Later, Marc is contacted by a girl named Reggie Osborne (Huffman), who also survived a multiple slaying like the one he escaped. Reggie is also on the trail of the mysterious supernatural killer, masquerading as a reporter who investigates ritual crimes. Leo, Marc, and Reggie form

an unlikely team to investigate the serial/ritual killings.

Local psychic Ben Magnus (Freeman Williams), who has helped Leo with other "weird investigations," contacts the lieutenant and tells him he has something for him. When the team arrives at Magnus's house, however, they find it deserted and stripped of furniture and belongings, except for a box of old books labeled "STUFF FOR LEO." In the box is a sealed note for the lieutenant warning, "Leo, he's coming back! I'm leaving! I suggest you do the same." Also in the box is a copy of the *Necronomicon* with a gray cloth cover. There is also a black folio-sized book called *The Gate and the Key* (Yog-Sothoth?) by C. W. Ward (Charles Dexter Ward?) with the title and a stylized key beautifully stamped or engraved on the cover in gold, and another volume entitled *Lost Gods*. At the bottom of the stack is another folio-sized book entitled *The Chronicles of Yog-Kothag* (Yog-Sothoth again?) that is (you guessed it!) a grimoire and book of worship for Yog-Kothag, who is (right again!) a God once worshiped by an ancient cult. Inside the book are two old newspaper clippings, one about the theft of a sacrificial dagger dedicated to Yog-Kothag from a museum in 1920, the other about the ritual murder of a family the same year. Among the pages of *The Chronicles* is an illustration of an ugly demon leaping out from the center of an inverted pentagram, probably intended to represent old Yog himself. Leo skeptically rejects the idea that the books could reveal anything useful to the investigation, but Marc and Reggie are more open-minded and take the books when they leave the abandoned house.

Marc's study of *The Chronicles* reveals that Yog-Kothag was "an ancient God so incredibly awful that the other gods ganged up on him and imprisoned him on a star—the quasar—and his cultists, what few of them remain, have been trying to bring him back ever since." His investigation of the serial killings, and his knowledge of astronomy, have convinced Marc that Yog-Kothag is imprisoned on a quasar called the "Ghost Quasar," whose rare radio frequency transmissions coincide perfectly with the times of the cult murders. The investigators mark a map with pins to indicate the sites of the ritual murders and discover that the pattern forms an inverted pentagram like the one in the grimoire. This gives them the location of the next murder. The only individual linked to each of the killings is Marc's former real estate agent, Parker Nash (Jacobsen), whose personal records turn out to be falsified to hide his advanced age—he was born in 1874.

Sure enough, Nash is a priest of Yog-Kothag and plans to conduct the final sacrifice to bring his God back to Earth as the Ghost Quasar begins its transmissions. Nash kills Leo, sics his pet zombie on Reggie and Marc, and even kills Marc in order to use him as a replacement for the revenant he destroyed. This is all to no avail, because Marc rebels, even in death, and kills Nash with his own ceremonial dagger. Reggie is the only survivor.

Shot on location in Houston and Coldsprings, Texas, this independent feature went straight to video, and though it presents a few intriguing ideas, it was badly hampered by a very low budget. The whole movie gives the impression of being an experimental film put together by college students. Camera work is generally stagnant and mostly unimaginative, and the special effects are crude. (There was, however, an effectively repulsive "demon baby" designed by Luis Ibarra.) The plot is erratic, inconsistent, and overly complicated. For instance, we are never sure whether the murders are being committed by zombies, a monster, cultists with a dagger, or the Thing they were trying to summon (Yog-what's-his-name). I'm not sure what the "B&S" in B&S Productions means—perhaps it stands for "Bull Shit."

The *Necronomicon* makes only a brief appearance in this film—a mere "walk-on" part. In an act of misplaced creativity, the dread tome is cast aside in favor of a book made up by the filmmakers themselves, which doesn't differ fundamentally from the *Necronomicon* itself. Why bring in the *Necronomicon* at all? And why, in the name of common sense, did they change Lovecraft's Yog-Sothoth into "Yog-Kothag"? Were they trying to prevent possible copyright infringement, or merely suffering from brain drain? However, the notion of a Great Old One imprisoned on a quasar whose rare emissions coincide with the activities of its cult is an amusing variant on the old quasi-astrological "stars come right" plot device seen in "The Call of Cthulhu" and other Mythos stories. Otherwise, there's enough cheese in this movie to cure a calcium deficiency.

The Unnamable. 1988. Yankee Classic Pictures.
Director: Jean-Paul Oulette. Screenplay: H. P. Lovecraft, Jean-Paul Oulette. Starring: Charles King, Mark Kinsey Stephenson, Alexandra Durrell.
This film begins in 1710, with the death of elderly wizard, Joshua Winthrop (Delbert Spain). Though he is never named in the original tale, Winthrop is undoubtedly "the childless, broken old man" of Lovecraft's "The Unnamable" (1923). As a thunderstorm rages outside his house, Winthrop lays aside his copy of the *Necronomicon* and tries to quiet the howling of his hideously deformed daughter, whom he keeps confined in the attic with the 18th-century equivalent of maximum security; a room with a heavy wooden door secured with log chains and a huge padlock. In an excess of fatherly concern, Winthrop unlocks the door to comfort his malformed offspring . . . and she tears out his heart. We are next shown a burial party of local yokels from "the Puritan age in Massachusetts" who are reluctant to inter the reputed sorcerer, Winthrop, in "hallowed ground," but finally decide to bury him in a crypt on the grounds of his house. The hasty funeral is conducted by a dour Puritan clergyman called Mr. Craft (Colin Cox), who commands that the house be sealed up and shunned by all and sundry. Or, as Lovecraft put it: "They never unlocked the attic door, but left the whole house as it was, dreaded and deserted."

We next flashforward to the 1980s, where folklore major Randolph Carter (the perfectly cast Stephenson) is sitting in the ancestral Winthrop graveyard telling his Miskatonic University classmates Howard Damon (King) and Joel Manton (Mark Parra) the legend set down by Puritan witch-hunter Cotton Mather, upon which Lovecraft actually based "The Unnamable." Some of the dialog here is actually taken from the story itself, and helps to enhance the atmosphere beautifully. Just as in Lovecraft's original tale, Joel is a scientific materialist who is unwilling to accept the notion that anything is "unnamable," since he believes everything can be quantified by science and mathematics.

Randolph, on the other hand, is more open-minded, claiming historical documentation for a New England folktale in which a boy goes insane after seeing the image of an "unnamable" creature imprinted like a photograph on a pane of glass. He insists that the windows of old houses can permanently retain the images of those who sat in front of them. Randolph has even written a published article about the subject (perhaps for *Fate* or the *Fortean Times*). Naturally, Joel ribs him about this, calling him Miskatonic's "best-published student."

Howard points out that the story can be proved (or disproved) by simply going to the house in question and looking for the arcane window pane with a monster's face frozen on it. Joel, the science major, agrees to this empirical approach, and asks where the house is. Just as in Lovecraft's tale, Carter tells them they've already seen it—they have been sitting in front of the shunned house all along! Joel insists they spend the night in the haunted house so he can prove that Randolph is "full of it." Randolph refuses to rush in where angels fear to tread, and goes back to the campus, with the hesitant Howard reluctantly tagging along.

So far, so good. At this point, however, screenwriter and director Jean-Paul Ouellette has used up most of Lovecraft's original short story. After such a promising start, with the hero, authentically named after Lovecraft's Randolph Carter, speaking lines of dialog actually taken from the text of Lovecraft's original tale, the film rapidly degenerates into a teen slasher movie whose only distinction is that it has the *Necronomicon* and a monster thrown in for good measure.

Joel, whose "scientific" approach consists of wandering aimlessly through the Winthrop house, finds nothing to discredit Randolph's tale . . . but something finds him. The unnamable (and still unseen) creature decapitates Joel and hangs his headless corpse upside down in the attic. Meanwhile, at Miskatonic University, Howard is worried when Joel doesn't show up for class the next day, and insists that they go back to the Winthrop place to check on him. Skeptical Randolph thinks Joel is just pulling a prank, but finally agrees to go.

Just as Randolph and Howard are gearing up for their expedition to spook central, Bruce and John (Eben Ham and Blane Wheatley), two obnoxiously arrogant fratrats, are also planning to visit the Winthrop house. These preppy studs are more interested in fornication than folklore, however. Since the nightlife in Arkham is nothing to write home about (unless you're writing horror fiction), they con two naive coeds—hot campus bimbo Wendy (Laura Albert) and her more conservative friend Tanya (Durrell)—into spending the night with them at Winthrop manor.

Unaware of the creepy folklore surrounding the old house, these four expect an evening of fun and games. What they get instead is more like a walk in the park . . . Jurassic Park! The proceedings begin with a candlelight tour of monster mansion to provide an excuse for the two couples to—er—couple. While Bruce tries to date-rape Tanya, John and Wendy find a cozy place to do the wild thing. No sooner does Wendy get naked, however, than she finds Joel's severed head on the floor. This isn't exactly the kind of "head" that Wendy wanted John to give her, so naturally, she runs through the house half-naked and shrieking. The monster then rips out John's throat while Wendy and Tanya scream in the key of B-movie soprano. Tanya runs downstairs and tries to open the big front door and run outside. The doors of Winthrop house, however, have a way of magickally locking themselves to keep anyone (or any *thing*) from getting out.

The door only opens when the nerdy rescue party of Randolph and Howard enter to save Tanya. Howard tends to the hysterical girl while Randolph discovers the dusty remnants of Winthrop's library. Like a true Lovecraft hero, the bookish Randolph spends more time researching occult lore than thrashing monsters. While his classmates are dropping like cheerleaders in a *Friday the 13th* sequel, Randolph scans through the books and sends Howard upstairs to search for the missing students. To his delight and amazement, he discovers a copy of the *Necronomicon* (what was he expecting to find, *Demonology for Dummies*?). He also finds the diary of Joshua Winthrop. As Randolph reads through the old sorcerer's journal, we are shown a flashback in which Winthrop (who always wears a white nightcap for some reason) explains more about the origins of the unnamable creature than Lovecraft did in his original tale. It seems that Winthrop was a precursor of Old Wizard Whateley (of "The Dunwich Horror"), impregnating his wife during his forbidden magickal experiments. She died giving birth to the monstrous half-human/half-demon creature that he later locked up in the attic. Since the unnamable creature is immortal, Winthrop's plan was to keep it imprisoned forever. Winthrop knew, however, that the house would eventually rot away, so his magick took a Druidical twist. He planted enchanted trees in the yard so that the "tree spirits" would imprison his demonic daughter. But "trees grow very slowly," and Winthrop died before the spellwork could be completed.

Meanwhile, in another part of the house, the unnamable monster crushes Bruce's skull, spilling his meager supply of brains on the floor. Howard finds Wendy, who has now lost her mind as well as her panties. Imagining him to be the killer, she attacks him with a sickle. The monster saves Howard by breaking Wendy's neck, and dragging her dead (but still attractive) body off into another room.

Back in the library, Randolph has finally found the spell to activate the "tree spirits" in the "Better Tomes and Gardens" chapter of the *Necronomicon*. Climbing down into Winthrop's crypt, he recites the incantation:

> Yggdrasil, Father of all trees, awaken the spirits of these trees Joshua Winthrop has planted here. Protect us forever from the evil that dwells within this place—*Yikes!!!*

"Yikes!" isn't part of the original spell; it's just what Randolph yells when the stone slab falls, trapping him inside the tomb.

Howard and Tanya have now ended up in the attic where they find Joel just hanging around—upside down and headless. They also come face to face with the supposedly "unnamable" creature, which is actually very recognizable and quite easily *named!* It looks like a classic demon from any medieval woodcut of a Hellmouth or witch's Sabbat—hooves, horns, wings, and tail are all there. And yet, the creature is distinctly female, and has an odd feminine grace. Composed of Goddess, goat, and gargoyle in equal parts—stunted, flightless wings jut from her shoulders; stubby, black horns sprout from her head; her face a wrinkled, wattled horror. Her white mane bristles down her back to a short satyr's tail, overlapping an unmistakably girlish derriere. Shapely female thighs disappear into shaggy goatish lower legs and cloven hooves. Designed by Debra Swihart and acted by Katrin Alexandre, the two bring to life the creature Lovecraft only described by tracks and marks left on its victim's bodies: "marks of horns on his chest and of ape-like claws on his back." This hideous result of a mating between man and beast was inspired from an account Lovecraft read in Cotton Mather's *Magnalia Christi Americana.* Whatever it is, it is moving in for the kill.

Carter's incantation has now born fruit. Or should I say, "spread branches"? Just in the nick of time, the tree spirits have activated the trees around the Winthrop house, and their branches come snaking through the windows like leafy tentacles to drag the she-demon away before it can make chutney out of Howard and Tanya. The couple staggers outside to find Randolph crawling out of the ground after his brief sojourn in Winthrop's crypt. The three jauntily stroll off together (hopefully to file a police report), and seem a bit too chipper for folks who have just seen three of their friends-butchered by an "unnamable" creature. Sanity loss just ain't what it used to be!

While this film gives a whole new meaning to the term "student body," there's not much that's new or original otherwise. It is so predictable that these kids are going to be killed, they might as well have each taken a number and sat in a waiting room till the monster could get to them. Randolph uses the terrible tome to help his two surviving friends escape the house, but only after the prettiest coed has done her obligatory nude scene and been predictably splattered by the monster. Like most films of the slasher subgenre, this one smugly reinforces society's traditional, Puritanical mores—the young folks seem to get killed only when engaged in rebellious activities like sex, beer drinking, and taking dares. The only female survivor is the one who won't "put out." The others are butchered because they are guilty of being young and sexually active. Perhaps there's a televangelist lurking behind the mask of the demon. This movie is a monument to wasted potential, in which originality was cast aside in favor of banal formula.

The prop *Necronomicon* in this film is a suitably large folio with an iron hasp on it. The lighting is so dim that I cannot tell whether the covers are leather or cloth. We are never given a close-up of the actual text on the pages, but Carter calls it "the *Necronomicon* of Abdul Al Hazred," which could be interpreted to mean that it's written in Arabic. One of the incantations he reads out of the book contains the words "Cthulhu" and "R'lyeh." Others are not so Lovecraftian. In one sequence, Carter reads a passage from the book to open a magickally sealed door. Another time, he speaks a chant containing the name of the Greek Goddess Eris—"Nigal etois Eris"—and three candles blow out. Then he repeats the same chant replacing Eris (Goddess of chaos) with the Norse Goddess Freya, and the three candles spontaneously light again. He also uses the *Necronomicon* to summon up the shade of Joshua Winthrop, and to gain the help of the tree spirits (the passage used contained the name "Yggdrasil") to fight the demon.

Use of the *Necronomicon* in this film seems to be every bit as half-baked as everything else about this ill-conceived opus. I probably don't have to remind Lovecraft fans that the dread grimoire never appears in Lovecraft's original tale, "The Unnamable" (1923). But that's par for the cinematic course, since filmmakers perversely love to insert the *Necronomicon* into movie versions of Lovecraft stories where it doesn't belong, and leave it out of the ones where it does. I'm not sure why the mad Arab would mix invocations to Classical Hellenic and Norse deities with those devoted to the Cthulhu Mythos. Tree spirits? Oh, please!

Exorsister series. 1995. Japanese.
Director: Takao Nakano. Starring: Ban Ippongi, Yumika Hayashi, Anri Inoue.
This series of movies was originally made for Japanese television by infamous director Nakano, who has a penchant for blending genres. The heroine "Exorsister" of the title is named Maria Cruel (played tongue-in-cheek by famed female manga illustrator, Ban Ippongi). She wears a miniskirt and a flat-brimmed, Clint Eastwood-style cowboy hat, rides a motorcycle, carries a water pistol filled with holy water, and a huge cross with knife blades in the arms. Between fights and car chases, she battles gangsters and evil wizards who summon demons through the *Necronomicon*, without ever crumpling her cigar or getting a run in her fishnets. There also seem to be at least three hard-core porn sequences per movie—each ten minutes long. As is typical of Japanese pornography, actual penetration is edited out with pixels.

The "plots" of these low-budget features (shot in Betacam) are there only to facilitate opportunities for cute girls to appear nude, and for Ms. Cruel to do battle with tentacled, pseudo-Lovecraftian sex-monsters. In the first installment; for example, *White Uniform Hell*, a tentacled monstrosity that shoots white streams of a fluid that look a lot like semen, attacks nurses in a hospital.

Use of the *Necronomicon* in these features is fairly correct, but minimal at best. In fact, it would probably be *best* if it weren't used at all.

Cast a Deadly Spell. 1991. HBO Pictures.
Director: Martin Campbell. Screenplay: Joseph Dougherty. Starring: Fred Ward, David Warner, Julianne Moore, Clancy Brown, Alexandra Powers.
The story is set in an alternate fantasy version of Los Angeles in 1948 where "Everybody used magic." Everybody, that is, except the hero of the tale, a hard-boiled, Sam

Spade–like ex-policeman and private detective named H. Phillip Lovecraft (Ward), who introduces his own story via *Maltese Falcon*–style narration. Like his namesake, Lovecraft the detective is a mechanistic materialist who is very uncomfortable with the occult. And there's lots of the occult to be uncomfortable with: police use magick to solve crimes, criminals use it to commit them, there are werewolves, vampires, unicorns, gremlins, and so on.

A wealthy magician and real estate magnate named Amos Hackshaw (perennial villain David Warner) hires Lovecraft (the detective) to find his stolen copy of the *Necronomicon*. Hackshaw describes the book as "bound in leather, finished in gold" and about the size of a "large photo album." Though he tries to pass his anxiety off as mere concern over an expensive collector's item, we soon realize that Hackshaw is hot to recover his copy of the *Al Azif* for more sinister reasons. He is also abnormally protective of his virginal, but flirtatious, daughter Olivia (Powers). As Lovecraft the P.I. drives away from their first interview, Hackshaw dispatches a magickally animated flying gargoyle to follow him.

To further complicate matters, Lovecraft's worst enemy and former partner, the gangster Harry Borden (Brown), is also after the book. (Borden runs a nightclub called *The Dunwich Room*.) In the second scene, we see a frightened, small-time con artist try to scam Borden with a fake *Necronomicon* (I guess we could call him a "Necronomi-Con"), and get himself magickally snuffed by Borden's sorcerer/hitman, Mr. Tugwell (the slightly Peter Lorre–like Raymond O'Conner), as a result. Borden even sends Tugwell to assassinate Lovecraft with a rune-summoned, carnivorous demon (an homage to M. R. James's "Casting the Runes" and Jaques Tourneur's *Curse of the Demon*). When that fails, Borden sends Lovecraft's old girlfriend Connie (Moore) to throw him off the track. And as if that weren't bad enough, there are zombie bouncers, stubborn cops, and the aforementioned gargoyle, all out to obstruct the slouch-hat-wearing gumshoe in his quest for the forbidden tome.

When Lovecraft finally nabs the *Necronomicon*, he is double-crossed by Connie, and loses the book to Borden. Borden has made a secret deal with Hackshaw in return for a piece of the cosmic action. The stars are about to "come right" and Hackshaw plans to sacrifice his daughter, Olivia (whom he has kept a virgin for just this purpose), to Yog-Sothoth. The ritual will enable the Great Old Ones to break through again, and Hackshaw believes they will give him infinite power and immortality.

After the final round of double-cross, in which Connie shoots Borden, Hackshaw forces Lovecraft and Connie to watch as he prepares to sacrifice the struggling Olivia, and summons Yog-Sothoth with the incantation from the *Necronomicon*:

> *From the wells of night to the gulfs of space, ever the praises of great Cthulhu and of Tsathoggua and of him that is not named. Ever praises and abundance to the Black Goat of the Woods, Ia Niggurath, the Goat with a Thousand Young. For thou hast seen the dark universe yawning, the lost place where the black planets roll without aim. Too long hast thou dwelt in that cold captiv-*

ity. . . . The way is clear, return and rule! Yog-Sothoth is the key and the guardian of the gate. . . . Crack the bands of formlessness, take shape and come forth! . . . And so forth.

This incantation is taken from both "The Dunwich Horror" (1928) and "The Whisperer in Darkness" (1930), with a sprinkle of innovation. When Yog-Sothoth finally appears, it bursts up out of the earth looking like a giant tortoise with the head of an anteater, and has long secondary jaws that it can extrude out of its head like H. R. Giger's *Alien*. Somehow the ritual goes wrong (or should I say right?) and Yog-Sothoth devours Hackshaw instead of his daughter, Olivia. We later discover the reason: Olivia Hackshaw is no longer a virgin, thanks to the timely services of one of Lovecraft's buddies on the police force. Thank heaven for postwar morality!

Joseph Dougherty's delightful script for *Cast a Deadly Spell* isn't based on any particular Lovecraft story, it's more like what you'd get if Raymond Chandler or Dashiell Hammett collaborated on a Lovecraft pastiche with Woody Allen. The hero's name, H. Phillip Lovecraft, is a nod to Chandler's fictional shamus Phillip Marlowe, as well as to Lovecraft. Instead of *The Big Sleep*, however, we go "Beyond the Walls of Sleep" in this hard-boiled whodunit. This film might just as well have been entitled *The Maltese Necronomicon*. What Sam Spade said of the Maltese Falcon definitely applies to Lovecraft's imaginary spellbook—"It's the stuff that dreams are made of"—or, in this case, nightmares! The deliberate parody of Bogart's version of Dashiell Hammett's Sam Spade is lots of fun, if sometimes a little self-conscious. The chain-smoking Lovecraft even gets to send his ex-girlfriend "up the river" for killing his no-good former partner. Raymond O'Conner is there to stand in for Peter Lorrie, and David Warner is a thinner substitute for Sidney Greenstreet. About the only thing missing is Elisha Cook Jr. waving a pair of .45 automatics. In the masterful hands of director Martin Campbell, however, these venerable elements are nostalgic rather than cliche—homage, not imitation. So, if you're up for a stylish blend of pulp fiction, *film noir,* and horror/comedy, this is the movie for you. Frankly, I loved it!

The gaudy *Necronomicon* prop in this movie looks almost as big as *Webster's Unabridged Dictionary*—definitely big enough to fit Lovecraft's 800–1,000-page estimate of the vile volume's probable length. It has gilt-edged pages and black or dark-brown leather covers held together with hasps of "solid gold." The front cover is embossed with a huge, insectoid-looking star with seven wavy rays, and has what appears to be a bird's skull set into the center. When Hackshaw opens the book and reverently runs his hands down the pages, the text and illustrations inside look as though they might have come out of a reference book on Roman Catholic vestments. I thought I recognized some of the pictures from a book in my own library.

Use of the *Necronomicon* in this film seems to be more or less in line with Lovecraft (I'm talking about the *real* Lovecraft now, not some cigarette-smoking Bogart clone). Hackshaw's reading of the Yog-Sothoth invocation has enough King James Bible "thees" and "thous" to sound convincingly like Dr. John Dee's English translation. However, I know from reading "The Dunwich Horror" that Dee's version is missing the invocation to Yog-Sothoth.[21] Which leads us to the only other problem with this version: The *Necronomicon* becomes a kind of anti-Bible in this film. When the detective mentions the *Necronomicon* in front of his "state-licensed Witch" landlady, Hypolite (the gorgeous Black actress, Arnetia Walker), she spits on the ground and quotes "Revelations" [sic] 5:1—"And I saw in the right hand of him that sat on the throne a book written within and on the backside, sealed with seven seal." The detective is both sobered and nonplussed: "They talk about the *Necronomicon* in the Bible?" Here the plot takes a Christianesque twist, and the dread book becomes a sort of Derlethian anti-gospel sought only by those with a Faustian blend of cynicism and naïveté (cynical enough to sacrifice Earth itself, naive enough to expect the Old Ones actually to reward them). In this respect, the film conflicts with Lovecraft's idea of the *Necronomicon*. The *Kitab Al Azif* could be many things: the dark sister of the *Arabian Nights*, or *The Lesser Key of Solomon* as written by Lovecraft's id. But it is not the *Book of Seven Seals* spoken of in "The Revelation of Saint John the Divine."

Cast A Deadly Spell was followed two years later by a sequel entitled *Witch Hunt*, which featured Dennis Hopper in the lead, but contained no Lovecraft references other than the name of the detective hero.

The Unnamable II: The Statement of Randolph Carter. 1992. Yankee Classic Pictures/Prism Films.

Director: Jean-Paul Oulette. Screenplay: H. P. Lovecraft, Jean-Paul Oulette? Starring: Mark Kinsey Stephenson, John Rhys-Davies, Maria Ford, David Warner.

As the title indicates, the plot is an adaptation of two Lovecraft stories: "The Unnamable" (1923) and "The Statement of Randolph Carter" (1919). After surviving the massacre at the old Winthrop house in the first *Unnamable* film, Randolph Carter (Stephenson) sneaks the *Necronomicon* past the Arkham police, who are investigating all the murders that occurred there. Ambulances are hauling away various members of the student body (or should I say dismembered student bodies?) Carter is taken to the Arkham hospital, where he is visited in his room by the shade of the old sorcerer Joshua Winthrop. (Winthrop is still wearing that damn nightcap from the first movie, and looks a bit like the ghost of Jacob Marley from Dickens's *A Christmas Carol*.) But Winthrop's ghost isn't there to herald the Spirit of Christmas Past. Instead, he asks Carter to use the *Necronomicon* to free his daughter Alyda (whose name means "winged woman") from the terrible curse he brought upon her by foolishly using her in his magickal experiments. It seems that old Winthrop used a spell from the *Necronomicon* that blended the molecular structure of a demon with the molecular structure of his daughter's body. For three hundred years she has been trapped as a hideous half-human/half-demon hybrid (shades of *The Exorcist*!) in the old Winthrop mansion, where he locked her away. In all that time, she has been unable to either die or escape.

Carter enlists the help of his favorite Miskatonic U. faculty member, occult scholar Professor Warren (Rhys-Davies of *Indiana Jones* fame). Together they explore a secret tunnel leading from the graveyard to the Winthrop house, and discover an underground altar stone inscribed, not only with Arabic text from the *Necronomicon*, but also a "quantum physics" equation written in the strange glyphs of the R'lyehian language. They also find the demon entangled in magickal tree roots (those crazy tree spirits again!). John Rhys-Davies reads Necronomiconian incantations with his *basso* at its most *profundo*. Warren and Carter examine the demon and discover that it is indeed two creatures compressed into one. The professor separates the two entities by injecting the demon with insulin! (Diabetic demons must be his special area of occult expertise.) The demon is then "exorcised," leaving only the young, beautiful—and stark naked—body of Alyda Winthrop (Maria Ford) in its place. Subsequently, Warren is slain by the newly exiled and very irate demon. And this, unfortunately, is the only section of the movie that bears any resemblance to Lovecraft's "The Statement of Randolph Carter."

After separating her from the demon, Carter quickly discovers that he too would like to join himself to lovely Alyda (if only at the groin), and the gorgeous but ancient ingenue is instantly devoted to our nerdy hero. (Three hundred years locked in an attic will limit your dating experience.) Alyda is not just another three-hundred-year-old pretty face, however. It's love-at-first-fright for Carter when he discovers that she speaks "the language of Cthulhu" (R'lyehian?) as taught to her by her magician father, Joshua Winthrop. The only chill on their budding romance is the demon, which is hunting her down in order to merge its body with hers again so that it can continue its stay on Earth. The desperate couple rush to the special collections department of Miskatonic University's library where Carter hopes to find the pages containing the spell to get rid of the demon, which are missing from his stolen copy of the *Necronomicon*. Alyda and Carter unsuccessfully try using incantations from the *Necronomicon* to battle the monstrosity that wants to rejoin its molecular structure with hers. Finally, Carter defeats the demon's attempt to weld itself back to Alyda by trapping its molecules in a wooden chair. (And to think Solomon only imprisoned evil genies in brass bottles!) Unfortunately, the monster's symbiotic relationship with the girl was the source of her immortality. With the ugly demon destroyed, the beautiful Alyda dies and crumbles into dust in a matter of seconds. (Shades of H. Rider Haggard's *She*.)

This sequel is superior to its predecessor in some ways. A bigger budget, if not more brainpower, went into this production than into that of the first *Unnamable* film. It features a splendid cast, including professional villain David Warner in a fleeting cameo role as the chancellor of Miskatonic University. And though there is plenty of delightful nudity, courtesy of the lovely Ms. Ford, this is not a slash-the-teens formula film a la *Friday the 13th*. Ironically, the body count is even higher, as the demon literally rips through anyone who stands in its path.

The prop *Necronomicon* used in this film is a huge, moldy, cloth-bound, parchment-paged folio-sized tome with a text of beautiful pseudo-Arabic calligraphy, which the actors in the film authentically scanned from right to left when pretending to read it. This *Necronomicon* also contains pseudo-Egyptian hieroglyphic writing and some magickal sigils and diagrams. One of Carter's colleagues in the Miskatonic dorms discovers that the book contains a mathematical equation for quantum mechanics, which is somehow encoded in hieroglyphic numerals. The equation is a magickal formula for blending the molecular structure of a demon with that of a human, thus turning the two creatures into one being—"two bodies occupying the same space."

Though the book is supposed to be Abdul Alhazred's text in the original Arabic, it is never referred to as the *Kitab Al Azif*. And why does the hero find a copy of the *Necronomicon* in Arabic at all? According to Lovecraft, all the Arabic versions were destroyed by 1228 in the reign of Pope Gregory IX, though one may have been destroyed in Oakland, California, in 1906.[22] Most of the survivals were in Latin, followed by Dr. John Dee's English translation. The intrusion of a quantum physics formula in the *Necronomicon* is what really does violence to Lovecraft's concept of the medieval grimoire, however. Screenwriter Andy Bark was probably trying to emulate Lovecraft's blend of supernatural horror with science fiction (meta)physics. While the forbidden book definitely contains elements of strange science—the witch Keziah Mason found weird geometric patterns in it that enabled her to travel at will across space-time in "The Dreams in the Witch House"[23]—there should be nothing recognizable as modern physics in its alien erudition. The *Necronomicon* is a compendium of frightful folklore, it is a grimoire of gruesome magicks, it is even a book of weird science—but it is not a book of *modern science.*

Why is the mathematical equation in the book encoded in some sort of hieroglyphic writing? If an Arab author in the early Middle Ages were going to write a mathematical equation, he would certainly have done so using *Arabic* numerals. This is the same base ten numerical system—nine digits and a zero—that we use today. The Arabs learned it from the mathematicians of India, and were using it throughout the Islamic world by the seventh or eighth century. A scholar like Abdul Alhazred, writing in the year 730 C.E. would have used so-called Arabic numerals to transcribe an equation in the *Al Azif/Necronomicon*, not a series of silly-looking "hieroglyphic" hen tracks.

Otherwise the use of the *Necronomicon* in this film aligns fairly well with Lovecraft's vision of it as a book of alchemical science as well as magick. In the Lovecraftian universe, the line between science and magick was often blurred, which is to be expected of a writer with a genius for mixing genres.[24] I hardly need to remind Lovecraft fans that the *Necronomicon* never appears in either "The Unnameable" or in "The Statement of Randolph Carter," another example of how moviemakers perversely love to impose the dread grimoire on film treatments of Lovecraft stories where it doesn't belong.

Army of Darkness. 1993. Universal/Renaissance Pictures.
Director: Sam Raimi. Screenplay: Sam Raimi, Ivan Raimi. Starring: Bruce Campbell, Embeth Davidtz, Marcus Gilbert, Ian Abercrombie.

Taking up where the last film in the *Evil Dead* series left off, Ash (Campbell) is dumped (literally) into a quasi-late-medieval world. We are never quite sure if it is supposed to be in our own medieval/Renaissance past from Earth history, or if it is part of the history of some alternate universe. Ash is no historian, so how can he tell? From most of the armor and weapons, I'd say the period was late-15th-century War of the Roses Britain, but for this sort of movie, historical authenticity is the least of the viewer's concerns.

Ash is captured by the medievals and taken back to the castle of Arthur (Marcus Gilbert), the local feudal lord, for execution in a near-tragic case of mistaken identity. When the locals throw Ash into a pit with hungry zombies (deadites) and see a demonstration of his modern chain saw and shotgun, however, they decide to enlist him in a quest to find the *Necronomicon* and fight the "deadites," the demon-animated corpses that now plague their kingdom just as they plagued Ash in the first two films. Ash may not be as—er—*handy* as he once was, since losing his right mitt in the second *Evil Dead* movie, but he's still a mean shot with a sawed-off twelve gauge. Ash only agrees to "quest" for the book after the Wise Man (Abercrombie)—the lord's advisor—promises him that the *Necronomicon* contains a spell that can return him to his own time and space in the late 20th century. So Ash replaces his lost right hand with a servo-powered steel gauntlet from a suit of armor and rides forth.

Ash is warned that he can only handle the *Necronomicon* successfully if he speaks the magickal words "Klaatu barada nikto"—which just happen to be the "safe words" used in the science fiction classic *The Day the Earth Stood Still*—as he picks it up. Of course, Ash botches the simple incantation ("Okay, so maybe I didn't say every little syllable!") and accidentally opens the gateway for a mass invasion of deadites that sweeps across the countryside as an organized military force under the command of Ash's own dark side, "Bad Ash," whom he tried unsuccessfully to kill in the course of the quest. Bad Ash reanimates himself as a rotting corpse with a serious underbite, resurrects every dead soldier he can find, and leads his army of deadites against the castle. Bad Ash is so disgustingly evil that he even kidnaps Ash's medieval girlfriend, Sheila (Embeth Davitz), for some necrophilic necking that turns her into a zombie.

What Bad Ash and his deadites are really after is the *Necronomicon*, which they believe will give them absolute power over humankind and Earth. Ash and his medieval friends are determined to keep the book from falling into their bony clutches. Having finally become interested in something besides going home, Ash takes charge of defending the castle and uses his technological knowledge to good advantage. The good guys finally save the book and the castle, thanks to Ash's ingenuity at making gunpowder and weapons, and to an unexpected alliance with a border reaver called Duke Henry the Red (Richard Grove). Bad Ash is blasted into bone fragments, and Sheila is restored to life after her brief career as a zombie bimbo.

In the final scenes, Ash has returned to his own modern time and his old job at S-Mart. His right hand has been miraculously restored, and his new girlfriend thinks his fantastic stories are cute. When he gets to the part about the magick spell that sent him back to the present, she asks if he got the words right this time. As if in answer, a store customer transforms into a rampaging deadite, and Ash kills it with a rifle from sporting goods, ("Shop smart, shop S-Mart."), thus saving the girl ("Say 'hail to the king', baby!").

When genre fans heard that Sam Raimi was working on a sequel to his *Evil Dead* movies, they were overjoyed. What they expected was a more-of-the-same sequel to the first two films with the same splatterpunk images repeated ad nauseam. What they got was more like *The Road Warrior Meets Excalibur Meets Return of the Living Dead III*, with a script treatment by the writers of *Monty Python and the Holy Grail*. *Army of Darkness* is a raucous, bawdy, swords-and-sorcery adventure fantasy with spectacular special effects, combat choreography, makeups, prosthetics, and huge doses of slapstick surrealism, but comparatively little of the splatterpunk style of the first two movies. There is still a lot of delightfully "inappropriate" humor; however, even Bad Ash and his evil deadites wisecrack and slapstick their way through rape and pillage as though they were the Three Stooges of the Apocalypse. If fans were disappointed, it was their own fault. They should have known better than to expect a by-the-numbers sequel from a filmmaker as brilliantly unpredictable as Sam Raimi. Fans who want an assembly-line product will have to search elsewhere.

No less versatile than Raimi, the director, is Bruce Campbell, the actor, whose incredible range is demonstrated throughout the film's frenetic comedy sequences, where he raves and twitches like a young Bob Hope high on amphetamines, blustering with heroic bravado one second, and whimpering with cowardly self-doubt the next.

Army of Darkness begins, as did *Evil Dead II*, with an imposing narrative account of the supposed origins of the *Necronomicon*. The dread grimoire hangs in space before our eyes as the waves of a red ocean roll in the background. Again, an invisible hand inks the pages with the same disturbing, slightly Spare-like illustrations and sigils (which simply must be watched in slow motion to be appreciated) as Bruce Campbell's voice-over elucidates:

> *Necronomicon Ex Mortis, Book of the Dead*; bound in human flesh and inked in blood, this ancient Sumerian text contained bizarre burial rites, funerary incantations and demon resurrection passages. It was never meant for the world of the living.

As before, the book is bound in a kind of rugose leather. The front cover bears the raised impression of a stretched, wrinkled, distorted, flattened, frowning face—human or otherwise. This *Necronomicon* is a sentient entity that can literally attack the would-be user; in one sequence, the face on the cover of the book comes alive and bites Ash's hand with the teeth concealed in its frowning mouth. The book can also take on multiple forms in order to camouflage itself from a would-be seeker. In his quest for the book, Ash is confronted by, not one, but three *Necronomicon*s (sort of like a modern shopper in any large bookstore), only one of which is real. The other two are traps. One of the "trap" books opens itself into a kind of vortex that threatens to suck Ash into an interdimensional void and temporarily warps parts of his body. The book can only be handled safely by using the words "Klaatu barada nicto." Unless these words are pronounced, there is the danger of opening an interdimensional doorway—an invasion route for evil entities. This *Necronomicon* also contains spells and even recipes for alchemical formulae that can send people back and forth through time and space (shades of Keziah Mason). This version of the *Necronomicon* also contains a prophecy that a "promised one" (who bears a marked resemblance to Bruce Campbell) will "fall from the skies" and defeat the deadites.

I find it difficult to comment seriously on the authenticity of this cinematic *Necronomicon* other than to say that Lovecraft never describes the book as being bound in human skin, nor is it actually a sentient entity that physically attacks its users. How seriously am I supposed to take a *Necronomicon* that can only be handled when saying "Klaatu barada nicto"—the code words used to appease Gort, the killer robot in *The Day the Earth Stood Still*? How seriously can I take a *Necronomicon* that prophesies that Bruce Campbell will show up with shotgun and chain saw to save a bunch of medieval Englishmen and Scots from an army of zombies?

Not seriously at all! Because this is a post-Spielberg action/adventure/fantasy/comedy in which the top priority is to maintain a constant level of hyperkinetic action. Intellectual considerations, even of the most modest sort, are subordinate to keeping the attention of an audience with an attention span stunted by constant exposure to television commercials. Bemusing as this screen *Necronomicon* is, it ultimately becomes a mere McGuffin for the heroes and villains to fight over—and the audience to laugh at—in the course of the action. The "Sumerian" reference in the introduction—lifted from the Simon book—the lack of any reference to Lovecraft's Cthulhu Mythos entities, and any other conflicts with Lovecraft's vision of the book are purely incidental. After all, it's only a prop!

Necronomicon: Book of the Dead. 1993, Necronomicon Films. 1996, New Line Home Video.
Directed by Brian Yuzna, Christophe Gans and Shusuke Kaneko. Screenplays: Brent V. Friedman and others. Starring: Jeffery Combs, Bruce Payne, Belinda Bauer, Bess Meyer, David Warner, Signy Coleman, Richard Lynch, Dennis Christopher.
This collection of three stories is introduced by a "wraparound" scenario that connects them all: *The Library*. In this section, H. P. Lovecraft is played by Jeffrey Combs, star of *From Beyond* (1986) and the *Reanimator* (1985–89) movies, the most famous (or infamous) Lovecraft adaptations every made. Lovecraft becomes a kind of literary Indiana Jones (action figures sold separately!), in search of forbidden books. As a

taxi delivers him to a huge, imposing building with Moorish architecture, a voice-over of Combs narrates:

> It was in the fall of 1932 when I discovered that a copy of the fabled *Necronomicon* was here in America, being guarded by a clandestine order of Ommiade[25] monks. Obtaining this legendary tome was vital; not only to my writings, but to all mankind . . . for within the pages of the *Necronomicon* lie the very secrets of the universe and future.

This is Lovecraft, not as the skeptic he was, but as most Lovecraftian occultists would love to imagine him. When the librarian monk accuses him of "dealing in fiction," the fictional Lovecraft indignantly responds, "My work is wrongly construed as fiction by the lesser-minded. In fact, I take pride in presenting fictional possibilities. It is my duty as a human being . . . to expose certain secrets unjustly hoarded by others."

The crafty Mr. Lovecraft steals keys from the librarians (Tony Azito and Juan Fernandez) that open the Special Collections vault where the dreaded *Al Azif* is secretly stored. There, he lifts the book out of the magickal safe that guards it, and reverently opens it. This *Necronomicon* is a huge book with what appear to be black leather covers completely embossed with an alien arabesque of sinister-looking filigree work of dull gray metal, like parkerized steel or lightly tarnished silver. The covers, though held together by a hasp, open easily, buckling out toward Lovecraft's hand and crackling electrically to his touch. Lovecraft begins taking notes, but his notes don't seem to taken from the text of the *Necronomicon* as much as from psychometric impressions taken off the book itself, as if it could tell him where it's been and where it's going. The historical inaccuracy of the film will spoil the fun for many Lovecraft fans: If the date is 1932, why is Lovecraft taking notes on stories he has already written, like "Cool Air" (1926) and "The Whisperer in Darkness" (1930)?

At any rate, the three stories in this movie trilogy unfold as Lovecraft/Combs clandestinely writes.

Part #1 The Drowned. (Director: Christophe Gans. Screenplay: Christophe Gans. Starring: Bruce Payne, Belinda Bauer, Maria Ford, Richard Lynch.) Edward Delapoer (Payne) is the last scion of an old New England family originally from the Netherlands. He has just returned from Europe to claim his inheritance, a crumbling old clifftop mansion overlooking the sea that has most recently been used as a hotel. The beautiful real-estate agent (Bauer) shows Edward around the mansion of doom while discretely trying to seduce him. Thwarted in her amorous efforts, she leaves, giving him another part of his inheritance, a sealed letter from his ancestor, the sea captain Jethro Delapoer (Lynch), who was the original owner of the house. Edward breaks the old wax seal and reads the yellowed document, which tells of the tragic loss of Jethro Delapoer's wife and son in a shipwreck. The tale of loss affects Edward deeply because of his own recent loss of his lover Clara (Ford) in a drowning accident for which he blames himself.

In a flashback, we are shown how Jethro Delapoer, unable to accept the deaths of his wife and child, burns the family Bible and drives the funeral mourners away, screaming that any God who would take his loved ones is not welcome in his house. Alone in the house with his grief and the bodies of his wife and son, Jethro is visited by a Deep One[26]—a member of a race of amphibious, humanoid, fish-creatures who worship Cthulhu and Dagon. The Deep One tells him he is not alone in his time of loss and leaves him a gift—the *Necronomicon*. The book falls open to a spell entitled "Towards the Remedy of Untimely Loss," complete with a diagram of a magickal sigil in the form of an inverted pentagram. Jethro chalks the sigil on the floor, splashes blood from his own opened veins into the center of the pentagram, and works the spell, chanting the couplet "That is not dead which can eternal lie! And with strange eons even death may die."

Faster than you can say "Reanimator," the corpses of Jethro's wife and son begin to show horrid signs of "life." Though his loved ones momentarily appear to be resurrected, they have an unpleasant tendency to extrude octopoid tentacles from their mouths—a dead giveaway (no pun intended) that they are mere carcasses animated by Cthulhu. Unable to face the despair of losing his wife and child twice in one day, Jethro Delapoer throws himself from the balcony of his clifftop house to the sea-washed rocks below.

Unintentionally, Jethro's letter has provided a clue to the location of the hidden copy of the *Necronomicon* within the house. Edward finds the book and determines to try the spell for himself—his grief outweighing his good judgment. Once again, the *Necronomicon* technically yields results, but not as desired. "Clara" visits Edward as he rests after the (literally) draining spell. He is at first overjoyed, but soon realizes that "she" is literally a puppet of Cthulhu. To free himself from her slimy clutches, he slashes at her with a sword, and her body morphs back into a Cthuloid tentacle. Great Cthulhu itself emerges from the underwater caves beneath the house (it must have been a long swim from R'lyeh!) and smashes up through the ground-level floor of the mansion. This version of Cthulhu is truly cyclopean—literally—it has only one eye! Tentacles sprout from its head, Medusa-like. With its prognathous snout and its long incisors and canines, it looks like the skull of a bear. After a desperate struggle, Edward drops a metal chandelier into Cthulhu's eye, which blinds the Old One. Edward escapes, but barely. Like the Ancient Mariner, he has become a sadder but a wiser man.

This engaging pastiche is not based on any one Lovecraft story, but is a composite of elements from several different tales, among them "The Shadow over Innsmouth" (1931), "Dagon" (1917), "The Rats in the Walls" (1923), "The Call of Cthulhu" (1926), and even a Robert E. Howard story called "The Hoofed Thing," in which the hero fights a tentacled Mythos monster with his ancestor's crusader sword. In this story, the Old Ones have become perhaps more loathsome than ever before. Prostituting the grief of the bereaved in order to break through is sinking lower than R'lyeh, if you ask me.

Nevertheless, this "Monkey's Paw"[27] effect is perfectly consistent with Lovecraft's idea of the *Necronomicon* as a sinister grimoire that never brings anything but destruction in its wake. Though Lovecraft never mentions a spell with the title of the one in the story, use of the "death may die" couplet automatically makes this film's depiction of the *Necronomicon* more consistent with Lovecraft than any of the published *Necronomicon* forgeries on the market today.

As for having the book delivered by a Deep One . . . the *Al Azif* is a tough old grimoire, but I'm not sure it's waterproof.

Part # 2 The Cold. (Director: Shusuke Kaneko. Screenplay: H. P. Lovecraft, Kazunori Ito. Starring: David Warner, Bess Meyer, Millie Perkins, Dennis Christopher.) This is an adaptation of a Lovecraft story called "Cool Air." Lovecraft's Hispanic hero, Dr. Munoz, has been replaced by a very English Dr. Madden (Warner), and the action has been moved from 1920s New York to contemporary Boston. Emily Osterman (Meyer), a young runaway girl, rents an apartment in an old brownstone building run by a woman named Lena (Perkins). Immediately, as Emily moves in, Lena warns her never to disturb the mysterious Dr. Madden, who lives in the penthouse apartment above. When Emily's sexual-molester stepfather (Gary Graham) tracks her down and tries to resume their "family affair" by savagely attacking her, Madden rescues her from rape, killing the stepfather in the process.

It is then that Madden is trapped into taking her into his confidence and revealing the truth about his bizarre lifestyle. He shows Emily his copy of the *Necronomicon* and explains, "Within these pages is the secret of preserving life." The pages also contain crude drawings of alchemical devices, and some kind of hairy-looking arthropod. Madden goes on to explain that he depends upon abnormally cold temperatures to survive—part of a strange life-extension (or death-preservation) program of cryptobiosis he learned from the *Necronomicon*. Though he has cheated death, he lives as a hermit because of his constant need for cold temperatures. His apartment is kept freezing cold by an elaborate refrigeration system. Lena, the landlady, who protects Madden from the outside world and runs his errands for him, is the only other person who knows about his condition. Madden is also forced to find victims, like Emily's stepfather, to supply himself with (gasp!) spinal fluid to keep his nervous system functioning. Without those spinal fluid cocktails, he would lose his ability to feel things—like Emily, for instance. Faster than you can say "Mountains of Madness," Emily and Madden fall in love—and make love—in his cool (downright frigid) penthouse pad.

Emily isn't the only one who has the hots for Dr. Cold, however! Lena is also just mad about Madden—and heartbroken over his affair with the younger woman. (I guess these people never heard of polyamory.) Meanwhile, Emily gets "cold feet," so to speak, because of Lena's jealousy, and leaves Madden, until she discovers that she is pregnant with his baby. When Emily returns, she and Lena quarrel hysterically over Madden's murderous spinal fluid addiction, causing a laboratory fire that kills Madden by literally melting him alive. The scene is much more graphically grue-some than the one described in Lovecraft's original tale, in which Munoz simply dies in a New York heat wave, leaving behind "a dark, slimy trail" and "a terrible little pool." Lena shoots Emily with a shotgun (shades of Granny in *The Beverly Hillbillies!*), mortally wounding her. Lena decides not to finish her off, however, when Emily reveals that she is carrying Madden's lovechild. So Emily stays on, practicing Dr. Madden's system of cryogenic life-extension with Lena's help, and injecting herself with spinal fluid, while posing as her own daughter to hide her longevity. After twenty-two years, she is still pregnant. So much for the health benefits of the *Necronomicon!*

Emily tells the story in flashbacks to a sleazy blackmailing journalist (Christopher), who gets his comeuppance when the ladies slip a sedative into his tea, and use him for an unwilling spinal fluid donor.

Lovecraft's original tale was based on the friendship between two men: the narrator and Dr. Munoz. Nevertheless, "Cool Air" was done once before as a boy-meets-girl love story in a 1971 episode of Rod Serling's "Night Gallery." Frankly, Serling's television version was far superior to this mess. It's arguable that the tale works just as well as a love story—but not as the sort of love *triangle* found in cheap romance novels. *The Cold* is essentially a "daytime drama" version of Lovecraft—it's what you'd get if you blended "Cool Air" with a couple of episodes of *The Young and the Restless*. The girl-fight between Lena and Emily is about as poignant as a mud-wrestling match, and only trashes up the storyline—as does the plight of Madden as a spinal fluid junkie. The pathos of tragedy becomes lost in soap opera sleaze. For Yog's sake, folks, this is supposed to be Lovecraft, not *Days of Our Lives!*

Warner's Madden character is rather less sympathetic than Lovecraft's Dr. Munoz, yet the audience still feels more pity than loathing for him. Warner fits Lovecraft's description of the good doctor as "a man of birth, cultivation, and discrimination," but not especially the part about "a high-bred face of masterful though not arrogant expression." Warner's trademark arrogance is not as over-the-top as usual, but it's still pretty blatant. The charm of the original Munoz was further enhanced by the simple fact that he wasn't a spinal fluid vampire.

At first glance, Lovecraft's original story, "Cool Air," has no reference to the *Necronomicon*. Or does it? Note the following passage from the tale itself:

> After that I paid him frequent overcoated calls . . . trembling a bit when I examined the unconventional and astonishingly ancient volumes on his shelves. . . . It seems he did not scorn the incantations of the mediaevalists, since he believed these cryptic formulae to contain rare psychological stimuli which might conceivably have singular effects on the substance of a nervous system from which organic pulsations have fled.[28]

Could not one of those "unconventional and astonishingly ancient volumes" on the shelves of the good doctor have been the *Necronomicon*? And where else would the doctor have learned those "incantations of the mediaevalists"? Though this use of the *Necronomicon* departs from its usual role as an evil encyclopedia of malignant magick, the idea of a medieval alchemical/magickal grimoire containing information about cryogenics and cryptobiosis is not as absurd as it may first appear. The ancient Romans had a crude form of refrigeration using chopped ice, and by the late 15th century, the Ottoman Turks were building insulated ice houses stocked with ice harvested on the Anatolian plateau. Once again, the *Necronomicon* blurs the line between magick, alchemy, and science. As Arthur C. Clarke noted, any sufficiently advanced technology would be indistinguishable from magic.

In "Cool Air," Lovecraft seems to have predicted the cryogenic preservation of dead bodies. As a plot device, the notion of cold as a life-extension (or resurrection) method has some basis in reality. Gerontologists and biochemists now believe that, if they can lower the human body temperature by just a few degrees, they can greatly extend the human life span. Just another example of Lovecraft as a writer of good science fiction as well as good horror stories.

Part #3 The Whispers. (Director: Brian Yuzna. Screenplay: H. P. Lovecraft, Brian Yuzna. Starring: Signy Coleman, Obba Babatunde, Don Calfa, Judith Drake.) Contrary to the title, there's a lot more yelling, screaming, and gun waving than "whispering" going on in this disjointed film treatment. Though ostensibly an adaptation of Lovecraft's "The Whisperer in Darkness," this uneven pastiche is more like "The Horror at Red Hook" (1925), since it revolves around a cop in New York who is investigating ritual atrocities. The cop in question, however, is a policewoman named Sarah (Coleman), who has become pregnant by her partner Paul (Babatunde). As the story opens, Paul and Sarah are arguing about her pregnancy, and she manages to roll and total their squad car in pursuit of a serial killer called "the Butcher." When Sarah regains consciousness, she realizes that she is injured and that Paul is missing from the wrecked vehicle.

She follows the bloody trail of drag marks made by Paul's body as someone pulled him into an old warehouse. Inside, she meets a disturbing man and woman: Mr. and Mrs. Benedict (Calfa and Drake). They tell her that they know who "the Butcher" is, that he dwells in the lower section of the building, and that he is an alien who has been there since "before the dinosaurs." They lead her through their trailer-trash living quarters, where there is a copy of the *Necronomicon* on a table (I suppose we could call this copy the "Red Neck-ronomicon"). After much screaming, threatening, and gun waving, Sarah makes them take her down into the lower depths of the building, where she sees ancient stone passageways sculpted in Pre-Columbian-looking bas-reliefs. One frieze depicts humans being sacrificed Aztec-style, and fed piece by piece to monstrous creatures. She finds gruesome piles of human remains, including those of her boyfriend, Paul. But Paul has become more than a mere monster snack. She discovers a rookery of flying creatures like airborne manta rays clinging to the walls. One of them speaks to her with Paul's voice and tells her that the things have taken his mind—in fact, she can see his brain floating in the creature's transparent abdomen. (Lovecraft's Mi-Go actually put human brains in metal cylinders instead.) He also tells her that the creatures need humans in order to breed. (Kinky!) Just as we are hoping to see a Mi-Go *menage-a-trois,* we learn that the creatures also have a "sweet tooth for bone marrow." They have long, rigid, serrated tongues, or beaks, like the snouts of sawfish or the blades of electric hedge trimmers, with which they saw off their victim's limbs and (eeek!) ream out the bone marrow.

Mr. and Mrs. Benedict eventually reveal that they too are aliens. Mrs. Benedict announces that she is going to take Sarah's baby, since she is "not worthy to be a mother." Sarah awakens screaming, with her arms hacked off and both legs amputated at the hip—no doubt to serve as confections for the hungry aliens. Shrieking helplessly, she watches one of the creatures slurp the marrow from her severed leg through its sawtoothed tongue, like a kid sucking soda through a straw.

In spite of its position at the end of the film anthology, where one would expect to find the piece de resistance, "The Whispers" has the look of something thrown together out of mismatched parts. Despite the excellent stop-motion-animation monster effects, the elaborate sets made to look like ancient Mayan stonework, and a hilarious performance by Calfa, this section still looks as if it were tacked onto the movie as an afterthought. I expected much more from Brian Yuzna, who is normally a very clever and entertaining director.

The most disturbing thing about this segment of the movie is not its horror element, but its politics. The era of "political correctness" has made overt chauvinism unacceptable, so some filmmakers have found a middle path by creating a fiercely independent female character and then having her brutally degraded. This is an attempt to satisfy both the audience members who admire this kind of woman, and those who secretly yearn to see her taken down. Signy Coleman is put through the meat grinder in this movie. Adding to the misogynistic overtones of the film is the way the alien creatures squawk in obnoxious voices through vagina-like vertical mouths in their thoraxes.

There's really very little of Lovecraft in "The Whispers": no Vermont folklore, no Akeley, no mention of Cthulhu, Azathoth, Shub Niggarath, or any of the Mythos Gods, no reference to the *Necronomicon,* nor are the Mi-Go (if that's what these ray critters are supposed to be) ever mentioned by name. Lovecraft fans will remember that the Outer Ones, Lovecraft's *Mi-Go*—the fungi from Yuggoth in his original story, "The Whisperer in Darkness"—may have stolen a brain or two, but never ate bone marrow. They looked nothing like rays, but appeared to be huge flying crustaceans, like giant crabs with wings, which he described as: ". . . a great crab with a lot of pyramided fleshy rings or knots of thick, ropy stuff covered with feelers where a man's head would be." He described them as having:

crustaceous bodies bearing vast pairs of dorsal fins or membraneous wings and several sets of articulated limbs, and with a sort of convoluted ellipsoid, covered with multitudes of very short antennae, where a head would normally be.

So why, in this film, has the Mi-Go become a mutant manta ray with a Freudian *vagina dentata* in its chest? Though Clark Ashton Smith is never mentioned in the credits, this screenplay was probably inspired by a sci-fi horror story by Smith called "The Vaults of Yoh-Vombis" (1932), in which a group of Earth archaeologists exploring a ruined city on Mars find subterranean stone catacombs (Strike one!), where they are attacked by flying mantalike creatures (Strike two!) that suck out their brains (Strike three! You're out!). Mi-Go or not, if these manta ray–like monsters are hunting for brains, they won't find any in this movie!

What does any of this have to do with the *Necronomicon*? Not much! Though it was mentioned in Lovecraft's original tale, the dread grimoire is never spoken of here, and only appears once, sitting on a nightstand, as though it had been lost in the shuffle.

After these three mini-movies, we are brought back to the framing story of the library, where Lovecraft/Combs is discovered in the forbidden vault with the forbidden book. First, he is attacked by a tentacled thing slithering in the water below an iron grating in the floor, and then by the nonhuman librarian-monk (Tony Azito). Years of rewriting pulp fiction must have imparted expert swordsmanship to Lovecraft, who dispatches them both with his swordcane. (The real Lovecraft would never have carried a cane—but let's not even go there!) Lovecraft tears the human face off the librarian, revealing him to be an alien, and feeds him (or it) to the interdimensional guardian in the magickal safe. Unconcerned about karmic debts—or overdue book fines—Lovecraft snatches up the *Necronomicon* and rushes out of the library to board a waiting taxi. The cabbie (Brian Yuzna himself) asks him if he found what he was looking for. Lovecraft answers enigmatically "It found me!" Why didn't they just call this movie *Lovecraft and the Library of Doom,* or *Raiders of the Lost Necronomicon*?

Necronomicon: Book of the Dead was not altogether satisfying. For example, Jeffery Combs doesn't look much like Lovecraft, no matter how big a prosthetic chin you glue onto his face. I daresay, however, that most fans would like to see more films of this kind. "The Drowned" seemed the best of the three from my perspective, but that was probably because it was not based directly on an original Lovecraft story that had been butchered—er, I mean *adapted*. Perhaps of greatest interest is the cast, several of whom—David Warner, Maria Ford, and the ubiquitous Jeffery Combs—are veterans of other Lovecraft film treatments. *Necronomicon* met with unjustified problems on the road to release in the U.S. Though completed in 1993, the film did not get a U.S. release until 1996. Even then, it was sent straight to video by New Line Home Video with no theatrical release. American film companies have a history of prejudice against horror films, but in this case, the situation was probably made worse by the episodic nature of the movie. Perhaps distributors don't trust anthology films that use the short story rather than the novel as their literary model.

(My) Necronomicon. 1997. Independent.

Director: Aaron Vanek. Starring: Page Hearn.

(My) Necronomicon is a one-minute-and-forty-six-second short feature shot in black and white on 16mm film by independent filmmaker Aaron Vanek. As the film opens, a bald, bespectacled man (Hearn) in a trenchcoat rushes into his house with a cloth-covered parcel under one arm. Moving with a sense of urgency, the bald man doffs his hat and coat, locks the outside door, and bustles into his office. A layout of tarot cards on his desk clearly indicates that he is an occultist. He carelessly sweeps the cards off onto the floor in order to make room for the all-important package. As he unwraps the white cloth of the bundle, he uncovers a copy of (what else?) the *Necronomicon*.

The cover of the folio-sized book is in bas-relief, as though molded from clay. The raised shapes on the cover are suggestive of the fossilized impressions of once-living creatures, sculpted faces silently scream from among the misshapen arabesques. The word "Necronomicon" is embossed in a black uneven font at the center of an eye-shaped cartouche at the top of the cover. Opening the book, the bald man runs his hands over what appear to be lines of Arabic text interspersed with diagrams and/or sigils. There is definitely an upright pentagram inside a circle.

As the obsessed scholar reads from the text, he appears to chant aloud, whether deliberately or absent-mindedly. Suddenly, he notices that the walls of the room are streaked with a thick, dark, viscous fluid that streams from floor to ceiling in defiance of gravity. When he reaches out to touch the bloodlike liquid, his hand sinks into the wall, as if it had turned into water. The chain reaction set off by the incantation is irreversible and the man is driven mad and absorbed by the force he has foolishly evoked. Vanek creates this impression by solarizing the image of the man until it disappears from the screen. In the last scene, the room is empty; there is no sign of the man, the walls have returned to normal. But the *Necronomicon* remains on the desk, at the center of its white wrapping cloth, as though awaiting another victim.

Vanek's method of short-feature filmmaking shows a type of artistic economy that is lacking in most mainstream cinema. Like the makers of television commercials, he packs the maximum amount of action, imagery, and information into the minimum amount of time. Tightly paced, suspenseful, and dramatically effective, there is no dialog in *(My) Necronomicon* to distract from the action, and the stark black-and-white format matches its grim subject matter. As fans of older films like *Curse of the Demon* (1958) can attest, it is often easier to create atmosphere with a black and white chiaroscuro than with color. Perhaps this type of short feature is uniquely suited to making film versions of Lovecraft's shorter fiction. Vanek's use of the *Necronomicon* in the plot is consistent with Lovecraft's idea of the dread grimoire's ability to bring magickal results without the intent of its user. The bald, bespectacled scholar absently reads aloud from the evil tome and dooms himself before he realizes what he has done, like a less fortunate version of Dr. Willett in *The Case of Charles Dexter Ward*. The prop *Necronomicon* itself was designed by Kristen Hageleit Denny. Aaron Vanek and his work first came to my attention through the 1997 edition of the NecronomiCon—the yearly Lovecraft convention.

Mystery of the Necronomicon. 1999. Anima 187/Central Park Media (Japanese) Director : Hideke Takayama. Screenplay: Abogado Powers. Japanese language with English subtitles.
Mystery of the Necronomicon is a cartoon (*anime*) feature, done in two parts; "Book of the Dead" and "Black Chapter," each of which consist of two episodes.

Book of the Dead. Episode #1: This animated feature begins with a bang—literally. Shrill female shrieks and blasts of thunder echo, and lightening streaks across the night sky. A rainstorm is raging around an old dark house, and the lightening flickers strobe-like over a gray stone statue that appears to be a likeness of H. P. Lovecraft. We move POV (Point of View) style down a dark stone corridor to a room at the end of the hall, where we see a close-up of the forbidden book lying on a desk. A voice-over explains what it is we are seeing:

> Necronomicon, *730* A.D. *This is the path of an evil book, written by Abdul Alhazard [sic] in Damascus. This book is described as being very complicated and mysterious, containing the secrets of magic... But is known to also carry the very essence of evil. The greatest book ever on the path of evil. It's considered the king of all books of magic. Therefore in 1050* A.D. *Archbishop Michael of Byzantine [sic] had the book condemned and sealed forever. Some believe that the book does not exist, intact, anywhere in the world.*

After that send-up, we are immediately assaulted with a series of strange and grisly images: a dead baby with an octopus on its chest, a woman rising out of a pool of blood, a man stabbing a woman in silhouette (accompanied by disturbingly wet sound effects), and a flashing amulet of aquamarine. A naked man stands over two bodies, while a young girl stands sobbing in the doorway before him. The man turns one of the bodies over, and discovers that the face of the corpse has been skinned away and the eyes removed from the sockets. He looks down to see the bloody eyeballs in the palms of his own hands—they are looking back at him! Suddenly, the sobbing girl's hair morphs into tentacles that reach out to grab him.

Abruptly, our hero (the naked man in the dream) awakens screaming and sweating in a bed. It was a nightmare! He looks down at his hands, however, just to make sure there are no eyeballs there. This is a recurring nightmare that has haunted him for years; it seems to be linked to some repressed memory.

Our hero is a tough, muscular private detective named Satoshi Suzusaki, who wears a Steven Segal ponytail, sunglasses, and an attitude, so he isn't one to let a little thing like oneiric terror get him down. Satoshi is staying at a ski resort on vacation with his "little sister," Asuka Kashiwagi, who is drawn like a typical "cute"anime girl—with eyes bigger than her mouth. She calls Satoshi "Chief" at his insistence. The two are trying to enjoy this rare getaway in spite of a series of grisly murders that mirror the killings in Satoshi's dreams. The victims' faces are skinned and their eyes removed. The murders panic the other guests at the resort, who are understandably afraid of er—losing face, and most try to leave. To make things worse, a blizzard has closed the roads leading to the resort. Only the police can get in and out using snowplows and helicopters, but nobody can call them because the telephone lines are down.

The elderly resort manager, Yashunori Shibusawa, turns to macho P. I. Satoshi for help, as the . . . um . . . face-off continues. Satoshi runs a computer check on all guests at the resort, and interrogates them to check their alibis. Oddly, the murder victims all have some connection to a corporation called M. M. Pharmaceuticals.

Among the "usual suspects" is a reclusive man named Toshiaki Nezu. At the sight of Nezu's face, Satoshi has a strange feeling of déjà vu. Nezu collects rare books (Hmmm!), and rants that modern science is inferior to "the ancient knowledge of magic." Nezu asks Satoshi if he has heard of the *Necronomicon* (Da Da Duuum!), saying that it contains the real secret of eternal life. "To be more precise, it's a way to bring the dead back to life." The hypnotic gaze of the mystery mage brings on a flashback of one of Satoshi's nightmares, thus ending the interview.

Satoshi's girlfriend, Mina Shizu (drawn as a sloe-eyed beauty with Betty Page bangs and long shapely legs), shows up unexpectedly. Mina is a "professional information collector," and, between gratuitous sex scenes, she sets up her computer and satellite array and hacks into the police files, revealing that the killer was left-handed and used an ice pick to gauge out his victims' eyes.The only left-handed suspect is (you guessed it!) Mr. Nezu, the book-collector. Satoshi goes to ask Nezu some questions before the police arrest him, but finds Nezu's corpse, the face skinned like the others. The phone rings in the dead man's room and Satoshi answers it. A sinister voice on the other end asks him who the next suspect will be, now that the "most likely person" is dead. Blood from the telephone stains Satoshi's hands, and the police rush in to see him standing over the corpse. He thus becomes "the most likely person"!

Book of the Dead. Episode #2: Mina and little sister Asuka (remember her?) wait anxiously while the police question Satoshi. Despite Satoshi's brilliant alibi ("I didn't do it!"), the police are understandably skeptical about his innocence. They point out that Satoshi was a suspect in a murder case six years ago, in a place called River Banks, Maine, where a Japanese couple and a Caucasian woman were killed—their faces skinned off. The Caucasian woman was his girlfriend. After the murder, Satoshi was sent to the Maine State Mental Institution. Because he suffered from amnesia—having lost all memory of the murders—he was not charged. He then returned to Japan with Asuka, whom he adopted. She is not actually his sister, but the daughter of the murdered Japanese couple.

Satoshi is released because of lack of evidence (or bad screenwriting), and because he was with Mina and Asuka at the time of the murder. Mina uses a little sexual persuasion to make Satoshi let the police handle the case. Satoshi continues his investigation, however, interrogating Ms. Sakimizu, a resort guest who confesses that she is a lesbian and was sexually blackmailed by a man named Hiruta (one of the murder victims) to protect her student and love object, Nozomi. She claims she didn't kill Hiruta, but the police have found a button from Sakimizu's blouse at the crime scene and arrest her. Satoshi promises to take care of the little Nozomi until her return.

Suddenly, Satoshi realizes Nezu must be behind all this. He remembers that the old manager, Mr. Shibusawa, somehow became left-handed after their first meeting and knows that "Nezu became Shibusawa." Asuka and Nozomi have suddenly gone missing, and Satoshi takes a snowmobile to the base of the mountain resort, convinced that Nezu has kidnapped the two girls.

Arriving at the base of the mountain, he finds that his girlfriend, Mina, has taken Asuka hostage at gunpoint. She tells him that Nezu is long gone with the captive Nozomi. When he accuses her of being Nezu's partner, she tells him she sent a fax to the police confessing that she and Nezu were the murderers. While Nezu actually did the killings, her job was to make sure that he, Hiruta, and all the other intended victims were gathered at the resort. Then she blew up the laboratory at M. M. Pharmaceutical Co. according to Nezu's plan. Meanwhile, the police move in via helicopter and the chief detective entreats Mina to turn herself in and release Asuka. Mina explains that she "protected Asuka from Nezu," because he was planning to kill her too. It seems that Nezu holds an undying grudge against Satoshi for interrupting an important black magick ritual six years ago (the source of Satoshi's nightmares), and has sworn to kill everyone related to Satoshi, including Asuka. Nezu really only needs Nozomi for a sacrificial victim to complete his "family circle." Mina says Nezu uses "strange magic," that he cuts off human faces to impersonate his victims (Shades of Hannibal Lector!), and controls human minds through hypnosis. She says she teamed with Nezu only for revenge. Twenty-one years ago, Mina worked in the development division of M. M. Pharmaceuticals, along with Hiruta and the other victims murdered at the resort. They were looking for the key to immortality (Nezu's pet obsession). The head of the department, Mina's boyfriend, wanted to shut down the experiments, so Hiruta and his accomplices killed him by injecting him with the untested drug. Hiruta and his partners then gang raped Mina, and injected her with the drug, thinking it would kill her too. Instead, the drug prolonged her life and youth. Afterward, Mina went underground as an information broker and planned her revenge. Enter Nezu, who employed Mina to help him eliminate all who knew about the drug and destroy the lab where it was created. Mina then releases Asuka, and asks Satoshi to forgive her and rescue Nozomi, before turning the gun on herself.

Black Chapter. Episode #1: Mina's confession has now freed Satoshi and Ms. Sakimizu (remember her?) of suspicion in the murder case. Satoshi deduces that the only place to look for Nezu—and Nozomi—is the Half-Acre Mansion in Maine, USA, the place where frightful events made him lose his memory six years ago, and where Nezu must be planning to use Nozomi in an unspeakable ritual. After flying to the United States with Asuka and Ms. Sakimizu in tow, Satoshi heads for the mansion, where he reunites with his old friend, Bill Toargia, a hulking American who also survived the terrible events of six years ago and likewise lost his memory of them. Bill says he feels an uncanny attachment to place, and now runs the Half-Acre Mansion as a hotel.

At dinner, Bill introduces Satoshi to the rest of the guests, who all seem to have interesting sexual predilections. One is a Japanese exchange student named Rumiko Higuchi, who is studying at "Miskatonik" University and writing a dissertation on the *Necronomicon*. Another is a man named Clark Ashton (ha!), who is accompanied by his insatiable girlfriend, Amy. The oddest of the lot is a German "site scholar" named Karl Ihiman, who claims to be looking for "some important historical spot." Rumiko, the occult scholar, convinces Satoshi that Nezu's ritual is going to take place on Beltane, the 30th of April—the same date as the terrible ritual that wiped his memory six years ago. Rumiko tells him Beltane is the best time "to cast magick spells related to life and death . . ." (Most Pagans would agree about the "life" part at least.)

Satoshi knows that he, Nezu, and Nozomi are connected in some way. He takes Asuka and Ms. Sakimizu to the County Library, where he goes through microfilms of old newspapers to trace the story of the murder six years ago. The news stories relate how three people were killed at the mansion; one of them was Satoshi's girl-friend, Nora Defarlane, who had been a student at Miskatonic University. Also mur-dered were Professor Kashiwagi of Miskatonic University and his wife, Akiko, (Asuka's parents). In fact, the Kashiwagis were also Nozomi's parents—she and Asuka are sis-ters. After the murders, Satoshi and Bill were found in a cemetery about a kilome-ter from the crime scene—both had lost all memory of the events. Satoshi was released by the authorities, who accepted the diagnosis of amnesia and sent him to the state mental hospital. This flood of information causes Satoshi to have a flash-back memory of the beautiful blond Nora leaping in front of him to save him from Nezu's dagger and taking the blade in her own heart.

Meanwhile, Asuka and Ms. Sakimizu have discovered that Half-Acre Mansion was built by a man named Herbert West, a professor of the medical department of Miskatonic University who retired to the town of River Bank after he left the university in 1940. The fifty-year-old picture of West looks exactly like Nezu, who must be over a hundred years old. Triggered by this information, Satoshi recalls that, six years ago, the dean of Miskatonic University hired him to investigate Professor Kashiwagi. Kashiwagi claimed to have found the *Necronomicon,* and the dean asked Satoshi to locate the dreaded book. Satoshi figures that another talk with Rumiko, the occult student, will answer a lot of his questions. Ms. Sakimizu points out that they'd better hurry—there only three more shopping days left till Beltane.

Further conversations with Rumiko are unlikely, alas, because she and her les-bian sex partner have been murdered back at Half-Acre Mansion. Marshall Perkins is unhappy to see Satoshi at the crime scene: "This is the same as it was six years ago. People die everytime you show up in this peaceful town." The two girls were grotesquely impaled and hung from the ceiling of their room, but when the corpses are lowered, they reanimate and attack the patrol officers, killing one. The two zombies are finally killed by gunshots to the head.

Black Chapter. Episode #2: Marshall Perkins and Satoshi interrogate the other guests, and the only one without an alibi is Ihiman, the German historian, who claims he was doing research all night. Ihiman says he heard the two women were still "alive" when found, and the police shot them in self-defense, "so it's not a murder." (I guess that's one way to look at it.) Other murders soon occur at the Mansion, however, and Bill discovers that the phone lines have been cut, making it impossible to call the police. Meanwhile, Marshall Perkins finds an old newspaper article about the "private research facility" established at the Mansion by Herbert West in 1942. A bit of computer enhancement on the old newspaper photo reveals that West and Nezu are one and the same. Satoshi searches Karl Ihiman's room, and finds a human-face mask and Nozomi's handbag—Ihiman is actually Nezu.

Meanwhile, Nezu, alias Ihiman, alias Herbert West, lurks in his secret chamber, and gloats over Nozomi, who is nude and shackled spread-eagled on a stone slab. He tells the terrified girl that he is her father, because he took her father's soul into his body, and that she too will soon be part of him. (Not exactly your typical family reunion.) Nezu whips out his copy of the *Necronomicon,* which he says is "the most definitive magick book in the world," and is also called *Kuro No Dansho* ("Book of the Devil"). Nezu says the book can "protect itself with its own power" and "erases the memory of people who are against it." Satoshi's and Bill's minds were sealed by the *Necronomicon*'s power, but their memories will be restored on Beltane, when the book's power temporarily wanes. Nezu knows that Satoshi and Bill will come to save Nozomi, and plans to kill them when they do. After this tirade, Nezu does some very *unfatherly* things to Nozomi. Bill and Satoshi now remember the way to Nezu's ritual chamber below the mansion. There is a romantic interlude here, where Asuka tells Satoshi that she loves him, even though there is a chance he killed her parents. She thanks him for the aquamarine amulet, once worn by Nora, that he gave her for protection from evil. (Let's hope it works better for Asuka than it did for Nora.) The two make love, in what is one of the most graphic sex scenes in the entire feature.

On the afternoon of Beltane, Bill, Satoshi, and the two girls go down the steps to Nezu's underground lair, where they are attacked by more of Nezu's reanimated corpses. Bill opens the heavy sliding door to Nezu's inner sanctum so that Satoshi and the girls can enter while he stays behind to fight the zombies. On the other side is Nezu, preparing to plunge a sword into Nozomi, who is still naked on the slab. Nezu helpfully explains that he is about to re-enact the ritual of six years ago, when the two people on the stone table were Asuka's and Nozomi's father and mother. Soon, he says, he will combine Nozomi's soul with his and complete the "family circle." Again, Nezu waves his copy of the *Necronomicon* and touts it's magickal secrets of immortality. Satoshi realizes that Nezu has killed everyone involved with the book.

Suddenly an unexpected guest arrives—Marshall Perkins—who points out that Nezu's real name is Herbert West, and that he was dismissed from Miskatonic University when the medical department disapproved of his experiments in reanimating the dead. West left the university with his assistant, Toshiaki Nezu, then killed Nezu and stole his body. Just as the Marshall threatens to arrest Nezu/West for murder, another of the evil sorcerer's zombies attacks Perkins—this time, it is the rather badly decayed corpse of Nozomi's mother, Akiko. With superhuman strength, the corpse of the slim woman picks up both Perkins and Bill, and throws them across the room, then puts Satoshi in a hammerlock. Nezu (or whoever he is) continues his ritual. Pouring nasty, gray oil over Nozomi's body, he chants a strange mantra over her, and odd glyphs form themselves in the gray sludge. Some maternal drive must remain deep inside the zombified Akiko, because when Nozomi cries out to her, she releases Satoshi. Satoshi tackles Nezu and runs him through with his own sword. Nezu, however, is unaffected by the stabbing, and he tries to tear out Satoshi's heart magickally. Asuka leaps in front of Satoshi to defend him, and her aquamarine amulet temporarily paralyzes Nezu with fear. Satoshi, however, remembers what happened to Nora six years ago. Little Nozomi, piping up from the altar, tells him that Nezu is afraid of "real fire." It's lucky that Satoshi is a smoker; he throws his lighter at Nezu, and both the evil wizard and his dreaded book burst into flames. Akiko then throws herself on the burning sorcerer. As the *Necronomicon* burns, it releases a swarm of moaning spirits that flutter away like burning butterflies. As the entire mansion bursts into Universal/AIP style flames, Satoshi, Asuka, Marshall Perkins, Bill (injured, but still alive), Ms. Sakimizu, and the newly freed Nozomi all rush from the doomed building. As they all stand outside watching the mansion burn (and wishing they had some marshmallows), Satoshi and Asuka share a passionate kiss. Bill casually observes, "Perkins, nobody will believe what happened here today." Perkins just stares into the flames and says, "I know." I'm not sure I believe it myself, but so ends *Mystery of the Necronomicon.*

Mix H. P. Lovecraft's "The Horror at Red Hook" and "Herbert West—Reanimator" in a medium-sized saucepan. Add two heaping spoonsful of "The Thing on the Doorstep" and *The Case of Charles Dexter Ward.* Throw in your favorite porn video. Add a dash of *Silence of the Lambs* and a pinch of *The X-Files.* Stir ingredients into a medium of Japanese anime at room temperature. Pour into a Hentai blender and liquefy at high speed, until the contents are of a slimy, disgusting consistency. Serve chilled. And there you have the recipe for *Mystery of the Necronomicon.*

Like Lovecraft's police detective, Thomas Malone, in "The Horror at Red Hook," Satoshi investigated ritual crimes so horrible that he blocked out the traumatic memories and temporarily checked into a mental institution—or, in Malone's case, took a leave of absence for "psychological convalescence." Like the villain, Robert Suydam, of the same story, Nezu seeks immortality via magick—including the "resurrection" of dead bodies. This idea overlaps "Reanimator" with Nezu's abominable practice of reanimating corpses. Lovecraft would probably be shocked, however, to find that Herbert West had turned Japanese and started using the forbidden book. Neither of the above two stories involved the *Necronomicon*. However, Nezu also had the ability to transfer his consciousness into other people's bodies, like the sorcerer Ephraim Waite in "The Thing on the Doorstep," which does mention the dreaded book. And he could also stay young indefinitely, like Joseph Curwen of *The Case of Charles Dexter Ward,* who also used the *Necronomicon*. So screenwriter Abogado Powers has updated, Japanized, and sexualized elements of these four Lovecraft stories for this script, replacing Lovecraft's Irish Malone with a cool Nipponese P. I. who, beneath his Sam Spade slouch hat, is a rogue Samurai at heart.

Though Lovecraft never described the terrible tome as bound in human skin, this cartoon *Necronomicon* has a cover pieced together from human hide, complete with mummified mouths and sightless eyes. The more traditional accessories of iron hinges, hasps, and a lock are also included. Powers has added to the book's magickal repertoire the ability to blank out the memory of anyone who works against it. (Wouldn't Simon love to have that!) It's use as a sourcebook for alchemy is fairly accurate according to Lovecraft's fiction, but the alternate title of *Kuro No Dasho* (Book of the Devil) is a uniquely Japanese twist, as is the flight of imprisoned souls from the burning book. For all his zealous practice of black magick, Nezu never evokes any of the Great Old Ones, and the two main Lovecraft stories cannibalized for the script are not part of the Cthulhu Mythos. I'm not sure why the Dean of Miskatonic University would hire a Japanese detective to find the *Necronomicon*, since the university is supposed to have a copy in its library already. Then again, I'm not sure why Miskatonic was misspelled with a "k" in the subtitles either.

Hideke Takayama is the famous (or infamous) director of *Urotsukidoji: Legend of the Overfiend,* the first adult (XXX) pornographic horror/fantasy animation from Japan. With the increasing popularity of Lovecraft in Japan, it was probably inevitable that Takayama would invade Lovecraft territory sooner or later. Those who have seen his *Overfiend* series probably expected to see wailing anime maidens violated by the tentacles of demons in every scene (not to mention every orifice). Surprise! *Mystery* is virtually tentacle-free, and the only demon is disturbingly human. The sex and violence are both fairly pedestrian by Takayama standards—but Takayama barely knows the difference between sex and violence, so for most people, *Mystery* would seem like a visual catalog of depravity. This feature is available only on VHS and DVD. Forget about seeing it in a movie theater. Saturday morning television is right out!

The quality of the anime art in *Mystery* runs from good to barely adequate. Some of the secondary characters in this feature are so expendible that they are given almost no facial expression, and look like amine versions of Mt. Rushmore. We're not talking *Ghost in the Shell* here, folks! Like many mystery movies and slasher films, *Mystery of the Necronomicon* has an overly complicated plot and a list of characters long enough to rival a telephone book. At 127 minutes of hopelessly tangled plotline and swarming cast, there is no such thing as a "brief synopsis" of this movie—you either explain it, or you don't. Most of the characters, however, are only there to add to the body count, the sex orgy, or both. In fact, almost everything about this feature is gratuitous, including the plot itself. The events in the first half—*Book of the Dead*—have little to do with the resolution in the second half. I don't understand Takayama's fetish for scenes of corpses with their faces cut away either. Wouldn't it be easier for the villain to change his appearance with a latex mask? However, Lovecraft did use the idea of an alien creature surgically removing a human face and using it for a disguise in "The Whisperer in Darkness." Face the facts!

Close, but no Grimoire

Many films show the influence of Lovecraft's *Necronomicon,* but never mention it by name. Some of these films are not even "horror movies" in the conventional sense, yet their makers subscribe—perhaps even unconsciously—to Lovecraft's archetypal concept of a powerful and dangerous supernatural book, or of a book for which men will kill and die.

Some Lovecraftian film treatments should mentioned the *Necronomicon* in their scripts but do not, while other filmmakers perversely enjoy inserting the blasphemous book into film treatments of Lovecraft stories where it doesn't belong, as we have already seen. Of the two movies discussed below, the first uses some very Lovecraftian ideas in its version of another author's horror story. The second film makes use of concepts and symbols from a modern *Necronomicon* forgery—the Simon book—as plot devices.

Curse of the Demon (also *Night of the Demon*). 1958. Columbia Pictures (British). Director: Jaques Tourneur. Screenplay: Charles Bennett. Starring: Dana Andrews, Peggy Cummins, Niall MacGinnis, Maurice Denham, Athene Seyler, Liam Redmond. The film begins with a long shot of Stonehenge, on Salisbury Plain in Wiltshire, England, followed by close-ups of some of the individual megaliths that make up the ancient cromlech. A voice-over narration tells us that, since ancient times, men have known how to summon demons from hell by magick.

In the opening scenes, Professor Harrington (Denham) visits cult leader Julian Karswell (McGinnis) in order to beg for his life. Harrington had brazenly promised the newspapers to expose the "Karswell Devil Cult" at an upcoming international scientist's convention, thus creating a media scandal. Karswell retaliated by putting a curse on the meddling professor that will cause him to be attacked and killed by a demon at a preordained time. The formerly skeptical Harrington has waited too late to become a believer, and there is no way to reverse the curse. Harrington is confronted by the hideous demon, which materializes at the preset time and mangles him. Fleeing the demon, Harrington rams his car into a power line pole and the police attribute his death to electrocution.

Harrington's American colleague, Dr. John Holden (Andrews), is newly arrived in England for the convention for "Investigation of International Reports on Paranormal Psychology" and is surprised to hear of the professor's death. Harrington's niece, Joanna (Cummins), is not satisfied with the pat conclusions of the police and is investigating Harrington's enmity with Karswell. Joanna points out that, if Harrington had died by electrical shock, his body would only have been burned and not mutilated as it was. Holden's new colleagues at the convention are not so sure either: Professor O'brien (Liam Redmond) points out crude drawings made by one of Karswell's uneducated cultists that look remarkably similar to medieval wood-cuts of demons. When asked his opinion about demons, Dr. Kumar of Bombay (Peter Elliot) replies "Oh I believe in them, absolutely!"

Holden is smugly skeptical, however, and immediately resumes Harrington's project to expose Karswell's black magick cult. His first step is to visit the library of the British Museum in search of a book mentioned in Harrington's notes called *True Discoveries of Witches and Demons*. Said to be more than four hundred years old, the strange book is supposed to exist only in its earliest manuscript form in the Museum Library. When Holden submits a request to see the book, however, it is mysteriously missing. Holden meets Julian Karswell at the library in an encounter that cannot be coincidental. Karswell tells Holden that he has a copy of *True Discoveries of Witches and Demons* in his private collection, and offers him the loan of it. Holden bitingly assures Karswell that this good turn will in no way prevent him from prosecuting the planned investigation/expose of Karswell's cult. Karswell invites Holden to visit his estate where the book is. He entreats Holden almost pleadingly, "If I could make my point, I could persuade you." Holden condemns himself with his own mouth: "I'm not open to persuasion." Karswell then knocks Holden's notes to the floor and hands them back to him with a magickal parchment bearing a spell in runes secreted inside. It is these runes that will send the demon to attack their bearer at a prescribed time. Karswell then informs Holden of the exact date and time of his impending death.

Holden accepts Karswell's invitation to visit him at Lufford Hall, but Karswell's offer to loan the book is merely bait. *True Discoveries of Witches and Demons* is written in a mysterious cipher and would be useless to Holden without a translation, which Karswell is not about to provide. The book itself is a huge folio tome with pages of crackling parchment illustrated with strange diagrams and odd text. The keen-eyed viewer may notice the Theban Alphabet, Malachim Script, and Celestial Script—alphabets sometimes used as code by occultists, the last two of which are based on Hebrew.[29] The book also contains a drawing of a demon on the facing page. Karswell infers that the book is of much greater antiquity than its 15th-century date of publication: "A remarkable work! The few men who really understood it learnt many strange and terrifying secrets. . . . I've spent my life trying to decipher it. The ancient sorcerers who wrote it knew their information was too valuable to entrust to any known language."

Evidence for the reality of the curse mounts: The cursed runic parchment tries to burn itself in a fireplace, fluttering though there is no wind. Holden experiences hallucinations and a constant sensation of cold. An eerie tune plays in his head, which O'brien and Kumar identify as a folksong about the devil. Karswell even weatherworks a storm in front of Holden, yet the stubborn psychologist still clings to his superstition of materialism. The hardheaded Holden will not believe in the danger of his situation, even after he is dragged to a seance where the medium (Reginald Beckworth) channels the spirit of Harrington who warns Holden that, "Karswell has the key. He's translated the old book! The answer is there!" Joanna convinces Holden to break into Karswell's house to search for the translation of the book. There, Holden is attacked by one of Karswell's minor demons ("nothing like the real thing when you meet it"), and chased through the woods by the smoky apparition of the demon Karswell uses as an assassin. Holden is surprised to find runes like those on the cursed parchment carved on one of the megaliths at Stonehenge. The truth is finally penetrating Holden's thick skull! Under hypnosis, Rand Hobart (Brian Wilde), a member of Karswell's cult, reveals that the only way to escape the demon is to return the cursed parchment to its original sender.

Barely in time to save himself, Holden corners Karswell on a train and tricks him into taking possession of the cursed parchment again. The deadly parchment flies out of Karswell's grip. Running down a train track, Karswell pursues the fluttering parchment, until it spontaneously ignites, burning itself to ashes and finalizing the curse. In vain, Karswell flees from the demon looming ominously on the horizon like a storm. The demon monster seizes Karswell and tears him apart, dropping his corpse on the railroad tracks to create the illusion that he was hit by a train.

This blend of film noire and horror/fantasy by the great director Jacques Tourneur has much in common with the suspense-building work of Val Lewton—Tourneur's film-making mentor—and Alfred Hitchcock—for whom screenwriter Charles Bennett had written several scripts. Brilliant use of lighting, timing, and plot development are all Tourneur hallmarks. Unfortunately, different schools of magick and religion—witchcraft, ceremonial magick, demonolatry, and Satanism—are indiscriminately lumped together in the screenplay. This brand of ignorance was typical of the 1950s, however, whereas more recent films that are guilty of the same mistakes have less excuse.

Dana Andrews's characterization of a man in transition from bluff skepticism to grudging belief is perhaps too good to let Holden pull much sympathy from the audience. He is a chain-smoking, bigoted, academic nincompoop with far more pride than intellect. We cannot admire him as a seeker of truth, because he routinely ignores evidence whenever it conflicts with his expectations. His religion of "scientific skepticism" is as narrowly prejudiced as the beliefs of any tribal witchdoctor. Early in the film, Holden crosses the line between good-natured skepticism and arrogant cynicism, so that halfway through the movie, the audience would love to see him ripped apart by the demon, if only to wipe that nauseating smirk off his face.

Of course, the Karswell character is just as disgusting as Holden, but in a totally different way. Like a demonic televangelist, he keeps his followers in fear to bilk money out of them and make himself powerful. Nial MacGinnis is nothing short of brilliant as the sinister but mercurially charming Dr. Karswell—a character obviously modeled after Aleister Crowley—one of the most fully developed characterizations of all horror film villains. Though there is no shortage of fictional and filmic villains inspired by Crowley, few of them have ever so closely matched Crowley's actual personality and mannerisms—including his habit of calling other men "dear boy."

Curse of the Demon was based on M. R. James's short story "Casting the Runes"[30] and the Karswell character was intentionally modeled after Crowley by the author. The ancient and powerful grimoire *True Discoveries of Witches and Demons*—so pivotal to the plot of the movie—does not, however, appear in James' original story. The rune-casting spell in the story came out of a book written by Karswell himself from undisclosed sources. The title of the movie grimoire seems to be a weird mix of the titles of *A True and Faithful Relation* (1659, Dr John Dee's diaries as published by Meric Casaunon), *Discoverie of Witches* (1647, written by Matthew Hopkins, Oliver Cromwell's Witchfinder General,though it was a witch-finding manual and not a magickal book), *The Discoverie of Witchcraft* (1584, by Reginald Scot, who sought to prove that witches didn't exist), and Montague Summers's *The History of Witchcraft and Demonology*.

The nature of Karswell's grimoire is too much like Lovecraft's *Necronomicon* to be a coincidence—as is the nature of the demon itself, which materializes out of a cloud of smoke as though burning an interdimensional hole in space, like Frank Belknap Long's demonic *Hounds* in "The Hounds of Tindalos"(1929).[31] Long's story of a man who was—well—*hounded* by interdimensional demons may have been at least partly inspired by Lovecraft's "The Hound" (1922), the first story in which the *Necronomicon* appears.[32] I admit that it is unlikely for a book written in medieval Damascus to contain a spell using Norse runes of the Elder Futhark. However, the *Necronomicon* also contains information about R'lyeh, the sunken city of Cthulhu in the Pacific Ocean, so perhaps its lore is so cosmopolitan and cosmic that it transcends provincial boundaries. Another very Lovecraftian element comes when hypnotized cultist Hobart reveals Karswell's mission statement:

> Those of us who believe that evil is good and good evil. Who blaspheme and desecrate. In the joy of sin can mankind, at its last, find itself again.

Compare this to the statement of Cthulhu cultist Old Castro from "The Call of Cthulhu":

> For then mankind would have become as the Great Old Ones; free and wild and beyond good and evil, with laws and morals thrown aside and all men shouting and killing and reveling in joy.

Though Lovecraft's literature would not become fashionable with the masses until the mid-to-late 1960s, it should be noted that many publishers were putting out cheap editions for the Armed Services through the forties and fifties. The same intelligentsia who write scripts for movies also tend to read books. Though filmed at an earlier date than the first movies overtly based on Lovecraft stories, *Curse of the Demon* definitely seems to show influence from Lovecraft and his fictional grimoire.

Ghostbusters. 1984. Columbia Pictures.
Director: Ivan Reitman. Screenplay: Dan Akroyd, Harold Ramis. Starring: Bill Murray, Dan Akroyd, Harold Ramis, Sigourney Weaver, Ernie Hudson, Annie Potts.
Three maverick scientists and scholars—Dr. Peter Venkman (Murray), Dr. Ray Stantz (Akroyd), and Dr. Egon Spengler (Ramis)—form a team to investigate paranormal phenomena. When they lose their academic backing, they offer their services to the public as commercial supernatural troubleshooters, and unexpectedly become a colossal success. They later hire on an adventurous and intelligent gentleman named Winston Zeddmore (Hudson). Together, they are the *Ghostbusters*, national celebrities to rival Elvis, Billy Graham, and the astronauts. As paranormal activity accelerates at a frightening rate, they intrepidly wade into it like the Four Stooges of the Apocalypse, trapping and containing negative spirits.

Dana Barrett (Weaver) calls the Ghostbusters when she opens her refrigerator one day and sees a vision of a ziggurat-like temple inside. She also sees an ugly, doglike demon that roars the word *Xul*. (See the definition of *xul* on page xlix "Common Sumerian Words and Phrases in English" from Simon's *Necronomicon*. In ancient Sumerian, the word *hul* means "evil.") Dr. Peter Venkman defines *Xul* from a reference book called *Tobin's Spirit Guide* as "'a demigod worshiped around 6,000 B.C. by the'—what's that word?—*Hittites!* 'Hittites, Mesopotamians and Sumerians.' Xul was a minion of Goser . . . Goser was very big in Sumeria." Dana just wants to know "What's he doing in my icebox?" Peter immediately wants to get into Dana's apartment (not to mention her pants). When he checks out her place, however, the spooks are lying low.

As her situation declines, Dana becomes possessed by the spirit, which calls itself "Xul, the Gate-keeper," a rather obvious spoof of the "Gates" of the Simon *Necronomicon*. Xul speaks through Dana to announce that it is preparing the way for Gozer the Destroyer. Both the possessed Dana and her possessed neighbor (Rick Moranis) are metamorphosed into giant, ogreish, horned dog-demons (Hounds of Tindalos?)—servitors of Gozer. Compare this to the dog-faced demons on page 49 of the Simon *Necronomicon*, described as "Messengers of the Gods of Prey."[33] Peter wants to save Dana, not only because she's a babe, but because of the unique challenges of her case. The possessed girl's apartment is in an old high-rise structure built of exotic materials and with weird (non-Euclidian? R'lyehian?) architecture. According to Ray's research, "the whole building is a huge superconductive antenna that is designed and built expressly for the purpose of pulling in and concentrating spiritual turbulence." According to Egon, "something terrible is about to enter our world and this building is obviously the door." Does all of this sound familiar?

The architect of the building was an evil magician named Ivo Shandor (shades of Anton *Szandor* LaVey?). He was also a doctor rumored to have performed much unnecessary surgery (shades of "Herbert West—Reanimator"). Shandor built the structure in 1920 (the era of both Lovecraft and Crowley) so that his Gozer cult could conduct their bizarre rituals on the top floor, which had been built to look (sort of) like a Sumerian temple. (The building itself looks more like Pieter Bruegel the Elder's *The Tower of Babel* than a real ziggurat.) Shandor's cult sought to summon the pseudo-Old One, Goser, to bring about the end of the world. Now, thanks to the stupidity of an EPA bureaucrat named Peck (William Atherton) who shut off the Ghostbusters' containment grid, all the negative psychic energy in NYC—plus Gozer itself—is concentrated in Shandor's art deco/Mesopotamian penthouse temple. The entire city will be destroyed unless the Ghostbuster boys can save the day. Accidentally summoning Gozer in the form of the "Stay Puft Marshmallow Man"—who looks like a giant demon-possessed version of the Pillsbury Doughboy—they nevertheless melt him down like a titanic smuller with blasts from their proton beams.

Ghostbusters was the first big-budget blend of horror and comedy. The movie is so much fun that the viewer cannot help but laugh at subject matter that might otherwise be considered a bit grim. Magnificent special effects by Richard Edlund contrast hilariously with the goofily doctrinaire nonchalance of Murray, Akroyd, and Ramis. Far from losing their sanity (assuming they ever had any) at the sight of a Lovecraftian monster, the Ghostbusters handle mind-blasting horrors as if they were all in a day's work.

I have included this movie for two reasons: because it shows some decidedly Lovecraftian influences, and because I believe much of its satire is aimed squarely at the Simon *Necronomicon*, although the "N" word is never spoken anywhere in the screenplay. Though there is no mention of the Cthulhu Mythos, there are some very Lovecraftian plot devices in this film, including its basic premise. Yes, it was Lovecraft who wrote the first story about scientific "ghostbusters" who try to shoot a supernatural entity with high-tech weapons. In "The Shunned House" (1924), the unnamed narrator and his uncle invade a "haunted" house, armed with a flame-thrower and a Crookes tube (a contraption invented by Sir William Crookes that creates an emission of electrons between two electrodes), to do battle with its hideous inhabitant.

It is doubtful that this movie will ever have a cult following from the Simon *Necronomicon* crowd. Simonian cliches are treated with light-hearted irreverence, if not utter contempt. When the pseudo-Mythos, quasi-Simonian Gozer morphs into a giant Marshmallow Man and gets blasted into gooey white chunks by the Ghostbusters, it becomes obvious how much respect screenwriters Dan Akroyd and Harold Ramis have for the little black book.

Another note of *Necronomicon*-related synchronicity that comes from *Ghostbusters* is the use of a fictional book called *Tobin's Spirit Guide* in the screenplay.

Akroyd and Ramis were using the old Lovecraft trick; there never was a real book entitled *Tobin's Spirit Guide*. The huge popularity of *Ghostbusters*, however, led to the marketing of a roleplaying game called *Ghostbusters International*,[34] which printed its own version of *Tobin's Spirit Guide*[35] as a supplement to the game. The "Guide" even contains an introduction from the imaginary Dr. Ray Stantz. This is just another object lesson in how easily a nonexistent book can artificially become a "real" book when profit margins rise high enough.

Favorite funny quote:

> Possessed Dana: *I want you in me!*
> Peter Venkman: *Sounds like you've got at least two people in there already.*

Call of the Cathode Ray Tube: The *Necronomicon* on Television —John Wisdom Gonce III

11

*Of the Shining Trapezohedron he speaks often, calling
it a window on all time and space.*
—HOWARD PHILLIPS LOVECRAFT,
"THE HAUNTER OF THE DARK"

Now every home contains its own Shining Trapezohedron. The fiendish artifact wasn't made on the planet Yuggoth, but manufactured in Japan or Mexico by a company like Toshiba or Zenith. It's hardly "a window on all time and space," but it does show abominable situation comedies, unnamable soap operas, and unspeakable commercials. It's called a television set. The ubiquitous grim grimoire of Lovecraft's imagination has also turned up on television, or *The Glass Teat*, as Harlan Ellison would call it. Even Saturday-morning cartoon television has been haunted by an appearance of the *Necronomicon*. It remains to be seen whether the *Necronomicon* will make the "vast wasteland" of television any vaster or more wasted.

Dark Legacy. "Thriller" series. 1961. (Black & White) Hubble Robinson Productions. Director: John Brahm. Starring: Harry Townes, Ilka Windish, Richard Hale, Doris Loyd, Henry Silva. Hosted by Boris Karloff.
The wealthy and famous old stage magician Radan Asparos (Townes) is also a real magician. He is preparing for his imminent death by planning to bequeath the frightful grimoire, which is the real secret of his theatrical success, to one of his few surviving relatives. Just before his demise, Radan works a ritual in which the archdemon Astaroth—who is associated with the book—chooses Radan's nephew, Mario Asparos (also Townes), as its heir. Cousin Anna Pringel[1] (Loyd) and cousin Lars Eisenhardt (Hale) are very disappointed that Radan has decided to leave his "secrets" to his nephew Mario, who is also a stage magician—though a far less successful one. Mario's current career status is self-described as "scratching around cheesy nightclubs at $150 plus drinks."

While Radan's will is being read at the Asparos estate during a freak thunderstorm, the book mysteriously appears on a table in Mario's house, accompanied a sensation of nameless dread that sends Mario's wife, Monica, into screaming hysterics. The front cover of the dark hardcover, dictionary-sized tome is engraved with a sigil that is almost identical to, but more symmetrical than, the "seal of Astaroth" from the *Goetia* as incorrectly reproduced by A. E. Waite in *The Book of Black Magic.*[2] Mario and his friend Toby Wolfe, a former stage hypnotist now studying psychology, rush home to look at this exotic find. Ignoring the question of how the book materialized out of blank space, the two friends pore over the tome for hours in an attempt to understand why Radan thought it so valuable. Eventually, Wolfe gives up on finding the secrets of Radan's stage illusions in the book and declares that what they have found is nothing more than a medieval grimoire. Mario, however, finds something that fascinates him—a note written in a margin of the book by Radan himself: "The magickal circle or pentagram used in Goetic theurgy according to the *Lesser Key of Solomon* useful for summoning Astaroth who gives great skill." Wolfe sarcastically quips, "I guess he meant to make you a great magician by passing along one of his pet demons," and advises Mario to sell the book as he leaves.

Mario, however, will try anything to save his sinking magic career—even real magick. Making a ceremonial dagger out of a letter opener and chalking a circle on the floor, Mario evokes Astaroth, who appears as a pair of eyes glowing out of a cloud of smoke. Though Astaroth kills the family dog, the archdemon also confers great magickal skill on the desperate Mario.

In the days that follow, Mario's illusionist act improves so greatly that his audiences are now applauding wildly, and the nightclub owner who once threatened to fire him is now begging him to stay on. Mario's old friend, Toby Wolfe, is leery of the hazardous tricks in Mario's new stage act and worried that they may endanger Monica, who is Mario's stage assistant as well as his wife. Mario then makes the startling claim that none of the "tricks" he now performs are illusions, but are actually manifestations of real magick. Mario takes Wolfe's skepticism as a challenge and promises, "I'm going to show you Astaroth!" Mario claims that Astaroth is "very fearful to behold . . . and very powerful. He serves me, however, because I possess his book."

Mario forces Wolfe and Monica to watch as he summons Astaroth into their presence. Wolfe's skepticism withers at the sight of Astaroth, and he begs Mario to "send it back." Mario, however, cannot send the archdemon anywhere, because he has made a pact with it subject to his ownership of the book. When Wolfe insists that he destroy the book, Mario orders Astaroth to kill both Wolfe and Monica. Wolfe then hurls the book into the fireplace, where it burns, effectively banishing Astaroth. The frustrated demon leaves, killing Mario as it departs.

This teleplay, though a bit melodramatic, is intriguing for a number of reasons. More research than average seems to have gone into the screenplay, but the use of magick in "Dark Legacy" is about as absurd and inaccurate as it is in most films. For example, "AGLA" is a Qaballistic Notarikon for "Ateh Gibor LeOlahm Adonai" or

"Thou art great forever, my Lord."It is not the name of a demon. The way in which the story links stage magic with occult magick is echoed by Clive Barker in *Lord of Illusion* more than twenty years later, proving that old ideas never die, but simply get recycled with flashier special effects.

Though "Dark Legacy" may owe something to Jaques Tourneur's *Curse of the Demon*, and to research on old grimoires, it probably owes a good deal more to Lovecraft. The lethal book of magick in the story is never identified as the *Necronomicon*—but it is never identified at all! The book is not the *Goetia*, which is only mentioned in the notes that Radan himself scribbled in the margins of the book. Though the Cthulhu Mythos is never mentioned, the archdemon Astaroth—whose name is unmistakably similar to Lovecraft's "Azathoth"—is pivotal to the plot. If we only knew the actual extent of the influence Waite's books and treatments of old grimoires had on Lovecraft, we might know whether or not the name of *Astaroth*, the Goetic demon, was an inspiration for Lovecraft's choice of the name *Azathoth* for his God of chaos. It probably wasn't, since the name *Azathoth* first appears in Lovecraft's writings in 1919. The name *Azathoth* is also remarkably similar to the word "Azoth," a name used in medieval alchemy for the Stone of the Philosophers. Perhaps Lovecraft encountered the word in his vast readings and it became submerged in his subconscious mind, only to reemerge in a slightly different form.

Though Lovecraft's fiction would not become popular with the masses until the mid-to-late 1960s, Arkham House, established in 1939, had been republishing his works throughout the forties and fifties. It is more than likely that John Tomerlin, who wrote the screenplay, was familiar with Lovecraft's work—and with his use of the *Necronomicon* as a plot device. The *Thriller* series also filmed a version of "Pigeons from Hell," a short story by Lovecraft's good friend Robert E. Howard, thus demonstrating the willingness of its writers to borrow from pulp fiction sources. The odds are good that this "Dark Legacy" was just another inheritance from Grandpa Ech-Pi-El.

"Return of the Sorcerer." *Rod Serling's Night Gallery* series. 1972. Universal\MCA-TV. Director: Jean Szwarc. Teleplay: Halsted Welles. Starring: Bill Bixby, Patricia Sterling, Vincent Price. Hosted by Rod Serling.

This is the strange tale of skilled linguist and professional nerd Noel Evan (Bixby), who replies to an advertisement for a translator of Arabic. Noel's future employer is a sinister, preoccupied man named Carnby (Price) who lives in a rambling old mansion cluttered with enough Satanic bric-a-brac to gladden the heart of Anton LaVey. Carnby offers Noel a huge advance on his salary and insists that he stay at the Carnby estate while working on the translation. Supposedly, the only other inhabitant of the house is Carnby's beautiful female "assistant" Fern (Sterling). Yet Noel keeps hearing disturbing noises of something dragging or shuffling through the halls—something too big to be rats. In spite of Noel's initial misgivings, the seductive Fern convinces him to stay.

At dinner, seated opposite a black goat, whom Carnby claims is his reincarnated father (another dysfunctional horror film family), Noel realizes that his hosts are not only occultists, but Satanists as well. Fern pontificates about the Black Mass, saying that it was an act of rebellion against the political and ecclesiastical oppression of medieval Europe. Carnby will not give Noel a straight answer as to just exactly *how* Fern "assists" him, only saying that, in sorcery, the female is always dominant. (Whips, chains, and pentacles. Oh my!)

Carnby's frustration is conspicuous as he reveals a huge tome with beautiful Arabic calligraphy and explains to Noel the importance of the translation:

> Much of the practice of sorcery is based on the Latin work, the *Necronomicon*. But that was based on this Arabic work. But you see, some of the most—I mean this literally—fiendish passages were never rendered into Latin.

Noel quickly discovers why the last two translators abruptly quit and tries to quit himself before Carnby forces him to finish the horrific translation at gunpoint:

> It is verily known by a few that the will of a dead sorcerer has powers upon his own body and can raise it up from the tomb and perform therewith whatever actions were unfulfilled in his life. Such resurrections are invariably for the detriment of others. But he can only do this damage to another person if that person knows of his peculiar power. There are cases in which the will of the wizard was so powerful that even though his body had been hewn into many fragments, these fragments can rise either separately or in concert to serve the wizard's end.

But it is the preamble curse that really makes Noel queasy:

> By all the dark powers of this world, may he who reveals this secret be flayed slowly over burning coals and thoroughly dismembered.

Carnby looks rather comatose after hearing the translation, and Fern explains that it's because Carnby killed and dismembered the body of his twin brother—a more powerful sorcerer than he—and now realizes that his fears of his brother's return are well founded. Noel panics at hearing this grisly news, but Fern, the alluring post-hippie sorceress, rebukes him for his squeamishness: "Cool it, man! Believe in the oneness. Terror is joy, joy is terror. Life is death and torture is ecstasy. We're holding a Black Mass later; I'll see you then."

Carnby later reveals to Noel that it is Fern who actually caused his brother's death by playing him and his brother against each other as competitors, and leading him to murder his sorcerer rival. It was always Fern's desire to be more powerful than both brothers. By the time Noel can pack his bags to escape, Carnby's twin brother has reconstituted his mutilated body and exacted a similar revenge on his perfidious sibling. As Fern puts it, the two brothers are now "fragmented, but together." Though Noel wants to leave, the beguiling Fern (you guessed it!)

convinces him to stay. Desperate for reassurance, Noel asks her if the "flaying" curse in the *Necronomicon* might not be powerless after all. Fern answers with a less-than-comforting silence.

In this story, based on a tale by Clark Ashton Smith, the use of the *Necronomicon* is nearly perfect with regard to the visions of both Smith and Lovecraft himself. However, the book is never referred to as the *Kitab Al Azif*, even though it is supposed to be in Alhazred's original Arabic text. The exotic atmosphere, unrelenting morbidity, and mordant humor are all Smith trademarks that are admirably carried over into this feature. There is the typical blurring of ceremonial magick, witchcraft, and Satanism that one sees in all too many horror films, but the mistakes somehow don't seem as flagrant as usual. Among the jumble of occult decor on the set, for example, there is a huge panel depicting the Ace of Cups from Aleister Crowley's *Thoth* Tarot deck. Of special interest is the way the plotline links the *Necronomicon* with Satanism, but this is part of the original story and thus is probably not connected to Anton LaVey's publication of Lovecraftian ceremonies in his *Satanic Rituals*, published before this episode was made. The enormous influence of the Decadent movement writers on Clark Ashton Smith may explain the apparent links between Satanism and the *Necronomicon* in this tale.

"Professor Peabody's Last Lecture." *Rod Serling's Night Gallery* series. 1972. Universal\MCA-TV. Director: Jerrold Freeman. Written by Jack Laird. Starring: Carl Reiner. Hosted by Rod Serling.
Professor Peabody (Reiner) is teaching a kind of comparative religions course dealing with "pagan religious cults." The professor's most annoying questioners have names like Bloch, Derleth, and Lovecraft. Today, however, Peabody has decided to devote the entire lecture to what he calls "indisputably the most outlandishly preposterous of all the ancient cults"—the *Cthulhu Mythos*. The good professor deals in turn with Nyarlathotep, Umr atTawil [sic], Hastur, Cthulhu, Azathoth, Shub Niggurath and Yog-Sothoth. At the prompting of a student named Lovecraft, Peabody produces the "grand grimoire" of the cultus, "a manuscript of that most infamous of Qaballistic treatises, the *Necronomicon* by Abdul Alhazred," which he says he has brought from the library at Miskatonic University. This version of the blasphemous book is only about octavo-sized or smaller, no bigger than a prayer book, with cracked brown covers held together by a metal hasp. The professor recites a brief (and correct) history of the text's major translations and publications, up to the "Black Letter edition, Germany, circa 1400" and admits that what he has for them is the "equivalent of a paperback edition," though nevertheless very rare.

Peabody has decided to read aloud from the *Necronomicon* in the belief that a sample of the actual text will convince his class of its absurdity far better than any secondhand description:

> Never is it to be thought that man is either the oldest or the last of the masters of earth, nor that the greater part of substances walks alone. The Old

Ones were, the Old Ones are, and the Old Ones shall be. They walk calm and primal, of no dimension and to us unseen. They walk foul in lonely places where the words have been spoken and the rites howled through at their seasons, which are in the blood and differ from the seasons of man. The winds gibber with their voices . . .

As the reading continues, a freakishly unseasonable storm is brewing on campus. Professor Peabody's reading becomes unconsciously more dramatic—even frenzied—as the eldritch storm blows the windows open and whips through the classroom:

Soon they shall rule again where man rules now. They shall return, and on this returning shall Great Cthulhu be freed from R'lyeh beneath the sea. And him who is not to be named shall come forth from his city which is Carcosa near the Lake of Hali. And Shub Niggurath shall come forth and multiply in her hideousness. Then Nyarlathotep shall carry the words of the Great Old Ones to their minions. And Yog-Sothoth, who is all in one and one in all, shall lay his hand on all who oppose them and destroy. Then from the black-litten caverns within the earth where all is chaos and destruction shall come the noxious Azathoth. And together they shall take possession of all things that live upon the earth.

Faster that you can say "shoggoth," Professor Peabody is bathed in an eerie green light and transformed before his gaping students into a creature that looks like a pile of spinach pasta with one lidless eyeball peering out from inside the heap. Unaware of his sudden metamorphosis, the old prof gamely closes his lecture: "And now if there are no further questions . . . "

Though the Catholic missal-sized *Necronomicon* looks a little too small to be Alhazred's 800-page grimoire, the "paperback edition" comment is probably an allusion to T. E. D. Klein's famous quip (see the quotation at the beginning of chapter 2 in part 1). The *Necronomicon* is definitely a grimoire, but I would hesitate to classify it as a "Qaballistic treatise," and I'm sure many Jewish viewers would agree. As opposed to the occult material, the Lovecraft scholarship in the script of "Professor Peabody" is unexpectedly good, considering that the teleplay was a comedy that veteran Carl Reiner hams up to the best of his vaudevillian ability.

Critics of the *Night Gallery* series have noted that the producers often insisted on framing the serious dramas featured on the show with fatuous comedy "blackout" vignettes, in imitation of Rowan and Martin's *Laugh-In*.[3] This was probably the fate of "Professor Peabody's Last Lecture," which, in other hands, might have become genuinely horrible instead of merely silly. Serling himself had little control over how scripts were mangled by nearly illiterate TV network executives. The observant viewer watching reruns of *Night Gallery* may notice that Serling often seems impatient and angry while introducing episodes over which he had no artistic control.

"The Collect Call of Cathulhu." *The Real Ghostbusters* cartoon series. 1986. RCA/ Columbia Pictures. Written by Michael Reaves. Based on the characters created by Dan Akroyd and Harold Ramis.

The name of *Cthulhu* is deliberately misspelled in the title card. Possibly this was done to avoid any possible copyright problems.

The *Necronomicon* is on display at the New York Public Library on the insistence of a librarian named Clark Ashton (Smith?) and over the objections of a man from Miskatonic University named Ted Klein, who claims that the book is too dangerous to be on public display. This cartoon *Necronomicon* appears to be bound in covers of dark brown, tooled leather with the word "*Necronomicon*" stamped or engraved in gold leaf, running vertically down the front cover. Also on the front cover is an upright pentagram inside a circle (elder sign?), also in gold. That night, the *Necronomicon* is stolen out of its case by an octopoid Spawn of Cthulhu that easily overpowers the guard. The following morning, just as the Ghostbusters are planning to view the dread grimoire on display, they receive word that it has been stolen. Rushing to the library, where they get "high paranormal readings" off the smashed display case, they begin to search for the book. Clark Ashton protests the efforts of the Ghostbusters, but Klein entreats them to try to find it immediately, for the safety of the entire world. Egon agrees that Klein is right to worry, because this is "the only English translation of the *Necronomicon*. If someone were to read the spells aloud, the results could be catastrophic." Egon explains, "The *Necronomicon*'s spells are like sonic keys that can open portals to other dimensions where the Great Old Ones wait to take over the earth."

The Ghostbusters track the Spawn of Cthulhu, which they assess as "a class-seven corporeal entity," into a sewer, where they find themselves quickly surrounded by the mollusk-like minions of Cthulhu. The huge octopoid creatures are only temporarily wounded by the beams from the Ghostbusters' proton packs and regenerate themselves almost instantly. The boys only escape by boiling the sewer water with their proton beams and fleeing under cover of the steam clouds. Peter loses a shoe extricating his leg from a tentacle's embrace. After their disappointing shoot-out with the Spawn, the Ghostbusters retreat to headquarters to do some research.

Ray discovers that, for the first time in sixty years, "the stars are right" for a resurrection of Cthulhu by the cult who stole the book. Egon insists they must find the book at once. He orders Ray and Winston to check the *Book of Dzyan* [sic] and the *Pnakotic Manuscripts* for more information, while he and Peter travel to Arkham, Massachusetts to consult a woman named Alice Derleth. Alice Derleth is not only a "renowned academician and scholar with a Ph.D. in the "occult sciences"[4]; she is also a stunningly beautiful woman. (Cartoon magick has not only given August Derleth, cofounder of Arkham House, a sex-change, but has turned him into a really hot babe to boot!) As soon as they meet Dr. Derleth at Miskatonic University, Peter tells her about the theft of the forbidden tome. The beautiful scholar quotes the "That is not dead which can eternal lie, and with strange eons even death may die" couplet, explaining that it's a quote from the *Necronomicon* about Cthulhu. She agrees to accompany the boys back to NYC to help search for the book, and the cult who stole it.

Back in New York, the Ghostbusters team, accompanied by Ms. Derleth, track the *Necronomicon* to "Wagner's Occult Shop," where Cthulhu cultists in long purple robes and tentacled Ku Klux Klan hoods are chanting "Ia Ia Cthulhu fhtagn." (At least they're not burning crosses.) When the Ghostbusters attack, the cultists sic an enormous shoggoth on them, but Alice turns it to stone with a handy spell. The cultists escape with the *Necronomicon* during the attack. In desperation, Ray leads the team to consult some old copies of *Weird Tales* in an antiquarian bookshop, claiming that he remembers a story that reveals how to defeat Cthulhu. Winston is incredulous at the notion that "those old science fiction stories" could help them save the world. Alice supports the idea, however, with the rationale that H. P. Lovecraft and his friends studied the *Necronomicon* as a basis of their tales.[5] At the shop, the team sifts through stacks of old pulps until they find the story Ray remembers from his childhood, a tale called "The Horror From the Depths,"[6] which they adopt as their battle plan. Egon calculates that the most likely place for the cult to summon Cthulhu is the southern tip of Brooklyn—Coney Island.

After a flat tire and a long subway ride, the team finally arrives at the wharf, only to see Cthulhu rising gigantically out of the sea, having just been summoned by the cultists. Blasts from the Ghostbusters' proton beams only piss off Great Cthulhu, and a spell from Alice Derleth, in which she calls on the God Nodens ("Etakka fotura Nodens!"), has no effect. Consulting the plot of the pulp fiction story from *Weird Tales*, they decide to lure Cthulhu into a rollercoaster (no tourist visiting Coney Island can resist the rides) hoping to make lightning strike it by "ionizing it" with their proton beams.[7] Peter teases Big C into crashing into the structure just as the boys—plus lightning—pump multiple gigavolts of electricity through it. Cthulhu melts down into a quivering puddle of seafood gumbo. The Cthulhu cultists—still robed and hooded like KKK members—are furious and ready to retaliate. Before they can take revenge, the police arrive to bust them. The cult leader (as you've guessed by now) is the librarian, Clark Ashton, who threatens to come back in a sequel as the cops drag him away. The *Necronomicon* is taken back to Miskatonic U, Ray dates Alice, and everyone but Egon lives happily ever after.

Some critics hate this little feature, but I must shamelessly confess that I thoroughly enjoy it. One reason for its "guilty-pleasure" status on my video shelf is the way in which writer Michael Reaves gives August Derleth a well-deserved sex-change—a fitting karmic retribution for his basic male chauvinism, his bastardization of Lovecraft's Mythos, and his violation of Lovecraft's unwritten story ideas with bogus "posthumous collaborations." Besides, I really enjoy Japanimation—even when it's done by Americans!

The feature does have its problems, of course. The cartoonists depict Great Cthulhu as red, whereas Lovecraft described him as "the green, sticky spawn of the

stars."[8] And where are the "long, narrow wings"[9] Lovecraft described? The anima-
tors also made Big C look too much like Godzilla with his head being eaten by a
giant squid. Then again, Lovecraft does describe Cthulhu's crypt on R'lyeh as bearing a "dragon-squid bas-relief,"[10] says that Cthulhu has "a scaly, rubbery-looking
body" (hmmm, sounds pretty Godzilla-like to me), and later describes Cthulhu as
"The awful squid-head with writhing feelers."[11] The worst boner in this cartoon is
the statement that Lovecraft and his Circle studied the *Necronomicon*, and based
their stories on it.

Scriptwriter Michael Reaves was a long-time fan of the Lovecraft Mythos. So
was *Ghostbusters* story editor, J. Michael Straczynski, of *Babylon 5* fame, who helped
get the script into production largely intact.[12] So an above-average amount of research
went into the screenplay for this cartoon feature. Not only are names of prominent
writers in the Lovecraft Circle—Clark Ashton Smith and August Derleth—used for
characters, but even the relative newcomer T. E. D Klein is incorporated. (These
kinds of in-jokes were a Lovecraft Circle tradition.) The Cthulhu cultists chant real
R'lyehian incantations, and Ms. Derleth quotes the celebrated "death may die" couplet that actually derives from Lovecraft's fictional grimoire. More obscure Mythos
inventions—the *Eltdown Shards* and *the Pnakotic Manuscripts*—are also mentioned,
as well as the pseudo-Lovecraftian Theosophical (actually written by Blavatsky)
Book of Dzyan, even though its title is mispronounced. More interesting still is the
spell that Alice Derleth casts against Cthulhu, calling upon the name of the God
Nodens, an obscure Mythos deity said to be Cthulhu's enemy.[13] All of this suggests
a more-than-casual acquaintance with the works and background of Lovecraft and
his Circle.

If you can get past the obligatory cartoon goofiness, you realize that this is as
close as anyone has yet come to making a film adaptation of "The Call of Cthulhu."
However, it is a version of the story as Robert E. Howard might have written it. The
four macho Ghostbusters and the gorgeous female intellectual are atypical of
Lovecraft's neurasthenic (and all-male) heroes, as is the spectacular way the team
blasts Cthulhu back to R'lyeh with nary a sign of sanity loss. All in all, for a cartoon
tailored to a juvenile audience, it's not bad.

In fact, it's not bad compared to a lot of live-action studio releases. The quality
of the animation is far above the average of planoform Hannah Barbarian crudity,
and is on the level of some Japanimation features. The plot is reasonably intelligent
and packs more action into thirty minutes than I've seen in some ninety-minute
films—particularly those early AIP atrocities chock full of stalking-through-the-fog
filler. The use of the *Necronomicon* in the story line is perfectly consistent with
Lovecraft's concepts, including his idea of the automatic effectiveness of spells spoken
aloud from the terrible tome. Though it is only a short cartoon feature made for a
Saturday morning television series, "Collect Call of Cathulhu" has a better grip on
the Cthulhu Mythos than some live-action movies by supposedly serious filmmakers.

Favorite funny quotes:

Egon: Cthulhu! Peter: Gudsundheit.

Winston: Cthulhu. I heard of him. He's bad, right?
Egon: He makes Gozer look like little Mary Sunshine!

Peter: Something the size of Godzilla wearing an octopus hat won't be hard to find.

Peter: Okay Squid face, I'm gonna make calamari out of you!

Alice Derleth: I'll take the *Necronomicon* back to Miskatonic University with me, where it can't be used for evil.

Out of Mind: The Stories of H. P. Lovecraft. 1998. Cine Qua Non Films. (Canadian)
Director: Raymond Saint-Jean. Screenplay: Raymond Saint-Jean
Starring: Christopher Heyerdahl, Art Kitching, Pierre Leblanc, Peter Foarbridge, Michael Sinelnikoff. And the voice of Sheena Larkin as Aunt Annie.
This feature begins with what appears to be an old, grainy, black-and-white film-clip of H. P. Lovecraft seated at a desk, with a 1920s microphone stand in front of him. Adding to the documentary feel of the sequence is the superimposed title at the bottom of the screen: H. P. LOVECRAFT, PROVIDENCE, RHODE ISLAND. Lovecraft seems to be giving an interview. And though his delivery is somewhat stiff and formal, he candidly sums himself in a nutshell, saying that he is mainly interested in three things: the fantastic, abstract truth, and that which is ancient and permanent. "Sundry combinations of these three will probably account for my odd tastes and eccentricities." Explaining himself a little further, he states:

> I could never write about ordinary people because I'm not the least bit interested in them, and without interest there can be no art. Man's relation to man does not captivate my fancy. It is man's relation to the cosmos, to the unknown, that arouses in me the spark of creative imagination.

This is followed by a color sequence of Lovecraft (Christopher Heyerdahl) in brown suit and homburg hat walking through the woods rehearsing the sound of the name "Cthulhu." He rolls the word off his tongue and growls it out of his throat in a variety of ways.

Back in documentary B&W, Lovecraft explains the strange spelling and eerie phonetics of the name of the Cthulhu—a name that cannot be properly pronounced by human vocal organs. He pronounces it once again, with a disquieting earnestness.

Back in color, we join Lovecraft in his study, where we hear him reading aloud from his manuscript of "The Call of Cthulhu," relishing his own prose description of "the green, sticky spawn of the stars."

Next we flashforward to the present day, to the workshop/studio of a young artist named Carter (Art Kitching), who welds metal sculptures. As he is working, a knock comes at the door. An unseen messenger has disappeared, leaving an envelope on the ground from the local law firm of Barlow and Associates. At the law office, Barlow (Pierre Leblanc) tells Carter that his mysterious great-uncle, George Angell, has left him an inheritance. The sleepy Barlow asks Carter if he actually knew his uncle. When Carter says he didn't, Barlow sarcastically replies; "Then you're in for a treat!" It seems that Barlow's firm was made executor of George Angell's will, but his Uncle George disappeared without a trace; no body was found, so there was no death certificate. The will states that the legacy is to be given, on his twenty-seventh birthday, "to the one who is born on the summer solstice of 1970." (That's Carter.) The law firm has had to keep track of Carter for almost three decades. Barlow pulls a box wrapped in plain brown paper out of a safe, and hands it to Carter. ("That's it?") But when Carter starts to open it and satisfy his curiosity, he is told that the will also stipulates that he must only open the package when he is alone. (Dum Da Dum Duuum!)

At home at last, Carter tears away the paper to find an old wooden box with a book inside. The book is the *Necronomicon* (you were expecting maybe a Harlequin romance novel?). It is an ancient-looking, vellum-bound volume full of parchment pages written in strange script, some interesting woodcuts, the Malachim script alphabet, and other occultic scribbles. Between the pages, he finds two envelopes; one contains a picture of H. P. Lovecraft; the other, addressed to Dr. Henry Armitage of Miskatonic University, contains a piece of paper bearing a strange inscription in an unknown language. He also finds an old, yellowed photograph of a young man in 1920s-period clothing, whose face looks identical to his. On the back of the photo is a strange incantation that he foolishly reads aloud. (Don't these people ever learn?)

With the words of the incantation still ringing in his ears, Carter goes to bed and enters the Dreamlands, where he finds himself dressed in 1920s garb, walking down a deserted city street. He meets another man in Twenties dress who is the spittin' image of his pal, Blake (Peter Farbridge), but insists that his name is Harley Warren. He calls Carter "George Angell," and thanks him for saving his life during World War I. It seems that he amputated one of Warren's legs when he served in the medical corps. Warren assures him (a little too earnestly) that he never believed any of those sinister rumors about "too many amputations—none of that 'Dr Stump' stuff!" He then asks Carter/Angell to help him talk some sense into his crazed twin brother. ("But Blake, you don't have a brother!") It seems the other Warren "got hold of this damned book" and dropped everything for some "fundamental research." This other Warren has a hysterical mop of hair, a smile like a crazed weasel, and a basement laboratory where he experiments with creatures assembled from human body parts. (He also says he has no brother.) From behind a hospital curtain, Warren raves over the growls of his creations; "You remember the book, the *Necronomicon*! It can keep these creatures alive, and I know where to find it." Warren shows him a misshapen, humanoid arm, and tells him to watch the curtain. As he steps forward to open the curtain, Carter wakes up.

Shaken by his dream, Carter decides to do some research, and takes the picture of Lovecraft to Blake, who works behind the counter at a Goth boutique that specializes in ceramic skulls, swords, music, T-shirts, and books for the terminally hip. Blake identifies the man in the picture as H. P. Lovecraft, and gives Carter a used paperback anthology of Lovecraft's stories, and a t-shirt with Lovecraft's picture on it. ("They're not selling anyways[sic].")

Now we briefly return to Lovecraft, in newsreel black-and-white, talking about his childhood nightmares of Nightgaunts. This segues into Carter, sitting in his home, reading the biographical material on Lovecraft in the paperback anthology. There is also a brief description of Lovecraft's imaginary *Necronomicon* as an "encyclopedia of evil compiled by the mad Arab poet, Abdul Alhazred." Now Carter knows what he has inherited from his mysterious uncle. His readings of the dread book have not only brought him disturbing dreams, these disturbances have begun to intrude on his waking mind as well.

Carter decides to visit Professor Armitage (Michael Sinelnikoff) at his home. The tweedy old gentleman is delighted to meet Carter, and says he studied anthropology under his great-uncle, George Angell, when he was Carter's age. The joviality comes to a screeching halt, however, when Carter shows Armitage his copy of the *Necronomicon*, and the professor examines it and realizes it is the real thing. He asks Carter if he has read the book, and, more important, "Have you spoken any of its contents aloud?" He explains that, "Legend has it that some of the words can act as keys which open invisible doors—doors which cross the wall of sleep." Armitage adds that some people doubted the book's existence, but that his uncle George did believe in it. In the hands of certain individuals, he warned, it can be a potent tool. "He believed that H. P. Lovecraft was such a person." Armitage asks Carter how his uncle died, and Carter admits he doesn't know. Armitage ominously hints that Angell may have proved his theory, and illustrates with the story of Alhazred being devoured by an invisible monster before a crowd: "The book suggests some . . . repulsive things." When Carter asks about Harley Warren, Armitage looks stunned and wants to know how he knows about Warren. Carter ingenuously admits he "met him last night." Armitage explains that Warren is a "dangerous maniac" with whom his uncle worked in the trenches of WWI and later, in the 1920s. He warns him to be very careful around Warren. Carter, then gives Armitage the cipher note in the envelope addressed to him. Armitage asks for the loan of the book, and promises to have the note deciphered by tomorrow.

That night, Carter dreams of a red-eyed, tentacled, cthuloid monster that pulls him under the bed by his head and devours him. Upon going to the sink, he sees his look-alike uncle staring back at him from the mirror, and saying; "You're not dreaming—I'm back!" Back to Lovecraft in B&W, commenting on the "titanic significance of dreams."

Carter returns to Armitage's house, and finds the professor downstairs, where his brain is being sucked out by a tentacled monster like the head-sucking horror in his dream. Carter grabs the *Necronomicon* and makes a panicky dash before he too becomes an hors d'ourve for the spawn of Cthulhu. Back at his workshop, Carter starts to torch the book, but hesitates. He translates the writing on the back of Uncle George's photograph: "That is not dead which can eternal lie . . ."

Carter in the 1990s, and Lovecraft in the 1920s, are both shown lying down to sleep. Lovecraft is resting from his work on a manuscript. Carter has another dream/flashback as George Angell, and finds himself in a cemetery with his friend (or is it fiend?) Harley Warren, where they are searching for a mausoleum that holds a copy of the *Necronomicon*. Warren is obsessed with the book, and says he needs precise pronunciations of the incantations to keep his reanimated corpses alive. Just as in Lovecraft's story, Warren goes down into the tomb, leaving Carter above with a field telephone. Just as in Lovecraft's original tale, Warren is overwhelmed and devoured by some unspeakable horror, and Carter's frantic cries are answered by a hideous voice that says, "YOU FOOL, WARREN IS DEAD!" Carter jolts awake in his apartment, picks up the phone, and calls Blake. The same hideous voice answers, "YOU FOOL, BLAKE IS DEAD!"

Carter next finds himself dreamwalking through the New England woods, where he meets none other than H. P. Lovecraft himself. Carter is wearing his Lovecraft T-shirt, and Lovecraft wants to know, "What am I doing on your shirt?" Carter tries to explain that he, Lovecraft, is a popular author in his time and space. Lovecraft remarks that he must be dreaming. Carter points out that they both are. In any case, Lovecraft is delighted to meet "Randolph Carter," one of his own characters, "the traveler in the world of dreams." He quotes an observation he made the day before in his commonplace book: "All of life is only a set of pictures in the brain, in which there is no difference between those born of real things and those born of dreams." He invites Carter back to his place for some of his Aunt Annie's lemonade.

Once more, Lovecraft, in black-and-white documentary mode, comments about the literary merit of his work, which he humbly states is redeemed only by its sincerity.

As he and Carter walk back to his place, Lovecraft remarks that he had an odd visit from two strange men in black that appeared at his door and asked how he had learned about the *Necronomicon*. When he told them he imagined it, they suddenly left. Carter suggests that Lovecraft somehow guessed of its existence. Carter insists that it exists, and that he has a copy. Lovecraft takes this in stride, with the statement that perhaps for a thing to exist, it is only necessary to imagine it. Then Lovecarft launches into an enthusiastic discussion of a new story idea of his about an evil alchemist who decides to use the dread book as a key with which to take over his nephew's body through dreams. This sounds remarkably like what is happening to Carter himself, and Lovecraft is nonplussed when Carter suddenly vanishes, leaving him standing alone on the deserted road.

Carter awakens to the sound of a familiar voice commanding him to go to the mirror. When he does, he sees the now-familiar face of George Angell beckoning him. "You pronounced the ancient words. You called me back!" Carter and Angell both speak the words "I'm Back!" as the two have become one. Meanwhile, Lovecraft starts awake at the sound of these words in his own head. Having awakened from this "magnificent nightmare," he begins writing.

In black suit and hat, Lovecraft walks through a cemetery, and meditates upon the arrogance of those mammals called humans, who are convinced of their own superiority in spite of the brevity of their existence. As he ponders the inevitability of oblivion, he gazes down upon his own grave with a kind of melancholy satisfaction.

Part of the splendid impact of *Out of Mind* comes from its deliberate "documentary" effect, in which most of Christopher Heyerdahl's dialog is taken directly from Lovecraft's letters. The effect is almost eerie, in that we feel we are watching an old film of Lovecraft being interviewed. The fictional elements in *Out of Mind* are a mix of "The Statement of Randolph Carter" and *The Case of Charles Dexter Ward*, with bits of "Herbert West—Reanimator" thrown in. By not basing his screenplay on any one particular Lovecraft story, Raymond Saint-Jean avoids the pitfall of having to reproduce one of Lovecraft's tales "perfectly." Perfection is a subjective concept, but that has never kept Lovecraft fans from savagely criticizing even the honest attempts of well-intentioned filmmakers.

Saint-Jean seems to have taken Lovecraft's maxim, "atmosphere, not action" to heart. *Out of Mind* is composed almost entirely of atmosphere—the plotline is obscured and submerged beneath a tangled thicket of Lovecraftian characters and situations, and the film seems more like a nostalgic ramble through Lovecraft country than a story in its own right. Sometimes I felt as if I were watching a film version of *Selected Letters* mixed with snippets from an anthology of Lovecraft pastiches. Saint-Jean also plays fast and loose with Lovecraft's characters: Harley Warren was not a "dangerous maniac" who experimented with dead bodies à la Herbert West, nor was George Angell (investigator of the Cthulhu cult) an evil alchemist. And, of course, the tombstone shown at the end of the film looks nothing like the one over Lovecraft's grave in Providence.

But these are petty criticisms when we consider the great effort that Saint-Jean and his cast and crew take to capture the haunting, tragic, dreamlike atmosphere, not only of Lovecraft's tales, but of Lovecraft the man. Farbridge and Sinelnikoff were especially inspired in their roles. I can also see (or rather hear) why Greatan Gravel and Serge LaForest won the Gemini Award for best original score for this unique production. And Serge Ladouceur's photography is excellent. The standout performance came from Heyerdahl, however, who was perfectly cast as the gaunt young Lovecraft. Indeed, his physical resemblance to Lovecraft is uncanny. Heyerdahl even mastered the Old Yankee dialect that Lovecraft must have spoken, so that his quotes from Lovecraft's letters and tales make us think we are listening to the voice of the master himself. This screen Lovecraft has just the sort of pathetic dignity that the Old Gent from Providence must have really had. He is human enough to gain our sympathy, but too wise and stoic for us to pity. His dream encounter with Carter conveys both the philosophical conversationalism that fascinated Lovecraft's friends, and the kindly charm and generosity that delighted them. *Out of Mind* is unmistakably a labor of love.

Conclusion
—Daniel Harms

The *Necronomicon* is more in the public eye than ever before. Players of the computer game *Doom II* may notice sigils from the Simon *Necronomicon* on the walls of its alien dungeons. A biennial Lovecraft convention called "NecronomiCon" attracts hundreds of fans of the master's work. A recent column in the *Denver Post*[1] made the tongue-in-cheek suggestion that an updated *Necronomicon* may have information on the "faked" Moon landing and the hordes of U.N. soldiers in our national forests. There has been a film called *Necronomicon*, in which Lovecraft steals the dread book from a sect of inhuman monks. *Fate* magazine has even named it as one of their top 100 paranormal phenomena of the 20th century.[2] The *Necronomicon* has grown from a horror writer's invention into an independent entity that has impacted many people's lives. At this point, when the myth is beginning to grow too large to be deciphered by an outsider, it seems proper to step in and separate the truth from the hype.

We have concentrated mainly on how the *Necronomicon*'s fame has grown through publishing and films, but perhaps more important than these are those informal discussions we have come to call the "great *Necronomicon* debate." At one time this only occurred in isolated instances when a few Lovecraft fans or magicians pooled their (limited) knowledge on the subject. With the Information Age now upon us, hundreds of people from across the world meet in such forums as the Usenet group alt.necronomicon and engage in heated debates over this topic. I have observed these arguments for years, and believe that I have identified one major source of confusion—the definition of the word *real*—that may defuse many such arguments.

When someone asks, "Is the *Necronomicon* real?" the first thing we must do is to turn the question around and ask, "What do you mean by 'real'?" From my own experience in the debate, there are three different meanings for this single word, and much of the debate is a misunderstanding over which definition each side is using.

First, "real" can mean that a book called the *Necronomicon* exists. This is the easiest to confirm (except perhaps for those who believe that reality itself is an illusion). A trip to any library or bookstore will turn up evidence of a number of *Necronomicon*s. Even if no such book existed, anyone could write a manuscript on any subject and entitle it *Necronomicon*, and it would meet these requirements. This viewpoint on "reality" is taken most often as a knee-jerk reaction to one of the viewpoints outlined below.

Second, "real" can refer to whether a published *Necronomicon* is an authentic pre-Lovecraft manuscript or a modern hoax. This viewpoint is that of many Lovecraft scholars and fans. This book has given adequate support to their position; most of the *Necronomicon*s are acknowledged fakes that appeared at times when Lovecraft was exceedingly popular, and the rumors that Lovecraft was inspired by such a book remain unsubstantiated. Though some may argue that the *Necronomicon* does exist in this sense, either hidden away in some library or held by a secret cult, the burden of proof lies with them. In this case, it is fairly clear that the *Necronomicon* is "imaginary."

Third, the various published *Necronomicon*s may be considered "real" if they work in a magickal sense. Of course, many would say that magick itself does not exist, but there are many who believe it does and who judge such a work by its perceived usefulness in accomplishing these goals. This is not a haphazard process—as their preference for the Simon edition over the others shows—but is based on similarities between the system outlined in the books and other systems of magick, as well as the magician's personality and goals. If there are enough similarities, they say, then the system probably works. It should be noted that even though a person may think a system works, that does not mean they use it themselves—many magicians object to the Simon book because it is usable and yet, according to the same comparative method, is not "safe." Still, on the matter of its power, most occultists are in agreement.

These ideas of "reality" are not really as cut-and-dried as all this. A few Lovecraft fans and magicians alike cling to the notion of a pre-Lovecraft *Necronomicon*. Some magicians object to the various *Necronomicon*s because they do not reflect a true ancient tradition, while some Lovecraft fans say that an inauthentic book cannot possibly have any magickal power (their personal experiences are usually not noted). While individuals may consider any or all of these to be valid, the groups as a whole tend to hold one definition of "reality" as important over all others.

I believe that this illuminates a great deal of how the debate progresses on the Internet. When someone asks whether the *Necronomicon* is "real," the sides are drawn between the Lovecraft fans, who believe that the *Necronomicon*s on the market are inauthentic, and the magickal practitioners, who insist that these *Necronomicon*s may be useful magickally even if they are of recent origin. Unfortunately, both sides use the word "real" to mean these things, so the two sides are pared off against each other upon what is essentially a non-issue. Soon another person objects to the Lovecraftians' statements that the *Necronomicon* is not "real" (after all, they own a copy!), and the debate becomes dirty and confusing. The irony is that many on each side actually agree on the points being debated, and are only in confusion over the meaning of the terminology.

By this time, some readers may have dismissed the *Necronomicon* as a mass delusion brought about by authors and hucksters, a product of the superstitious times into which civilization is slowly sliding. Others have decided that all of this is merely an elaborate smokescreen, that my co-author and I are pawns of some shadowy organization dedicated to keeping the secret of the *Necronomicon* to ourselves. And a number are probably sitting on the fence.

Most of the people who read this will put it aside and never give the issues another thought. That's perfectly fine—they got what they came for, and there are more important matters in life than the *Necronomicon*. Still, there will be those who want to go further and take a look for themselves. Unfortunately, training people to think critically is not a high priority in most societies. Much as we like to think of ourselves as free individuals, we are nonetheless educated to hold certain views by our upbringing, and are rarely taught how to question them, save in the light of another, largely unquestioned belief system. To provide some aid, I'm going to give some guidelines for looking into these questions. Unlike many "debunking" books, the goal of *The Necronomicon Files* is not to produce believers, but to give you the tools to investigate for yourself.

1. ***Be your own worst critic.*** Many times, we are told that it's best to "keep an open mind" and "wait until the facts are in" to pass judgment. In reality, the facts don't always come in, and most people make up their minds on such questions quickly. Anyone who has taken the time to read this far in the book most likely has opinions or beliefs about the *Necronomicon* question, whether pro or con. Forming these views is a regular part of life.

    The key to investigation is not to avoid believing anything, but to use your beliefs as a springboard. Examine them critically, and be prepared to argue both for and against them. Thus, even though John and I do not believe in a pre-Lovecraft *Necronomicon*, we spent a great deal of time operating as if we did—following up rumors, checking library catalogs, and researching in such a way that some may mistake us for supporters of the *Necronomicon*'s existence. This can provide a number of interesting avenues to explore, and leaves open the possibility of finding information that contradicts what we hold dear.

2. ***Get back to the original sources.*** Always try to follow a rumor as far back as you can. *Necronomicon* rumors have a tendency to become

entangled with both fact and fiction as time goes on. The original source is likely to have more information that will help you evaluate the claim—or may be willing to let you in on the joke. I am always surprised by the people who pontificate on what Lovecraft said about the *Necronomicon*, then admit they've never read his stories!

3. *Go to alternate sources for corroborating information.* Does Lovecraft say that John Dee translated the *Necronomicon*? Start looking for biographies of John Dee, descriptions of his library, and and other relevant information. Too many people have placed their trust in a single source without investigating whether it is true. The Internet is a useful source for this sort of crosschecking, but requires a great deal of judgment and considerable breadth of researching.

4. *Break the rumor into smaller parts, and verify each one individually.* Taking their cue from Lovecraft, many hoaxers blend fact with fiction, and it is necessary to evaluate each statement individually. Just because John Dee was a real person doesn't mean that he translated the *Necronomicon*. Even if you do find out that one part is false, it often helps to do more research to bolster your argument.

5. *If you can't be certain, assess the probabilities.* It is almost impossible to disprove the existence of anything. A few people have asked skeptics to prove that a pre-Lovecraft *Necronomicon* doesn't exist. This is impossible; one would have to search every place on Earth where such a book might be hidden at the same instant (to make sure no one moved it while the search was on). Still, hundreds of people have searched for it for three-quarters of a century, and no such book has ever been found, so it is quite improbable. It is better to ask if anyone has any proof that such a book does exist.

6. *Recognize your limitations.* I've been looking over *Necronomicon* hoaxes for years, yet if someone brought me a Greek or Latin manuscript and said it was the *Necronomicon*, I would be unable to evaluate it for myself. Know when you need to call in someone else to help you.

7. *Don't burn bridges for others.* Be polite, return books and documents to libraries and collections, and make your research into a pleasant experience for everyone involved. Sometimes, we become so engrossed in our own doings that we forget we're dealing with other living, breathing people, with whom someone else might want to deal in the future. If someone won't talk to you, or you can't take that treasured

book home, don't ruin the chance for someone else to do so next week or a few years down the road. I apologize to those of you who don't need to hear this, but many do.

I should also comment on two other "ways of knowing" that may come up in a *Necronomicon* search. One of these is through knowledge that comes from within us, whether through intuition, contact with a higher power, or divination and fortune-telling. These can be the source of deep personal revelation and significance, and should not be dismissed lightly. However, don't expect this knowledge to be accepted by anyone else. Too many people have a spiritual realization and then are disappointed that everyone else doesn't accept it on their say-so. Your "solution" may be substituting one improbability for another; one person told me that the best way to find if the *Necronomicon* exists is to summon a demon! If you do have an experience like this, and want to convince others, look for proof in the physical world.

The other sort of information that may present itself is secret knowledge. On one hand, you might be stonewalled by a person who refuses to talk or gives as their justification, "That's a secret we've been told to keep." On the other, you may learn something, with the condition that you keep it to yourself or not divulge your source. Unfortunately, when it comes to convincing others, most such evidence is useless without a source to back it up. While you may be tempted to pry into others' lives or give out such information, this is always a bad idea. When John and I have been given secret pointers, we have asked, "How else could we find this out?" and tried to find it another way. If we can't, we don't use it.

When John and I set out to write this book, our intention was to take all of these factors into account when discussing the *Necronomicon*. Some readers may object that, in doing so, we spread ourselves thin, and that we should have concentrated on one aspect of the phenomenon (preferably that which interests them). The following story should illustrate, though, why all of these matters are important.

About a year ago, a friend of mine posted to the alt.necronomicon Usenet group asking if anyone had had any supernatural experiences with the *Necronomicon* that they would like to share. One young man replied that his life had changed forever after reading the *Necronomicon*—or rather, skimming over its pages—in the rare books room of the UCLA library. He had felt the urge to write and edit Cthulhu Mythos–related poetry, and his life had become unbelievably chaotic, yet full of purpose since then. He attributed all of this to the book's power.

When I read his piece, it immediately became clear to me that he was talking about De Camp's *Al Azif* published by Owlswick Press, a book written as a joking hoax in an imaginary script. It wasn't a manuscript kept tucked away by some secretive cult for ages, but a book created during the seventies by a small press that wanted to provide knowledgeable Lovecraft fans with a faux copy of the book. Yet at the same time, it had a meaning to this young man who had handled it, and by its very existence changed his way of thinking.

I have always been of an empirical turn of mind. While I think that a supernatural being or beings exist, I have insisted on keeping the realms of religion and science separated. For a person such as myself, the factual element is the one that is most important in this debate. Even though some may gloss over matters of authenticity, they are nonetheless important. For those who would hold that they are not, I would merely point to the large number of readers whose entire knowledge of Lovecraft, Crowley, and Sumerian mythology is taken from the Simon *Necronomicon*. Even if they choose to accept the tenets of this book, they should at least be made aware of these problems so that they can make an informed choice. Recent controversies, ranging from global warming to cold fusion, have shown how questions of authenticity can impact large numbers of people. Even though the *Necronomicon* is not likely to have such a wide-ranging effect, it should nonetheless be treated with caution and skepticism.

At the same time, even if we dismiss the claims that the published *Necronomicon*s are sources of magickal power, we cannot dismiss that they do have the power to change people's beliefs and their perceptions of the world. History is filled with examples of the power of fiction. H. Rider Haggard's novel *King Solomon's Mines* was so convincing that a group of adventurers actually mounted an expedition across Africa to search for the diamonds of Solomon. Arthur Machen's short story, "The Bowmen," became the nucleus for the legend of the "Angels of Mons" who appeared over a battlefield in World War I to help the British beat back the Germans. On a more sinister note, a German occult society called the Vril Group, which based many of its practices on Lord Bulwer-Lytton's novel, *Vril: The Coming Race*, were the most powerful branch of the Thule Gesselschaft, which some say gave birth the Nazi Party. None of these authors were deliberately constructing a hoax, but their stories were taken as fact nonetheless, and provided some who read them a sense of meaning and purpose that cannot be dismissed because their sources were not "authentic." We are thus advised to make our inquiries into the subject of the *Necronomicon* with both respect and skepticism.

APPENDIX:
History of the *Necronomicon*[1]
—H. P. Lovecraft
with annotations by Daniel Harms

Original title *Al Azif*—azif being the word used by the Arabs to designate that nocturnal sound (made by insects) suppos'd to be the howling of daemons.[2]

Composed by Abdul Alhazred, a mad poet of Sanaá, in Yemen, who is said to have flourished during the period of the Ommiade caliphs,[3] circa 700 A.D. He visited the ruins of Babylon & the subterranean secret of Memphis[4] & spent ten years alone in the great southern desert of Arabia—the Roba El Khaliyeh or "Empty Space" of the ancients—& "Dahna" or "Crimson" desert of the modern Arabs, which is held to be inhabited by protective evil spirits & monsters of death. Of this desert many strange & unbelievable marvels are told by those who pretend[5] to have penetrated it. In his last years Alhazred dwelt in Damascus, where the *Necronomicon* (Al Azif) was written, & of his final death or disappearance (738 A.D.) many terrible & conflicting things are told. He is said by Ebn Khallikan (12th cent. biographer)[6] to have been seized by an invisible monster in broad daylight & devoured horribly before a large number of fright-frozen witnesses. Of his madness many things are told. He claimed to have seen the fabulous Irem, or City of Pillars,[7] & to have found beneath the ruins of a certain nameless desert town[8] the shocking annals & secrets of a race older than mankind.[9] He was only an indifferent Moslem, worshipping unknown entities whom he called Yog-Sothoth & Cthulhu.[10]

In A.D. 950 the *Azif*, which had gained a considerable tho' surreptitious circulation among the philosophers of the age, was secretly translated into Greek by Theodorus Philetas[11] of Constantinople under the title *Necronomicon*. For a century it impelled certain experimenters to terrible attempts, when it was suppressed and burnt by the patriarch Michael.[12] After this it is only heard of furtively, but (1228) Olaus Wormius[13] made a Latin translation later in the Middle Ages, & the Latin text was printed twice—once in the 15th century in black-letter[14] (evidently in Germany) & once in the 17th—(prob. Spanish) both editions being without identifying marks, & located as to time & place by internal typographical evidence only. The work (both Latin & Gk.) was banned by Pope Gregory IX in 1232,[15] shortly after its Latin translation, which called attention to it.[16] The Arabic original was lost as early as Wormius' time as indicated by his prefatory note[17] & no sight of the Greek copy (which was printed in Italy bet. 1500 & 1550) has been reported since the burning of a certain Salem man's library in 1692.[18] A translation made by Dr. Dee[19] was never printed, & exists only in fragments recovered from the original MS.[20] Of the Latin texts now existing one (15th cent.) is known to be in the British Museum under lock & key,[21] while another (17th cent.) is in the Bibliotheque Nationale at Paris.[22] A 17th cent. edition is in the Widener Library at Harvard,[23] & in the library of Miskatonic University at Arkham.[24] Also in the library of the Univ. of Buenos Ayres.[25] Numerous other copies probably exist in secret, & a 15th century one is persistently rumoured to form part of the collection of a celebrated American millionaire.[26] A still vaguer rumour credits the preservation of a 16th cent. Greek text in the Salem family of Pickman; but if it was so preserved, it vanished with the artist R. U. Pickman, who disappeared early in 1926.[27] The book is rapidly suppressed by the authorities of most countries, & by all the branches of organized ecclesiasticism. Reading leads to terrible consequences. It was from rumours of this book (of which relatively few of the general public know) that R. W. Chambers is said to have derived the idea of his early novel "The King in Yellow."[28]

H. P. Lovecraft

Chronology

Al Azif written circa 730 A.D. at Damascus by Abdul Alhazred

Tr. to Greek 950 A.D. as *Necronomicon* by Theodorus Philetas

Burnt by Patriarch Michael 1050 (i.e., Greek Text)—Arabic text now lost

Olaus translates Gr. to Latin 1228

1232 . . . Latin Ed. (& Gr.) suppr. by Pope Gregory IX

14 . . . black-letter edition published (Germany)

15 . . . Gr. text printed in Italy

16 . . . Spanish printing of Latin text

In the name of Ganesa, Elephant-headed Lord of Wisdom, Remover of Obstacles, and Protector of Books. In the name of Inanna/Ishtar, Queen of Heaven and Earth, Lady of the Morning and the Evening Star, She who bestows fertility and prosperity, Lady of Battles and Mistress of the Chariot, She who bestows kingship and grants victory, Lady Luck! In the name of Yeshua of Nazareth, Christ of the Crusaders, in the name of Saint Andrew, Saint Michael, Saint George, and Sant Joan of Arc. In the name of Mother Durga the Invincible, She who annihilates evil. In the name of Mother Bagla Mukhi the Powerful One, She who paralyzes and silences the enemies of the sadhak., In the name of Mother Saraswati, Patroness of the Arts, She who grants fluency to the sadhak. In the name of Mother Lakshmi, She who prospers the yogi. In the name of Mother Tara, She who is swift to rescue the sadhak. In the name of Lord Shiva who balances creation and destruction in His dance. In the name of Lord Krishna who destroys ignorance and illusion, In the name of Pallas Athena, Goddess of war and wisdom who crushes the enemies of truth. In the name of Tyr, God of war, justice, and trial by combat, who bound Fenris, the Wolf of Chaos. In the name of Crom Cruach, Lord of the Mound, He of terrible vengeance called Old Crom of the Mountain. In the name of Nodens, Lord of the Abyss. And in the names of other angels, Goddesses, and Gods that I shall not reveal.

A GEAS IS PLACED ON ALL WHO READ THIS.

This book will cause great displeasure to purveyors of occult "disinformation." While all are free to criticize it verbally, no one may attack the authors of this book psychically, astrally, or magickally. Should you seek to attack the authors of this book, their mates, families, friends, agents, heirs, pets, or property by telepathic poisoning, foul thought forms, ensouled elementals, sendings of demons and Qlippothic entities, psychic or astral vampirism, or by any other means whatsoever, fierce modes of defense shall return all entities and energies back to you, the senders, multiplied sevenfold, there to wreak whatever vengeance is karmically just. If you persist thereafter in your attacks, the foul things that you seek to control will devour you so that the horror of your destruction will become the stuff of legend, a tale to frighten children in the night, and a proverb for generations yet unborn.

CAVEAT MALFACTORES!

ISHTAR LAMASSU UMANISHU!

(Ishtar is the Guardian Angel of Her Warriors!)

DIVA VULT! DEUS VULT!

Endnotes

Preface

1   Ellie Howe, *The Magicians of the Golden Dawn* (London: Routledge & Kegan Paul), p. 127.

Introduction

1   *Encyclopedia of Claims, Frauds, and Hoaxes of the Occult* (New York: St. Martin's Press, 1995).
2   *Satanism: The Seduction of America's Youth* (Nashville, TN: Nelson Publishers, 1989), pp. 138–9.
3   Larson, *Satanism,* p. 117.
4   John and I suggest that those who want to know more about occult subjects not use books, tapes, or cartoons written by Christian "occult experts." We don't say this because of the authors' religious persuasion—instead, every such work we've ever read is poorly researched and highly inaccurate, passing on rumor as fact and quoting similar books without looking back at the sources. One could say the same of many occult authors, of course, but most of these can be counted on to have a decent knowledge of their own tradition.

Initiation

I tend to use the old-fashioned word *cult* rather than the more fashionable and politically correct term "New Religious Movement" (NRM). Sociologists adopted the term NRM because the word *cult* has become a prejudicial term loaded with negative connotations. Unfortunately, the term New Religious Movements is misleading at best, and often totally inaccurate. Many cults are not new, but are based on heretical versions of standard world religions. Some cults are not religious, as in the case of political extremist groups and street gangs. And many cults are too small to be considered "movements," as is the case with most *Necronomicon*-related groups. NRM may be "politically correct," but it is incorrect in every other way. Also, I use the word *cult* so that readers will know what I'm talking about. I've always found that it is wiser to call a spade a spade, rather than referring to it as an "agricultural instrument."

Chapter 1: H. P. Lovecraft and the *Necronimicon*

1   Fritz Leiber, "A Literary Copernicus," in *H. P. Lovecraft: Four Decades of Criticism.* S. T. Joshi, ed. (Athens, OH: Ohio University Press. 1980), p. 61.
2   S. T. Joshi, *H. P. Lovecraft: A Life* (West Warwick, RI: Necronomicon, 1996), p. 6.
3   Colin Wilson, "Introduction to the *Necronomicon*," in *The Necronomicon: The Book of Dead Names,* George Hay, ed. (London: Skoob Esoterica, 1992), pp. 13–55.
4   H. P. Lovecraft, "Letter to Frank Belknap Long, October 26, 1926," *Selected Letters II,* ed. August Derleth and Donald Wandrei (Sauk City, WI: Arkham House, 1968), p. 88.
5   H. P. Lovecraft, Letter to J. Vernon Shea, May 29, 1933, *Selected Letters IV,* ed. August Derleth and James Turner (Sauk City, WI: Arkham House, 1976), p. 191.
6   S. T. Joshi, *H. P. Lovecraft,* p. 19.
7   Lyon Sprague de Camp, *H. P. Lovecraft: A Biography* (New York: Barnes and Noble, 1996), p. 18.

8 John Gonce will comment further on the influence of the *Thousand and One Nights* later in this book.

9 H. P. Lovecraft, Letter to Virgil Finlay, October 24, 1936, *Selected Letters V,* ed. August Derleth and James Turner (Sauk City, WI: Arkham House, 1976), p. 335.

10 H. P. Lovecraft, Letter to Reinhardt Kleiner, November 16, 1916, *Selected Letters I,* ed. August Derleth and Donald Wandrei (Sauk City, WI: Arkham House, 1965), p. 35.

11 H. P. Lovecraft, *Selected Letters V,* p. 335.

12 Edgar Allan Poe, *Complete Stories and Poems* (Garden City, NJ: Doubleday, 1966), p. 185.

13 Thomas Ollive Mabbott, ed., *Collected Works of Edgar Allan Poe* (Cambridge, MA: Harvard University Press, 1978), vol. 2, p. 421 n25.

14 Poe, *Complete Stories and Poems,* p. 185.

15 Poe, *Complete Stories and Poems,* p. 185. Despite this characterization, the actual contents of this manuscript are reported to be orthodox. See Mabbott, *Collected Works of Edgar Allan Poe,* p. 421 n25. This theory was originally proposed in Steven J. Mariconda's "'The Hound'—A Dead Dog?" (*Crypt of Cthulhu,* Eastertide, 1986, pp. 3–7). When writing the previous version of this book, I was not aware of this essay save in the revised form (omitting the reference in question) that appears in Mariconda's *On the Emergence of "Cthulhu" and Other Observations* (West Warwick, RI: Necronomicon Press, 1995), pp. 45–49.

16 S. T. Joshi, *H. P.Lovecraft,* p. 63.

17 H. P. Lovecraft, "The Statement of Randolph Carter," in *At the Mountains of Madness,* Corrected printing. (Sauk City,WI: Arkham House, 1985), p. 300.

18 George T. Wetzel, "The Cthulhu Mythos: A Study," in *H.P.L.,* ed. Meade and Penny Frierson (Birmingham, AL: The Editors, 1972), p. 36.

19 S. T. Joshi, *H. P. Lovecraft,* p. 231–32.

20 S. T. Joshi, ed., *Miscellaneous Writings* (Sauk City, WI:Arkham House, 1995), p. 90.

21 Letter from David Goudsward to the author, February 21, 1999.

22 H. P. Lovecraft, "The Nameless City," in *Dagon and Other Macabre Tales.* Corrected printing (Sauk City, WI: Arkham House, 1987), p. 99.

23 H. P. Lovecraft, "Nameless City," p. 103.

24 H. P. Lovecraft, Letter dated October 17, 1930, *Selected Letters III,* ed. August Derleth and Donald Wandrei (Sauk City, WI: Arkham House, 1971), p. 193.

25 H. P. Lovecraft, *Dagon and Other Macabre Tales,* p. 174.

26 Lovecraft, *Dagon and Other Macabre Tales,* p. 175.

27 Wetzel, "The Cthulhu Mythos: A Study," p. 36.

28 S. T. Joshi, *H. P. Lovecraft,* p. 285

29 H. P. Lovecraft, *Selected Letters V,* p. 418.

30 Wetzel, "The Cthulhu Mythos: A Study," p. 36.

31 Joan C. Stanley, *Ex Libris Miskatonici* (West Warwick, RI: Necronomicon, 1993), p. 54.

32 S. T. Joshi, *H. P. Lovecraft,* p. 285.

33 H. P. Lovecraft, Letter to Henry O. Fischer, late February 1937, *Selected Letters V,* p. 418.

34 The stages of the *Necronomicon*'s development proposed in this essay were first proposed in Robert M. Price's "Lovecraft's *Necronomicon*: An Introduction" (*Crypt of Cthulhu.* St. John's Eve, 1984). Instead of using them as examples of the *Necronomicon*'s uncertainty of meaning, I believe it is more useful to use them as stages the book passed through chronologically.

35 H. P. Lovecraft, *Dagon and Other Macabre Tales,* p. 211.

36 H. P. Lovecraft, *Dagon and Other Macabre Tales,* p. 214.

37 H. P. Lovecraft, *Dagon and Other Macabre Tales,* p. 216.

38 Price, *Lovecraft's Necronimicon,* p. 27.

39   H. P. Lovecraft, Letter dated October 9, 1925, *Selected Letters II*, p. 27.

40   Examples of Lovecraft's writing on this subject include "Science Versus Charlatanry" (in S. T. Joshi, ed., *Miscellaneous Writings* (Sauk City, WI: Arkham House, 1995), pp. 500–1) and "The Fall of Astrology" (*Miscellaneous Writings*, pp. 502–5.)

41   H. P. Lovecraft, "Letter dated October 9, 1925," *Selected Letters I–III*, p. 28.

42   H. P. Lovecraft, "Letter dated October 9, 1925," *Selected Letters I–III*, p. 28.

43   Letter dated October 11, 1926. *Selected Letters II*, p. 76.

44   A letter from Smith to Virgil Finlay, dated June 13, 1937, recommends Montague Summer's *The Geography of Witchcraft* and *The History of Demonology and Witchcraft* (actually *The History of Witchcraft and Demonology*), and Grillot de Givry's *Witchcraft, Magic and Alchemy* (from the Eldritch Dark website, http://members.xoom.com/ eldritchdark/wri/non-fict/letter_virgil_2.html). None of these were published at the time Lovecraft wrote Smith, save for de Givry's work in the original French. It is my opinion that Smith was not familiar with much magickal literature, as many of these works are intended as popularized accounts on the subject.

45   H. P Lovecraft, "Letter dated June 1, 1933," *H. P. Lovecraft: Letters to Robert Bloch*, ed. David E. Schultz and S. T. Joshi (West Warwick, RI: Necronomicon Press, 1993), p. 17. Sadly, this work is extremely hard to find, and the entries are not clear. For the inter- est of future scholars, these are the books listed as "Occult." I have expanded on their titles, as these are not always clear. *The Arabian Nights*; Sabine Baring-Gould, *Curious Myths of the Middle Ages*; Richard Blakeborough, *The Hand of Glory and Further Grandfather's Tales and Legends of Highwaymen and Others Collected by the Late R. Blakeborough*; Thomas Bulfinch, *The Age of Fable, or Beauties of Mythology*; John Fiske, *Myths & Myth-Makers: Old Tales and Superstitions Interpreted by Comparative Mythology*; Camille Flammarion, *Haunted Houses*; Harry Houdini, *A Magician among the Spirits*; John Henry Ingram, *The Haunted Homes and Family Legends of Great Britain*; Johann Heidrich Jung-Stilling, *Theory of Pneumatology, in Reply to the Question, What Ought to be Believed or Disbelieved concerning Presentiments, Visions, and Apparitions according to Nature, Reason, and Scripture*; John MacPhilpin, *The Apparitions and Miracles at Knock*, also, the *Official Depositions of the Eye-Witnesses*; Sir Walter Scott, *Letters on Demonology and Witchcraft Addressed to J. G. Lockhart, Esq*; Lewis Spence, *An Encyclopaedia of Occultism*. In the same book, in a letter dated January of 1935, Lovecraft also mentions reading the *Malleus Maleficarum* (p. 40).

46   H. P. Lovecraft, Letter dated July 29, 1936, *Selected Letters V*, p. 286. I should note that *The History of Magic* was another of Waite's translations of Eliphas Levi, and that the Rohmer book was most likely *The Romance of Sorcery*.

47   Willis Conover and H. P. Lovecraft, *Lovecraft at Last* (Arlington, VA: Carrolton-Clark, 1975), p. 30.

48   H. P. Lovecraft, Letter dated October 11, 1926, *Selected Letters II*, p. 76.

49   Some may point out that Lovecraft was reading a great deal of horror fiction for his essay "Supernatural Horror in Literature," and that one of these pieces may have inspired him to make this change. Although this is possible, I point out that Lovecraft devotes much space in his essay to the stories that impressed him more, and no "book of spells" appears in any of these. Even within this document, we find signs of his new knowledge of the occult; he mentions such classic books as the *Claviculae* (or *Keys*) *of Solomon* and Francis Barrett's *The Magus,* and even briefly discusses *Cabala*, a type of Jewish mysticism adopted by many occultists.

50   Ja'far Sharif and Gerhard Andreas Herklots, *Qanoon-e-Islam, or, The customs of the Moosulmans of India comprising a full and exact account of their various rites and cere- monies, from the moment of birth till the hour of death* (London: Parbury, Allen, 1832.

Lovecraft seems to have gotten his knowledge of this book secondhand from the article on "Magic" in the 9th edition *Encyclopedia Britannica,* from which he derived the material for "The Horror at Red Hook." As a result, he seems not to have known that the book was published nearly a full century after Merritt saw the fake copy in Curwen's library.

51   H. P. Lovecraft, *At the Mountains of Madness,* p. 121

52   Arthur Edward Waite, *The Mysteries of Magic: A Digest of the Writings of Eliphas Levi* (London: George Redway, 1886), p. 162. Thanks to S.T. Joshi for this information.

53   H. P. Lovecraft, *Selected Letters II,* pp. 201–2.

54   H. P. Lovecraft, *The History of the Necronomicon* (West Warwick, RI: Necronomicon Press, 1989).

55   It was formerly thought that "azif" was not a true Arabic word, but research conducted by Kevin Van Bladel, Dan Clore, Peter Levenda, and myself has corroborated it.

56   H. P. Lovecraft, *The History of the Necronomicon.*

57   S. T. Joshi, "Lovecraft, Regner Lodbrog, and Olaus Wormius," in *Crypt of Cthulhu, Eastertide,* 1995), pp. 3–7.

58   Conover and Lovecraft, *Lovecraft at Last,* pp. 104–5.

59   H. P. Lovecraft, *The Dunwich Horror and Others.* Corrected printing (Sauk City, WI: Arkham House, 1984), p. 167.

60   Lovecraft, *Dunwich Horror,* p. 170.

61   Frank Belknap Long, *Tales of the Cthulhu Mythos,* 2nd ed. (Sauk City, WI: Arkham House, 1990), p. 88.

62   Some editions of "History" include a sentence about this copy, but this was a later insertion by Wilson Shepherd, the first person to publish the essay, and did not turn up in Lovecraft's original manuscript.

63   Clark Ashton Smith, *The Abominations of Yondo* (Sauk City, WI: Arkham House, 1960), p. 3.

64   Conover and Lovecraft, *Lovecraft at Last,* p. 33.

65   Lovecraft, *Dunwich Horror,* p. 219.

66   H. P. Lovecraft, *Dunwich Horror,* p. 223.

67   H. P. Lovecraft, *At the Mountains of Madness,* p. 106.

68   S. T. Joshi, *H. P. Lovecraft,* p. 615.

69   I have been unable to locate this item, but it seems to have appeared during late 1936. See *H. P. Lovecraft, Letters to Henry Kuttner,* ed. David E. Schultz and S.T. Joshi (West Warwick, RI: Necronomicon Press, 1990), p. 27.

70   H. P. Lovecraft, Letter to William Frederick Anger, dated August 14, 1934, *Selected Letters V,* p. 16.

71   H. P. Lovecraft, Letter to Willis Conover, dated July 29, 1936, *Selected Letters V,* p. 285.

72   H.P. Lovecraft, *Uncollected Letters,* ed. S.T. Joshi (West Warwick, RI; Necronomicon Press, 1986), p. 38.

73   H. P. Lovecraft, *Uncollected Letters,* p. 37.

74   H. P. Lovecraft, Letter dated May 7, 1932, *Selected Letters IV,* pp. 39–40.

75   H. P. Lovecraft, *Uncollected Letters,* p. 38.

76   H. P. Lovecraft, *Uncollected Letters,* p. 38.

77   H. P. Lovecraft, *The Horror in the Museum and Other Revisions.* Corrected printing. (Sauk City, WI: Arkham House, 1989), p. 217.

78   H. P. Lovecraft, *At the Mountains of Madness,* p. 431.

79   Price's original draft has recently been published as "The Lord of Illusion" (In *Tales of the Lovecraft Mythos,* Minneapolis,WI: Fedogan and Bremer, 1992), pp. 137–52.)

80   S. T. Joshi, *H. P. Lovecraft,* p. 629.

81   See Umberto Eco, *Foucault's Pendulum* (New York: Ballantine, 1990), p. 493.

82   See Jose Luis Borges, "There are More Things," in *El Libro de Arena* (Buenos Aires:

Emece Editores, 1975), pp. 65–77.

83   Lynn Thorndike, *History of Magic and Experimental Science* (New York: Columbia University, 1923), vol. 2. p. 815.

84   Roger Bryant, "Stalking the Elusive Necronomicon," in *H. P. L.,* Meade and Penny Frierson, eds. (Birmingham, AL, The Editors, 1972), pp. 42–3.

85   H. P. Lovecraft, "The Brief Autobiography of an Inconsequential Scribbler,"in *Miscellaneous Writings,* p. 527.

86   Don Burleson, *Passages from the American Notebooks of Nathaniel Hawthorne* (New York; Houghton, Mifflin and Co., 1896), p. 26.

87   H. P. Lovecraft, "Letter to Clark Ashton Smith dated May 12, 1927," *Selected Letters I–III,* p. 127.

88   H. P. Lovecraft, Letter to E. Hoffman Price dated February 15, 1933, *Selected Letters IV,* p. 153.

89   H. P. Lovecraft, Letter dated November 30, 1936, *Letters to Henry Kuttner,* p. 27.

90   H. P. Lovecraft, Letter dated November 30, 1936, Letters to Henry Kuttner, p. 27.

91   Simon, *Necronomicon* Workshop Tapes (New York: Magical Childe, 1981).

92   S. T. Joshi, *H.P. Lovecraft,* p. 217.

93   Simon, "Introductory Essay," *Necronomicon* (New York; Avon Books, 1980), pp. xvii–xx.

94   Conover and Lovecraft, *Lovecraft at Last,* p. 103. Last update: June 3, 2001.

Chapter 2: The *Necronicom* Made Flesh

1   T. E. D. Klein, "Black Man with a Horn," in *New Tales of the Cthulhu Mythos,* Ramsey Campbell, ed. (Sauk City, WI: Arkham House, 1980), p. 174.

2   Willis Conover and H. P. Lovecraft, *Lovecraft at Last* (Arlington, VA: Carrollton-Clark, 1975), p. 103.

3   Conover and Lovecraft, *Lovecraft at Last,* p. 103.

4   Conover and Lovecraft, *Lovecraft at Last,* p. 103.

5   Conover and Lovecraft, *Lovecraft at Last,* p. 103.

6   Conover and Lovecraft, *Lovecraft at Last,* p. 103.

7   Thanks to Darrell Schweitzer for this information.

8   E. P. Berglund, "What Was the Sussex Manuscript?" *Crypt of Cthulhu, Hallowmass,*1985. pp. 23–5, 27.

9   Fred Pelton, *A Guide to the Cthulhu Cult* (Seattle: Pagan Publishing, 1998).

10   Pelton, *A Guide to the Cthulhu Cult,* p. 148.

11   Pelton, *A Guide to the Cthulhu Cult,* p. 148.

12   Pelton, *A Guide to the Cthulhu Cult,* p. 81.

13   Jacob Blanck, "News from the Rare Book Sellers," *Publishers' Weekly,* December 22, 1945, p. 2727.

14   H. P. Lovecraft and August Derleth, "History and Chronology of the *Necronomicon,* Together with some Pertinent Paragraphs," *Arkham Sampler,* Winter, 1948, pp. 17–18.

15   Lovecraft and Derleth, "History and Chronology of the *Necronomicon,*" p. 19.

16   August Derleth, "The Making of a Hoax," in *The Dark Brotherhood and Other Pieces* (Sauk City, WI: Arkham House, 1966), p. 265.

17   Mark Owings, *The Necronomicon: A Study* (Baltimore, MD: Mirage, 1967), p. 19.

18   Phillippe Druillet, "Leaves from the Necronomicon," *Anubis,* Autumn 1966,. pp. 12–15.

19   Phillippe Druillet, "Excerpts from the Necronomicon," *Heavy Metal,* October 1979, pp. 56–61.

20   Since I first visited the site *(www.imaginet.fr/~reve/HPL/),* it has vanished.

21   Druillet, "Leaves from the *Necronomicon,*" p. 12.

22   Druillet, "Leaves from the *Necronomicon,*" p. 12

23 Thanks to E. P. Berglund for this information.
24 Owings, *The Necronomicon*, p. 3.
25 Owings, *The Necronomicon*, p. 11.
26 Owings, The Necronomicon, p. 19.
27 Owings, The Necronomicon, p. 3.
28 Lyon Sprague de Camp, "Preface to *The Necronomicon*," *Crypt of Cthulhu, St. John's Eve 1984*, p. 17.
29 Letter from George Scithers to the author, October 4, 1997.
30 A friend of mine once saw a larger copy of the Owlswick Press edition, bound in black and containing a few differences from the more popular version. This was most likely a custom photocopy, as Owlswick knows nothing about it. The only known copy was sighted at a now-defunct bookstore in Nashville several years ago. If anyone knows any more about this variant edition, please contact me.
31 "Abdul Alhazred" *Al Azif: The Necronomicon* (Philadelphia, PA: Owlswick, 1973), p. iv.
32 Letter from George Scithers to the author.
33 For more information on Jay Solomon (a.k.a. Yaj Nomolos), see John Gonce's "Nameless Cutlery" in this book.
34 Anthony Raven, *The Occult Lovecraft* (Saddle River, NJ: Gerry de la Ree, 1975).
35 "Augustus Rupp," *The Necromantic Grimoire of Augustus Rupp* (Waldwick, NJ: Bob Lynn, 1974), p. 3.
36 Rupp, *The Necromantic Grimoire*, p. 4. Both the *Grimoire of Honorius* and the *Heptameron* are authentic grimoires—or rather, about as authentic as grimoires can be.
37 Rupp, *The Necromantic Grimoire*, pp. 4–5.
38 Rupp, *The Necromantic Grimoire*, p. 6.
39 Rupp, *The Necromantic Grimoire*, p. 3.
40 Rupp, *The Necromantic Grimoire*, p. 5.
41 Michael Drayton, *Nymphidia, or the Court of Faery* (London: George Routledge and Sons 1906), p. 20.
42 Rupp, *The Necromantic Grimoire*, Book II, Plate IV. The title given to Hastur is somewhat unusual, as in the Cthulhu Mythos it is Nodens who is known as the "Lord of the Great Abyss."
43 Rupp, *The Necromantic Grimoire*, Book II, Plate VII.
44 Robert M. Price, Introduction to "The Papyrus of Nephren-Ka," in *The Nyarlathotep Cycle*, Price ed. (Oakland, CA: Chaosium, 1997), p. 215.
45 Price, *The Nyarlathotep Cycle*, pp. 216–23.
46 Robert Culp, *The Necronomicon* (Fort Myers, FL: Robert Culp, 1975).
47 Thanks to E. P. Berglund for this information.
48 H. R. Giger, *H R Giger Arh+* (Cologne: Benedikt Taschen Verlag GmbH, 1992), p. 40.
49 Giger, *H. R. Giger*, p. 40.
50 H. R. Giger, *The Necronomicon* (Beverly Hills, CA: Morpheus, 1991), title page.
51 Giger, *Necronomicon*, title page.
52 H. R. Giger, *Necronomicon II* (Beverly Hills, CA: Morpheus, 1985), title page.
53 Simon, *Necronomicon* (New York, NY: Avon Books, 1980), p. iv.
54 Simon, *Necronomicon*, p. vii.
55 Simon, *Necronomicon*, p. li.
56 Simon, *Necronomicon*, pp 4–5.
57 "Two Unfrocked 'Byzantine Priests' Held in Yale Rare-Book Thefts," *New York Times*, March 17, 1997, pp. 1:3, 37:1.
58 Simon, *Necronomicon Spellbook* (New York, NY: Magickal Childe, 1987), p. 6.
59 *New York Times*, January 21, 1976. p. 41:4.

60   Simon, *Necronomicon Spellbook.* pp. 1–7.

61   *home.flash.net/~khem/Simonomicon.html.*

62   Khem Caigan, letter to Dan Clore, October 20, 1997.

63   Letter from L. K. Barnes to *Fate* magazine, January 27, 1978. American Religions Collection, ARC Mss 1, Department of Special Collections, University Libraries, University of California, Santa Barbara..

64   Document registration number TX 2-582-633. The *Necronomicon* itself has not been registered, but it is nonetheless protected under U.S. law.

65   Simon, *Books of Rune & Magickal Alphabet & Cypher* (NY: Earth Religions Supply, 1975), p. 4.

66   Simon, *Books of Rune,* title page.

67   Simon, *Books of Rune,* table of contents.

68   Simon, *Necronomicon,* p. iv.

69   Peter Levenda, interview in *Dagobert's Revenge,* vol. 2, no. 2, p. 31.

70   Levenda, interview in *Dagobert's Revenge,* vol. 2, no. 2, p. 32.

71   Email received 19 April 1997 00:25:18–0400

72   Untitled article, American Religions Collection, ARC Mss 1, Department of Special Collections, University Libraries, University of California, Santa Barbara.

73   Public records search.

74   Simon. *Necronomicon,* p. xix.

75   One of the ingredients for this spell is "the grass Olieribos." On a tape released from the Magickal Childe, Simon states that this substance is nettle, and that the name is a Greek term found in a medieval herbal.

76   Simon, *Necronomicon,* pp. 104–5.

77   Simon, *Necronomicon,* p. 111.

78   Simon, *Necronomicon,* p. 218.

79   Simon, *Necronomicon,* p. liii.

80   See John Gonce's essay, "Magic and the *Necronomicon*" in this book.

81   Simon, *Necronomicon,* p. xxxiii.

82   Simon, *Necronomicon,* p. 30.

83   Simon, *Necronomicon,* pp. xix–xx.

84   I omit the Sumerian night-demon Lilith here, as she gained greater importance in the Hebraic tradition much later.

85   Adapa, "The Necronomicon and Ancient Sumer: Dubunking [sic] the Myth." Posted at *http://amavart.com/~adapa/Index.html. 1996* (?). See also Jeremy Black and Anthony Green. *Gods, Demons, and Symbols of Ancient Mesopotamia* (Austin, TX; University of Texas Press, 1992), p. 63.

86   Black and Green, *Gods, Demons, and Symbols,* p. 106.

87   Black and Green, *Gods, Demons, and Symbols,* pp. 147–8.

88   Ioan Petru Culiani, *Psychodania I: A Survey of the Evidence Concerning the Ascension of the Soul and Its Relevance* (Leiden: E. J. Brill, 1983).

89   Simon, *Necronomicon,* p. 19.

90   Simon, *Necronomicon,* page 26.

91   Alasdair Livingston, *Mystical and Mythological Explanatory Works of Assyrian and Babylonian Scholars* (Oxford: Clarendon Press, 1986), p. 177

92   Livingston, *Mystical and Mythological Explanatory Works,* p. 182.

93   Livingston, *Mystical and Mythological Explanatory Works,* p. 177.

94   The Simon Tapes, Magickal Childe.

95   Culiani, *Psychodania I,* p. 20.

96   Morris Jastrow, *Religion of Babylonia and Assyria* (Boston: Ginn and Company, 1898), p. 618.

97   Culiani covers these mistakes at great length in the work mentioned above.

98   R. C. Thompson, *The Devils and Evil Spirits of Babylonia* (London: Luzac, 1904), v. 1, p. 51.

99   James B. Pritchard, *Ancient Near Eastern Texts Relating to the Old Testament* (Princeton, NJ: Princeton University Press, 1955), p. 391.

100   Markham Geller, *Forerunners to Udug-Hul: Sumerian Exorcistic Incantations* (Stuttgart: Franz Steiner Verlag Wiesbaden GMH. Freiburger altorientalische Studien 12, 1985).

101   Geller, *Forerunners to Udug-Hul*, p. 41. As Thompson makes clear (p. 51), he has made a decision to translate the mentions of Namtar (the plague-God) in this incantation as plural, even though the grammar indicates a single entity. Oddly enough, Simon makes the same decision.

102   Simon, *Necronomicon*, p. xxxii.

103   Simon, Necronomicon Spellbook, p. 167

104   Letter from Peter Levenda to the author, April 22, 1997.

105   Robert C. Carey, "The Case of Simon's Necronomicon," in *Crypt of Cthulhu*, St. John's Eve 1984, pp. 21–22, and Tim Maroney, post to Usenet group *alt.magick*. December 5, 1995.

106   Simon, *Necronomicon*, p. vii.

107   Simon, *Necronomicon*, p. vii.

108   Colin Wilson, "The Mythos Writers: Colin Wilson," in *Fantasy Macabre*, Sept. 1980, p. 20.

109   Colin Wilson, "The Necronomicon: The Origin of a Spoof," *Crypt of Cthulhu*, St. John's Eve 1984, p. 15.

110   Wilson, "The Necronomicon: The Origin of a Spoof," p. 16.

111   Letter from Peter Levenda to the author, April 22, 1997.

112   Robert M. Price, "Hexes and Hoaxes," *Rod Serling's The Twilight Zone Magazine*, December 1984, p. 65.

113   Wilson, "The Necronomicon: The Origin of a Spoof," p. 14.

114   Lars Lindholm, *Pilgrims of the Night: Pathfinders of the Magical Way* (St. Paul, MN: Llewellyn, 1993), p. 170.

115   *The R'lyeh Text* (London: Skoob Esoterica, 1995), p. 120.

116   *The R'lyeh Text*, p. 129.

117   Elizabeth Ann St. George, *Casebook of a Working Occultist* (London: Rigel Press, 1972), pp. vii–viii.

118   St. George, ed., *Necronomicon* (London: Spook Enterprises, 1983), p. 1.

119   St. George, ed., *Necronomicon*, p. 3.

120   Merlyn Stone, *The Necronomicon*, 1999, p. 3.

121   Stone, *The Necronomicon*, p. 16.

122   Stone, *The Necronomicon*, p. 5.

123   Stone, *The Necronomicon*, p. 4.

124   Letter to the author, 4/24/2000

125   Personal communication from Kingsword, March 16, 1997.

126   *Candlemas*, 1990 issue.

127   Price, *Necronomicon*, pp. 130–98.

128   Thanks to Tani Jantsang for this information.

129   Price, *Necronomicon*, p. 178.

130   Price, *Necronomicon*, p. 181.

131   George Hay, ed. *The Necronomicon: The Book of Dead Names* (London: Skoob Esoterica, 1992), pp. 123, 125.

132   Price, *Necronomicon*, pp. 166–8.

133   Hay, *Necronomicon*, p. 113.

134   Price, *Necronomicon*, back cover.

135   Andy Black, *Necronomicon: The Journal of Horror and Erotic Cinema* (London: Creation Books, 1996), p. 5.

136   Internet document (*www.cs.utk.edu/~mclennan/BA/NN.html*).

137   *psorcereezee.future.easyspace.com/grimoire/grimoire.html.*

138   *psorcereezee.future.easyspace.com/grimoire/intro.html.*

139   *psorcereezee.future.easyspace.com/grimoire/primum.html.*

140   *psorcereezee.future.easyspace.com/grimoire/secundum.html.*

141   *psorcereezee.future.easyspace.com/grimoire/tertium.html.*

142   *psorcereezee.future.easyspace.com/grimoire/quartum.html.*

143   *necronomiconfiles.tripod.com/ripel.htm.*

144   *www.fanucci.it/.*

145   *www.eerie.eerie.fr/~alquier/.*

146   Laurent Alquier, *Chaosium Digest*, May 18, 1997. Last updated August 11, 2001.

Chapter 3: Evaluating *Necronomicon* Rumors

1   Letter from Colin Low to the author, November 12, 1996.

2   As quoted in post to alt.magick by valis, February 18, 1996.

3   Post by Mark Gibson on alt.horror.cthulhu, January 28, 1997.

Chapter 4: The Evolution of Sorcery

1   S. L. MacGregor Mathers, trans., *Book of the Sacred Magic of Abramelin the Mage* (New York: Dover, 1975), p. 50.

2   Aleister Crowley, *Magick in Theory and Practice*. Reprint as an electronic file. Fairfax, CA: Ordo Templi Orientis, 1989.

3   Henry Cornelius Agrippa, *Three Books of Occult Philosophy*. James Freake, trans. Edited and annotated by Donald Tyson (St. Paul: MN Llewellyn Publications, 1993).

4   Bill Whitcomb, *The Magician's Companion* (St. Paul, MN: Llewellyn, 1993).

5   Francis Barrett, *The Magus* (London: Lackington, Allen & Co., 1801).

6   J-K Huysmans, *La-Bas*. K. Wallis, trans. (New York: University Books, 1958).

7   For a detailed account of this magickal feud between two Decadent period factions(the Abbe Boullan and his friend Huysmans, versus the Marquis Stanislas de Guaita, a puritanical morphine addict with delusions of godhood), see Richard Cavendish, *The Black Arts* (New York: Perigee Books, 1983), pp. 34–37.

8   It has been debated whether Crowley actually founded any magickal groups of his own, as opposed to just taking them over by political piracy. Crowley did actually found a few small groups toward the end of his life. And then there was the Abbey of Thelema at Cephalu. It must also be noted that Crowley profoundly changed any organization under his leadership. The OTO groups of today are very different from the Lodge headed by Theodor Reuss. The A.˙.A.˙. also definitely bears the indelible mark of the Great Beast, and is not simply the Golden Dawn continuing under Crowley's banner (unless you think the Golden Dawn was a Thelemic organization). Whether you call it the Argenteum Astrum or the Aurum Aurorum, the A.˙.A.˙. is definitely Crowley's own.

9   Aleister Crowley, *Liber 77 vel Oz The Rights of Man* (York Beach, ME: Weiser, 1994).

10   There is a legend in the magickal community that Crowley did spellwork to make himself famous, but forgot to specify what kind of fame he wanted.

11   "Women, like all moral inferiors, behave well only when treated with firmness, kindness and justice."—quote from Crowley found in Lars B. Lindholm, *Pilgrims of the Night* (St. Paul, MN: Llewellyn, 1993), p. 111. Crowley often wrote of rape in glowingly heroic or romantic terms, as in his famous "Hymn to Pan." The entries in Crowley's

magickal diaries are also rather telling: "6 Sept. Christine Rosalie Byrne ('Peggy Marchmount') Piccadilly prostitute. . . . The girl is a sturdy bitch of 26 or so." in *The Magical Record of the Great Beast 666,* edited and annotated by John Symonds and Kenneth Grant (London NW 1: Gerald Duckworth & Co. Ltd., 1972), p. 4.

12 Ten was not an arbitrary choice for the number of Sephiroth in the traditional Hebrew system of Kabbalah. Since everything in the Kabbalistic universe was believed to be an emanation from the Sephiroth, the Kabbalists deduced the number of Sephiroth from the number of elemental forces ruling the natural world: every force has three degrees, every object three dimensions (height, depth, width), plus gravity makes ten. Numerologically $1 + 0 = 1$, the number of God. Crowley's addition of one to this balanced traditional system, making the total eleven, amounted to a metaphysical monkey wrench. See Erich Bischoff, *The Kabbala* (York Beach, ME: Weiser, 1995).

13 Pascal Beverly Randolph, *Sexual Magic.* Translated, edited and introduced by Robert North (New York, Magickal Childe 1988). See also Margo Anand, *The Art of Sexual Magic* (New York: Tarcher/ Putnam, 1995), p. 30.

14 Lars B. Lindholm, *Pilgrims of the Night* (St. Paul, MN: Llewellyn, 1993), p. 112.

15 Isaac Bonewits, *Real Magic; An Introductory Treatise on the basic Principles of Yellow Magic* (York Beach, ME: Samuel Weiser, 1993), p. 221–22.

16 H. P. Lovecraft, "From a letter to Emil Petaja, March 6, 1935," *Selected Letters IV–V,* ed. August Derleth and Donald Wandrei (Sauk City, WI: Arkham, 1976), p. 120.

17 Bonewits, *Real Magic,* pp. 14–15.

18 Bonewits, *Real Magic,* pp. 14–15.

19 Lindholm, *Pilgrims of the Night,* p. 137.

20 Adrian Savage, *An Introduction to Chaos Magick* (New York, NY: Magickal Childe, 1988).

21 Bonewits, *Real Magic.*

22 Phil Hine, *Condensed Chaos* (Tempe, AZ: New Falcon Publications, 1996), p. 80.

23 Linda Blood, *The New Satanists* (New York, NY: Warner Books, 1994), p. 72.

24 Erik Davis, "Calling Cthulhu," *Gnosis,* Fall 1995. The same article was expanded and circulated on the Internet.

25 Anand, *Sexual Magic,* pp. 171–95.

26 Bonewits, *Real Magic.*

27 Lindholm, *Pilgrims of the Night,* p. 171.

Chapter 5: Lovecraftian Magick: Sources and Heirs

1 W. H. Muller, *Polaria: The Gift of the White Stone* (Albuquerque, NM: Brotherhood of Life Publishing, 1995).

2 Anthony Raven, "Lovecraft and Black Magic," in *The Occult Lovecraft* (Saddle River, NJ: Gerry De la Ree, 1975), pp. 32–40.

3 Lovecraft, H. P., *Lord of a Visible World: An Autobiography in Letters,* ed. S. T. Joshi and David E. Schultz (Athens, OH: Ohio University Press, 2000), pp. vii.

4 Derleth idiosyncratically censored many references to fiction sales, politics, and other subjects from Lovecraft's published letters. It is a safe bet that he also expurgated most references to studies of occult subjects.

5 August Derleth, "Introduction" to *Selected Letters I* (Sauk City, WI: Arkham House, 1965), p. xxii.

6 Letter to Robert E. Howard, January 16, 1932. *Selected Letters IV* (Sauk City, WI: Arkham House, 1976), p. 8.

7 Letter to Robert E. Howard, January 16, 1932. Arkham House Transcripts. Quoted in S. T. Joshi, *H. P. Lovecraft: A Life* (West Warwick, RI: Necronomicon Press, 1996), p. 19.

8 S. T. Joshi, *Lovecraft: A Life,* p. 19.

9   "It is not likely that the Providence *Picatrix* of Winfield Lovecraft (mentioned in G. Hay ed., *The Necronomicon*, London 1978, p. 50) ever existed." See David Pingree, *Picatrix, The Latin Version* (London: The Warburg Institute, 1986), p. *xv.* Despite some hoaxed rumors, Lovecraft never read the *Picatrix*, and was apparently unaware of its existence.

10   Robert Irwin, *The Arabian Nights: A Companion*(London: The Penguin Press, 1994), p. 203.

11   Robert Irwin, *The Arabian Nights: A Companion*, pp. 206–207.

12   Robert Irwin, *The Arabian Nights: A Companion*, p. 205.

13   Robert Irwin, *The Arabian Nights: A Companion*, p. 178.

14   Robert Irwin, *The Arabian Nights: A Companion*, p. 186.

15   H. P. Lovecraft, *Selected Letters I*, ed. August Derleth and Donald Wandrei (Sauk City, WI: Arkham House, 1965), p. 33.

16   H. P. Lovecraft, Letter to Clark Ashton Smith, December 13, 1933, *Selected Letters IV,* ed. August Derleth and James Turner (Sauk City, WI: Arkham House, 1976), p. 335.

17   Letter to Edwin Baird, February 3, 1924, from the John Hay Library, Brown University. Quoted in Lovecraft's *Lord of a Visible World,* edited by Joshi, and Shultz, p. 14. Also found in "A Confession of Unfaith" in *Miscellaneous Writings* (Sauk City, WI: Arkham House, 1995), pp. 534–535.

18   H. P. Lovecraft, *Lord of a Visible World*, p. 14.

19   Paul F. Memoli, *Lovecraft Sorceror*[sic] (a pamphlet privately published in Woodbridge, CT, October 1979).

20   H. P. Lovecraft, *Lord of a Visible World,* 85.

21   Found at the website for The Writings of C. S. Lewis, *www.westminster.edu/staff/mackypw/rel30pwm.htm.*

22   Jack Sullivan, ed., *The Penguin Encyclopedia of Horror and the Supernatural* (New York: Viking Penguin, Inc., 1986), p. 276.

23   H. P. Lovecraft, "The Call of Cthulhu," in *the Dunwich Horror and Others* (Sauk City, WI: Arkham House, 1963), p. 136.

24   Letter to Robert Bloch, June 1, 1933. S. T. Joshi and David Schultz, eds., *H.P. Lovecraft: Letters to Robert Bloch* (West Warwick, RI: Necronomicon Press, 1993), p. 14.

25   Felix Morrow, "Introduction" to Sax Rohmer, *The Romance of Sorcery* (New York: Causeway Books, 1973), p. *ix.* Also found in Kay Van Ash and Elizabeth Sax Rohmer, *Master of Villany: A Biography of Sax Rohmer* (Bowling Green, OH: Bowling Green University Press, 1972).

26   H. P. Lovecraft, Letter to Emil Petaja, March 6, 1935, *Selected Letters V,* ed. August Derleth and James Turner (Sauk City, WI: Arkham House, 1976), p. 120.

27   H. P. Lovecraft, Letter to Clark Ashton Smith, October 9, 1925, *Selected Letters II,* ed. August Derleth and Donald Wandrei (Sauk City, WI: Arkham House, 1971), p. 27.

28   Found at the Eldritch Dark website: *www.eldritchdark.com/wri/non-fict/letters/letter_virgil_2.html.*

29   H. P. Lovecraft, *Selected letters V,* p. 287.

30   H. P. Lovecraft and C. M. Eddy Jr., "The Cancer of Superstition" in *The Dark Brotherhood and Other Pieces* (Sauk City, WI: Arkham House, 1966), pp. 247–61.

31   H. P. Lovecraft, "The Call of Cthulhu" in *The Dunwich Horror and Others* (Sauk City, WI: Arkham House, 1963), p. 126.

32   H. P. Lovecraft, *Selected Letters IV,* ed. August Derleth and James Turner (Sauk City, WI: Arkham House, 1976), p. 155.

33   H. P. Lovecraft, *Selected Letters IV, p. 153.*

34   These included: *The Arabian Nights,* Sabine Baring-Gold's *Curious Myths of the Middle*

Ages, Richard Blakeborough's (coll.) *The Hand of Glory and Further Grandfather's Tales and Legends of Highwaymen and Others*, Bullfinch's *Age of Fable*, John Fiske's *Myths and Myth-Makers*, Camille Flammarion's *Haunted Houser*, Harry Houdini's *A Magician Among the Spirits*, John H. Ingram's *Haunted Homes and Family Legends of Great Britain*, Johann Heinrich Jung-Stilling's, *Theory of Pneumatology*, MacPhilpin's *Miracles at Knock*, Scott's *Demonology and Witchcraft*, and Lewis Spence's *An Encyclopedia of Occultism*.

35   H. P. Lovecraft, *Selected Letters IV*, p. 271.

36   Dirl W. Mosig, "Lovecraft: The Dissonance Factor in Imaginative Literature," *The Miskatonic*, v. 4, n. 8. 1985. As quoted in "Reluctant Prophet" from *Starry Wisdom: An Anthology of Essays from the Newsletter of the Dunwich [UK] Lodge of the Esoteric Order of Dagon* (Eugene, OR: Starry Wisdom Press, 1990), p. 36.

37   H. P. Lovecraft, *Supernatural Horror in Literature* (New York: Dover Publishing, Inc., 1973), p. 13.

38   Colin Wilson, "Tentacles Across Time," in *Skoob Esoterica Anthology* (London: Skoob Books, 1995), p. 14.

39   Sandy Robertson, *The Aleister Crowley Scrapbook* (York Beach, ME: Weiser, 1994), p. 95.

40   Actually, Lovecraft's idea of the Elder Sign looks nothing like a pentagram. His drawing of it consists of a curved upright line with a series of smaller lines projecting out from it like ribs from a spine. It looks like a leaf, the body of a centipede, or perhaps the skeleton of a fish. See H. P. Lovecraft, *Selected Letters III*, ed. August Derleth and Donald Wandrei (Sauk City, WI: Arkham House, 1971), p. 216.

41   Kenneth Grant, *Aleister Crowley and the Hidden God* (London: Frederick Muller Ltd., 1975), p. 95.

42   Kenneth Grant, *Outside the Circles of Time* (London: Muller, 1980), p. 59.

43   "The Cabala is often mystifyingly obscure and is so complicated that almost anything said about it is bound to be oversimplified."—Richard Cavendish, *The Black Arts* (New York: Perigee Books, 1983), p. 81.

44   Todoros Abulafia (second half of the 13th century) is generally thought to be the prime exponent of the doctrine of the ten Qlippoth (or Kelippoth). See Erich Bischoff, *The Kabbala: An Introduction to Jewish Mysticism and Its Secret Doctrine* (York Beach, ME: Samuel Weiser, 1985).

45   "But Coronzon (for so is the name of that mighty devil), envying man's felicity, and perceiving that the substance of man's lesser part was frail and began to assail man, and so prevailed." See John Dee, *The Enochian Magick of Dr. John Dee*. Edited and translated by Geoffrey James (St. Paul, MN: Llewellyn Publications, 1994), p. 1. (Previously published as *The Enochian Evocation of Dr. John Dee*, Gillette, NJ: Heptangle Books, 1984). Notice that the context in which Dee uses the name "Coronzon" makes it appear to be nothing more than an alternative name for Satan. It appears that Crowley simply ran with the name and used it as he saw fit.

46   Whitcomb, *The Magician's Companion*, p. 495.

47   H. P. Lovecraft, "The Dunwich Horror," in *The Dunwich Horror and Others*. Corrected printing (Sauk City, WI: Arkham House, 1984), p. 170.

48   Aleister Crowley, *The Equinox*, vol 1, no. 7, 1912, pp. 69–74.

49   Kenneth Grant, *Nightside of Eden* (London: Skoob Books, 1994), p. xii.

50   Grant, *Nightside of Eden*, pp. 137–255.

51   Lovecraft, "The Dunwich Horror," p.170.

41   H. P. Lovecraft, *The Horror in the Museum*. Corrected printing (Sauk City, WI: Arkham House, 1989), p. 230.

53   August Derleth, *The Watchers Out of Time* (Sauk City, WI: Arkham House, 1974), p.

147. Though often considered a "posthumous collaboration" between Lovecraft and August Derleth, "Lurker at the Threshold" contains little of Lovecraft other than perhaps the central theme, and is 99% Derleth.

54   Grant, *Outside the Circles of Time*, p. 167.

55   Grant, *Outside the Circles of Time*, p. 167.

56   Grant, *Outside the Circles of Time*, p. 166.

57   Grant, *Outside the Circles of Time*, p. 168.

58   Grant, *Outside the Circles of Time*, p. 169.

59   Grant, *Outside the Circles of Time*, p. 168. also Kenneth Grant, *Man, Myth & Magic*, No. 84, 1971.

60   Grant, *Outside the Circles of Time*, p. 169.

61   H. P. Lovecraft, *Selected Letters V*, p. 156.

62   H. P. Lovecraft, Letter to Clark Ashton Smith, October 9, 1925, *Selected Letters II*, p. 27.

63   "Lovecraft in Church of Satan," Post by Dr. Michael A. Aquino to newsgroup alt.satanism, November 21, 2000.

64   Michael A. Aquino, "Lovecraftian Ritual," *Nyctalops*, May 1977, pp. 13–15.

65   Michael A. Aquino, *The Satanic Rituals* (New York: Avon Books, 1972), pp. 181–93.

66   Aquino, *Satanic Rituals*, pp. 197–201.

67   Aquino, *Satanic Rituals*, pp. 108–10.

68   Aquino, *Satanic Rituals*, p. 117.

69   Aquino, *Satanic Rituals*, p. 119.

70   Letter to Daniel Harms, September 26, 1998 00:16:54 EDT.

71   Morris Doreal, *An Interpretation of the Emerald Tablets* (Sedalia, CA: Brotherhood of the White Temple, Inc., 1948), p. 31

72   Doreal, *Emerald Tablets*, p. 42.

73   Anton Szandor LaVey, "The Law of the Trapezoid," in *The Devil's Notebook* (Portland, OR: Feral House, 1992), pp. 113–14. See also Blanche Barton, "Angles of Madness," in *The Secret Life of a Satanist: The Authorized Biography of Anton LaVey* (Portland, OR: Feral House, 1992), pp. 159–66.

74   Aquino, *The Satanic Rituals*. p. 15.

75   Neville Drury, "An Interview With Michael Bertiaux," *www.geocities.com/Athens/Delphi/3527/bertiaux.html*.

76   Kenneth Grant, *Cults of the Shadow* (London: Skoob Books, 1994), p. 21.

77   Kenneth Grant, *Cults of the Shadow*, pp. 186-9.

78   *www.geocities.com/Athens/Delphi/3527/bertiaux.html*.

79   *www.geocities.com/erzulie_freda/chor.htm*.

80   Nina Crummet Peter Smith, and Alec Hidell, "The Veiled Continuum," in *The Silver Key*, No. 1, 1993.

81   Introduction to *Starry Wisdom* (Eugene, OR: Starry Wisdom Press, 1990), p. 2.

82   Introduction to *Starry Wisdon*, p. 2.

83   Frater Tenebrous, *Starry Wisdom*, v. 1, n. 1, e.v. Frater Tenebrous, Esoteric Order of Dagon, Dunwich Lodge, Leeds, England.

84   Frater Tenebrous, *Starry Wisdom*.

85   Frater Tenebrous, *The Aeon of Cthulhu Rising* (Logan, OH: Black Moon Publishing, 1990).

86   Tenebrous, *Aeon of Cthulhu*, p. 19.

87   The authentic earthly location of R'lyeh is believed by several Cthulhu Mythos magicians to be the ruins of an ancient stone city of indeterminate age called Nan-Matol, located on the Micronesian island of Ponape. Lovecraft actually mentions Ponape in "The Shadow over Innsmouth." He mentions both Ponape and "the megalithic masonry" of Nan-Matol in "Out of the Aeons" (with Hazel Heald), as well as the *Book of Eibon*,

the *Pnakotic Fragments* (Pnakotic Manuscripts), von Junzt's *Nameless Cults* (*Unaussprechlichen Kulten*), and, of course, the *Necronomicon*. He links them all vaguely to Ponape by way of a mysterious hieroglyphic inscription. Michael Aquino has written a fascinating study of Ponape/Nan-Matol, linking it to Lovecraft's fictional R'lyeh. See Aquino, "Expedition to R'lyeh" in *Starry Wisdom*, v. 1, n. 5 (first published in *The Cloven Hoof*, Church of Satan, VII/ 1972, available from Black Moon publishing). See also Chris Jarocha-Ernst, *A Cthulhu Mythos Bibliography* (Seattle, WA: Pagan Publishing, 1994), entries for Ponape and Nan-Matol.

88   Frater Tenebrous, "The Rite of the Communion of Cthulhu," in *Starry Wisdom* (Eugene, OR: Starry Wisdom Press, 1990), pp. 10–12.

89   *alt.horror* Cthulhu FAQ.

90   Ian Blake, *Eight Arms to Hold You* (Eugene, OR: Sepulchral Press, 1993).

91   Nina Crummett, *The Silver Key: The Journal of the Miskatonick Society*, Issue 1, 1993, p. 4.

92   "Announcement Of The Re-Emergence Of The Esoteric Order Of Dagon," issued by the Yaddith Lodge XXXIII*. *Crypt of Cthulhu* 94.

93   William Siebert (AshT ChOzar Ssaratu), "Some Brief Notes Regarding the On-Going Work of our Miskatonic Alchemical Expedition," Internet document, *www.crl.com/~tzimon/General/zchron2_1.txt*.

94   William Seibert, "Some Brief Notes."

95   William Seibert, "Some Brief Notes."

96   William Seibert, "Some Brief Notes."

97   William Seibert, "Some Brief Notes."

98   William Seibert, "Some Brief Notes."

99   Karl Mac McKinnon, "The Temple of the Vampire," Internet document, *www.io.com/~chimera/temple_vampire.html*. 1996. I advise anyone interested in communicating with the Temple of the Vampire to exercise caution. Reliable sources indicate that the TOV uses cult-style harassment techniques on their former members, some of whom report very negative experiences. Daniel and I sent fifty dollars to the TOV for a copy of their *Vampire Bible* more than three years ago and, as of the time of this writing, we have yet to receive anything in return for our money.

100   Davis, "Calling Cthulhu."

101   Davis, "Calling Cthulhu."

102   Phil Hine, *Pseudonomicon* (Irvine, CA: Dagon Productions, 1997).

103   Hine, *Pseudonomicon*, p. 17.

104   Hine, *Pseudonomicon*, p. 27. This ritual is undoubtedly the inspiration for Ryan Parker's "Rite of the Ghouls."

105   Micahel A. Aquino, "Lovecraftian Ritual," *Nyctalops*, 13, p. 13.

106   Hine, *Pseudonomicon*, p. 2.

107   Anonymous, "Return of the Elder Gods," *Cincinnati Journal of Magic*, Vol. 1, no. 3, 1978.

108   Anonymous, "Return of the Elder Gods," p. 17.

109   Anonymous, "Return of the Elder Gods," p. 18.

110   Anonymous, "Return of the Elder Gods," p. 22.

111   Grant, *Outside the Circles of Time*. In the chapters "Masks of Maat" and "The Forgotten Ones," Grant introduces these concepts.

112   Hine, *Pseudonomicon*, pp. 41–42. Hine points out that healing is not an application with which most practitioners would associate the Great Old Ones.

113   G. K. Chesterton, *The Everlasting Man* (1925) (San Francisco, CA: Ignatius Press, 1993), pp. 144, 148, 149.

114   Kenneth Grant, *Hecate's Fountain* (London: Skoob Books, 1992), p. 18.

115 Aleister Crowley, *Magick in Theory and Practice* (New York: Magickal Childe Publishing), p. 214.

116 John Carter, *Sex and Rockets, The Occult World of Jack Parsons* (Venice, CA: Feral House, 1999), p. 58.

117 John Carter, *Sex and Rockets*, p. 172.

118 H. P. Lovecraft and William Lumley, "The Diary of Alonzo Type," found in *The Horror in the Museum* (Sauk City, WI: Arkham House Publishers, Inc., 1989), p. 317.

119 John Carter, *Sex and Rockets*, p.95.

120 John Carter, *Sex and Rockets*, p. 150.

121 John Carter, *Sex and Rockets*, p. 150.

122 John Carter, *Sex and Rockets*, p. 187.

Chapter 6: A Plague of *Necronomicons*

1 Sloane MS. 3189, the "clean copy" of Dee's *Liber Mysteriorum Sextus et Sanctus* or *Liber Logaeth,* contains 65 folios with 101 complex magick squares, of which 96 are composed of 49 x 49 cells containing Latin letters and Arabic numerals. Nothing of the kind appears in the Hay/Wilson *Necronomicon!* Contrary to the claims of Hay, Turner, and Langford, the text of the manuscript is not entirely written in cypher, and partial translations already exist. Dee scholar Clay Holden is currently preparing a full transcription of *Liber Logaeth* that, when published, should prove embarrassing to the authors of the Hay book. Clay Holden points out that the proper spelling of *Logaeth* should be "Loagaeth," and that the currently common misspelling comes from an error in Meric Casaubon's book, *A True and Faithful Relation.* See "Introductory Bibliography of Enochian and Diary MSS of John Dee" (based on Peter French's bibliography with comments from the bibliography compiled by R. F. Buchanan (AZ0th) 1992, some information supplied by Adam McLean, Gionni di Gravio and Clay Holden.) Internet document.

2 Geoffrey James, *Angel Magic* (St. Paul, MN: Llewellyn, 1995), p. 188.

3 Kenneth Grant, *Outside the Circles of Time* (London: Muller, 1980), p. 166.

4 S. L. Mathers, MacGregor, trans., *The Grimoire of Armadel* (York Beach, ME: Samuel Weiser Inc., 1980).

5 The only example I have seen of the Hay\Wilson *Necronomicon* being used for actual magick is in the form of an Internet document by Ryan Parker. The essay instructs the reader in how to make his own shoggoth by means of masturbatory sex magick ("particularly suited for creating violently powerful and unpredictable entities"). The practitioner makes use of the Sign of the Elders, the Talisman of Yhe, the Sign of Koth, the Elder Sign, and the Voorish Sign, but uses none of the rituals in the Hay/Wilson book.

6 Simon, *Necronomicon* (New York, NY: Avon Books, 1980), pp. 17–61.

7 Geoffrey James, ed. and trans., *The Enochian Magick of Dr. John Dee* (St. Paul, MN: Llewellyn, 1994), pp. xx.

8 Simon, *Necronomicon*, p. iv.

9 Sandy Robertson, *The Aleister Crowley Scrapbook* (York Beach, ME: Samuel Weiser, Inc., 1994), p. 97.

10 Personal e-mail communication to Daniel Harms, April 22, 1997, 13:03:39 0400 (EDT).

11 Personal conversation, 17 August 1997.

12 Personal e-mail communication

13 Simon, *Necronomicon*, p. xxi.

14 Simon, *Necronomicon Spellbook* (New York, NY: Magickal Childe, 1987), p. 7. First published as *The Necronomicon Report.*

15 Lawrence Fellows, "2 Unfrocked Priests Held in Yale Rare-Book Thefts," *New York Times,* March 17, 1973, p. 1.

16 Simon, *Necronomicon*, p. xxxiii.

17 For more information about this fascinating archaeological scandal, see "Tracking the Shapira Case," *Biblical Archaeology Review*, v. 23, n. 3, May/June 1997 issue, pp. 32–42.

18 Personal e-mail communication.

19 Simon, *Necronomicon*, p. xi.

20 "Chaldea" was the term applied by 19th-century writers to Mesopotamia as a whole, but should be restricted to the area near the Persian Gulf and the period of the first millennium B.C.E. "Chaldeans" was the name inaccurately used to designate the Sumerians, but it should only be applied to the tribes that inhabited Lower Mesopotamia in the sixth and seventh centuries B.C.E. The term was sometimes applied to the Babylonians as well. See: Andre Parrot, *Sumer: The Dawn of Art* (New York: Golden Press, 1961), p. 344.

21 Aleister Crowley, *Magick Without Tears* (Las Vegas, NV: Falcon Press/Golden Dawn Publications, 1989), p. 80.

22 S. L. Mathers, MacGregor trans., *The Lesser Key of Solomon: Goetia, the Book of Evil Spirits* (Chicago: De Laurence, Scott & Co., 1916), p. 2.

23 F. L. Griffith and Herbert Thompson, *The Demotic Magical Papyrus of London and Leiden* (London: Grevel and Company, 1904), p. 4.

24 Aleister Crowley, "The Cephalodium Working," Internet document, Affe Lovbo, 1996.

25 Aleister Crowley, *Liber Aleph vel CXI: The Book of Wisdom or Folly* (York Beach, ME: Samuel Weiser, 1991), p. 151.

26 Personal e-mail communication, April 23, 1997, 02:33 AM.

27 H. P. Lovecraft, *Selected Letters V*, ed. August Derleth and James Turner (Sauk City, WI: Arkham House, 1965), p. 189.

28 Sir E. A. Wallis Budge, *Amulets and Talismans* (New York: University Books, 1968), pp. 406–9.

29 Personal e-mail communication April 22, 1997, 13:30.

30 Khem Caighan, "The Simonicon and Me," found at *www.bway.net/~frob/simonicon.htm*.

31 William S. Burroughs, *Cities of the Red Night* (New York: Henry Holt and Company, 1995), pp. xvii–xviii.

32 Burroughs, *Cities of the Red Night*, pp. xvii–xviii.

33 Obtained from the American Religions Collection, ARC mss.1, Department of Special Collections, Davidson Library, University of California, Santa Barbara.

34 American Religions Collections, ARC mss 1.

35 American Religions Collections, ARC mss 1.

36 Department of Special Collections, Davidson Library.

37 Department of Special Collections, Davidson Library.

38 Herman Slater, *Earth Religion News* (June, 1974).

39 Simon, *Earth Religion News* (June, 1974).

40 Department of Special Collections, Davidson Library.

41 Francis King, *The Grimoire of Armadel* (York Beach, ME: Samuel Weiser, 1980), p. 7.

42 Department of Special Collections, Davidson Library.

43 Kenneth Grant, *Outer Gateways* (London: Skoob Books, 1994), p. 27.

44 Grant, *Outer Gateways*, p. 27.

45 Robert Larson, *Satanism, the Seduction of American Youth* (Nashville, TN: Thomas Nelson Publishers, 1989), p. 139.

46 David Godwin, *Godwin's Cabalistic Encyclopedia* (St. Paul, MN: Llewellyn, 1994), pp. 41, 82.

47 William Whitcomb, *The Magician's Companion: A Practical Encyclopedic Guide to Magic & Religious Symbolism* (St. Paul, MN: Llewellyn Publications, 1994), pp. 494–95.

48   Whitcomb, *The Magician's Companion*, p. 495.

49   Whitcomb, *The Magician's Companion,* p. 495.

50   Erik Davis, "Calling Cthulhu," *Gnosis*, Fall 1995, p. 63.

51   Lars B. Lindholm, *Pilgrims of the Night* (St. Paul, MN: Llewellyn, 1993), p. 170.

52   Konstantinos, *Summoning Spirits: The Art of Magical Evocation* (St. Paul, MN: Llewellyn, 1995), p. 117.

53   Konstantinos, *Summoning Spirits,* p. 118.

54   Konstantinos, *Summoning Spirits,* p. 119.

55   Phil Hine, *Pseudonomicon* (Irvine, CA: Dagon Productions, 1997), p. 6.

56   Hine, *Pseudonomicon,* p. 34.

57   Donald Michael Kraig, *Modern Magick* (St. Paul, MN: Lewellyn, 2001), p. 530.

58   Kraig, *Modern Magick*, p. 530.

59   Kraig, *Modern Magick*, p. 530.

60   Highly respected Neopagan magician Isaac Bonewits's "Switchboard Theory" states that the older a magickal "circuit" the more power it will have.

61   Jeremy Black and Anthony Green, *Gods, Demons and Symbols of Ancient Mesopotamia* (Austin, TX: University of Texas Press, 1995), p. 126.

62   Kalyn Tranquilson, "Comments on the *Necronomicon* Excerpted from Babylonia," Internet document, 1996, *www.sonic.net/~tenwich/arcanum/chaos/simnecro.html*. See also David L Evens Internet document on alt.magick newsgroup, Saturday, December 10, 1994, 02:09:44 GMT.

63   Black and y Green, *Gods, Demons and Symbols,* p. 126.

64   Tranquilson, "Comments on the *Necronomicon.*

65   *Sixth and Seventh Books of Moses* (Arlington, TX: Dorene Publishing Co. Inc., 1997), p. 51.

66   *Sixth and Seventh Books of Moses*, p. 51.

67   Hans Sebald, "The Sixth and Seventh Books of Moses: The Historical and Sociological Vagaries of a Grimoire," *Ethnologia Europea,* 18, 1988, pp. 53–8. No such seal appears in any editions of the book we have checked.

68   Kurt E. Koch, *Occult ABC* (Grand Rapids. MI: Kregel Publications, 1981), p. 204. Also found in "The Books of the Damned" by Scott Corrales, *Fate,* July 2000, p. 24.

69   Adapa, "The *Necronomicon* and Ancient Sumer: Dubuking [sic] the Myth," Internet document, 1995. See also Lewis Spence, *Myths and Legends of Babylonia and Assyria* (London: Harrap, 1916), p. 264; E. Campbell Thompson, *The Devils and Evil Spirits of Babylonia* (London: Luzac 1904).

70   Simon, *Necronomicon*, pp. 79–80.

71   Black and Green, *Gods, Demons and Symbols,* p. 128.

72   Black and Green, *Gods, Demons and Symbols,* p. 128.

73   Black and Green, *Gods, Demons and Symbols,* p. 63. The Sumerian equivalent of *rabi su* (spirit) is *maskim.*

74   Marvin Meyer and Richard Smith, *Ancient Christian Magic: Coptic Texts of Ritual Power* (San Francisco: HarperCollins, 1994), pp. 160–61. Papyrus text Berlin 8325, translated by Marvin Meyer.

75   Black and Green, *Gods, Demons and Symbols,* p 41.

76   James B. Pritchard, *The Ancient Near East Volume II: A New Anthology of Texts and Pictures* (Princeton, NJ: Princeton University Press, 1992).

77   Black and Green, *Gods, Demons and Symbols,* p. 46.

78   Black and Green, *Gods, Demons and Symbols,* p. 36.

79   Alasdair Livingstone, *Mystical and Mythological Explanatory Works of Assyrian and Babylonian Scholars* (Oxford: Clarendon Press, 1986), p. 177.

80   Livingstone, *Mystical and Mythological Explanatory Works, p. 177.*

81   Simon, *Necronomicon*, p. 187.

82   Richard Aldington and Delano Ames, trans., *New Larousse Encyclopedia of Mythology* (New York and London: Prometheus Press/Hamlyn House, 1968), p. 68.

83   Black and Green, *Gods, Demons and Symbols*, pp. 17, 106.

84   Andre Parrot, N. K. Sandars, trans. and ed., *The Epic of Gilgamesh* (New York: Penguin Books, 1972), p.83.

85   Black and Green, *Gods, Demons and Symbols*, pp. 106, 147–48.

86   Personal e-mail communication from Peter Levenda, April 22, 1997, 13:30

87   Personal e-mail communication from Peter Levenda, April 22, 1997, 13:30

88   Mathers, *The Goetia* , p. 41.

89   Dan Clore, *Necronomicon Web Site,* found at *www.geocities.com/SoHo/9879/necpage.htm.*

90   Simon, *Necronomicon*, p. xviii.

91   H. P. Lovecraft, Letter to Duane Rimel, July 23, 1934, *Selected Letters V*, pp.10-11. "The actual sound—as nearly as human organs could imitate it or human letters record it—may be taken as something like *Khlul-hlooh*."

92   Khem Caighan, "The Simonicon and Me" at *http://home.flash.net/~khem/simonicon.html.*

93   Donald Michael Kraig, "Introduction" to Melita Denning and Osborne Phillips, *Planetary Magick*. (St. Paul, MN: Llewellyn, 1992).

94   Simon, *Necronomicon*, p. 19.

95   Tish Gattis, proprietor of *The Goddess and the Moon*. As an object lesson in what can happen to those who disregard the safety of circles and banishings, one of my close friends was working a ritual to summon a spirit from the *Goetia*. He was so inexperienced with magick that he believed his ritual had failed just because he saw no visible manifestation of the spirit. In disgust, he stepped out of the circle with no dismissal or banishing. For a month afterward, he suffered from severe depression, loss of appetite, loss of sex drive (remarkable in an eighteen-year-old man), and periodic attacks of hysterical blindness.

96   Simon, *Necronomicon*, p. 37.

97   Personal e-mail communication from Az0th, October 11, 1996

98   Benjamin Foster, *From Distant Days . . . Myths, Tales and Poetry from Ancient Mesopotamia* (Bethesda, MD: CDI Press, 1995).

99   Adela Yarbro Collins, "The Seven Heavens in Jewish and Christian Apocalypses," in *Death, Ecstasy, and Other Worldly Journeys,* edited by John J. Collins and Michael Fishbane (New York: State University of New York Press, 1995), p. 60.

100   Collins, "The Seven Heavens in Jewish and Christian Apocalypses," p. 60.

101   Richard Aldinton and Delano Ames trans., *New Larousse Encyclopedia of Mythology* (Feltham, UK: Hamlyn Publishing, 1968),p. 64. When the Goddess Innana/Ishtar descended into the underworld, she had to abandon an article of apparel at each of the seven gates until she was naked and trapped behind the last gate. Resurrected by the intervention of Enki, She emerged victorious over death.

102   Godwin, *Godwin's Cabalistic Encyclopedia*, p. 142 ("Hell"), pp. 242–43 ("Qlippoth"), p. 341 ("Yesod").

103   Simon adds the word "therefore" and changes the punctuation.

104   Posting to Usenet group alt.magick. Friday, October 20, 1995. The address is obviously not real, but was undoubtedly changed to protect the identity of the sender.

105   Posting to Usenet group *alt.magick*. Friday, October 20, 1995. The address is obviously not real, but was undoubtedly changed to protect the identity of the sender.

106   Black and Green, *Gods, Demons and Symbols*, pp. 77, 86, 180. Interestingly, *Ganzir* was often used to mean the *gate* to the underworld.

107   Simon, *Necronomicon*, pp. 6, 16, 174, 175, 178, 179.

108   Simon, *Necronomicon*, p. 16.

109   Melita Denning and Phillips, Osborne, *The Llewellyn Practical Guide to Astral Projection: The Out-of-the-Body Experience* (St. Paul, MN: Llewellyn 1993), pp. 223–25 (Appendix: An Example of Astral Combat). Denning and Phillips are adamant that these creatures come only from the lower astral plane. Such entities are too intelligent in their mode of attack to be actual dogs. There are stories of predatory dog spirits in the folklore of several cultures. Ironically, Lovecraft first used the *Necronomicon* in a story called "The Hound" (1922), which probably served as inspiration for Frank Belknap Long's Mythos tale of inter-dimensionally traveling dog-demons, "The Hounds of Tindalos."

110   Personal e-mail communication from Az0th, October 11, 1996, 14:37:57.

111   Personal e-mail communication from Az0th, October 11, 1996, 14:37:57.

112   Michelle Marie Hankins, *Re : Necronomicon* January 6, 1998. Posted to alt.religion.wicca newsgroups.

113   Hankins, *Re : Necronomicon*.

114   Donald Tyson, *Enochian Magic for Beginners* (St. Paul, MN: Llewellyn, 1997). See also *Tetragrammaton: The Secret to Evoking Angelic Powers and the Key to the Apocalypse* (St. Paul, MN: Llewellyn 1995).

115   Private e-mail from Donald Tyson to Daniel Harms and John Gonce, August, 2000.

116   Az0th, Internet document posted on alt.magick.newsgroup. NDG. Reposted by Tyagi Nagasiva, November 1995.

117   Az0th, Internet document posted on alt.magick.newsgroup. NDG. Reposted by Tyagi Nagasiva, November 1995.

118   Personal e-mail communication from Peter Levenda, April 22, 1997, 13:03 GMT.

119   Personal e-mail communication from Peter Levenda, April 22, 1997, 13:03 GMT.

120   Personal e-mail communication from Peter Levenda, April 22, 1997, 13:03 GMT.

121   Simon, *Necronomicon*, pp. 191.

122   *The Greek Herbal of Dioscorides, Illustrated by a Byzantine* A.D. *512, Englished by John Goodyer* A.D. *1655, Edited and First Printed* A.D. *1933 by Robert T. Gunther, M. A., Hon., LL.D.* Facsimile reprint of the 1934 edition (London and New York: Hafner Publishing Company, 1968), pp. 382, 383.

123   Agrippa, *Three Books of Occult Philosophy*, p. 112.

124   M. A. Grieve. *A Modern Herbal* (2 vol.) (New York: Dover Publishing, 1971).

125   H. P. Lovecraft, *The Case of Charles Dexter Ward* in *At the Mountains of Madness* (Sauk City, WI: Arkham House, 1964), p. 194.

126   Simon, "A Short Primer on Pagan Ceremonial Magick" in *Earth Religion News* (1974).

127   E. A. Wallis Budge, *The Egyptian Book of the Dead* at *www.sacred-texts.com/egy/ebod/* quoted by Simon in "A Short Primer on Pagan Ceremonial Magick" in *Earth Religion News* (1974).

Chapter 7: Simon, Slater, and the Gang—True Origins of the *Necronomicon*

1   Isaac Bonewits, *Real Magic* (York Beach, ME: Samuel Weiser, Inc., 1993), p. 163.

2   Bonewits, *Real Magic*, pp. 221–22.

3   Nestor to Phil Legard, personal e-mail communication November 4, 1998, 17:07:43 GMT, forwarded to Daniel Harms and John Wisdom Gonce III. Nestor asked that the message be forwarded to interested parties.

4   Nestor to Phil Legard, personal e-mail communication November 4, 1998, 17:07:43 GMT

5   Nestor to Phil Legard, e-mail November 4, 1998, 17:07:43 GMT

6   Nestor to Phil Legard, e-mail November 4, 1998, 17:07:43 GMT

7   Nestor to Phil Legard, e-mail November 4, 1998, 17:07:43 GMT

8   Nestor to John Wisdom Gonce III, personal e-mail communication January 21, 1999, 21:22:41.

9   Nestor to Phil Legard, personal e-mail communication, November 24, 1998, 17:07:43, forwarded to Daniel Harms and John Wisdom Gonce III.

10   Khem Caigan to Dan Clore, personal e-mail communication October 20, 1997 04:43:23—0400, forwarded to Daniel Harms and John Wisdom Gonce III.

11   Norman Fleck, interview, Monday July 26, 1999.

12   Nestor to author, personal e-mail communication January 21, 1999, 21:22:41 GMT.

13   Dick Sells, interview at the Circle of Raven Fain Mabon celebration, September 26, 1998.

14   Dick Sells to author, personal e-mail communication August 17, 1999, 17:33.

15   Dick Sells to author, personal e-mail communication August 17, 1999, 17:33.

16   Nestor to author, personal e-mail communication 1999.

17   Simon, *Necronomicon Spellbook* (New York: Avon Books, 1981), p.1.

18   Nestor to author, personal e-mail communication 1998.

19   Simon, *Necronomicon Spellbook*, pp. 32–49.

20   Simon, *Necronomicon Spellbook*,pp. 38–9.

21   Peter Levenda to author, personal e-mail communication April 30, 1997, 05:40 P.M.

22   Herman Slater, ed., *The Magickal Formulary* (New York: Magickal Childe, 1981), p. 90.

23   Darren Fox, *Necronomian: Workbook Guide to the Necronomicon* (Palm Springs, CA: I.G.O.S. Research Society, 1996), p. 37.

24   Fox, *Necronomian: Workbook Guide*, p. 38.

25   Simon, *Necronomicon*, p. 37.

26   Alric Thomas, *The Hidden Key of the Necronomicon* (Palm Springs, CA: I.G.O.S. Research Society, 1996), p. 15.

27   Tahuti, *Necronomicon Revelations Book I* (Palm Springs, CA: International Guild of Occult Sciences, 1996), p. ix.

28   Tahuti, *Necronomicon Revelations*, p. viii.

29   Markham J. Geller, *Forerunners to Udug-Hul: Sumerian Exorcistic Incantations* (Stuttgart: Franz Steiner Verlag Wiesbaden GMBH, 1985), p. 29, tablet III, line 164.

30   Found at the website Babylonian Magick, *www.angelfire.com/tx/tintirbabylon/*.

31   Scott Cunningham, *Cunningham's Encyclopedia of Magical Herbs* (St. Paul, MN: Llewellyn, 1994), pp. 160–61.

32   David Marcus, *A Manual of Akkadian* (Lanham, MD: University Press of America, 1978), p. 156.

Chapter 8: The Chaos of Confusion

1   Tish Gattis, quotation from September 20, 1995.

2   Colin Low to author, personal e-mail communication November 12, 1996, 10:22:22 GMT. Low's scenario involved Sonia Greene's supposed transmission of (imaginary) *Necronomicon* information from Aleister Crowley (who never was) her old lover, to Lovecraft, her new husband. None of it ever happened (other than her marriage to Lovecraft). Low's justification for his hoax was that naive individuals posting to alt.magick newsgroup asking where to find the *Necronomicon* were being cruelly abused for their gullibility. The hoax was meant to be revenge on the abusers. Supposedly, those who "knew their stuff would see through it . . . while those who were insulting others for sport would be cast into doubt and confusion."

3   Larry Kahaner, *Cults That Kill: Probing the Underworld of Occult Crime* (New York: Warner Books, 1988), pp. 30–1. Quote from detective Cleo Wilson.

4   Linda Blood, *The New Satanists* (New York: Warner Books, 1994).

5   Blood, *The New Satanists*, p. 94.

6 Carl A. Raschke, *Painted Black* (New York: Harper and Row, 1990), p. 183.

7 Paul Nehib, "Utilizing the Vril With the Aid of Magickal Foci," posted to the Internet.

8 Paul Nehib, "The Book of the Absu," Posted to the Internet.

9 Black and Green, *Gods, Demons and Symbols of Ancient Mesopotamia* (Austin, TX: University of Texas Press, 1995), p. 27.

10 Allen Mackey, "Disciples of Zann," *Crypt of Cthulhu* 89 (Eastertide, 1995), p. 13.

11 Marilyn Manson and Neil Strauss, *The Long Hard Road Out of Hell* (New York: Harper Collins, 1998), p. 45.

12 "NARR MARRATU" is used as a synonym for "Abyss" in the Simon *Necronomicon* (p. 73.) Nar Maratu is actually a marshy area at the junction of the Persian Gulf and the three rivers.

13 Sinister, "Awaiting the Absu," in *Hate* (Millersville, PA: Nuclear Blast America, 1995).

14 David K. Sakheim and Susan E. Devine, E. *Out of the Darkness: Exploring Satanism and Ritual Abuse* (New York: Lexington Books (Macmillan, 1992), p. 60.

15 Lupo the Butcher, "The Alt.Satanism FAQ," Posted to *alt.satanism* March 18, 1993, 20:36:10.

16 Lupo the Butcher, "The Alt.Satanism FAQ," Posted to *alt.satanism* March 18, 1993, 20:36:10.

17 More information about Xastur can be found on *Succubus-L* website at *www.necronomi.com/elists/succubus-l/*.

18 Steven Hassan, *Combating Cult Mind Control* (Rochester, VT: Park Street Press, 1990).

19 Usenet poster to Daniel Harms, personal e-mail communication 5/24/97.

20 Frank Stanfield, "Occult Shadows Lurk: Ferrell's Lawyers Want to Withhold Videos," in *The Orlando Sentinel*, February 15, 1998.

21 Simon, *Necronomicon*, p. 70.

22 Robert Rickard, "The Devil Worshippers," in *Fortean Times, The Journal of Strange Phenomena*, no. 98, June 1997, p 26.

23 Michael Schneider, "Vampire Cult Trial To Begin Monday," Associated Press, 02-01-98 1646 EST1997.

24 Rickard. *Fortean Times*, June 1997, p. 25. While "Vassago" is the name of a demon in *The Goetia: The Lesser Key of Solomon the King* (*Clavicula Salomonis Regis*), I doubt that Roderick Ferrell was scholarly enough to be familiar with it. He undoubtedly got the name from the film *Hideaway*.

25 Jorge Casuso, "Murder in a Santa Monica Squat," found at *www.laweekly.com/ink/99/36/news-casuso.shtml*.

26 Peter Levenda to author, personal e-mail communication April 22, 1997.

27 Peter J. Carroll, *Liber Chaos* (York Beach, ME: Samuel Weiser, 1992), pp. 147–59.

28 Doreen Valiente, "Necronomicon—the Ultimate Grimoire" found in *Prediction* (Croydon, UK: Link House Publications, April 1982), vol 48, number 4, p. 12.

29 Isaac Bonewits to John Wisdom Gonce III, personal e-mail communication Saturday, June 28, 1997, 01:31:34—0400.

30 *http://.member.tripod.com/necronomiconfiles*.

31 Letter to John Wisdom Gonce III dated February 17, 1997.

32 Tim Maroney, "Science Fiction and the Mythic Future," *Gnosis*, Summer 1994), p. 28.

33 Allen Mackey, "Disciples of Zann," p. 19.

34 Colin Low, Internet document 1997, found at *www.geocities.com/soho/9879/necfaq.htm*.

Chapter 9: The *Necronomicon* and Psychic Attack

1 Dion Fortune, *Psychic Self-Defense* (York Beach, ME: Samuel Weiser, Inc., 1996), p. 194.

2 Fortune, *Psychic Self-Defense*, pp. 194–7.

3   Fortune, *Psychic Self-Defense*, p. 196.

4   See the section on "High School Metaphysics" in Chapter 8.

5   Michelle A. Belanger, "Spirit Guide: A Primer of Otherworldly Beings," in *Fate* St. Paul, MN: Llewellyn Publications May 1998), p. 53.

6   Peter Levenda to the author, personal e-mail communication April 22, 1997.

7   Az0th to the author, personal e-mail communication Saturday, July 19, 1997, 12:06:49 EDT. Az0th's warnings were predicated on his belief that the magick in the Simon book really is an ancient—even prehuman—system dating back to the dawn of human history. Because of my studies, I do not share this belief. If this investigation has proven anything, it has proven that the Simon book is of recent origin and, despite the few snatches from ancient texts found in it pages, its magick bears little or no resemblance to that practiced in ancient Mesopotamia.

8   Ordinarily, defense will be easier than attack, and in many cases a good defense will automatically become a counterattack when the destructive force sent by the attacker rebounds upon him. In other cases, it is necessary to retaliate. In this case, the target should be the *Necronomicon* egregore itself, not its human dupe.

Chapter 10: Unspeakable Cuts—The *Necronomicon* on Film

1   Phil Hine, *The Pseudonomicon* (Irvine, CA: Dagon Productions, 1997), p. 9.

2   Robert Rickard, "The Devil Worshippers," *Fortean Times: The Journal of Strange Phenomena*, no. 98, June 1997, pp. 23–6, "known to use the name Vesago [sic]."
      Ferrell probably got the name from the 1995 movie in which the "Vassago" character—a Satanist who was brought back from the dead (and back through the gates of hell) by his father, See, S. L. Mathers, MacGregor Mathers, and Aleister Crowley, *The Goetia: The Lesser Key of Solomon the King (Clavicula Salomonis Regis)* (York Beach, ME: Samuel Weiser Inc., 1997), p. 28.

3   Thanks to Tony Kail for this information. Tony is a professional investigator of occult crime, and of gang- and cult-related crime. Much of his work consists of educating law enforcement officers about the differences between Neopaganism, Afro-Caribbean religions, and Satanism. He teaches an excellent workshop entitled *Law Enforcement and the Pagan Community* at both Pagan gatherings and training sessions for police officers.

4   In his excellent introduction to Migliore and Strysik's wonderful book *Lurker in the Lobby,* Joshi mistakenly states, "this book is a valuable first step in tracing Lovecraft's influence upon film and television." Actually, it is a valuable *second* step. Since this present work, *The Necronomicon Files,* was published in its first edition in October 1998, and *Lurker in the Lobby* didn't see the light of print until January 2000, *The Necronomicon Files* is technically the first work to systematically examine the subject of Lovecraft on film. Our book is, however, limited in its scope to appearances of the *Necronomicon*, whereas *Lurker* is a broad (and vastly entertaining) survey of all kinds of Lovecraftian film pastiches. Migliore's and Strysik's reviews are endlessly clever and insightful, and backed by excellent scholarship. Their book features not only movie reviews, but also interviews with directors and actors, and many photographs from Lovecraftian films. I heartily recommend it to anyone interested in the subject.

5   When I say "folio-sized," I am using traditional printer's jargon to describe the physical dimensions of the book. The size of a book is traditionally determined by the number of times the sheets of paper, which constitute its pages, have been folded. The first books were large "folios" whose pages were formed by simply folding huge sheets of paper in half and stitching them together to form a crude binding. Smaller books called "quartos"(quarter) were made by folding the sheets a second time. By 1501, the famous printer Manutius had created a demand for the even smaller "octavo"(eighth), half the size of the

quarto. Other printers later introduced the "half-quarto," or "sexto-decimo," and the even smaller "twenty-fourmo," or "small twelve," made by folding an octavo three times. According to the Scale of the American Library Association, a folio averages a page size of 12" by 19," with an outside head-to-foot cover height of 30cm. Folios can actually measure from 10" X 15" to 12.5" X 20" or larger. (Some of the earliest printed books were enormous, and these archaic terms cannot be used as precise indicators of size.). *Quartos* usually range from 7.5" X 10" to 10" X 12.5" and *octavos* are usually between 5" X 7.5" and 6.25" X 7.5". Most editions of the *Necronomicon* seem to be folio-sized.

6   Andrew Black, *Necronomicon: The Journal of Horror and Erotic Cinema, Book One.* (London: Creation Books International, 1996), p. 112.

7   Cathal Tohill and Peter Tombs, *Immoral Tales, European Sex and Horror Movies 1956–1984* (New York, NY: St. Martin's Press, 1995), p. 93.

8   Tohill and Tombs, *Immoral Tales.*

9   Tohill and Tombs, *Immoral Tales,* p. 94.

10   H. P. Lovecraft, "The Dunwich Horror," in *The Dunwich Horror and Others* (Sauk City, WI: Arkham House, 1963), p. 160.

11   Lovecraft, "The Dunwich Horror," p. 169.

12   Lovecraft, "The Dunwich Horror," p. 171.

13   Lon Milo DuQuette, *The Magick of Thelema* (York Beach, ME: Samuel Weiser Inc., 1993), pp. 63, 91, 106.

14   Adrian Savage, *An Introduction to Chaos Magick* (New York, NY: Magickal Childe Inc., 1988), pp. 26–27.

15   Simon, *Necronomicon* (New York, NY: Avon Books, 1980), pp. xlii (definition), xliv, 53, 73, 79–81, 85, 88, 108, 185.

16   Andrew E. Rothovius, "Lovecraft and the New England Megaliths," in *The Dark Brotherhood and Other Pieces* (Sauk City, WI: Arkham House, 1966), pp. 179-197.

17   Kenneth Grant, *Aleister Crowley and the Hidden God* (New York, NY: Samuel Weiser, 1974), plates 7, 10, 12, 17.

18   Stephen Hugh Chan, *Evil Dead II: Dead by Dawn,* transcription, Internet document 1995, *www.geocities.com/evildeadpage/EVILDEAD2HTM.*

19   Chan, *Evil Dead II: Dead by Dawn.*

20   H. P. Lovecraft, *History of the Necronomicon* (West Warwick, RI: Necronomicon Press, 1986).

21   Lovecraft, *The Dunwich Horror and Others,* pp. 167, 169.

22   Lovecraft, *History of the Necronomicon.* See also Clark Ashton Smith, "The Return of the Sorcerer," in *Tales of the Cthulhu Mythos.* Second Edition. (Sauk City, WI: Arkham House, 1990). (First printed in *Strange Tales,* September 1931.)

23   H. P. Lovecraft, "The Dreams in the Witch House," in *At the Mountains of Madness and Other Novels.* Corrected printing. (Sauk City, WI: Arkham House, 1985), pp. 263, 264.

24   For a good essay on Lovecraft's genius at blending the genres of fantasy, horror, and science fiction, see "Through Hyperspace with Brown Jenkin," by Fritz Leiber, in *The Dark Brotherhood and Other Pieces* (Sauk City, WI: Arkham House, 1966).

25   There is no order of "Ommiade monks" of any religion, anywhere in the world. The word "Ommiade" was probably borrowed from Lovecraft's mention of the Ommiade Caliphs in his *History of the Necronomicon.*

26   For a more thorough description of the Deep Ones, accounts of their history, lifestyle, and abominable sexual habits, see H. P. Lovecraft, "The Shadow over Innsmouth," in *The Dunwich Horror and Others.* See also Daniel Harms, *Encyclopedia Cthulhiana* (Oakland, CA: Chaosium Inc., 1994), entry for "Deep One," pp. 51–2.

27   W. W. Jacobs, "The Monkey's Paw," in *Tellers of Tales: 100 Short Stories.* Selected and

with an introduction by W. Somerset Maugham (New York, NY: Doubleday, Doran & Co. Inc., 1940), p. 436.

28   Lovecraft, "Cool Air," in *The Dunwich Horror and Others*, p. 203.

29   Janet and Stewart Farrar, *Spells and How They Work* (Custer, WA: Phoenix Publishing Inc., 1990), pp. 176–78.

30   M. R. James, "Casting the Runes," in *The Ghost Stories of M. R. James* (New York, NY: St. Martin's Press, 1976), p. 235. The story was first published in *Ghost Stories of an Antiquary* (Messrs. Arnold, 1904).

31   Frank Belknap Long, "The Hounds of Tindalos," *Weird Tales*, vol. 13, no. 3, March 1929.

32   H. P. Lovecraft, "The Hound," in *Dagon and Other Macabre Tales*. Corrected printing (Sauk City, WI: Arkham House, 1987).

33   Simon, *Necronomicon*, p. 49.

34   *Ghostbusters International* (Honesdale, PA: West End Games).

35   Kim Mohan, *Tobin's Spirit Guide: A Supplement for use with the Ghostbusters International Roleplaying Game* (Honesdale, PA: West End Games, 1989).

Chapter 11: Call of the Cathode Ray Tube

1   I wonder if this character's name—Anna Pringel—is a pun on the mythical Anna Springel, a mysterious and almost certainly fictional character created by Dr. Wynn Westcott when he forged the letters giving him permission to create the Golden Dawn as a branch of an imaginary German occult society.

2   Arthur Edward Waite, *Book of Black Magic* (York Beach, ME: Samuel Weiser, Inc., 1993), p. 201.

3   Jack Sullivan, *The Penguin Encyclopedia of Horror and the Supernatural* (New York, NY: Viking/Penguin Inc., 1986), p. 422.

4   To the best of my knowledge, the only person who has ever gotten a bona fide degree in magick is Isaac Bonewits. But this is a Saturday-morning cartoon, so what do you expect?

5   How many little kids came away from this episode of *The Real Ghostbusters* believing that the *Necronomicon* is a historic book rather than an invention of Lovecraft's imagination?

6   "The Horror from the Depths" was an actual story written by August Derleth and Mark Schorer, but it was first published (as "The Evil Ones") in *Strange Stories* in October 1940, not in *Weird Tales*.

7   At first, I thought the Derleth/Schorer story, "The Horror from the Depths," might have influenced Michael Reaves's script for *The Collect Call of Cathulhu*, but Reaves told me that he had never read the story before he wrote the script. "I simply made up a Lovecraftish title and went from there. That the story contains similar points to my script is pure serendipity" (personal e-mail communication 1/20/99). Although Cthulhu does not appear in "The Horror from the Depths" (much less get fried by an electrified roller coaster), the tale does feature the Spawn of Cthulhu breaking *out* of a display in the Chicago museum (not *into* the NYC Public Library), rising from the depths of Lake Michigan (not the Atlantic), and invading the Grounds of the Chicago World's Fair (not Coney Island). See "The Horror from the Depths" in *Colonel Markesan and Less Pleasant People* (Sauk City, WI: Arkham House, 1966), p. 225.

8   H. P. Lovecraft, "The Call of Cthulhu," in *The Dunwich Horror and Other Stories*. Corrected Printing (Sauk City, WI: Arkham House, 1984), p. 152.

9   Lovecraft, "The Call of Cthulhu," p. 152.

10   Lovecraft, "The Call of Cthulhu," p. 151.

11   Lovecraft, "The Call of Cthulhu," p. 151.

12   Michael Reaves to the author, personal e-mail communication 1/20/99 6:52 PM. Those
      wishing to read the original screenplay for *The Collect Call of Cathulhu* should go to
      Michael Reaves' website at *www.mindspring.com/~michaelreaves/callpreface.htm.*
13   Daniel Harms, *Encyclopedia Cthulhiana* (Oakland, CA: Chaosium Inc., 1994),see entry
      for Nodens, p. 147.

Conclusion

1   Jack Kisling, "Secret plans are seldom secret enough," *The Denver Post*, June 27, 1995.
2   *Fate*, vol. 52, no. 12, pp. 42–3.

Appendix: History of the *Necronomicon*

1   The text given here was taken from a facsimile of the original printing in 1938 by Wilson
     H. Shepherd's The Rebel Press in Oakman, AL. I have corrected it to reflect Lovecraft's
     original manuscript, printed on pages 102–3 of Willis Conover and H. P. Lovecraft's
     Lovecraft at Last (Arlington, VA: Carrolton Clark, 1975). Lovecraft's draft of "History"
     was written over a single-page letter from William L. Bryant of the Roger Williams
     Park Museum in Providence dated April 27, 1927. In the top right-hand corner appears
     the dedication "To the Curator of the Vaults of Yoh-Vombis, with the Curator's (?)
     compliments." This suggests that it eventually went to Lovecraft's friend Robert Barlow,
     whose cluttered archives of his favorite author's works were referred to as "The Vaults
     of Yoh-Vombis," after the Clark Ashton Smith story of the same name.
2   Lovecraft took this word from the notes to Samuel Beckford's *Vathek*.
3   The caliphs were the early rulers of the Islamic state that arose after Muhammed's
     death. The Ommiade, or Umayyad, Caliphate lasted from 661–750.
4   Capital of Egypt during the 3rd millennium B.C. This could be a passing reference to
     two matters in Lovecraft's stories—the subterranean passages that Houdini explores
     in "Under the Pyramids" (or "Imprisoned with the Pharaohs"), and a reference to a
     "Darke Thing belowe Memphis" that one wizard sends to another in *The Case of Charles
     Dexter Ward*.
5   Marked out in the original: "have pretended."
6   Ebn Khallikan: Shams Ad-Din Al-'Abbas Ahmad Ibn Muhammed Ibn Khallikan
     (1211–82), scholar who spent much of his life in Damascus and wrote a biographical
     dictionary describing many of the eminent men of his time. It is unlikely that a man
     like Abdul Alhazred, living five centuries before, would be included in this work.
7   Irem: Mythical lost city of the desert, built by the prince Shaddad in imitation of the
     Garden of Eden. When it was completed, Allah destroyed Shaddad and his entourage
     with a "noise from heaven." Lovecraft probably encountered this city through the
     description given in *The Arabian Nights*. Irem is now thought to be the recently dis-
     covered ruins of Ubar, though some debate that equation.
8   Marked out: "[illegible] town."
9   Shepherd adds the following: "(Editor's Note: A full description of the nameless city,
     and the annals and secrets of its one-time inhabitants will be found in the story THE
     NAMELESS CITY, published in the first issue of Fanciful tales, and written by the
     author of his [sic] outline)." *Fanciful Tales of Time and Space* was a fanzine published
     by Shepherd and Donald Wollheim that saw only one issue in fall of 1936.
10   Yog-Sothoth and Cthulhu: Yog-Sothoth is a powerful being who is referred to in "The
     Case of Charles Dexter Ward," and Cthulhu turned up first in Lovecraft's *The Call of
     Cthulhu*. Both stories were written within a year and a half of "History."
11   Theodorus Philetas, a fictional character.
12   Patriarch Michael, Michael Cerularius (c. 1000–59), Patriarch of Constantinople and

a key figure in the split between the Roman Catholic and Greek Orthodox Churches.

13   Olaus Wormius, Olaus Worm (1588–1654), Danish physician for whom the Wormian bones in the skull were named. For an explanation of why Lovecraft was off by four centuries on the clergyman's life, see "Lovecraft, Regner Lodbrog, and Olaus Wormius," *Crypt of Cthulhu*, Eastertide 1995, pp. 3–7.

14   Black-letter, a medieval style of handwriting, used in early printed works (such as those published by Gutenberg).

15   Pope Gregory IX (c. 1170–1241), one of the most active popes of all time and the founder of the Holy Office, or Inquisition.

16   This sentence was probably added as an afterthought, as it appears in the margins of the text.

17   Shepherd adds the following: ". . . (there is, however, a vague account of a secret copy appearing in San Francisco during the present century, but later perished in fire)." This refers to C. A. Smith's "The Return of the Sorcerer." This line turns up in many publications of this essay, even though it does not appear in the original.

18   This event is probably fictional—no evidence has emerged that anyone at Salem had a library on the occult sciences.

19   John Dee (1527–1608), English astrologer, spy (?), and magician.

20   This sentence was written in later, after Lovecraft had read Frank Belknap Long's "The Space-Eaters," which featured the Dee edition for the first time.

21   British Museum, London museum opened in 1769. Its collection of books became part of the British Library in 1973.

22   Bibliothèque Nationale, France's largest library, which operates in much the same way as the United States' Library of Congress.

23   Widener Library, library founded in 1915 and named after Harry Elkins Widener (–1910), who went down with the *Titanic*. Most of the rare books were moved to the Houghton Library in 1942.

24   Miskatonic University and Arkham are creations of Lovecraft that appear first in "Herbert West—Reanimator" and "The Picture in the House," respectively.

25   University of Buenos Ayres, founded in 1821. No one is sure why Lovecraft chose this as a spot for the *Necronomicon*.

26   Celebrated American millionaire, Lovecraft never explains who this individual is.

27   Richard Upton Pickman, artist in Lovecraft's "Pickman's Model" and "The Dream-Quest of Unknown Kadath." Lovecraft never mentions the *Necronomicon* in connection with him anywhere else.

28   *The King in Yellow*, both a fictional play invented by Robert W. Chambers (1865–1933), and a real book that includes the play in its stories. This sentence has led many to believe that the *Necronomicon* was inspired by Chambers's book *The King in Yellow*, even though Lovecraft had been writing about it for years before he read Chambers's work. It should be noted that *The King in Yellow* is not a novel, but a collection of short stories.

Index

(f) designates items found originally in a work presented as fiction. Individual works are listed under their own names, rather than that of their authors.

777 (Crowley), 77, 153, 195
93 Current, 136
A∴A∴, 81, 316
Abbey of Thelema, 316
Absu, 199; (band), 200
Abulafia, Todoros, 319
Ab-Ul-Diz Working (Crowley), 102
Abyss, 106, 110; Working (Crowley), 125
Adad, 161
Adam, ix
Adar, 187
Adytum Azothos Lodge, OTOA, 115
Aeon of Cthulhu Rising (Tenebrous), 115
Aeon of Horus, 74, 136
Agape Lodge, OTO, 124, 126
Age of Fable, The (Bulfinch), 91, 309, 318
Agla, 282
Agrippa von Nettesheim, Henry, 71–74, 79, 81, 103
Aiwass/Aiwaz, x, 103, 135–36, 157
Akashic Records, 103, 110, 119, 142
Akeley, Henry (f), 19
Akroyd, Dan, 278–79
Al Azif (Arabic Necronomicon) (f), 15, 18, 99, 102, 110, 285, 303; (de Camp), 34–35, 38, 49, 127, 209, 301
Albertus Magnus, 14, 128
Aleister Crowley and the Hidden God (Grant), 103
Alexandre, Katrin, 248
Al-Hazred, Abd (f), 57
Alhazred, Abdul (f), 7, 9, 12, 15, 20–21, 52–54, 57–59, 64, 88, 90, 99, 110, 129, 133, 142, 156, 212, 214, 243, 249, 254, 285–86, 303–04, 333, origin of 5
Alice in Wonderland (Carroll), 124
Alien, 38
Allen, Zadok (f), 146
Alquier, Laurent, 58
Al-Raschid of Sothis, 52–53
alt.horror.cthulhu Usenet group, 66–67
alt.magick Usenet group, 80, 164, 167
alt.necronomicon Usenet group, 297, 301
alt.religion.wicca Usenet group, 165
alt.satanism FAQ, 200–01
Amazing Stories, 124
American International Pictures, 228–29, 234–35

American Library Association, 330
Amulets and Talismans (Budge), 136
Anand, Margo, 83
Anarchist's Cookbook, The, 169
Anchor Books Doubleday, 222
Ancient Near Eastern Texts Relating to the Old Testament (Pritchard), 47
Ancient Ones (f), 41, 47, 118, 147, 157, 182, 191–92, 194, 196, 212
Anderson, Howard, 204
Andrews, Dana, 275
Angell, George (f), 12, 291–94
Angels of Mons, 302
Angerstein, 149
Anonymous, Rev. Dr. Johnny, xvi, xxii
Antiquarian Bookman, 33
Anu, 161, 163, 192
Anubis, 33
Anz, 162
Apollonius of Tyana, 94
Apparitions and Miracles at Knock, The (MacPhilpin), 310, 318
Aquino, Michael, 78, 81, 111, 112, 120, 198, 320
Ar nDriocht Fein (ADF), 80
Arabian Nights, The, 4, 87–90, 252, 308–09, 318, 333, editions, 88
Arabian Nights, The: A Companion (Irwin), 89–90
Aradia (Leland), 175
Argentum Astrum, 316
Argosy, 6
Aristotle, 162
Arkham (f), 16, 227, 234, 246, 252, 287, 304, 333
Arkham House, 23, 31–32, 34–35, 87, 158, 283, 287
Arkham Sampler, 54
Armadel, 14, 129, 141
Armitage, Henry (f), 16–17, 232–33, 236, 291–92
Armstrong, Neville, 50
Army of Darkness, 255–57
Arnold, Arnold, 129
Aryan race, 195
Asatru, 78, 210
Asheville Gazette-News, 9
Ashtoreth, 156
Asmodeus, 36
Assaku, 154
Assurbanipal,191
Assyria, 43
Astaroth, 156, 282–83

Astral Love (Conway), 161
Astrology, 12, 46, 97, 135, 153, 159, 164
"Astronomicon" (Manilius), 9
"At the Mountains of Madness" (Lovecraft), 20
Aurum Aurorum, 316
Autocephalous Slavonic Orthodox Catholic Church, 39
Avon Books, 27, 40, 134, 179, 181, 201
Az0th, 160, 164–65, 208, 220, 329
Azag-Thoth, 43, 154
Azagthoth, Trey, 200
Azathoth (f), 19, 110, 144, 154, 157, 208, 234, 263, 283
Azonei, 41–43, 147
Azoth, 283
B&S Productions, 245
Babalon, 125–26
Babalon Working, 125–26, 237
Babylon, 41–43, 46, 147–48, 150, 159, 162–63, 169, 180, 191, 303
Babylon 5, 289
Babyloniaca (Berossus), 188
Bacon, Roger, 65, 79
Baker, Alfred, 5, 88
Ballantine, 54
Bardo Thodol, 119
Bark, Andy, 254
Barlow, Robert, 21, 23, 332
Barnes, Larry, 40, 133, 139–40, 142, 176
Batwing (Rohmer), 93–94
Baylor, Walter, 33
Beaumont, Charles, 229
Beinecke Library, Yale, 65
Belanger, Michelle, 218
Bell Murru, 190
Bennett, Charles, 275
Berglund, Edward, 32
Berlin Film Festival, 232
Bertiaux, Michael, 113–15
"Beyond the Wall of Sleep" (Lovecraft), 100, 111
Beyond the Mauve Zone (Grant), 110, 142
Bibliotheque Nationale, 16, 304, 333
Bierce, Ambrose, 10, 30, 110
Biomechanics (Giger), 38
Black, Jeremy, 152
Black Magic (Bowen), 124
Black Mass, xii, 53, 123, 284
Black Moon Publishing, 143
Black Pilgrimage, 125
Blackwood, Algernon, 12, 27, 93, 191

Blanck, Jacob, 32
Blavatsky, Helena, x, 26, 73, 97–98, 110
Blish, James, 22
Bloch, Robert, 8, 13, 21, 32, 94, 110
Bodleian Library, Oxford, 64
Bogart, Humphrey, 251
Bokrug XIII, Frater, 116
Bonewits, Isaac, 77, 79–80, 145, 173, 209–10, 324, 331
"Book of Babalon" (Parsons), 125
Book of Black Magic and of Pacts (Waite), 15, 96, 151, 282
Book of Dzyan, x, 26, 98, 110, 287, 289
Book of Eibon (f), 320
Book of Enoch, 160
Book of Mormon, 68
Book of Shades (Saint George). *See* Necronomicon (Saint George)
Book of Shadows, 59
Book of St. Dunstan, ix, 141
"Book of the Absu, The" (Nehib), 199
Book of the Arab (Geoffrey) (f), 64–65
Book of the Great Logos, The, 131
Book of the Law (Crowley). *See Liber Al vel Legis*
Book of the Sacred Magic of Abramelin the Mage, The (Mathers, trans.) x, 160, 173, 175, 187
Book of Thoth, The (Crowley), 94, 110, 124, 167
Books in Print, 183
Books of Rune & Magickal Alphabet & Cypher (Gulevitch, Levender, and Slater), 40
Borges, Jose, 24
Boullan, Abbe, 73, 316
Bousset, 162
"Bowmen, The" (Machen), 302
Bradbury, Ray, 8
Bradford Review and East Haven News, 30
Bradley, Marion, 209
British Library, 333
British Museum, 16, 50, 134, 304, 333
Brood of the Witch-Queen (Rohmer), 94
Brotherhood of the White Temple, 112
Brown University, 87, 111
Bruegel, Pieter the Elder, 278
Bryant, William, 332
Buczynski, Edward, 174, 178
Buddhism, 74, 83, 93, 103, 119, 209
Burleson, Don, 25
Burroughs, William, 40, 68, 83, 118, 138–40,
Burton, Richard, 89
Butler Hospital, Providence, 4
Cagliostro, 49
Caigan, Khem, 40, 132, 134, 138, 158, 176, 192

Calder, Kim, 207
Calfa, Don, 263
Calif Haroun Alraschid and Saracen Civilization (Palmer), 89
Call of Cthulhu role-playing game, 55
"Call of Cthulhu, The" (Lovecraft), 12, 17, 94, 97–98, 100, 117, 125, 245, 259, 276–77, 289–90, 333
"Call to Cthulhu" (Aquino), 111–12
"Calling Cthulhu" (Davis), 144
Cameron, Marjorie, 126, 237
Caminecci, Pier, 231–32
Campbell, Bruce, 241, 256–57
Cancer of Superstition (Eddy, Houdini, and Lovecraft) 13, 97
Carnacki, Ghost-Finder (Hodgson), 112
Carranza, Venustiano, 58
Carroll, Peter, 81, 83, 197, 208
Carter, Lin, 31, 54, 55
Carter, Randolph (f), 7, 245–48, 252–54, 293
Case of Charles Dexter Ward, The (Lovecraft), 14, 94, 96, 100–01, 171, 227, 229, 241, 266, 271–72, 294, 332–33
Casebook of a Working Occultist (Saint George), 52
Cassell and Company, 5
Cast a Deadly Spell, 250–52
Castaigne, Hildred (f), 25
"Casting the Runes" (James), 250, 276
Castings (Dominguez), 221
Cavendish, Richard, 103
Celestial Script, 274
"Cephaloedium Working, The" (Crowley), 135
"Ceremony of the Nine Angles, The" (Aquino), 111
Chaldea, 135, 323
Chaldean Magic: Its Origin and Development (Lenormant), 37
Chaldean Oracles of Zoroaster, 163–64, 187
Chalker, Jack, 33
Chambers, Robert, 25–6, 30, 110, 304
Chaosium Books, 55, 132
Chaplin, Charlie, 226
Chapo, Steven, 133
Chariots of the Gods? (Von Daniken), 188
"Children of the Night, The" (Howard), 18
Chopra, Deepak, 79
Chorazin, 125
Choronzon. *See* Coronzon
Choronzon Club, 113
Christianity, 78, 92, 123, 143, 148, 153, 163, 166, 186, 203, 209, 211, 216, 252, 307
Chronicles of Narnia (Lewis), 103
Church of All Worlds, 177
Church of Satan, 78, 111–13, 200, 237

Cincinnati Journal of Ceremonial Magick, 120
Cities of the Red Night (Burroughs), 138–39
Clarke, Arthur, 79, 262
Clore, Dan, 133, 157, 310
Coleman, Matt, 212
Coleman, Signy, 263
"Collect Call of Cthulu, The," 287–90, 332
"Colour Out of Space, The" (Lovecraft), 124
Combating Cult Mind Control (Hassan), 202
Combs, Jeffrey, 258, 264
Commentaries on Witchcraft (Mycroft) (f), 32
Commonplace Book (Hawthorne), 25
Commonplace Book (Lovecraft), 7
Communism, 166
Compendium of Herbal Magick (Beyerl), 170
Complete Rituals of the Golden Dawn (Regardie), 201
Conan (f), 18
Condensed Chaos (Hine), 221
Confraternity of Oblates of the Monastery of the Seven Rays, 113
Conover, Willis, 13, 19, 28, 30, 94, 96
Conservative, The, 7
Constant, Alphonse. *See* Levi, Eliphas
Consumer Reports, 211
"Cool Air" (Lovecraft), 258, 260–62
Cooper, Dana, 204
Corgi Books, 50
Corman, Roger, 229, 235–36
Coronozon/Choronzon, 106, 109, 125, 319
Corrigan, Ian, 80
"Count Magnus" (James), 125
Crawling Chaos (Lovecraft), 56
Creation Press, 56, 122
"Critical Commentary on the Necronomicon, A" (Price), 55
Critical Dissertation on the Poems of Ossian (Blair), 15
Crookes, Sir William, 278
Crowley, Aleister (Edward Crowley), x, 26, 52, 53, 57, 64, 71, 74, 76–79, 81, 83, 89, 91, 95, 102–03, 106, 110–11, 115, 117, 120, 123–26, 131–32, 134–38, 143, 157–59, 173, 177, 189, 197–98, 212, 220, 237, 276, 278, 285, 302, 316, 319, 327; and Sumer, 134–36
Crummett, Nina, 116
Crypt of Cthulhu, 32, 50–51, 54–55
Crystal Dawn Press, 53

Cthulhu (f), 12, 31, 38, 41, 50, 94, 96, 103, 112, 115–19, 131, 144, 148–49, 158, 218, 243, 249, 259, 263, 276, 285, 278–90, 293–94, 303, 332–33

Cthulhu Mythos, 17, 23–24, 29, 31–32, 34, 37, 50, 54–57, 65, 97, 101–02, 106, 109–10, 112, 114, 118–21, 125, 133, 144–48, 154, 156–58, 165, 186, 208–09, 212–13, 218, 229, 231, 245, 249, 257, 272, 278, 283, 285, 289, 301, 313, 320

Cthulhu News, 38

Cthulhu Rising, 116

Culianu, Ioan, 162

Culp, Robert, 37

cult, term, 307–08

Cults of the Shadow (Grant), 114

Cults That Kill (Kahaner), 199

Cultus Maleficarum (Pelton), 31–32, 55

Curious Myths of the Middle Ages (Baring-Gould), 309, 318

Current of Maat, 120

Curse of the Demon, 250, 265, 273–77, 283

Curwen, Joseph (f), 14, 101, 123, 171, 212, 227–29, 272, 310

Cutha, 148–49

cyberpagans, 80

Daath, 77, 106, 109–10, 115, 125

Daemonolatreia (Remy), 10, 17

Dagobert's Revenge, 40

Dagon, 115, 259

"Dagon" (Lovecraft), 259

Damascius, 7

Danforth (f), 20

Daoloth (f), 58

"Dark Legacy," 281–83

Darker Than You Think (Williamson), 124–25

Das Necronomicon, 51–52, 127

Davidson Library, University of California at Santa Barbara, 41

DAW Books, 30

Dawkins, Richard, 166

Dawn, Crystal, 184–85

Day the Earth Stood Still, The, 194, 255, 257

de Camp, Lyon, 34–35, 49, 86

de Guaita, Marquis Stanislas, 73, 316

De Heptarchia Mystica (Dee), 129

"De Homunculo Epistola" (Crowley), 237

De la Ree, Gerry, 158

de Metz, Gauthier, 7

de Sade, Marquis, 49

De Vermis Mysteriis (Prinn) (f), 32, 98

"Death of Halpin Frayser, The" (Bierce), 10

Decadent Movement, 73–74, 77, 95, 128, 217, 285

deconstructionism, 55

Dee, Doctor John, ix–x, 16–18, 50, 54, 56–57, 62, 64, 72–74, 79, 81, 94, 106, 127, 129, 131, 141, 159, 166, 176, 198, 252, 254, 276, 300, 304, 319, 322, 333

Dee, Sandra, 234–36, 238

Deep Ones (f), 114, 119, 123, 146, 237, 259–60, 331

Deicide, 200

Denny, Kristen, 266

Denver Post, 297

Derleth, August, 17, 23–24, 31–32, 34, 49, 51, 54, 87, 109, 114, 129, 157, 186, 229, 252, 287–89, 317

"Descendant, The" (Lovecraft), 11

Descent of Inanna, The, 163, 186

Demons and Evil Spirits of Babylonia, The (Thompson), 47–48

Devil's Lake, 114

Devil's Notebook (LaVey), 112

Dharma, 74

"Diary of Alonzo Typer, The" (Lovecraft and Lumley), 22, 99, 125

"Die elektrischen Vorspiele" (LaVey), 112

Die Goldene Dammerung, 26, 74

Die Monster Die, 234

Dills, Robert, 35

"Dim-Remembered Story, A" (Barlow), 21

Discoverie of Witches (Hopkins), 276

Doeden, April, 205

Doom II, 297

"Doom of Yakthoob, The" (Carter) 54

Dore, Gustave, 5

Doreal, Morris, 112

Dougherty, Joseph, 251

Dracula (Stoker), 101, 124

"Dream-Quest of Unknown Kadath, The" (Lovecraft), 5, 90, 334

"Dreams in the Witch-House" (Lovecraft), 20, 97, 100, 254

Druids, 53, 78, 83, 210

Druillet, Philippe, 33

Drury, Neville, 113, 115

Dumuzi, 153

Dungeons and Dragons, 202

Dunsany, Lord, 27, 124, 137

Dunwich (f), 16–17, 233–34

Dunwich Horror, The, 226, 229, 232–38

"Dunwich Horror, The" (Lovecraft), 16, 19, 109, 114, 123, 125, 192, 247, 251–52

Dunwich Lodge, EOD, 116

Dupin, C (f), 33

Durga, 216

Duriac language (f), 35

Duschnes, Phillip, 32

Dwyer, Bernard, 136

Dyer, William (f), 20

Ea, 46, 150, 153, 161, 186

Earth Religion News, 140, 171, 200

Ebn Khallikan, 303, 333

Ecbatana, 46

Ecclesia Gnostica Catholica, 113

Eco, Umberto, 24

Eddy, C. M., 13, 97

Editions du Terrain Vague (f), 33

Edlund, Richard, 278

egregore, 145, 165, 216, 221

Egyptian Book of the Dead (Budge, trans.), 171, 175

Einstein Factor, The (Wenger and Poe), 166–67

Elder Gods (f), 31, 120, 150, 186, 191, 227, 228, 229

Elder Ones (f), 17

Elder Sign (f), 102, 116, 192, 319

Elder Things, 160

elementals, 216, 218

Elizabeth I, Queen, x, 17, 72

Elizabethan Magick (Turner), 129

Ellison, Harlan, 281

Eltdown Shards (f), 289

Emerald Tablets (Doreal), 112

Encyclopedia Britannica, 13, 95, 310

Encyclopedia Cthulhiana (Harms), xvi, xxii

Encyclopedia of Claims, Frauds, and Hoaxes of the Occult (Randi), xvi, 142

Encyclopedia of Occultism, An (Spence), 99, 310, 318

Enki, 46, 136, 153, 161, 186, 192, 325

Enkidu, 154

Enlil, xv, 43, 46, 154–55, 161

Enmeshara, 46, 153

Enoch, ix–x

Enochian language, 17, 73, 129, 198

Enochian Magic for Beginners (Tyson), 80

"Entombed with the Pharaohs" (Houdini and Lovecraft). *See* "Under the Pyramids"

Enuma Elish, 151, 180, 186, 188

Epic of Anzu, 148

Epic of Gilgamesh, 43, 154–55

Equinox, The (Crowley), 106

Ereshkigal, 37, 135, 148

Eris, 249

Esoteric Buddhism (Sinnett), 26

Esoteric Order of Dagon (amateur press organization), 37; (f), 123; (magickal group), 115–18, 143, 198

Etana, 161–63

Evangelista, Benjamino, 65–66

Evil Dead II, 241–43, 255–56

Evil Dead, The, 240–43, 255–56

Exorcist, The, 43, 158

Exorsister series, 249
Extreme Evil (Larson), 143
"Fall of the House of Usher, The" (Poe), 6
Fanciful Tales of Time and Space, 333
Fantasy Macabre, 50
Fanucci Editors, 57
Faraday review, 30
Faraday, W. (f), 30
Farbridge, Peter, 294
Farrar, Janet, 78
Farrar, Stewart, 78
Fate magazine, 139, 140, 145, 218, 297
Faust, 214
Feint Type, 40
Fellini Satyricon, 231
Fellini, 231
Ferrell, Roderick, 203–07, 226, 328–29
"Festival, The" (Lovecraft), 10–12, 14, 96
Finlay, Virgil, 96, 309
First Baptist Church of Providence, 92
Fischer, Robert, 38
Fleck, Norman, 176–77
Flying Rolls, Golden Dawn, 74, 77
Ford, Henry, 213
Ford, Maria, 264
Forerunners to Udug-Hul (Geller), 47, 190
Forever Evil, 243–45
Forgotten Ones, 120
Fortune, Dion (Violet Firth), 94, 216, 220
Fourth Book of Agrippa, 73
Fox, Darren, 181
Fragments of a Faith Forgotten (Mead), 159
Franco, Jess, 231–32
Fraternitas Saturni, 51
Frederic I, Baron of Sussex (f), 31
Freemasonry, 4, 38, 49, 73, 81, Egyptian, 4, 49, 111, Memphis-Misraim rite, 113
Freya, 249
From Beyond, 258
Fu Manchu (f), 14, 93
Ganzir, 164–65, 183, 206, 326
Gardner, Gerald, 78, 80, 176, 209
Gardner, Martin (f), 65
Gates of the Necronomicon (Simon), 39, 180–81, 196
Gattis, Tish, 325
Gehenna, 163
Geoffrey, Justin (f), 64
Geoghegan, Shevawn, 206–07
Geography of Witchcraft, The (Summers), 309
Germer, Karl, 126
Ghayat al-Hakim, 89. See also *Picatrix*

Ghostbusters International, role-playing game, 279
Ghostbusters, 277–79
Ghoulies, 226
ghouls, 89
Giger, Hans, 38, 240
Giger's Necronomicon, 240
Gilgamesh, 154
Glanvil, Joseph, 10
Gnosis, 144
Gnosticism, 148, 159, 165, 185
Goddess and the Moon, The, 325
Godwin's Cabalistic Encyclopedia (Godwin), 144
Goetia, x, 50–51, 136, 151, 153, 156, 170, 179, 195, 282–83, 325, 328. See also *Lesser Key of Solomon*
Golden Bough, The (Frazer), 13, 97
Golowin, Sergius, 38
Gonce, John III, xiii, xvi, 63, 299, 301, 307–08
Goodman, John, 205
"Gorge Beyond Salampunco, The" (Derleth), 32
Grand Albert, 128
Grand Grimoire. See *Red Dragon*
Grant, Kenneth, 86, 102–03, 106, 109–11, 113–15, 117, 119–20, 122, 125–26, 129, 135–37, 142, 145, 160, 163, 168, 182, 189, 208–09, 212–13
Gravel, Greatan, 294
Graves, Robert, 78
Great Beast 666. See Crowley, Aleister
"Great God Pan, The" (Machen), 91, 125–26
Great Old Ones (f), 17, 31, 37, 96, 102, 106, 112, 118–21, 138, 150, 186, 218, 229, 232–33, 243, 245, 272, 287, 321
Great One of the Night of Time, 102
Greek Herbal of Dioscorides, The, 170
Green, Anthony, 152
Greene, Sonia. See Lovecraft, Sonia
Greenwood, Steven, 115–16
Gregorius, Gregor. See Grosche, Eugen
Gregory IX, Pope, 15, 254, 304, 333
Grieve, M., 170
Grimoire of Honorius, 36
Grimoire of Zos (Spare), 241
grimoires, 128, 168, 192, 195, 198
Grimoirium Imperium (Legard), 56–57
Grosche, Eugen (also Gregor Gregorius), 51
Grove Street Bookstore, 32
Guide to the Cthulhu Cult, A (Pelton), 31–32
Gulevitch, Vladimir, 40
Hadith, 102
Hagin, Kenneth, 221–22

Halfpenny, Kate, 205
Hali (f), 10
Haller, Daniel, 229, 236
Hammett, Dashiell, 251
Hancock, Graham, 155
Hand of Glory, The (Blakeborough), 309, 318
Hanson, Lee, 236
Haramullah, 83, 198
Harms, Daniel, xiii, xxii, 133–34, 149, 178, 186, 211, 212, 218, 219, 321
Harre, T., 137
Harrington, Curtis, 237
Harvard University, 39, 304
Hastur (f), 36, 144, 285, 313
Haunted Homes and Family Legends of Great Britain (Ingram), 309, 318
Haunted Houses (Flammarion), 309, 318
Haunted Palace, The, 227–28, 230, 234
"Haunter of the Dark, The" (Lovecraft), 22, 65, 98, 100, 112
Haverhill incident, 7
Hawthorne, Candice, 204
Hawthorne, Nathaniel, 24–25
Hay, George, 49–50, 322
Hazard family, 5, 88
"He" (Lovecraft), 11
Heavy Metal, 33
Hecate's Fountain (Grant), 122, 142, 182
Heptameron (d'Abano), 36, 73
"Herbert West—Reanimator" (Lovecraft), 271–72, 278, 294, 333
Hermes Trismegistus, 14
Hermetic Order of the Golden Dawn, x, 13, 26–27, 46, 72–74, 78, 80–81, 83, 93–94, 102, 129, 131, 136, 159, 175, 191, 208, 220, 316, 331
Herodotus, 46
"Hexes and Hoaxes" (Price), 55, 141
Heyerdahl, Christopher, 294
Hidden Key of the Necronomicon (Thomas), 182–83
Hideaway, 205, 226, 328
Hieroglyphic Monad (Dee), ix–x
Hinduism, 74, 103, 216
Hine, Phil, 119–21, 221, 225–26, 321
Hinterstoisser, Stanislaus (f), 49–50
History of Magic (Levi), 310
History of Magic and Experimental Science (Thorndike), 24
"History of the *Necronomicon*" (Lovecraft), 15, 18, 25, 30, 33–34, 38, 303–04, 331
History of Witchcraft and Demonology, The (Summers), 276, 309
Hitchcock, Alfred, 275

H. P. Lovecraft: A Life (Joshi), 85
Holden, Clay, 322
Holographic Universe, The (Talbot), 79, 145
Holy Trinosophia (St. Germain), x
"Hoofed Thing, The" (Howard), 259
Hopper, Dennis, 237, 252
"Horror at Red Hook, The" (Lovecraft), 11, 12, 86, 95, 111, 178, 262, 271, 310
"Horror from the Depths, The" (Derleth and Schorer), 331–32
"Horror in the Museum" (Heald and Lovecraft), 22, 109
Houdini, Harry (Erich Weiss), 13, 94, 97
Houghton Library, Harvard, 333
"Hound, The" (Lovecraft), 8–9, 14, 95, 276, 326
"Hound—A Dead Dog?, The" (Mariconda), 308
Hounds of Tindalos (f), 277
"Hounds of Tindalos, The" (Long), 112, 276, 326
House of the Seven Gables, The (Hawthorne), 24–25
Hoven, Adrian, 231
Howard, Robert, xi, 18, 22, 50, 64, 67, 289
Huback, Michael, 133
Hubbard, L. Ron, 124–26
Humwawa. *See* Huwawa
Hunchback of the Morgue, The, 238–39
Huwawa (Humwawa), 43, 154–55, 170, 182
Huysmans, Joris-Karl, 73, 316
"Hymn to Pan" (Crowley), 91, 316
I Ching, 215
"I Know What You Need" (King), 24
Iak Sakkath, 194
Ibarra, Louis, 245
Ifa, 115
Iff, Simon (f), 131–32
Il Trigono Libreria Esoterica, 57
Iliad, 4
Illuminates of Thanateros, 81
Ilyth'la (f), 31
Image-Maker of Thebes, The, 226
In the Mouth of Madness, 219
Inanna, xxii, 41–42, 147, 153, 160–62, 186–88, 192, 195, 211, 325. *See* Ishtar
*Index Expurgatorius,*15
"Inhabitant of Carcosa, An" (Bierce), 10
Innsmouth (f), 123
Inquisition, 36, 64, 168, 210, 238, 241, 333
Interceding Against the Powers of Darkness (Hagin), 221
International Guild of Occult Sciences, 181–85, 222

"Into the Depths of Severity and All Beauty" (Frisvold), 115
Irem, 303, 333
Ishniggarab, 157
Ishtar, xxii, 46, 147, 153, 161–62, 186, 192, 211, 325. *See* Inanna
Isis Unveiled (Blavatsky), 26
Islam, 52, 88–89, 153, 186, 211, 254, 303, 332
Ithaqua (f), 31
James, Geoffrey, 129, 159
Jastrow, Morris, 46
Jean-Maine, Doctor Lucien-Francois, 113
Jenkin, Brown (f), 20
Jesus, ix, 186, 216, 222
Joshi, S., 7, 9, 15, 85–88, 310, 329
Journeys Out of the Body (Monroe), 165
Judaism, 90, 148, 186
Julius II, Pope, 149
Jung, Carl, 82, 100, 213
Kabbalah. *See* Qaballah
Kadath (f), 102
Kaddish, 190
Kail, Tony, 140, 329
Kalem Club, 27, 191
Kali, 207
"Kathulu Majik" (Nagasiva), 118
Kelley, Edward, ix–x, 56, 72, 141, 159, 166, 198
Kessler, Donald, 5
Key of Solomon the King, 14, 50, 151, 203, 310
KGB, 52
Khem Set Rising, 40
kia, 237
King in Yellow, The (Chambers), 25, 304, 334
"King in Yellow, The" (f), 25, 334
King Solomon's Mines (Haggard), 302
King, Francis, 141
Kingsport (f), 10
Klein, Theodore, 286, 289
Kleiner, Rheinhardt, 226
Knights of St. John, 81
Knowledge Lectures, Golden Dawn, 74
Koch, Kurt, 149
Koenig, H., 14
Kraig, Donald, 79, 159, 175
kundalini, 131
Kurten, Peter, 49
Kuttner, Henry, 21, 26
Kutu, 148–49. *See* Cutha
Kutulu, 41, 43, 138, 150, 158, 170, 211
La Magia Estelar: El Verdadero Necronomicon (Ripel), 57
La-Bas (Huysmans), 73, 217
Ladouceur, Serge, 294
LaForest, Serge, 294
Lake, Professor (f), 20
Lamashtu, 154

Lane, Edward, 88
Lang, Fritz, 232
Langford, David, 50, 129, 322
Larson, Bob, 143–44, 200, 203
Last Ten Million Years, The (f), 66
"Last Test, The" (Castro and Lovecraft), 15
LaVey, Anton, 78, 81, 111–13, 198, 200, 203, 237, 278, 283
Law of the Trapezoid, 112
Le Couleuvre Noire, 113–14
Leadbeater, Charles, 220
"Leaves from the Necronomicon" (Druillet), 33
Legard, Phil, 56
Lemuria, 54
Lenormant, Francois, 146
Lesser Banishing Ritual of the Pentagram, 80–81, 150, 190, 202, 216, 218, 221
Lesser Black Magic, 81
Lesser Key of Solomon, 152, 173, 180, 252. *See also* Goetia.
Letters on Demonology and Witchcraft (Scott), 310, 318
Levenda, Peter, 40–41, 48, 132, 135, 138, 155–56, 168–69, 175, 178, 180–81, 186, 199, 207, 218–19, 310
Levi, Eliphas (Alphonse Constant), x, 13, 73, 96
Leviathan, 158, 189
Lewis, C., 92
Lewton, Val, 275
Leyden Papyrus, 135
Li, 122
Liber 418: The Vision and the Voice (Crowley), 159
Liber 555 (Bell), 59
Liber Al vel Legis (Crowley), x, 74, 102, 120, 136, 157
Liber Aleph vel CXI (Crowley), 135
Liber Azif, 143
Liber CCXXXI (Crowley), 106, 109
Liber Kaos (Carroll), 208
Liber Loagaeth, 50, 127, 129, 322
Liber Muqarribun (Legard), 57
Liber Mysteriorum Sextus et Sanctus (Dee), 322
"Liber V vel Reguli" (Crowley), 237
Library of Congress, 333
Library of Daath, 116
Lilith (MacDonald), 124
Lilith, 36, 314
Lindholm, Lars, 84
Live-action role-playing (LARP) games, 59
Llewellyn Practical Guide to Astral Projection (Denning and Phillips), 165
Llewellyn Practical Guide to Psychic Self-Defense and Well-Being (Denning and Phillips), 221

Llewellyn Publications, 221
Lloigor (f), 31
Long, Frank, xi, 18, 112, 137
Lord of a Visible World (Joshi and Schultz), 87
Lord of Illusion (Barker), 283
"Lord of Illusion, The" (Price), 311
Lord of the Rings trilogy (Tolkien), 120
Los Angeles Science Fantasy Society, 124
Lovecraft at Last (Conover and Lovecraft), 30, 332
Lovecraft Circle, xxii, 87, 99, 110, 118, 124, 141, 158, 212, 289
Lovecraft, H. P., (f), 250–51
Lovecraft, Howard Phillip, x–xii, xvi–xviii, xxi–xxii, 3–25, 28–29, 31, 37–38, 40, 42, 48–50, 54–56, 62, 64–68, 82, 85–86, 88, 92–94, 100, 102–03, 106, 109–11, 114–16, 118, 121–23, 125, 127, 129, 131, 134–35, 137–38, 141–44, 146, 156–58, 160, 165, 167, 174, 185, 191, 197–99, 208–09, 212–14, 225, 229–36, 238–39, 241, 243, 245–46, 248, 251–52, 254, 257–64, 266, 273, 276, 278, 281, 283, 286, 288–94, 297–302, 310, 317, 319, 326, 331–34; and dreams, 5, 101; and occultism, 12–15, 26–27, 86–87, 89–91, 94–99; and Sumer, 136; death, 23; on Aleister Crowley, 74, 77, 137; on film, 226; religious views, 99
Lovecraft, Sarah (Susie), 3–4, 8, 92
Lovecraft, Sonia, 13, 64, 111, 123, 197, 327
Lovecraft, Winfield, 3–4, 49, 111
Lovecraft: A Biography (de Camp), 35
Lovecraft: A Look Behind the Cthulhu Mythos (Carter), 54
Lovecraft: Sorceror (sic) (Memoli), 91
"Loved Dead, The" (Eddy and Lovecraft), 123
Loveman, Samuel, 6
Low, Colin, 64, 197, 214, 327–28
Lucifer Principle, The (Bloom), 166
Lugh, 216
Lumley, William, 22, 99
"Lurker at the Threshold, The" (Derleth and Lovecraft), 109, 319
Lurker in the Lobby, The (Migliore and Strysik), 329–30
Lynn, Bob, 36
Machen, Arthur, 27, 93, 110, 191
Macotta University, 67–68
Mage's Guide to the Internet, 80
Magical Revival, The (Grant), 102, 111, 136
Magician Among the Spirits, A (Houdini), 97, 309, 318

Magician's Companion, The (Whitcomb), 106, 144
Magick in Theory and Practice (Crowley), 74, 89, 124
Magick Without Tears (Crowley), 135
magick, xviii, 71, 101, 167; and dreams, 99–100, 201–02; and geometry, 99–100; and letters, 90; and truth 80; and words, 99–100; ceremonial, 78–81, 90, 113, 300, 210; chaos, 79, 82–84, 118, 198, 208, 237; definition of, 71; dogmatic, 80–81, 83–84, 198; Enochian, 72–73, 106, 125, 129, 159, 166, 194, 208; Lovecraftian/Necronomicon, xxii, 84–85, 111, 114–15, 119–22, 124–26, 197, 208, 213; Maat, 160; Neopagan, 79–80; planetary, 152, 208; Satanic, 78, 80; sex, 122–23, 200; spelling of, 71; Thelemic, 123, 125, 158, 160, 176
"Magick and the Necronomicon" (Harms and Gonce), 146
Magickal Childe bookshop, 39–40, 46, 48, 51, 113, 132, 134, 140, 149, 171, 174–75, 179–81, 185, 188, 314
Magickal Formulary, The (Slater, ed.), 181
Magnalia Christi Americana (Mather), 12, 123, 248
Magus, The (Barrett), 73, 80, 310
Maklu Text. See Maqlu Text
Malachim Script, 274, 291
Malleus Maleficarum (Kramer and Sprenger), 310
Malone, Thomas (f), 95, 271–72
"Man and the Snake, The" (Bierce), 10
Man, Myth, and Magic (Cavendish, ed.), 110
mandalas, 187
Mangham, Elizabeth, 207
Manichaenism, 186
"Mannikin, The" (Bloch), 32
Manson, Charles, 206
Manson, Marilyn, 199–200
Manutius, 330
Maqlu Text, 42, 162, 191
Marduk, 39, 42–43, 145, 148, 151–52, 154, 161, 179–80, 184, 186, 189, 192–93; (band), 200
Maroney, Tim, 213
Marshall, Sir William, xii
Martinist Order, 113
Marvel Comics, 189–90
Marvells of Science (Morryster) (f), 10
Mason, Glen, 206–07
Mason, Keziah (f), 20, 100, 254, 257
Master of Villainy (Rohmer), 94
Math of the ChRyStAL HUMM, 117–18

Mather, Cotton, 12, 246
Mathers, Samuel "MacGregor," x, 26, 73–74, 77, 110, 135, 189
Mauve Zone, 105–06
Maxwell, Frank, 229
McCarthy, Jim, 199
McGinnis, Nial, 276
"Medusa's Coil" (Bishop and Lovecraft), 19
Melton, J, 139–40
meme theory, 166–67
Memphis, 303
Meon, 114
Merritt, John, 14, 310
Metal Hurlant, 33
Metamorphosis (Ovid), 91
Metempsychosis, 110
Michael, Archangel, 216
Michael, Patriarch of Constantinople, 15, 304, 333
Midul Path, 83, 198
Mi-go (f), 263–64
Miller, William, 22
Mind Parasites, The (Wilson), 49
Mirage Press, 33–34
Miskatonic (f), 158
Miskatonic Alchemical Expedition, 117–18
Miskatonic University (f), 10–11, 16–17, 19–20, 33, 232, 234, 236, 246, 253–54, 269, 271–72, 285, 287, 291, 304, 333
Miskatonick Society, 116
Mithra, 186
Modern Magick (Kraig), 145–46, 221
Modern Sex Magick (Kraig), 79
Mohammed, 89, 332
Moloch, Frater, 181–82. *See also* Fox, Darren
Monastery of the Seven Rays, 113
"Monkey's Paw, The" (Jacobs), 167, 260
Moonchild (Crowley), 125, 131, 237
Moorcock, Michael, 82, 208
Morbid Angel, 200
Morrigu, 216
Morse, Richard, 137, 226
Morton, James, 6
Mortuorum Demonto (f), 243
Moses, ix, 81
Mosig, Dirk, 86, 100
Mulge, 37
Muller, W., 86
Mummu, 191
Munoz, Doctor (f), 260–61
Murray, Bill, 278
Murray, Margaret, 78, 80, 96–97
(My) Necronomicon, 265–66
Myers, Dru, xxii
Myers, Wade III, 204
Mysteries of Magic (Levi), 14, 96
Mystery of the Necronomicon, 266–73

Mystery Science Theater 3000, 185, 227

Mythos, 56

Myths and Myth-Makers (Fiske), 97, 309, 318

Nader, Ralph, 210

Nagasiva, Tyagi, 118–19, 209

Nameless City (f), 12

"Nameless City, The" (Lovecraft), 7, 12, 18

Nameless Cults (f), 320

Namtar, 37, 48, 314

Nan-Matol, 320

Nanna, 151, 161, 187

Nar Mat(t)aru, 328

Naschy, Paul, 238–39

Nathan of Gaza, 64

National Union Catalog, 67

Nazis, 52, 64, 112, 116, 302

Nebo, 161

Necromantic Grimoire of Augustus Rupp, The (Raven), 36–37, 158

Necronomian (Fox), 181–82, 222

Necronomical Exmortis (Betrayer), 200

Necronomicon (books)

Carter, 54–55, 127

Culp, 37, 127

Fanucci, 57–58

Giger, 38, 49, 127, 142, 209

Lovecraft creation, xi–xii, xvi, 3–4, 8–14, 16–21, 23, 28–30, 48, 64, 98–99, 127, 167, 212, 230, 254, 326; fictional history, 15; first appearance, 7; origin, 5–6, 24–26; possibility of Lovecraft writing, 22

Owlswick Press. *See Al Azif* (de Camp)

Pizzari, 57

Price, ed., 32, 54–55, 127

Quine (f), 66–8

Simon, xi–xii, 27, 37, 39–43, 46–53, 58, 67, 118, 127, 131–34, 138–71, 173–86, 188–201, 203–12, 214–16, 218–19, 226, 237, 241, 257, 273, 277–78, 297–98, 313, 328, 329; and cults, 201–203; and psychic attack, 215; gatewalking ceremony, 41, 43, 46, 151, 153, 159–65, 169, 181–84, 187–88, 190, 193–95, 201, 206, 220; origins 39–41, 174–78

St. George, 52–53, 127

Stone, 53, 184–85

NecronomiCon (convention), 266, 297

Necronomicon (film, also called *Succubus*), 230–32

"Necronomicon" (song by Hypocrisy), 200

Necronomicon 2: The Tomb of Alhazred, 58

Necronomicon, The: A Study (Chalker and Owings), 33–34, 38, 127

Necronomicon: Book of the Dead, 257–65, 297

Necronomicon: The Book of Dead Names (Hay), 38, 49–52, 54–55, 58, 65, 127, 129–31, 141–45, 157, 209, 322

Necronomicon: The Journal of Horror and Erotic Cinema (Black, ed.), 56

"Necronomicon Anti-FAQ" (Low), 64–65, 198

Necronomicon egregore, 219–20, 329

Necronomicon Ex Mortis, 243

"*Necronomicon* FAQ" (Chua), 80, 144

Necronomicon Files, The (Harms and Gonce), xxi–xxii, 61, 178–79, 299, 329–30

Necronomicon Gnosis, 110

Necronomicon II (Giger), 38, 127

Necronomicon Mythos, 110

Necronomicon Novum (Opsopaus), 56

Necronomicon Press, 87

Necronomicon Project (Alquier, ed.), 58

Necronomicon Report (Simon), 39

Necronomicon Revelations I (Tahuti), 83–84

Necronomicon rumors, 61–67

Necronomicon Spellbook (Simon), 39–40, 48, 132–33, 151, 178–81, 184–85

Necronomicon tapes (Simon), 185–96

"*Necronomicon*—The Ultimate Grimoire?" (Valiente), 209

Nehib, Paul, 199

Nekromantik, 241

Nema, 160

"Nemesis" (Lovecraft), 110

Neopaganism, xxi, 77–80, 91, 147, 155, 173, 209, 213, 324, 329

Neoplatonism, 90, 186

Nephilim, 198

Nergal, 148, 152–53, 161, 182

Nergal (band), 200

Nestor, 174–78, 327

Neville Spearman Limited, 50

New Age movement, 78–80, 138, 210, 213

New Isis Lodge, 114, 122

New Line, 264–65

New Religious Movement, term, 307–08

New Republic, The (Blow), 210

New Satanists, The (Blood), 199

New York Public Library, 132

New York Times, 40, 133

New York Times Index, 66

Nielsen, Bonny, 40

Nietzsche, Friedrich, 83

"Night-Gaunts" (Lovecraft), 5

Night of the Demon. See Curse of the Demon

Night of the Living Dead, 194

Night Tide, 237

Nightside of Eden (Grant), 107–09

Ninib. *See* Ninurta

Ninnghizidda, 193, 200

Ninurta (also Ninib), 46, 147–48, 153, 161–62, 187, 192

Nippur, 147

Nixon, Richard, 225

Nodens, 288–89, 313

Nomolos, Yaj (Jay Solomon), 35

Norbar the Arab, 24

Northam, Lord (f), 12

Nostradamus, 94

Nuctemeron of Apollonius, x

Nyarlathotep (f), 57, 106, 115, 119, 144, 157, 200, 285

"Nymphidia" (Drayton), 36

Oannes, 188

Obsculum Obscenum (album by Hypocrisy), 200

Occult Lovecraft, The (Raven), 36, 86, 158

Odin, 216

Oedipus Aegytiacus (Kircher), 104

Old Ones (f), xiv, xvi, 12, 17, 20, 43, 50, 54, 115, 120, 198, 205, 252, 259–60

Oldest History of the World (Evangelista), 65–66

Olieribos, 160

Ommiade caliphs, 303, 331–32

One Thousand Nights and One Night. See Arabian Nights

On-Line Computer Library Catalog, 36, 65, 67

Order of the Absu, 199, 208, 212

Order of the Crystal Dawn, 184

Order of the Cubic Stone, 49

Order of the Trapezoid, 112

Ordo Rosae Mysticae, 57

Ordo Templi Orientis (OTO), 52, 81, 124, 131, 237, 316; Calipate, 173, 176; Cthonic-Auranian, 117–18; Typhonian, 102, 117, 168, 208, 212, 213

Ordo Templi Orientis Antiqua, 113, 115

Oriental Magic (Shah), 151

Orne, Simon (f), 171, 228

Orridge, Genesis, 83, 118

OTO. *See* Ordo Templi Orientis

Out of Mind, 290–95

"Out of the Aeons" (Heald and Lovecraft), 22, 320

Out of the Darkness (Sakheim and Devine), 200

Outer Gateways (Grant), 142

Outside the Circles of Time (Grant), 110

Outsider, The (Wilson), 49
Outsider and Others, The
    (Lovecraft), 23
Owings, Mark, 33–34
Owlswick Press, 34–35, 301, 312
Oxford University Press, 96
Oz series (Baum), 120
Pagan Publishing, 32
Paganism, 92, 93, 138, 176, 190, 195, 216
Painted Black (Raschke), 199
Pan, 91, 138, 157
"Papyrus of Nephren-Ka, The"
    (Culp), 37
Paracelsus, 79
Paradise Lost (Milton), 5
Parker, Ryan, 322
Parsons, John, 124–26, 237
Path to Power (Heisler), 221
Patton, 225
Pazuzu, 43–44, 138, 153–55, 158, 195
Pelton, Fred, 31–32
Persephone, 186
Peter, Apostle, 132
Phantagraph, The, 30
Philetas, Theodorus (f), 15, 303–04, 333
Phillips, Whipple, 4, 6, 91
Philosopher's Stone, The (Wilson), 49, 65
Picatrix, xii, 24, 89, 317
Pickman, Richard (f), 304, 334
"Pickman's Model" (Lovecraft), 89, 334
"Picture in the House, The"
    (Lovecraft), 333
"Pigeons from Hell" (Howard), 283
Pigwiggin (f), 36
Pilgrims of the Night (Lindholm), 51, 144
planets, seven, 43, 46, 162–63
Plato, 162
Pliny, 170
Pnakotic Manuscripts (f), 287, 289, 320
Pneumatologia Occulta et Vera, 95
Poe, Edgar, 3, 5–6, 33, 228–29
Polansky, Roman, 234, 237
"Polaris" (Lovecraft), 111
Ponape, 320
Pope, Alexander, 4
Powers, Abogado, 272
Prediction, 209
Presson, Audrey, 204
Price, Edgar, 23, 26, 98, 110, 124
Price, Robert, 11, 51, 55, 132, 141–42, 309
Price, Vincent, 228
Prime Chaos (Hine), 208
Princeton University, 66
Prinn, Ludvig (f), 110
Process Church, 78

"Professor Peabody's Last Lecture,"
    285–86
Providence Journal, 33
Pseudonomicon (Hine), 119, 145, 208
Psychic Self-Defense (Fortune), 216, 220
Psycho, 234; (Bloch), 21
Ptolemy, 153, 162
Publisher's Weekly, 32
Qaballah, 53, 64, 72–74, 82, 90, 100–01, 103, 106, 108–09, 113–14, 119, 131, 159, 161, 163, 165, 169, 180, 190, 195, 200, 209, 221, 282, 285–86, 310, 316
Qanoon-e-Islam (Sharif and Herklots), 14, 310
Qlippoth, 103, 106, 108–09, 120, 153, 163–65, 170, 190, 206, 216, 218, 222, 319
Queen of the Damned (Rice), 204
Quine, Antonius (f), 66–68
Raimi, Sam, 256
Raising Hell (Newton), 199
Rambo, 225
Ramis, Harold, 278–79
Randi, James, xvi, 142
Randolph, Paschal, 77, 176
"Rats in the Walls, The" (Lovecraft), 125, 259
Raven, Anthony, 36
Ravenwood, 177
Reagan, Ronald, 225
Real Ghostbusters, The, 287, 331
Real Magic (Bonewits), 79
Reanimator, 258
Reaves, Michael, 288–89, 332
Rebel Press, The, 332
Red Dragon, The (or *Grand Grimoire*), xii, 149, Simon translation, 39
Regardie, Israel, 26
Reiner, Carl, 286
Remembering Aleister Crowley (Grant), 137
Remigius. *See* Remy, Nicolas
Remmington, Sarah, 204
Remy, Nicolas, 10
"Repairer of Reputations, The"
    (Chambers), 25
Report on the Necronomicon
    (Simon), 179
"Return of the Elder Gods"
    (Anonymous), 120
"Return of the Sorcerer," 283–85;
    (Smith), 18, 333
Reuss, Theodor, 316
Revelation, Book of, 166, 252
revisionism, historical, 80
Reynaud, Janine, 231
Rig-Veda, 26
Ripel, Frank, 57
R'lyeh (f), 36, 116, 119, 249, 253, 259–60, 276–77, 289, 320

R'lyeh Lodge, EOD, 116
R'lyeh Text (f), 51, 157
R'lyeh Text, The (Turner, ed.), 51, 55, 129
Roba El Khaliyeh, 303
Robertson, Sandy, 102
Rod Serling's Night Gallery (ck. *Night Gallery*), 261, 283, 285–86
Rod Serling's The Twilight Zone Magazine, 55, 141
Roger Williams Park Museum, 332
Rohmer, Sax (Arthur Sarsfield Ward), 13, 93–94
Roman Catholic Church, 78
Romance of Sorcery, The (Rohmer), 94, 97, 310
Rops, Felicien, 73–74
Rosemary's Baby (Levin), 234, 237
Rosenbaum, Henry, 236
Rosicrucianism, 73, 81, 93–94
Ruby Toad, The (Raven), 36
Rudolph, Emperor of Bohemia, 73
Runes of Nug-Soth, 54
runes, 215
Rupp, Augustus (f), 36
Ruzo (f), 52
Sacred Grove Press, 53
Sacred Grove Press, 184
Saduscismus Triumphatus (Glanvil), 10
Saint George, Elizabeth, 52
Saint-Jean, Raymond, 294
"Salem Horror, The" (Kuttner), 21
Salem witch trials, 12
Samuel Weiser, 40, 141, 220–21
Sanskrit, 143
Sapere Aude, 164. *See also* Westcott, William
SapFire Productions, 221
Satan, 158
Satanic Bible, The (LaVey), 198–99, 207
Satanic Rituals, The (LaVey), 111–12, 120, 198, 285
Satanism, xii, 53, 72, 77–78, 80, 83, 95, 198–201, 203, 207–08, 226, 237, 284–85, 329
Satanism (Larson), xvii, 143
Saul, Barnabus, 56
Sauthenerom, 57
Scarlet Letter, The (Hawthorne), 24
Schlangekraft, 40, 131, 139, 142, 208
Schweitzer, Darrell, 312
Science Occult: La Magie chez les Chaldeens (Lenormant), 37
Scientology, 124
Scimitar of Barzai, 54
Scithers, George, 35, 312
Scorpion Man, 183, 202
Scotland Yard, 83
Scott, Dennis, 207
Scott, Stan, 204
Scott, Winfield, 33

Sebittu, 150

Secret Chiefs, 26

Secret Doctrine, The (Blavatsky), 26, 209

Secret Lore of Magic, The (Shah), 151

"Secret of the Tomb, The" (Bloch), 21

Selected Letters (Lovecraft), 87, 110, 294

Sellers, Sean, 143

Sells, Richard, 177

Senzar, 26

Sephiroth, 73, 77, 103, 106, 109, 131, 163, 165, 316

Serling, Rod, 261, 286

Setna and the Magic Book, 124, 167

Set-Thoth, 102

Sex and Rockets (Carter), 124, 237

Shaddad, 333

"Shadow Kingdom, The" (Howard), 112

"Shadow Out of Time, The" (Lovecraft), 22, 49

"Shadow over Innsmouth, The" (Lovecraft), 37, 114, 123, 259, 320

Shadow over Innsmouth, The (Lovecraft), 20

Shakespeare, William, 225

Shamanism, 82–83, 117, 120, 165

Shamash, 153, 161, 169

shantaks, 90

Shapira, Moses, 134

She (Haggard), 253

Shepherd, Wilson, 310, 332–33

shew-stone, 72

Shining Trapezohedron (f), 112, 198, 281

Shinto, 114

shoggoths (f), 20, 160, 218, 239, 288, 322

Shore, Patricia, 129

"Short Primer on Pagan Ceremonial Magick, A" (Simon), 171

Shub-Niggurath (f), 31, 50, 131, 144, 157, 263, 285

"Shunned House, The" (Lovecraft), 278

Siebert, Bill (AshT ChOzar Ssaratu), 117–18

Silent Dragon, The, 182

Silkosky, Ronald, 236

Silver Key, The, 116

Silver's Spells for Protection (Ravenwolf), 221

Simon, 27, 39–41, 43, 46, 48, 51, 132, 135–36, 140–41, 148–50, 153, 157–59, 163–65, 170–71, 178, 185–96, 200, 208, 211, 272, 314, 325; (Peter), 174, 177–78

Sin, 41, 160–61, 164

Sinelnikoff, Michael, 294

Sirius Mystery, The (Temple), 209

Sitchin, Zecharian, 188

Sixth and Seventh Books of Moses, The, 148–50, 207

Skoob Esoterica, 51, 55, 130

Slater, Herman, 39–40, 132, 140–41, 163, 174, 176–78, 187

Smith, Clark, xi, 8, 12–13, 15, 18, 50, 85, 95–96, 98–99, 110–11, 124, 137, 264, 285, 289, 309

Smith, Peter, 116

Society of the Inner Light, 94

Solomon, ix–x, 81, 214

Sorcerer's Handbook, The (Stone), 184

Sothis (Sirius), 52

"Space Eaters, The" (Long), 18, 333

Space Vampires, The (Wilson), 49

Spade, Sam (f), 251

Spare, Austin, 81–83, 103, 198, 237, 241, 243, 256

Sphinx-Verlag, 38

Spiritual Cleansing (Mickaharic), 220

Spiritualist movement, 73

Spook Enterprises, 52

Sprengel, Anna, 26, 74, 331

Stallone, Sylvester, 225

"Star Ruby, The" (Crowley), 237

Star-Treader and Other Poems, The (Smith), 95

Starry Wisdom, 56, 64, 65, 115, 122; Oil, 181

Starwood Festival, 146, 190

"Statement of Randolph Carter, The" (Lovecraft), 7, 252–54, 294

Sting, 225

Stockdale, Carter (f), 36

Stockwell, Dean, 235–37

Stoker, Bram, 101

Stone, Merlyn, 53, 184

Story of Atlantis and the Lost Lemuria, The (Scott-Elliot), 26

Straczynski, J, 289

Strange Stories, 332

Strange Story, A (Bulwer-Lytton), 124

Strength to Dream, The (Wilson), 49

Studio 31 Graphics, 40

Stuttgart University, 36

Subculture Project, 140

Succubus, 230, 232. See also *Necronomicon* (film)

Sullivan, Tom, 241, 243

Sumer, and Crowley, 134–36; and Lovecraft 27, 136; civilization of, 41, 43, 67, 147, 187–88; language of, 143, 147–48, 188, 195; magic of, 48, 147, 150–53, 156, 162, 186, 191, 193, 196; mythology of, 27, 37, 42, 46, 144, 148, 161, 180, 302; religion of, 147

Summoning Spirits (Konstantinos), 145

Sun Tzu, 222

Suns of the Light (al-Hajj), 89

Sun-Tzu Speaks (Bruya, trans.), 222

Supernatural Horror in Literature (Lovecraft), 5, 25, 94, 101, 310

Sussex Manuscript. See *Cultus Maleficarum*

Suydam, Robert (f), 272

Swift, Jonathan, 4

Swihart, Debra, 248

Switchboard theory (Bonewits), 82, 146, 324

Sword of Hubur, 206

Symonds, John, 135

Tablets of Destiny, xv

Tahuti, 183

Takayama, Hideke, 272–73

Tales of the Genii (Morrell), 89

Talk-Back, 143

Tall Cedar (f), 49

Talman, Wilfred, 13–14, 95

Tanglewood Tales (Hawthorne), 25, 91

Tantra, 77–78, 82, 103, 115, 131, 208, 210, 216

Taoism, 77, 82

Tarot, 119, 124, 215, 285

"Tarot of the NecronomIcon" (Mat-A), 143

Tausk, Carl, 49

Tehuti (Thoth), 154

Templars, 81

Temple of Set, 78, 81, 111–13

Temple of the Vampire, 118, 321

Tenebrous, Frater, 115

terma, 119, 209

Terror of the Threshold, 161

Teutonic Knights, 81, 238

Theban Alphabet, 274

Thee Temple ov Psychick Youth, 83, 118

Thelema, 120, 125

Thelemites, 102, 115, 120, 123, 134, 157, 177, 189, 208, 212, 316

Theory of Pneumatology (Jung-Stilling), 309–10, 318

Theosophical Society, 26, 73

Theosophy, 78–79, 97, 114, 200

Therion, Master. *See* Crowley, Aleister

"Thing on the Doorstep, The" (Lovecraft), 271–72

Thompson, R, 314

Thoth, xv, 154

Thousand and One Nights. See *Arabian Nights*

Three Books of Occult Philosophy (Agrippa), 72–73, 80, 170

Thriller, 281, 283

Throbbing Gristle, 83⁻

"Through the Gates of the Silver Key" (Lovecraft and Price), 22–23

Thuggee, 207

Thule Gesselschaft, 302

Tiamat, 42–43, 148, 186, 189, 191, 205–06

Tiamat (band), 200
Tibetan Book of the Dead. See Bardo Thodol
Tishku, 37
"To Charlie of the Comics" (Lovecraft), 226
"To Hell in a Breadbasket" (Simon), 200
Tobin's Spirit Guide (f), 279
Tobler, Li, 240
Tomerlin, John, 283
Tourneur, Jacques, 250, 275, 283
Tree of Death, 106, 108–09
Tree of Life, Qabbalistic, 72–73, 103–06, 109, 113, 163, 182
Tree of Lights, 131
Trip, The, 235
True and Faithful Relation, A (Casaubon), 159, 176, 276, 322
Tsathoggua (f), 19, 121
Tunnels of Set, 107–10, 142, 163
Turner, Robert, 49–51, 129, 157, 322
Tylor, Edward, 95
Typer, Alonzo (f), 125
Tyr, 216
Tyson, Donald, 142–43, 166
Ubaid culture, 41, 147
Ubar, 333
Unaussprechlichen Kulten (f), 66, 67
"Under the Pyramids" (Houdini and Lovecraft), 13, 94, 97, 332
Unholy Alliance (Levenda), 199
Unicorn Grove, 177
Unification Church, 202
Universal, 234
Universe B, 114
University of Buenos Aires, 16, 304, 334
University of Chicago, 39
University of Mexico City (f), 58
University of Notre Dame, 39
Unnamable, The, 245–49, 252–53
"Unnamable, The" (Lovecraft), 123, 245–46, 249, 252, 254
Unnamable II, The, 252–55
Ur, 187
Urotsukidoji: Legend of the Overfiend, 272
Uruk, 147, 188
Usher, Roderick (f), 6
Utu, 153. *See also* Shamash
Valiente, Doreen, 119, 209
Vampire Bible, 321
Vampire Clan, 203–06
Van Bladel, Kevin, 310
Van Doren Stern, Philip, 93
Vanderbilt University, xvi
Vanek, Aaron, 265–66
Vassago, 205, 226, 328–29
Vathek (Beckford), 15, 332
"Vaults of Yoh-Vombis, The" (Smith), 264, 332
Vedas, 98

Venus, 160
Verlag Richard Schikowski, 51
Vigiliae Mortuorum secundum Chorum Ecclesiae Maguntinae, 6
Vir sign, 76, 237
Von Junzt, Friedrich (f), 67
Voodootronics, 114
Voudon, 113–15
Voudon-Gnostic Workbook, The (Bertiaux), 113, 115
Voynich Manuscript, 65
Vril (Bulwer-Lytton), 302
Waite, Arthur, 13–15, 73–74, 96, 151, 283
Waite, Ephraim (f), 272
Wandrei, Donald, 23, 32
"War of the Gods and Demons" (Chesterton), 121
Ward, Charles (f), 14, 123, 227–29, 244
Warlock Shop (Magickal Childe), 39, 174, 176, 200
Warner, David, 253, 264
Warnke, Michael, 203
Warren, Harley (f), 7, 294
Wasserman, James, 40, 133, 176
Watcher, 42, 160–62, 171, 182, 189–93, 196, 216, 218
Weeden, Ezra (f), 227
Weird Tales, 8, 17–18, 20–21, 32, 97, 112, 124, 288
Weiss, Erich. *See* Houdini, Harry
Wendorf, Heather, 204, 206
Wendorf, Naoma, 203
Wendorf, Richard, 203
West, Herbert (f), 269–72, 294
Westcott, William (also Sapere Aude), 26, 74, 81, 164, 331
Wetzel, George, 7, 9
Whateley, Lavinia (f), 232–36
Whateley, Wilbur (f), 16–17, 212, 232–37
Whateley, Wizard (f), 16, 232–36, 247
When God Was a Woman (Stone), 184
"Whisperer in Darkness, The" (Lovecraft), 19, 251, 258, 262–63, 273
White Uniform Hell, 249
Whitmore, J. (f), 33
Wicca, 59, 78, 80, 97, 143, 159–60, 163, 177, 197, 209–10, 216, 221
Widener Library, Harvard, 16, 304, 333
Widener, Harry, 333
Wildside Press, 35
Willet, Marinus (f), 101, 228–29, 241, 266
"Willows, The" (Blackwood), 93
Wilmarth, Albert (f), 19
Wilson, Colin, 4, 49–51, 65–77, 129, 243
Witch Hunt, 252

Witchcraft and the Shamanic Journey (Johnson), 80
Witchcraft movement, 78, 82
Witchcraft, Magic and Alchemy (de Givry), 309
Witch-Cult in Western Europe, The (Murray), 13, 96–97, 209
Witch's Guide to Fairy Folk (McCoy), 221
Wolfe, Jane, 126
Wollheim, Donald, 30, 333
Wolverine, 7
Wonder Book (Hawthorne), 25, 91
Wonder's Child (Williamson), 125
Woodman, W., 26, 74
Wooley, Sir Leonard, 187
Wormius, Olaus, 11–12, 15, 30–33, 37, 64, 243, 304, 333
Wright, Farnsworth, 21
Xastur, 154, 170, 202, 328
Xul, 277
Yaddith Lodge, EOD, 116
Yakthoob (f), 54
Yale University, 39, 66
Yeats, William, 74, 93
"Yellow Sign, The" (Chambers), 25
Yezidis, 136, 189
Yoakum, Jason, 207
yoga, 77–78, 82, 100
Yog-Sothoth (f), 38, 50, 101–02, 106, 109–10, 123, 194, 227–29, 232, 234, 237, 243–45, 250–52, 285, 303, 333
Yuggoth (Pluto), 19, 281
Yuzna, Brian, 263
Zauber-Bibliothek (Horst), 95
Zerkov, Tanya, 207
Ziggurats, 46, 187–88
Zonei, 41–43, 147, 151, 183
Zoroastrianism, 148, 186
Zos Kia Cultus, 81